American Women Writers

A Critical Reference Guide
from Colonial Times to the Present

*A Critical
Reference Guide
from Colonial Times
to the Present*

**ABRIDGED EDITION

IN TWO VOLUMES

VOLUME 2: M TO Z**

AMERICAN WOMEN WRITERS

Langdon Lynne Faust

Editor

Frederick Ungar Publishing Co.
New York

Library of Congress Cataloging in Publication Data
Main entry under title:

American women writers.

  Includes bibliographies.
  1. American literature—Women authors—History and
criticism. 2. Women authors, American—Biography.
3. American literature—Women authors—Bibliography.
I. Faust, Langdon Lynne.
PS147.A42 1983   810′.9′9287   82-40286
ISBN 0-8044-6165-1 (pbk. : v. 2)

Abbreviations of Reference Works

AA   *American Authors, 1600–1900: A Biographical Dictionary of American Literature* (Eds. S. J. Kunitz and H. Haycraft, 1938).

AW   *American Women: Fifteen-Hundred Biographies with Over 1,400 Portraits* (2 vols., Eds. F. E. Willard and M. A. Livermore, 1897). This is a revised edition of *A Woman of the Century* (1893).

CA   *Contemporary Authors: A Bio-Bibliographical Guide to Current Authors and Their Works* (various editors, 1962–present).

CAL   *Cyclopaedia of American Literature, Embracing Personal and Critical Notices of Authors and Selections from Their Writings* (2 vols., Eds. E. A. Duyckinck and G. L. Duyckinck, 1866).

CB   *Current Biography: Who's News and Why* (Eds. M. Block, 1940–1943; A. Rothe, 1944–1953; M. D. Candee, 1954–1958; C. Moritz, 1959–present).

DAB   *Dictionary of American Biography* (10 vols., Eds. A. Johnson and D. Malone; 5 suppls., Eds. E. T. James and J. A. Garraty; 1927–1977).

FPA   *The Female Poets of America* (Ed. R. W. Griswold, 1849).

HWS   *History of Woman Suffrage* (Vols. 1–3, Eds. E. C. Stanton, S. B. Anthony, and M. J. Gage; Vol. 4, Eds. S. B. Anthony and I. H. Harper; Vols. 5 and 6, Ed. I. H. Harper; 1881–1922).

LSL   *Library of Southern Literature, Compiled under the Direct Supervision of Southern Men of Letters* (16 vols., Eds. E. A. Alderman and J. C. Harris; Suppl., Eds. E. A. Alderman, C. A. Smith, and J. C. Metcalf, reprinted 1970).

NAW   *Notable American Women, 1607–1950: A Biographical Dictionary* (3 vols., Eds. E. T. James, J. W. James, and P. S. Boyer, 1971).

NCAB   *National Cyclopedia of American Biography: Being the History of the United States As Illustrated in the Lives of the Founders, Builders, and Defenders of the Republic, and of the Men and Women Who Are Doing the Work and Moulding the Thought of the Present Time* (various editors, Vols. 1–57, 1892–1976; Vols. A–M, Permanent Series, 1930–1978).

20thCA *Twentieth Century Authors: A Biographical Dictionary of Modern Literature* (Eds. S. J. Kunitz and H. Haycraft, 1942).

20thCAS *Twentieth Century Authors, First Supplement: A Biographical Dictionary of Modern Literature* (Eds. S. J. Kunitz and V. Colby, 1955).

WA *World Authors, 1950–1970: A Companion Volume to Twentieth Century Authors* (Ed. J. Wakeman, 1975).

Abbreviations of Periodicals

In the bibliographies, periodicals have been abbreviated in conformity with the Modern Language Association master list of abbreviations. Newspapers and magazines not in that list are abbreviated as follows:

AHR   American Historical Review
CathW   Catholic World
CSM   Christian Science Monitor
EngElemR   English Elementary Review
JSocHis   Journal of Social History
KR   Kirkus Review
NewR   New Republic
NYHT   New York Herald Tribune
NYHTB   New York Herald Tribune Books
NYT   New York Times
NYTMag   New York Times Magazine
NYTBR   New York Times Book Review
PW   Publisher's Weekly
SatEvePost   Saturday Evening Post
ScribM   Scribner's Magazine
VV   Village Voice
WallStJ   Wall Street Journal
WLB   Wilson Library Bulletin
WrD   Writer's Digest
WSCL   Wisconsin Studies in Contemporary Literature

American Women Writers

A Critical Reference Guide
from Colonial Times to the Present

Mary Margaret McBride

B. *16 Nov. 1899, Paris, Missouri; d. 7 April 1976, West Shokan, New York*
D. *of Thomas Walker and Elizabeth Craig McBride*

M., the daughter of a modestly successful farming couple, always knew she would be a journalist. Two relatives whose interest had permanent influence on M. were her maternal grandfather, a Baptist minister, who schooled her in bible readings, and her paternal grandfather, a scholar, who gave her an appreciation of Greek and Latin poetry. The first woman in her family to aspire to a career, she attended the University of Missouri, graduating in two and a half years, and financing her education by working on the Columbus *Times*. Successive feature-writing positions on the Cleveland *Press* and the New York *Mail* catapulted her to a syndicated column, a woman's-page editorship, and extensive magazine freelance work.

A second and third career for M. emerged from the Depression years when periodicals ceased publication or could no longer pay her prices. She turned to producing books and to conducting a daily program on radio (and ultimately on television), earmarking each media venture with her special vitality, her wide-ranging interests, her candor, and her respect for facts.

Though, on the one hand, M.'s work was characterized by deep-seated religious and moral convictions, plus sincere and un-self-conscious sentimentality, she was at the same time a tough and searching reporter. And though she struggled against and never conquered deep feelings of guilt and insecurity, she numbered among her close friends heads of state and celebrities in diverse fields in the U.S. and abroad. Testaments to her personal popularity and magnetism were the quarter of a million letters she received annually from listeners and a party on her tenth anniversary in radio, held at Madison Square Garden and attended by 125,000 "Mary Margaret" fans.

M.'s newspaper assignments were, for the most part, self-selected. She managed, whether the story involved a parade, a political convention, or a luncheon, to make the reader feel like a ringside spectator by introducing particulars of texture, smell, and other detail. Her acute sensory awareness coupled with searching curiosity and a zealot's concern for the truth contributed to M.'s being one of the most sought-after and highest-paid journalists in the country.

When the magazine market suffered reverses in the late 1920s, M. completed four travel books with coauthor and journalist, Helen Josephy. Though the books sold well because European travel was becoming popular, they have little value today except as social documents. Their preoccupation with where celebrities dined, resided, and shopped, made these books highly palatable to middle America and were a harbinger of M.'s modus operandi and subsequent success in radio and television.

Several other volumes are autobiographical, nonintellectual, nonliterary, but highly readable. *A Long Way from Missouri* (1959) and its sequel, *Out of the Air* (1960), recount with modesty and pride the events of M.'s life. Both books are replete with names and anecdotes, her successes and her setbacks, all treated honestly and with the utmost simplicity.

Her shift in media to radio, and later to television, made no difference in the persona of M., though, for contractual reasons, she assumed initially the "radio name" of Martha Deane. The same buoyancy, frankness, and cozy confidentiality prevailed. Her selection of guests, books, professions, and hobbies were examined like feature stories, utilizing, for the first time, newspaper techniques in radio presentation. To the extent that material was written, she prepared it herself, including the commercials. Products were always personally pretested for acceptability before she agreed to their sponsorship. *Printer's Ink,* authoritative bible of the marketing world, commenting on the slavish acceptance of her listeners, described the response to her program and her merchandising prowess as "the most outstanding example of reliance upon the word of a human being in the commercial field."

With the death in 1954 of her friend and manager, Stella Karn, M. gave up her own program and restricted herself to guest appearances. Six years later she moved permanently to a refurbished barn in West Shokan, New York. Her own assessment of her career was characteristically candid and self-effacing: "I've enjoyed my life and don't regret any of it. But I can see that, taken altogether it is faintly, sometimes even blatantly ridiculous. I wanted to be a great writer, and now I never shall be."

WORKS: Jazz: A Story of Paul Whiteman (with P. Whiteman, 1926). *Charm* (with A. Williams, 1927). *Paris Is a Woman's Town* (with H. Josephy, 1929). *The Story of Dwight Morrow* (1930). *London Is a Man's Town* (with H. Josephy, 1931). *New York Is Everybody's Town* (with H. Josephy, 1931). *Beer and Skittles: A Friendly Modern Guide to Germany* (1932). *Here's Martha Deane* (1936). *How Dear to My Heart* (1940). *America for Me* (1941). *Tune in for Elizabeth* (1945). *How to be a Successful Advertising Woman* (edited by McBride, 1948). *Harvest of American Cooking* (1957). *Encyclopedia of Cooking* (1959). *A Long Way from Missouri* (1959). *Out of the Air* (1960). *The Giving Up of Mary Elizabeth* (1968).

BIBLIOGRAPHY: For articles in reference works, see: *CB* (1954; June 1976). *Ladies of the Press,* I. Ross (1974). *Successful Women,* I. Taves (1943). *Whatever Became of . . . ?,* R. Lamparski (1970).

Other references: *American Mercury* (Jan. 1949). *Life* (4 Dec. 1944). *NY* (19 Dec. 1942). *NYT* (8 April 1976). *SatR* (1 March 1947). *Scribner's* (March 1931).

ANNE S. BITTKER

Mary Therese McCarthy

B. *21 June 1912, Seattle, Washington*
D. *of Roy Winfield and Theresa Preston McCarthy; m. Harold Johnsrud, 1933; m. Edmund Wilson, 1938; m. Bowden Broadwater, 1946; m. James Raymond West, 1961*

M. graduated from Vassar in 1933 and then settled in New York City, where she began her writing career. M.'s early book reviews appeared in *The New Republic* and *The Nation,* and in 1937 she became drama editor of the *Partisan Review.* She quickly attracted the attention of the literary establishment, which she often sharply attacked.

Known primarily as a novelist, M. is a very fine expository writer, who covers a wide range of subjects, from theories of the novel to travel observations to art history. Many of her essays are on political subjects. Her prose is graceful and precise, showing the influence of her classical education. M. dislikes slang and often uses Latinate diction as well as long, balanced structures, but her writing is generally informal. M.'s sentences are often barbed, sometimes given to startling generalizations; but she is usually concrete, meticulous, and reasonable.

M. began writing fiction at the suggestion of her second husband, the critic Edmund Wilson, and published her first story in 1939. She was long admired by a small readership, but *The Group* (1963) was an enormous bestseller and vastly enlarged her public. The novel recreates an era as it follows the lives of eight Vassar girls of the class of 1933 during the seven years after their graduation. It details their experiences with sex, psychiatry, domesticity, and politics; a description of one character's defloration is both funny and shockingly graphic. The book has a unique third-person point of view: The narrative "voice" is that of the Group, sometimes in chorus, sometimes individually. The girls are comic characters by M.'s definition—ineducable, unchanging, and therefore immortal.

M. is an extremely personal writer whose uses of her acquaintances in fiction are often unflattering. *The Oasis* (1949), a prize-winning *conte philosophique* about a utopian experiment, is a case in point; Philip Rahv and Dwight Macdonald were the "originals" of two satiric portraits which expose the dishonesty and pretentiousness of liberals whose high ideals and rhetoric offer no immunity against human frailty. M. is no gentler with herself than with her friends. Some readers have mistaken "Artists in Uniform" for fiction, probably because of the uncomplimentary light it casts upon the author, but it is fact. So, M. says, are two of the short stories about Margaret Sargent, heroine of M.'s first novel, *The Company She Keeps* (1942), which is actually a collection of stories unified by Margaret's quest for self. Other characters based to some extent on M. include Kay (*The Group*), Martha Sinnott (*A Charmed Life*, 1955), and Rosamund Brown (*Birds of America*, 1971). These characters are self-consciously "superior" but at times self-doubting, and relentlessly honest with themselves, believing that if action is sometimes compromised, thought should never be. Although liberal intellectuals, they believe in ritual and ceremony and abhor the common, the cheap, and the ugly.

These characteristics are discernible in the child described in *Memories of a Catholic Girlhood* (1957), M.'s autobiography. A collection of memoirs brought together with an introduction and epilogues, the book derives its unity chiefly from the character of the young Mary and from its themes of education, Catholicism, Jewishness, the quest for superiority, and the difficulty of doing the right thing for the right reason.

In *The Groves of Academe* (1952), Henry Mulcahy, a physically and morally repulsive man, fights his dismissal from a "progressive" college by falsely confessing to membership in the Communist Party, thereby cynically enlisting the support of faculty liberals. The novel moves with relentless logic from Mulcahy's letter of dismissal to the resignation of Hoar, blackmailed by the triumphant Mulcahy. In conforming to liberal conventions, Hoar and the faculty override their own good sense and powers of observation.

Yet even when not self-deceived, the liberal in M.'s fiction finds moral integrity difficult to achieve. In *Birds of America*, Peter Levi, a nineteen-year-old egalitarian and literary kinsman of Candide, sees that the things he most loves—nature, tradition, art—are threatened by the advance of the thing he believes in most—equality; yet the evils of injustice and poverty persist undiminished. In *Cannibals and Missionaries* (1979) a committee of liberals en route to Iran to investigate the Shah's regime and a tour group of American art collectors are hijacked by an international terrorist group and held in Holland while the collectors are exchanged for their priceless paintings and a farmhouse is turned into an unlikely gallery. Liberals and paintings are then offered in exchange for Holland's withdrawal from NATO and severing of relations with Israel. The novel's moral center is a senator who comes to the recognition that terrorism is a "kid brother" of minority electoral politics; both are equally ineffectual against the inertia of facts. The outcome is grim, but the mode is comic; people and their institutions are impervious to these events, and at the end, the Reverend Mr. Frank Barber, among others, has survived to go on counting his blessings.

M.'s ear is true, and her fiction is rich with the sounds of authentic voices, heightened but not distorted. If her characters are often ridiculous, she tolerates their absurdities even as she exposes them, although she is merciless with self-professed intellectuals who exempt themselves from responsibility to facts. Her most malevolent characters—Henry Mulcahy and Norine Schmittlapp (*The Group*)—thrive in personal and moral squalor with no foothold in truth.

As social critic and moralist, M. has consistently and scrupulously sought truth. Neither hopeful nor sentimental, M.'s messages often fall on unwelcoming ears. Like most satiric writers, she sometimes writes about the topical. But her range is wide, her eye and ear are keen, and her literary commitment is to the durable and universal facts of human life candidly and often caustically recorded.

WORKS: *The Company She Keeps* (1942). *The Oasis* (1949). *Cast a Cold Eye* (1950). *The Groves of Academe* (1952). *A Charmed Life* (1955). *Sights and Spectacles: 1937–1956* (1956). *Venice Observed* (1956). *Memories of a*

Catholic Girlhood (1957). *The Stones of Florence* (1959). *On the Contrary: Articles of Belief, 1946–1961* (1961). *The Group* (1963). *Mary McCarthy's Theatre Chronicles, 1937–1962* (1963). *Vietnam* (1967). *Hanoi* (1968). *The Writing on the Wall, and Other Literary Essays* (1970). *Birds of America* (1971). *Medina* (1972). *The Mask of State: Watergate Portraits* (1974). *The Seventeenth Degree: How It Went, Vietnam, Hanoi, Medina, Sons of the Morning* (1974). *Cannibals and Missionaries* (1979).

BIBLIOGRAPHY: Auchincloss, L., *Pioneers and Caretakers: A Study of Nine American Women Writers* (1965). Goldman, S., *Mary McCarthy: A Bibliography* (1968). Grumbach, D., *The Company She Kept* (1967). Hardwick, E., *A View of My Own: Essays in Literature and Society* (1963). McKenzie, B., *Mary McCarthy* (1966). Mailer, N., *Cannibals and Christians* (1966). Stock, I., *Mary McCarthy* (University of Minnesota Pamphlets on American Writers, No. 72, 1968).

For articles in reference works, see: *CA*, 5–8 (1969). *20thCAS*.

Other references: *Columbia University Forum* 6 (1973). *Esquire* (July 1962). *JAmS* 9 (1975). *Paris Review* (Winter-Spring 1962).

WILLENE S. HARDY

Helen McCloy

B. 6 June 1904, New York City
Writes under: Helen Clarkson, H. C. McCloy, Helen McCloy
D. of William Conrad and Helen Worrell Clarkson McCloy; m. David Dresser, 1946

M.'s father was managing editor of the New York *Evening Sun;* her mother wrote short stories under her maiden name. A Quaker, M. studied at the Brooklyn Friends School in New York. At fourteen, she published a literary essay in the Boston *Transcript;* at fifteen, she published verse in the *New York Times.* M. lived in France for eight years, studying at the Sorbonne in 1923 and 1924. M. was Paris correspondent for the Universal News Service (1927–31) and the monthly art magazine *International Studio* (1930–31). She also was London correspondent for the Sunday *New York Times* art section and wrote political sketches for the London *Morning Post* and the *Daily Mail.*

M. returned to the U.S. in 1931 and spent several years writing magazine articles and short stories. In 1938, she published her first mystery novel, *Dance of Death*. She has one daughter. She was divorced in 1961 from her husband, who writes mysteries under the name Brett Halliday.

M. has been rather prolific, writing twenty-eight novels of detection and suspense, many short stories, and newspaper and magazine articles. She won Ellery Queen Mystery Magazine awards for the short stories "Through a Glass, Darkly" (reprinted in *The Singing Diamonds*, 1965) and "Chinoiserie" (reprinted in *20 Great Tales of Murder*, 1951), and the Edgar Award from the Mystery Writers of America for the best mystery criticism. M. was the first woman president of the Mystery Writers of America.

Dance of Death features her detective, Dr. Basil Willing, a psychiatrist and an expert in forensic medicine; he appears in many of what are considered her strongest novels. The social satire in such novels as *Cue for Murder* (1942) and *Two-Thirds of a Ghost* (1956), as well as the fine presentation of New York society in *Alias Basil Willing* (1951) and *Unfinished Crime* (1954), suggests, as Erik Routley has indicated, that M. is one of those mystery writers in whom "there is a good deal of straight novel-writing." Anthony Boucher believes that M. "has always resembled the best British writers of the Sayers-Blake-Allingham school in her ability to combine a warm novel of likeable people with a flawless deductive plot."

M.'s choice of a psychiatrist-detective as hero reveals her interest in psychology, especially in its more paranormal manifestations, as is evident in *Through a Glass, Darkly* (1949), *Who's Calling?* (1942), and *The Slayer and the Slain* (1957). Her interest in the fragile structure upon which an individual's personality is based is shown in *The Changling Conspiracy* (1976), which deals with political kidnapping and brainwashing. This and other recent novels reflect M.'s interest in contemporary affairs; *The Goblin Market* (1943) and *Panic* (1944), which were written during World War II and deal with problems created by the war, suggest that this interest is not new.

In general, critics have preferred M.'s novels of detection to the novels of suspense or terror. M. herself believes that the current popularity of detective stories is related to "some lack in the accepted literary diet." The "moral understanding of common minds which results in sympathy for common lives" and the themes "that mean so much to the common man—love and death"—are missing from modern novels. In her best works, M.'s success in providing interesting characters and themes is matched with her ability in plotting.

WORKS: *Dance of Death* (1938). *The Man in the Moonlight* (1940). *The Deadly Truth* (1941). *Cue for Murder* (1942). *Who's Calling?* (1942). *Do Not Disturb* (1943). *The Goblin Market* (1943). *Panic* (1944). *The One That Got Away* (1945). *She Walks Alone* (1948). *Through a Glass, Darkly* (1949). *Alias Basil Willing* (1951). *20 Great Tales of Murder* (edited by McCloy, with B. Halliday, 1951). *Unfinished Crime* (1954). *The Long Body* (1955). *Two-Thirds of a Ghost* (1956). *The Slayer and the Slain* (1957). *The Last Day* (1959). *Before I Die* (1963). *The Singing Diamonds* (1965). *The Further Side of Fear* (1967). *Mister Splitfoot* (1968). *A Question of Time* (1971). *A Change of Heart* (1973). *The Sleepwalker* (1974). *Minotaur Country* (1975). *The Changling Conspiracy* (1976). *The Imposter* (1977). *The Smoking Mirror* (1979). *Burn This* (1980).

The papers of Helen McCloy are at the Boston University Library, Boston, Massachusetts.

BIBLIOGRAPHY: Routley, E., *The Puritan Pleasures of the Detective Story* (1972).

For articles in reference works, see: *CA*, 25-28 (1971). *A Catalogue of Crime*, J. Barzun and W. H. Taylor (1971). *Encyclopedia of Mystery and Detection*, Eds. C. Steinbrunner and O. Penzler (1976). *WA*.

Other references: *NYHTB* (28 Nov. 1943; 7 Oct. 1956). *NYT* (27 Feb. 1938; 11 Oct. 1942; 18 June 1950).

DIANA BEN-MERRE

Anne O'Hare McCormick

B. *16 May 1880, Wakefield, England; d. 29 May 1954, New York City*
Wrote under: Anne O'Hare, Anne O'Hare McCormick
D. of Thomas and Teresa Beatrice O'Hare; m. Francis J. McCormick, 1910

As an infant M. was brought from England to Columbus, Ohio, by her American-born parents. Intellectually influenced by her Catholic mother, a poet and woman's-page editor, M. was educated in private schools in Ohio, graduating from the College of St. Mary of the Springs. Following in her mother's footsteps, she published children's feature articles and soon became an associate editor for her mother's employer, Cleveland's weekly *Catholic Universe Bulletin*.

After her marriage to an engineer and importer, M. resigned her editorship and traveled with her husband on his European business trips. She wrote several impressionistic articles about European countries in the aftermath of World War I for the *New York Times Magazine*.

In 1921, her dispatches from Europe, serious assessments of the rise of fascism in Italy and of the role of Benito Mussolini (a figure then dismissed as a "posturing lout" by most journalists) impressed *Times* managing editor Carr V. Van Anda. He hired her as a foreign correspondent in 1922. She was the first woman hired as a regular contributor to the *Times* editorial page (1936) and the second woman to receive a Pulitzer Prize for journalism (in 1937, for her European correspondence).

Through the early 1950s she lectured in major U.S. cities, made radio broadcasts, and wrote "Abroad," a column based on reportage in Europe, Asia, and Africa. She also published editorials commenting on the American political scene.

The Hammer and the Scythe: Communist Russia Enters the Second Decade (1928) is based on articles M. originally wrote for the *Times* while traveling in Russia in the 1920s. M. reports her impressions of the Russian people, their conditions, and the clash of new and old. *The Hammer and the Scythe* is among the best of the books written by American journalists visiting Russia in the 1920s, but *The World at Home* (1956), one of two collections of M.'s *Times* columns posthumously edited by her personal friend, Marion Sheehan, better withstands the passage of time. Like other writers in the 1930s, M. "rediscovered America" in the pieces included in *The World at Home*. Her generalizations about the nation are convincing, particularly when examined together with the essays on Franklin Roosevelt. She connects small details that blend into larger patterns of the nation's character and dramatizes "that curious community . . . between the mind of the President and the mind of the people."

M. considered herself above all else a newspaperwoman. Aside from her book on Russia, she preferred to write "on top of the news while people were listening." Her reporting of foreign and domestic events was clear, incisive, and authoritative. It embodied her commitment to moral absolutes and professional standards of reporting. The body of correspondence (especially, warnings about fascism's rise in Europe), achievements as an influential political columnist, and eighteen years of service on the editorial board of America's most prestigious newspaper, secure M. an important place in the ranks of American journalists.

WORKS: *The Hammer and the Scythe: Communist Russia Enters the Second Decade* (1928). *The World at Home: Selections from the Writings of Anne O'Hare McCormick* (Ed. M. T. Sheehan, 1956). *Vatican Journal: 1921–1954* (Ed. M. T. Sheehan, 1957).

BIBLIOGRAPHY: Filene, P. G., *Americans and the Soviet Experiment: 1917–1933* (1967). Hohenberg, J., *Foreign Correspondence: The Great Reporters and Their Times* (1964). Marzolf, M., *Up from the Footnote: A History of Women Journalists* (1977). Talese, G., *The Kingdom and the Power* (1966).

For articles in reference works, see: *Catholic Authors: Contemporary Biographical Sketches, 1930–1947,* Ed. M. Hoehn (1952). *Ohio Authors and Their Books,* Ed. W. Coyle (1962). *20thCA. 20thCAS.*

Other references: *CathW* (Oct. 1954). *NYT* (30 May 1954). *SatR* (19 June 1954).

JENNIFER L. TEBBE

Carson Smith McCullers

B. 19 Feb. 1919, Columbus, Georgia; d. 29 Sept. 1967, Nyack, New York
Wrote under: Carson McCullers, Lula Carson Smith
D. of Lamar and Marguerite Waters Smith; m. Reeves McCullers, 1937;
divorced 1940; remarried McCullers, 1945

M.'s childhood was remarkable more for imaginative activity than for external events. She knew firsthand the monotony and dreary heat of a small southern town, which later provided settings for her novels. Her family was very supportive of her artistic talents, which gave early promise in both writing and music.

In 1935, M. went to New York City to study music. She lost her tuition money to the Julliard School of Music, however, and took part-time jobs while studying writing at Columbia University. She married a young army corporal, whom she divorced in 1940 but remarried five years later.

Her health, always delicate, deteriorated steadily from a tragic series of paralyzing strokes, breast cancer, and pneumonia. Yet she received visitors, traveled, and worked at her writing while half paralyzed until a final stroke killed her when she was about fifty.

M. received immediate acclaim with her remarkable first novel, *The Heart Is a Lonely Hunter* (1940), written when she was twenty-two. She became one of the most controversial writers in America and had many prominent friends, including Tennessee Williams, W. H. Auden, Louis MacNiece, and Richard Wright.

With *The Heart Is a Lonely Hunter*, M. established the themes that concerned her in all subsequent writings: the spiritual isolation of the individual and the individual's attempt to transcend that loneliness through love. The action centers on a deaf-mute, John Singer, to whom an odd assortment of characters turn as to a being especially wise and benevolent. The adolescent Mick speaks to him passionately of music, although Singer has never heard music. Dr. Copeland, a black physician, confides desperately his dreams for educating his race. Jake Blount, an ineffectual agitator, rants about the workers' revolution. Biff Brannon, quiet observer of men, is fascinated by Singer because of his effect on all the others. But Singer loves another mute: an indolent, retarded Greek named Antonapoulos, who can never respond in kind to the outpourings of communication from Singer's expressive hands. Thus, each man creates a god fashioned after his own need—but such gods fail. When Antonapoulos dies in a mental hospital, Singer commits suicide. His death signals the fading of a dream for each of those who revered him. This novel, like many of M.'s works, is highly symbolic yet rich in concrete detail. A number of allegorical meanings have been suggested for the story, of which M.'s own, concerning fascism, seems least appropriate.

Reflections in a Golden Eye (1941) is technically more polished and controlled than the first novel but more grotesque in character and event. In the static, ingrown environment of a southern army post, Captain Penderton, a latent homosexual, is impotent with his beautiful wife, Leonora, but infatuated with their neighbor, Major Langdon, who is her lover. The catalyst is Private Williams, an inarticulate young man with an affinity for nature and horses, especially Leonora's high-spirited stallion, Firebird. Captain Penderton both loves and hates Private Williams with a repressed sado-masochism reminiscent of D. H. Lawrence's "The Prussian officer." Williams glimpses the naked Leonora through an open door, and thereafter he creeps into the Penderton house at night and crouches reverently beside Leonora's bed simply to watch her sleep. Captain Penderton discovers him there and shoots him. The influence of Freud is unmistakable in this novel; M. was one of the first American writers to deal openly with homosexual impulses. The approach is consistently objective and nonjudgmental, as though reflected in the disinterested eye of nature.

M.'s novella *The Ballad of the Sad Café* (1951) achieves more successfully the mode of archetypal myth she approached in *Reflections in a Golden Eye*. It combines realistic detail with the legendary quality of folk ballad, in a tale of love at once melancholy and sardonically humorous. Surely no more incongruous pair exists in literature than the manlike, independent, cross-eyed Miss Amelia and her self-centered little hunchback, Cousin Lyman. Singlehandedly running an excellent distillery and the only general store, Miss Amelia is the leading citizen of a tiny backwoods community. The townsfolk, like a stupid and malicious Greek chorus, have no recreation but observing her colorful career. Miss Amelia once married a local bad boy but quickly threw him out when he tried to augment their partnership with sexual attentions. The humiliated lover made threats, turned to crime, and landed in the penitentiary. Now, a pathetic, homeless dwarf who claims kinship to Miss Amelia straggles into town. Contrary to all expectations, she takes in the stranger and builds her life around him. She opens a café, which becomes the social hub of the community, and the misshapen Cousin Lyman becomes a strutting little prince in her modest castle. Eventually, however, her despised husband returns from prison. Ironically, the dwarf becomes enamored with Macy, who uses him to harass Miss Amelia. The competition culminates in a public fistfight between Miss Amelia and Macy. Miss Amelia is actually winning when the dwarf leaps savagely upon her back and turns her victory into physical and emotional defeat. The two men vandalize her café and distillery and then get out of town. Miss Amelia becomes a recluse, and the town seems to share in her emotional death. There is nothing to do there now but listen to the melancholy singing of the chain gang.

M. hardly surpassed the skill and originality of *The Ballad of the Sad Café*, but many people prefer her mood piece, *The Member of the Wedding* (1946). It is certainly the most autobiographical of M.'s novels, and may seem closer to everyday experience, although the view of life as painful and frustrating is consistent with her more bizarre creations. The story concerns a motherless adolescent girl's abortive attempt to outgrow her childhood and create a platonic bond of love with a dimly understood adult world. Frankie Addams wants to find the "we" of "me" and thus escape the prison of selfhood; she decides to go away with her brother and his bride at their forthcoming marriage. This preposterous dream is born of endless conversations in the kitchen with Berenice, the black maid who is her only adult companion, and her seven-year-old cousin, John Henry, who represents the relatively untroubled childhood she wishes to discard. The little boy dies unexpectedly at the end of the novel, suggesting not only that childhood passes but that even children are not exempt from tragedy. Frankie, of course, is denied her dream of the perfect threesome on the honeymoon. She does not die of this traumatic rejection, but something rare and fragile is broken. M. converted this novel into an award-winning play, which ran for 501 performances in New York.

M.'s other works include a number of significant short stories ("A Tree, A Rock, A Cloud," sometimes compared in theme to "The Rime of the Ancient Mariner," was chosen for *O. Henry Memorial Prize Stories of 1942*); some poetry for children; another, less successful play (*The Square Root of Wonderful*, 1958, with fifty-five performances on Broadway); and one other novel, written in the veritable shadow of death. *Clock without Hands* (1961) concerns a man who faces death from leukemia.

In the foreword to *The Square Root of Wonderful*, M. wrote: "I suppose a writer writes out of some inward compulsion to transform his own experiences (much of it unconscious) into the universal and symbolical. . . . Certainly I have always felt alone." She admired, and to some extent emulated, some of the very greatest writers: Tolstoy, Dostoevsky, and Flaubert. M.'s works do not have the psychological insight or concentrated impact of the European masters, but they still cherished Christian redemption as the answer to human failure, which M. cannot do. For her, there is only human love to pit against the indifferent universe—and that love is tragically flawed.

WORKS: *The Heart Is a Lonely Hunter* (1940; film version, 1968). *Reflections in a Golden Eye* (1941; film version, 1967). *The Member of the Wedding* (1946; dramatization, 1951; film version, 1952). *The Ballad of the Sad Café* (1951; dramatization by E. Albee, 1963). *The Square Root of Wonderful* (1958). *Clock without Hands* (1961). *Sweet As a Pickle and Clean As a Pig: Poems* (1964). *The Mortgaged Heart* (Ed. M. G. Smith, 1971).

BIBLIOGRAPHY: Carr, V. S., *The Lonely Hunter, a Biography of Carson McCullers* (1975). Eisinger, C. E., *Fiction of the Forties* (1963). Evans, O., *The Ballad of Carson McCullers* (1966). Schorer, M., in *The Creative Present*, Eds. N. Balakian and C. Simmons (1963).

For articles in reference works, see: *American Writers*, Ed. L. Unger (1972). *CA*, 5–8 (1969); 25–28 (1971). *Contemporary American Novelists*, M. Felheim (1964). *20thCA. 20thCAS.*

Other references: *CE* (Oct. 1951). *GaR* (12, 1958; Summer 1963). *Jahrbuch fur Amerikastudien* 8 (1963). *Kenyon Review* (Winter 1947). *SAQ* 56 (1957). *WSCL* (1, 1960; Feb. 1962).

KATHERINE SNIPES

Betty Bard MacDonald

B. 26 March 1908, Boulder, Colorado; d. 7 Feb. 1958, Seattle, Washington
Wrote under: Betty MacDonald
D. of Darsie and Elsie Sanderson Bard; m. Robert Eugene Heskett, 1927;
  m. Donald Chauncey MacDonald, 1942

The second of five children, M. lived in Mexico, Idaho, and Montana before her mining-engineer father transferred the family to Seattle. After his death, the children were raised by M.'s mother and paternal grandmother. In 1927, M. abandoned art studies at the University of Washington to marry an insurance salesman, who brought her to a chicken ranch on the Olympic Peninsula. They separated in 1931, eventually divorcing in 1935. M. remained with her two daughters in her mother's home, holding a variety of jobs until her second marriage.

In 1943, at her sister Mary's urging, M. took a day from work to prepare a book outline for a visiting publisher's representative. That book became *The Egg and I* (1945), and her writing career was launched.

M. lived with her husband on Vashon Island, Puget Sound, until they purchased a California ranch in 1955. Stricken with cancer in 1957, she returned to Seattle for treatment and died at the age of forty-nine.

M.'s major books are autobiographical and are written in high humor. *The Egg and I*, her witty account of life on a primitive chicken ranch, achieved immediate popularity; one million copies were sold in the first year of publication. In 1947, Universal International released the movie, starring Fred MacMurray and Claudette Colbert and featuring Marjorie Main and Percy Kilbride as Ma and Pa Kettle.

Much of M.'s charm as author-character lies in her zealous determination to do the right thing. Nevertheless, her homemade bread is a disaster and her autopsies of spraddled chick carcasses futile ("Cause of death: Eggzema"). Amid the humor, M. probes the loneliness of the farm wife, discovering in a fair exhibit of knotted gunnysacks a pathetic symbol of what isolation can do to a woman. Behind her parade of outlandish characters, she offers carefully muted evidence of her crumbling marriage.

The Plague and I (1948) details M.'s battle against tuberculosis at age thirty. Confined in a sanatorium, she sketches other inmates with an artist's precision, barely touching on her own fears. *Anybody Can Do Anything* (1950) encompasses her years as a career woman during the Depression, and *Onions in the Stew* (1955) depicts family life on Vashon Island.

A born humorist with a fine sense of timing, M. knows how to tell a story. Her observations are succinct ("piddocks are clams with some sort of neurosis that makes them afraid to face life"), her caricatures barbed ("a small sharp-cornered woman with a puff of short gray hair like a gone-to-seed dandelion"), and her language friendly and pleasantly earthy. Less generally recognized is her affinity to nature. In M.'s almost lyric descriptions of mountains in the mist, damp green rain forests, and the earth itself, the eye of the art student never deserts her.

M.'s humor is frequently self-deprecatory. Actually quite competent, M. creates an impression of hopeless ineptness, at the same time praising courageous women like her mother and sister. Her ambivalence toward housework and domesticity is striking. She genuinely loves children and displays a gregarious nature, yet one senses in her writing a barely repressed undercurrent of frustration, almost anger, at the subordinate role that wife and mother must play in society.

Critically dismissed as a "regional" and "popular" writer, M. still projects an easy warmth and familiarity that draw her reader close. Though her popularity has waned since the 1950s, M.'s work is worthy of rediscovery; her comments are as pungent, her characters as delightful as ever.

WORKS: *The Egg and I* (1945; film version, 1947). *Mrs. Piggle-Wiggle* (1947). *The Plague and I* (1948). *Mrs. Piggle-Wiggle's Magic* (1949). *Anybody Can Do Anything* (1950). *Nancy and Plum* (1952). *Mrs. Piggle-Wiggle's Farm* (1954). *Onions in the Stew* (1955). *Hello, Mrs. Piggle-Wiggle* (1957). *Who, Me? The Autobiography of Betty MacDonald* (1959).

BIBLIOGRAPHY: Spacks, P. M., *The Female Imagination* (1975).
Other references: *NYT* (8 Feb. 1958). *SatR* (14 May 1955). Tacoma *News Tribune* (28 Aug. 1977).

JOANNE McCARTHY

Jessica Nelson North MacDonald

B. 7 Sept. 1894, Madison, Wisconsin
Writes under: Jessica Nelson North
D. of David Willard and Elizabeth Nelson North; m. R. l. MacDonald, 1921

Early in life M. showed signs of the literary potential that would bring her recognition as poet, novelist, critic, and editor. A precocious child, she memorized and recited poetry from the time she could speak. By the age of five, she read the newspaper and composed rhymes. In her youth M. competed successfully with other young poets, including Edna St. Vincent Millay, in the contests conducted by Mary Mapes Dodge, editor of St. Nicholas Magazine.

M. discovered Poetry Magazine while a student at Lawrence College, from which she was graduated in 1917. When M. moved to Chicago in 1920, she began to contribute poems to Poetry; through the next few decades, she placed poems in such magazines as the Dial, the Forge, Atlantic Monthly, the London Mercury, the Double-Dealer, Nation, The New Yorker, Voices, the Lyric, and the Saturday Evening Post. In 1927 she was awarded the Reed Poetry prize.

M.'s best poetry is finely crafted, and even the weakest shows inventiveness. Her first volume, A Prayer Rug (1923), while evincing control of traditional techniques and forms, reveals modernist influences. As Elizabeth Tietjens pointed out, M. creates images with the best of her peers, but knows that "a single image is not enough to make a poem." M. treats a wide range of everyday topics, and a number of the poems shed light on the complexity of woman's role in society. Her calm ironic voice registers clearly in such poems as "Hunger Inn," "The Marionette," and "The Sleeper."

The poems in The Long Leash (1928) demonstrate M.'s growth as a poet. The volume exhibits what Horace Gregory calls her "technique of restraint." The selections focus on the power of the creative woman to capture and examine intensely dramatic male-female relationships. The title poem, considered one of her best, treats the confidence with which reciprocated love enables the creative woman to face life's realities and fulfill her artistic potential. "A Sumerian Cycle" and "Hibernalia" illustrate the breathless emotion M. is capable of producing through understatement. M. succeeds best in the longer poems, where she develops and multiplies dramatic scenes.

M.'s artistic control and keen sensibility appear again in *Dinner Party* (1942), although this volume seems to lack the modernity of her other poetry of that period. As late as 1982, she was at work on a fourth volume of poetry.

Although M. is primarily a poet, she has also produced two successful novels: *Arden Acres* (1935) and *Morning in the Land* (1941). *Arden Acres* draws upon her observations of life in a suburban area outside Chicago during the Depression years. The narrator depicts the lives of the Chapin family, plagued by poverty and shocked by the father's murder. Although the emotional impact of the novel is effective, its real strength lies in the characterization of women from three generations —Gram, Loretta, and Joan—each of whom demonstrates unusual resilience and aptitude for survival.

Morning in the Land, based on the recollections of M.'s father, is a fictional account of an English immigrant family in Wisconsin between 1840 and 1861, when the son is about to leave for service in the Civil War. The novel centers on the frontier achievements of the protagonist, Dick Wentworth, but it also calls attention to the difficulties both Indian and white women endured within the male-oriented social structure.

Throughout the period in which her prose and poetry were being published, M. also gained a reputation as editor and critic. She began by editing the Chicago Art Institute *Bulletin* under the direction of Robert Harshe. Learning on the job, M. prepared catalogues for exhibits and published many articles describing various holdings of the institute. In 1927, she moved to *Poetry*, where over the next twenty years, under the tutelage of Harriet Monroe, she helped make *Poetry* a showcase for the best young American and British authors. M. filled various editorial posts and, in later years, served as a member of the advisory committee. During this period she wrote twenty-one articles and fifty book reviews. Her contributions ranged from caustically critical pieces such as "The Wrong-Headed Poets," "The Hungry Generations," and "Quality in Madness," to the gently appreciative tribute commemorating the death of Harriet Monroe. In her criticism, as in her poetry, M. displays a sharp eye for honesty of emotion and perfection of form.

WORKS: *A Prayer Rug* (1923). *The Long Leash* (1928). *Arden Acres* (1935). *Morning in the Land* (1941). *Dinner Party* (1942). *Paintings: An Introduction to Art* (with C. J. Bulliet, 1934). *History of Alpha Delta Pi* (1929).

LUCY M. FREIBERT

Katherine Sherwood Bonner McDowell

B. 26 Feb. 1849, Holly Springs, Mississippi; d. 22 July 1883, Holly Springs, Mississippi
Given name: Catherine Sherwood Bonner
Wrote under: Sherwood Bonner
D. of Charles and Mary Wilson Bonner; m. Edward McDowell, 1871

As a young teenager, M. experienced the harsh realities of the Civil War, when Union troops occupied Holly Springs and even her family home. M. also suffered personal losses during the war years, with the deaths of her youngest sister in 1863 and her mother in 1865. In 1871, M. married another native of Holly Springs; their only child was born in 1872. The McDowells separated in 1873; finally, M. established residence in Illinois and obtained a divorce in 1881.

In 1873, M. moved to Boston to pursue a career in writing; there Nahum Capen, who had published her first story in 1864, recommended her to Henry W. Longfellow, with whom she worked and established a close friendship. During 1876, M. sent from Europe a number of travel articles for the Memphis *Avalanche* and the Boston *Times*. Her only novel, *Like Unto Like,* was published in 1878.

M. returned to Holly Springs in the fall of 1878 and nursed her father and brother through fatal illnesses with yellow fever. In 1881, as her writing career was gaining momentum, M. learned that she had breast cancer. Until her death, she continued to write and to prepare her short stories, which had appeared in such magazines as *Lippincott's, Harper's Weekly,* and *Youth's Companion,* for publication in two volumes, *Dialect Tales* (1883) and *Suwanee River Tales* (1884).

M.'s Gran'Mammy tales present a distinctive element of southern life; M. creates one of the finest literary portraits of the black mammy, who sustained and taught the members of her white family. "Gran'Mammy's Last Gifts" (1875) may well be the first example of black dialect published in a northern magazine. The most successful story of the group is "Coming Home to Roost" (1884), in which M. perceptively treats slave superstition. The child narrator has a significant role in the story's action, for her chance remark causes Aunt Beckey to believe she has been bewitched. The story is humorous, yet suspense builds as Beckey weakens spiritually and physically. She is cured by the brash young medical student, Henry, who is able to deal with the "trickery" on Beckey's level. M.'s detailed and accurate descriptions are effective, as is the realistic attitude of the rest of the white family, who can view Henry's actions only as a "fraud."

A study of M.'s fiction does not reveal any sustained development from purely regional to more sophisticated realistic works. Even though she began writing as a teenager, M. wrote for too short a period of time to develop her talents fully. *Like Unto Like* was reviewed favorably, but M. is appreciated today chiefly for her short stories, especially for her realistic use of dialects—lower-class midwestern, southern mountain, and black—and her humor. Many readers also enjoy her characterizations and plots. She is important as a forerunner of later southern women writers like Flannery O'Connor and Eudora Welty.

WORKS: *Like Unto Like* (1878). *Dialect Tales* (1883). *Suwanee River Tales* (1884). *Gran'Mammy* (1927).

BIBLIOGRAPHY: Frank, W. L., *Sherwood Bonner* (1976). McAlexander, H. H., *The Prodigal Daughter: A Biography of Sherwood Bonner* (1981).

For articles in reference works, see: *AA. DAB*, VI, 2. *NAW* (article by L. J. Budd).

Other references: *ALR* (Winter 1972). *MissQ* (Winter 1963–64). *NMW* (Spring 1968; Spring 1969).

MARTHA E. COOK

Phyllis McGinley

B. 21 March 1905, Ontario, Oregon; d. 22 Feb. 1978, New York City
D. of Daniel and Julia McGinley; m. Charles L. Hayden, 1937

Beginning her career as a teacher in New Rochelle, New York, M. wrote poetry in her spare time. Her success in publishing it in magazines enabled her to give up teaching. To keep going, M. held various other positions, including poetry editor for *Town and Country* and copywriter for an advertising agency. According to an interview in *Newsweek*, she started writing in the style of Swinburne, but switched to light verse when she found out that that was what *The New Yorker* wanted from her.

Faithful to the eastern seaboard, although brought up in Colorado and Utah, she hymned New York to begin with and then, when she moved to Westchester County, the suburbs. In a volume of essays, *The Province of the Heart* (1959), she speaks out in favor of the Easterner and praises the village in which she lives for the way the neighbors love one another. A suburban housewife and mother was what she was and what she was happy to be.

Her first volume of verse, *On the Contrary*, was published in 1934. It contains mainly occasional verse—light comments on contemporary events. It was followed by *One More Manhattan* (1937), in which M. developed more of the tone we associate with her—light, astringent, and witty. There are times when M. comes close to Emily Dickinson, but she deliberately avoids total seriousness. *A Pocketful of Wry* (1940) contains a fair amount of political comment. In *Husbands Are Difficult; or, The Book of Oliver Ames* (1941), M. pokes fun at her husband, but her mockery is very mild and loving. In *Stones from a Glass House* (1946), she comments on the war but refuses to hate. *The Love Letters of Phyllis McGinley* (1954) shows her improving and maturing, and won several awards.

M. won the Pulitzer Prize in 1961 for her volume of collected poetry, *Times Three* (1960), which was prefaced by W. H. Auden. The collection starts with the poems of the 1950s and works backward through the 1940s and 1930s. Some of the most charming poems are about saints and reformers, bearing testimony to her religious convictions as a Catholic but also to her moderation and warmhearted reasonableness. In a second volume of essays, *Sixpence in Her Shoe* (1964), M. writes of the trials and rewards of a wife and mother, a state which she accounted woman's most honorable profession.

A Wreath of Christmas Legends (1967) and *Saint-Watching* (1969) show her more deeply entrenched in the Catholic faith. In *Saint-Watching*, M. deliberately brings out the human side of the saints, whom she treats as people endowed with a special form of genius; it is a delight to read and can be described without irony as heartwarming. M. also wrote a number of children's books, but these do not have the distinction of her writing for adults.

Staunchly traditional, M. believed in lifelong vows and in the special vocation of women to motherhood. She also believed in the reality of sin, but was sure it could be forgiven. For her, manners were morals. Her lightness of touch was always backed by an acute intelligence and the feeling that she had found her proper place. She was probably a happy woman.

WORKS: *Mary's Garden* (1927). *On the Contrary* (1934). *One More Manhattan* (1937). *A Pocketful of Wry* (1940). *Husbands Are Difficult; or, The Book of Oliver Ames* (1941). *The Horse Who Lived Upstairs* (1944). *The Plain Princess* (1945). *Stones from a Glass House* (1946). *All Around the Town* (1948). *A Name for Kitty* (1948). *The Most Wonderful Doll in the World* (1950). *Blunderbus* (1951). *The Horse Who Had His Picture in the Paper* (1951). *A Short Walk from the Station* (1951). *The Make-Believe Twins* (1953). *The Love Letters of Phyllis McGinley* (1954). *The Year without a Santa Claus* (1957). *Merry Christmas, Happy New Year* (1958). *Lucy McLockett* (1959). *The Province of the Heart* (1959). *Sugar and Spice: The ABC of Being a Girl* (1960). *Times Three: Selected Verse from Three Decades with Seventy New Poems* (1960). *Mince Pie and Mistletoe* (1961). *The B Book* (1962). *Boys Are Awful* (1962). *A Girl and Her Room* (1963). *How Mrs. Santa Claus Saved Christmas* (1963). *Sixpence in Her Shoe* (1964). *Wonderful Time* (1966). *A Wreath of Christmas Legends* (1967). *Wonders and Surprises* (1968). *Saint-Watching* (1969). *Confessions of a Reluctant Optimist* (1973).

BIBLIOGRAPHY: Auden, W. H., Foreword to *Times Three* by P. McGinley (1960).

For articles in reference works, see: *CB* (Nov. 1961). *20thCAS*.

Other references: *Commonweal* (9 Dec. 1960). *Newsweek* (26 Sept. 1960). *SatR* (10 Dec. 1960).

BARBARA J. BUCKNALL

Sister Madeleva

B. 24 May 1877, Cumberland, Wisconsin; d. 25 July 1964, Boston, Massachusetts
Given name: Mary Evaline Wolff
D. of August and Lucy Arntz Wolff

The daughter of a German-born harness maker and a former teacher, M. grew up in a mill town in rural Wisconsin. After a year at the University of Wisconsin, M. transferred to St. Mary's College at Notre Dame, Indiana, from which she graduated in 1909. She received an M.A. from the University of Notre Dame and a Ph.D. in English from the University of California. By 1908, she had joined the Congregation of the Holy Cross which conducts St. Mary's, taking the name Sister Mary Madeleva, and her entire life was devoted to educating women. From 1934 to 1961, M. served as president of St. Mary's; during this time she was responsible for the founding of the first American Catholic graduate school of theology for the laity. From 1942–48 she was president of the Catholic Poetry Society of America.

Her prose works include essays and addresses on education as well as literary criticism. M.'s best-known study is "Chaucer's Nuns" (1925), in which she interprets details of the portrait of the prioress in the prologue to the *Canterbury Tales* by observing her in the context of religious life.

With the publication of *Knights Errant, and Other Poems* (1923), M. became the first of the modern "nun-poets"—a peculiarly American phenomenon.

Most of M.'s poems are short lyrics, usually under twenty lines. M.'s only leisure, she explained, came in recuperating from illnesses; other moments were snatched between tasks, in walking from building to building, or during nights of insomnia.

Only occasionally do her poems focus on secular themes: her visits to Oxford and the Holy Land, glimpses of nature, or literary interests. "Marginalium," for example, protests the death of the Lady of Shalott. The great bulk of M.'s work deals with religious experience.

M.'s religious poetry is always personal and devotional, never didactic or public. By dealing with her own experience, M. avoids the pious and the platitudinous. Her verse abounds in nature imagery of an amiable sort. "My Windows," from *Penelope, and Other Poems* (1927), describes two "wonder-windows": One lets in "tranquillity and noon . . . magic and the moon"; the other looks on a garden with "a sudden rose, / A poppy's flame. . . ." It is through these windows that the poet sees God. Here as always M.'s theme is constant love and serene beauty; images of horror or despair are absent.

Even the tone of religious longing is usually carefully modulated. In "Petals and Wings," from *Four Girls, and Other Poems* (1941), field flowers—"Silent, at peace, and beautiful"—are contrasted with "wild, unlettered birds, / Song-silver things." The poet's question as to whether "petalled peace" or "wilding flight / Into the sun" is ultimately preferable remains unanswered, except in the hidden mind of God.

The mystical "The King's Secret" (in *Penelope*), generally recognized as M.'s best poem, is unlike almost all her other work. In this poem, her longest, M. abandons her usual reticence and in explicitly erotic language, inspired by and even echoing the Song of Songs, speaks ecstatically of union with "this King Who is God and your Lover." Some critics, presumably not recognizing the biblical precedent, were critical of this breach of nunly decorum, and the poem was not included in *Selected Poems* (1939). In her later published work M. returned to the ascetic restraint of her first volume.

WORKS: *Knights Errant, and Other Poems* (1923). *Chaucer's Nuns, and Other Essays* (1925). *Pearl—A Study in Spiritual Dryness* (1925). *Penelope, and Other Poems* (1927). *A Question of Lovers, and Other Poems* (1935). *The Happy Christmas Wind, and Other Poems* (1936). *Christmas Eve, and Other Poems* (1938). *Gates, and Other Poems* (1938). *Selected Poems* (1939). *Four Girls, and Other Poems* (1941). *Addressed to Youth* (1944). *A Song of Bedlam Inn, and Other Poems* (1946). *Collected Poems* (1947). *A Lost Language, and Other Essays on Chaucer* (1951). *American Twelfth Night, and Other Poems* (1955). *The Four Last Things* (1959). *My First Seventy Years* (1959). *Conversations with Cassandra* (1961). *A Child Asks for a Star* (1964).

BIBLIOGRAPHY: For articles in reference works, see: *CB* (1942; 1964). *NCAB*, 51. *20thCA*. *20thCAS*.

Other references: *America* (57, 1937; 58, 1938). *Catholic Library World* (12, 1940). *Commonweal* (63, 1956). *Spirit* (6, 1939; 15, 1948). *Thought* (23, 1948).

ARLENE ANDERSON SWIDLER

Theresa Serber Malkiel

B. 1 May 1874, Bar, Russia; d. 17 Nov. 1949, New York City
M. Leon A. Malkiel, 1900

M. emigrated to the U.S. with her family in 1891. Her political activity began when she became a member of the Russian Workingmen's Club. In 1892, she helped organize the Woman's Infant Cloak Maker's Union, was elected its first president, and served as its delegate to the Knights of Labor. In 1893, she joined the Socialist Labor Party and was a delegate to the first convention of the Socialist Trade and Labor Alliance in New York City. M. split from the Socialist Labor Party in 1899 and joined the Socialist Party, in which she continued to be active for many years. M.'s interest in the relationship between feminism and socialism became central to her political work in 1907 when she helped organize the Women's Progressive Society of Yonkers, New York. When a vacancy occurred in the National Woman's Committee, she was elected a member by the national committee of the Socialist Party.

In addition to extensive labor-union organizing throughout the northeast and midwest, M. was an ardent champion of "women's issues." She wrote of the coming "free woman," whose goals could be realized only within the framework of a socialist future. Similarly, M. disagreed with party members who claimed that feminism detracted from the class struggle; to M., the woman question was an important key to the emancipation of all humanity. Throughout her career, M. wrote extensively in such party-affiliated journals as *Socialist Woman, Progressive Woman,* and *Coming Nation* and such periodicals as New York *Call,* Chicago *Daily Socialist,* and *Daily Forward* (New York). She also edited a woman's column in the *Jewish Daily News* (New York).

Both *Woman of Yesterday and Today* (1915) and *Woman and Freedom* (1915) vigorously argue the implicit relationship and politically necessary connection between feminist and socialist goals. Both works establish the historical connections between the women's rights movement and the entrance of women into the wage-earning labor force. In

Woman of Yesterday and Today, M. writes a brief history of the changing economic status of American women since the revolutionary war, focusing on how working conditions and experiences create a new self-definition for women and a concomitant desire for expanded rights. In *Woman and Freedom*, M. links this new consciousness with the history of political advancement of all working people. M. also underscores the double oppression of the working woman: "Under the present system the working man has only one master—his employer, the workingwoman must bow to the will of husband as well." Both pamphlets stress the importance of a direct and personal involvement in political activity on the part of American women: "She who would be free must herself strike the blow."

In *Diary of a Shirtwaist Striker* (1910), a fictionalized account of the New York shirtwaist maker's strike, M. dramatizes both the obstacles faced and the triumphs attained through direct and personal political activism. Written from the point of view of a native-born American woman who works not for survival but for extra money, the novel depicts the heroine's conversion, first to the immediate goals of the strike and eventually to the wider goals of the Socialist Party. It provides an excellent introduction to many of the problems that were central to the unionization of women during the early years of the 20th c.: the tensions between native and immigrant workers, the hostility of male trade unions, the class bias of the Women's Trade Union League, and the questions about "woman's place" raised by parents and lovers when their daughters and fiancées were on picket lines. M.'s main focus is on the self-respect, comradeship, and capabilities that develop among young women as a result of their strike experiences. Her heroine becomes a vividly portrayed mouthpiece for M.'s vision of the woman of the future, a woman for whom the goals of feminism and socialism have become inseparable.

The resurgence of attention paid to the connection between issues of sex and class has generated a new interest in M.'s writings. Her tireless investigation of the relationship between a woman's personal and political self-definition will strike many readers as surprisingly modern. *Diary of a Shirtwaist Striker* should prove of invaluable interest to any reader interested in questions about the relationship between social movements and literary representation.

WORKS: *Diary of a Shirtwaist Striker* (1910). *Woman and Freedom* (1915). *Woman of Yesterday and Today* (1915).

BIBLIOGRAPHY: Blake, F., *The Strike in the American Novel* (1972). Buhle, M. J., "Feminism and Socialism in the United States, 1820–1920" (Ph.D. diss., Univ. of Wisconsin, 1974). Dancis, B., "Socialism and Women in the United States, 1900–1917," in *Socialist Revolution* (1976). Hill, V., "Strategy and Breadth: The Socialist-Feminist in American Fiction" (Ph.D. diss., SUNY at Buffalo, 1979). Maglin, N., "Rebel Women Writers, 1894–1925" (Ph.D. diss., Union Graduate School, 1975).

Other references: *Progressive Woman* (May 1909).

VICKI LYNN HILL

Catherine Marshall

B. 27 Sept. 1914, Johnson City, Tennessee; d. March 1983
D. of John Ambrose and Leonora Whitaker Wood; m. Peter Marshall, 1936;
  m. Leonard Earle LeSourd, 1959

M.'s father was a pastor of a Presbyterian church in Canton, Mississippi, and later in Keyser, West Virginia. M. earned a B.A. in history from Agnes Scott College. Her first husband was already a well-known pastor in Atlanta when they were married. In 1937, they moved to the New York Avenue Church in Washington, D.C., and in 1946 Peter became chaplain of the U.S. Senate. After her husband's death in 1949, M. became an editor and writer in order to support herself and her son. Her second husband was editor of *Guideposts*, an inspirational magazine that has published many of M.'s shorter articles. M. was woman's editor of the *Christian Herald* from 1958 to 1960, when she became a roving editor for *Guideposts*.

In 1953, M. was named "Woman of the Year" in the field of literature by the Women's National Press Club. She is a member of Phi Beta Kappa, has served Agnes Scott College as a trustee, and has received honorary doctorates from Cedar Crest College and Taylor University.

M.'s first independent work was editing a few of Marshall's sermons and prayers, which were published as *Mr. Jones, Meet the Master* (1949). *Mr. Jones* stayed on the nonfiction best-seller list for almost a year and led to the contract for her most important work, *A Man Called Peter* (1951), a bestseller for many years.

MARSHALL, CATHERINE □ 29

A Man Called Peter has been categorized as "a biography, an auto-biography-biography, a fairy story with a sad ending, a Horatio Alger novel, a how-to book on successful marriage, and a straight-from-the-shoulder devotional on God." Whatever its genre, this book sold over four million copies during its first twenty years and is still selling well. With M. assisting in production, it was made into a successful movie (1955), and it has been translated into Dutch, printed in a large-print edition, and recorded for the blind.

This "autobiography-biography" is, of course, the story of Peter Marshall, the Scotsman who grew up in poverty, emigrated to America, and became one of the most widely admired preachers of the 20th c. The prose is clear, concise, concrete; and the book is saved from excessive sentiment by its simple sincerity, honesty, and forthrightness.

M.'s novel, *Christy* (1967), features a protagonist whose fortitude grows from her faith, much as Marshall's does in *A Man Called Peter*. Based on the experiences of the author's mother, *Christy* is the story of a nineteen-year-old woman who, in 1912, leaves her comfortable home to spend a year teaching in the Smoky Mountains of Tennessee. The clear style and obvious sincerity that mark all of M.'s works enable this long novel to maintain its charm, even though it sometimes moves very slowly.

M. has also written or edited fourteen other book-length works, including several children's books, and many articles for popular and religious magazines. Her latest publication, *The Helper* (1978), is a series of forty devotionals about the Holy Spirit, which M. says "has been written out of my own spiritual need to speak to those who share my longing for thirst-quenching quaffs of the Living Water." Probably everything M. has ever published could be prefaced by those words.

WORKS: *The Mystery of the Ages* (with P. Marshall, 1944). *Mr. Jones, Meet the Master: Sermons and Prayers of Peter Marshall, D.D.* (edited by Marshall, 1949; rev. ed., 1950). *A Man Called Peter: The Story of Peter Marshall* (1951; film version, 1955). *Let's Keep Christmas* by P. Marshall (introduction by Marshall, 1953). *God Loves You: Our Family's Favorite Stories and Prayers* (with P. Marshall, 1953; rev. ed., 1967). *The Prayers of Peter Marshall* (edited by Marshall, 1954). *Friends with God: Stories and Prayers of the Marshall Family* (1956). *The Heart of Peter Marshall's Faith: Two Inspirational Messages from "Mr. Jones, Meet the Master"* (introduction by Marshall, 1956). *To Live Again* (1957). *The First Easter* (by P. Marshall, edited and introduction by Marshall, 1959). *John Doe, Disciple: Sermons for the Young in Spirit* (by P. Marshall, edited and introduction by Marshall, 1963). *Beyond Ourselves* (1966). *Christy* (1967). *Claiming God's Promises:*

Selections from "Guideposts" by Catherine Marshall and Others (1973). *Something More: In Search of a Deeper Faith* (1974). *Adventures in Prayer* (1975). *The Helper* (with P. Marshall, 1978). *My Personal Prayer Diary* (with E. LeSourd, 1979). *Meeting God at Every Turn* (1980).

BIBLIOGRAPHY: Davis, E. L., *Fathers of America: Our Heritage of Faith* (1958). Hosier, H. K., *Profiles: People Who Are Helping to Change the World* (1977).
    For articles in reference works, see: *CA* (1976). *Something about the Author*, Ed. A. Commire (1971).
    Other references: *Newsweek* (4 April 1956). *PW* (18 Oct. 1971). *SatR* (10 April 1954).

PEGGY SKAGGS

Paule Marshall

B. 9 April 1929, Brooklyn, New York
D. of Samuel and Ada Burke; m. Kenneth E. Marshall, 1957; m. Nourry Menard, 1970

A first-generation American born of Barbadian parents, M. spent her childhood in Brooklyn. At the age of nine, she visited the native land of her parents and discovered for herself the quality of life peculiar to that tropical island. After writing a series of poems reflecting her impressions, M. began a long period of reading. She graduated Phi Beta Kappa from Brooklyn College (1953) and attended Hunter College (1955) for postgraduate study.

M. has worked in libraries and, as a staff writer for *Our World* magazine, has traveled on assignment to Brazil and the West Indies. She has lectured at several colleges and universities within the U.S. and abroad and has contributed short stories and articles to various magazines and anthologies. M. has been the recipient of several awards and grants.

In her first novel, *Brown Girl, Brownstones* (1959), M. explores the coming of age of Selina Boyce and the struggle for survival of a black immigrant family and community. Divided into four sections, the novel functions on several imaginative levels and devotes some attention to the ramifications of power as experienced by the dawning political consciousness of a small black community.

M.'s consistent use of imagery and symbolism, and her concise, rhythmic, and passionate style dramatically define and technically underscore themes of rebirth and self-definition. The end result is a picture of a world not blurred by racial bitterness, but sharply focused in its unabashed honesty and deliberate confrontation of Western cultural values.

Her language is strikingly beautiful and powerfully effective, capturing the essence of black language as a weapon of survival and revealing how spoken communication can itself be a form of art. M. adopts and adapts the West Indian dialect, fusing it with biblical and literary allusions to create a language that compels imaginative associations and entertains with the sheer delight of sound.

Soul Clap Hands and Sing (1961), a collection of short stories, borows its title from Yeats's "Sailing to Byzantium." Thematic connections are obvious as we read the accounts of four men of different national origins experiencing the inevitable decline of age.

Caught up in the Western credo of amassing wealth and prestige, the characters have developed a hardened exterior impervious to meaningful human relationships. When the submerged need for love and acceptance emerges, they can only respond by reaching out to the young. That itself remains a selfish motivation, and the implications of their wasted lives are recognized too late. Unable to translate harsh reality into lyrical song, their dying moments sound the notes of lamentation and doom, as Marcia Keiz observes in *Negro American Literature Forum*.

The Chosen Place, the Timeless People (1969) is a massive epic novel recapitulating and expanding upon themes developed in earlier works. The main story line concerns a small group of Americans who travel to the Caribbean island of Bournehills. Sponsored by a philanthropic foundation, they intend to design a project to assist an "underdeveloped" but curiously unified people. Juxtapositions and correspondences give the novel its texture, but the cohesive element is achieved through the paradoxical characterization of the native woman Merle Kinbona. With her, we explore the political, sociological, and psychological dimensions of power not only as it influences racial and sexual roles, but also as it shapes cultural patterns and assumptions.

Never sacrificing art to propaganda, M. sustains full human portraiture within a racially turgid atmosphere and concludes with the vision of a world not solely defined by territorial boundaries or even by cultural distinctions.

M. has exceptional talent born of solid scholarship and careful craftsmanship. By choosing to depict West Indian-American culture, M. makes a valuable contribution toward helping contemporary society understand the multidimensional aspects of the black experience.

WORKS: *Brown Girl, Brownstones* (1959; dramatization by CBS Television Workshop, 1960). *Soul Clap Hands and Sing* (1961). *The Chosen Place, the Timeless People* (1969).

BIBLIOGRAPHY: For articles in reference works, see: *Black American Writers Past and Present,* T. Rush, C. Myers, and E. Arata (1975). *Contemporary Novelists,* Ed. J. Vinson (1976).
   Other references: *CLAJ* 16 (1972). *Encore American and Worldwide News* (23 June 1975). *Journal of Black Studies* 1 (1970). *Negro American Literature Forum* 9 (1975). Trinidad *Guardian* (12 Sept. 1962).

DOROTHY L. DENNISTON

Margaret Mead

B. 16 Dec. 1901, Philadelphia, Pennsylvania; d. 15 Nov. 1978, New York City
D. of Edward Sherwood and Emily Fogg Mead; m. Luther Cressman, 1923;
m. Reo Fortune, 1928; m. Gregory Bateson, 1935

M. was the eldest of five children. Her father was a professor at the Wharton School of Finance and Commerce. She was educated informally at home by her grandmother until high school. After a disappointing year at DePauw University, M. transferred to Barnard College, where she studied anthropology under Franz Boas and Ruth Benedict (B.A. 1923). Her Ph.D. is from Columbia University (1929). M. held almost forty positions, including professor of anthropology at Columbia. She was the recipient of many honorary degrees and some thirty-five awards. M. was married three times and was the mother of one daughter.

M.'s long and productive career as an author-anthropologist blossomed with the publication of her first and most popular book, *Coming of Age in Samoa* (1928). It has since been translated into seven languages and has reappeared in seven editions. The book is based on M.'s first field-work, undertaken at the age of twenty-three, in which she set out to discover whether the problems that trouble American adolescents are due to the biological nature of adolescence or to culturally learned attitudes. Her study of the individual within a culture was unique. M. vividly de-

scribes the basic character of Samoan life and how attitudes and behavior are shaped from birth to maturity. The results of her nine months
of work showed that much of individual behavior is culturally learned.
Stripped of the technical jargon of anthropology, M.'s clear presenta-
tions of life in Samoa and her answers to a fascinating anthropological
question have reached a wide and enthusiastic audience.

Sex and Temperament in Three Primitive Societies (1935), which
has been translated into twelve languages, was the outcome of fieldwork
in three villages in New Guinea. When going into the field in 1931, M.'s
original intentions were to study the cultural conditioning of the personalities of the two sexes. After working for two years in three different
villages, M. discovered that her findings revealed more about differences
in human temperament than about gender. Among the Mountain Arapesh, both men and women are gentle and maternal; among the Mun-
dugumor, both sexes are fierce and virile; and among the Tchambuli, the
roles of men and women are reversed from our traditional roles. Thus,
gender is only one of the ways in which a society can group its social
attitude toward temperament.

In 1949, M. wrote *Male and Female: A Study of the Sexes in a Changing
World*. It is based on fourteen years of fieldwork in seven different societies, and was written at a time when traditional roles of male and female were undergoing scrutiny in our society. M. discusses ways in which
physical similarities and differences are the basis on which we learn
about our own sex and our relationship to the other sex. M. includes a
discussion of how societies develop myths to answer the questions about
differences between men and women, and about how children grow up
to be a member of one or the other group. In the final section M. brings
her knowledge back to America and discusses ways in which we can
make improvements in our society.

Culture and Commitment: A Study of the Generation Gap, written in
1970 and revised extensively in 1978, is written in the belief that if we
know and understand enough, our knowledge will breed optimistic and
constructive thinking. M. feels that we are experiencing an irreversible
evolutionary change brought about by modern technology, population
explosion, and destruction of the natural environment, and that it is a
change of which, for the first time in human history, we have a full
awareness.

M.'s autobiography, *Blackberry Winter: My Earlier Years* (1972), is
perhaps her most interesting book, providing the reader with some insight into the person behind the prolific and influential personality. In

the first and third sections, M. writes about her family life, first from her early point of view as a granddaughter and then from her later view as a grandmother. The middle section is devoted to her field experiences.

M.'s contributions as an anthropologist have been unparalleled. She taught us about the behavior of other human beings—human beings like ourselves in everything but their culture—and in so doing gave us a better understanding of ourselves within a broad perspective. M. applied the results of her studies in primitive cultures to the questions of the day in our rapidly changing world. With the insight and knowledge she gained as a granddaughter and a grandmother, M. was able to span the gaps between the generations to which she spoke. As a person who watched children from isolated primitive societies grow up into a modern world, M. gained and shared a knowledge of cultural change and continuity. M. was a person who made her home the entire world and who communicated what she learned in such a felicitous, direct, and vivid style that people everywhere have benefited from her insights.

WORKS: *Coming of Age in Samoa: A Psychological Study of Primitive Youth for Western Civilization* (1928). *An Inquiry into the Question of Cultural Stability in Polynesia* (1928). *Growing Up in New Guinea: A Comparative Study of Primitive Education* (1930). *Social Organization of Manu'a* (1930). *The Changing Culture of an Indian Tribe* (1932). *Kinship in the Admiralty Islands* (1934). *Sex and Temperament in Three Primitive Societies* (1935). *Cooperation and Competition among Primitive Peoples* (edited by Mead, 1937). *The Mountain Arapesh* (Vol. 1, *An Importing Culture*, 1938; Vol. 2, *Supernaturalism*, 1940; Vol. 3, *Socio-Economic Life*, 1947; Vol. 4, *Diary of Events in Alitoa*, 1947; Vol. 5, *The Record of Unabelin with Rorschach Analysis*, 1949). *From the South Seas: Studies in Adolescence and Sex in Primitive Societies* (1939). *And Keep Your Powder Dry: An Anthropologist Looks at America* (1942). *Balinese Character: A Photographic Analysis* (with G. Bateson, 1942). *Male and Female: A Study of the Sexes in a Changing World* (1949). *Growth and Culture: A Photographic Study of Balinese Childhood* (with F. C. MacGregor, 1951). *The School in American Culture* (1951). *Soviet Attitudes toward Authority* (1951). *Cultural Patterns and Technical Change: A Manual Prepared by the World Federation for Mental Health* (edited by Mead, 1953). *Primitive Heritage: An Anthropological Anthology* (edited by Mead, with N. Calas, 1953). *The Study of Culture at a Distance* (edited by Mead, with R. Metraux, 1953). *Themes in French Culture: A Preface to a Study of French Community* (with R. Metraux, 1954). *Childhood in Contemporary Cultures* (edited by Mead, with M. Wolfenstein, 1955). *New Lives for Old: Cultural Transformation—Manus, 1928–1953* (1956). *An Anthropologist at Work: Writings of Ruth Benedict* (1959). *People and Places* (1959). *The Golden Age of American Anthropology* (edited by Mead, with R. L. Bunzel, 1960). *Anthropology, a Human Science: Selected Papers 1939–1960* (1964). *Continuities in Cultural Evolution* (1964). *American Women* (edited by Mead, with F. B. Kaplan, 1965). *Anthropologists and What They Do* (1965). *Family* (with K. Heyman, 1965). *The Wagon and the Star: A Study of American Community Initiative* (with M. Brown, 1966). *Science and the Concept of Race* (edited by Mead, with T. Dobzhansky, E. Tobach, and R. E. Light, 1968). *The Small Conference: An Innovation in Communication* (with P. Byers, 1968). *Culture and Commitment: A Study of the Generation Gap* (1970; rev. ed., 1978). *A Way of Seeing* (edited by Mead, with R. Metraux, 1970). *A Rap on Race* (with J. Baldwin, 1971). *Blackberry Winter: My Earlier Years* (1972). *To Love or to Perish: The Technological Crisis and the Churches* (edited by Mead et al., 1972). *Twentieth Century Faith: Hope and Survival* (1972). *Ruth Benedict: A Biography* (1974). *World Enough: Rethinking the Future* (with K. Heyman, 1975). *The Atmosphere: Endangered and Endangering* (edited by Mead, with W. W. Kellogg, 1977). *Letters from the Field, 1925–1975* (1977). *Aspects of the Present* (with R. Metraux, 1980).

BIBLIOGRAPHY: Cottler, J., and H. Jaffe, in *More Heroes of Civilization* (1969). Gordan, J., ed., *Margaret Mead: The Complete Bibliography 1925–1975* (1976). Moss, A., *Shaping a New World: Margaret Mead* (1963). Rossi, A. S., *The Feminist Papers from Adams to de Beauvoir* (1973). Stoddard, H., in *Famous American Women* (1970). Yost, E., in *American Women of Science* (1955).

For articles in reference works, see: *Britannica Yearbook of Science and the Future* (1971). *NCAB*, 1. *20thCA. 20thCAS.*

Other references: *Louisiana Academy of Sciences Proceedings* 31 (1968). *New York Magazine* (13 Aug. 1973). *NY* 97 (1961). *NYTMag* (26 April 1970). *SatR* 4 (1977). *Science* 184 (1974). *Science Year: The World Book Science Annual* (1968).

MIRIAM KAHN

Cornelia Lynde Meigs

B. 6 Dec. 1884, Rock Island, Illinois; d. 10 Sept. 1973, Hartford County, Maryland
Wrote under: Adair Aldon, Cornelia Meigs
D. of Montgomery and Grace Lynde Meigs

The strong sense of family tradition that pervades much of M.'s writing for young people comes naturally from her own appreciation of kinship and its values. A descendant of Commodore John Rogers of Revolutionary fame, M. grew up in a close-knit family on the Mississippi, where her father was a government engineer.

Graduating from Bryn Mawr College in 1907, M. taught in Davenport, Iowa (1912–1913), where she began "to tell stories to the younger children . . . finding quickly just what sort they liked and what they would have none of." M.'s first book of short stories, *The Kingdom of the Winding Road* (1915), resulted from this experience. Novels, two plays (*The Steadfast Princess* won the Drama League prize in 1915), and four pseudonymous adventure stories followed during the next two decades.

From 1932 to 1950 M. taught English at Bryn Mawr. M.'s work as a literary scholar culminated in her editing and contributing to the landmark book *A Critical History of Children's Literature* (1953; rev. ed., 1969). Ann Pellowski refers to it as "a definitive survey of the literature," and Frances Sayers says that M.'s section "The Roots of the Past" has the "storyteller's narrative pace, the novelist's eye for endearing detail, and the scholar's control of historic perspective."

These talents are evident in most of the fiction, history, and biography that M. wrote. Her historical romances, beginning with *Master Simon's Garden* (1916), are compelling narratives. This first novel is suitable for an adolescent audience and traces the vicissitudes and final triumph of puritan Master Simon's family and garden ("a symbol of tolerance and understanding" according to Constantine Georgiou) through several generations. The sense of continuity of family ideals is strong, and the many characters are clearly individualized.

Invincible Louisa: The Story of the Author of Little Women (1933) won the Newbery Medal in 1934. "A thoroughly readable and satisfactory life," Bertha Miller called this labor of scholarship and love. In her acceptance paper for the prize, M. stated that she read Alcott's letters and journals "over and over again through my growing years" and in times of difficulty for "the stimulation of courage" they brought. Her biography carries this same "stimulation of courage," as does her last major work, *Jane Addams: Pioneer for Social Justice* (1970), another excellent biography of a strong woman.

M.'s young heroines, although brave and sensible, often play a comparatively passive role, but of the two real-life models that M. chose for her biographies, each, like Alcott, "gallantly went her own way and won her own triumph." M.'s talents seem fully realized only in her biographies. However, her books, of whatever type, have, as Bertha Miller notes, "given expression to America's best in thought, feeling and action."

WORKS: *The Kingdom of the Winding Road* (1915). *Master Simon's Garden* (1916). *The Steadfast Princess* (1916). *The Island of Appledore* (1917).

The Pirate of Jasper Peak (1918). *The Pool of Stars* (1919). *At the Sign of the Heroes* (1920). *The Windy Hill* (1921). *Helga and the White Peacock* (1922). *The Hill of Adventure* (1922). *The New Moon: The Story of Dick Martin's Courage, His Silver Sixpence, and His Friends in the New World* (1924). *Rain on the Roof* (1925). *As the Crow Flies* (1927). *The Trade Wind* (1927). *Clearing Weather* (1928). *The Wonderful Locomotive* (1928). *The Crooked Apple Tree* (1929). *The Willow Whistle* (1931). *Swift Rivers* (1932). *Invincible Louisa: The Story of the Author of Little Women* (1933). *Wind in the Chimney* (1934). *The Covered Bridge* (1936). *Young Americans: How History Looked to Them While It Was in the Making* (1936). *Railroad West* (1937). *The Scarlet Oak* (1938). *Call of the Mountain* (1940). *Mother Makes Christmas* (1940). *Vanished Island* (1941). *Mounted Messenger* (1943). *The Two Arrows* (1949). *The Violent Men: A Study of Human Relations in the First American Congress* (1949). *The Dutch Colt* (1952). *A Critical History of Children's Literature: A Survey of Children's Books in English from Earliest Times to the Present* (edited by Meigs, 1953; rev. ed., 1969). *Fair Wind to Virginia* (1955). *What Makes a College? A History of Bryn Mawr* (1956). *Wild Geese Flying* (1957). *Saint John's Church, Havre de Grace, Md. 1809–1959* (1959). *Mystery at the Red House* (1961). *The Great Design: Men and Events in the United Nations from 1945 to 1963* (1964). *Glimpses of Louisa: A Centennial Sampling of the Best Short Stories* (edited by Meigs, 1968). *Jane Addams: Pioneer for Social Justice* (1970). *Louisa M. Alcott and the American Family Story* (1971).

BIBLIOGRAPHY: Georgiou, C., *Children and Their Literature* (1969). Pellowski, A., *The World of Children's Literature* (1968).

For articles in reference works, see: *CA*, 9–12 (1974); 45–48 (1974). *Junior Book of Authors*, Eds. S. J. Kunitz and H. Haycraft (1934; 1951). *Newbery Medal Books, 1922–1955*, Eds. B. M. Miller and E. W. Field (1955).

Other references: *Horn Book* (Sept. 1944). *LJ* (July 1934). *PW* (30 June 1934; 25 April 1936).

CELIA CATLETT ANDERSON

Marguerite Merington

B. ca. 1860, Stoke Newington, England; d. 19 May 1951, New York City
D. of Richard Whiskin Crawford Merington

Although born in England, M. spent most of her life in America after her father emigrated because of business interests. M. was teaching Greek at the Normal College in New York City when she wrote her most famous work, *Captain Lettarblair*, for the prominent actor E. H. Sothern.

The play was produced by Daniel Frohman at the Lyceum Theatre in 1891 and revived during the next two seasons.

Captain Lettarblair Litton of the Irish Fusilliers has been scrimping to pay off a debt to clear the name of his wronged, deceased father. He hopes to marry Fanny Hadden. So strongly does she desire a proposal from him that she contrives to send him a large sum of money as though it came from his estate. However, in order to do so, she must press for payment of an old debt owed to her estate, not realizing that the debtor is Lettarblair himself.

The captain is forced to sell all his possessions, including his mare, and to renounce hope of marrying Fanny. The check that Fanny sends him is stolen from the mail pouch by the villainous Merivale, a rival for Fanny's hand, who leads her to believe that Lettarblair has squandered the money. By such complications is the flimsy plot sustained until the lovers are united in act 3. It is further buoyed up by moments of farcical business, such as the scene in which Lettarblair negotiates a sale through the window of his quarters while his valet tries to hold the door against the collection agent, or the scene in which Fanny is stranded in Lettarblair's room with her skirt caught in the door and the knob fallen off out of reach.

The popularity of *Captain Lettarblair* may be attributed to the performance of Sothern. To the modern reader, the play is belabored and contrived, but it won critical acclaim from the *New York Times*: "Miss M. has a knack of devising pictures which is a valuable theatrical gift, and she writes dialogue with great facility. Some of the Hibernicisms of the hero are delightful." In 1906, it was published in an elaborate book edition with numerous photographs from the production.

Love Finds the Way (1898) was M.'s last professionally produced play and the one M. considered her best. Thereafter, M. turned to writing mostly fairy-tale plays for young children and literary adaptations and historical dramas for high-school students. M.'s sincere dedication to these audiences is evident in her article "The Theatre for Everybody" in *The World's Work* (December 1910): "I regard the stage, rightly employed, as part of a broad general training. To language it is invaluable —and what trade is there, what calling, in which language is not a tool? . . . The theatre was part of the national life of the Greeks in their civilization's heyday—and there are matters in which we have yet to outstrip the wisdom of the Greeks."

Although M.'s children's plays now seem dated, they were popular in their time. *Snow White* (1905), written for the dramatic department of the Hebrew Educational Alliance, drew hundreds of children to each Sunday matinee.

In addition to M.'s several collections of fairy-tale plays and plays for holidays, one collection of particular interest is her *Picture Plays* (1911). These are very short one-act plays based upon famous paintings: *The Last Sitting* (da Vinci's "Mona Lisa"), *A Salon Carré Fantasy* (Titian's "Man with the Glove"), *His Mother's Face* (Watteau's "Une Fête champêtre"), and so forth. *Scribner's* magazine published many of M.'s sonnets, which, she later told an interviewer, one editor liked to call "Merington's 57 Varieties of Love, Life, and Death."

M. had met Elizabeth Bacon Custer, the widow of General George A. Custer, in 1894. They became close friends, and when Mrs. Custer died, M. was her literary executor. M.'s only major nondramatic work was an edition of the letters of General Custer and his wife, published in 1950. At the time of M.'s death, she was working on a book of recollections of the pianist Paderewski.

The success of M.'s fifty-nine-year career as a writer may be attributed to the dedication and sincerity of purpose by which she labored at her craft.

WORKS: *Captain Lettarblair* (1891). *Oh, Belinda* (1892). *Goodbye* (1893). *An Everyday Man* (1895). *Daphne; or, The Pipes of Arcadia* (1896). *Bonnie Prince Charlie* (1897). *Love Finds the Way* (1898). *Old Orchard* (1900). *The Gibson Play* (1901). *Cranford* (1905). *The Lady in the Adjoining Room* (1905). *Snow White* (1905). *The Turn of the Tide* (1905). *Scarlet of the Mounted* (1906). *The Vicar of Wakefield* (1909). *Holiday Plays* (1910). *Picture Plays* (1911). *The Elopers* (1913). *Festival Plays* (1913). *More Fairy-Tale Plays* (1917). *A Dish o' Tea Delayed* (1937). *Booth Episodes* (1944). *The Custer Story: The Life and Intimate Letters of General George A. Custer and His Wife Elizabeth* (1950).

Ten undated plays in typewritten manuscripts are at the New York Public Library.

BIBLIOGRAPHY: *NYT* (23 Oct. 1891; 21 May 1951). *NYTBR* (12 Feb. 1950). *Theatre Magazine* 6 (Oct. 1906).

FELICIA HARDISON LONDRÉ

Elizabeth Avery Meriwether

B. 19 Jan. 1824, Bolivar, Tennessee; d. ?1917, Memphis, Tennessee
Wrote under: George Edmunds, Elizabeth Avery Meriwether
D. of Nathan and Rebecca Avery; m. Minor Meriwether, 1850

In her autobiography, M. reveals little about her childhood other than to note that her family moved from Bolivar to Memphis when she was eleven. It is obvious, however, that M. was well educated, for after the death of her parents, she became a teacher. When the Civil War began, her husband, a civil engineer, joined the army, leaving M. in Memphis. The city was occupied by the Union army in 1862, and after several unpleasant encounters with Northern generals, M. decided to seek refuge in Alabama.

While in Tuscaloosa, M. resumed her childhood pastime of writing. She won a competition sponsored by the Selma *Daily Mississippian* offering $500 for the best story dealing with the war. "The Refugee" is based partly on her own experiences traveling through Alabama and Tennessee. Encouraged by this success, M. wrote "The Yankee Spy," which the newspaper planned to publish as a book. However, when the Confederacy fell, these plans were abandoned.

After the war, M. combined writing with an interest in social reform. In 1872, she edited and published a weekly newspaper, *The Tablet*, which lasted for a year. A strong believer in woman suffrage, M. "cast a vote" in the Memphis elections of 1872 and began a correspondence with leading feminists. In 1881, M. joined Elizabeth Cady Stanton and Susan B. Anthony on a speaking tour of New England. There she met Henry George and became a supporter of his "single tax" theory of economics.

M.'s first novel, *The Master of Red Leaf*, was published in 1872. It is basically a description of life on a southern plantation before the Civil War and a justification of secession. Her other works include novels, a play, and several works of popular history. M.'s autobiography, *Recollections of 92 Years*, was published the year before her death.

In many ways, M. can be considered a "professional Confederate." Not only do most of her works deal with the antebellum South, but unlike other postwar southern authors, M. refused to acknowledge that slavery had been a moral or social evil. M.'s fiction is replete with stereotyped black characters—happy, carefree, childlike, and unable to govern themselves without the discipline of slavery.

However, with the end of slavery, M. saw her ordered world turned upside down. "Life in the South," M. wrote, "became one long nightmare; then a miracle happened—for surely the way the South escaped from that frightful nightmare was little short of miraculous." The "miracle" was the Ku Klux Klan. M. writes about the Klan with an insider's knowledge and sympathy, for her husband was a member. She witnessed its night raids, terrorism, and destruction of black property, claiming that the corruption of the carpetbaggers and the insolence of "uppity" blacks justified any actions by disfranchised whites. M. concludes: "No doubt many abuses were committed by the Ku Klux. In large bodies of men some unwise ones, some mean ones will inevitably be found. But considered as a whole the work of the Ku Klux was done in a patriotic spirit for patriotic purposes, and I rejoice to see . . . that History is beginning to do justice to that wonderful secret movement. At the time it was misunderstood; in the North it was reviled. But in truth it accomplished a noble and necessary work in the only way in which that work was then possible."

Despite M.'s obvious prejudices, her works are enjoyable. She had a knack for telling a good story and making her characters real. M.'s descriptions of poor white hill people are charming and convey the spirit of these people.

WORKS: *The Master of Red Leaf* (1872). *The Ku Klux Klan; or, The Carpet-bagger in New Orleans* (1877). *English Tyranny and Irish Suffering* (1881). *Black and White: A Novel* (1883). *The Devil's Dances: A Play* (1886). *The Sowing of Swords* (1910). *Recollections of 92 Years* (1916).

BIBLIOGRAPHY: Horn, S. F., *Invisible Empire: The Story of the Ku Klux Klan* (1939). Patton, J. W., *Unionism and Reconstruction in Tennessee, 1860–1869* (1934).

                                                    JANET E. KAUFMAN

Annie Nathan Meyer

B. *19 Feb. 1867, New York City; d. 23 Sept. 1951, New York City*
D. *of Robert Weeks and Annie Florance Nathan; m. Alfred Meyer, 1887*

Born in New York City, the youngest of four children, M. proudly claimed her heritage in a prominent Jewish family that dated to the revolutionary era. After the 1875 stock-market crash, her family moved to the Midwest, where M. lived until just before her mother's death in 1878, when the three youngest children were sent to New York to live with M.'s grandfather. Later M. lived with her father until her marriage; she spent the rest of her life in New York City.

In 1885 she secretly studied for and passed the entrance examinations for Columbia University's collegiate course for women. At that time women were not allowed to attend Columbia's classes but could be admitted to the collegiate course for women and allowed to study independently for the same examinations taken by men. When her father learned of her activities, he warned, "You'll never marry" because "men hate intelligent wives." Undaunted by his criticism, she decided "to forego all chances of winning a husband." This potential sacrifice, described in her autobiography, *It's Been Fun* (1951), and in her account of the founding of Barnard College, *Barnard Beginnings* (1935), proved unnecessary. She described her husband, Dr. Meyer, as sympathetic to her literary ambitions.

Although M. felt continuation of the Columbia course no longer necessary for her literary ambitions, she did begin campaigning for a women's college affiliate of Columbia that would allow women the full advantages of a collegiate education comparable to that available to Columbia's male students. As an incorporator and trustee of Barnard College, M. continued throughout her life to support the college she had helped found in 1889.

M. also pursued her own literary career, writing novels, plays, and short stories; articles on education, art, and feminism; and frequent letters to the editors of various publications. Her stories and articles appeared in such periodicals as *Bookman, Critic, Harper's Bazaar, North American Review, Putnam's,* and *Century.*

Many of M.'s works deal with the special problems resulting from women's search for new roles in the late 19th and early 20th centuries. After expressing her concern for the improvement of education for women in the late 1880s, she turned to the special problems of the women who entered the professions in *Woman's Work in America* (1891), a collection of essays by prominent women, such as Mary Putnam Jacobi, Frances Willard, and Clara Barton.

In 1892 M. anonymously published *Helen Brent, M.D.*, a novel about the special problems of a woman doctor. The heroine refuses to surrender her career to marriage and insists that she has as much right to ask a man to give up his ambition as he does to demand such a sacrifice from her. Until she can find a man willing to accept a wife who will continue her career, she will forgo marriage. Of all of M.'s works, this one stirred the most controversy among reviewers.

Several of M.'s plays also addressed complexities faced by the new woman. M. did not, however, maintain any consistent prowoman philosophy. In *The Dominant Sex* (1911), she satirizes the club woman who ignores her own child while she campaigns for child-protection legislation. This play also satirizes the tendency of some women to assume that they are the superior sex. Eventually chastened by the knowledge that her husband represents the dominant sex, the club woman gives up her club work and returns to her proper role at home.

The Dominant Sex dramatizes the strong antisuffrage views M. presented in "Woman's Assumption of Sex Superiority" (*North American Review*, Jan. 1904), which rejects both the ideas that women could combine marriage and career and that women represent a morally superior group. Although M. claimed in her autobiography that *Helen Brent, M.D.* and *The Advertising of Kate*—a play about the "delicate adjustment of the claims of sex to the work of the business woman," written in 1914 and produced on Broadway in 1922—were ahead of their times, other works seem very dated in their opposition to the new woman.

Among her approximately twenty-six plays, several addressed other social issues. In *The New Way*, a comedy directed by Jessie Bonstelle at the Longacre Theatre in New York in 1923, M. treated humorously the complexities of marriage and divorce. Her more serious *Black Souls* (1932), directed by James Light in 1932 at the Provincetown Playhouse in New York and including members of Zora Neale Hurston's choral group, dealt with the horrors of the lynching of blacks and the hypocrisy of white attitudes toward blacks.

In addition to numerous published works, M.'s unpublished manuscripts and correspondence reveal both her wide-ranging social interests and her occasionally contradictory convictions about the issues of her day.

WORKS: *Woman's Work in America* (1891). *Helen Brent, M.D.* (1892). *My Park Book* (1898). *Robert Annys, Poor Priest* (1901). *The Dominant Sex: A Play in Three Acts* (1911). *The Dreamer: A Play in Three Acts* (1912). *P's and Q's: A Play in One Act* (1921). *The New Way: A Comedy in Three Acts* (1925). *Black Souls: A Play in Six Scenes* (1932). *Barnard Beginnings* (1935). *It's Been Fun: An Autobiography* (1951).

The papers of Annie Nathan Meyer are at the American Jewish Archives, Cincinnati, Ohio.

BIBLIOGRAPHY: Askowith, D., *Three Outstanding Women: Mary Fels, Rebekah Kohut, and Annie Nathan Meyer* (1941).

For articles in reference works, see: *AW*.

Other references: *Harper's Bazaar* (4 June 1892). *NY* (23 Oct. 1943; 30 Oct. 1943). *NYT* (2 April 1911; 9 May 1922; 31 March 1932; 24 Sept. 1951; 25 Sept. 1951).

JEAN CARWILE MASTELLER

Josephine Miles

B. 11 June 1911, Chicago, Illinois
D. of Reginald Odber and Josephine Lackner Miles

M. is descended from an English business family which came to America on the Mayflower. M.'s mother studied history and education with John Dewey and Colonel Parker at the University of Chicago.

M. attended grammar and high school in Los Angeles and graduated Phi Beta Kappa from the University of California at Los Angeles in 1932. She took graduate degrees from the University of California at Berkeley and joined the Berkeley faculty in 1940. She retired, university professor emerita, in 1978.

M. began writing poems at age eight. In high school, she gained a strong foundation in Latin and Greek poetry, followed in college by rigorous training in literary history. During early graduate study, M. developed her compelling interests in poetic language and form. The metaphysical poets and Yeats led her own early verse in a direction counter to that of a number of her contemporaries. Later, the writing of Neruda and Rilke offered in subject and approach modern alternatives to the more oblique expression of the metaphysical poets. The contemporary poets she has regarded most highly include Eberhart, Rukeyser, Levertov, Dickey, Stafford, Nathan, and Ammons. Those characteristics M. identifies as important in their verse—incisiveness, factualness, simplicity, power, and lyricism—are evident in her own finest poems. M. has received distinguished awards for her poetry and for her literary scholarship.

M.'s approach to what she calls "verse composition" is often determined by "the idea of speech . . . people talking . . . as the material from which poetry is made." In an early poem, "Speaker," the voice admits: "My talking heart talked less of what it knew / Than what it saw." What is known in many of M.'s poems is conveyed obliquely by what is observed in commonplace landscapes. Long a city resident, M. includes in these landscapes the repeated sights of urban life. In "Entry," the quantifiable city where "the small matter is put down already / To depreciation" is contrasted with the country, a place of hints and expectation.

M.'s poetry has not received the critical attention it deserves. It is difficult to generalize about M.'s writing except to note its condensation, craft, unexpected juxtaposition of images, pleasure in "the space and active interplay of talk," and—in recent volumes—willingness to employ more irregular form and an increasingly more direct political and ethical stance. Negative criticism of her work has centered on a miscellaneous quality of a number of the poems, as well as a control which has seemed to some to force a too moderate, reasonable, and civil response. However, longer poems, such as "Two Kinds of Trouble (for Michelangelo)," "Ten Dreamers in a Motel," and "Views from Gettysburg," show M. capable of sustaining and varying form.

M.'s doctoral dissertation, "Wordsworth and the Vocabulary of Emotion," was published in 1942. In this systematic study, M. establishes a historical and quantitative approach to criticism based on a method which she later refined and applied to other poets and eras and to prose style as well. By "counting the number of previously established names of emotion and standard signs of emotion in every poem, group, and in the complete poetical works" of a poet, the literary scholar could, M. demonstrates, formulate a more scientific, evidential basis for analyzing the relationship of thought and feeling in an era and the specific vocabulary a poet considered "poetic." In *Style and Proportion* (1966), by tabulating numerous British and American writers' use of adjectives, nouns, verbs, and connectives, M. recognizes "three styles distinguishable on the basis of structural choice: the predicative, the connective-subordinate, and the adjectival." At times reluctant to acknowledge the prior necessity of such tabulation, some scholars have praised M.'s aesthetic criticism and insight into the social nature of language at the expense of appreciation of the scientific method she employed in describing English poetry from the 16th c. to the present.

WORKS: *Lines at Intersection* (1939). *Poems on Several Occasions* (1941). *Pathetic Fallacy in the Nineteenth Century* (1942). *Wordsworth and the Vocabulary of Emotion* (1942). *Local Measures* (1946). *The Vocabulary of Poetry: Three Studies* (1946). *Criticism: The Foundations of Modern Literary Judgment* (edited by Miles, with M. Schorer and G. McKenzie, 1948; rev. ed., 1958). *The Continuity of English Poetry from the 1540's to the 1940's* (1951). *Prefabrications* (1955). *Eras and Modes in English Poetry* (1957; rev. ed., 1964). *The Poem: A Critical Anthology* (edited by Miles, 1959; rev. and abridged ed., *The Ways of the Poem*, 1969; rev. ed., 1973). *Poems, 1930–1960* (1960). *Renaissance, Eighteenth-Century, and Modern Language in English Poetry: A Tabular View* (1960). *Classic Essays in English* (edited by Miles, 1961; rev. ed., 1965). *Ralph Waldo Emerson* (1964). *Civil Poems* (1966). *Style and Proportion* (1966). *Kinds of Affection* (1967). *Fields of Learning* (1968). *Poetry and Change: Donne, Milton, Wordsworth, and the Equilibrium of the Present* (1974). *To All Appearances: New and Selected Poems* (1974). *Coming to Terms* (1980).

BIBLIOGRAPHY: Bogan, L., in *A Poet's Alphabet* (1970). Dickey, J., in *Babel to Byzantium* (1968). Smith, L., in *Rereadings*, Ed. G. Kuzma (1978).

For articles in reference works, see: *CA*, 1–4 (1967). *Contemporary Poets*, Ed. R. Murphie (1970). *Contemporary Poets*, Eds. J. Vinson and D. L. Kirkpatrick (1975). *20thCAS*.

Other references: *PrS* (Winter 1958–9). *TLS* (25 April 1975).

THEODORA R. GRAHAM

Margaret Millar

B. 5 Feb. 1915, Kitchener, Ontario, Canada
D. of William and Lavinia Ferrier Sturm; m. Kenneth Millar, 1938

M. studied at the University of Toronto; her early interests were classics, archeology, music, and psychiatry. M.'s husband writes mysteries under the name Ross Macdonald. M. is a former president of the Mystery Writers of America and widely known as an environmentalist. *The Birds and the Beasts Were There* (1967) recounts the difficulties and the pleasures of a major current interest, bird watching.

Primarily known as a mystery writer, M. created two series detectives. Dr. Paul Prye, psychiatrist and witty amateur sleuth, appears in *The Invisible Worm* (1941) and *The Weak-Eyed Bat* (1942), which details Prye's search for a killer and his courtship of clever, brash Nora Shane. Their wedding, in *The Devil Loves Me* (1942), is complicated by a murder and allows for the introduction of the second continuing character, Detective-Inspector Sands.

Sands, unprepossessing but perceptive and humane, is more typical of M.'s characters and appears in two other novels. *Wall of Eyes* (1943) uses an important M. device—characters who are not what or who they seem. The relationship between the Heath sisters, pliant Alice and blind, shrill Kelsey, asks who is prey and who is predator. *The Iron Gates* (1945) finds Sands investigating the disappearance of Lucille Morrow, one of M.'s most successfully complex characters. The novel also features another important M. motif, dream imagery, and a key theme, the evil power of love.

Fire Will Freeze (1944) and *Rose's Last Summer* (1952) are comedy-mysteries. *Fire* provides amusing characters, a measure of terror, and a clever surprise ending. All the early novels employ the "closed circle of suspects" technique.

Psychotic personalities are the focus of *The Cannibal Heart* (1949) and *Beast in View* (cited as best mystery of 1955 by the Mystery Writers of America). In *The Cannibal Heart*, the relative innocence of young Jessie Banner and adolescent Luisa Roma contrasts with the corruption of Janet Wakefield as she attempts to compensate for disappointment in marriage and motherhood. *Beast in View* is the study of Helen Clarvoe, rejected and repressed as a child and dangerous as a woman. Hurtful family impact is a central theme, and the novel employs yet another pattern, the outsider drawn into a turmoil of family entanglements.

Perhaps M.'s best novels are *Vanish in an Instant* (1952) and *The Fiend* (1964). The former compares the relationship between Virginia Barkley, accused of a murder, and her overprotective mother with that between Earl Loftus, who confesses to the killing, and his alcoholic mother. *The Fiend*, compassionate and unsentimental, probes the interactions within and between five families as Charlie Gowen, former child molester, struggles against his interest in little Jessie Brant. The characterizations are vivid, and M. uses a variation of the mother-child theme here, as a childless woman interferes with another's daughter.

The Listening Walls (1959) compares the self-protective instincts of a Mexican hotel maid with those of a pampered California matron. *Beyond This Point Are Monsters* (1970) and *Ask for Me Tomorrow* (1976) have fine Southern California settings, and in each M. provides sensitive examinations of the position of Mexican-Americans within that culture.

How Like an Angel (1962) interweaves two plots—a disappearing husband and the fate of the True Believers, a strange religious cult. The Believers' impact on the elderly Sister Blessing and teenaged Sister Karma are of especial interest, as is the portrait of Charlotte Keating, the seemingly controlled, competent, independent physician of *Do Evil in Return* (1950). The detectives in these novels, Quinn and Easter, are imperfect but decent men doing their best to cope with murder and with love.

Experiment in Springtime (1947), *Wives and Lovers* (1954), and *A Stranger in My Grave* (1960) treat failed marriages. In each, recognition of failure and termination of the marriage symbolize growth toward maturity for at least one partner. *Experiment in Springtime* contrasts the "second youth" of Martha Pearson and Steve Ferris, reunited lovers, with the realistic adolescence of Laura Shaw, who also loves Steve. *A Stranger in My Grave* effectively combines gothic overtones with a search for self-definition as Stevens Pinata discovers factual reasons for Daisy Harker's nightmares.

M. is considered a novelist of skill and power, especially noted for her effective imagery and excellent characterizations.

WORKS: *The Invisible Worm* (1941). *The Weak-Eyed Bat* (1942). *The Devil Loves Me* (1942). *Wall of Eyes* (1943). *Fire Will Freeze* (1944). *The*

Iron Gates (1945). *Experiment in Springtime* (1947). *It's All in the Family* (1948). *The Cannibal Heart* (1949). *Do Evil in Return* (1950). *Rose's Last Summer* (1952). *Vanish in an Instant* (1952). *Wives and Lovers* (1954). *Beast in View* (1955). *An Air That Kills* (1957). *The Listening Walls* (1959). *A Stranger in My Grave* (1960). *How Like an Angel* (1962). *The Fiend* (1964). *The Birds and the Beasts Were There* (1967). *Beyond This Point Are Monsters* (1970). *Ask for Me Tomorrow* (1976). *The Murder of Miranda* (1979). *Mermaid* (1982).

BIBLIOGRAPHY: For articles in reference works, see: *CA*, 13–16 (1975). *Encyclopedia of Mystery and Detection*, Eds. C. Steinbrunner and O. Penzler (1976). *WA*.

Other references: *The Armchair Detective* (Jan. 1970). *NYT* (13 Oct. 1976). *NYTBR* (30 May 1954; 21 June 1964).

JANE S. BAKERMAN

Edna St. Vincent Millay

B. 22 Feb. 1892, Rockland, Maine; d. 19 Oct. 1950, Steepletop, New York
Wrote under: Nancy Boyd, Edna St. Vincent Millay
D. of Henry and Cora Buzzelle Millay; m. Eugen Boissevain, 1923

M. was the oldest of three daughters. Her father, a schoolteacher and school superintendent, left the household when M. was seven. Her mother supported the family by working as a practical nurse. She also did her utmost to encourage all three girls to develop their creative talents.

M. first received recognition as a poet when her long poem "Renascence" was selected in 1912 for inclusion in *The Lyric Year*. However, "Renascence" narrowly missed receiving one of the three prizes awarded for the best poems in the volume. Publication of the anthology brought forth a storm of protest. Readers maintained that M.'s youthful statement of despair, rebirth, and affirmation was the strongest in the book.

M.'s success brought her to the attention of Caroline Dow, who made it possible for the poet to attend Vassar College. In 1917, soon after graduation, M. moved to Greenwich Village, where she quickly became a legend.

Several images of M. during this period emerge: the serious artist living on limited funds; the bohemian, careless of health and propriety; the passionate woman involved in brief, intoxicating love affairs. During her

Village years, M. published *Renascence, and Other Poems* (1917) and *A Few Figs from Thistles* (1920). The latter, with its famous "candle" quatrain (beginning "My candle burns at both ends; / It shall not last the night") and flippant love poems, captured the imaginations of the "emancipated" youth of the early 1920s. At the same time, M. finished the poems that would appear in *Second April* (1921), and wrote and directed a pacifist verse play, *Aria da Capo* (1920).

In 1922, M. received the Pulitzer Prize for *The Ballad of the Harp-Weaver*, an expanded edition of *Figs* with eight new sonnets. The following year, she married a Dutch businessman. Boissevain's first wife had been Inez Milholland, the famous suffragist, who died in 1916. M., who had admired Milholland at college, dedicated to her a sonnet honoring the women's rights movement.

Eventually, Boissevain gave up his coffee business to manage M.'s highly successful poetry-reading tours, and to superintend Steepletop, their farm in upstate New York. Their marriage lasted twenty-seven years, until Boissevain's death in 1949. During these years, M. produced several books of poems—*The Buck in the Snow* (1928), *Fatal Interview* (1931), *Wine from These Grapes* (1934)—that are more subdued and more contemplative in tone than her earlier work.

In 1927, M. became active in the movement to save Sacco and Vanzetti. She signed petitions, demonstrated, and, in a futile interview, tried to persuade the governor of Massachusetts to grant clemency. Her involvement in this case is reflected in several poems, most notably "Justice Denied in Massachusetts."

Growing increasingly concerned about the spread of fascism throughout Europe and the start of World War II, M. renounced her former pacifism in the late 1930s. In a series of political poems, she argued for American military preparedness and aid to France and England. Unfortunately, these poems are quite poor, relying on jangling rhythms and trite language. Collected in *Make Bright the Arrows* (1940), they drew a barrage of adverse criticism.

M. is particularly interesting because, at a time when modern poetry was abandoning traditional forms, she chose to write ballads, lyrics, and sonnets. Though M.'s later work is somewhat more experimental, she usually stayed within familiar structures, adapting them to her own use. M.'s strongest poems work precisely because of the balance maintained between the emotional intensity of her subjects and the disciplined craftmanship of her forms. As Floyd Dell said, "She learned the molds first, into which she poured her emotions while hot."

Many of her first poems ("Renascence," "God's World") reveal innocence and youthful exuberance. In "Recuerdo," the young lovers, after
riding "back and forth all night on the ferry," impulsively give bags of
fruit and "all our money but our subway fares" to an old woman newspaper seller. Other early verses, however, exhibit a mocking, skeptical
attitude toward life and love. In many of the poems from *A Few Figs
from Thistles*, M. creates a bold, unconventional woman persona who is
frankly attracted to men and who initiates and terminates love affairs at
will. In *Sonnet xi*, for instance, she tells her lover: "I shall forget you
presently, my dear, / So make the most of this, your little day." The
poem ends with the forthright statement: "Whether or not we find what
we are seeking / Is idle, biologically speaking." In another poem, the persona glories in being a "wicked girl" and declares: "if I can't be sorry,
why, / I might as well be glad."

A more serious note appears in *Second April* (1921). The skepticism remains, but the lightness is gone. In "Spring," M. states that "Life
in itself / Is nothing" and compares the month of April to "an idiot, bab-
bling and strewing flowers." The love poems in this book are somber.
Sonnet xix, for example, begins: "And you as well must die, beloved
dust / And all your beauty stand you in no stead."

Throughout all of M.'s poetry runs the message that life is short
and love ephemeral. Human relationships, however sweet, cannot last.
The theme of death constantly recurs. The early "Passer Mortuus Est"
begins "Death devours all lovely things" and the late "Epitaph for the
Race of Man" mourns, "Earth, unhappy planet, born to die."

M. has been criticized for writing only of herself and her love affairs, but many of her poems reflect wider concerns. However, her love
poems, far from being sentimental effusions, are central to her vision of
life's brevity and impermanence.

The recipient of much acclaim in the 1920s, M. is less popular today.
Feminist readers tend to dismiss her work as old-fashioned and conventional. This is unfortunate because M., though no structural innovator,
is in many ways close to the feminist-oriented poets of the 1970s. Certainly M.'s use of highly personal material; her fresh, forthright language; and her creation of strong female personae anticipate modern
women's poetry. M.'s finest poems, moreover, ensure her position as an
important American woman poet.

WORKS: *Renascence, and Other Poems* (1917). *Aria da Capo* (1920). *A Few
Figs from Thistles* (1920). *The Lamp and the Bell* (1921). *Second April* (1921).
Two Slatterns and a King (1921). *The Harp-Weaver, and Other Poems* (1923).

Distressing Dialogues (1924). *The King's Henchman* (1927). *The Buck in the Snow* (1928). *Poems Selected for Young People* (1929). *Fatal Interview* (1931). *The Princess Marries the Page* (1932). *Wine from These Grapes* (1934). *Flowers of Evil* by Baudelaire (translated by Millay, with George Dillon, 1936). *Conversation at Midnight* (1937). *Huntsman, What Quarry?* (1939). *Make Bright the Arrows* (1940). *Collected Sonnets* (1941). *Invocation to the Muses* (1941). *The Murder of Lidice* (1942). *Collected Lyrics* (1943). *Poem and Prayer for an Invading Army* (1944). *Mine the Harvest* (1954). *Collected Poems* (1956).

BIBLIOGRAPHY: Atkins, E., *Edna St. Vincent Millay and Her Times* (1936). Bogan, L., *Achievements in American Poetry* (1951). Cheney, A., *Millay in the Village* (1975). Dash, J., *A Life of One's Own* (1973). Dell, F., *Homecoming: An Autobiography* (1933). Gould, J., *The Poet and Her Book* (1969). Gray, J., *Edna St. Vincent Millay* (Univ. of Minnesota Pamphlets on American Writers, 1967). Gurko, M., *Restless Spirit* (1962). Sheean, V., *The Indigo Bunting* (1951). Wilson, E., *I Thought of Daisy* (1929). Wilson, E., in *The Shores of Light* (1952).

For articles in reference works, see: *NAW* (article by J. M. Brinnin). *NCAB*, B.

ENID DAME

Kate Millett

B. *14 Sept. 1934, St. Paul, Minnesota*
D. *of James and Helen Feely Millet; m. Fumio Yoshimura, 1965*

The second of three daughters, M. attended parochial schools in St. Paul. Her father, a contractor, abandoned the family when M. was fourteen. Her mother took a job selling insurance, and the girls helped support the family. M. was graduated from the University of Minnesota, magna cum laude and Phi Beta Kappa, in 1956. She studied literature for two years at St. Hilda's College, Oxford, and earned first honors.

M. taught briefly at the Women's College of the University of North Carolina, but later resigned her post and went to New York to paint and sculpt. In 1961, M. moved to Japan, where she taught English and sculpted.

On returning to New York in 1963, M. exhibited "pop furniture," such as chairs with human legs. She joined the civil rights and peace movements, and in 1966 became one of the first members of the National Organization for Woman (NOW). Her first book, *Token Learning* (1967), was a pamphlet for NOW, challenging the validity of the curricula at women's colleges.

In 1968, M. was hired to teach at Barnard College, and began work on a Ph.D. in English and comparative literature at Columbia. M.'s activism in the causes of women's liberation and student rights led to her being relieved of her teaching post in December of her first year. However, a speech M. delivered to a women's group at Cornell became the germ of her doctoral thesis.

M.'s thesis may be considered the first major literary criticism of the new wave of feminism. She sets forth the postulate that the oppression of women is essentially political, and then discredits religious, literary, philosophical, and "scentific" constructs erected by male supremacists to justify their advantage. A second section documents the feminist revolution and male chauvinist counterrevolution in the history of ideas, and the third section exposes the phallic supremacism of three modern male literary idols: D. H. Lawrence, Henry Miller, and Norman Mailer. Finally, M. sets up Jean Genet, the French homosexual writer, as master social critic who reverses every status hierarchy in western culture, including that of masculine and feminine.

In March 1970, M. was awarded the doctoral degree with distinction, and in August her thesis was published by Doubleday. It sold 80,000 copies in the first six months of publication. *Sexual Politics* offered the public a major new concept, and many reviewers merely used the title as a springboard for their personal tirades against feminism. The media both praised and lambasted the book and its author, seizing upon them as a reification of "women's lib."

The Prostitution Papers began as a chapter for Vivian Gornick's *Woman in a Sexist Society* (1971). M. edited oral narratives from two prostitutes and a feminist lawyer, and added an essay of her own arguing that prostitution is only one salient example of the ways in which femaleness has been reduced to a commodity. M. called the chapter "a quartet for four voices," and had the four statements printed side by side in columns; but when the chapter was published separately as a book, the experimental layout was abandoned. The 1976 edition includes M.'s firsthand account of the 1975 French prostitutes' revolt.

M.'s experience with spoken language led her to make the film *Three Lives*, and inspired her fourth book. Frankly confessional, *Flying* (1974) was M.'s response to the enforced two-dimensionality of being created as a media feminist and showed M.'s need to bring together disparate private and public selves. M. had originally planned to write a scholarly treatise in defense of homosexuality, but wrote instead a supremely vulnerable book about her own sexuality, her work, her feelings, her friends, and the movement. Using the writing of the book itself as a framework, M. intercuts scenes from other periods of her life, giving the effect of a sculptural assemblage.

Sita (1977) resembles *Flying* stylistically, but it is focused on a narrower theme. M. takes the reader on a *tour de force* of a dissolving romance between herself and an older woman. Again, M. makes sculpture out of confession. She repeatedly reconstructs her theme, each time from a slightly different perspective, building up the paradigm of emotional attitudes toward a single set of facts. More tightly controlled than *Flying*, *Sita* conveys a relentless progressive present that both encompasses and reshapes history.

M.'s capacity for obsession drives her art. For ten years, she sculpted almost nothing but cages, her response to a newsmagazine article about the murder of a sixteen-year-old girl by her female guardian and a group of kids. *The Basement: Meditations on a Human Sacrifice* (1979) is a cage of words. M. verbalizes the bars of the cage—her subjects' poverty, their isolation from societal restraints, their rationalizations and guilts and enjoyment of petty drama—and fills the cage with monologues representing the interior voices of torturer and victim. There is a constant sliding back and forth between M.'s ideas and voice and those of her characters, as the author performs the ritual of becoming them, the self-abasement of taking on their impoverished language and brutal experience. Much of the tension of the book results from M.'s continual refusal to permit herself to explain the deed cleanly away.

A pacifist and international feminist activist, M.'s politics are frequently denigrated and her works sometimes harshly reviewed in the major press. Nevertheless, her influence is pervasive, and a generation of feminist writers has taken her for its model. She has set a standard for powerful feminist criticism, and provoked reevaluation of confessional and journal writing as artistic literary forms.

WORKS: *Token Learning* (1967). *Sexual Politics* (1970). *The Prostitution Papers* (1971; rev. ed., 1976). *Flying* (1974). *Sita* (1977). *The Basement: Meditations on a Human Sacrifice* (1979). *Going to Iran* (1981).

BIBLIOGRAPHY: Chrysalis (1977; 1978). *Harper's* (1970). *Ms.* (1974).

FRIEDA L. WERDEN

Jessica Mitford

B. 11 Sept. 1917, Batsford Mansion, Gloucestershire, England
D. of David and Sydney Bowles Mitford; m. Esmond Romilly, 1936;
m. Robert E. Truehaft, 1943

M. is the daughter of the second baron of Redesdale. Her eccentric siblings include Nancy, the biographer, Diana, the wife of fascist Oswald Mosley, and Unity, disciple of Hitler. After receiving a private education at home, M. ran away with her second cousin, Esmond Romilly, in 1936 to assist the Loyalist cause in Spain. They worked briefly as journalists before returning to England, where M. was a market researcher for an advertising agency. M. and her husband emigrated to the U.S. in 1939, where each took odd jobs while traveling along the eastern seaboard.

M. worked in Washington, D.C., for two years in the Office of Price Administration after Romilly was killed in action during World War II. She married a lawyer in 1943, and became a naturalized U.S. citizen in 1944. After moving to Oakland, California, M. worked as executive secretary for the Civil Rights Congress, where she pressed for the investigation into charges of police brutality. In 1973, M. was appointed distinguished visiting professor in sociology at San Jose State College, where she taught a class on "The American Way" and a seminar on muckracking.

M.'s first book, *Lifeitselfmanship*, was privately published in 1956. Her autobiography, *Daughters and Rebels* (1960), hilariously recounts her childhood and marriage to Romilly.

M.'s first investigative study, *The American Way of Death* (1963), exposed the greed and commercialism of the funeral industry. Relying on extensive research and quotations from the industry's own publications, M. satirically deflated the pretentious hypocrisy of such establishments as Forest Lawn Memorial-Park. Although the book was viciously denounced by the industry, it was used as the basis for a television documentary.

M.'s second investigative study, *The Trial of Dr. Spock, William Sloane Coffin, Jr., Michael Ferber, Mitchell Goodman, and Marcus Raskin* (1969), concluded with the observation that conspiracy laws threatened personal and civil rights: "Does not the cherished concept of due process of law, the foundation of our system of jurisprudence, become merely an elaborate sham to mask what is in reality a convenient device to silence opponents of governmental policies?"

M. next attacked the Famous Writers School in a lengthy article entitled "Let Us Now Appraise Famous Writers" (*Atlantic*, July 1970). M. charged the Westport, Connecticut, school with deception in advertising and criticized writers who allowed the school to use their names.

Kind and Usual Punishment: The Prison Business (1973) exposes the atrocities of the penal system. In a chapter entitled "Clockwork Orange," M. listed the techniques used in prisons to modify behavior and reform "antisocial personalities," including chemotherapy, aversion therapy, neurosurgery, and drugs. M. points out that prisons have become the "happy hunting ground for the researcher." M. condemns lengthy and indeterminate sentences, the parole system, and the use of prisoners in psychological and physiological research, while supporting the idea of a prisoners' union. M. concludes that prisons are "inherently unjust and inhumane," institutions that demean all people in society.

M. published the sequel to her autobiography *Daughters and Rebels* in 1977. *A Fine Old Conflict* traces M.'s involvement with the Communist Party in America. As M. puts it, being fiercely anti-Fascist and antiracist, the Communist Party seemed to her the only practical outlet for her political and social beliefs. Recreating the ambience of the "witchhunting" 1950s, M. recalls such activities as her trip to Mississippi in 1951 to appeal the conviction of a black rapist and her efforts to raise money for the party by organizing chicken dinners. After defecting from the party after twenty years, M. describes it as "an embattled, proscribed (and, to me, occasionally comical) organization." The appendix reprints her previously unavailable spoof of party jargon, *Lifeitselfmanship*.

In addition to her book-length studies, M. has published extensively in *Life, Esquire, The Nation*, and the San Francisco *Chronicle*. A staunch supporter of civil liberties, M. has often been accused of communist sympathies and "un-American" activities. All M.'s writings, however, reveal a satirical perspective on the fraud and corruption of organizations that victimize and exploit human beings.

WORKS: *Lifeitselfmanship* (privately published, 1956). *Daughters and Rebels* (1960; published in England as *Hons and Rebels*). *The American Way of Death* (1963). *The Trial of Dr. Spock, William Sloane Coffin, Jr., Michael Ferber, Mitchell Goodman, and Marcus Raskin* (1969). *Kind and Usual Pun-*

ishment: *The Prison Business* (1973). *A Fine Old Conflict* (1977). *Poison Penmanship: The Gentle Art of Muckracking* (1979).

BIBLIOGRAPHY: For articles in reference works, see: *CA* (1967). *CB* (1974).
DIANE LONG HOEVELER

Penina Moise

B. *23 April 1797, Charleston, South Carolina; d. 13 Sept. 1880, Charleston, South Carolina*
D. *of Abraham and Sarah Moise*

M. was the sixth of nine children of parents who had fled to Charleston during the slave insurrections in Santo Domingo. The death of M.'s father forced M. to abandon formal education and help support the family by needlework, but she nevertheless continued to study and write, publishing poems and stories in newspapers and periodicals. Devoutly religious, M. served as superintendent of the religious school of Beth Elohim beginning in 1842. After the Civil War, although ill and nearly blind, M. founded a school for girls and conducted literary salons.

Fancy's Sketch Book (1833) was probably the first published book to which a Jewish woman appended her full name. Primarily a volume of verse, it includes light satires, epigrams, lyrics, and occasional poems commemorating prominent events. Conventional themes of love, death, and nature predominate, but in many instances they are distinguished by charming poignancy, delicate wit, and clever word play. For example, in "The Disconcerted Concert" M. uses the double meaning of musical terms to describe a quarrel among the instruments.

Serious themes are not neglected, and the book reveals a wide range of interests and knowledge, including Greek mythology, the Bible, Shakespeare, music, art, and history. Women are generally presented in terms of love or motherhood, but in one instance M. writes movingly of the women who donated their wedding rings to support Koscivszko's efforts to liberate Poland.

Hymns Written for the Use of Congregation Beth Elohim, first published in 1842 and enlarged in three subsequent editions, is primarily the work of M. The art of hymn writing, which requires decided meter with little variation, simple language that conveys an immediate sense of emotion, and above all sincere devoutness, brought out M.'s talents to the fullest—her hymns are still included in modern hymnals. In writing the lyrics, M. often added images that echoed many parts of the service, and her dramatic images greatly enhance the effectiveness of the prayer.

Although the bulk of M.'s writings still lies buried in the numerous newspapers and periodicals to which she contributed, a selection of her poems and hymns was collected in *Secular and Religious Works of Penina Moise* (1911). Some of the verses from the earlier volumes were included, but the collection is notable for works on specifically Jewish subjects and a number of previously uncollected poems dealing with political and social issues. The refusal by the British House of Lords to grant constitutional rights to Jews became for M. "that dark deformity from Freedom's code," and when the Jews of Damascus were being persecuted, she reproached the rest of the world that could "the suppliants scorn / From whose inspired relics revelation was born."

Limited by poverty, by social tradition, by illness, and by blindness, M. nevertheless produced a substantial body of poems and hymns. Much of M.'s work reveals an excessive concern for the poetic diction and conventions of her time, but several of her satiric pieces can still delight readers. M.'s poems on serious subjects reveal an unusual awareness of social and moral problems. Her hymns, expressing a deep, sincere faith in God's mercy, continue to evoke a solemn piety. All contemporary accounts of M. emphasize her cheerfulness, good humor, and wit, despite the hardships under which she lived. The mark of suffering which found no voice in her poetry was expressed only in the lines M. wrote for her epitaph: "Lay no flowers on my grave. They are for those who live in the sun, and I have always lived in the shadow."

WORKS: *Fancy's Sketch Book* (1833). *Hymns Written for the Use of Congregation Beth Elohim* (1842). *Secular and Religious Works of Penina Moise* (1911).

BIBLIOGRAPHY: Elzas, B. A., *The Jews of South Carolina* (1905). Moise, H., *The Moise Family of South Carolina* (1961). Reznikoff, C., and U. Z. Engleman, *The Jews of Charleston* (1950).

For articles in reference works, see: *AA. DAB*, VI, 2. *NAW* (article by C. Reznikoff).

Other references: *American Jew's Annual* (1885–86). *American Jewish Yearbook* (1905–06). *Critic* (28 Dec. 1889). *Southern Jewish Historical Society* (1978).

CAROL B. SCHOEN

Harriet Monroe

B. 23 Dec. 1860, Chicago, Illinois; d. 26 Sept. 1936, Arequipa, Peru
D. of Henry Stantan and Martha Mitchell Monroe

Poet, editor, and journalist, M. was an influential force in the publication of modern poetry in the U.S. and an important figure in the Chicago Renaissance. Both her parents had moved to the growing city shortly before their marriage in 1855: her father, who became a prominent lawyer, from western New York and her mother from Ohio. Decidedly more erudite and socially ambitious than his beautiful but uneducated wife, Monroe inspired in his daughter a keen interest in literature, painting, music, and the theater; and much of her early education was acquired from reading in his substantial library.

The tensions in her parents' marriage, increased after 1871 by her father's business reverses, contributed along with frail health to M.'s reserved, nervous character as a girl. At the Georgetown Visitation Convent in Washington, D.C. (1877–79), she outgrew her former reticence, forming lifelong friendships with several affluent classmates and discovering the satisfactions of an independent, critical mind. She also blossomed into an aspiring poet.

During the 1880s involvement in the Fortnightly, a literary women's club, and publication of occasional art and drama reviews provided M. entrée into the world of Chicago's writers and journalists, among them Margaret Sullivan and Eugene Field, who became her friends and sponsors. While she had several opportunities to marry, she chose not to.

M. spent the winter of 1888–89 with her sister Lucy in New York as an art, drama, and music correspondent for the Chicago *Tribune*. At E. C. Stedman's Sunday evenings, she tasted the culture of the New York art and literary scene, meeting such luminaries as W. D. Howells and Joseph Pulitzer. Yet, despite her growing knowledge of contemporary art and theater, she considered journalism always second to her poetry and worked during her free time that winter on the verse play *Valeria*.

On her return to Chicago she was commissioned by a group of businessmen to write a cantata for the dedication ceremony of Louis Sullivan's new Auditorium in 1889. After a visit to London and northern

France in 1890, she established herself as a free-lance art and music reviewer and, from 1909 to 1914, worked as art critic for the *Tribune*. Her most public success as a poet came in 1892: the performance of her "Columbian Ode," a long poem composed (with music for lyric passages by G. W. Chadwick) for the World's Columbian Exposition in Chicago. *Valeria, and Other Poems* appeared in a private edition in 1891 and a memoir of her brother-in-law, the Chicago architect John Wellborn Root, in 1896.

M. traveled extensively in the U.S., Europe, and Asia. On her return from a P.E.N. congress in Buenos Aires in 1936, she traveled to Peru intending to view the Inca ruins at Machu Picchu. During a stop at Arequipa, however, she died and was buried in the Andean village.

Although M.'s poetry never gained the wide audience and critical notice she hoped for, she continued thoughout her life to write occasional verse, competent but largely conventional in sentiment and language. Among her more interesting poems are short lyrics about the deserts and mountains of the American southwest; longer descriptions of foreign locations she visited—among them, Constantinople, Peking, the Parthenon; and a few ironic observations of modern society like "The Hotel."

M.'s most distinguished and lasting achievement was the founding of *Poetry: A Magazine of Verse* in October 1912 and editing the monthly for twenty-four years. In June 1911, at the suggestion of her friend H. C. Chatfield-Taylor, M., then fifty-one, began the arduous task of soliciting subscriptions of fifty dollars a year for five years from 100 Chicago business leaders and professionals to establish a magazine "which shall give the poets a chance to be heard." To develop a public "interested in poetry as art" became her persistent aim.

The circular and personal letter she sent to many poets, established and unknown, discovered through ardent research—and through Elkin Mathews's fortuitous presentation to her in London in 1910 of two of Ezra Pound's early books—drew favorable response to her ambitious venture. It also stimulated a flow of letters from Pound, who became the magazine's unpaid foreign correspondent with the second issue. Along with Alice Corbin Henderson, her associate editor, Pound influenced M. to include in *Poetry*'s early years the writing of Yeats, Lawrence, Frost, William Carlos Williams, his own work, and in 1915, Eliot's "The Love Song of J. Alfred Prufrock."

Ellen Williams locates the great years of *Poetry* in 1914 and 1915, when M. opened the publication to controversy over Imagism, experimental verse, and the poet's relation to his audience. In general, M.'s preference for democratic and more accessible American poetry led her to espouse Lindsay, Masters, and many lesser poets. But the contribution she made, despite criticism and financial difficulties, in gaining recognition for poets in the U.S., in articulating modern standards in opposition to those of the powerful established outlets, and in calling attention to new writing and ideas in editorials and reviews was invaluable.

WORKS: *Valeria, and Other Poems* (1891). *The Columbian Ode* (1893). *John Wellborn Root: A Study of His Life and Work* (1896). *The Dance of the Seasons* (1911). *You and I* (1914). *The New Poetry: An Anthology* (edited by Monroe, with A. C. Henderson, 1917; rev. ed., 1932). *The Difference, and Other Poems* (1924). *Poets and Their Art* (1926). *A Book of Poems for Every Mood* (edited by Monroe, with M. D. Zabel, 1933). *Chosen Poems: A Selection from My Books of Verse* (1935). *A Poet's Life: Seventy Years in a Changing World* (1938).

Manuscripts, diaries, letters, and personal papers are located in the Harriet Monroe Collection, University of Chicago Library.

BIBLIOGRAPHY: Cahill, D. J., *Harriet Monroe* (1973). Duffey, B., *The Chicago Renaissance in American Letters* (1956). Hoffman, F. J., et al., *The Little Magazine* (1947). Redle, K. G., "Amy Lowell and Harriet Monroe: Their Correspondence" (Ph.D. diss., Northwestern Univ., 1968). Williams, E., *Harriet Monroe and the Poetry Renaissance: The First Ten Years of Poetry, 1912–22* (1977).

For articles in reference works, see: *DAB*, Suppl. 2; *NAW* (article by M. D. Zabel); *20thCA*.

Other references: *JML* 5 (1976). *Illinois Quarterly* 37 (1975). *Poetry* (Jan. 1961).

THEODORA R. GRAHAM

Marianne Craig Moore

B. 15 Nov. 1887, Kirkwood, Missouri; d. 5 Feb. 1972, New York City
Wrote under: Marianne Moore
D. of John Milton and Mary Warner Moore

M. was raised by her mother and grandfather, a Presbyterian minister. M. was seven when her grandfather died, and her mother moved the two children to Carlisle, Pennsylvania. She became an English teacher in the Metzger Institute, where M. was educated before entering Bryn Mawr college (B.A. 1909). In college M. specialized in biology and histology, but also submitted poetry to the campus literary magazine.

For four years after graduating from the Carlisle Commercial College in 1910, M. taught stenography, typing, and bookkeeping at the U.S. Indian School in Carlisle.

M.'s publishing career began in 1915 when the *Egoist*, a London journal dedicated to the new Imagist movement in poetry, accepted "To the Soul of Progress," a short satire on war. The same year, *Poetry* published M. for the first time in a U.S. magazine of general circulation.

In Greenwich Village, where M. lived with her mother, she became part of a literary group that included poets William Carlos Williams, Wallace Stevens, and Alfred Krembourg. *Poems* (1921) was published without M.'s knowledge by her admirers in England. M. added several poems, including the long *Marriage* (issued first as a pamphlet in 1923), before the collection was published in the U.S. as *Observations* (1924). It won the $2,000 Dial Award for "distinguished service to American letters," and M. was asked to become acting editor of the *Dial*, where she worked from 1926 until the magazine ceased publication in 1929. Thereafter, her vocation was solely poetry and writing.

M. was the recipient of many honorary degrees and awards, including the Bollingen and Pulitzer prizes for her *Collected Poems* (1951). In 1955, M. was elected to the American Academy of Arts and Letters.

Observations shows clearly M.'s celebrated innovations in prosody, formal structuring of verse, and poetic vision of animals and of man. In "The Fish," M.'s sharp powers of close observation enable M. to render vividly the world of the ocean. That poem also reveals M.'s intense interest in design and pattern, indicated by the distinctive forms of typography, and her new emphasis on the whole stanza as a formal unit, rather than on the line. In the first few lines of "Poetry," M. tells us that she, too, dislikes poetry, but that by reading it, one may discover "the genuine." This poem includes M.'s famous description of poetry as seeing real toads in imaginary gardens.

In his introduction to M.'s *Selected Poems* (1935), T. S. Eliot linked her with the Imagist poets, yet pointed out unique characteristics of her work. He acknowledges her as the greatest master of *light* rhyme, admiring her intricate forms and patterns. Eliot recognizes M.'s work as being part of a small number of durable poems from our time.

In "The Mind Is an Enchanted Thing" (from *Nevertheless*, 1944), M.

argues, through her own intricate form of syllabics, that contemplation of art has the power to transform spiritual dejection into spiritual joy. The most emotional of all M.'s poems is "In Distrust of Merits." It has been called the best poem to come out of World War II; the theme is the tragedy of war, and the poem reflects M.'s profound hope that contagion, so effective in sickness, may also become effective in creating trust.

M.'s major scholarly work, on which she spent nine years, is a translation of the fables of La Fontaine (1954). The fables are all slyly satirical and entertaining in their striking wisdom and new typographical forms. M.'s criticism, collected in *Predilections* (1955), is eclectic; her topics include Louise Bogan, D. H. Lawrence, Sir Francis Bacon, Ezra Pound, Henry James, and Anna Pavlova. She also wrote a play, *The Absentee: A Comedy in Four Acts* (1962), based on the 1812 Irish novel by Maria Edgeworth. M.'s most popular book, *A Marianne Moore Reader* (1961), includes selections from her best prose and poems.

M.'s main literary contribution is the development of the artful flexibility of direct language in poems. She is remembered as a genius of invention in poetry, for humane wit and intellectual energy, and as a loved and gracious literary artist.

WORKS: *Poems* (1921). *Marriage* (1923). *Observations* (1924). *Selected Poems* (1935). *The Pangolin, and Other Verse* (1936). *What Are Years* (1941). *Nevertheless* (1944). *Rock Crystal, a Christmas Tale* by A. Stifter (translated by Moore, with E. Mayer, 1945). *A Face* (1949). *Collected Poems* (1951). *The Fables of La Fontaine* (translated by Moore, 1954). *Gedichte* (1954). *Predilections* (1955). *Like a Bulwark* (1956). *Idiosyncrasy & Technique: Two Lectures* (1958). *Letters from and to the Ford Motor Company* (1958). *O to Be a Dragon* (1959). *A Marianne Moore Reader* (1961). *The Absentee: A Comedy in Four Acts* (1962). *Puss in Boots, the Sleeping Beauty, and Cinderella* by Charles Perrault (translated by Moore, 1963). *The Arctic Ox* (1964). *Poetry and Criticism* (1965). *Tell Me, Tell Me; Granite, Steel, and Other Topics* (1966). *The Complete Poems of Marianne Moore* (1967). *The Accented Syllable* (1969).

BIBLIOGRAPHY: Abbott, C. S., *Marianne Moore: A Descriptive Bibliography* (1977). Engel, B. F., *Marianne Moore* (1964). Garrigue, J., *Marianne Moore* (University of Minnesota Pamphlets on American Writers, No. 50, 1965). Hadas, P. W., *Marianne Moore: Poet of Affection* (1977). Hall, D., *Marianne Moore: The Cage and the Animal* (1970). Jennings, E., in *American Poetry*, Ed. I. Ehrenpreis (1965). Nitchie, G. W., *Marianne Moore: An Introduction to the Poetry* (1969). Sheehy, E. P., and K. A. Lohf, *The Achievement of Marianne Moore: A Bibliography, 1907–1957* (1958). Stapleton, L., *Marianne Moore: The Poet's Advance* (1978). Thérèse, Sister Mary, *Marianne Moore:*

A Critical Essay (1969). Tomlinson, C., ed., *Marianne Moore: A Collection of Critical Essays* (1969). Watts, E. S., *The Poetry of American Women from 1632 to 1945* (1977).

For articles in reference works, see: *CA*, 33 (1973) *CB* (Dec. 1952; April 1968). *20thCA. 20thCAS.*

Other references: *CE* (Feb. 1953). *Harper's* (May 1977). *Quarterly Review of Literature* (4, 1948; 16, 1969).

ROBIN JOHNSON

Sarah Parsons Moorhead

M. lived during the tumultuous Great Awakening, the religious revival of the 1740s which shook New England. M.'s one slender published work, *To the Reverend James Davenport on His Departure from Boston by Way of a Dream* (1742), is an extended poetic comment on the controversy that occurred in Boston over Davenport's theological opinions and religious practices.

Davenport, deeply affected by the religious zeal of the 1740s, deserted his congregation of Southold, Long Island, and began itinerant preaching. He attacked the piety and sincerity of local ministers, creating internal dissension in many congregations. M. comments sharply on his behavior and admonishes backsliding and bickering Bostonians. Her public criticism of the clergy is significant because it was published contemporaneously with the events discussed in the poem. That is, a woman writer had been accepted as a critic of current events as early as 1742.

Stylistically, M. mimics the poetical taste of the day. Paradoxically, although her subject is religious, M. speaks with the voice of a distressed sentimental lover. M. also employs the technique of a dream vision. She interjects a femine feeling through florid description, creating an elaborate tapestry quality. Perhaps M. recognized that using such sugared language would make her severe criticism acceptable to the public. Her style and subject matter thus appear as a strange but well-presented mixture of the religious and the secular, the pious and the sentimental.

M.'s criticism, perhaps influenced by Charles Chauncy, the conservative minister of the First Church of Boston, focuses on the extremist elements of the Great Awakening and on a prevalent religious hypocrisy. She also discusses free grace. Dealing with a major problem among the Puritans—the difficulty of differentiating between moral action and faith—M. depicts the good-deeds churchgoers, who salve their conscience while actually remaining "immers'd in the black Gulph of sin, / . . . Pleas'd with the fancy'd Freedom of their Will." She believed that salvation can be secured only through the gift of free grace.

The poem also emphasizes the breakdown of morale in the Congregationalist churches—a result of continued quarreling over theological differences, notably among the ministers. M. admonishes the New England churches to remain united against external opposition if they are to survive. She restates this notion in a short poetic postscript published with the longer Davenport verse.

M.'s two poems have historical importance as well as poetic merit. They indicate a general easing of social and religious restraints among New England's Puritans, which allowed women a wider range of subjects and an emergent, if limited, public voice in the New England colonies.

WORKS: *To the Reverend James Davenport on His Departure from Boston by Way of a Dream: With a Line to the Scoffers at Religion Who Make an Ill Improvement of His Naming Out Our Worthy Ministers* (1742).

BIBLIOGRAPHY: Benedict, A., *A History and Genealogy of the Davenport Family* (1851).

JACQUELINE HORNSTEIN

Lillian Mortimer

D. *18 Dec. 1946, Petersburg, Michigan*
Wrote under: Lillian Mortimer, Naillil Remitrom
M. J. L. Veronee

M.'s date of birth is unknown, but she was acting in her own plays by 1895. M. began producing her plays and achieved her greatest success with *No Mother to Guide Her* (1905). For a number of years, M. played the comic soubrette Bunco in that melodrama. M. evidently had a repertoire of *lazzi* to use whenever her stage directions indicated "funny business," and she must have been able to put across lines such as this: "Christopher Columbus! Burglars! I thought dere was somethin' crooked about dat guy. De oder one didn't want to do it. Hully gee—what'll I do? Guess I'll have to take my trusty and go after dem. Dey're comin' back." *No Mother to Guide Her* was revived in 1933 for thirteen performances with a cast of fifteen midgets.

The popularity of *No Mother to Guide Her* can scarcely be comprehended by the reader of the published text. The dialogue is little more than a framework on which to hang innumerable bits of comic business, scuffles, pratfalls, abductions, faintings, fisticuffs, knife fights, and revolver shots. The stage directions at the ends of the acts illustrate the genre: At the end of act 2, "they fight. Livingstone gets the better of the knife fight—stabs Jake and throws him off. Livingstone starts for Jake again with knife, to give him another thrust, and as he does so, Bunco enters from R., shoots him; he staggers. During all this action there is a terrible storm raging."

In 1915, M. left the popular-priced melodrama theater circuit to become a headliner in vaudeville. In an interview about her plans for the future, M. said, "I shall write again—when I get time . . . I've got enough scenarios to keep me busy for the next year if I should make plays of all the plots that I have in mind; but I'm always waiting for a little 'leisure,' and then along comes a new contract, and I jump to the road again." Although M. remained on the Keith Circuit for twenty years, she found leisure time during the 1920s to write three to five full-length "comedy-dramas" each year. Most were published for use by amateur theater groups.

In these plays, M. frequently used ethnic characters for the secondary roles—Irish, German, and Jewish "types," country folk, and blacks. In *Mammy's Lil' Wild Rose* (1924), M. specified that Mammy be "made up with minstrel black (not mulatto) and mammy wig." *Headstrong Joan* (1927) includes a courtship between the lovable middle-aged Irish maid Honora and Abie, a "typical Jewish peddler," who wears a paper collar and his derby pulled down to make his ears stand out. This subplot spoofs the long-running Broadway hit *Abie's Irish Rose*. The various dialects M. used provide a counterpoint to the bright, slangy speech of the lively young couples.

The plot formula that M. found most useful set up a confrontation between two young couples. The more attractive pair is virtuous and romantically idealized. The other two, motivated by greed or jealousy, create obstacles for the innocent lovers. But the lovers are so young and appealing that the plotters finally repent and accept the ethics and values that will enable them to live happily ever after.

The photograph of M. in the New York *Dramatic Mirror* (12 May 1915) is of a self-assured middle-aged woman, flamboyantly dressed. She stands with hand on hip and chin tilted back, archly gazing from heavy-lidded eyes. It is hardly the image one would expect of the author of more than forty moral dramas that reaffirm the values of girlish innocence and of decency and noble self-abnegation for young men.

WORKS: *No Mother to Guide Her* (1905). *A Man's Broken Promise* (1906). *The City Feller* (1922). *Little Miss Jack* (1922). *The Path Across the Hill* (1923). *The Road to the City* (1923). *Yimmie Yonson's Yob* (1923). *Mammy's Lil' Wild Rose* (1924). *That's One on Bill* (1924). *An Adopted Cinderella* (1926). *The Bride Breezes In* (1926). *Mary's Castle in the Air* (1926). *Nancy Anna Brown's Folks* (1926). *Ruling the Roost* (1926). *Headstrong Joan* (1927). *He's My Pal* (1927). *Nora, Wake Up!* (1927). *The Winding Road* (1927). *His Irish Dream Girl* (1928). *Love's Magic* (1928). *Paying the Fiddler* (1928). *Two Brides* (1928). *The Open Window* (192–?, by Naillil Remitrom, pseud.). *Manhattan Honeymoon* (1929). *The Gate to Happiness* (1930). *The Wild-Oats Boy* (1930). *Jimmy, Be Careful!* (1931). *Mother in the Shadow* (1936).

BIBLIOGRAPHY: Leverton, G. H., ed., *America's Lost Plays* (Vol. 8, 1940). Mantle, B., ed., *The Best Plays of 1933–34* (1934).

Other references: New York *Dramatic Mirror* (12 May 1915). *NYT* (26 Dec. 1933; 20 Dec. 1946).

FELICIA HARDISON LONDRÉ

Martha Morton

B. *10 Oct. 1865, New York City; d. 18 Feb. 1925, New York City*
M. *Hermann Conheim*

M.'s family included two playwrights and several novelists and journalists. Her mother encouraged M. to write poems and short stories, some of which were published in magazines. Since the stories were mostly in dialogue, M. was persuaded to try writing a play. Unable to interest any managers in her first effort, *Hélène*, she mounted it at her own expense, for one performance, in 1888. The *New York Times* called it "a lugubrious and ill-made though not wholly ineffective drama," but actress Clara Morris revived it in 1889 for a two-year run that returned fifty thousand dollars to the novice playwright.

M.'s second produced play, *The Merchant*, won the New York *World* Play Contest. M. described the prejudice she had to face while directing a rehearsal: "The men shook their heads. They said the drama was going to the dogs. Then they crept in through the stage door and watched that 'green girl' direct the rehearsal and one of them came up to me and said, 'Are you going to make a business out of this?' . . . I looked him straight in the eyes and answered fervently, 'God help me, I must!' Then he put out a friendly hand, crushed my fingers into splinters and gave me the comforting assurance that a woman would have to do twice the work of a man to get one-half the credit."

Because women were barred from membership in the American Dramatists' Club, M. organized the Society of Dramatic Authors. Thirty women constituted its charter membership, but male playwrights were also invited to join. In 1907, the older group proposed consolidation, and the result was the Society of American Dramatists and Composers.

By 1910, M. was called "America's pioneer woman playwright," "the first successful woman playwright," and "the dean of women playwrights." She wrote about thirty-five forgotten plays, fourteen of which were professionally produced in New York City between 1888 and 1911.

M.'s most successful plays were written for the popular comedian William H. Crane: *Brother John* (1893), *His Wife's Father* (1895), *A Fool of Fortune* (1896), and *The Senator Keeps House* (1911). These were considered "good and clean, not too subtle and not too obvious." M.'s favorite subjects were marital adjustments, ups and downs in the business world, and the foibles of high society. *A Bachelor's Romance* (1896) showed members of the frivolous social élite redeemed by exposure to rural life. M.'s plays pleased audiences despite the critics' continual readiness to point out their hackneyed qualities.

M. traveled widely in Europe, and was well read in French and German literature. Her most ambitious work was an adaptation of Leopold Kampf's *On the Eve* (1909), about revolutionary unrest in Russia. For the part of the heroine, M. sent for German actress Hedwig Reicher, who made a personal triumph of her first English-speaking role. Of that character, M. said: "Woman is the tragic element in the social body. . . . The chief woman figure in *On the Eve* symbolizes the woman of today, the universal woman seeking her work and finding it." Critics called this play "a collection of antiquated theatrical effects," but M.'s professionalism afforded her a degree of prestige attained by few other women playwrights.

WORKS: *Hélène* (1888). *The Triumph of Love: The Merchant* (1891). *Geoffrey Middleton* (1892). *Brother John* (1893). *His Wife's Father* (1895, produced in London as *The Sleeping Partner*, 1897). *A Bachelor's Romance* (1896). *A Fool of Fortune* (1896). *The Diplomat* (1902). *Her Lord and Master* (1902). *A Four Leaf Clover* (1905). *The Truth Tellers* (1905). *The Movers* (1907). *On the Eve* (1909). *The Senator Keeps House* (1911).

BIBLIOGRAPHY: *Bookman* (Aug. 1909). *Green Book Magazine* (May 1912). *Theatre Magazine* (10, 1909; 18, 1913). *World To-Day* (July 1908).

FELICIA HARDISON LONDRÉ

Sarah Wentworth Apthorp Morton

B. *Aug. 1759, Boston, Massachusetts; d. 14 May 1846, Quincy, Massachusetts*
Wrote under: Constantia, Sarah Wentworth Apthorp Morton, Philenia
D. *of James and Sarah Wentworth Apthorp; m. Perez Morton, 1781*

M. was the scion of two influential, wealthy early New England families. She had a thorough education, evidenced in the literary quality of her verses. When the revolution started, M.'s family was accused of Tory loyalties, but she expressed strong patriot sentiments in her post-revolutionary verse. In 1781, M. married a Harvard graduate, a patriot lawyer during the revolution and a prominent figure in state government in the Republic's early years. During their early married life, M. and her husband headed Boston's socialites and remained leading figures in Massachusetts' social and political life. Five of their six children lived to maturity, but all died before M.

In 1788, Perez had an affair with M.'s sister Frances, ending in her sister's suicide. This affair appeared fictively in the first American novel, *The Power of Sympathy; or, The Triumph of Nature* (1789), by William Mill Brown.

M. and her husband led the fight for repeal of Massachusetts's antitheater laws in 1793, subscribing to Boston's first theater. M. supported the earliest American abolitionist groups. In later life she was a patron to young writers.

M.'s subject matter is wide-ranging. Her earliest poems are sentimental plaints or elegies filled with neoclassic devices. Her post-1800 works are mainly occasional poems. Themes throughout focus primarily on moral and political issues.

In much of her work, M. speaks through a languishing, affected female persona, whose sentimental sufferings are suffused with the soft glow of flowery diction. M.'s interest in sentimental neoclassicism also appears in "Ode to Mrs. Warren," a notable example of one early American female poet praising another. In her concern for female attitudes and behavior, M. was a "Sappho," the woman's poet.

However, M. was also an "American" poet, for she wrote verse about the new nation's ideological issues. Her best works in this vein demonstrate a well-developed social and moral conscience, independent thought, and notable poetic scope.

M.'s poem "Beacon Hill" (*Columbian Centinal*, 4 Dec. 1790), written in neat neoclassic couplets, celebrates the sacred, solemn events which transpired on Boston Hill during the revolution. With revisions and enlargements, this poem reappeared as *Beacon Hill: A Local Poem, Historic and Descriptive, Book I* (1797). Here M. tries to revitalize and mythologize the revolutionary era. The poem's introductory section reviews early events: Warren's death, Bunker Hill, Washington's camp at Cambridge. The central section discusses the "natural, moral, and political history" of the colonies. Book One closes with a shepherd-soldier figure defending "his hereditary farm," while the prophetic Columbian muse bears the message of "Equal Freedom" around the earth. Although thoroughly nationalistic in this work, M. also presents a critique of southern slavery.

M.'s "sister" poems, *Ouâbi; or, The Virtues of Nature: An Indian Tale in Four Cantos* (1790) and *The Virtues of Society: A Tale Founded on Fact* (1799), show further interest in moral and social issues. They exemplify her mixed vision of the sentimental-domestic and historical-heroic. *Ouâbi*, perhaps the first American "Indian" poem, discusses a contemporary problem: the survival of simple American virtues beset by luxury and sophistication. *The Virtues of Society*, a spin-off of the failed epic *Beacon Hill*, is a romantic tale based on an incident in the American Revolution.

My Mind and Its Thoughts, in Sketches, Fragments, and Essays (1823) is M.'s only work to appear under her real name. It consists of numerous aphorisms, short essays, and poems—some previously published and rewritten, others new to print. Her "Apology" explains that she made the collection to ease her distress (her son had recently died). The book is a curious mixture of the public and private, the patriotic and sentimental, summarizing M.'s life's interests.

M. was quite popular in the 1790s, but she outlived the vogue for her neoclassical style and post-revolution themes. Her last book was praised nostalgically, not for innate achievement. Her reputation as a poet died with her.

WORKS: *Ouâbi; or, The Virtues of Nature: An Indian Tale in Four Cantos* (1970). *Beacon Hill: A Local Poem, Historic and Descriptive, Book I* (1797). *The Virtues of Society: A Tale Founded on Fact* (1799). *My Mind and Its Thoughts, in Sketches, Fragments, and Essays* (1823).

BIBLIOGRAPHY: Evans, C., *American Bibliography* (1912). Field, V. B., *Constantia: A Study of the Life and Works of Judith Sargent Murray* (1931). Otis, W. B., *American Verse, 1625–1807: A History* (1909). Pearce, R. H., *The Savages of America* (rev. ed., 1953). Pendleton, E., and Milton Ellis, *Philenia: Life and Works of Sarah Wentworth Morton* (1931). Watts, E. S., *The Poetry of American Women from 1632 to 1943* (1977).

For articles in reference works, see: *AA. CAL. DAB*, VII, 1. *NAW* (article by O. E. Winslow).

JACQUELINE HORNSTEIN

Lucretia Coffin Mott

B. 3 Jan. 1793, Nantucket Island, Massachusetts; d. 11 Nov. 1880, Roadside, Pennsylvania
D. of Thomas and Anna Folger Coffin; m. James Mott, 1811

Born to a hearty, seafaring Quaker family, M. was sent to a Friends' school in New York, where she subsequently served as an assistant teacher. There she met her husband, with whom she had six children. M. was designated a minister of the Society of Friends in 1821. During the Great Separation of the Society in 1827, she allied herself with the liberal Hicksite faction. Within the next decade she became a vocal abolitionist who helped found the Philadelphia Female Anti-Slavery Society. Within the abolitionist movement, M. backed the radical faction of William Lloyd Garrison, which urged immediate emancipation of the slaves.

The diary in which M. recorded her experiences at the 1840 World's Anti-Slavery Convention in London, where, because of her sex, she was denied recognition as a delegate of the U.S., has been edited by Frederick B. Tolles (*Slavery and "The Woman Question,"* 1952). M. describes the political wrangling among abolitionists and Quakers, her meeting with English female reformers, her conversations with Elizabeth Cady Stanton, and her travels throughout the British Isles. M.'s friendship with Stanton, begun at the convention, resulted in a decision to call the first women's rights convention in 1848 at Seneca Falls, New York.

A preacher and reformer, M.'s literary corpus consists almost entirely of recorded sermons and discourses. Her appeal to reason and moral principle, powerful delivery, and personal presence gave M.'s words great impact. Her preaching was shot through with the liberal religious belief that practical righteousness was more important than theological speculation. In *A Sermon to the Medical Students* (1849), M. laid out her self-proclaimed heretical view that true religion is not mysterious, but is based on the universal and self-evident conviction that the kingdom of God is within. Humanity is not depraved, and does not need to be brought to righteousness by the atonement of Christ. The work of the present age is to reveal the nobility, and hence the divinity, of humanity through works of reform.

In response to a lecture by Richard Henry Dana, M. delivered her logical and powerful *Discourse on Woman* (1849), in which she shows that the present position of woman is neither her natural nor original one. Her equality with man is established by God, but she is everywhere in subjection to man. Woman's natural ability is illustrated historically in the lives of great women, but society promotes her inferiority. Woman, like the slave, has no liberty. She is subject to laws she does not make, excluded from a pulpit that disciplines her, and bound by a marriage contract that degrades her. She asks for no favors, but for the right to be acknowledged as a moral, responsible being.

In *A Sermon at Yardleyville* (1858), M. affirms the divinity of human instincts and claims that the attempt to create greater equality among people is characteristic of the work of the real Christian. In *A Sermon at Bristol* (1860), she urges Christians to be nonconformists like Jesus, and women to reject sectarianism, which sets limits on the divinity within them. M. maintains in *Discourse at the Friends' Meeting, N.Y.* (1866) that human progress is really moral progress and that skepticism and critical thinking are religious duties.

"Truth for authority, rather than authority for truth" was M.'s central concern. In her preaching and speaking M. attempted to uncover truth. Through her personal involvement in a myriad of reform movements she tried to live truth and help realize it in her own time. In her home, where M. offered hospitality to hundreds of fellow reformers and society's most oppressed, she helped sustain truth and those who sought it.

WORKS: *Discourse on Woman* (1849). *A Sermon to the Medical Students* (1849). *A Sermon at Yardleyville* (1858). *A Sermon at Bristol* (1860). *Discourse at the Friends' Meeting, N.Y.* (1866). *Discourse at the Second Unitarian Church, Brooklyn* (1867). *Sermon on the Religious Aspects of the Age* (1869). *Life and Letters of James and Lucretia Mott* (Ed. A. D. Hallowell, 1884). *Slavery and "The Woman Questions": Lucretia Mott's Diary of her Visit to Great Britain to Attend the World's Anti-Slavery Convention of 1840* (Ed. F. B. Tolles, 1952). *Lucretia Mott: Complete Sermons and Speeches* (Ed. D. Greene, 1980).

The letters of Lucretia Mott are in the Friends Historical Library, Swarthmore College, and the Sophia Smith Collection, Smith College Library.

BIBLIOGRAPHY: Bacon, M., *Valiant Friend: The Life of Lucretia Mott* (1980). Cromwell, O., *Lucretia Mott* (1958).

For articles in reference works, see: *AW. DAB*, VI, 1. *HWS*, 1. *NAW* (article by F. B. Tolles). *NCAB*, 2.

Other references: *American Scholar* (Spring 1951). *Bulletin of the Historical Society of Montgomery County, Pa.* (April 1948).

DANA GREENE

Louise Chandler Moulton

B. *10 April 1835, Pomfret, Connecticut; d. 10 Aug. 1908, Boston, Massachusetts*
Wrote under: Ellen Louise Chandler, Louisa Chandler, A Lady, Ellen Louise,
   Louise Chandler Moulton
D. *of Lucius Lemuel and Louisa Rebecca Clark Chandler; m. William Upham*
   Moulton, 1855

M. was born on a farm outside a town settled by her Puritan ancestors. Her parents were wealthy, conscientious Calvinists. M.'s childhood was solitary and circumscribed, but reasonably happy. Precocious, M. published her first verses at fifteen. When she entered Emma Willard's Female Seminary in Troy, New York, fellow students knew her as "Ellen Louise," editor of *The Book of the Boudoir* (1853) and author of *This, That, and the Other*, a collection of sentimental stories and sketches which appeared in 1854 and sold 20,000 copies.

Soon after M.'s graduation in 1855, she married the editor and publisher of *The True Flag*, a Boston literary journal. Members of the city's literary society, the Moultons entertained Whittier, Longfellow, Holmes, and Emerson. In 1870, M. became the Boston literary correspondent for the New York *Tribune*. She began contributing stories to magazines such as *Harper's*, *Galaxy*, and *Scribner's;* her poem "May-Flowers" achieved great popularity after appearing in the *Atlantic*. Other works during this period include *June Clifford* (1855), a novel; *Some Women's Hearts* (1874), short stories; and *Bed-Time Stories* (1873), the first in a series of children's books.

After an initial trip to Europe in 1876, M. divided her life between the two continents. Her overwhelming success in London literary society began in 1877 with a letter of introduction to Lord Houghton (Richard Monckton Milnes) from "the Byron of Oregon," Joaquin Miller. From this time, M. was firmly established in European artistic circles.

Although she had published an earlier volume of poetry in America, *Swallow-Flights* (1877) brought M. her first wave of extravagant praise. Professor William Minto compared her to Sir Philip Sidney; other critics mentioned the lyric poets of the 16th and 17th centuries. *In the Garden of Dreams* (1890) and *At the Wind's Will* (1899) confirmed her reputation. Critics rated her love poetry close to Mrs. Browning's and considered her sonnets second only to Christina Rossetti's. During these years, M. also brought out two delightful volumes of Irvingesque travel sketches and a book of social advice culled from her newspaper column in *Our Continent*.

Certainly any assessment of M.'s achievements must cite her "genius for friendship." Her correspondence, now in the Library of Congress, fills fifty-two volumes; its index is a virtual directory of late Victorian authors. M.'s library, bequeathed to the Boston Public Library, comprised nine hundred books, many of them rare editions and autographed presentation copies. However, M.'s greatest legacy stemmed from her critical astuteness and sympathy. As a European literary correspondent for the Boston *Sunday Herald* and the New York *Independent* during the

1880s and 1890s, M. gained recognition in the U.S. for the Pre-Raph-aelites, Décadents, and French Symbolist poets.

Like many late Victorians, M. wrote in traditional forms such as the sonnet, the French ballade, triolet, and rondel. She was known for her polished metrics, sensuous imagery, and meticulous workmanship. While critics appreciated her spontaneity, rarely do her emotions burst their poetic form; poise is all. However, M.'s meditations on love and ap-proaching death hint at deep feeling below the restrained surface.

Upon her death, M.'s reputation reached its crest. According to Whit-ing, she "had left a place in American letters unfilled and that no succes-sor is in evidence will hardly be disputed." M. lamented half-seriously that she seemed to have only two themes: love and death. But, as her biographer Lilian Whiting commented, these are surely two of the very greatest. As a poet, her contribution was small, but worth noting. As a critic and literary publicist, she played a valuable role in American let-ters. As a woman, her social success and "feminine" artistry reveal a great deal about late Victorian expectations.

WORKS: *The Waverly Garland: A Present for All Seasons* (edited by Moulton, 1853). *The Book of the Boudoir; or, A Momento of Friendship* (edited by Moulton, 1853). *This, That, and the Other* (1854). *June Clifford: A Tale* (1855). *My Third Book* (1859). *Evaline, Madelon, and Other Poems* (1861). *Bed-Time Stories* (1873). *Some Women's Hearts* (1874). *More Bed-Time Stories* (1875). *Jessie's Neighbor, and Other Stories* (1877). *Swallow-Flights* (American title, *Poems*, 1877). *New Bed-Time Stories* (1880). *Random Rambles* (1881). *Poems* (1882). *Firelight Stories* (1883). *Garden Secrets* by Philip Bourke Marston (edited, with biographical sketch, by Moulton, 1887). *Ourselves and Our Neighbors* (1887). *Education for the Girls* (1888). *Miss Eyre from Boston* (1889). *A Ghost at His Fireside* (1890). *In the Garden of Dreams* (1890). *Stories Told at Twilight* (1890). *A Last Harvest* by Philip Bourke Marston (edited, with biographical sketch by Moulton, 1891). *Col-lected Poems of Philip Bourke Marston* (edited by Moulton, 1892). *Arthur O'Shaugnessy, His Life and His Work* (1894). *In Childhood's Country* (1896). *Lazy Tours in Spain and Elsewhere* (1896). *Against Wind and Tide* (1899). *At the Wind's Will* (1899). *Four of Them* (1899). *The American University Course (State Registered): Second Month Conduct of Life* (1900). *Jessie's Neighbor* (1900). *Her Baby Brother* (1901). *Introduction to the Value of Love and Its Compiler Frederick Lawrence Knowles* (1906). *Poems and Son-nets of Louise Chandler Moulton* (Ed. H. P. Spofford, 1908).

The papers of Louise Chandler Moulton are at the Library of Congress and the American Antiquarian Society.

BIBLIOGRAPHY: Howe, J. W., *Representative Women of New England* (1904). Spofford, H. P., *A Little Book of Friends* (1916). Spofford, H. P., *Our Famous Women* (1884). Whiting, L., *Louis Chandler Moulton, Poet and*

Friend (1910). Winslow, H. M., *Literary Boston of Today* (1902).

For articles in reference works, see: *AW. CAL. DAB*, VII, 1. *Female Prose Writers of America* (1857). *NAW* (article by L. M. Young). *NCAB*, 3.

Other references: Boston *Transcript* (12 Aug. 1908). *Poet-Lore* (Winter 1908).

SARAH WAY SHERMAN

Mary Noailles Murfree

B. 24 Jan. 1850, Murfreesboro, Tennessee; d. 31 July 1922, Murfreesboro, Tennessee
Wrote under: Charles Egbert Craddock, R. Emmet Dembury
D. of William Law and Fanny Dickinson Murfree

Born at the family plantation, M. was the daughter of a lawyer and author and a mother whose love of music greatly influenced the family. Illness at the age of four left M. with permanent lameness.

In 1855, M. spent the first of fifteen summers at Beersheba Springs in the Cumberland Mountains, which she fictionalized as New Helvetia Springs. Soon the family moved to Nashville, where M. and her sister Fanny were educated at the Nashville Female Academy. After the Civil War, which the Murfrees spent in Nashville, M. continued her education at Chegary Institute in Philadelphia, a French finishing school.

M.'s writing career began in earnest with the publication of "The Dancin' Party at Harrison's Cove" in the *Atlantic Monthly* (May 1878) under the pseudonym Charles Egbert Craddock. M.'s mountain fiction was very well received; by 1885, when *The Prophet of the Great Smoky Mountains* was being serialized, her popularity had led to increased speculation about the author's identity, and the sensation following its revelation gained M. invaluable publicity.

Although the modern reader may find M.'s decorous mountain fiction more romantic than realistic, and may be bored by the lack of individualization in her characters, contemporary readers were fascinated by the minute detail, often gleaned through research, with which M. portrayed people and their activities. The dominant feature of M.'s earlier work is the mountains themselves. The juxtaposition of florid prose with dialect is probably its weakest trait.

In spite of M.'s desire for realism, her characters tend to be stereotypes. Most of the young "mountain-flower" girls, such as Cynthia Ware in "Drifting Down Lost Creek" and Clarsie Giles in "The 'Harnt' That Walks Chilhowee," are almost indistinguishable. " 'Harnt,' " probably M.'s best-known work, is notable for its theme of the superiority of mountain life.

M.'s greatest achievement is her first volume of stories, *In the Tennessee Mountains* (1884), with its emphasis on the picturesque details of regional life. M.'s stories appealed to the awareness of sectional differences which had been heightened by the Civil War, as the popularity of this volume indicates.

Except for M.'s first novel, *Where the Battle Was Fought* (1884), based on personal experiences during the Civil War, M.'s work through the late 1890s focuses on mountain places and themes. When the popularity of local-color writing waned, M. turned to historical subjects in undistinguished novels such as *The Story of Old Fort Loudon* (1899) and *The Amulet* (1906). By 1910, M.'s public appeal had diminished to the point that Houghton-Mifflin rejected a proffered novel and collection of stories.

M. has been favorably compared to local colorists such as Bret Harte, Sarah Orne Jewett, and fellow southerner George Washington Cable. Her reputation is based on her mountain stories and novels; the body of her work is flawed by M.'s tendency to repeat characters and plots. However, *In the Tennessee Mountains* remains an important contribution to regional literature in the late 19th c.

SELECTED WORKS: *In the Tennessee Mountains* (1884). *Where the Battle Was Fought* (1884). *The Prophet of the Great Smoky Mountains* (1885). *In the "Stranger People's" Country* (1891). *The Mystery of Witch-Face Mountain, and Other Stories* (1895). *The Phantoms of the Foot-Bridge, and Other Stories* (1895). *The Story of Old Fort Loudon* (1899). *A Spectre of Power* (1903). *The Amulet* (1906). *The Fair Mississippian* (1908). *The Raid of the Guerilla, and Other Stories* (1912). *The Story of Duciehurst* (1914).

BIBLIOGRAPHY: Cary, R., *Mary Noailles Murfree* (1967). Parks, E. W., *Charles Egbert Craddock (Mary Noailles Murfree)* (1941). Wright, N., Introduction to *In the Tennessee Mountains* (1970).

For articles in reference works, see: *AW. CAL. DAB*, VII, 1. *NAW* (article by E. W. Parks).

Other references: *ALR* (Autumn 1974). *Appalachian Journal* (Winter 1976). *MissQ* (Spring 1978).

MARTHA E. COOK

Judith Sargent Murray

B. 1 May 1751, Gloucester, Massachusetts; d. 6 July 1820, Natchez, Mississippi
Wrote under: Constantia, Honoria, Honoria-Martesia, Judith Sargent,
  Judith Stevens
D. of Winthrop and Judith Saunders Sargent; m. John Stevens, 1769;
  m. John Murray, 1788

M. was the oldest child of a well-to-do merchant who was active during the Revolution on the colonists' side. M. was better educated than most women of her time, because her father permitted her to study with a brother who was preparing for Harvard. She spent most of her life in Gloucester, where she was married twice: to a sea captain and, two years after his death, to Murray, founder of the American Universalist Church. Two children were born of the second marriage, a son who died shortly after birth and a daughter who survived her mother. Financial difficulties marked the final years of both marriages.

In 1798, M. collected many of her writings into a three-volume work called *The Gleaner*. These volumes include one series of essays that appeared originally from 1792 to 1794 in the *Massachusetts Magazine*, additional essays previously unpublished, and two plays—*Virtue Triumphant* and *The Traveller Returned*, produced with little success at the Federal Street Theatre in Boston. There remain uncollected a number of essays and poems published in periodicals and a catechism for children, which was published as a book under the name of Judith Stevens. In addition, M. edited Murray's letters and autobiography.

M. is best known for her periodical essay series, "The Gleaner." These essays purport to be written by Mr. Vigilius, a well-off, philanthropic man of reason and sensibility who has adopted the pen name of the Gleaner to write about moral, religious, political and family matters. M. reveals her liberal religious views, federalism, cultural nationalism, concern for the special problems of bringing up daughters, and commitment to education, about which she had modern views. Much of the interest, however, centers less on discussions of general issues than on the Gleaner's accounts of his family. Because the story of his daughter is so fully developed, this series has been referred to as a novel of sensibility. In a subplot there is, in contrast with traditions of 18th-c. sensibility, an unusually realistic cameo view of women's experience.

M. is also known for her feminist statement "On the Equality of the Sexes," which she claimed to have written in 1779, before Wollstonecraft's *Vindication of the Rights of Woman* appeared, although it was not published until 1790 in the *Massachusetts Magazine*. Concerned here with arguing the intellectual equality of women, M. went on in the later *Gleaner* essays to elaborate her defense of women's abilities.

M.'s essay series has attracted some scholarly attention in the past, and her plays, which combine American settings and sentiments with traditions of the Restoration stage, read surprisingly well and are of historic interest. Recently, her essays have attracted attention because of M.'s feminist defense of women's intellectual potential and her insistence on the importance of education and economic independence for women. M.'s work reflects an acceptance of the literary and intellectual traditions of her time and the strength of mind to reject tradition when she believed it incorrect or unfair.

WORKS: *Some Deductions from the System Promulgated* (1782). *The Gleaner* (3 vols., 1798). *Letters and Sketches of Sermons*, by John Murray (3 vols., edited by Murray, 1812–13). *Records of the Life of the Rev. John Murray, Written by Himself, with a Continuation by Mrs. Judith Sargent Murray* (edited by Murray, 1816).

BIBLIOGRAPHY: Benson, M. S., *Women in Eighteenth Century America* (1935). Field, V. B., *Constantia: A Study of the Life and Works of Judith Sargent Murray* (1933). Hanson, E. R., *Our Women Workers* (1882).

For articles in reference works, see: *DAB*, VII, 1. *NAW* (article by J. W. James).

Other references: *AL* 12 (1940). *AQ* 28 (1976). *EAL* (9, 1975; 11, 1976–77). *SP* 24 (1927).

PHYLLIS FRANKLIN

Pauli Murray

B. 20 Nov. 1910, Baltimore, Maryland
D. of William Henry and Agnes Georgianna Fitzgerald Murray

Orphaned at the age of three, M. was raised by her mother's sister, an elementary school teacher in a small black school. M. attended her aunt's classes and learned to read and write at an early age.

M. received a B.A. from Hunter College in New York. In 1938, she applied to the graduate school of the University of North Carolina but was denied admission to the white institution. During this period, M. wrote prose and poetry under the guidance of Stephen Vincent Benét. M. suspended her literary work to serve as special field secretary for the Workers Defense League. After Benét's death in 1943 she resumed her efforts to write the epic poem which he had urged her to write about blacks in America. She finished the first version of "Dark Testament" during the Harlem riot of 1943.

In 1944, M. was graduated with honors from Howard University Law School in Washington, D.C. As a woman, she was denied admission to Harvard Law School in 1944 and 1946, but received an M.A. in 1945 from the University of California Law School at Berkeley and a Ph.D. from Yale in 1965. From 1948 to 1960, she was in private practice in New York. In 1960 and 1961, M. was senior lecturer on constitutional and administrative law at the Ghana School of Law. While in Accra, she joined Leslie Rubin in the writing of *The Constitution and Government of Ghana* (1961). M. has practiced law, taught law and political science, and served on numerous national committees.

Dark Testament, and Other Poems (1970) includes poems originally published in several magazines. The longest and best is "Dark Testament." Part 1 of "Dark Testament" questions the possibility of hope but ends on a note of determination, saying ". . . let the dream linger on." M. contends that universal brotherhood must be the goal of humanity. Part 2 contains poems dealing with specific historical events: a Detroit riot, the lynching of Mack Parker, and the death of Franklin Roosevelt. The third part focuses upon the universal human predicament and has no racial emphasis. Neither has the fourth part, which takes images from nature for poems dealing with love, friendship, death, and loneliness.

Proud Shoes: The Story of an American Family (1956) is the story of M.'s ancestors. Asserting that "true emancipation lies in the acceptance of the whole past, in deriving strength from all my roots, in facing up to the degradation as well as the dignity of my ancestors," M. traces the family back to great-grandparents who were slaves. But the major portion of *Proud Shoes* is devoted to her greatest source of pride, her grandfather, who taught M. that she ought to cherish "courage, honor, and discipline."

Though she knew her parents only briefly during early childhood, M. found great sources of pride in her mother's family. *Proud Shoes* does more than account for the pride that has made M. such a successful black woman. It analyzes miscegenation as a social phenomenon and examines its bearing on race relations. It attacks stereotypes of the black family as broken and matriarchal. Thus, it is a valuable social document as well as an interesting biography of an American family.

Though M. has chosen to make her social contribution primarily though service rather than literature, her small oeuvre is significant. Her legal writing establishes her as a scholar, *Proud Shoes* proves her a capable biographer, and *Dark Testament* reveals a talented poet whose lines combine the skills of both biographer and lawyer—precision of language and vision—with the compression of poetic forms to achieve powerful effects.

WORKS: *All for Mr. Davis* (with M. Kempton, 1942). *States Law on Race and Color* (1950). *Proud Shoes: The Story of an American Family* (1956). *The Constitution and Government of Ghana* (with L. Rubin, 1961). *Dark Testament, and Other Poems* (1970).

BIBLIOGRAPHY: Diamonstein, B., *Open Secrets* (1972).

For articles in reference works, see: *Black American Writers Past and Present*, T. G. Rush, C. F. Myers, and E. S. Arata (Vol. 2, 1975).

Other references: *Afro-American* (20 Jan. 1968).

GWENDOLYN THOMAS

Alice Ruth Moore Dunbar Nelson

B. *19 July 1875, New Orleans, Louisiana; d. 18 Sept. 1935, Philadelphia, Pennsylvania*
Wrote under: *Alice Dunbar, Alice Dunbar-Nelson, Alice Ruth Moore*
D. *of Joseph and Patricia Wright Moore; m. Paul Laurence Dunbar, 1889; m. Robert John Nelson, 1916*

The younger of two daughters of middle-class working parents, N. attended public schools and Straight College, New Orleans. After graduation, she began to teach and to submit poetry to the Boston *Monthly Review*.

One of these poems and the accompanying photograph of N. attracted Dunbar, then a young poet. He wrote N., conversationally raising literary issues, and enclosed a copy of his "Phyllis." This began a friendship that led to marriage.

N. separated from Dunbar after a quarrel in 1902, and returned to teaching—she had taught kindergarten at Victoria Earle Matthews's White Rose Mission in New York—becoming head of the English Department at Howard High School in Wilmington, Delaware. She retained this position for eighteen years until she was fired for defying an order to abstain from political activity.

During World War I, N. became involved in organizing black women on behalf of the U.S. Council of National Defense. N. was the first black woman to serve on Delaware's Republican State Committee.

N. became associate editor of the *Wilmington Advocate,* a weekly newspaper published by her second husband and dedicated to the achievement of equal rights for blacks. She also wrote a weekly column for the Washington, D.C., *Eagle* and contributed occasional pieces to the *American Methodist Episcopal Church Review.* Her later years were devoted to social work, especially with delinquent black girls, and to the cause of world peace.

N.'s reply to Dunbar's first letter to her set forth her views on the literary use of "the Negro problem:" "I haven't much liking for those writers that wedge the Negro problem and social equality and long dissertations on the Negro in general into their stories. It is too much like a quinine pill in jelly. . . . Somehow when I start a story I always think of my folk characters as simple human beings, not of types of a race or an idea, and I seem to be on more friendly terms with them." N.'s letter also mentioned the forthcoming publication of her first book, *Violets, and Other Tales* (1895). In accord with her philosophy, the book presents "simple human beings" caught in universal dilemmas such as poverty and love betrayed.

While many of the twelve poems and seventeen tales and sketches in *Violets, and Other Tales* are romantic and slight, they give evidence of a fresh, lively style. Noteworthy in this collection for their sprightliness and originality are the humorous "In Unconsciousness," a mock-epic inspired by a tooth extraction, and "The Woman," a lively meditation on the independent woman. This piece decries "this wholesale marrying of girls in their teens, this rushing into an unknown plane of life to avoid work," and reassures readers that an independent, intelligent woman, a lawyer or doctor, does not lose her ability to love when she gains a vocation.

During the period of her marriage to Dunbar, N. published her second collection, *The Goodness of St. Rocque, and Other Stories* (1899), fourteen local-color stories of New Orleans life. These are crisply written sketches, portraying struggling, heroic characters trapped in difficulties. Most have a surprise twist at their conclusions.

While teaching at Howard High School, N. edited two collections of poems and prose for oratory students, *Masterpieces of Negro Eloquence* (1914) and *The Dunbar Speaker and Entertainer* (1920). Included in the latter are several pieces by N., many of them (such as the one-act play *Mine Eyes Have Seen*) expressing conventional patriotic sentiments and racial pride. The short lyric "I Sit and Sew," while sharing the conventional patriotism of the others, is also a statement of a woman chafing at the limited range of appropriate female activity; it has an intensity, freshness, and power which the other pieces lack.

N. was a pioneer in the black short-story tradition. Her second volume shows an increase in power, which promised further development, had she continued to write in this genre. Instead, N., an energetic woman of diversified talents, devoted her later life to journalism and political and social activism.

WORKS: Violets, and Other Tales (1895). *The Goodness of St. Rocque, and Other Stories* (1899). *Masterpieces of Negro Eloquence* (edited by Nelson, 1914). *The Dunbar Speaker and Entertainer* (edited by Nelson, 1920).

BIBLIOGRAPHY: Bernikow, L. *The World Split Open: Four Centuries of Women Poets in England and America* (1974). Brawley, B., *Paul Laurence Dunbar* (1936). Brown, H. Q., *Homespun Heroines, and Other Women of Distinction* (1926). Kerlin, R. T., *Negro Poets and Their Poems* (1935). Loggins, V., *The Negro Author* (1931). Martin, J., ed., *A Singer in the Dawn* (1975). Whiteman, M., *A Century of Fiction by American Negroes, 1853–1952: A Descriptive Bibliography* (1955).

For articles in reference works, see: *NAW* (article by N. A. Ford).

Other references: *Delaware History* 17 (Fall–Winter 1976).

KAREN F. STEIN

Eliza Jane Poitevent Nicholson

B. *11 March 1848, Pearlington, Mississippi; d. 15 Feb. 1896, New Orleans,*
Louisiana
Wrote under: Pearl Rivers
D. *of Captain William James and Mary Amelia Russ Poitevent;*
m. Alva Morris Holbrook, 1872; m. George Nicholson, 1878

N. was raised by an aunt near the Louisiana-Mississippi border. She entertained herself by roaming the piney woods along the Pearl River, developing in her youth an affectionate regard for nature.

In 1867, N. began submitting the poems she had been writing since age fourteen to newspapers and magazines. Her first published poem appeared in the New Orleans literary sheet *The South* in 1868. Soon poems by "Pearl Rivers" appeared in the New York *Home Journal*, the New York *Ledger*, and the New Orleans *Times* and *Daily Picayune*.

In 1868, N. met A. M. Holbrook, owner and editor of the *Daily Picayune*. He offered her a job as literary editor for $25 a week. Over the strenuous objections of her family, N. accepted, becoming New Orleans' first female journalist. Her lively prose and intelligent selections markedly improved the paper's literary section. In 1872, she married Holbrook, divorced and forty years her senior. (His angry ex-wife returned from New York a month after the wedding and proceeded to attack N. with a pistol and a bottle of rum. The subsequent trial was covered in scandalous detail by the *Daily Picayune*.)

When Holbrook died, four years later, N. assumed ownership and management of the *Picayune*, which was eighty thousand dollars in debt. At twenty-seven, she thus became the first woman ever to own and operate a metropolitan daily paper. With the assistance of a loyal staff, including the part owner and business manager, George Nicholson, whom she married in 1878, N. transformed the *Picayune* into a profitable paper and the first general-interest daily in the South. N.'s most significant innovations were directed at women. She introduced a society column, personal notes, fashion news, home and medical advice columns, children's pages, and plentiful illustrations. N. also employed talented writers, including several women. N.'s own poetry and prose also appeared, including columns of her personal and imaginative commentary. In 1884, N. became president of the Women's National Press Association and was the first honorary member of the New York Women's Press Club.

In N.'s only volume of poetry, *Lyrics* (1873), the theme is almost without exception nature and seasonal change. N.'s rhymed quatrains are characterized by personifications of the months and seasons and by fairylike perspectives of plants and animals. Occasionally, she writes of feminine heartbreak. Technically pedestrian, N.'s poems reveal a delight in nature and an eye for authentic detail. To N., poetry was a "gift of song," intended to cheer and please her audience.

Two later poems, "Hagar" and "Leah," published first in *Cosmopolitan* in 1893 and 1894, suggest a richer dimension of N.'s talent. Long dramatic poems in blank verse, they are uneven but vivid and insightful evocations of their heroines' bitterness and jealousy as overlooked women. "Hagar" is the stronger of the two poems, with an effective use of meter and imagery.

Although her early pastoral poetry is slight, N.'s later poems reflect an ability to dramatize emotion effectively. But it is N.'s journalistic ability that distinguishes her. Her columns are filled with a sure, lively prose, whose mark was entertaining dialogue and reflective commentary. Her paper stands as a model of innovative and responsible publishing. A remarkable and sensitive woman, N. is said to have possessed little confidence in her abilities. Nevertheless, her strong sense of duty and courage often substituted for self-confidence and forged the means by which her creativity and discriminating intelligence were expressed.

WORKS: *Lyrics* (1873). *Four Poems by Pearl Rivers* (1900). *Two Poems by Pearl Rivers* (1900?).

The papers of Eliza Jane Poitevent Nicholson are at the Howard-Tilton Library, Tulane University, New Orleans, Louisiana.

BIBLIOGRAPHY: Dabney, T. E., *One Hundred Great Years* (1944). DeMenil, A. N., *The Literature of the Louisiana Territory* (1904). Farr, E. S., *Pearl Rivers* (1951). Gill, H. M., *The South in Prose and Poetry* (1916). Harrison, J. H., *Pearl Rivers, Publisher of the Picayune* (1932). Holdith, W. K., "The Singing Heart: A Study of the Life and Work of Peark Rivers," SoQ 22 (Winter 1982). Mount, M., *Some Notables of New Orleans* (1896). Ross, I., *Ladies of the Press* (1936).

For articles in reference works, see: *DAB*, VII, 1. *Dictionary of American Authors*, Ed. O. F. Adams (1904). *Living Female Writers of the South*, Ed. M. T. Tardy (1872). *The Living Writers of the South*, J. W. Davidson (1869). *NAW* (article by W. Wiegand). *NCAB*, 1.

Other references: *Louisiana Historical Society* (Oct. 1923). New Orleans *Daily Picayune* (16 Feb. 1896). New Orleans *Times-Democrat* (16 Feb. 1896). *Teachers' Outlook* (Feb. 1901).

BARBARA C. EWELL

Marjorie Hope Nicolson

B. 18 Feb. 1894, Yonkers, New York; d. 9 March 1981, White Plains, New York
D. of Charles Butler and Lissie Hope Morris Nicolson

The daughter of a newspaper editor, N. spent most of her adult life in an academic environment, studying at Michigan, Yale, and Johns Hopkins, and teaching at Minnesota, Goucher, Smith, Columbia, and Claremont. She was a member of the Institute for Advanced Studies at Princeton from 1963 to 1968, and now resides in White Plains, New York.

N. earned many honors during her long and distinguished career and blazed many new trails for academic women. As the first woman president of the United Chapters of Phi Beta Kappa (1940), she explained that most academic women had not been able to distinguish themselves because it was hard to be "both scholars and ladies," in that women scholars "have no wives to look after social contacts and to perform the drudgery for them." She was the first woman to be elected president of the Modern Language Association, the first woman to receive Yale's John Addison Porter Prize for original work, and the first woman to hold a full professorship on Columbia University's graduate faculty.

N. was fascinated with the impact on the literary imagination made by science and philosophy, especially in the 17th and 18th centuries. As early as 1935, N.'s lifelong interest surfaced in a study of *The Microscope and English Imagination*, in which she describes how the invention of the microscope had stimulated both serious and satiric themes in literature, even influencing the remarkable technique of Swift's *Gulliver's Travels*.

Several of her best volumes focus on the way scientific advances alter aesthetic judgments and hence modify literary treatments. For instance, *A World in the Moon* (1937) describes the changing attitudes toward the moon brought about by the telescope; *Mountain Gloom and*

Mountain Glory (1959) describes humanity's shift from abhorrence of mountains as reflecting sin's disruption to attraction to mountains as symbols of the infinite; and *Breaking of the Circle* (1950) describes the dislocating insecurity caused by the Copernican Revolution as reflected in the works of John Donne and his contemporaries. Although this latter was her most influential book, it also caused considerable scholarly controversy because many argued that N. had overestimated the importance of scientific theory to people who were accustomed to finding their security not in science but in religion. *Newton Demands the Muse* (1946), a study of how Newtonian optics affected 18th-c. poets, merited the Rose Mary Crawshay Prize of the British Academy.

It is not surprising that a woman so interested in science and literature should turn her attention to John Milton, who was similarly attracted to the advanced scientific thought of his day. Accordingly, Nicolson edited a volume of Milton's major poems and published *A Reader's Guide to Milton* (1963), which has proved popular on many campuses.

This Long Disease, My Life: Alexander Pope and the Sciences (1968), written with G. S. Rousseau, after N.'s retirement, includes a detailed medical history of the poet, a study of five medical themes or episodes in his work, an extensive section on Pope and astronomy, and a concluding section on Pope's interest in the other sciences of his day, especially geology.

In addition to her books, N. was a frequent contributor to periodicals. She edited *American Scholar* from 1940 to 1944 and served on the editorial board of the *Journal of the History of Ideas* for many years. Her work is never academic in the "dry-as-dust" sense; it pulsates with the fascination, wry wit, and human involvement she feels toward her subject. It is N.'s flair for making her point memorably that ensures her a continuing influence among lovers of literature.

WORKS: *The Art of Deception* (1926). *Conway Letters* (1930). *The Microscope and English Imagination* (1935). *A World in the Moon* (1937). *Newton Demands the Muse* (1946). *Voyages to the Moon* (1948). *Breaking of the Circle* (1950; rev. ed., 1960). *Science and Imagination* (1956). *Mountain Gloom and Mountain Glory* (1959). *Milton: Major Poems* (edited by Nicolson, 1962). *A Reader's Guide to Milton* (1963). *Pepys' Diary and the New Science* (1965). *This Long Disease, My Life: Alexander Pope and the Sciences* (with G. S. Rousseau, 1968).

BIBLIOGRAPHY: *CA* (1964). *CB* (1940).

VIRGINIA RAMEY MOLLENKOTT

Josephina Niggli

B. 13 July 1910, Monterrey, Mexico
D. of Frederick Ferdinand and Goldie Morgan Niggli

N.'s father, of Swiss and Alsatian ancestry, left Texas in 1893 to manage a cement plant in the village of Hidalgo, Mexico; her mother was a concert violinist from Virginia. In 1913 and in 1925, when revolutions broke out in Mexico, the family fled to San Antonio, Texas, where N. had her only formal schooling. She graduated from Main Avenue High School in 1925 and from Incarnate Word College in 1931.

N. studied playwriting at the University of North Carolina, a center for the development of regional and folk drama. She wrote a three-act play, *Singing Valley*, for her thesis, and received her M.A. degree in drama in 1937. N.'s work with Professor Frederick H. Koch's Carolina Playmakers was a major influence on her writing. Koch himself edited an anthology of her work, *Mexican Folk Plays*, in 1938. Since then, N. has lived in North Carolina, except for sojourns with Bristol University and the Bristol Old Vic in England and with the Abbey Theatre in Dublin. N. has taught English and radio scriptwriting at the University of North Carolina, and she established a drama department at Western Carolina University in Cullowhee.

N.'s one-act plays of Mexican folk life have long been favorites of discerning high-school drama groups. These plays enliven a small cast and simple scenic requirements with abundant stage action, sound effects, and opportunities for characterization. N.'s special skill is her ability to blend closely observed local color and customs with universally understood emotions and humor. Although written in the 1930s, her plays have not become dated.

In *This Bull Ate Nutmeg* (1937), N. drew upon her childhood memories of a one-man sideshow attraction and of mock bullfights. The play includes folk music, a romantic rivalry, and a climactic backyard bullfight, underscored by the cheers and laughter of village spectators.

This is Villa! (1939) is a portrait of the murderous Pancho Villa. N. created an incident that reveals his sentimental and childlike side as well as his cruelty. Despite momentary lapses into swashbuckling melodrama, the play, like all N.'s dramatic and narrative fiction, has a convincing documentary quality.

N.'s most frequently performed play is *Sunday Costs Five Pesos* (1939). In her book *New Pointers on Playwriting* (1945), N. commented: "My *Sunday Costs Five Pesos* has made me more money than a best-selling novel, primarily because it is presented again and again in contests."

N.'s first narrative fiction work, *Mexican Village* (1945), a collection of ten stories of daily life in the village of Hidalgo, using recurrent characters, was uniformly praised by critics. *Step Down, Elder Brother* (1947) is set among the aristocracy in Monterrey. N. again studied the impact of social and historical change in Mexico in *Farewell, Mama Carlotta* (1950) and *Miracle for Mexico* (1964). If her writing is occasionally criticized as "excessively romantic," that is also its strength, for it ensnares the reader with the devices of good storytelling and vividly conveys N.'s warm affection for the people of northern Mexico.

WORKS: *Mexican Silhouettes* (1931). *Tooth or Shave* (1936). *Singing Valley* (1937). *This Bull Ate Nutmeg* (1937). *Mexican Folk Plays* (1938). *Sunday Costs Five Pesos* (1939). *This is Villa!* (1939). *Miracle at Blaise* (1944). *Mexican Village* (1945). *New Pointers on Playwriting* (1945). *Pointers on Radio Writing* (1946). *Step Down, Elder Brother* (1947). *Farewell, Mama Carlotta* (1950). *Miracle for Mexico* (1964).

BIBLIOGRAPHY: Spearman, W., *The Carolina Playmakers: The First Fifty Years* (1970).

For articles in reference works, see: *American Novelists of Today*, H. R. Warfel (1951). *CB* (1949). *National Playwrights Directory*, Ed. P. J. Kaye (1977).

Other references: *NYT* (21 Jan. 1939).

FELICIA HARDISON LONDRÉ

Anaïs Nin

B. 21 Feb. 1903, Paris, France; d. 14 Jan. 1977, Los Angeles, California
D. of Joaquin and Rosa Culmell Nin; m. Hugh P. Guiler, 1923

N. was the eldest of three children of a Spanish composer and concert pianist and a French-Danish mother. N. began keeping a diary after her father's desertion. N.'s departure with her mother and brothers for New York, her return to Paris, and her home in Louveciennes in the outskirts of Paris were all delineated. Purposely omitted was her marriage to Guiler, a bank and financial consultant who was also known as the engraver and filmmaker Ian Hugo.

D. H. Lawrence: An Unprofessional Study (1932) marked N.'s entrée into "creative criticism." N. was an enemy of naturalism, realism, positivism, and rationalism, which she felt distorted reality; what was of import for her was the catalytic effect of Lawrence's work on the reader's senses and imagination. To know Lawrence, she maintained, was to take a fantastic voyage: to "flow" forward with his characters and situations, to follow their feelings as manifested in impulses and gestures.

N.'s feelings of timidity and inadequacy became so disruptive that in 1932 she consulted the psychiatrist René Allendy, who encouraged her to begin The House of Incest (1936). "It is the seed of all my work," N. wrote, "the poem from which the novels were born." Affinities with Lawrence, Joyce, Woolf, and the surrealists were evident in her reliance upon dream sequences and in her use of stream-of-consciousness style.

Dr. Otto Rank's attitude to the problem of creativity was more to N.'s liking, and she became his patient in 1933. When he moved his offices to New York in 1934, he invited N. to practice as a lay analyst. Although successful, N. understood that her mission in life was artistic and not therapeutic. She returned to France, where she lived until the outbreak of World War II. Her friends included Miller, Artaud, Brancusi, Supervielle, Orloff, Durrell, Breton, Dali, Barnes, Young, Varèse, Varda, and many more.

In New York, artistic and financial setbacks encouraged N. to print her own works: Winter of Artifice (1939) and Under a Glass Bell (1947). To probe her heroine's dream world in Winter of Artifice, N. chose the anti-novel technique, with its pastiches, repetitions, omissions, and ellipses, instead of the structured characters and plot of the psychological novel.

Cities of the Interior (1959), a "continuous novel," includes six short works: *Ladders to Fire* (1946), *Children of the Albatross* (1947), *The Four-Chambered Heart* (1950), *A Spy in the House of Love* (1954), *Solar Barque* (1958), and *Seduction of the Minotaur* (1961). Labeled "space fiction," *Cities of the Interior* is centered in the unconscious, upon clusters of visual configurations. In this inner space, characters confront, respond, act, and react to each other like multiple satellites. N.'s deepening psychological acumen and intuitive faculties, her heightened powers of observation are brought into play in the recording of minute vibrations in nuanced and counterpuntal relationships.

The Diary of Anaïs Nin (7 vols., 1966–78) is a "woman's journey of self-discovery," which Henry Miller placed "beside the revelations of St. Augustine, Petronius, Abélard, Rousseau, Proust." The *Diary* is a historical document in that it reports and deals with events chronologically. It is of psychological import because it analyzes inner scapes (dreams, reveries, motivations) and a variety of approaches to the unconscious; it is of aesthetic significance because it introduces readers to the world of the novelist, poet, musician, painter, and the artistic trends of the day: cubism, realism, surrealism, op, pop, and minimal art.

It was with her *Diary* that N. won an international reputation. She was called upon to lecture throughout North America at universities, poetry centers, and clubs. N. synthesized and elaborated her earlier statements of her artistic credo—*Realism and Reality* (1946)—in *The Novel of the Future* (1968), in which she endorses the dictum of C. G. Jung: "Proceed from the Dream Outward."

N.'s writings express an inner need; truth shaped and fashioned into an art form. Thought, feeling, and dream are captured in metaphors, images, and alliterations, which are interwoven in complex designs. The techniques of free association and reverie enable her to penetrate the inner being, evoke a mood, and arouse sensations in an impressionistic and pointilliste manner. N.'s work offers readers perpetual transmutations of matter and spirit. Hers is a very personal, authentic, and innovative talent, unique in her time.

WORKS: *D. H. Lawrence: An Unprofessional Study* (1932). *The House of Incest* (1936). *Winter of Artifice* (1939). *Under a Glass Bell* (1944). *Ladders to Fire* (1946). *Realism and Reality* (1946). *Children of the Albatross* (1947). *On Writing* (1947). *The Four-Chambered Heart* (1950). *A Spy in the House of Love* (1954). *Solar Barque* (1958). *Cities of the Interior* (1959). *Seduction of the Minotaur* (1961). *Collages* (1964). *The Diary of Anaïs Nin* (7 vols., 1966–78). *The Novel of the Future* (1968). *A Woman Speaks: The Lectures, Seminars, and Interviews of Anaïs Nin* (1975). *In Favor of the Sensitive Man, and Other Essays* (1976). *Delta of Venus: Erotica* (1977). *Waste of Timelessness, and Other Early Stories* (1977). *Linotte: 1914–1920* (1978). *The Early Diary of Anaïs Nin: 1920–1923* (1982).

BIBLIOGRAPHY: Evans, O., *Anaïs Nin* (1968). Franklin, V. B., and D. Schneider, *Anaïs Nin: An Introduction* (1979). Harms, V., ed., *Celebration with Anaïs Nin* (1973). Hinz, J. E., *The Mirror and the Garden* (1971). Hinz, J. E., *The World of Anaïs Nin* (1978). Knapp, B. L., *Anaïs Nin* (1979). Spencer, S., *Collage of Dreams* (1977).

BETTINA L. KNAPP

Kathleen Thompson Norris

B. *16 July 1880, San Francisco, California; d. 18 Jan. 1966, San Francisco, California*
Wrote under: Jane Ireland, Kathleen Norris
D. *of James Alden and Josephine E. Moroney Thompson; m. Charles Gilman Norris, 1909*

The second of six children, N. grew up in rural Mill Valley, where her father, a San Francisco bank manager, commuted daily by ferry. In 1899, both parents died within a month, leaving the children to shift for themselves. N. worked as clerk, bookkeeper, librarian, and newspaper reporter to help support the family. While covering a skating party, she met her future husband, a writer. She followed him to New York City when he became arts editor for the *American* magazine.

N. published fiction in the New York *Telegram*, winning fifty dollars for the best story of the week. Her husband encouraged N. to send out others, and the *Atlantic* accepted "The Tide-Marsh" and "What Happened to Alanna" in 1910. N. began *Mother* (1911) for another story contest, but it grew too long; it was enlarged to become a popular novel.

For the next half century, despite crippling arthritis, N. wrote ninety books, numerous stories and magazine serials, a newspaper column, and a radio soap opera. A pacifist, she campaigned vigorously against capital punishment and foreign involvement.

Much of N.'s writing is rooted in her own life and California background. Typical is *Little Ships* (1921), centering on a large nouveau-riche Irish-Catholic family and its less fortunate relatives, including a fine old peasant grandmother. Although the book is marred by sentimentality and prejudice, N. creates deft characterization and effective dramatic tension in her family scenes.

Certain People of Importance (1922) is considered N.'s most ambitious work. In this impressive family chronicle spanning more than a century, descendants of Forty-niner Reuben Crabtree invent a "first family" history not in the least based on fact. Scandals and intrigues worthy of any soap opera are plentiful, yet no one lifts an eyebrow. Although N. denies a "knowledge of those dark forces which fascinate modern writers," the novel's true subject seems to be human greed, hypocrisy, and deceit.

One of the book's strengths is its precise attention to forgotten detail —fashions, furnishings, eating habits, and amusements. N. writes sympathetically of independent young women who chafe under the restrictions of parents or brother. She also offers a grim reminder of the risks of pregnancy, childbirth, and poverty. This, N.'s most realistic book, was not well received.

Through a Glass Darkly (1957) is noteworthy only because its first half depicts a Utopia where war does not exist, the government feeds anyone who needs it, and people take care of each other. Those who die on earth "arrive" in Foxcrossing to live happily. But the protagonist, who longs to "go back" to our world to help suffering children, loses her life trying to rescue hurricane victims and is reincarnated in the book's second half. The story moves disappointingly into N.'s familiar formula of a working girl's struggle to survive. The Utopian world is forgotten.

N. also published two sometimes conflicting autobiographies, *Noon* (1925) and *Family Gathering* (1959). Many of her books remain in print, but most of these are frothy romances with pink-and-gold heroines and contrived endings. These characters seem suspended in an eternal 1910, regardless of the real year. N.'s best writing shows more depth: family warmth, sincerity, and pettiness; condemnation of the self-centered rich; and vivid accounts of early California. She portrays men and women of another generation, almost another world, meeting life however they can—with love, with humor, with desperation.

WORKS: Mother (1911). *The Rich Mrs. Burgoyne* (1912). *Poor, Dear Margaret Kirby* (1913). *Saturday's Child* (1914). *The Treasure* (1914). *The Story of Julia Page* (1915). *The Heart of Rachael* (1916). *Martie, the Unconquered* (1917). *Undertow* (1917). *Josselyn's Wife* (1918). *Sisters* (1919). *Harriet and the Piper* (1920). *The Beloved Woman* (1921). *Little Ships* (1921). *Certain People of Importance* (1922). *Lucretia Lombard* (1922). *Butterfly* (1923). *Uneducating Mary* (1923). *The Callahans and the Murphys* (1924). *Rose of the World* (1924). *Noon* (1925). *The Black Flemings* (also published as *Gabrielle*, 1926). *Hildegarde* (1926). *The Kelly Kid* (1926). *Barberry Bush* (1927). *The Fun of Being a Mother* (1927). *My Best Girl* (1927). *The Sea Gull* (1927). *Beauty and the Beast* (1928). *The Foolish Virgin* (1928). *Home* (1928). *What Price Peace?* (1928). *Mother and Son* (1929). *Red Silence* (1929). *Storm House* (1929). *Beauty in Letters* (1930). *The Lucky Lawrences* (1930). *Margaret Yorke* (1930). *Passion Flower* (1930). *Belle-Mère* (1931). *Hands Full of Living: Talks with American Women* (1931). *The Love of Julie Borel* (1931). *My San Francisco* (1932). *Second-Hand Wife* (1932). *Treehaven* (1932). *Younger Sister* (1932). *The Angel in the House* (1933). *My California* (1933). *Walls of Gold* (1933). *Wife for Sale* (1933). *Maiden Voyage* (1934). *Manhattan Love Song* (1934). *Three Men and Diana* (1934). *Victoria: A Play* (1934). *Beauty's Daughter* (1935). *Shining Windows* (1935). *Woman in Love* (1935). *The American Flaggs* (1936). *Secret Marriage* (1936). *Bread into Roses* (1937). *You Can't Have Everything* (1937). *Baker's Dozen* (1938). *Heartbroken Melody* (1938). *Lost Sunrise* (1939). *Mystery House* (1939). *The Runaway* (1939). *The Secret of the Marshbanks* (1940). *The World Is like That* (1940). *These I Like Best* (1941). *The Venables* (1941). *An Apple for Eve* (1942). *Come Back to Me, Beloved* (1942). *Dina Cashman* (1942). *One Nation Indivisible* (1942). *Star-Spangled Christmas* (1942). *Corner of Heaven* (1943). *Love Calls the Tune* (1944). *Burned Fingers* (1945). *Motionless Shadows* (1945). *Mink Coat* (1946). *Over at the Crowleys'* (1946). *The Secrets of Hillyard House* (1947). *High Holiday* (1949). *Morning Light* (1950). *Shadow Marriage* (1952). *The Best of Kathleen Norris* (1955). *Miss Harriet Townshend* (1955). *Through a Glass Darkly* (1957). *Family Gathering* (1959).

BIBLIOGRAPHY: Kilmer, J., *Literature in the Making: By Some of Its Makers* (1917). Woollcott, A., *While Rome Burns* (1934).

For articles in reference works, see: *Catholic Authors: Contemporary Biographical Sketches 1930–1947*, Ed. M. Hoehn (1948). *20thCA. 20thCAS.*

Other references: *Bookman* (Sept. 1922). *NR* (11 Oct. 1922). *NYT* (19 Jan. 1966). *NYTBR* (6 Feb. 1955).

JOANNE McCARTHY

Joyce Carol Oates

B. *16 June 1938, Lockport, New York*
D. *of Frederick J. and Caroline Bush Oates; m. Raymond J. Smith, 1961*

One of three children, O. was born into an Irish-Catholic working-class family in a rural area near Millerport, New York, the "Eden County" country of many of her stories and novels. O., who attended a one-room schoolhouse, graduated Syracuse University, phi beta kappa, in 1960 with a B.A. in English, and earned an M.A. from the University of Wisconsin in 1961.

O. taught English for six years at the University of Detroit. She was in Detroit during the race riots, an event she documents in *them* (1969). Winner of many awards, O. has been elected to the National Academy and Institute of Arts and Letters.

From 1967 to 1977, O. and her husband taught literature at the University of Windsor, Ontario. They now live in Princeton, where they publish *Ontario Review* and run the Ontario Review Press and where O. is writer-in-residence at Princeton University.

In O.'s fiction, the individual is always viewed in the perspective of the larger world. O.'s protagonists strain to escape the world in which they live, but they do not succeed, except in madness or death. As O. drives her characters into a recognition of the boundaries of the real, the ideal is collapsed into the actual, the hope for freedom is converted into a hope for initiation, and the isolated self is confronted with its otherness.

With Shuddering Fall (1964) begins with idealized, romantic characters—a godlike, paternal figure, Herz; his virginal, religious daughter, Karen; and the violent rebel, Shar. The novel relates the story of Karen's initiation, which is effected not by a complete submission to an authoritarian order represented by her father, but by a rejection of the rootless freedom represented by Shar.

A Garden of Earthly Delights (1967), *Expensive People* (1968), and *them* constitute a trilogy exploring rural, suburban, and urban America. *A Garden of Earthly Delights* focuses on the condition of alienation, a condition O. views as rooted in the circumstances of American history and intensified by the American ideals of autonomy and self-sufficiency.

As in *them* and in *Wonderland* (1971), the Depression dislodges the characters from their paternal roots. Clara, the daughter of a migrant laborer who was forced from his land, maniacally and successfully plots to marry a man for his money and land to bequeath to her son a name that wields power. Ironically, rather than accept the world his mother has usurped for him, her son is possessed by a sense of alienation so intense that he finally commits suicide.

Matricide is the solution that Richard, child-hero of *Expensive People* (1968), finds for his mother's narcissistic assertion of freedom that denies him love and recognition. O. portrays affluent suburbia as an antithetical "paradise" into which one is admitted by virtue of greed; the dominant metaphor of the novel is gluttony, which stands not only for excessive material acquisition but for an inflated sense of self that leads to a denial of the world.

Although O. has not overtly associated herself with the women's movement, *Do With Me What You Will* (1973) attests to her sympathy with its cause. Elena, the novel's heroine, who tries to avoid reality by an almost psychotic passivity, finally reenters time and history when she leaves her husband and escapes with a lover. For O., the mask of passivity is as narcissistic as the mask of megalomania: The world must be confronted, not avoided or overcome.

O.'s later fiction demonstrates her increasing interest in the novel as an aesthetic object. In these works, form *is* theme. The monistic absolutists who populate the world of *The Assassins: A Book of Hours* (1975) are revealed through their streams of consciousness. Each consciousness is isolated from the others in a separate section of the novel, just as each character is isolated from the living totality of being by virtue of a stubborn adherence to a personal version of reality. A character's refusal to accommodate to the pluralistic universe is a surrender to Thanatos, an "assassination" of reality.

In *Bellefleur* (1980), a best-selling novel, O. employs the gothic to create a haunting fictional world perched between the fantastic and the real. Indeed, O. has woven a shimmering tapestry made of odd and contradictory threads: A hermaphrodite birth, a vulture who devours an infant, a dwarf with "powers," and a vampire are harmoniously woven into a history of the powerful Bellefleur family whose significance is not only historical but sociological, psychological, and mythic.

O. is a much anthologized short-story writer. A favorite of anthologists is the haunting "Where Are You Going, Where Have You Been" from *The Wheel of Love* (1970). It concerns an encounter between

Arnold Friend, a demon-lover figure, and the adolescent Connie. The same volume contains the powerful "The Region of Ice," the film version of which won an Academy Award in 1977.

All of O.'s fiction affirms that humanity is located in a universe that it cannot avoid, transcend, or control, and from which there is no separation or redemption. She is a writer obsessed with reconciling an age convinced that the isolated self is the final authority of reality and value to experiential plurality and human reciprocity, to time, history, and the manifest world.

Although O.'s fiction has received a good deal of critical attention, much of it intelligent and probing, some critics have tended to catalogue the novels' violent events, ignoring the careful structure of the works and the moral vision that informs them.

WORKS: *By the North Gate* (1963). *With Shuddering Fall* (1964). *Upon the Sweeping Flood* (1966). *A Garden of Earthly Delights* (1967). *Expensive People* (1968). *Women in Love, and Other Poems* (1968). *them* (1969). *Anonymous Sins, and Other Poems* (1969). *The Wheel of Love, and Other Stories* (1970). *Love and Its Derangements, and Other Poems* (1970). *Wonderland* (1971). *Marriages and Infidelities* (1972). *The Edge of Impossibility: Tragic Forms in Literature* (1972). *Do With Me What You Will* (1973). *Angel Fire* (1973). *Dreaming America* (1973). *The Goddess and Other Women* (1974). *The Hungry Ghosts: Seven Allusive Comedies* (1974). *Where Are You Going, Where Have You Been?: Stories of Young America* (1974). *New Heaven, New Earth: The Visionary Experience in Literature* (1974). *The Assassins: A Book of Hours* (1975). *The Poisoned Kiss, and Other Stories* (1975). *The Seduction, and Other Stories* (1975). *The Fabulous Beasts* (1975). *Childwold* (1976). *The Triumph of the Spider Monkey: The First Person Confession of the Maniac Bobby Gotteson, as Told to Joyce Carol Oates* (1976). *Crossing the Border: Fifteen Tales* (1977). *Son of the Morning* (1978). *All the Good People I've Left Behind* (1978). *Women Whose Lives Are Food, Men Whose Lives Are Money* (1978). *Unholy Loves* (1979). *Bellefleur* (1980). *Angel Light* (1981).

BIBLIOGRAPHY: Bellamy, J. D., ed., *The New Fiction: Interviews with Innovative American Writers* (1974). Creighton, J. V., *Joyce Carol Oates* (1979). Friedman, E. G., *Joyce Carol Oates* (1980). Friedman, E. G., "The Journey from the 'I' to the 'Eye': Joyce Carol Oates' *Wonderland*," in *Studies in American Fiction* (1980). Wagner, L. W., ed., *Critical Essays on Joyce Carol Oates* (1979). Waller, G. F., *Dreaming America: Obsession and Transcendence in the Fiction of Joyce Carol Oates* (1978).

Other references: *AL* (43, 1971; 49, 1977). *Commonweal* (5 Dec. 1969). *Critique* 15 (1973). *NYTBR* (28 Sept. 1969). *Paris Review* 74 (1978). *Soundings* 58 (1975). *Spirit* 39 (1972). *Studies in the Novel* 7 (1975).

ELLEN G. FRIEDMAN

Flannery O'Connor

B. 25 March 1925, Savannah, Georgia; d. 3 Aug. 1964, Milledgeville, Georgia
Given name: Mary Flannery O'Connor
D. of Edward Flannery and Regina Cline O'Connor

O. was the only child of parents whose Georgia manners and Catholic background influenced her deeply. She began writing at an early age and after graduation from Georgia State College for Women in 1945 attended the Writers' Workshop at the University of Iowa (M.F.A. 1947). "The Geranium" was accepted by *Accent* in 1946. Publication of other stories followed, and O.'s first novel, *Wise Blood*, triggered by the stories from the Iowa thesis, appeared in 1952.

Described by O. as "a comic novel," *Wise Blood* is the story of Haze Motes, a religious fanatic in an electric blue suit who preaches that "there was no Fall because there was nothing to fall from and no Redemption because there was no Fall and no Judgment because there wasn't the first two. Nothing matters but that Jesus was a liar." In his insistence that "there's only one truth and that is that there's no truth," Motes ricochets from a pseudo-blind prophet and his libidinous daughter, to the company of the moronic Enoch Emery, the one with "wise blood," to a final resting place with a rapacious landlady who plots to marry him. In his desperate quest for meaning, Motes mutilates himself with broken glass in his shoes, blinds himself with lye, and finally dies in a squad car on the way back to the landlady's bed. His physical humiliations and self-flagellations are enacted without hope of redemption; at the end of the novel, he has become a new and distorted Christ who can offer no salvation, even to himself.

Although the book was received with mixed reviews and an uneasy feeling that the cast of characters was too grotesque even for a public used to Faulkner's southern Gothics, the critics were aware that a new talent had indeed appeared. But in 1950, O. had learned that she, like her father, had lupus. She moved back to Milledgeville to a farm where she could raise herds of peacocks and have time to write. She received a *Kenyon Review* Fellowship in 1953, and published her first book of short stories, *A Good Man Is Hard to Find*, in 1955.

The title story of this book is described by O. as "the story of a family of six which, on its way driving to Florida, gets wiped out by an escaped convict who calls himself the Misfit." The Misfit is another Haze Motes, who also equates himself with Jesus and who realizes he is damned if Jesus did what He is said to have done and doomed to an absurd life in which there is "no pleasure but meanness" if Jesus didn't.

Motes and the Misfit, as well as a myriad of O.'s protagonists, are psychic cripples with what Hawthorne called "ice in the blood." They have become consumed with an image of Christ, and hence have lost all human feelings. O. commented in a 1960 lecture that "while the South is hardly Christ-centered, it is most certainly Christ-haunted."

The character in "Good Country People" who is preoccupied with religion in order to deny it is a one-legged spinster Ph.D., O.'s most obvious caricature. The lumpish young maid entices a young Bible salesman into a loft with plans to seduce him and instead has her wooden leg stolen by him. The Bible salesman, Manley Pointer, is thus one of the conmen who appear in O.'s fiction with as much regularity as her mad prophets. In "The Life You Save May Be Your Own," the con man, who steals an old woman's car by marrying her daughter, is named Tom T. Shiftlet—or possibly Aaron Sparks or George Speeds—since the identity of these opportunists shifts with equal regularity.

This lack of a secure identity for the characters is also apparent in O.'s use of the double. In countless stories, the protagonist is not only a distorted double for Christ but also has another character who is his own double. In some cases the double can even be an animal, generally a pig, but in "The Displaced Person," the double of the displaced person/Christ figure is a peacock. This story also demonstrates O.'s most skillful use of dramatic irony, and the reader anticipates helplessly as the survivor of a Nazi concentration camp becomes an obsession to the Georgia locals and is finally crushed, literally beneath a tractor, by another collection of good country people.

In 1959, O. received a Ford Foundation grant for creative writing, and in 1960 her second novel, *The Violent Bear It Away*, appeared. The fanatics are back, and this book contains three: old Tarwater, a mad prophet; young Tarwater, his grandson with an obsession to rid himself of Jesus by baptizing his idiot second cousin, Bishop; and his atheist uncle Rayber, who is equally obsessed by preventing the baptism. The violent clashes between the Tarwaters and Rayber become a struggle for young Tarwater's soul, and Rayber loses when the boy drowns Bishop and flees. Young Tarwater tries, with the desperation of a Motes, to convince himself that all old Tarwater had told him was false. But as he flees the murder of Bishop, he is picked up, drugged, and seduced by a man in a lavender car—which the old man had warned him was possible. The book ends as Tarwater gives in to his terrible destiny of prophecy, becoming as mad as his grandfather.

The title story of *Everything That Rises Must Converge* (1965) has as its central conflict the struggle between children and their parents, most often the mother, that appears in some of O.'s best work. The best story in the collection, "Revelation," shows O.'s child-parent conflict at its finest. This story presents another of the maimed and ugly daughters, this time characterized by ferocious acne, and another of those good country people, Mrs. Turpin, so complacent about their own virtue that they become almost evil in their selfishness. In the final story, "Parker's Back," the last story O. wrote before she died, the ubiquitous reversed Christ appears as a tattoo on Parker's back.

In 1972, *The Complete Stories* appeared and received the National Book Award. This book included all the previously published stories as well as those from O.'s Iowa thesis never before published.

The Habit of Being (1979), O.'s selected letters, presents a composite portrait of a writer who constantly emphasized this necessity of seeing. When one newspaper put her in the "realistic school," O. wrote to reject that label, insisting, "I am interested in making up a good case for distortion, as I am coming to believe it is the only way to make people see." The letters, edited by her longtime friend Sally Fitzgerald, offer brilliant glimpses of O.'s personality while they provide invaluable insights into her methods and fiction.

To call O.'s stories of death and destruction comic seems a contradiction in terms, but as she says blithely in the introduction to *Wise Blood*, "all comic novels that are any good must be about matters of life and death." O. will simply not allow identification with a single character, even when that character is so blatantly O. herself. With her sharp cartoonist's eye, O. has etched the outlines of her characters in stone, and they stonily resist all empathy. O. consistently utilizes the dramatic point of view in which she presents her characters as though on a stage, and the reader is never allowed to see the innermost thoughts of the character's head—or heart.

This lack of heart thus becomes central to O.'s themes, and the single-minded self-centeredness of the characters who are concerned only with their own salvation makes those characters essentially grotesque. As O. said: "whenever I'm asked why Southern writers particularly have a penchant for writing about freaks, I say it is because we are still able to recognize one." In creating her gallery of freaks, O. has eschewed not only the heroic but the normal.

The fact that her comic characters must suffer mentally and physically gives O.'s fiction overtones of tragedy, and it is perhaps significant that O. read *Oedipus Rex* just before completing the blinding episode in *Wise Blood*. Yet in the final analysis, O.'s work is more comic than tragicomic. Her comedy is not merely that of technique, but of vision; ultimately, the fiction becomes positive despite all its horrors and doubts. There is basically a maturation in the stories, an essential growing up in which the dreadful children do learn from their equally dreadful mothers and perhaps become equipped to cope and accept a moment of grace. In the southern ability to recognize a freak, there is the implicit idea of what a whole man must be, and ultimately this Swiftian view of man as capable of reforming—once his freakishness and his grotesqueness are revealed to him—breaks through the clouds of O.'s bleak fiction to show the pale light of hope.

WORKS: *Wise Blood* (1952). *A Good Man Is Hard to Find* (1955). *The Violent Bear It Away* (1960). *Everything That Rises Must Converge* (1965). *Mystery and Manners* (Ed. S. and R. Fitzgerald, 1969). *The Complete Stories* (1972). *The Habit of Being* (Ed. by S. Fitzgerald, 1979).

BIBLIOGRAPHY: Drake, R., *Flannery O'Connor* (1966). Driskell, L. V., and J. Brittain, *The Eternal Crossroads* (1971). Eggenschwiter, D., *The Christian Humanism of Flannery O'Connor* (1972). Feeley, K., *Flannery O'Connor* (1972). Friedman, M. J., and L. A. Lawson, eds., *The Added Dimension* (1966). Golden, R. E., *Flannery O'Connor and Caroline Gordon: A Reference Guide* (1977). Hendin, J., *The World of Flannery O'Connor* (1970). Hyman, S. E., *Flannery O'Connor* (1966). Martin, C. W., *The True Country* (1969). May, J. R., *The Pruning Word* (1976). McFarland, D. T., *Flannery O'Connor* (1976). Muller, G. H., *Nightmares and Visions* (1972). Reiter, R. E., ed., *Flannery O'Connor* (1968). Walters, D., *Flannery O'Connor* (1973).

Other references: *Bulletin of Bibliography* (1967). *Critique* (Fall 1958). *Esprit* (Winter 1964). *Flannery O'Connor Bulletin*.

PAT CARR

Lillian O'Donnell

B. 15 March 1926, Trieste, Italy
D. of Zoltan D. and Maria Busutti Udvardy; m. J. Leonard O'Donnell, 1954

O. is a New Yorker; she grew up in the city, where she attended parochial and public schools, pursued a career in the theater, married, and continues to live in the city. With a minor role in *Pal Joey*, O. became involved in Broadway productions as an actress and dancer. Later, she appeared in television productions, and then moved on to direct summer stock, becoming one of the first women managers. After her marriage, O. left the theater and decided to try writing novels.

O.'s early mystery stories reflect a gothic dimension in exotic settings, country-estate motifs, and genteel characters. *Death Schuss* (1963), for example, takes place in Canada at the height of the ski season amid the luxurious environs of an heiress's home. This unlucky young lady becomes the victim in this murder puzzle which is fraught with romantic entanglements and glamour. These early works are too filled with cliches to be unique.

The turning point in O.'s literary career occurred when she cast off the trappings of the mystery cum gothic style and moved into the real world of the police thriller to create Norah Mulcahaney of the New York City Police Department as her serial heroine. Norah Mulcahaney is a credible character. O. gives her heroine ethnic roots and a strong moral fiber. Norah is also appropriately attractive: tall and slim, with long dark tresses. Norah makes her first appearance in *The Phone Calls* (1972); she is just learning the ropes in the department when she is assigned to the case of a psychopathic killer who preys on women. In *Don't Wear Your Wedding Ring* (1973), Detective Mulcahaney becomes more self-assured; this time she is in pursuit of a female prostitution ring. "The chase" as well as the nature of the crime lives up to the tradition of the thriller as Norah eludes a murderous gang. Her relationship with Sgt. Joe Capretto develops in this case; the reader perceives a match is in the making. (Ultimately Norah marries Joe, but she neither retires nor loses her individuality; they do not become a "crime team.")

The crimes which O. chooses for her heroine are usually crimes

against women, such as rape (*Dial 577 R-A-P-E*, 1974). Norah Mulcahaney meets all challenges with conviction—she is a feminist who is
concerned with the plight of other women (other policewomen in *No
Business Being a Cop*, 1978).

O. learned about the inner workings of the police world through observation and careful research. Amid growing concern for the victims
of crime, O. chose another dimension to investigate and a different
kind of heroine. Mici Anhalt, an investigator for the New York City
Victim/Witness Project, makes her debut in *Aftershock* (1977). A combination social worker and detective, she often experiences personal danger. She too is attractive; though a liberated thirtyish female, she has the
youthfulness and enthusiasm of a teenager.

In both *Aftershock* and *Falling Star* (1979), Mici does her sleuthing by
assignment and under less than optimum conditions. She experiences on-
the-job harassment and departmental jealousies, not to mention the perils
of attack from malevolent assailants. But, like Norah Mulcahaney, she
endures, proving that a resilient female can make her own way in a tough
world.

O.'s novels have achieved success not because her characters are profound or unusual, or because her plots are mind-boggling or aesthetically
interesting. Hard-core realism, neither sweetened by gingery femininity
nor leavened by blood or brutality, is O.'s metier. Her unadorned literary
style is honest and appropriate to the street crimes she depicts.

WORKS: *Death on the Grass* (1959). *Death Blanks the Screen* (1960). *Death
Schuss* (1963). *Murder Under the Sun* (1964). *Death of a Player* (1964). *The
Babes in the Woods* (1965). *The Sleeping Beauty Murders* (1967). *The Tachi
Tree* (1968). *The Face of the Crime* (1968). *Dive into Darkness* (1971). *The
Phone Calls* (1972). *Don't Wear Your Wedding Ring* (1973). *Dial 577
R-A-P-E* (1974). *The Baby Merchants* (1975). *Leisure Dying* (1976). *After-
shock* (1977). *No Business Being a Cop* (1978). *Falling Star* (1979). *Wicked
Designs* (1980).

BIBLIOGRAPHY: Booklist (15 July 1977). *KR* (1 July 1979). *LJ* (Aug
1973). *Ms.* (Oct. 1974). *NYTBR* (8 Aug. 1976). *SatR* (29 Jan. 1972).

PATRICIA D. MAIDA

Cora Miranda Baggerly Older

B. 1875, Clyde, New York; d. 26 Sept. 1968, Los Gatos, California
Wrote under: Mrs. Fremont Older
D. of Peter and Margaret Baggerly; m. Fremont Older, 1893

O. was a Syracuse University student on vacation when she met and married her journalist husband, who was soon fighting both corporations and labor as editor of the San Francisco *Bulletin* and later of the *Call*. In her early married years, O. wrote reviews, society news, and celebrity interviews for her husband's paper. Her first novels were fictionalized versions of muckraking journalism. When the family moved to a ranch in the Santa Clara foothills in 1915, O. took charge of managing the property and its staff of paroled convicts.

O. wrote in three distinct genres. O.'s early novels were social melodramas that reflected current events. In *The Socialist and the Prince* (1903), Paul Stryne whips up resentment of cheap Chinese labor into a string of workingmen's clubs, a paramilitary organization, and an enormous political influence, but ultimately loses all for a beautiful, self-willed society girl who flirts with socialism. *The Giants* (1905) plays off the free children of the West against the railroad-monopoly capital of the East. *Esther Damon* (1911) is mildly utopian. The hero, a Civil War veteran reduced to alcoholism through wartime pain and postwar bitterness, reforms and begins a cooperative community. His protégée wins her way back to a place in society after she has been ruined by her parents' excessive Methodism and has had an illegitimate child.

During this period, O. also wrote magazine articles on social questions, including a long account of the San Francisco graft prosecutions for *McClure's*. Her novels were, for the most part, condemned as too sensational, stark, and evident of purpose. Turning away from fiction, O. wrote plays (none of which have been published), and in the 1930s "authorized" and highly laudatory biographies of William Randolph Hearst (who was her husband's employer) and his father George.

O.'s last works took up the matter of California in a more sophisticated fashion. *Savages and Saints* (1936), a novel, two collections of short stories, and a book about San Francisco combine carefully researched history with fictionalized versions of the lives and legends of Hispanic and Anglo pioneers.

O.'s style was not far removed from that of the dime novel. She wrote a spare, journalistic prose, with short simple sentences and abrupt paragraphs; she aroused emotion with predictable confrontations, duels, and love scenes played out on cliffs beside the sea during a thunderstorm. Yet although she shared the western naturalist's admiration for the successful—even brutal—man, she also wrote about women who took action instead of simply being acted upon. Flirtatious, dependent, clinging women are assigned to the villainous role; happy women generally earn a place of their own before marrying. Many of the stories in *California Missions and their Romances* (1938) and *Love Stories of Old California* (1940) tell of women who endured enormous hardship to keep the flames of religion and civilization alive in an unwelcoming land.

WORKS: *The Socialist and the Prince* (1903). *The Giants* (1905). *Esther Damon* (1911). *George Hearst, California Pioneer* (with F. Older, 1933). *Savages and Saints* (1936). *William Randolph Hearst, American* (1936). *California Missions and their Romances* (1938). *Love Stories of Old California* (1940). *San Francisco: Magic City* (1961).

The diary of Cora Miranda Baggerly Older is in the Bancroft Library, Berkeley, California.

BIBLIOGRAPHY: Older, F., *My Own Story* (1926).
Other references: *Bancroftiana* 59 (1974). *NYT* (29 Sept. 1965). *Time* (27 April 1936).

                                                    SALLY MITCHELL

Rose Cecil O'Neill

B. 25 June 1874, Wilkes-Barre, Pennsylvania; d. 6 April 1944, Springfield,
 Missouri
Wrote under: Rose O'Neill, Rose Cecil O'Neill, Mrs. H. L. Wilson
D. of William Patrick and Alice Asenath Cecelia Smith O'Neill;
 m. Gray Latham, 1896; m. Harry Leon Wilson, 1902

O. was educated in parochial schools in Omaha, Nebraska. Her professional career began at thirteen, when she won a children's drawing contest sponsored by the Omaha *World-Herald*, which then engaged her to do a weekly cartoon series. O. later moved to New York City, where her work found a ready market. At nineteen, she was a nationally known illustrator and later was also a regular contributor of stories and poems to women's magazines. In 1896, she married Gray Latham, whom she divorced in 1901. The next year she married Wilson, the novelist and playwright; that marriage ended in 1907.

O. is best remembered for the Kewpies, sentimentalized "little cupids" whose illustrated adventures in verse appeared first in the 1909 Christmas issue of the *Ladies' Home Journal* and later in other magazines and in several books. In 1913, O. patented the design, and Kewpie dolls and other Kewpie-decorated articles earned a fortune in royalties.

The first of four novels, *The Loves of Edwy* (1904), shows O.'s characteristic charm, humor, and tenderness; it reveals much about her own childhood and youth in a large, needy family. *The Lady in the White Veil* (1909) is a farcical mystery story in which a stolen Titian portrait is repeatedly recovered and lost anew. In spite of prodigious energy and O.'s unremitting mirth, it soon becomes tedious. *Garda* (1929) presents a fantasy world both beautiful and bizarre. Garda and her twin brother, Narcissus, symbolize a single mystical being represented as body and soul, the one joyously sensual, the other sensitive and suffering. They are in conflict over and ultimately reconciled by a common passion. *The Goblin Woman* (1930) is unsuccessful in attempting to combine a theme of sin and redemption with a milieu of contemporary sophistication.

The Master-Mistress (1922) is a collection of poems, varying in quality from excellent to trivial, on many moods and aspects of natural and supernatural love. Like all O.'s works, it is illustrated by the author.

In spite of substantial critical appreciation, none of the works for adults had a second edition. Their conspicuous merits were overwhelmed by excesses of whimsy and sentimentality. O.'s Irish forebears were given both credit and blame for qualities in her writing described as "Celtic." A modern reader will find much wit, originality, and beauty of language and atmosphere in O.'s works.

WORKS: *The Loves of Edwy* (1904). *The Lady in the White Veil* (1909). *The Kewpies and Dotty Darling* (1912). *The Kewpies: Their Book: Verse and Pictures* (1913). *Kewpie Kutouts* (1914). *The Master-Mistress* (1922). *The Kewpies and the Runaway Baby* (1928). *Garda* (1929). *The Goblin Woman* (1930).

BIBLIOGRAPHY: Brooks, V. W., *Days of the Phoenix* (1957). Kummer, G., *Harry Leon Wilson* (1963). McCanse, R. A., *Titans and Kewpies: The Life and Art of Rose O'Neill* (1968). Wood, C., *Poets of America* (1925).

Other references: *Independent* (15 Sept. 1904). *International Studio* (March 1922). *NY* (24 Nov. 1934).

EVELYN S. CUTLER

Sarah Osborn

B. 22 Feb. 1714, London, England; d. 2 Aug. 1796, Newport, Rhode Island
Wrote under: Sarah Osborn
D. of Benjamin and Susanna Haggar; m. Samuel Wheaton, 1731;
 m. Henry Osborn, 1742

O. emigrated to America with her family in 1722. They first settled in Boston, Massachusetts, and later moved to Newport, Rhode Island, where O. spent the remainder of her life. In Newport, O. met and married a seaman, who was lost at sea in November 1733. O. cared for their child alone, sometimes through great hardships, until she remarried.

O. was admitted to the Congregationalist church in Newport in 1737, an event of great significance to a Puritan in the early part of the 18th c. O.'s spiritual autobiography, *The Nature, Certainty, and Evidence of True Christianity* (1755), was evidently written in retrospect over a ten-year period from 1743 to 1753. It was originally couched in terms of a letter from one friend to another "in great Concern of Soul." This fifteen-page work reappeared in later editions and reprints in 1793, and apparently was expanded by or with the help of her minister, Samuel Hopkins, as *Memoirs of the Life of Mrs. Sarah Osborn* (1799). The *Life* was meant as an example of piety for a younger generation.

O.'s work is characterized by foreshadowings of the sentimental, moralistic fiction of the late 18th and early 19th centuries. The work is replete with tear-stained emotion and signs of O.'s sensibility. O.'s moments of doubt are linked to hysterics and excessive agitation. She relates that she could neither eat nor sleep for a week after Satan had suggested to her that the state of her soul was hopeless. Typically, O. weeps when asking her minister for church admittance, a change from the austere intellectualizing of earlier spiritual autobiographies by New England women.

O.'s writing evidences a notable stylistic as well as contextual change from earlier spiritual autobiographies. In her conscious attempt to tell a life story, O. increases the cast of characters to include not only the self, the savior, and the devil, but also family, friends, ministers, and various incidental personages. She includes a variety of incidents and events to carry the story forward. Thus, while the narrative still focuses on her saving experience, it is broadened to contain plot, action, and dialogue. There is even an echo of the English novel of sentiment.

O. shows an ambitious desire to create a lengthy, complex story. As such, her memoirs have importance. Although the content often appears unexceptional or repetitive to the modern reader, it stands out as an early attempt by a woman writer to use available, socially acceptable materials to fabricate a readable and entertaining story.

WORKS: *The Nature, Certainty, and Evidence of True Christianity* (1755). *Memoirs of the Life of Mrs. Sarah Osborn* (Ed. S. Hopkins, 1799).

JACQUELINE HORNSTEIN

Frances Sargent Locke Osgood

B. 18 June 1811, Boston, Massachusetts; d. 12 May 1850, New York City
Wrote under: Ellen, Florence, Kate Carol, Frances Sargent Osgood
D. of Joseph and Mary Ingersoll Foster Locke; m. Samuel Stillman Osgood,
1835

O. was the daughter of a Boston merchant. She was educated primarily at home. O.'s parents encouraged her to write, and she also benefited especially from the influence of a half-sister, Anna Maria Foster Wells, and an older brother, Andrew Aitchison Locke, both of whom became writers. O. began publishing verse at the age of fourteen in the first American children's monthly, *Juvenile Miscellany*.

O. lived in England (1835–40) with her husband, an artist; her success there in turn commended her to readers at home. She was estranged from her husband in 1844, but they were reconciled, even though there was much gossip about her literary "romance" with Edgar Allan Poe.

The major subject of O.'s poetry and prose sketches is the relationship between men and women. Love—passionate, spiritual, seductive, secret, instant, eternal, consummated, holy, pious, true, false, forbidden, self-denying, transforming, transcendent, destructive—receives such a variety of expression that it cloys the appetite.

Although O. is adept in the traditional forms—songs, sonnets, ballads, rhymed narratives, and dramatic blank verse—her meters often lack the force or tension of the inevitable line; her rhymes are conventional, so that blank verse is her best measure. She frequently runs symbol and abstraction together. The poems are customarily straightforward; emotions are often stated directly.

More interesting are her verses about children. Several of the poems describe O.'s own daughters: one of them sleeping with "beautiful abandonment" on a downy carpet; Fanny smiling for the first time; May trying to lift the sun's rays, or inquisitively playing with a watch. The best of these poems is "A Sketch," which describes two little, careless girls—their straw bonnets flung among the leaves—as, silent with delight, they make garlands for one another, and think of nothing but their own sweet play.

It is also in poems about children and their fate that O. reveals a view of life she rarely allowed herself to express. In "The Daughter of

Herodias," O. imagines Salomé, a light and blooming child, without trouble or care, suddenly bewildered and terror-struck as her revengeful mother snares her in an unspeakable woe. The change in Salomé's character is dramatically realized: "Now, reckless, in her grief she goes / A woman stern and wild." Chilled with fear, the once thoughtless girl curses her fatal grace.

During a period of literary nationalism, as well as an age of sentiment, O. was the most popular and most admired of American women poets. There is little of excruciating or evil design in O.'s work; she wished "to live in blessed illusion." As a writer, she idealizes almost every image and sentiment that engages her attention. But O. deserves the appreciation she enjoyed for her verses about children.

WORKS: *Philosophical Enigmas* (183?). *A Wreath of Wild Flowers from New England* (1838, reissued as *Poems*, 1846). *The Casket of Fate* (1839). *Flower Gift* (1840, reissued as *The Poetry of Flowers and the Flowers of Poetry*, 1841, reissued again as *The Floral Offering*, 1847). *The Rose: Sketches in Verse* (1842). *The Snow-drop* (1842?). *Puss in Boots, and the Marquis of Carabas* (1844). *The Flower Alphabet in Gold and Colors* (1845). *The Cries of New York* (1846). *A Letter About Lions* (1849). *Poems* (1849, reissued as *Osgood's Poetical Works*, 1880).

BIBLIOGRAPHY: Hewitt, M. E., ed., *The Memorial: Written by Friends of the Late Mrs. Osgood* (1851). Griswold, R. W., ed., *The Literati* by E. A. Poe (1850). Mabbott, T. O., *Collected Works of Edgar Allan Poe, Poems I* (1969). Moss, S. P., *Poe's Literary Battles* (1963). Quinn, A. H., *Edgar Allan Poe: A Critical Biography* (1941).

For articles in reference works, see: *American Female Poets*, C. May (1848). *FPA. NAW* (article by J. G. Varnet). *The Poets and Poetry of America*, Ed. R. W. Griswold (1847).

Other references: *Godey's* (March 1846; Sept. 1846). *Graham's* (Jan. 1843). *Southern Literary Messenger* (Aug. 1849).

ELIZABETH PHILLIPS

Sarah Margaret Fuller Ossoli

B. 23 May 1810, Cambridgeport, Massachusetts; d. 19 July 1850, off Fire
  Island, New York
Wrote under: Margaret Fuller, S. M. Fuller, S. Margaret Fuller, J.
D. of Timothy and Margaret Crane Fuller; m. Giovanni Angelo, Marchese
  d'Ossoli, 1850

O.'s father was a lawyer and politician; her mother bore nine children,
seven of whom survived infancy. Having hoped for a son, Fuller gave
his oldest child a masculine education. Pushed by her father's ambitions
and by her own growing sense that she could achieve greatness, O. read
Horace, Ovid, and Virgil in the original at seven and continued reading
widely in her father's library until she first attended school at fourteen.
Two unhappy years at school in Groton, Massachusetts, made clear the
social problems caused by what she herself considered her lack of a normal childhood. Back in Cambridge, she studied French, German, Italian,
Greek, and philosophy, and made friends with future Transcendentalists
Frederick Henry Hedge and James Freeman Clarke. In 1833, O.'s father
retired from public life and moved his family to a farm at Groton, forty
miles from Boston. For two years, O. took care of the house and of
her younger brothers and sisters while teaching four of the children five
to eight hours a day. She also continued her ambitious "self-culture,"
reading widely in history, literature, philosophy, and religion.

When O.'s father died in 1835, she became breadwinner and head of
the family. She taught at Bronson Alcott's school in Boston (1836–37)
and the Greene Street School in Providence, Rhode Island (1837–39). In
1839, she moved her family to Jamaica Plain and began her "Conversations" in Boston and Cambridge, which continued until 1844. From July
1840 until July 1842, at the urging of Emerson and other Transcendentalist friends, she edited the Dial.

In 1843, O. accompanied James and Sarah Clarke on a trip to Illinois
and Michigan. In December 1844, she went to New York City as a
correspondent for Horace Greeley's Daily-Tribune. In part because of
an unfortunate romantic involvement with James Nathan, O. sailed in

August 1846 for Europe and subsequently traveled in England, Scotland, and France, still acting as a *Tribune* correspondent. In Rome, in 1847, she met her future husband, the Marchese d'Ossoli. Her son Angelo was born in September 1848. Ossoli supported the Roman Republic, and the family stayed in Rome throughout the French siege. O. directed a hospital and cared for the wounded. After the Republic fell, the family went to Florence and then sailed for America. All three were drowned when their ship broke up in a storm off Fire Island.

O. began writing with translations of Eckermann's *Conversations with Goethe* (1839) and the *Correspondence of Fräulein Günderode and Bettina von Arnim* (1842); some unhappy attempts at fiction; and rhapsodic, sentimental verse of little merit. Her first successful and original work, *Summer on the Lakes* (1844), used the frame of her western visit with the Clarkes for a mixture of realistic reporting, autobiography, historical and philosophical musings, and literary criticism. The result resembles Thoreau's later *A Week on the Concord and Merrimack Rivers* (1849).

Using a journal she had kept on the trip, O. provides fresh and perceptive comments on places and people from Chicago and the prairie settlements of Illinois to Milwaukee and Mackinaw. Whatever is rhapsodic or overly Romantic in her approach to the West usually succumbs before her own observations and her commonsense good will. O. admires the spirit of the new land, even as she recognizes the cruelty with which the native American has been forced from his country.

Papers on Literature and Art (1846) collected O.'s critical pieces, but the only other book she wrote was *Woman in the Nineteenth Century* (1845), a revision and amplification of her July 1843 *Dial* article, "The Great Lawsuit—Man *versus* Men; Woman *versus* Women." O.'s Transcendental tract endorses above all the idea that the powers of each individual should be developed through his or her apprehension of an ideal. Her insistence on the godlike possibilities of *all* humans differs little from the same radical idealism in the writings of Emerson and Thoreau, but O. emphasizes that the fullest possible development of man will not come without the fullest possible development of woman.

O. says that women must not wait for help from men, continuing their old, bad habits of dependence, but must help themselves; self-reliance and independence are the best ways of aiding themselves and their sisters. The capacity for economic independence is prerequisite to moral and mental freedom, and the freedom to choose celibacy over a degrading or unequal and merely convenient marriage is essential. Late in her book she makes her famous statement that women should be able to do anything for which their individual powers and talents fit them —"let them be sea-captains if they will."

The myths that have grown up around O.'s brief life and her relatively small oeuvre make her contributions difficult to assess. Some contemporary and many later critics have maintained that the genius she displayed in conversation, whether natural or guided, never became fully evident in her writings: "Ultimately she should be remembered for what she was rather than what she did" (Blanchard). The *Dial* has always been seen as central to the Transcendentalist movement; some contend that the magazine reflects O. more than it does "the generality of Transcendentalist thought" (Rosenthal). O.'s writings for the *Dial* and the *Tribune* gave her a chance to introduce European culture to America, to promote American literature, and to diffuse her social ideals while contrasting them with harsh reality. With Poe she must be considered America's first major literary critic, but her reporting gives evidence of a livelier, more supple prose that might have matured given time. Undoubtedly, she contributed much to American Romanticism and the feminist movement.

WORKS: Conversations with Goethe by J. P. Eckermann (translated by Ossoli, 1839). *Correspondence of Fraulein Günderode and Bettina von Arnim* (translated by Ossoli, 1842). *Summer on the Lakes* (1844). *Woman in the Nineteenth Century* (1845). *Papers on Literature and Art* (2 vols., 1846). *Memoirs of Margaret Fuller Ossoli* (Eds. R. W. Emerson, W. H. Channing, and J. F. Clarke; 2 vols., 1852). *At Home and Abroad* (Ed. A. B. Fuller, 1856). *Art, Literature, and the Drama* (Ed. A. B. Fuller, 1860). *Life Without and Life Within* (ed. A. B. Fuller, 1860). *Margaret and her Friends* (Ed. C. W. H. Dall, 1895). *Love-Letters of Margaret Fuller, 1845–1846* (1903). *The Writings of Margaret Fuller* (Ed. M. Wade, 1941).

The papers of Margaret Fuller, Marchesa d'Ossoli, are at the Boston Public Library and the Houghton Library, Harvard.

BIBLIOGRAPHY: Blanchard, P., *Margaret Fuller: From Transcendentalism to Romanticism* (1978). Boller, P. F., *American Transcendentalism 1830–1860: An Intellectual Inquiry* (1974). Brown, A. W., *Margaret Fuller* (1964). Buell, L., *Literary Transcendentalism: Style and Vision in the American Renaissance* (1973). Cooke, G. W., *An Historical and Bibliographical Introduction to Accompany the Dial* (2 vols., 1961). Deiss, J. J., *The Roman Years of Margaret Fuller* (1969). Durning, R. E., *Margaret Fuller, Citizen of the World* (1969). Emerson, R. W., *The Journals and Miscellaneous Notebooks of Ralph Waldo Emerson* (Eds. W. H. Gilman et al.; 14 vols. to date, 1960–   ). Hawthorne, N., *The American Notebooks* (Ed. C. M. Simpson, 1972). Miller P., *The American Transcendentalists* (1957). Miller, P., *The*

Transendentalists (1950). Myerson, J., *Margaret Fuller: A Descriptive Bibliography* (1978). Myerson, J., *Margaret Fuller: A Secondary Bibliography* (1977). Rosenthal, B., in *ELN* 8 (Sept. 1970). Stern, M. B., *The Life of Margaret Fuller* (1942). Swift, L., *Brook Farm* (1900). Thoreau, H. D., *The Correspondence of Henry David Thoreau* (Eds. W. Harding and C. Bode, 1958). Wade, M., *Margaret Fuller: Whetstone of Genius* (1940). Wilson, E., *Margaret Fuller: Bluestocking, Romantic, Revolutionary* (1977).

For articles in reference works, see: *AA. The Female Prose Writers of America*, Ed. J. S. Hart (1855). *NAW* (article by W. Berthoff).

Other references: *SAQ* 72 (Autumn 1973).

SUSAN SUTTON SMITH

Mary White Ovington

B. *11 April 1865, Brooklyn, New York; d. 15 July 1951, Newton, Massachusetts*
D. *of Theodore Tweedy and Louise Vetcham Ovington*

The daughter of a well-to-do New York family, O. was raised by abolitionists and radicals. O.'s education at Radcliffe College (1891–93) was followed by two years in society, after which O. worked as registrar at the Pratt Institute, and then opened the Greenpoint Settlement of the Pratt Institute Neighborhood Association, where she served as headworker from 1895 to 1903.

O.'s fifty years of work in the cause of full equality for black Americans began with *Half a Man: The Status of the Negro in New York* (1911). Begun by O. while she was a Greenwich House fellow in 1904–05, the interviews and research in New York and in the South continued for seven years. Meanwhile, O. had also convinced Henry Phipps to build The Tuskegee in New York City as an experiment in model housing for blacks; had caused a national sensation as the central white female participant in the 1908 interracial Cosmopolitan Club dinner at Peck's Restaurant; had cofounded the Lincoln Settlement for Negroes with Verina Morton-Jones, a black physician; and had been the leading figure in the founding of the National Association for the Advancement of Colored People (NAACP) in 1909.

Work with the NAACP was to consume O.'s energies for the rest of her life. O. was dubbed "Fighting Saint," "Saint Mary," and "Mother of the New Emancipation" by people in and out of that organization. Able to get along with almost everyone, O. was described by co-workers as sensitive, modest, shy, retiring, but fearless and unshakable wherever she encountered injustice, poverty, or exploitation.

O.'s major writing can be grouped into sociological study, children's books, fiction, drama, and biography/autobiography. *Half a Man* is a highly readable and insightful sociological study of what was in 1911 a nearly invisible minority populace. It gives a thorough picture of the differences between white and black women's roles early in the 20th c., and provides a rare early depiction of the peculiar burdens and strengths of the American black woman.

O. wrote two books and helped edit another to fill the gap she perceived in literature for black children. *Hazel* (1913), a novel for girls, was dramatized and performed at the YWCA in Brooklyn in 1916. *Zeke: A School Boy at Tolliver* (1931), was written for boys. With Myron Thomas Pritchard, O. compiled *The Upward Path: A Reader for Colored Children* (1920), an excellent collection of stories and poems by black writers.

Notable in O.'s fiction is a short story, "The White Brute," printed in *The Masses* in 1915 and also in her autobiography. Based on actual incident, the story seeks to realistically reverse the image of the "black brute" so often touted in the South as excuse for lynching. Dialogue and description are effectively done. *The Shadow* (1920) combines O.'s interests in race problems and the labor movement.

Of O.'s two plays, *The Awakening* (1923) and *Phillis Wheatley* (1932), the latter, shorter play remains the less dated. *The Awakening* is primarily a propaganda piece for the NAACP. *Phillis Wheatley* is based on letters of the 18th-c. black poet to her friend Obour Tanner, and on the biographical notes prefacing editions of Wheatley's poems.

O.'s other two long books, *Portraits in Color* (1927) and *The Walls Came Tumbling Down* (1947), show again the clear, appealing writing style evident in *Half a Man*. *Portraits in Color* depicts the life and work of twenty black men and women. *The Walls Came Tumbling Down* is O.'s autobiography, concentrating not so much on the inward person as on O.'s political activities. It provides an excellent personalized picture of the early days of the NAACP and the people, black and white, who helped push down walls of discrimination and exploitation.

WORKS: *Half a Man: The Status of the Negro in New York* (1911). *Hazel* (1913). *The Shadow* (1920). *The Upward Path: A Reader for Colored Children* (edited by Ovington, with M. T. Pritchard, 1920). *The Awakening: A Play* (1923). *Portraits in Color* (1927). *Zeke: A School Boy at Tolliver* (1931). *Phillis Wheatley: A Play* (1932). *The Walls Came Tumbling Down* (1947).

Most of the papers of Mary White Ovington are in the NAACP papers, Library of Congress Manuscript Division.

BIBLIOGRAPHY: Archer, L., *Black Images in the American Theatre: NAACP Protest Campaigns—Stage, Screen, Radio, and Television* (1973). Hughes, L., *Fight for Freedom: The Story of the NAACP* (1962). Kellogg, C. F., Introduction to *Half a Man* by Ovington (1969). Kellogg, C. F., *NAACP: A History of the National Organization for the Advancement of Colored People* (1967). Ross, B. J., *J. E. Spingarn and the Rise of the NAACP, 1911–1939* (1972).

CAROLYN WEDIN SYLVANDER

Mary Alicia Owen

B. 29 Dec. 1858, St. Joseph, Missouri; d. 5 Jan. 1935, St. Joseph, Missouri
Wrote under: Mary Alicia Owen, Julia Scott
D. of James Alfred and Agnes Jeannette Cargill Owen

The daughter of a midwestern lawyer and financial writer, O. was educated in private schools and at Vassar College. She began her career by submitting verses, reviews, and travel sketches to a weekly newspaper in St. Joseph; eventually she became its literary editor. Under the pseudonym "Julia Scott," O. published short stories in *Peterson's Magazine, Overland Monthly, Century,* and *Frank Leslie's Illustrated Newspaper.* However, O.'s most important work stemmed from her lifelong study of folklore.

O.'s native Missouri sheltered four groups that deeply influenced each other: the native Musquakie (Sacs) Indians, the French and English settlers, and the transplanted African slaves. Raised among these disparate peoples, O. began collecting folklore, customs, and mythology. In 1888, she announced her findings on the voodoo magic practiced by ex-slaves; in 1891, she presented a paper on the Missouri-Negro tradition before the

International Folk-Lore Congress in London. In 1893, with the encouragement of folklorist Charles Godfrey Leland, O. published *VooDoo Tales*.

O. cast this book in a form similar to Joel Chandler Harris's *Uncle Remus:* Five old slave women gather around the cabin fire to share their tales with little "Tow Head," the plantation owner's daughter. "Big Angie" carries her eagle-bone whistle with her missal, her "saint's toe on her bosom and the fetish known as a 'luck-ball' under her right arm." Rendered in dialect appropriate to each speaker, the exploits of Woodpeckeh, Ole Rabbit, and Blue Jay have the flavor of true oral tradition. Although the form of *VooDoo Tales* suffers from the effort to combine serious research with literary entertainment, O.'s materials are compelling and accurate and the plots, language, and imagery are fresh.

O. describes gypsy tribes in *The Daughter of Alouette* (1896). The Musquakie Indians, who granted O. tribal membership in 1892, are described in a paper presented before the British Association at Toronto in 1897. O. later expanded this paper into a monograph, published by the English Folk-Lore Society in 1904. Accompanying the text is a catalogue of O.'s extensive collection of Musquakie artifacts.

Folk-Lore of the Musquakie Indians (1904) is a formal anthropological description of the tribe during a critical "clash of cultures." After carefully surveying their myths and yearly festivals, O. introduces the catalogue of her collection. Although she rejects the merely picturesque or aesthetically pleasing artifact in favor of the sacred or ceremonial, O. also recognizes that "to the wild man surrounded by civilization and making a stand against it, everything that pertains to his free and savage past has become a ceremonial object."

Among O.'s other works are *The Sacred Council Hills* (1909), a "folk-lore drama" portraying the Indian's plight, and *Home Life of Squaws*, of which no extant copy has been located.

O.'s writing, like the cultures it described, was influenced by many different traditions: regional humor, pastoral romanticism, the reform spirit, and the pioneering research of other folklorists. Although *VooDoo Tales* retains considerable charm, O.'s books are most interesting for their eclectic blend of literature and science. In an age when specialization was less narrow, O. synthesized several elements of late-19th-c. thought. A member of numerous scientific societies, she based her work on professional, firsthand observations; her conclusions were guided by deep respect for the people of the Mississippi Valley and their ways of life.

WORKS: *VooDoo Tales, as Told among the Negroes of the Southwest, Collected from Original Sources by Mary Alicia Owen* (1893; English title, *Old Rabbit, the Voodoo, and Other Sorcerors*; reissued as *Ole Rabbit's Plantation Stories*, 1898). *The Daughter of Alouette* (1896). *Oracles and Witches* (1902). *Folk-Lore of the Musquakie Indians of North America* (1904). *The Sacred Council Hills: A Folk-Lore Drama* (1909). *Home Life of Squaws* (n.d.). *Messiah Beliefs of the American Indians* (n.d.). *Rain Gods of the American Indians* (n.d.).

BIBLIOGRAPHY: Dorsen, R. M., *The British Folklorists* (1968). Hartland, E. S., Preface to *Folk-Lore of the Musquakie Indians* by M. A. Owen (1904). Leland, C. G., Preface to *VooDoo Tales* by M. A. Owen (1893).

For articles in reference works see: *AW. Dictionary of American Authors Deceased before 1950*, Ed. W. S. Wallace (1951). *NCAB*, 13.

SARAH WAY SHERMAN

Rochelle Owens

B. *2 April 1936, Brooklyn, New York*
D. *of Maxwell Bass and Molly Adler Bass; m. George Economou, 1962*

The daughter of a postal inspector, O. graduated from Lafayette High School and then attended the Herbert Berghof Studio. O. then moved to Greenwich Village and held numerous clerical positions; while on the job, she wrote poetry. O. also attended the New School and traveled extensively.

In 1967, O. received wide critical attention for her play *Futz* (1962; revised version, 1968), which established her career as a playwright. The same year, *Futz* received an Obie committee citation as one of the distinguished new plays of 1966–67. In 1973, *The Karl Marx Play* was nominated for an Obie. In addition to her theater pieces, O. is the author of six books of poetry.

Futz opened at the Tyrone Guthrie Workshop, Minnesota Theatre Company, in 1965. It is a violent and controversial tragicomedy, dealing with a simple farmer, Cy Futz, who is emotionally and sexually in love with his pig Amanda. He lives with her in domestic bliss until "the world" invades their privacy.

Majorie Satz, a promiscuous townswoman, seduces Futz and participates in his lovemaking with Amanda. Later, shamed by her actions, she denounces him to the town. Oscar Loop and Ann Fox inadvertently discover Futz and Amanda cavorting together. Oscar becomes mad, beats Ann to death, and blames his violence on what he has seen. The community rises up against Futz. The sheriff places him in protective custody, but Futz cannot escape his fate. Ned Satz enters Futz's cell and stabs him to death.

The emotional center is Futz's relationship to Amanda. Futz is an instinctual being, and his affection for his sow is contrasted to the brutal and bitter relationships among the other characters. Futz says, "I like Amanda because she is good," and, ironically, Futz is the only character in the piece to display a sensitive and deep emotional life. Thus, Futz's murder at the end tragically symbolizes the destructive force of society's rigid, puritanical, and repressive codes. *Futz* is characterized by O.'s crude and passionately intense poetry. She employs words for their alliterative and associative impact, and her images are surreal and shocking.

By working outside the conventions of stage realism, O. underlines the idea that *Futz* is a modern morality fable. Above all, the inventiveness of her story and the raw power of her language make *Futz* an arresting and vibrant theater composition.

In *Homo* (1968), O. explores the unconscious sexual, racial, and economic fantasies of men and women. Each scene depicts a master/slave relationship in which one individual or group is manipulated, threatened, and humiliated by another. This dream, O. suggests, is the root of people's primordial drives.

In *The Karl Marx Play* (1974), the characters do not relate to each other through the story and dialogue but through the subject and theme. At each moment and in each segment the same images and ideas recur. Thus, the piece is "a play with music whose story is told as much by its imagery and tonal 'meanings' as it is by its plot."

O. focuses on Marx's painful physical debilities, his financial dependence on Engels, his rejection of his Jewish heritage, his lust for his wife, and his emotional need to complete his writings. Through this technique, therefore, we do not see the journey of Marx through his life, but the critical threads which constitute the fabric of his existence in the mid-1850s.

O.'s aim in this piece is to create "a theatrical experiencing of the extreme humanness of Karl Marx." She sacrifices a complex portrait of Marx to a theatrical concept. Thus, despite the play's verbal and musical richness, the text lacks the immediacy and power of O.'s other works.

All O.'s plays are characterized by a fluid and free use of language and time. She is a poet of the stage. Her dramatic imagination and verbal creativity mark O. as a notable modern writer.

WORKS: *Not Be Essence That Cannot Be* (1961). *Futz* (1962; revised version, *Futz and What Came After*, 1968). *Homo* (1968). *Salt and Core* (1968). *I Am the Babe of Joseph Stalin's Daughter* (1971). *Spontaneous Combustion: Eight New American Plays* (edited by Owens, 1972). *Poems from Joe's Garage* (1973). *The Joe 82 Creation Poems* (1974). *The Karl Marx Play, and Others* (1974). *The Widow and the Colonel* (1977). *The Joe Chronicles/Part 2* (1977).

BIBLIOGRAPHY: Brustein, R., *The Third Theatre* (1969). Kerr, W., *God on the Gymnasium Floor* (1969). Novick, J., *Beyond Broadway* (1968). Poggi, J., *Theatre in America: The Impact of Economic Forces, 1870–1967* (1968).

For articles in reference works, see: *Contemporary Dramatists*, Ed. J. Vinson (1977). *Notable Names in the American Theatre*, Ed. R. D. McGill (1976).

TINA MARGOLIS

Dorothy Myra Page

B. ca. 1899, Newport News, Virginia
Given name: Dorothy Gary
Wrote under: Dorothy Page Gary, Dorothy Markey, Dorothy Myra Page, Myra Page
D. of Benjamin Roscoe and Willie Alberta Barham Gray; m. John Markey

P.'s interest in writing was explicitly tied to her sense of art as social commentary. Her earliest memories are of accompanying her doctor father in his carriage as he made rounds. It was here that P. first recognized the severe extremes of class and race that characterized her town. When she was told that her brother, not she, would be encouraged to pursue a career in medicine, her sense of social inequity deepened. Writing became her vehicle for social investigation and self-expression.

P. published her first poem at age nine in the Richmond *Times* and wrote fiction throughout high school. In 1918, she graduated from Westhampton College in Richmond, where she edited the yearbook and won an award for her short story, "Schuman's Why." After an unsatisfying year teaching literature and history in a local junior high school, P. went to Columbia University. She received her Master's degree in political science, writing a thesis on yellow journalism. During the months in New York City, P. also became familiar with the goals of the trade union movement and revolutionary socialism.

P. returned to Virginia as an industrial secretary for the YWCA. Her job was to organize women working in department stores and silk mills into cultural and educational clubs to prepare them for unionization, but P. became disenchanted with the conservative attitude of the local YWCA leadership. She began to work with the Amalgamated Clothingmakers Union in Philadelphia, St. Louis, and Chicago. Her writing, primarily as a journalist covering labor issues, continued sporadically during this period.

In the late 1920s, P. received a teaching fellowship at the University of Minnesota. While in Minnesota she worked with the Minnesota Federation of Labor and the Farmers' Labor Party and married another graduate student. P. earned her Ph.D. in 1928, majoring in sociology and minoring in economics and psychology. Her dissertation was published as *Southern Cotton Mills and Labor* in 1929. Although she taught briefly at Wheaton College, most of P.'s time was given to her political work and her writing. She was a contributor to *Nation, New Masses, New Pioneer,* and *Labor Age* and a member of the Revolutionary Writers' Federation.

Gathering Storm (1932) is a fictional dramatization of several of the most significant events in the history of the American labor movement. The novel begins with an aging woman telling her spirited granddaughter about how the North Carolina hill people originally came to work in the cotton mills, and then traces the various characters through their involvement in and impressions of the 1910 shirtwaist makers' strike in New York City, the Russian Revolution, the political repression that accompanied patriotic zeal after World War I, the political debate between the Socialist Party and the IWW, the Chicago meatpackers' strike, and the formulation of an American Communist Party. The novel culminates with the cotton mill workers' strike in Gastonia, North Carolina, in 1929. Although heavily didactic, *Gathering Storm* is interesting because of P.'s attempts to make the problems of both women and black workers central to her discussion of the events and their possible resolution.

In the early 1930s, P. went to Europe to study and write about teachers' unions, and went from there to the Soviet Union. In the Soviet Union P. worked as a journalist and lived in a thriving artists' community. *Soviet Main Street* (1933) describes the changes which occur in Poldolsk, a small factory town outside of Moscow, as the residents adjust to the new life made possible by the revolution. *Moscow Yankee* (1935), a fictionalization of P.'s impressions of life in postrevolutionary Russia, is especially memorable for its portrayal of the personal dimensions of the conversion to Communism, most significantly the evolution of sexual relationships in a changing political climate.

With Sun in Our Blood (1950) is a fictionalized biography of Dolly Hawkins, the daughter, wife, and mother of coal miners in the Cumberland Mountains of Tennessee. P.'s admirable blend of local-color realism, lyrical, often ballad-like descriptions, and astute social commentary make the novel one of lasting significance.

Blacklisted during the repressive literary and political climate of the 1950s, P. adopted her husband's name when she could not get work published under her own. As Dorothy Markey, she wrote two biographies of American scientists for adolescent readers: *The Little Giant of Schenectady* (1956), a biography of Charles Steinmetz, and *Explorer of Sound* (1964), a biography of Michael Pupin.

P. is currently working on the first two volumes of her fictionalized autobiography, *Soundings* and *Midstream*. She writes in her preface to *Soundings*: "A man's reach must exceed his grasp, what then about a woman's?"

WORKS: *Southern Cotton Mills and Labor* (1929). *Gathering Storm: A Story of the Black Belt* (1932). *Soviet Main Street* (1933). *Moscow Yankee* (1935). *It Happened on May First* (1940). "The March on Chumley Hollow," *100 Non-Royalty Plays* (Ed. W. Konzlenko, 1941). *With Sun in Our Blood* (1950; reprinted as *Daughter of the Hills: A Woman's Part in the Coal Miners' Struggle*, 1977). *The Little Giant of Schenectady* (1956). *Explorer of Sound* (1964).

BIBLIOGRAPHY: Blake, F., *The Strike in the American Novel* (1972). Hill, V., "Strategy and Breadth: The Socialist-Feminist in American Fiction" (Diss., SUNY at Buffalo, 1979). Rideout, W., *The Radical Novel in the United States, 1900–1954* (1956).

Other references: *In These Times* (May 1978). *Mountain Heritage* (May 1978). *Social Research* (1971). *Westchester Gannet* (23 Jan. 1978).

VICKI LYNN HILL

Phoebe Worrall Palmer

B. *18 Dec. 1807, New York City; d. 2 Nov. 1874, New York City*
D. *of Henry and Dorothea Wade Worrall; m. Walter Clark Palmer, 1827*

Author and evangelist of the "Holiness" movement, P. was the fourth of ten children of an American Methodist mother and an English father. In 1827, P. married a doctor and fellow Methodist. Both were lifelong New Yorkers. The Palmers had six children, only three of whom survived infancy.

In the 1840s, P. distributed tracts in the slums and regularly visited the Tombs, the legendary New York prison. For eleven years she was corresponding secretary of the New York Female Assistance Society for the Relief and Religious Instruction of the Sick Poor. P.'s most lasting contribution was the founding of the Five Points Mission in 1850 in the city's worst slum. Supported by the Methodist Ladies' Home Missionary Society, it was the forerunner of later settlement houses.

P.'s sister Sarah Worrall Lankford (1806–1896, who became the second wife of Walter Palmer in 1876) experienced "entire sanctification" in 1835. Though the experience was one testified to by many early Methodists in response to John Wesley's teachings on Christian perfection, it had not been stressed by American Methodists. In August 1835, Sarah founded the Tuesday Meeting for the Promotion of Holiness, which met in the home the Palmers and Lankfords shared. This weekly meeting for prayer, Scripture reading, and testimony, which continued for more than sixty years, was widely copied and became the catalyst for the "Holiness" or "Lay" revival of 1857–58, which eventually led to the formation of such holiness denominations as the Church of the Nazarene and such Pentecostal groups as the Assemblies of God.

P. testified to the same experience in 1837. Her writing and speaking, as well as her leadership in the Tuesday Meeting, soon made P. the more prominent sister. For six months each year "Dr. and Mrs. Phoebe Palmer" spoke in churches and camp meetings throughout the eastern U.S. and Canada. In 1859, they took the revival to the British Isles. Magazine reports on this trip were published as a book, *Four Years in the Old World*, in 1865.

P. was also a frequent contributor to the *Guide to Christian Perfection*, founded in Boston in 1839. Rechristened the *Guide to Holiness* in 1843, it was merged with the *Beauty of Holiness* when the Palmers purchased both in 1864. P. became editor, a post she held until her death. P.'s series of articles, "Fragments from My Portfolio," were collected as *Faith and Its Effects* in 1849.

Revivalist Charles G. Finney and his colleague at Oberlin College, President Asa Mahan, began in 1836 and 1837 to develop what came to be known as "Oberlin Perfectionism." Finney had transformed the old Puritan notion of religious conversion as an agonizing process contingent on divine election into a simple decision of human free will, an act, and an event.

P. transformed Wesley's idea of perfection as a lifelong process into an act and an experience. In response to a Presbyterian elder's question as to whether "there is not a *shorter way* of getting into the way of holiness?" P. replied in the *Christian Advocate and Journal*, "THERE IS A SHORTER WAY!" Her articles became her most famous work, *The Way of Holiness* (1843). P. begins with the premise that "God requires *present* holiness." Using Finney's logic that God would not command something people cannot do, P. declares that a person must consecrate all to God. (For eighty descriptions of this by ministers who have experienced it, see P.'s *Pioneer Experiences*, 1868.) Using rather dubious biblical exegesis, P. termed this "laying all upon the altar." She declared that the altar was Christ and that "whatever *touched* the altar became holy, virtually the *Lord's property, sanctified to His use*." Since God has declared this to be true, any person who consecrates everything to God can simply claim sanctification and testify to it publicly, whether or not he or she receives any inner confirmation from the Holy Spirit (as Wesley taught) or has any emotional experience. A person simply claims holiness on the basis of faith in God's promise.

P.'s other significant work was *Promise of the Father* (1859), in which she argued from Scripture, church history, and biographical example for the right of women to preach. Although P. never considered herself a "woman's rights" advocate or sought ordination for her own ministry, she strongly supported the right, and even Christian duty, of women to publicly testify to their religious experience and to become full-time preachers if they felt that to be God's call.

P.'s understanding of holiness, despite her very controversial "altar terminology," transformed the notion from one of process to one of experience. The movement P. helped give birth to left a lasting impact on American religious culture. P.'s defense of women's ministry was the first of many in the holiness-Pentecostal tradition, which led such churches to ordain women more than fifty years before "mainline" Protestantism.

WORKS: *The Way of Holiness* (1843). *Faith and Its Effects* (1849). *Present to My Christian Friend on Entire Devotion to God* (1853). *The Useful Disciple; or, A Narrative of Mrs. Mary Gardner* (1853). *Incidental Illustrations of the Economy of Salvation* (1855). *Promise of the Father* (1859). *Four Years in the Old World* (1865). *Pioneer Experiences* (1868). *A Mother's Gift* (1875).

BIBLIOGRAPHY: Wheatley, R., *The Life and Letters of Mrs. Phoebe Palmer* (1876). Hughes, G., *The Beloved Physician, Walter C. Palmer, M.D.* (1884). Hughes, G., *Fragrant Memories of the Tuesday Meeting* (1886). Roche, J., *The Life of Mrs. Sarah A. Lankford Palmer* (1898). Peters, J. L., *Christian Perfection and American Methodism* (1956). Smith, T., *Revivalism and Social Reform in Mid-Nineteenth Century America* (1957). Dayton, D. W., *Discovering an Evangelical Heritage* (1976).

For articles in reference works, see: *NAW* (article by W. J. McCutcheon).

NANCY A. HARDESTY

Helen Waite Papashvily

B. *19 Dec. 1906, Stockton, California*
Writes under: *Helen Papashvily, Helen Waite Papashvily*
D. *of Herbert and Isabella Findlay Lochhead Waite; m. George Papashvily, 1933*

P. was educated in public schools and at the University of California at Berkeley. She graduated in 1929, and then opened a bookstore. The next year she met her husband, an immigrant from Kobiankari in Soviet Georgia who had come to the U.S. in 1923. About the same time P. began her writing career with a variety of short pieces.

In 1933, the Papashvilys moved to New York City, where P. collected books for private libraries and wrote short stories, works for children, and articles. In 1935, they bought the Ertoba Farm in Bucks County, Pennsylvania, where P. still lives.

It was P.'s idea to set down her husband's accounts of his involved and colorful twenty-year Americanization. *Anything Can Happen* (1945) quickly sold 600,000 copies, was translated into fifteen languages, and was made into a film.

Anything Can Happen looks back to a period early in this century, just before the National Origins Act (1924) cut off the large wave of immigration from southern and eastern Europe. The book, told from a personal perspective, constitutes a "psychological case-study in the adjustment of the alien" (H. Fields). P. approaches the immigrant's quest for food, shelter, and matrimony with wit, enthusiasm, honesty, and gracious old-world manners. His story presents a version of the old theme of innocence encountering experience—with not all the innocence on the immigrant's side.

Part of the book's popularity originally stemmed from its optimistic portrayal of life in America, its tone being one of philosophic acceptance rather than rebellion against injustices. Consequently, the book lends credence to the vision of America as a melting pot. Its appeal, however, is also attributable to its vivid, charming, and often poetic use of language. This can be credited in part to P., who set out to capture the rhythm and flavor of her husband's English rather than his exact speech.

The Papashvilys' five joint works constitute total and perfect collaboration. Papashvily supplied the material; his wife, seeing its potential, transformed it from verbal anecdotes into written words. (Papashvily, coming from a rural, oral tradition, and involved in tactile rather than verbal pursuits, eventually learned to read English, but never to write it.) Moreover, as an American married to an immigrant, P. sensed how best to present her husband's material to an American audience. Perhaps because the collaboration was so successful, the extent of P.'s contribution to it is often glossed over.

Of the Papashvilys' other works the most important is *Yes and No Stories* (1946), one of the few books to render the folklore of Georgia, a country inaccessible both geographically and linguistically, into a language other than Russian. Because Georgian history involves recurrent invasions that resulted in the grafting of diverse ethnic cultures upon native materials, the tales, "though circumscribed in their locale, merge with the main stream of Indo-European folk matter" (H. Wedeck).

P.'s most important independent effort, *All the Happy Endings* (1956), was the first book to study in detail the enormous quantities of popular 19th-c. American fiction written by, for, and about women; to discuss its authors individually; and to assess the relationship of their work to

feminism. Treating domestic fiction as a social and psychological phenomenon, P. concluded that while the suffragists of the period waged
outright rebellion, the novelists engaged in surreptitious warfare "to destroy their common enemy, man." As Nancy Cott notes, P. thus found
"the roots of feminism, in a shrewdly adapted form, in domesticity
itself."

WORKS: *Anything Can Happen* (with G. Papashvily, 1945; film version,
1952). *Yes and No Stories: A Book of Georgian Folk Tales* (with G. Papashvily, 1946). *Thanks to Noah* (with G. Papashvily, 1951). *Dogs and People*
(with G. Papashvily, 1954). *All the Happy Endings: A Study of the Domestic
Novel in America, the Women Who Wrote It, the Women Who Read It,
in the Nineteenth Century* (1956, 1972). *Louisa May Alcott* (1965). *Russian
Cooking* (with G. Papashvily and the editors of Time-Life Books, 1969).
Home, and Home Again (with G. Papashvily, 1973). *George Papashvily:
Sculptor, A Retrospective Catalogue* (1979).

BIBLIOGRAPHY: Cott, N., *Bonds of Womanhood* (1977). Fields, H., in
Saturday Review (13 Jan. 1945). Wedeck, H., in *NYTBR* (1 Dec. 1946).
  Other references: *Christian Science Monitor* (22 Oct. 1956; 4 Nov. 1965; 17
Oct. 1973). *New Republic* (15 Jan. 1945). *NYHTB* (5 April 1951; 21 Oct.
1956). *NYT* (21 Nov. 1954). *NYTBR* (31 Dec. 1944; 21 Oct. 1956). San
Francisco *Chronicle* (8 Nov. 1946). *SatR* (9 Nov. 1946; 10 Nov. 1956).

JANET SHARISTANIAN

Dorothy Rothschild Parker

B. 22 Aug. 1893, West End, New Jersey; d. 7 June 1967, New York City
Wrote under: "Constant Reader," Dorothy Parker, Dorothy Rothschild
D. of Henry and Eliza A. Marston Rothschild; m. Edwin Pond Parker, 1917;
  m. Alan Campbell, 1933

P. was the only daughter of a Jewish father and a Scottish mother who
died while P. was still an infant. After a very restricted youth and
adolescence, P. entered the publishing world in a minor editorial position
at *Vogue* in 1916. A year later, she became drama critic for *Vanity
Fair* and married Parker, whose name she retained even after their divorce in 1928.

P. became the acknowledged leader of the (Hotel) "Algonquin Round Table," surrounded by such notables as Edna Ferber, Robert Benchley, and Alexander Woollcott. She left *Vanity Fair* in 1926, after her first volume of poetry, *Enough Rope*, became a bestseller.

The opening poems of *Enough Rope* are composed of love lamentations and reiterate the desire for death in a dismal, often dirgelike tone. However, the tender lovers and passive victims soon give way to the carefree adventuress and the jaundiced "flapper." The poems are characterized by regular lines of alternating rhyme and lapidary verse. Romance is often countered by a satiric thrust: "All of my days are gray with yearning. / (Nevertheless, a girl needs fun.)"

Sunset Gun (1928) achieves a solidarity through alternating voices of melancholy and seriousness. The cavalier tone often reveals the comic dimensions of sorrow, but various poems, such as those concerning Mary's pain at the loss of Jesus, touch on the universal nature of tragedy. *Death and Taxes* (1931) emphasizes the artistic integrity of the poetry by moving even further into the realm of the dramatic monologue. The usual caustic verse alternates with statements by various historical and literary figures. The contemplative verse shows a fine mastery of mood and tone and a manipulation of public myths, which places P. far above the level of light entertainer. Poems from all three volumes were collected in *Not So Deep as a Well* (1936).

In 1927, P. began writing stories and a book-review column signed "Constant Reader" for *The New Yorker*. P. wrote for many popular magazines, but her most sustained critical endeavor was the "Constant Reader" column. Like her play reviews of the same period, the forty-six pieces are characterized by an easy conversational tone that seems to effortlessly interweave epigrams, puns, and personal anecdotes. Notwithstanding the subjective mode of approach, sound literary commentary and insightful critical evaluations distinguish most of P.'s work.

P. published stories in *Laments for the Living* (1930) and *After Such Pleasures* and collected them in *Here Lies* (1939). The stories reveal her as a master of cutting, ironic fiction.

"Big Blond," won the O. Henry Prize for 1930. Hazel Morse works hard at being a "good sport." However, when near thirty, she marries Herbie and delights in being able to relax and give in to her moods. Unfortunately, he tires of her and leaves. The need to be a "good sport" again prevails. Hazel is provided for by a succession of men, but always in a mist of alcohol, depressed and longing for peace. The four-part presentation traces the progressive disintegration from contentment through despair over a number of years with an admirable unity of effect. The analogy made between the nonintrospective, passive victim and a "beaten driven, stumbling" horse struggling "to get a footing" is the heart of the narrative and is all the more vivid for the stark rendering of the background details.

"A Telephone Call" (1930) provides a striking example of P.'s proficiency in the modified stream-of-consciousness technique. As a woman futilely awaits a promised telephone call, the shifting phases of desperation and pain are revealed through a superb rhetorical display that encompasses rushing prayers, meandering introspections, and angry threats.

"Clothe the Naked" (1939) concerns Big Lannie, a stoic black laundress whose only surviving daughter dies in childbirth leaving her with a blind grandson. The distanced narrative tone imparts a sense of sustained suffering throughout.

Although P.'s reputation has suffered a sharp decline, the literary merit of her short stories and much of her poetry can scarcely be contested. The perennial concerns of alienation and loss of love are treated with an irony that only barely masks the sense of deep tragedy beneath. The economy of language, flawless dialogue, and sharp eye for detail that characterize the short stories is directly attributable to P.'s poetic sense. The crystalline, concise sentences set the tone and sum up the characters as aptly as the measured, polished verse.

WORKS: *Enough Rope* (1926). *Sunset Gun* (1928). *Laments for the Living* (1930). *Death and Taxes* (1931). *After Such Pleasures* (1933). *Not So Deep as a Well* (1936). *Here Lies* (1939). *Dorothy Parker* (1944).

BIBLIOGRAPHY: Keats, J., *You Might As Well Live: The Life and Times of Dorothy Parker* (1972). Wilson E., *Classics and Commercials* (1950).

Other references: *EJ* 23 (1934). *Esquire* 70 (1968). *Horizon* 4 (1962). *Paris Review* 13 (1956). *Poetry* (30, 1927; 33, 1928; 39, 1931). *Rendezvous* 3 (1968). *Revue de Paris* 54 (1947).

FRANCINE SHAPIRO PUK

Elsie Worthington Clews Parsons

B. 27 Nov. 1875, New York City; d. 19 Dec. 1971, New York City
Wrote under: John Main
D. of Henry and Lucy Madison Clews; m. Herbert Parsons, 1900

P. was the daughter of wealthy and socially prominent parents. She was educated in New York City, receiving from Columbia University a B.A. in 1896, M.A. in 1897, and Ph.D. in 1899. In 1900, she married a New York attorney who became a Congressman and a leader in the Republican Party. The marriage lasted until his death in 1925 and seems to have been unusual in the degree of autonomy P. achieved within it. There were six children born of this marriage, four of whom survived P.

Primarily a researcher and writer, P. taught only briefly, from 1899 to 1905 at Barnard College and then at the New School for Social Research in 1919. But her professional achievements were well recognized: She presided over the American Folklore Society (1918), the American Ethnological Association (1923–25), and the American Anthropological Association (1940–41); she was also associate editor of the *Journal of American Folklore* (1910–1941) and vice-president of the New York Academy of Sciences (1936).

P.'s career may be divided into two periods, the first beginning in 1899 when she undertook speculative work in sociology, committed to the belief that individuals have the right to self-development, and that civilized society must allow for and benefit from such development. Occasionally, P.'s objective observations of her own society made readers uncomfortable. For example, a college textbook titled *The Family* (1906) attracted unusual attention because it was directed at both students and "intelligent mothers" of daughters, and discussed not only the family but also the inequities of the double standard and the advantages of trial marriage.

P.'s next five books also dealt with social oppression, but from a broader perspective. *The Old-fashioned Woman* (1913) is a book written with wit and quiet irony. Here P. reviews attitudes and customs relating to women in so-called primitive societies and in her own society so that the limitations of her society are revealed as being painfully like the limitations of primitive societies. In *Social Freedom* (1915) P. explores the negative effects of such social categorization by age and sex on the development of individual personality. In *Social Rule* (1916) she argues that social categories are used as a way of controlling such groups as women, children, employees, and "backward peoples." Of special interest in this book is P.'s view of the ideal role of feminism.

The second stage of P.'s career began about 1915, when she became interested in the anthropological approach of Franz Boas. P. did not abandon her commitment to self-development, but turned from speculating about the way society functioned to collecting ethnographic data that could indicate how a specific culture functioned. After 1915, P. undertook at least one field trip a year to study various groups, though her chief work was done with American and West Indian blacks and with Indians of the southwest Pueblos. On occasion, she returned to her earlier speculations and her interest in feminist-related issues when she wrote journal articles.

Boas and other anthropologists cite two works of this period as having special significance—*Pueblo Indian Religion* (1939) and *Mitla: Town of the Souls, and Other Zapoteco-speaking Pueblos of Oaxaca, Mexico* (1936)—but these books are aimed at the specialist reader.

Vital to any assessment of P. is a consideration of her character, which was marked by an uncompromising commitment to her work and to living in accordance with her beliefs. She was, Boas wrote: "intolerant towards [herself], tolerant towards others, disdainful of selfish pettiness and truthful in thought and action." So strong was her personality that Robert Herrick, a novelist of the period, used it as the basis for several characterizations in *Wanderings* (1925), *Chimes* (1926), and *The End of Desire* (1932).

Since P.'s death, her work has attracted little general attention, though at the time of her death the value of her work and the significance of her support of the American Folklore Society and of the field work of other anthropologists were acknowledged by many.

WORKS: *Educational Legislation and Administration of the Colonial Governments* (1899). *The Family* (1906). *The Old-fashioned Woman* (1913). *Religious Chastity* (1913). *Fear and Conventionality* (1914). *Social Freedom: A Study of the Conflicts between Social Classifications and Personality* (1915). *Social Rule: A Study of the Will to Power* (1916). *Notes on Zuñi* (1917). *Folk-tales of Andros Island, Bahamas* (1918). *Notes on Ceremonialism at Laguna* (1920). *Winter and Summer Dance Series in Zuñi in 1918* (1922). *Folk-lore from the Cape Verde Islands* (1923). *Folk-lore of the Sea Islands, South Carolina* (1923). *Laguna Genealogies* (1923). *The Scalp Ceremonial of*

Zuñi (1924). *The Pueblo of Jemez* (1925). *Tewa Tales* (1926). *Kiowa Tales* (1929). *The Social Organization of the Tewa of New Mexico* (1929). *Isleta, New Mexico* (1932). *Folk-lore of the Antilles, French and English* (1933). *Hopi and Zuñi Ceremonialism* (1933). *Mitla: Town of the Souls, and Other Zapoteco-speaking Pueblos of Oaxaca, Mexico* (1936). *Taos Pueblo* (1936). *Pueblo Indian Religion* (2 vols, 1939). *Taos Tales* (1940). *Notes on the Caddo* (1941). *Pequche, Canton of Otavelo, Province of Imbabura Ecuador: A Study of Andean Indians* (1945).

BIBLIOGRAPHY: Boas, F., in *The Scientific Monthly* 54 (May 1942).

Other references: *American Anthropologist* 45 (1943). *Journal of American Folk-lore* 56 (1943). *Proceedings of the American Philosophical Society* 94 (1950).

PHYLLIS FRANKLIN

Louella Oettinger Parsons

B. 6 Aug. 1893, Freeport, Illinois; d. 9 Dec. 1972, Beverly Hills, California
D. of Joshua and Helen Wilcox Oettinger; m. John Parsons, 1910;
m. Dr. Harry Martin, 1931

As a youngster, P. showed an interest in writing and had her first story published in the Freeport *Journal-Standard* before she reached high-school age. While in high school, P. acquired her first newspaper job, working as the dramatic editor and assistant to the city editor on the Dixon, Illinois, *Morning Star*. P. received most of her journalism education through such practical experiences.

In 1910, P. married a real-estate agent. The couple soon moved to Burlington, Iowa, where P. became frustrated and bored. After the birth of a daughter in 1911, P. left with the child to visit an uncle in Montana. From then on, P. and her husband drifted apart.

After the death of her husband in 1914, P. took her daughter to Chicago and worked as a reporter for the *Tribune*. P. soon became involved in the movie business and took a job with the Essanay Company reading scripts and writing scenarios.

P. was later able to convince the Chicago *Record-Herald* to run a series of her articles on how to write for the movies. These articles were well received, and P. realized that if people were interested in a behind-the-scenes look at films, they would also be interested in a more surface view—a look at the movie stars.

In 1918, P. moved with her daughter to New York City. She became the movie critic for the *Morning Telegraph*, where she remained until 1924. During her five years with the *Telegraph*, P. was made editor of the motion picture section and was presented with an all-female staff nicknamed the "Persian Garden of Cats."

P. started writing for the Hearst papers in 1924. In 1925, P. discovered that she had tuberculosis; she spent a year (on full salary) resting. After she recovered from the illness, Hearst sent P. to California, and she wrote her stories from Hollywood. At this time P.'s column became syndicated.

In 1931, P.'s work expanded to the broadcast field when she was hired by the Sunkist Orange Company to do a thirteen-week radio show. She began a second radio show in 1934, on which she interviewed movie stars. For four years, "Hollywood Hotel" was one of the leading radio programs.

Throughout the 1940s, P. continued to write her column, which was by then widely syndicated. Even at the age of sixty-four, P. was still doing a weekly radio show, writing her column, covering hard news events, writing stories for *Photoplay* and *Modern Screen*, and reviewing movies for *Cosmopolitan*. She retired in 1964.

Besides writing columns and doing radio shows, P. was also the author of three books. The first, *How to Write for the Movies*, was published in 1915 and used as a text in early film classes at Ohio State University. With the advent of the "talkie," however, the book became dated.

The Gay Illiterate (1944) is a delightful account of P.'s life until 1939. P.'s entertaining style of writing makes the book a pleasure to read even today.

Tell It to Louella (1961) is an account of some of P.'s more memorable celebrity interviews. Her quick and often acerbic wit provides greater insight into P.'s life and personality than into the personalities of the stars she covered.

P. was the first widely read gossip columnist in the U.S. She once wrote that she would "do almost anything" in order to get a scoop. Her columns were largely devoted to interviews with the most popular movie stars and reports on weddings, divorces, and births; she was most proud of "scooping" the divorces of famous stars. P. maintained a colorful reputation throughout her career.

WORKS: *How to Write for the Movies* (1915). *The Gay Illiterate* (1944). *Tell It to Louella* (1961).

BIBLIOGRAPHY: Eells, G., *Hedda and Louella* (1972). For articles in reference works, see: *CA* 37 (1973). *CB* (1940).

SANDRA CARLIN GUIN

Sara Payson Willis Parton

B. 9 July 1811, Portland, Maine; d. 10 Oct. 1872, New York City
Wrote under: Olivia Branch, Fanny Fern
D. of Nathaniel and Hannah Parker Willis; m. Charles Eldredge, 1837;
*   m. Samuel Farrington, 1849; m. James Parton, 1856*

P. preferred her talented mother to her harsh, narrowly religious father; she believed that her mother would have distinguished herself in literature had she not had such a large family. P. said her pen name, "Fanny Fern," was inspired by happy childhood memories of her mother picking sweet fern leaves.

When P. was a small child, her family moved to Boston, where her father established a religious newspaper. P. attended Boston schools and Catharine Beecher's famous seminary in Hartford, Connecticut, at the time when Harriet Beecher was a student teacher. Despite a lack of studiousness, P. wrote witty essays at the Beecher school and on her return to Boston contributed to her father's new publication, *Youth's Companion.*

In 1844, P.'s mother died, and in the next two years she lost the older of her three daughters and her first husband, a bank cashier. P. was reduced to relative poverty, with only grudging support from her father and in-laws. She tried marriage to a Boston merchant, but he soon left her. Although P. attempted to forget her second marriage, never directly referring to it, she later used Farrington as a model for one of her characters. In *Rose Clark* (1856), a "hypocrite" and "gross sensualist" tricks a reluctant widow into marriage and then slanders her and leaves her penniless.

When P. failed in her attempts to earn a living teaching and sewing, she appealed unsuccessfully to her brother, a successful poet and editor in New York, for help in launching a literary career. P. began to write short sketches, and by 1851 she was placing her work in small Boston magazines. Her magazine pieces were so popular that in 1853 J. C. Derby published a collection of them as *Fern Leaves from Fanny's Portfolio*. P. continued the next year with a second series and a juvenile, *Little Ferns for Fanny's Little Friends*. The three books sold an astonishing 180,000 copies in America and England, and P. was suddenly rich and famous.

Based very closely upon P.'s own experience, *Ruth Hall* (1855) recounts the struggles of a widow to support herself and her children. Ruth Hall finds few opportunities open to women and is treated shabbily by her relatives, who can tolerate neither a passive dependent nor the successful and assertive writer Ruth finally becomes. *Ruth Hall* caused a sensation in the literary world. P. had apparently thought herself protected by her pseudonym and neglected to disguise the characters, who were obviously based on P.'s relatives. P.'s true identity was discovered and the family quarrel aired in public.

Ruth Hall was admired by Hawthorne, and attacked by the critics for the same reasons he praised it—its lack of restraint and "female delicacy"; one critic referred to it as "Ruthless Hall." Soon after the publication of *Ruth Hall*, the anonymous *Life and Beauties of Fanny Fern* appeared, satirizing P. as a spendthrift, adventuress, and ingrate to her family.

In the meantime, P. moved to New York City and was engaged by Robert Bonner, publisher of the New York *Ledger*, to write a weekly column for the then outlandish sum of $100 a week. For the next twenty years, P. wrote weekly for the *Ledger*, never missing a column. P. lived a relatively quiet life with her third husband, James Parton, a well-known biographer eleven years her junior.

After *Ruth Hall*, P. wrote only one more novel, *Rose Clark* (1856), but her talent was not for fiction, and after *Rose Clark* she stuck with the form she was best at—the informal essay, sometimes lightly fictionalized but always short. She published several collections of these from her *Ledger* columns.

Because her early work is best known, P. has been mistakenly classified as a sentimentalist. However, P.'s writing changed and developed significantly after her initial success. In the first series of *Fern Leaves* there are two parts: the first, which comprises about three quarters of the book, is indeed lachrymose, but the remaining quarter consists of humorous and satirical pieces. In the second series of *Fern Leaves* the proportion is exactly reversed.

In *Folly as It Flies* (1859), P. adopted a new voice, which she would maintain for the rest of her career. Her sentimentality and heavy-handed satire give way to relaxed, humorous philosophizing. She abandons the artificiality and straining for effect of her earlier pieces, and writes more naturally and spontaneously. While P.'s staple continued to be everyday domestic topics, like child care and the annoying habits of husbands, she became conscious of social conditions in New York City and began to depict poverty, prostitution, exploitation of workers, and prison life.

P. also became more direct and outspoken in her championship of women. Women's estate and the relationship between the sexes had always been P.'s major subject, but in her early fiction she protested injustice to women by portraying them as passive victims of male brutality. By the end of the 1850s, P. came to support the women's rights movement and encourage her readers to seek suffrage, better education, and wider fields of endeavor.

WORKS: *Fern Leaves from Fanny's Portfolio* (English title, *Shadows and Sunbeams;* 1st series, 1853; 2nd series, 1854). *Little Ferns for Fanny's Little Friends* (1854). *Ruth Hall* (1855). *Rose Clark* (1856). *Fresh Leaves* (1857). *Play-Day Book* (1857). *Folly as It Flies* (1859). *A New Story Book for Children* (1864). *Ginger-Snaps* (1870). *Caper-Sauce* (1872). *Fanny Fern: A Memorial Volume* (Ed. J. Parton, 1873).

BIBLIOGRAPHY: Adams, F. B., *Fanny Fern* (1966). Derby, J. C., *Fifty Years Among Authors, Books and Publishers* (1884). *The Life and Beauties of Fanny Fern* (1855).

For articles in reference works, see: *NAW* (article by E. B. Schlesinger).

Other references: *AL* (Nov. 1957). *Biblion* (Spring 1969). *Colophon* (Sept. 1939). *NY Historical Society Quarterly* (Oct. 1954). *WS* 1 (1972).

BARBARA A. WHITE

Elia Wilkinson Peattie

B. 1862, Kalamazoo, Michigan; d. 12 July 1935, Wellington, Vermont
Wrote under: Elia W. Peattie, Sade Iverson
Given name: Elia Wilkinson
M. Robert Burns Peattie, 1883

P.'s family moved from Michigan to Chicago shortly after the 1871 fire. They built a comfortable house, in which P. and her husband later raised their own children.

In 1884, P. became the first "girl reporter" on the Chicago *Tribune*. After ten years in Omaha, where P. wrote pot-boiler histories and her best stories while her husband managed the *World-Herald*, P. returned to Chicago in 1898, when she bore their third son. A daughter died in childhood; all three sons survived their parents, two becoming writers who married writers.

From 1901 to 1917, P. was Chicago *Tribune* literary critic, while also publishing prolifically. Invitations to the Peatties' Sunday afternoon gatherings represented acceptance into the Chicago literary establishment.

P. left Chicago in 1917, when her husband joined the *New York Times*. They retired to Tryon, North Carolina, in 1920, where P. remained after his death in 1930.

Many of P.'s publications were primarily commercial ventures. *The Story of America* (1889) has neither original interpretation nor careful writing to recommend it, yet P. published several editions and adaptations. Similarly commercial were the two poetry anthologies that the *Tribune*'s influential literary critic edited in 1903.

P.'s other historical works reflect her involvement in Chicago's cultural "uplift" movement. Her early historical romances and romanticized histories promoted the cultural establishment's fascination with knighthood's European flowering. P.'s one-act costume pageant of women's changing status from mythological to modern times, *Times and Manners* (1918), was written specifically for a Chicago Woman's Club production.

P.'s involvement with club theatricals also inspired several fine one-act plays late in her career. The title piece of *The Wander Weed* (1923) is probably her best, dealing with a Blue Ridge mountain girl's encounter with a sphinxlike old woman who breaks silence to convince Lu Constant of the need to accept the pains and joys of ongoing family relationships.

Family settings and themes are the common denominators for P.'s girls' books. *Azalea* (1912) is representative; its young heroine forsakes nomadic circus adventures for the everyday continuities and domestic affections of small-town family life. Such small-town virtues also win out over artistic ambition and urban wealth in *Lotta Embury's Career* (1915) and *Sarah Brewster's Relatives* (1916).

The best of P.'s early magazine short stories, collected in *A Mountain Woman* (1896), call domestic sentimentality into question. In "Jim Lancy's Waterloo," newly married Annie Lancy confronts the hard facts of premature aging and madness among neighboring Nebraska wives and of infant death in her own home. Generally, the *Mountain Woman* stories embody a conviction that city and frontier pose irreconcilable cultures, engendering psychic disorientation for intercultural migrants.

Similarly critical of domestic sentimentality are P.'s two adult novels. An implicitly erotic relationship between father and daughter informs the violent action of *The Judge* (1890), while *The Precipice* (1914) exposes patriarchal tyranny and neighborly hypocrisy underlying small-town family life. Nonetheless, Kate Barrington's search for independence in *The Precipice* is undercut by her friends' dramatizations of feminine limitations and the joys of motherhood. Kate's own social-work activities—modeled on those of Julia Lathrop, first head of the U.S. Children's Bureau—remain in the novel's background. The organizing marriage-versus-career theme ultimately resolves itself ambiguously in Kate's decision to relinquish "prideful" independence for marital commitment, yet to subordinate "womanly" fulfillment to civic duty by living in Washington, D.C., apart from her husband.

A few of P.'s short stories and one-act plays are fully realized literary works, and *The Precipice* is fascinating in its treatment of feminist issues. However, P.'s career was ultimately compromised by easy commercial productions and thematic contradictions. As a critic and romancer, she upheld derivative genteel standards of "noble" thoughts and "classic" forms. Yet her best fictions and plays are realistic, and "The Milliner" (1914), a pseudonymous free verse poem for *The Little Review*, met with deserved acclaim.

WORKS: The Story of America (1889; rev. eds., 1892, 1896; reprinted as *America in Peace and War,* 1898). *A Journey through Wonderland* (1890). *The Judge* (1890). *With Scrip and Staff* (1891). *The American Peasant* (with T. Tibbles, 1892). *A Mountain Woman* (1896). *Our Chosen Land* (1896). *The Pictorial Story of America* (1896). *Pippins and Cheese* (1897). *The Love of a Calaban: A Romantic Opera* (1898; adapted by E. Freer as *Massimillano,* 1925). *The Shape of Fear, and Other Ghostly Stories* (1898). *Ickery Ann, and Other Boys and Girls* (1899). *The Beleaguered Forest* (1901). *How Jacques Came into the Forest of Arden* (1901). *Castle, Knight, and Troubador* (1903). *The Edges of Things* (1903). *Poems You Ought to Know* (edited by Peattie, 1903). *To Comfort You* (edited by Peattie, 1903). *Edda and the Oak* (1911). *Azalea* (1912). *Annie Laurie and Azalea* (1913). *Azalea at Sunset Gap* (1914). *The Precipice* (1914). *The Angel with a Broom* (1915). *Azalea's Silver Web* (1915). *Lotta Embury's Career* (1915). *Sarah Brewster's Relatives* (1916). *The Newcomers* (1917). *Painted Windows* (1918). *Times and Manners* (1918). *The Wander Weed, and Seven Other Little Theater Plays* (1923). *The Great Delusion* (1932). *The Book of the Fine Arts Building* (n.d.).

BIBLIOGRAPHY: Atlantic 83 (1899). *Bookman* (April 1914; Jan. 1916). Boston *Transcript* (18 Feb. 1914). *NYT* (24 Dec. 1916).

SIDNEY H. BREMER

Julia Mood Peterkin

B. 31 Oct. 1880, Laurens County, South Carolina; d. 10 Aug. 1961,
  Fort Motte, South Carolina
D. of Julius Andrew and Alma Archer Mood; m. William Peterkin, 1903

The youngest of four children, P. spent several years with her grandparents in rural South Carolina after her mother's early death. Later, she lived in Sumter, South Carolina, with her father. After receiving her B.A. and M.A. degrees from Converse College, Spartanburg, South Carolina, P. taught at Fort Motte, a small, isolated community. She married the owner of Lang Syne plantation there. There were few whites and many blacks on the two-thousand-acre plantation. Because of her husband's ill health, P. took over most of the responsibilities of running Lang Syne until her son William was able to assume the actual management.

P. began writing in her early forties, and her work was centered around Fort Motte and Murrell's Inlet, a coastal village in South Carolina where she had a summer home.

Plantation stories were a popular genre from antebellum days until well into the 20th c., and it is one of P.'s contributions that she brought to this genre a sense of realism and dignity in her portrayal of the lives of black characters. In most of her work there is no stereotyped or affected local color, a common characteristic of plantation stories. P. also broke out of the southern pattern of sentimentality.

P.'s first works, which appeared in many magazines in the early 1920s, may be divided generally into two groups: Gullah-dialect sketches and more conventionally structured short stories. The former are usually dramatic monologues in the words of coastal South Carolina blacks, but the dialect at times becomes obtrusive. The larger group, in which P. departs from extended use of dialect but maintains the rhythm and syntax of the speech, are stark, powerful portrayals of the lives of these isolated people. The stories in *Green Thursday* (1924) continue in this vein, but there is more description of the land and the natural cycles, which always play an integral part in the lives of her characters. The stories may be read almost as a novel, centering on Killdee and his family.

Black April (1927), P.'s first novel, incorporates some of the incidents of the stories. The book is episodic rather than tightly plotted. It gives a convincing picture of the daily lives of the characters and a strong sense of community.

In *Scarlet Sister Mary* (1928), P.'s Pulitzer Prize–winning novel, P. creates a fully conceived heroine of modern fiction. Mary reveals a strong affirmation of life as she steers between the restrictive mores of the community and her sense of freedom and selfhood. Mary's guiding principle is, "Everybody has a selfness that makes the root of his life and being." Like many of Eudora Welty's women characters, Mary, intelligent but uneducated, frequently articulates her emotions through metaphorical identifications with the natural world.

Bright Skin (1932) is a sensitive portrayal of the developing relationship of a boy and girl as they mature.

Roll, Jordan Roll (1933) is P.'s commentary on photographs of blacks at Lang Syne. In this book, P. loses her artistic objectivity and becomes somewhat nostalgic. Interestingly, Doris Ullman's photographs capture much of the dignity and realism that is portrayed in P.'s fiction. In *A Plantation Christmas* (1934), P. seems overwhelmed by a sense of the past, and although there are fine descriptions, the total effect is local color for its own sake, nostalgic and sentimental. These two books are weakened by the presence of a white narrator; in P.'s best works, all the characters are black and events are viewed entirely through their eyes.

Though P. lived and wrote in isolation from the literary world, she was helped and encouraged by many literary figures who praised her economy of style, detachment, and compassion. P.'s characters live in an isolated but believable society in which folk beliefs and folk wisdom aid them in the struggle between personal responsibility and fate. Their lives reveal the drama and dignity of the ordinary events of life.

WORKS: *Green Thursday* (1924). *Black April* (1927). *Scarlet Sister Mary* (1928). *Bright Skin* (1932). *Roll, Jordan Roll* (with D. Ulmann, 1933). *A Plantation Christmas* (1934). *The Collected Short Stories of Julia Peterkin* (Ed. F. Durham, 1970).

BIBLIOGRAPHY: Clark, E., *Innocence Abroad* (1931). Davidson, D., in *The Spyglass: Views and Reviews, 1924–1930*, Ed. J. Fain (1963). Durham, F., Introduction to *The Collected Short Stories of Julia Peterkin* (1970). Landers, T. H., *Julia Peterkin* (1976).
Other references: *NYHT* (17 Jan. 1933).

ANNE NEWMAN

Ann Lane Petry

B. 12 Oct. 1908, Old Saybrook, Connecticut
Writes under: Ann Petry
D. of Peter Clark and Bertha James Lane; m. George D. Petry, 1938

P. was born into a poor black family of Old Saybrook, Connecticut, a predominantly white New England community. Her father was the local druggist. After receiving her Ph.G. in 1931 from the University of Connecticut, P. returned home to work as a pharmacist in the family drugstores from 1931 to 1938. In 1938, she married Petry (they have one daughter) and moved to New York City, becoming an advertising salesperson and writer for the *Amsterdam News* (1938–41), and then reporter and woman's-page editor for the rival *People's Voice* of Harlem (1941–44). P. was also a member of the American Negro Theater and wrote children's plays.

P. studied creative writing at Columbia University from 1944 to 1946 and published her first short stories in *The Crisis* and *Phylon*. In addition to writing, P. has lectured at Berkeley, Miami University, and Suffolk University, and was a visiting professor of English at the University of Hawaii (1974–75).

After P. had served her literary apprenticeship as a journalist, she began to publish short stories. "Like a Winding Sheet" was reprinted in *Foley's Best American Short Stories of 1946*, and another story led to a Houghton Mifflin Literary Fellowship, under which P. completed her first novel, *The Street* (1946). *The Street* is a naturalistic novel usually associated with the Wright school of protest fiction. The protagonist, Lutie Johnson, imbued with the American success ethic of Benjamin Franklin, is defeated in her attempts to improve her life by the detrimental influences of Harlem. Critics see the novel as gripping yet simplistic.

Country Place (1947) is an "assimilationist" novel set in the small town of Lennox, Connecticut. The major characters are white, and are enmeshed in a plot and setting reminiscent of a cross between *Winesburg, Ohio* and *Peyton Place*, as an apocalyptic autumn storm brings out the true natures of the townspeople. *Country Place* is considered P.'s most successful novel in scope and use of symbol and metaphor to parallel action and evoke character. The plot is unified and the prose clear and powerful.

The Narrows (1953) demonstrates a return to the theme of race. The plot revolves around the classic love conflict between heroic black man and rich white woman. Link Williams, the protagonist, is a fine portrayal of a young black man, an orphan and possessor of a college degree who has chosen to tend bar in the hub of the Narrows, the black section of Monmouth, Connecticut, rather than become a member of the black bourgeoisie. *The Narrows* is simultaneously sophisticated and melodramatic, as brilliantly conceived characters outshine a standard plot.

The rest of P.'s opus consists of four juvenile books and a collection of short stories, *Miss Muriel, and Other Stories* (1971). "In Darkness and Confusion" concerns a poor black couple's way of coping with their son's mistreatment in a segregated army by participating in looting and property damage during the Harlem riot of August 1943. The well-wrought title story is semiautobiographical, told from the perspective of a twelve-year-old black girl. Set in the drugstore of a New England town, the story treats the loss of innocence that comes with a growing awareness of maturity.

P.'s fiction is of a fine quality. Her stories succeed better than her novels, although the novels certainly belong in the mainstream of American naturalism and realism. P.'s work has not yet received thorough treatment by literary critics.

WORKS: *The Street* (1947). *Country Place* (1947). *The Drugstore Cat* (1949). *The Narrows* (1953). *Harriet Tubman* (1955). *Tituba of Salem Village* (1964). *Legends of the Saints* (1970). *Miss Muriel, and Other Stories* (1971).

BIBLIOGRAPHY: Bone, R. A., *The Negro Novel in America* (1958; rev. ed., 1965). Royster, B. H., "The Ironic Vision of Four Black Women Novelists: A Study of the Novels of Jessie Fauset, Nella Larsen, Zora Neale Hurston, and Ann Petry" (Ph.D. diss., Emory Univ., 1975).

For articles in reference works, see: *CB* (March 1946). *Great Black Americans*, Eds. B. Richardson and W. A. Fahey (1976). *Twentieth Century Children's Writers*, Ed. D. L. Kirkpatrick (1978).

Other references: *Crisis* 53 (1946). *Crit* (Spring 1974). *NEQ* 47 (1974). *NYHT* (16 Aug. 1953). *Opportunity* 24 (1946). *SBL* (Fall 1975).

ANN RAYSON

Almira Hart Lincoln Phelps

B. 15 July 1793, Berlin, Connecticut; d. 15 July 1884, Baltimore, Maryland
D. of Samuel and Lydia Hensdale Hart; m. Samuel Lincoln, 1817;
  m. John Phelps, 1832

P. and her elder sister, Emma Hart Willard, shared a love for study, an aptitude for teaching, and a desire to improve the intellectual status of women. Close association with the pioneering Troy, New York, Female Seminary has made Emma more celebrated than her equally productive but more eclectic sister. P.'s early schooling was in Berlin, and she later studied at Middlebury and Pittsfield, Massachusetts.

After teaching for several years, P. married a Federalist editor. Left a widow with two small daughters in 1823, she returned to teaching and to writing to earn a family income. After joining Emma at the Troy Female Seminary, she studied science with Amos Eaton, a professor of natural science at nearby Rensselaer Institute. In 1832, P. remarried. She continued to write, and in 1838 her husband urged her to accept the principalship of a promising new seminary in West Chester, Pennsylvania. After brief administrations in Pennsylvania and at the Rahway,

New Jersey, Female Institute, P. headed the Patapsco Female Institute in Ellicott's Mills, Maryland, from 1841 to 1855.

An imaginative and successful educator, P. was also a prolific writer. Her first textbook, *Familiar Lectures on Botany* (1829), was her most original and useful. Botany was a popular subject, and P.'s text provided a middle ground between the conversational style of many books written for young ladies and the formal presentation of scientific principles designed for advanced students. Traditional in its reliance on the Linnean artificial classification system, the book provides diagrams and suggestions for study designed to engage the student's participation in learning; appendixes provide all necessary reference material, including a description of genera and species, a dictionary of terms, and a common-name index. Frequently revised and used widely in academies for boys and girls, the volume went through twenty-eight editions (275,000 copies) by 1872. There were eighteen editions of an abridged version, *Botany for Beginners* (1833). Moral observations, literary references, and history were combined with sound science in a text designed to develop specific skills while integrating student learning. The success of the botanical text led P. to write books on chemistry, natural philosophy, and geology; but these were more derivative in content and less popular. *Familiar Lectures on Chemistry*, for example, used similar teaching techniques, but a reliance on household examples circumscribed its audience, and borrowed material caused the book to lack cohesion.

Most of P.'s writing was intended to educate and elevate young women. P.'s stories were in the popular, melodramatic, and didactic mode of antebellum novels. *Caroline Westerley; or, The Young Traveler from Ohio* (1833) presents a series of letters from an older sister to a younger; it is a guide through the New England landscape, an educational commentary on topics from plant life to housing styles, and a moral analysis of people encountered. Sarah Josepha Hale's review found this story "a charming picture of a young girl, engaged in improvement, and finding happiness. . . ." P.'s two other novels held more drama but similar purposes. Both *Ida Norman; or, Trials and Their Uses* (1848) and *The Blue Ribbon Society; or, The School Girls' Rebellion* (1879) were presented chapter by chapter for evening discussion at Patapsco Institute and were later published.

As educator and writer, P. could not resist contemporary discussion about the purpose and nature of education for young women, whether in public addresses, journal articles, or books. Although a domestic feminist, P. did not advocate a curriculum to develop household skills, but stressed classical subjects as well as the sciences. Her *Lectures to Young Ladies* (1833) stressed the need to study widely and to discipline the mind. Discussions of morality became more common in later editions. *The Female Student* (1836) emphasized the value of study but also stressed the need for a good diet, proper exercise, and proper clothing. This volume, like *Lectures*, was published as part of the School Library series, under the sanction of the Massachusetts School Board. P. moved with the vanguard of women educational reformers of the mid–19th c.

After the Civil War, P. retired from teaching but continued to write for national journals. Some of her essays explored the fine arts. P. also dedicated her energy to opposing the woman suffrage movement, although she continued to advocate educational equality for women. P.'s ideas and leadership, so significant to her own generation, were often disregarded or even dismissed by the suffragists and co-educational reformers of the late 19th c. Herself the model of the self-determination she taught, P. helped establish the possibility for women's public and political roles.

WORKS: *Familiar Lectures on Botany* (1829). *Address on the Subject of Female Education in Greece and the General Extension of Christian Intercourse among Females* (1831). *The Child's Geology* (1832). *Botany for Beginners* (1833). *Caroline Westerley; or, The Young Traveler from Ohio* (1833). *Lectures to Young Ladies* (1833). *Chemistry for Beginners* (1834). *The Female Student; or, Lectures to Young Ladies on Female Education* (1836; republished as *The Fireside Friend*, 1840). *Familiar Lectures on Natural Philosophy* (1837). *Lectures in Chemistry for the Use of Schools, Families, and Private Students* (1838). *Natural Philosophy for Beginners* (1838). *Ida Norman; or, Trials and Their Uses* (1848). *Christian Households* (1858). *Hours with My Pupils* (1859; republished as *The Educator*, 1868). *Foreign Correspondence in Relation to the Rebellion in the United States* (1863). *Our Country, in Its Relations to the Past, Present, and Future* (edited by Phelps, 1864). *Reviews and Essays on Art, Literature, and Science* (1873). *Women's Duties and Rights, the Woman's Congress: An Address to the Women of America* (1876). *The Blue Ribbon Society; or, The School Girls' Rebellion* (1879).

BIBLIOGRAPHY: Bolzau, E. L., *Almira Hart Lincoln Phelps: Her Life and Work* (1936). Lutz, A., *Emma Willard: Daughter of Democracy* (1929). Woody, T., *A History of Women's Education in the United States* (2 vols., 1929).

For articles in reference works, see: *DAB*, VII, 2. *NAW* (article by F. Rudolph). *NCAB*, 11.

SALLY GREGORY KOHLSTEDT

Elizabeth Stuart Phelps

B. 13 Aug. 1815, Andover, Massachusetts; d. 29 Nov. 1852, Andover,
  Massachusetts
Wrote under: E. S. Phelps, H. Trusta
D. of Moses and Abigail Clark Stuart; m. Austin Phelps, 1842

P.'s mother was a long-term invalid and her father a clergyman and professor of Greek and Hebrew literature at Andover Theological Seminary.
At age ten, P. began to compose tales to amuse family and servants.

P. was educated at Abbot Academy in Andover. At age sixteen, she
went to live in Boston with the Reverend Jacob Abbott, author of the
juvenile Rollo series, and attended the Mount Vernon School. P.'s first
publications—brief articles written over the name "H. Trusta," an ana-
gram of "Stuart"—appeared in a religious magazine edited by Abbott.
According to P.'s husband, P.'s early literary ambition was to gain her
father's approval. By 1834, P. was beginning to suffer from a "cerebral
disease" characterized by headache, partial blindness, and temporary pa-
ralysis. When P. began to write, her health improved, although she was
never again "for any long time" without symptoms of disease.

P.'s daughter, who became a successful author writing under her
mother's name, was born in 1844. P.'s father died in January 1852. She
herself followed within eleven months, never fully recovering from the
birth in August of her second son.

P. wrote newspaper and magazine articles as well as children's books,
the latter published anonymously and later not identifiable even by P.
After her marriage, P. kept a "Family Journal" as well as journals of her
children's lives. She reviewed contemporary books and continued to
write for children as well as older readers. From the late 1840s until
her death in 1852, P. wrote five juvenile books, two collections of short
fiction, and two novels.

P.'s husband located one of the strong motivations for P.'s juvenile
writing in her childhood sleeplessness from a deep fear of death. Finding
in children's Sunday-school literature an association of "early piety with
the necessity of an early death," P. wished to provide a counter to such
association in the depiction of "religious principle as it is in life." From
1851 to 1853, P.'s four "Kitty Brown" books appeared. In Little Kitty

Brown and Her Bible Verses (1851), anecdotes demonstrate to a juvenile reader the behavioral correlates of various biblical dicta. These highly didactic tales present numerous realistic details from everyday living. *Little Mary; or, Talks and Tales for Children* (1854) was probably written for P.'s own children.

All of P.'s short writings point clear morals, but they demonstrate a literary advance over P.'s juvenilia, first by leaving morals implied and second by achieving greater realism from increased attention to the documentation of daily life. *The Angel over the Right Shoulder* (1852), one of P.'s best works, describes the daily round of duties expected of a mother, develops the mother's deep concern for the future of her daughter, and reveals the conflict existing between these expectations and a woman's need to "cultivate her own mind and heart." P.'s two posthumously published collections consider a range of topics. *The Tell-Tale* (1853) includes six sketches concerning marital relationships, and one each about the relationships between father and daughter and between older women and younger women, as well as a satiric view of celebrating July 4th.

P.'s two anonymous novels sold well. *The Sunny Side; or, The Country Minister's Wife* (1851) received international recognition and by P.'s death claimed 300,000 to 500,000 readers. *A Peep at "Number Five"; or, A Chapter in the Life of a City Pastor* (1852), a partially autobiographical fiction and P.s favorite, sold 20,000 copies in less than one year. *The Sunny Side* first brought to P. renown as an author. The book follows Emily Edwards from wedding through marriage and motherhood to funeral, detailing her domestic and familial trials and triumphs. Undoubtedly the popularity of this book comes from its sympathetic and realistic presentation of a woman's daily life. *A Peep at "Number Five"* delineates the burdened life of Lucy Holbrook, who for the six years of the novel must meet parishioners' expectations at the expense of her own needs, but who nonetheless is relieved that her husband declines a call to a more prestigious position in favor of their remaining within the city parish. In both novels, P. presents a detailed view of a 19th-c. minister's household as seen through the eyes of his wife, and thus demonstrates the wife's excessive burdens and need for relief.

In her best work, P. depended little upon imaginative fabrication and largely upon meticulous observation. Along with her Andover neighbor Harriet Beecher Stowe, P. must be counted among the earliest depicters of the New England scene. She wrote at the beginning of the transition of American women's writing from domestic sentimentality to regional realism.

WORKS: *Little Kitty Brown and Her Bible Verses* (1851). *The Sunny Side; or, The Country Minister's Wife* (1851). *The Angel over the Right Shoulder* (1852). *Kitty Brown and Her City Cousins* (1852). *Kitty Brown and Her Little School* (1852). *A Peep at "Number Five"; or, A Chapter in the Life of a City Pastor* (1852). *Kitty Brown Beginning to Think* (1853). *The Last Leaf from Sunny Side* (1853). *The Tell-Tale; or, Home Secrets Told by Old Travellers* (1853). *Little Mary; or, Talks and Tales for Children* (1854).

BIBLIOGRAPHY: Hart, J. D., *The Popular Book* (1950). Kessler, C. F., "'The Woman's Hour': Life and Novels of Elizabeth Stuart Phelps, 1844–1911" (Ph.D. diss., Univ. of Pennsylvania, 1977). McKeen, P., and P. McKeen, *Annals of Fifty Years: A History of Abbot Academy* (1880). Phelps, A., "Memorial of the Author" in *The Last Leaf from Sunny Side* (1853). Robbins, S. S., *Old Andover Days: Memories of a Puritan Childhood* (1909). Ward, E. S. P., *Austin Phelps: A Memoir* (1891). Ward, E. S. P., *Chapters from a Life* (1896).

For articles in reference works, see: *AA. CAL. DAB*, X, 1. *NAW* (article by O. E. Winslow). *NCAB*, 9.

Other references: *Frontiers: A Journal of Women Studies* (1976; 1980).

CAROL FARLEY KESSLER

Josephine Lyons Scott Pinckney

B. *25 Jan. 1895, Charleston, South Carolina; d. 4 Oct. 1957, New York City*
Wrote under: *Josephine Pinckney*
D. *of Thomas and Camilla Scott Pinckney*

P.'s Charleston heritage is evident in most of her writing. During the 1920s, she was active in the Poetry Society of South Carolina, which she helped to found; she was also one of its leading poets. Some of P.'s work was published in *Poetry* before she gathered it together in *Sea-Drinking Cities* (1927).

P.'s poetry skillfully evokes scenes and moods of the Carolina Low Country; at times, however, it tends to be artificial and contrived. Realizing her limitations, P. soon turned to writing prose fiction. During the 1930s, P. published short stories in some of the better literary magazines.

Hilton Head (1941) is a fictionalized account of the life of Henry Woodward, one of the first English settlers of South Carolina. P.'s research into Woodward's life and into the Indian and Spanish, as well as early English, settlements of the period was painstaking. The prose style is at times marred by P.'s background as a poet of the imagist school, producing descriptions with the quality of stiff brocade. The major flaw is P.'s failure to dramatize the complex actions she presents. The novel's best passages are those which describe landscapes and personal interactions.

P. realized her inability to dramatize action, and in *Three O'Clock Dinner* (1945) she found a genuine fictional mode in the novel of manners, especially the manners of Charleston. A Literary Guild selection, this was the most popular of P.'s works and perhaps her best. Set in early 20th-c. Charleston, the story is of the inroads made by the daughter of a German immigrant family into one of the bastions of Charleston aristocracy, the Redcliff family. Although the girl fails to breech the family bulwark, she does shake and weaken its foundations. P.'s skillful description of Charleston manners displays both the charms and shortcomings of her characters, and she retains the ability to capture the scenery and moods of her native city.

Charleston is also the setting for *Great Mischief* (1948), but here it is the Charleston of the late 19th c. In addition to her careful research on the period, P. explores the superstitions of the time and includes a historically accurate account of 19th-c. witchcraft. These elements are woven together so skillfully that the line between fantasy and reality is blurred not only for the characters but also for the readers. The night of the witches' sabbath coincides with the great Charleston earthquake of 1886 so that both the main character and the reader are left to wonder if the witching was real or merely a dream.

In *My Son and Foe* (1952), P. abandons the Charleston setting to study the interactions of her characters in the crucible of a small, remote Caribbean island—interactions of love and jealousy, good and evil.

P. returned to a Charleston setting with *Splendid in Ashes* (1958). She chronicles the feelings of a generation of Charlestonians about the life and times of Augustus Grimshawe, recently deceased. Grimshawe's career and personality, as well as the personalities of those with whom he came into contact, are revealed as the characters react to the news of his death. P. ties the past to the present with a skillful combination of reminiscence and flashback.

P.'s first two books are the works of a literary novice. With her third book, P. found herself and became not only a writer with popular appeal but also a skillful delineator of the manners of the rigid Charlestonian society she knew so well. In her best novels, P. reveals the Charlestonian mind with wit and ironic humor.

WORKS: *Sea-Drinking Cities* (1927). *Hilton Head* (1941). *Three O'Clock Dinner* (1945). *Great Mischief* (1948). *My Son and Foe* (1952). *Splendid in Ashes* (1958).

BIBLIOGRAPHY: Davidson, D., *The Spyglass: Views and Reviews* (1963).
   For articles in reference works, see: *American Novelists of Today*, H. R. Warfel (1951). *20thCAS.*
   Other references: *NYHTBR* (20 Jan. 1952). *NYTBR* (23 Sept. 1945; 21 March 1948; 4 May 1958).

HARRIETTE CUTTINO BUCHANAN

Sylvia Plath

B. 27 Oct. 1932, Boston, Massachusetts; d. 11 Feb. 1963, London, England
Wrote under: Victoria Lucas, Sandra Peters, Sylvia Plath
D. of Otto Emil and Aurelia Schober Plath; m. Ted Hughes, 1956

P.'s father emigrated from the Polish corridor and became a biologist at Boston University; her mother, also a German immigrant, taught high-school English. P. was instilled with an achievement ethic which fueled her precocious talent for writing and drawing.

The facts of P.'s biography directly inform her writing, especially her idyllic yet menaced childhood by the sea, which ended abruptly with her father's death when P. was eight. His death, its dramatic circumstances, and the ensuing move inland to Wellesley affected P. profoundly. Writing poetry became "a new way of being happy." Sea, father, and childhood became a haunting amalgam of loss.

P.'s legend as superachiever began early. By the time she won a scholarship to Smith (1950), P. had drawings, poems, and stories in national publications, including *Seventeen*. Maintaining her momentum at Smith with school honors and steady publication, she won *Mademoiselle*'s College Fiction Contest, was named Guest Editor ("the literary woman's 'Miss America' "), and in June 1953 was initiated to "Mad"-ison Avenue.

Exhausted, demoralized, and at odds with her hard-won image as the all-American girl, P. had a mental breakdown and attempted suicide. After psychiatric treatment she returned to Smith, graduating summa cum laude (1955), again winning top awards and also a Fulbright to Cambridge for graduate work.

During her two years at Cambridge, P. married Hughes, a poet. Returning to Smith as English professor, she found the conflict between teaching and writing untenable. After another year attending Robert Lowell's poetry seminar and Yaddo, P. made her life in England, immersing herself in writing, Devon country life, and motherhood.

Worn down by competing pressures of motherhood and muse, chronic ill health, a cold winter, a failed marriage, and recurrent depression, P. gassed herself at the age of thirty-one.

In her apprentice work, P. submerges her specific concerns about identity, creation, death, and muse beneath detached, synthetic, allusive pieces on nature and art. P.'s early poems attest to her control, not only over form but over the emotion it contains. Her middle poems are best represented by *The Colossus* (1960), which spans her college, breakdown, scholar, and marriage phases of development. Painstakingly wrought, word by well-chosen word, the clenched poems elicit admiration for their mature technical virtuosity, and criticism (shared by P.) for their elaborate "checks and courtesies," "maddening docility," and "deflections."

Three Women: A Monologue for Three Voices (1962) is a transitional, formative work. Always obsessed by, and ambivalent about, female creativity, P. now presents her Darwinian value system: the mother is victor, for *she* produces, while the Girl and the Secretary are "empty," "restless and useless," creating "corpses." The three voices represent P.'s consciousness of her role conflict as artist, wife, and mother. The radio-play format opens up her style. After this, her poetry is dramatic rather than narrative or expository, written "all of one piece," to be read aloud; its imperfect cadences, careless-seeming rhymes, and impression of spontaneity and free association underlie P.'s new aesthetics, which demand of the poems that they be "possessed . . . as by the rhythms of their own breathing."

The poems in *Ariel* (1965), *Crossing the Water* (1971), and *Winter Trees* (1971) are the culmination of themes and images of P.'s previous works. They are different only in degree—"extremist" in their profound disillusionment in her idealized marriage and the "years of doubleness, smiles, and compromise." P. releases her long-suppressed rage and is, at the same time, disconcertingly gleeful and triumphant, gaily macabre, and erotically murderous. Vitality, not iambics, produces the rhythm, and the half, slanted rhymes sound like a drunk's.

While the poems appear autobiographical and private in imagery (the "toe" of "Daddy," one of P.'s best-known poems, refers to her father's amputated foot) and bare of artifice, years of practice with form and poetics underlie these outbursts, and the literal concrete metaphors universalize the meaning.

P.'s fiction contains the same preoccupation with her own experience, but it never loosens control as in her breakthrough poetry and hence never assumes the poetry's powerful voice. It was written throughout P.'s career, largely for the commercial market. Yet in these manufactured stories, with their studied moralistic formulas, P. gives candid expression to her own anxieties. In "The Fifty-ninth Bear," she projects a wife's canny hostility to her husband. "Den of Lions" reveals the Plathian voice at its best, where the persona is "game," wryly humorous, and self-deprecating about her traumas.

The engaging narrator of "Den of Lions" turns up again in *The Bell Jar* (1963), P.'s autobiographical novel about her mental breakdown. Again, disillusionment fuels the criticism P. now levels about growing up female in middle-class America. P.'s approach is satiric; the world's injustice is more absurd than evil. The heroine's summer on "Mad" Avenue is an initiation ritual into "the real world," which turns out to be a disillusioning joke. P.'s refusal to moralize and her naive insistence on the private nature of her vision effectively result in a moving book with tragic and universal overtones.

Her earnest effort to conform as woman and artist led to P.'s breakdown. As P. herself disengages the gagging mask of pleasing, pleased normalcy, her literature devolves from its disguised interest in landscapes and events to the subject of raw, terrifying self released from the pretense of objectivity: "Peel off the napkin / O my enemy. / Do I terrify?" ("Lady Lazarus"). Accompanying the unmasking of the subject is the conversion of duty-bound literary behavior to the exuberant anarchies of a released prisoner of style.

WORKS: *The Colossus* (1960). *A Winter Ship* (1960). *American Poetry Now* (edited by Plath, 1961). *The Bell Jar* (1963; film version, 1979). *Ariel* (1965). *Uncollected Poems* (1965). *Three Women: A Monologue for Three Voices* (1968; BBC television broadcast, 1962). *Crossing the Water* (1971). *Crystal Gazer* (1971). *Fiesta Melons* (1971). *Lyonesse* (1971). *Winter Trees* (1971). *Pursuit* (introduction by T. Hughes, 1973). *Letters Home: Correspondence 1950–1963* (edited by A. S. Plath, 1975). *The Bed Book* (1976). *Johnny*

Panic and the Bible of Dreams, and Other Prose Writings (edited by T. Hughes, 1978). *The Collected Poems* (Ed. T. Hughes, 1981).
The Sylvia Plath collection is at the Lilly Library, Bloomington, Indiana.

BIBLIOGRAPHY: Aird, E., *Sylvia Plath: Her Life and Work* (1973). Alvarez, A., *The Savage God* (1971). Butscher, E., *Sylvia Plath: Method and Madness* (1976). Butscher, E., ed., *Sylvia Plath, The Woman and Her Work* (1977). Gilbert, S. M., in *Shakespeare's Sisters,* Eds. Sandra M. Gilbert and Susan Gubar (1979). Howard, R., in *Alone With America: Essays on the Art of Poetry in the United Statest Since 1950* (1969). Kroll, J., *Chapters in a Mythology: The Poetry of Sylvia Plath* (1976). Lane, G., and M. Stevens, *Sylvia Plath: A Bibliography* (1978). Newman, C., ed., *The Art of Sylvia Plath: A Symposium* (1970). Rosenthal, M. C., "Confessional Poets" in *The New Poetry* (1975). Steiner, G., *Language and Silence* (1969).

For articles in reference works, see: Crowell's *Handbook of Contemporary American Poetry*, Ed. Karl Malkoff (1973). *WA.*

Other references: *London Magazine* (Feb. 1962). *Mademoiselle* (July 1975). *Ms.* (October 1975). *Southern Review* (Summer 1973).

BARBARA ANTONINA CLARKE MOSSBERG

Eleanor Hodgman Porter

B. 1868, Littleton, New Hampshire; d. 23 May 1920
Wrote under: Eleanor Stewart
D. of Francis H. and Llewella Woolson Hodgman; m. John Lyman Porter, 1892

When P. died, the headline of her brief obituary in *The New York Times* read simply: "Author of *Pollyanna* dies." P. had written four volumes of short stories and fourteen novels, but it was the phenomenal success of *Pollyanna* that had made her famous.

P. dropped out of high school to lead a more robust outdoor life. Later she studied music at the New England Conservatory in Boston, going on to make public appearances as a singer and traveling with church choirs. In 1892, P. married a businessman. Switching her profession from music to writing, P. began to submit stories to magazines, at first with little success, but finally with the publication of her novel *Cross Currents* (1907) the tide began to turn. P. wrote a sequel in 1908 called *The Turn of the Tide.* An even more significant turning point was reached in 1913, when *Pollyanna* appeared, an event described by one commentator as "only less influential than the World War."

Pollyanna, that incredibly cheerful champion of the Glad Game, who could find in even the grimmest situation something to be glad about (if you break a leg, "be glad 'twasn't two"), stirred the hearts and hopes of people of all ages all over the world. After selling a million copies in this country, the book appeared in editions in France, Germany, Holland, Poland, Czechoslovakia, Norway, Sweden, Switzerland, Scotland, and Japan.

Critics sang *Pollyanna*'s praises: "It is a wholesome, charming book, moral but not preachy," said the popular *Literary Digest*. The *Bookman* earnestly agreed: "If the *Pollyanna* books are read with the sympathetic comprehension they deserve, many a child's life will be made happier. . . ." With this end in view, Glad Clubs sprang up everywhere—and not just for children. One branch, "The Pollyanna Glad Kids," was started by inmates of a penitentiary. Mary Pickford paid the then astronomical fee of $115,112 for the silent screen rights for *Pollyanna*.

Although P. won instant celebrity, she was not thereby admitted to the ranks of serious authors. A growing number of readers irked by the sentimental and simplistic outlook would join in Aunt Polly's exasperated demand that Pollyanna "stop using that everlasting word. . . . It's 'glad'—'glad'—'glad'—from morning till night until I think I shall go wild." In a recent survey of girl's fiction, the authors dismiss Pollyanna as hopelessly "puerile" and "intellectually debilitating," her "imbecile cheerfulness" issuing from stupidity and an infuriating tactlessness, especially when she tells a chronic invalid to be glad other folks aren't like her—"all sick, you know"; or when she tells the elderly gardener, bent with arthritis, to be glad he doesn't have to stoop so far to do his weeding.

Some critics claim that P.'s later writing was not as relentlessly cheerful as her earlier works, but evidence provided by the posthumously published *Hustler Joe, and Other Stories* (1970) indicates otherwise. In each of the stories a downbeat plot works itself miraculously into an upbeat ending. Hustler Joe, for instance, who shoots his father in the opening chapter, discovers in the closing chapter that the bullet didn't kill him after all.

When accused of being overly optimistic, P. was quoted as saying, "I have never believed that we ought to deny discomfort and pain and evil. I have merely thought that it is far better to greet the unknown with a cheer." That she did, and—despite her critics—there are readers of Pollyanna even today who are still cheering.

WORKS: *Cross Currents* (1907). *The Turn of the Tide* (1908). *Miss Billy* (1911). *The Story of Marco* (1911). *Miss Billy's Decision* (1912). *Pollyanna* (1913). *Miss Billy Married* (1914). *Pollyanna Grows Up* (1915). *Just David* (1916). *The Road of Understanding* (1917). *Oh Money! Money!* (1918). *Dawn* (1919). *May-Marie* (1919). *Sister Sue* (1921). *The Tie that Binds: Tales of Love and Marriage* (1924). *Across the Years* (1924). *Money, Love, and Kate* (1924). *The Tangled Threads* (1924). *Hustler Joe, and Other Stories* (1970).

BIBLIOGRAPHY: Cadogan, M., and P, Craig, *You're a Brick, Angela! A New Look at Girls' Fiction from 1839–1975* (1976). Overton, G., *The Women Who Make Our Novels* (1918).

For articles in reference works, see: *20thCA*.

Other references: *Bookman* (60, 1914; 61, 1915; 63, 1916). *Good Housekeeping* (July 1947). *PW* (19 July 1941). *Woman's Home Companion* (April 1920).

JACQUELINE BERKE

Katherine Anne Porter

B. *15 May 1890, Indian Creek, Texas; d. 18 Sept. 1980, Silver Spring, Maryland*
D. *of Harrison Boone and Mary Alice Jones Porter; m. ?, 1906; m. Eugene Dove Pressly, 1933; m. Albert Russel Erskine, Jr., 1938*

P. was the fourth of five children, a descendant of pioneers. Her mother died as a young woman, and P. was raised by her father and paternal grandmother.

Although P. is generally acknowledged to be a master stylist, she rarely earned her living directly through her writing. Instead, she supported herself through a variety of related activities: as a reporter, writer of screenplays in Hollywood, translator, hack writer, and most often, as a lecturer, writer-in-residence, and guest speaker. She received a number of honorary degrees and an impressive range of prestigious literary awards, including Guggenheim fellowships in 1931 and 1938, Fulbright and Ford Foundation grants in the 1950s, an O. Henry Award in 1962, and the Pulitzer Prize in 1966 for her *Collected Stories* (1965).

P. traveled extensively, living often in Europe and Mexico; was married three times; and involved herself in political events. Yet these activities are only peripherally reflected in her stories. P. makes a clear distinction between *adventure*, something you do to find an "illusion of being more alive than ordinarily," and *experience*, which is "what really happens to you in the long run; the truth that finally overtakes you." The latter is the subject of P.'s prose. She delights in revealing through microcosmic events truths about human nature.

"The Downward Path to Wisdom" (*The Leaning Tower, and Other Stories*, 1944) is a pivotal story in understanding the etiology of disillusionment in P.'s work. The protagonist, a child named Stephen, is shuffled from adult to adult in an awkward and futile attempt to keep him unaware of his parents' quarreling. P. emphasizes Stephen's genuineness by continually alluding to his sensual awareness of being warm, bare, embraced, sticky, scrubbed roughly, etc. In contrast, P. shows us, through the overheard dialogue of the parents, that they experience him simply as a reminder of their growing antipathy. She deftly controls the emergence of Stephen's final decision to set himself emotionally apart from these people who "love" him by juxtaposing the child's motives with the adults' harsh judgments of him. Stephen's final rejection of them seems healthy, yet P. manages to convey that the act of rejection forecasts Stephen's own inability to love as an adult.

Some of P.'s best stories reflect the deterioration of relationships, especially of marriages, which are corrupted by the bitterness and anger accompanying dependence. P. has said that one's spouse is a "necessary enemy," for whom we cannot help but feel both love and hate because we resent our need for him or her. P. characterizes one such marriage in "Rope" (*Flowering Judas, and Other Stories*, 1930). The husband and wife quarrel over his purchase of some unneeded rope, and their discussion evolves into a destructive verbal battle about the entire relationship and their disappointments in one another.

P.'s portraits of relationships ring true because she has a perfect eye for the tiny, telling domestic detail. Time and again, a single incident conveys the character of an entire relationship. In "Noon Wine" (*Pale Horse, Pale Rider*, 1939), Mr. Thompson affectionately yet cruelly pinches his wife Ellie, and we are introduced to those notions about himself, his intense, masculine pride, that will make Mr. Thompson capable of killing a man later in the story. "Noon Wine" is a study of sources of violence and self-betrayal in essentially good people.

The disappointments that grow between people are evident in both men and women in P.'s stories, but perhaps because her own awareness is based so firmly in feminine realities, P. is especially effective in depicting the limitations in relationships as women experience them, or rather, the limiting relationships that she saw as the only ones allowed to women. In stories based around the experiences of Miranda (the character who seems most similar to P.), Miranda's grandmother (based on P.'s grandmother), and others, P. implies that for a woman the rejection of close and demanding relationships is virtually the only means of finding autonomy.

For all of P.'s thoughtful characters, life involves introspection, disappointment, and moral dilemmas. If her characters (like her married couples) stay in their oppressive relationships, resentment eats away at them. If they break free, they are terribly alone. It is not surprising that P. projects onto her primitive characters—such as the eponymous Mexican Indian in the story "María Concepción" (*Flowering Judas*) and the Spanish dancers in *Ship of Fools* (1962)—the very strengths which she believes introspective people cannot achieve: a passionate, unselfconscious, unquestioning spontaneity that carries with it no moral complications.

Ship of Fools, P.'s long-awaited novel, appeared in 1962. P. was deeply shaken by the two world wars and by world events that for decades threatened the human race with catastrophe. She tells us that much of her energy in those years was given to an attempt "to grasp the meaning of those threats, to trace them to their sources and to understand the logic of this majestic and terrible failure of the life of man in the Western world." P.'s allegorical novel became an exploration into the possible sources of human evil and particularly into the states of mind which could account for such horrors as the Holocaust.

The story takes place on a German freighter-passenger ship traveling from Veracruz, Mexico, to Bremerhaven, Germany, in late summer of 1931, with a passenger list representing various nationalities. To the degree that the characters become stereotypes for particular countries, the novel seems a failure, for its ironies are heavy-handed and the notes of prophecy seem contrived, written as they were long after World War II. But on the level of individual human encounters, P.'s portrayals are meticulous, vivid, and often engrossing. In depicting a range of individuals preoccupied with their narrow personal concerns, she shows acute perception of how we tend to blind ourselves to external realities and become culpable in evil events.

Ultimately, the pleasures we find in reading P.'s stories prove to be subtle ones: the frequent perfection of her choice of words and details and commentary on a character's behavior; the telling scenes; the recognitions about human nature; the ironic narrative; and P.'s understanding of the pleasures of childhood (always being crushed by somber adult realities), of the stories we tell ourselves to make our lives make sense, of the self-delusions, self-betrayals, and ultimate isolation of each of us. Her perceptions are acute, and her prose is often superb. P. severely limited the number of stories she would allow to be published, yet her choices seem to have been wise ones, for they offer us a surprisingly consistent vitality in their revelation of human truths.

WORKS: *Outline of Mexican Popular Arts and Crafts* (1922). *Flowering Judas, and Other Stories* (1930; republished with added stories, 1935). *Katherine Anne Porter's French Song Book* (1933). *Hacienda: A Story of Mexico* (1934). *Noon Wine* (1937). *Pale Horse, Pale Rider: Three Short Novels* (1939). *The Itching Parrot* (1942). *The Leaning Tower, and Other Stories* (1944). *The Old Order: Stories of the South* (1944). *The Days Before* (1952). *A Defense of Circe* (1955). *Holiday* (1962). *Ship of Fools* (1962). *The Collected Stories of Katherine Anne Porter* (1965). *A Christmas Story* (1967). *The Collected Essays and Occasional Writings of Katherine Anne Porter* (1970).

BIBLIOGRAPHY: Auchincloss, L., *Pioneers and Caretakers: A Study of Nine American Women Writers* (1965). Emmons, W. S., *Katherine Anne Porter: The Regional Stories* (1967). Hardy, J. E., *Katherine Anne Porter* (1973). Hartley, L., and G. Core, eds., *Katherine Anne Porter: A Critical Symposium* (1969). Hendrick, G., *Katherine Anne Porter* (1965). Kiernan, R. F., *Katherine Anne Porter and Carson McCullers: A Reference Guide* (1976). Krishnamurthi, M. G., *Katherine Anne Porter: A Study* (1971). Liberman, M. M., *Katherine Anne Porter's Fiction* (1971). Mooney, H. J., Jr., *The Fiction and Criticism of Katherine Anne Porter* (1962). Nance, W. L., *Katherine Anne Porter and the Art of Rejection* (1964). Waldrip, L., and S. A. Bauer, eds., *A Bibliography of the Works of Katherine Anne Porter, and A Bibliography of the Criticism of the Works of Katherine Anne Porter* (1969). Wescott, G., "Katherine Anne Porter, Personally," *Images of Truth: Remembrances and Criticism* (1962). West, R. B., Jr., *Katherine Anne Porter* (1963).

GAIL MORTIMER

Rose Porter

B. 6 Dec. 1845, New York City; d. 10 Sept. 1906, New Haven, Connecticut
D. of David and Rose Anne Hardy Porter

The author or editor of more than seventy books on religious themes, P. was descended from New England clergymen. Her father was a prosperous businessman and her mother an upper-class Englishwoman. P. attended a New York City private school and spent time in England. After her parents' deaths, she became a semiinvalid and lived alone in New Haven.

Besides her fifteen novels and her volumes of religious essays, P. produced devotional exercises; anthologies of consolatory verse, such as *Hope Songs* (1885) and *Comfort for the Mothers of Angels* (1881); prayer books for the sick, such as *In the Shadow of His Hand* (1892); and collections of texts from literature and scripture arranged on calendars or diaries. P. also edited selections from many poets.

Her first success was *Summer Driftwood for the Winter Fire* (1870). Presented as the diary of a nineteen-year-old girl, the book records a summer's travel, during which she falls in love and her lover dies. But most of the pages are occupied by the girl's meditations about Ruskin, heaven, her dead mother, and the beauties of nature. At the end, she is consoled in her single life because she has found work helping orphans.

Most of P.'s novels are similar: calm, retrospective, meditative, and told without suspense or emotional tension. P. seldom created a villain or even a character with whom the hero or heroine might have serious conflict. When she did attempt novels with more plot, P. used the conventions of sentimental melodrama.

In *Foundations; or, Castles in the Air* (1871), Alfred Merwin leaves his widowed mother in the country and goes off to be a city merchant's clerk. He falls into temptation—stays home from church, goes to "places of amusement" (unspecified), and gambles—and the farm is mortgaged to pay his debts. Ultimately, his mother's faith saves him; he prospers, gives to charity, returns to church, and marries his childhood sweetheart. The action is omitted; we do not see his debauchery or even his confession to his mother, but are told about both much later.

The masochistic elements of victory through suffering are most clearly visible in *Uplands and Lowlands* (1872). After an idealized relationship with his mother, orphaned Paul Foster goes to Rome and paints a magnificent holy picture. Because he will do no crass commercial work, he starves to death. His genius, of course, is recognized as soon as he has died.

The devotional books make P.'s basically conservative theology explicit. Her God is not human and domesticated but other and unfathomable. P. emphasizes faith rather than works. Most importantly, she extols weakness and submission and suffering, which subdue the individual will and open the mind to God, and which are also particularly suitable for women. In *Life's Everydayness* (1893), P. praises the daily annoyances and petty discouragements of the household because they enable one constantly to deny self and to exercise passivity and renunciation. Sympathy is woman's special vocation; many days may be well spent doing nothing but attending to the interests of others. P. also finds it important to fight discontent; a woman should daily count her blessings and be happy with the people and circumstances around her.

P.'s writing gave theological support to a conception of woman as domestic, virtuous, passive, weak, devoted to the trivial, inculcating morality by example, enforcing obedience by suffering, and utterly unfit for any sphere beyond house walls. Reviewers praised P.'s novels for their purity; they were often included in series for young readers; and, to judge from the sheer number of titles, they must have had a fairly steady sale.

SELECTED WORKS: *Summer Driftwood for the Winter Fire* (1870). *Foundations; or, Castles in the Air* (1871). *Uplands and Lowlands* (1872). *The Winter Fire* (1874). *The Years That Are Told* (1875). *Christmas Evergreens* (1876). *A Song and a Sigh* (1877). *In the Mist* (1879). *Charity, Sweet Charity* (1880). *Comfort for the Mothers of Angels* (1881). *Our Saints: A Family Story* (1881). *The Story of a Flower* (1883). *Foregleams of Immortality* (1884). *Honoria; or, The Gospel of a Life* (1885). *Hope Songs* (1885). *A Modern Saint Christopher* (1887). *Driftings from Mid-Ocean* (1889). *Looking toward Sunrise* (1890). *Open Windows, a Heart-to-Heart Diary* (1890). *Saint Martin's Summer; or, The Romance of the Cliff* (1891). *Women's Thoughts for Women: A Calendar* (1891). *In the Shadow of His Hand* (1892). *Life's Everydayness: Papers for Women* (1893). *My Son's Wife* (1895). *One of the Sweet Old Chapters* (1896). *The Pilgrim's Staff* (1897). *A Daughter of Israel* (1899). *The Everlasting Harmony* (1900).

BIBLIOGRAPHY: For articles in reference works, see: *NCAB*, 10. *A Woman of the Century*, Eds. F. Willard and M. Livermore (1893).
Other references: *Harper's* (Sept. 1870; June 1871). *NYT* (11 July 1870).

SALLY MITCHELL

Sarah Porter

P. lived during the late 18th c. and probably the early 19th c. She was probably a resident of Plymouth, Massachusetts, and a member of either a Congregationalist or a Presbyterian church.

P.'s slender volume of published poetry, *The Royal Penitent, in Three Parts, to Which Is Added David's Lamentation over Saul and Jonathan* (1791), contains work of such quality and interest that it seems probable that she produced other works. This work reveals ambition and talent in its three hundred and fifty-two lines, which deal with David's guilt and repentance for his seduction of Bathsheba and betrayal of her husband, his loyal general, Uriah. P.'s handling of this subject includes not only religious but also political and social themes relevant to contemporary interests of late-18th-c. Americans. The structure and content indicate at least a passing familiarity with Dryden's *Absalom and Achitophel* and the American poet Timothy Dwight's epic, *The Conquest of Canaan*.

P.'s poem presents two major themes: the workings of divine providence and the necessity for morality in government. The poem particularly emphasizes the concept that a country is only as good (moral) as its leaders. A decadent ruling class subverts national morals. P.'s was not a very veiled criticism of the contemporary political situation in the U.S. in the decade after the revolutionary war. During those years, a major complaint of those who remained staunch republicans was that the government and the nation as a whole were being subverted from the high ideals of the revolutionary era. This "subversion" was a result of an influx of new wealth, followed by a vulgar taste for luxury. P. shows this type of moral decay through the example of King David as he remembers his humble beginnings, his rise to power, and his subsequent immoral behavior, the result of his lust for material possessions. Thus, David's downfall becomes a warning for P.'s compatriots about their politics.

P.'s poetic ambitions appear also in her choice of style and form. She exhibits a thorough understanding of neoclassical poetic techniques and evidently possessed the training and ability to employ them with success.

P. produced a heroic poem in which characters of great personal and historical stature act against a background of national events as the super- natural and natural worlds mingle. The narrative alternates between descriptive passages and dialogue, producing an effective variety.

Published along with the successful *Royal Penitent* is a short work, a paraphrase of David's lament for Saul and Jonathan (2 Samuel 1:17). Taking full advantage of the substance of her biblical model, P. uses the elegy to convey both religious and political themes. Using the Puritan concept of America as the new Israel, P. draws an implied analogy be- tween the dead Hebrew heroes and the dead American revolutionary heroes, stressing the recurrent theme of late-18th-c. American literature— the necessity for national political unity in the face of anarchic and ex- ternal incursions.

P. made important contributions to the broadening thematic materials in the poetry of American women. She enlarged the scope of women's poetry to encompass current political and ideological interests through the device of the contemporaneously popular heroic verse form.

WORKS: *The Royal Penitent, in Three Parts, to Which is Added David's Lamentation over Saul and Jonathan* (1791).

JACQUELINE HORNSTEIN

Emily Price Post

B. 3 Oct. 1873, Baltimore, Maryland; d. 25 Sept. 1960, New York City
Wrote under: Emily Post
D. of Bruce and Josephine Lee Price; m. Edwin Post, 1892

P. was a member of New York society, raised in the well-educated and proper atmosphere of Tuxedo Park. Her early career was prescribed by the conventions of upper-class leisure and manners: governesses, trips to Europe, private schooling, and debutante balls. After being divorced and then forced by economic stress to explore and expand upon her native talents, P. began her public life with interior decoration schemes. She wrote travelogues and a series of light novels of manners about Ameri- cans vacationing in Europe and associating with the Continental gentry.

P. soon expanded her scope and wrote about American standards of manners, mores, and taste in manuals of etiquette and home decor.

The original dean of modern American decorum, P. was the first in a line of inventive women writers of handbooks on etiquette and manners. She remains a key figure in setting the tone for civil behavior in a rapidly changing world of styles, relationships, and attitudes—a kaleidoscopic social scene of shifting patterns in class, money, taste, and mobility, intensified by the departure from 19th- and early 20th-c. "laws" of social procedure, which had long been relied on as fixed and permanent. The need for more relaxed and flexible standards of behavior suited to the millions of upwardly mobile Americans after World War I made P.'s *Etiquette: The Blue Book of Social Usage* (1922) an immediate and long-lived success.

P.'s name quickly became a household word for "proper" manners, even if in a new key. Ironically, the conventions of formality and civility now associated so firmly with her were heartily opposed in all P.'s analysis and advice, her most famous aphorism being, "Nothing is less important than which fork you use."

P.'s *Blue Book* was the most popular and influential book of etiquette by a woman of social standing since Mary Sherwood's *Manners and Social Usages* (1884). P.'s easy readability and practical approach to the myriad problems of interpersonal relations posed by the unfamiliar contexts of changing times have made the *Blue Book* a perennial bestseller. In recent years, more progressive works by younger writers have supplanted the *Blue Book*, but P.'s emphasis on the spirit rather than the letter of the law of manners has made the *Blue Book* adaptable to change, assuring it a lasting place as a reference statement in the field. For example, in the 1940s, a supplementary edition was devised to deal with the special circumstances of wartime.

The book's success led to a newspaper column and a radio broadcast series, as well as many requests for P.'s endorsement of food, drink, and household products. The formulations P. established for diplomatic protocol were adopted by Washington offices as a uniform code, and *The Personality of a House* (1930), used as a text in courses about taste and decoration, is further evidence of her strong feeling for atmosphere and the quality of life. This feel for style informs such other works as *Children Are People* (1940).

To P., it was obvious that simplicity and grace are the fundamental precepts of manners, and that there is an urgent need to state this principle in detail, dramatizing its application in every conceivable setting and circumstance. Her writing ushered in a new era, which thought about etiquette not as a fixed system of gestures and words but as an ever-changing rule of thumb, based on a much more open, democratic, and classless view of society with an active sense of mobility and impermanence. P.'s interpretation of etiquette as a "science of living" sets the terms of discussion later taken up and developed in the contemporary scene by a core of women social arbiters including Jean Kerr, Peg Bracken, Amy Vanderbilt, Abigail Van Buren, and Ann Landers.

WORKS: *The Flight of a Moth* (1904). *Purple and Fine Linen* (1906). *Woven in the Tapestry* (1908). *The Title Market* (1909). *The Eagle's Feather* (1910). *By Motor to the Golden Gate* (1915). *Etiquette: The Blue Book of Social Usage* (1922; rev. ed., 1955). *Parade* (1925). *How to Behave Though a Debutante* (1928). *The Personality of a House* (1930; rev. ed., 1948). *Children Are People* (1940). *Emily Post Institute Cook Book* (with E. M. Post, Jr., 1949). *Motor Manners* (1950).

BIBLIOGRAPHY: For articles in reference works, see: *CB* (1941).
   Other references: *AH* (April 1977). *NYT* (27 Sept. 1960).

                                                            MARGARET J. KING

Mary Traill Spence Lowell Putnam

B. 3 Dec. 1810, Boston, Massachusetts; d. 1898, Boston, Massachusetts
Wrote under: M. L. P., Mary Lowell Putnam
D. of Charles and Harriet Brackett Spence Lowell; m. Samuel R. Putnam

P.'s mother imbued her Christian rectitude and love of learning in her children. Her father, a minister at West Church in Boston, was descended from Judge John Lowell, who was a member of the Continental Congress and a district and circuit court judge. Judge Lowell's benevolence toward black people, the family's proud New England heritage, and a fervent Christian faith are all reflected in P.'s work.

P. is noted for translating Fredrika Bremer's play, *The Bondmaid*, from Swedish (1844). Her fluency in French, coupled with her voracious reading, allowed P. to take on the editor of the *North American Review*, Francis Bowen, who had sharply criticized Kossuth and the Magyars after their revolution. In two essays in the *Christian Examiner* P. shreds Bowen's articles, taking them line by line and proving their inaccuracy and bad logic.

P.'s four chief works, all published anonymously and centered on the issue of slavery, are told from the vantage point of Edward Colvil, a New England farmer-poet transplanted to the South. *Record of an Obscure Man* (1861) and *Fifteen Days: An Extract from Edward Colvil's Journal* (1866) are filled with exposition and speculation about black history and alternatives to slavery. *Tragedy of Errors* (1862) and *Tragedy of Success* (1862), both plays, embody some of P.'s theories about the beauty of black music, the eloquence of black preaching, and black people's special capacity for loyalty and revenge.

Record of an Obscure Man is narrated by a friend of Colvil's who listened to Colvil's discussion of African history and theories about slavery and, after Colvil's death, arranged for publication of his two verse plays, *Tragedy of Errors* and its sequel, *Tragedy of Success*. Written "in the dramatic form, but not intended for the stage," the plays form the core of P.'s series.

Their plot is overly complicated. The intrigue of a jilted mulatto woman, Dorcas, catapults a young white woman, Hecate, into slavery. She has a child by her plantation owner, Stanley, switches her baby with that of his wife, and watches her illegitimate daughter, Helen, grow up as a generous, highly intelligent, free woman who endears herself with the slaves and longs to accomplish some great work but feels hampered by a weak-spirited husband. After the baby-switching comes to light, Helen takes her place as a slave, but escapes with her son when her husband tells her that he wants to keep her as his mistress. Just as he sees the light (encouraged by proof that Helen is white), Helen is captured and dies in jail from loss of hope (but not faith).

In contrast to P.'s very readable prose, the verse in the plays is only occasionally strong; but a few of the scenes have convincing dialogues: in one, Dorcas successfully confronts her remorseful accomplice, a slave trader, by skillfully reminding him of his self-doubts and mixed motivations. In another, Helen powerfully decries the severe limitations of woman's freedom to her sister-in-law Alice: "Restrained and cramped / In all her outward acts, she cannot know / The joys of self-possession,

—man's great bliss; / She only claims those of renunciation." Despite her limits, however, woman is "man's second conscience," and must speak "the word God printed on her soul."

Fifteen Days is the most unified work in the series. The journal starts on Good Friday, 1844, and describes Colvil's meeting with a charismatic figure, Harry Dudley, a young visiting botanist from Massachusetts who tries to buy a slave so that he can free him. *Fifteen Days* balances the joy of deepening friendship between Colvil and Dudley against the sense of looming tragedy. Colvil seems excessively anxious to live up to Dudley's expectation, but his anxiety is interestingly confirmed when Dudley is killed at the end, ironically by a good friend who was also the slave's former owner.

The central victims in P.'s tragic series are all young, perceptive, and white, but her exposition of African history shows a sensitivity to the intelligence and culture of black people. P.'s writings on Hungary show her capable of imagining herself in other people's shoes. Although her characters are scarce on flesh and blood, their sensibility is frequently compelling.

WORKS: The Bondmaid by Fredrika Bremer (translated by Putnam, 1844). *The North American Review on Hungary* (reprinted from the *Christian Examiner*, Nov. 1850; March 1851). *Record of an Obscure Man* (1861). *Tragedy of Errors* (1862). *Tragedy of Success* (1862). [*Memorial of William*] *Lowell Putnam* (1863). *Fifteen Days: An Extract from Edward Colvil's Journal* (1866). *Guépin of Nantes: A French Republican* (1874). *Memoir of Rev. Charles Lowell, D.D.* (1885).

BIBLIOGRAPHY: Adelman, J., *Famous Women* (1926). Dorland, W. A. N., *The Sum of Feminine Achievement* (1917). *Homes of American Authors* (1857).

For articles in reference works, see: *American Authors, 1795–1895: A Bibliography*, Ed. P. K. Foley (1897). *American Fiction, 1851–1875*, Ed. L. H. Wright (1965). *A Critical Dictionary of English Literature and British and American Authors*, Ed. S. A. Allibone (1872). *A Dictionary of American Authors*, Ed. O. F. Adams (1897). *DAB* (article on James Russell Lowell) VI, 1. *Index to Women of the World, from Ancient to Modern Times: Biographies and Portraits*, Ed. N. O. Ireland (1970). *Women's Record*, Ed. S. J. Hale (1870).

Other references: *North American Review* (Jan. 1862; April 1862).

KAREN B. STEELE

Ayn Rand

B. 2 Feb. 1905, St. Petersburg, Russia; d. 6 March 1982, New York City
M. Frank O'Connor, 1929

R.'s early life of relative comfort was abruptly terminated when the family business was nationalized after the Russian Revolution. An excellent student whose far-ranging interests included mathematics, literature, philosophy, and engineering, R. graduated from the University of Leningrad with a degree in history. Not able to adjust to the Communist regime, she accepted an invitation to visit relatives in New York in 1926.

R. went to Hollywood to write screen scenarios and was given a job as an extra by Cecil B. de Mille. Though de Mille rejected her first five scenarios as too romantic, unrealistic, and improbable, R. did eventually work as a screenwriter.

We, the Living (1936) received a lukewarm critical reception. The themes are the sanctity of human life and the evil of collectivism in Russia. Written at the same time, *The Night of January 16th* (1936) is an effective dramatic piece. The play's originality derives from the gimmick of allowing each night's audience to serve as the jury in a murder trial.

The Fountainhead (1943) established R. as a popular writer and is considered her best work. The world of contemporary architecture serves as the backdrop for this battle between the forces of individualism and collectivisim, between creativity and derivativeness.

The plot follows protagonist Howard Roark's career from the day he is expelled from architectural school, through his difficulties in establishing a career, to his professional and personal victory and vindication. The book ends with the triumph of the virtuous and the creative. The heavy moralizing has drawn negative reactions from some commentators.

The philosophies set forth in *The Fountainhead* were amplified in *Atlas Shrugged* (1957), the fullest novelistic treatment of R.'s theories. *Atlas Shrugged* established R. as an intellectual cult figure. A novel which can be read to satisfy many different tastes, it has been categorized by various critics as a mystery story, science fiction, a philosophical diatribe, a female fantasy novel, and a justification of capitalism.

The protagonist, Dagny Taggart, whose attempts to run a transcontinental railroad are complicated by networks of bureaus, councils, and committees that strangle productive initiatives, fights a losing battle against a group that wants to "stop the motor of the world" in order to rebuild a society of free enterprise, devoid of government controls. She inadvertently finds a projection of this society, Galt's Gulch, a utopia in a hidden valley in Colorado. Galt's Gulch was born as a reaction against the collectivist maxim, "From each according to his ability, to each according to his need"; its motto is "I swear by my life and my love of it that I will never live for the sake of another man nor ask another man to live for mine."

R. is also known as a philosopher. All of her publications since *Atlas Shrugged* have been nonfiction. During the 1960s she was a popular campus lecturer. In conjunction with *The Objectivist*, a newsletter published to explain R.'s philosophy, courses in Objectivism were taught by the Nathaniel Branden Institute.

R.'s novels, though popular, have received little serious consideration as works of literature; she is something of a cultural phenomenon. Though R.'s politics are anathema to most feminists, her commitment to self-actualization both as a philosopher and as creator of one of the most positive female protagonists in American literature (Dagny Taggart) suggests that perhaps her works need to be reevaluated by women.

WORKS: *We, the Living* (1936). *The Night of January 16th* (1936). *Anthem* (1938; rev. ed., 1946). *The Fountainhead* (1943; film version, 1949). *Atlas Shrugged* (1957). *For the New Intellectual: The Philosophy of Ayn Rand* (1961). *The Virtue of Selfishness* (1964). *Capitalism: The Unknown Ideal* (1966). *The Romantic Manifesto* (1969). *The New Left: The Anti-Industrial Revolution* (1971). *Introduction to Objectivist Epistemology* (1979). Newsletters: *The Objectivist Newsletter* (1962–65). *The Objectivist* (1966–71). *The Ayn Rand Letter* (1971–76).

BIBLIOGRAPHY: Branden, N., and B. Branden, *Who is Ayn Rand?* (1962). Ellis, A., *Is Objectivism a Religion?* (1968). O'Neill, W., *With Charity toward None* (1971).

Other references: *Commonweal* (8 Nov. 1957). *NY* (26 Oct. 1957). *College English* (Feb. 1978). *NYTBR* (16 May 1943). *Playboy* (March 1964). *SatR* (12 Oct. 1957).

MIMI R. GLADSTEIN

Marjorie Kinnan Rawlings

B. 8 Aug. 1896, Washington, D.C.; d. 14 Dec. 1953, Crescent Beach, Florida
D. of Arthur F. and Ida May Traphagen Kinnan; m. Charles A. Rawlings,
1919; m. Norton Sanford Baskin, 1941

Daughter of a U.S. patent examiner, R. graduated Phi Beta Kappa from
the University of Wisconsin in 1918 with a major in English. R. wrote
for the Louisville *Courier-Journal* and the Rochester *Journal-American*
from 1920 to 1928. Needing solitude, she bought an orange grove in
Hawthorn, Florida, near Cross Creek, where she farmed and wrote from
1928 to 1947. R. traveled in England, Alaska, and Bimini. Her marriage
to a journalist ended in divorce (1933). R.'s second husband was a hotel
owner in St. Augustine. Sued for libel, R. left Florida to buy a New
York farm.

R.'s earliest published story was "Cracker Chidlings" (1930) in *Scrib-
ner's*. Her humorous sketches about local figures contained accounts of
a squirrel feast at a church picnic, domestic squabbling, and an expla-
nation of "Cracker" as the whip-cracking country cattle driver. In 1931,
Scribner's published "Jacob's Ladder," a sensitive odyssey of a young
Cracker pair through storm-ridden piney woods and scrub. These were
R.'s continuing subjects: the human bond to the earth, and the Florida
Crackers with their folklore, language, and struggles.

South Moon Under (1933) received critical acclaim. Three generations of a Cracker family subsist in the Florida scrub. Old Lantry, an
irascible loner and moonshiner, moves his family into obscurity to elude
the law for murdering a Prohibition official. He gives up moonshining
and tries to farm. His grandson, Lant Jacklin, forced to early manhood
by his father's death, labors at farming and trapping. Hardships finally
compel Lant to moonshine. Betrayed, he repeats his grandfather's crime
and kills a man, condemning himself to a life of restless fear and flight.
The moon of the title symbolizes the powerful necessity laid upon all
creatures, men and animals, forcing them to act against their will. Moon
lore abounds. Deer feed in the moonlight. "South moon under" meant
that the moon was directly under the earth, unseen, and yet "it reached
through the earth" with a "power to move the owls and rabbits," and

drive a man to kill. Despite R.'s descriptions of the earth's beauty, these dark lunar forces, the treachery of kin, the legacy of family violence, and the intractability of the wilderness, convey her somber vision of the human lot.

Golden Apples (1935) describes an uneasy idyll between a frail ignorant Cracker girl and a callous, hard-drinking young English planter who comes to the fertile hummock to reclaim his father's homestead. R. deals more frankly than elsewhere with sexuality: Desire seems to rise up out of the steamy Florida undergrowth. But the man's real view of the land is that it is a "damn rotten crawling place," and when the girl he seduces looks "all eyes and belly" as she wordlessly kneels to clean his boots, he looks at her with repugnance. The girl dies in premature labor. A strange reconciliation takes place between her brother and her lover, as they join together to plant an orange grove.

The Yearling (1938) won the 1939 Pulitzer Prize for fiction. R.'s editor, Maxwell Perkins, liked her hunt and river scenes, and urged her to do a boy's book. *The Yearling*'s theme is the passage from childhood to manhood for fourteen-year-old Jody Baxter. The plot is based on Jody's adopting a baby fawn when its mother is slain. After thirteen months, the fawn is no longer a baby but a yearling that destroys the family's crops and whose wild nature cannot be subdued. Jody is at first unable to obey his father's directive to kill the yearling, which has become a part of himself, but is forced to do so when his mother's faulty aim wounds the creature. His grief drives him from home to a river journey, and he wishes for the death of his gentle father, who, it seems, has betrayed him. Jody's homecoming shows him ready to put a child's happiness behind him and embrace the lonely hardships of manhood.

R. creates a Floridian earthly paradise. With all its loveliness, however, this wilderness reveals to the growing boy many signs of nature's cruelty. This sacrifice of the wild creature is a gesture implying that to attain maturity a man must quell his own rapturous, irresponsible, animal nature. Biblical echoes reinforce the end of innocence.

When the Whippoorwill (1940) collects R.'s best magazine stories. Noteworthy is "Gal Young Un," about a gaunt gray woman married for her wealth by a flashing opportunist. Several stories introduce R.'s fine comic narrator, Quincey Dover, "a woman with a tongue sharp enough to slice soft bacon." Others treat of moonshining, alligator hunting, and family life.

In 1942, R. published *Cross Creek*, chronicling her years in this chosen spot. R. describes the farmhouse, the tall old orange trees, the coral honeysuckle twisting on the wire fence. She gathers materials that will feed her fiction: scenes, animals, anecdotes, personalities. Her portraits of the neighbors whose lives she shared, notably of black women, are both humorous and painful, revealing R.'s sure grasp on human realities. In "Hyacinth Drift," two women, R. and a friend, navigate several hundred miles of river in an eighteen-foot boat. Beset with cares, R. had momentarily "lost touch with the Creek"; this is a journey of renewal that enables R. once again to long for home. "Because I had known intimately a river, the earth pulsed under me." *Cross Creek* ranks as a classic of the American pastoral scene.

Although she was admired as a regional writer, R.'s ambivalence about this designation led her to approach new subjects. She believed that a "great" writer could write anywhere, and she broke from Cross Creek. R.'s last novel, *The Sojourner* (1953), about a Hudson Valley farm after the Civil War, lacks the power of her earlier work.

R. belongs to the tradition of Thoreau and Whitman. Nature for R. is cruel as well as beneficent, and she accepts the savagery as part of the cycle of living and dying. R.'s witty revelation of regional character and language places her in the mainstream of writers from Mark Twain on. R.'s typical fictional perspective is that of a male, usually naive, forced to acknowledge the sinister side of a seductive pastoral world.

WORKS: South Moon Under (1933). *Golden Apples* (1935). *The Yearling* (1938; film version, 1945). *When the Whippoorwill* (1941). *Cross Creek* (1942). *The Sojourner* (1953). *The Secret River* (1955).

BIBLIOGRAPHY: Bellman, S., *Marjorie Kinnan Rawlings* (1974). Berg, A. S., *Max Perkins, Editor of Genius* (1978). Bigelow, G. E., *Frontier Eden: The Literary Career of Marjorie Kinnan Rawlings* (1966). Bigham, J. S., Introduction to *The Marjorie Rawlings Reader* (1956).

Other references: *Collier's* 116 (29 Sept. 1945). *EJ* 64 (1975). *Family Circle* (7 May 1943). *NYT* Sunday Travel Section (27 Jan. 1980). *SLJ* 9 (1977).

MARCELLE THIÉBAUX

Lizette Woodworth Reese

B. 9 Jan. 1856, Waverly, Maryland; d. 17 Dec. 1935, Baltimore, Maryland
D. of David and Louisa Reese

R.'s life as a child and young woman in Waverly, a suburban village of Baltimore, provided the material for most of her writing, both poetry and prose. In R.'s poems and reminiscences, Waverly becomes the symbol for a time and a value system more stable than those of the present. R. not only grew up in Waverly but began her long teaching career in the local parish school. Her first poem, "The Deserted House," appeared in the *Southern Magazine* in June 1874. From that time until her death, R. continued to write lyric poetry that was of fairly consistent quality.

R.'s first volume of poetry, *A Branch of May* (1887), was privately printed through subscriptions from friends. This volume of thirty-three poems was sent to several of the leading critics of the day, all of whom received it favorably. R.'s reputation grew with *A Handful of Lavendar* (1891), which was published by a national publisher.

The subject matter and style of R.'s poetry remained constant through her subsequent volumes. Her subjects are the eternal truths of life and death—joy and sorrow, expressed in images drawn from her childhood experiences in the Maryland countryside and readings in English literature. Her best poems make arrestingly fresh use of images from ordinary experience. R.'s central images are of village and orchard. The orchard becomes a primary image, for, as R. says, "although not so open as the lane, or so secret as the wood, it keeps the free heart of the one, and somewhat of the privileged quiet of the other."

R. was generally praised for the freshness of her images in a time when most lyric poetry was marked by the tired conventions of excessive and archaic expression. Her forte was the short lyric, but she was also an accomplished sonneteer. Her best-known poem was the sonnet "Tears," which first appeared in *Scribner's* magazine in 1899 and was repeatedly anthologized. The poem presents a series of arresting metaphors about the futility of grieving over the fugitive cares of life.

Although primarily a lyric poet, R. published one successful long narrative poem, *Little Henrietta* (1927), and was at the time of her death working on another, which was published posthumously as *The Old*

House in the Country (1936). *Little Henrietta* probes the grief and eventual reconciliation over the death of a young child, and *The Old House* is an attempt to unify the diverse recollections of childhood memories.

Childhood memories form the substance of two volumes of autobiographical reminiscence, *A Victorian Village* (1929) and *The York Road* (1931). These prose works poetically present the recollections and associations brought to R.'s mind by people, places, and events from her childhood and young adulthood. At the time of her death, R. was reworking these experiences into an autobiographical novel, published posthumously as *Worleys* (1936).

R. is neglected today, although she was one of the finest poets writing during the last decade of the 19th c. and the first decade of the 20th. She is a transition figure between the stylized conventions of the Victorian poets and the free form and subject matter of the moderns. At its best, R.'s poetry is characterized by a striking intensity and freshness of image.

WORKS: *A Branch of May* (1887). *A Handful of Lavendar* (1891). *A Quiet Road* (1896). *A Wayside Lute* (1909). *Spicewood* (1920). *Wild Cherry* (1923). *The Selected Poems* (1926). *Little Henrietta* (1927). *A Victorian Village* (1929). *White April, and Other Poems* (1930). *The York Road* (1931). *Pastures, and Other Poems* (1933). *The Old House in the Country* (1936). *Worleys* (1936).

BIBLIOGRAPHY: Gregory, H., and M. Zaturenska, *A History of American Poetry, 1900–1940* (1946). Klein, L. R. M., "Lizette Woodworth Reese" (Ph.D. diss., Univ. of Pennsylvania, 1943). Rittenhouse, J. B., in *The Younger American Poets* (1906).

Other references: *Personalist* 31 (1900). *SAQ* (April 1930; Jan. 1957). *SUS* 8 (1969).

HARRIETTE CUTTINO BUCHANAN

Agnes Repplier

B. 1 April 1855, Philadelphia, Pennsylvania; d. 16 Dec. 1950, Philadelphia,
Pennsylvania
D. of John George and Agnes Mathias Repplier

R. did not learn to read until she was almost ten. Her formal education
was limited to two years at the Convent of the Sacred Heart and three
terms at Miss Irwin's School in Philadelphia. Both schools dismissed her
because of independent behavior, so that R. was entirely self-educated
after the age of sixteen. Her intensive reading was augmented by numerous trips (the first in 1890) and long periods of residence in Europe.

Urged by her mother, R. began publishing at sixteen to increase the
family's income when her father's fortune collapsed, and throughout
her life she loyally supported her family. R.'s first writings were stories
and sketches for Philadelphia newspapers. After publishing "In Arcady"
in Catholic World (1881), the editor urged R. to write essays, since she
knew a great deal about books and not much about life. This set the
direction of R.'s career, for she made the familiar essay distinctively
her own form—witty, graceful, and richly textured with allusions from
her vast reading.

In 1886, R. was accepted by the American literary establishment.
"Children, Past and Present" appeared in the Atlantic Monthly. Here
she continued to publish frequently—ninety essays in all, the last in 1940.
A highly disciplined writer, R. was determined from the start that her
work would have permanence. In 1888, R. arranged the first of many
collections, Books and Men, which included the first seven essays from
Atlantic Monthly. Similar volumes appeared throughout the years. R.
was a popular public lecturer, noted for her sharp perceptions, lively
manner, and witty expression.

A plain child and woman with an incisive mind and quick wit, R.
never married. She thought the feminist cause a just one and opposed
any kind of discrimination. She had, however, no use for reformers in
any area because of their excessive claims and simplistic and sentimental
solutions. "Woman Enthroned" presents her case, as do "The Strayed
Prohibitionist" and "Consolations of the Conservative." For R., happiness

was fleeting and lay in "the development of individual tastes and acquirements."

The urbane stance is typical of R. However, before U.S. involvement in World War I, R. argued passionately for several years against neutrality, collaborating with Dr. J. W. White on a pamphlet, *Germany and Democracy* (1914), and writing many essays, collected in *Counter-Currents* (1916).

A lifelong and devout Roman Catholic, R. wrote from a strong ethical code that provided a firm base for her relentlessly skeptical view of human performance. R.'s specifically Catholic writings are among her most successful and include a merry autobiography, *In Our Convent Days* (1905), and three distinguished biographies of American religious leaders: *Père Marquette* (1929), *Mère Marie of the Ursulines* (1931), and *Junipero Serra* (1933).

Addressing herself to a wide range of literary subjects and social change for more than half a century, R. was usually provocative but rarely inelegant in her commentary. Her familiar essays provide a distinctive and pleasing alternative to the prevailing realism of American literature. Perhaps R.'s most characteristic mode is epitomized by two collections separated by half her writing career, *A Happy Half-Century* (1908) and *In Pursuit of Laughter* (1936). R.'s range is broad, but her audience was always a select and patrician one.

WORKS: *Books and Men* (1888). *Points of View* (1889). *A Book of Famous Verse* (edited by Repplier, 1892). *Essays in Miniature* (1892). *Essays in Idleness* (1893). *In the Dozy Hours, and Other Papers* (1894). *Varia* (1897). *Philadelphia: The Place and the People* (1898). *The Fireside Sphinx* (1901). *Compromises* (1904). *In Our Convent Days* (1905). *A Happy Half-Century* (1908). *Americans and Others* (1912). *The Cat, being a Record of the Endearments and Invectives Lavished by Many Writers* (1912). *Germany and Democracy, the Real Issue* (with J. W. White, 1914). *Counter-Currents* (1916). *J. William White, M. D.: A Biography* (1919). *Points of Friction* (1920). *Under Dispute* (1924). *Père Marquette* (1929). *Mère Marie of the Ursulines* (1931). *Times and Tendencies* (1931). *To Think of Tea!* (1932). *Junipero Serra* (1933). *Agnes Irwin* (1934). *In Pursuit of Laughter* (1936). *Eight Decades* (1937).

BIBLIOGRAPHY: Repplier, E., *Agnes Repplier: A Memoir by Her Niece* (1957). Stokes, G. S., *Agnes Repplier: Lady of Letters* (1949).

For articles in reference works, see: *Catholic Authors: Contemporary Biographical Sketches, 1930–1947*, Ed. M. Hoehn (1948). *DAB*, Suppl. 4. *NAW* (article by G. S. Stokes). *NCAB*, 9.

Other references: *Nation* (29 Nov. 1933). *NYHTB* (13 Jan. 1929; 29 Nov. 1931). *SatR* (23 Dec. 1933). *YR* (March 1937).

VELMA BOURGEOIS RICHMOND

Alice Caldwell Hegan Rice

B. 11 Jan. 1870, Shelbyville, Kentucky; d. 10 Feb. 1942, Louisville, Kentucky
Wrote under: Alice Caldwell Hegan, Alice Hegan Rice
D. of Samuel Watson and Sallie Caldwell Hegan; m. Cale Young Rice, 1902

R. was born and raised in Kentucky, the setting for most of her fiction. She married Rice shortly after the publication of her first book. They traveled widely in Asia and Europe, associating with many of the most prominent literary figures of the 20th c. Their permanent home was Louisville. Though Rice was primarily a poet and R. a writer of fiction, they worked closely together, publishing short stories by each of them in three collections (*Turn About Tales*, 1920; *Winners and Losers*, 1925; and *Passionate Follies*, 1936). R. also published an autobiography (*The Inky Way*, 1940) and two collections of religious meditations (*My Pillow Book*, 1937, and *Happiness Road*, completed by her husband in 1942).

R.'s best works are set among Kentucky's poor, particularly the urban poor whom she came to know as a volunteer settlement worker. *Mrs. Wiggs of the Cabbage Patch* (1901), inspired by a real person and a slum area in Louisville, is noteworthy both for its fidelity to the facts of the lives of poor urban whites and for the gentle humor with which it depicts their characters. These are the "deserving poor," honest and willing to work. Mrs. Wiggs, a widow with five children, is poor and illiterate but wise and proud; she straightens out the personal lives of the wealthy young woman and man who, in turn, give her surviving children a chance to make something of themselves. The novel's humor comes from its use of dialect, from Mrs. Wiggs's malapropisms, and from the children's pranks and mishaps. *Lovey Mary* (1903) is a sequel about an orphan girl who flees the orphanage and is taken in by Mrs. Wiggs and her friends. Both novels are trite and sentimental in plot, but their restraint and gently comic tone keep them from becoming mawkish.

Four other novels center on poor but meritorious characters trying to make their way in a hostile world. *Sandy* (1905), loosely based on the experiences of the magazine editor S. S. McClure, tells of a Scottish waif finally lucky enough to be taken in by a wealthy Kentuckian. Also dealing with an adolescent boy is *Our Ernie* (1939), whose title character quits school at fourteen to support his loving but feckless family.

He rises in the business world, becoming entangled with the daughter of his employer, but in a reversal of the Horatio Alger motif, frees himself from her while retaining his position. A rather melodramatic subplot concerns German spies. R.'s dedication describes it as "a happy book about funny people," a valid description for most of her novels.

Mr. Pete & Co. (1933) tells of a middle-aged derelict who returns home to Louisville when he inherits a riverfront tenement. The unaccustomed responsibility for the building and its inhabitants regenerates him, and by novel's end he has instigated an urban-renewal project and transformed the lives of his tenants.

R.'s most ambitious attempt to depict urban poverty and inspire reform is *Calvary Alley* (1917), which recounts the life of Nance Molloy, at eleven a mistress of gang-fighting techniques, later a reform-school inmate, and then a factory worker. Through much of the novel her prime goal is to escape the slum, but she matures and through hard work and good luck becomes a nurse in a clinic serving her people. R. was disappointed that this book was generally received as another comic novel rather than as the serious indictment of slum conditions she intended.

Most of R.'s other novels concern family situations, the central characters bearing responsibility for unworldly and eccentric relatives. Particularly interesting is *The Buffer* (1929), which centers on Cynthia Freer, an aspiring writer who is strong and self-sacrificing but has a sense of humor. At the novel's conventional happy ending, she seems to be ready to subordinate her literary ambitions to marriage—but she takes the manuscript of her novel with her.

R.'s novels are readable and amusing, though lacking in roundness of characterization or thematic depth. Compared to the works of her naturalistic contemporaries, who used many similar materials, R.'s treatments seem shallowly optimistic. She had few pretensions, however, always considering her husband's serious poetry more important than her own light fiction. But his work is largely forgotten today, while at least one of her characters, Mrs. Wiggs, still lives.

WORKS: *Mrs. Wiggs of the Cabbage Patch* (1901; film version, 1934). *Lovey Mary* (1903). *Sandy* (1905). *Captain June* (1907). *Mr. Opp* (1909). *A Romance of Billy-Goat Hill* (1912). *The Honorable Percival* (1914). *Calvary Alley* (1917). *Miss Mink's Soldier, and Other Stories* (1918). *Turn About Tales* (with C. Y. Rice, 1920). *Quinn* (1921). *Winners and Losers* (with C. Y. Rice, 1925). *The Buffer: A Novel* (1929). *Mr. Pete & Co.* (1933). *The Lark Legacy* (1935). *Passionate Follies: Alternate Tales* (with C. Y. Rice, 1936). *My Pillow Book* (1937). *Our Ernie* (1939). *The Inky Way* (1940). *Happiness Road* (1942).

BIBLIOGRAPHY: Overton, G., *The Women Who Make Our Novels* (1919). Other references: *Book News Monthly* (Oct. 1909). *Boston Transcript* (31 Oct. 1917; 14 Sept. 1921; 23 Sept. 1933). *NYHTB* (10 Nov. 1940).

MARY JEAN DeMARR

Adrienne Cecile Rich

B. 16 May 1929, Baltimore, Maryland
D. of Arnold and Helen Rich; m. Alfred H. Conrad, 1953

R. was brought up in a southern, Jewish household which she has described as "white and middle-class . . . full of books, with a father who encouraged me to read and write." From her father's library R. read such writers as Rosetti, Swinburne, Tennyson, Keats, Blake, Arnold, Carlyle, and Pater, and as a child she was already writing poetry. Neither she nor her younger sister was sent to school until fourth grade: Dr. Rich, a professor of medicine, and Helen Rich, a trained composer and pianist, believed that they could educate their own children in a more enlightened, albeit unorthodox, way. In fact, most of the responsibility fell to the mother; she carried out the practical task of teaching them all their lessons, including music.

R.'s later education was conventional, and she graduated from Radcliffe in 1951. From 1953 to 1966, she lived in Cambridge, Massachusetts, with her three sons and her husband. These were years of personal and political growth and crisis for R. Her teaching career reflected her political commitment as she became involved in the SEEK and Open Admissions Programs of City College in New York City, where she took up residence after 1966. Her husband died tragically in 1970. R. continued teaching in the New York area until 1979, when she gave up her professorship at Rutgers University and settled in western Massachusetts with "the woman who shares my life."

W. H. Auden chose *A Change of World* (1951) for the Yale Younger Poets Award. Although Auden's tone in the preface has been criticized as condescending, he focused immediately on R.'s careful handling of form and clarity of thought: "The poems a reader will encounter in this book are neatly and modestly dressed, speak quietly but do not mumble, respect their elders but are not cowed by them, and do not tell fibs: that for a first volume is a good deal." Indeed, critic after critic has noted R.'s stylistic control and elegance as the hallmark of her early achievement.

This restrained style was to continue through the 1950s and be perfected in her second volume, *The Diamond Cutters* (1955). In a review of that volume, Randall Jarrell called her an "enchanting poet," an "endearing and delightful poet." But in the early 1960s, R. startled her critical audience with a shift to more political and feminist themes and an increasingly experimental style. Of her early experience, she has said, "In those years formalism was part of the strategy—like asbestos gloves, it allowed me to handle materials I couldn't pick up bare-handed . . . In the late Fifties I was able to write, for the first time, directly about experiencing myself as a woman."

R. wrote the title poem of *Snapshots of a Daughter-in-Law* (1963) "in a longer and looser mode than I'd ever trusted myself with before. It was an extraordinary relief to write that poem." This and other poems here, composed of irregular stanzas, are about madness, anger, waste, and failure in women's lives. "A Marriage in the 'Sixties," "End of an Era," "Novella," and "Readings of History" explore the self in relation to society, intimacy, war, violence, and pacifism.

In the 1970s, R.'s poetry revealed an urgent and driving tone that was expressive of her militant feminism. Critics worried that politics and ideology were undermining the poetry, but R. made no such distinction between politics and poetry. *Diving into the Wreck* (1973) is an attempt to start from the bottom, speaking of matters as yet unspoken in words as yet undefined. There are disturbing poems of pain, anger, and violence. Yet coexistent with this anger is a deep sorrow over our vulnerabilities and our frustrated ideals.

In *The Dream of a Common Language* (1978), R. begins to rebuild and to document the difficult process of re-vision. Expanding on an earlier method, she draws some of her material from historical figures: Marie Curie, Clara Westhoff (who married the poet Rainer Maria Rilke), and Elvira Shatayev (the leader of a women's mountain-climbing team). But her primary concern seems to be to provide mythic structures that will confirm and nourish the vital hopes and experiences of women. Thus in her latest phase R. has not abandoned form and restraint; rather she is searching for a new poetics defined by and for women.

R.'s concern with myth has also appeared in her prose. *Of Woman Born: Motherhood as Experience and Institution* (1976) is a carefully documented attempt to demystify motherhood as a patriarchal institution. She has also published widely on poetry, feminism, and lesbianism.

Among contemporary poets, R. is regarded highly. The integrity of her craft and the timeliness of her themes have earned her not only an academic audience but also a popular one. Above all her voice is directed towards other women, sharing her perceptions and partaking of a common experience.

WORKS: *A Change of World* (1951). *The Diamond Cutters* (1955). *Snapshots of a Daughter-in-Law* (1963). *Necessities of Life* (1966). *Selected Poems* (1967). *Leaflets* (1969). *The Will to Change* (1971). *Diving into the Wreck* (1973). *Poems: Selected and New* (1975). *Twenty-One Love Poems* (1975). *Of Woman Born: Motherhood as Experience and Institution* (1976). *The Dream of A Common Language: Poems 1974–1977* (1978). *On Lies, Secrets, and Silence: Selected Prose, 1966–1978* (1979). *A Wild Patience Has Taken Me This Far: Poems, 1978–1981* (1981).

BIBLIOGRAPHY: Gelpi, B. C., and A. Gelpi, *Adrienne Rich's Poetry: The Texts of the Poems, the Poet on Her Work, Reviews and Criticism* (1975). Juhasz, S., *Naked and Fiery Forms: Modern American Poetry by Women* (1976). Karp, S. H., "Beginning Here: A Reading of Adrienne Rich's *The Dream of a Common Language* as Feminist Manifesto and Myth," in *The Proceedings of the Second CUNY English Forum* (1981).

Other references: *Anonymous* 2 (1975). *Hollins Critic* (Oct. 1974). *The Island* 1 (May 1966). *Ms.* (July 1973). *Newsweek* (24 Dec. 1973). *NYT* (3 Feb. 1980). *The Ohio Review* 13 (1971). *Parnassus* (2, 1973; 4, 1975). *Poetry* 109 (Jan. 1967). *Salmagundi* 22–23 (1973). *SatR* (22 April 1972). *Southwest Review* 60 (Autumn 1975).

SHEEMA HAMDANI KARP

Lola Ridge

B. *12 Dec. 1873, Dublin, Ireland; d. 19 May 1941, Brooklyn, New York*
Given name: Rose Emily Ridge
Wrote under: Lola, L. R. Ridge, Lola Ridge
D. *of Joseph Henry and Emma Reilly Ridge; m. Peter Webster, 1895; m. David Lawson, 1919*

R. lived with her mother in Australia and New Zealand as a child. R.'s early interests included art and music, and when her marriage to the manager of a New Zealand gold mine proved unhappy, she moved to Sydney to study painting under Julian Ashton. R. later regretted having destroyed poems she wrote during this period, but a collection of her work has recently been discovered at the Mitchell Library in Sydney.

R. emigrated to San Francisco in 1907, and moved to New York City in 1908. She supported herself as a writer of fiction and poetry for popular magazines. She also served as one of the first organizers of Ferrer Association Modern School.

The Ghetto (1918), written during a five-year absence from New York City, was hailed as a book that seemed destined for greatness. Revolutionary in spirit and written in free verse, the title poem dwells on life among the Jewish immigrants of New York's Lower East Side and illustrates themes that recur throughout R.'s work—the moral courage of ordinary men and women, the paramount importance of liberty in human lives, and faith in the possibilities that America holds.

After the success of *The Ghetto*, R. edited a number of issues of *Others* and served as the American editor of *Broom*. She also toured the Midwest, speaking on subjects such as "Individualism and American Poetry" and "Woman and the Creative Will."

Sun-Up (1920) contains both personal and public poems. The title poem draws heavily on the author's own childhood. Technically, its flashing pictures resemble those of the Imagists; psychologically, it shares ground with the experiments of James Joyce. The public poems "Sons of Belial" and "Reveille" demonstrate R.'s sympathy with an exploited working class and affirm her function as a poet "[blowing] upon [their] hearts / kindling the slow fire."

Red Flag (1927) also includes poems saluting those who have fallen in the cause of freedom. "Red Flag" focuses on Russia and figures in the Russian revolution, and "Under the Sun" commemorates martyrs of other struggles. Most of the poems in this volume, however, are poems about natural and spiritual beauty and imagistic portraits of R.'s contemporaries.

R.'s last two books are characterized by an increasingly stylized language and growing mysticism. *Firehead* (1929), R.'s response to the executions of Sacco and Vanzetti in 1927, retells the story of the Crucifixion. The nine sections view the Crucifixion from a variety of points of view, including those of Judas, the two Marys, and Jesus himself; the Christ of the poem is viewed as "one who had proclaimed men equal— aye / Even unto slaves and women . . . / And babbled of some communal bright heaven." During her lifetime, *Firehead* was widely acclaimed as R.'s masterpiece.

On a visit to Yaddo in 1930, R. outlined a poem cycle, "Lightwheel," which was to occupy the greatest portion of her creative energies in her last years. "Lightwheel" was to include *Firehead* and five other books treating ancient Babylon, Florence during the Renaissance, Mexico at the time of Cortez and Montezuma, France during the Revolution, and Manhattan after World War I. R. traveled to the Near East (1931–32) and to Mexico (1935–37) to research her epic work, but the cycle remained unfinished at her death.

R.'s theory of history also shapes a sonnet sequence called "Via Ignis," the central poem in *Dance of Fire* (1935). But despite the poem's large theme—that we are at a crucial stage in history, but "may come forth, for a period, into a time of light"—its language is essentially private.

Though plagued by illness during much of her life, R. is remembered for her charisma. Her work attests to the continuous if not special concern that American women poets have had with social issues.

WORKS: *The Ghetto* (1918). *Sun-Up* (1920). *Red Flag* (1927). *Firehead* (1929). *Dance of Fire* (1935).

BIBLIOGRAPHY: Gregory, H., and M. Zaturenska, *A History of Modern Poetry: 1900–1940* (1946). Perkins, D., *A History of Modern Poetry: From the 1890s to the High Modernist Mode* (1976). Untermeyer, L., *The New Era in American Poetry* (1919).

For articles in reference works, see: *Living Authors: A Book of Biographies*, Ed. S. J. Kunitz (1931). *NAW* (article by A. Guttmann).

Other references: SatR (31 May 1941).

ELAINE SPROAT

Mary Roberts Rinehart

B. 12 Aug. 1876, Allegheny, Pennsylvania; d. 22 Sept. 1958, New York City
D. of Thomas Beveridge and Cornelia Gilleland Roberts; m. Dr. Stanley
  Marshall Rinehart, 1896

R. began her career in 1903, publishing short stories in magazines like *All-Story* and *Munsey's*. In three or four weeks in 1905, R. wrote *The Man in Lower 10* for serialization in *All-Story*, and she followed that the next year with *The Circular Staircase*. When Bobbs-Merrill published the *Circular Staircase* in 1908, R.'s long period of success began. These mysteries fleshed out the novel of deduction with fuller if somewhat stereotyped characters, a second, romantic plot line, a good deal of Gothic atmosphere, and frequently comic elements.

R. essentially stopped writing mystery novels after 1914, returning to the form in 1930 with *The Door*, her first novel to be published by her sons' new publishing house, Farrar and Rinehart. In the next twenty-three years, R. published eleven full-length mysteries in which she exploited fully the "buried story"—a sequence of events never narrated in the novel and emerging only as "outcroppings," places at which material about the past of the characters supplies clues to the solution of the mystery. R.'s "buried stories" most often center on errors of passion leading to sexual alliances across class lines and leading inexorably to crime some years later.

The villains in R.'s mysteries are frequently lower-class women who have ensnared richer, more aristocratic men. The heroines most often are unmarried young women with little money but of good family, who serve as the center of the romantic plot as well as the focus of the murder story. R.'s intention in establishing the young female narrator was to link her mystery plot as closely as possible with her romantic plot; however, the use of this central character type has had the effect of placing her work, erroneously, in the class of Gothics.

Although R. is remembered today as a writer of mysteries, she was more popular in her own time for her serious novels. Beginning with *The Street of Seven Stars* (1914) and *"K"* (1915), R. produced romances with some attention to contemporary problems. This emphasis became stronger with World War I; R. depicted life near the western front in *The Amazing Interlude* (1918) and sabotage and attempted insurrection on the home front in *Dangerous Days* (1919) and *A Poor Wise Man* (1920). Both critical and popular success eluded R. in her most serious attempt at fiction, *This Strange Adventure* (1929), a dark look at the life of a fairly typical married woman. R. recouped in 1931 with her fine autobiography, *My Story*.

R.'s humor was not restricted to isolated episodes in mystery novels. With the creation in 1910 of Letitia Carberry, "Tish," R. produced a character who would remain a staple of *The Saturday Evening Post* and a favorite of American readers for nearly thirty years. Tish is an undaunted spinster of about fifty who with her two companions travels America and Europe, resolving lovers' problems, rounding up bandits and kidnappers, once capturing an entire German company, and maintaining throughout her own slightly askew brand of absolute moral rectitude.

R. also achieved considerable success in the theater. In collaboration with Avery Hopwood, she wrote *Seven Days* (1909), with nearly four hundred performances, and *The Bat* (1920), with 878 performances and six road companies. *The Bat*, with close affinities to *The Circular Staircase*, mixes murder, romance, and comedy.

From 1910 to 1940, R. was America's most successful popular writer. Eleven of R.'s novels were among the ten top bestsellers of the year they were published, and in the 1930s mass-circulation magazines paid as much as $65,000 to serialize her novels. From its infancy the movie industry sought her work, and later radio and television used her material. Today, R.'s serious novels are dated by her cautious attitude toward popular morality; she was careful to offend neither editors nor audience. R.'s mystery novels have fared better with time, continuing to sell well in reissue. *The Circular Staircase* has achieved the status of a classic in the genre.

WORKS: *The Circular Staircase* (1908). *The Man in Lower 10* (1909). *When a Man Marries* (1909). *The Window at the White Cat* (1910). *The Amazing Adventures of Letitia Carberry* (1911). *Where There's a Will* (1912). *The Case of Jennie Brice* (1913). *The After House* (1914). *The Street of Seven Stars* (1914). *"K"* (1915). *Kings, Queens, and Pawns* (1915). *Through Glacier Park* (1916). *Tish* (1916). *The Altar of Freedom* (1917). *Bab: A Sub-Deb* (1917). *Long Live the King* (1917). *The Amazing Interlude* (1918). *Tenting Tonight* (1918). *Twenty Three and a Half Hours Leave* (1918). *Dangerous Days* (1919). *Love Stories* (1919). *Affinities* (1920). *Isn't That Just Like a Man? Well! You Know How Women Are!* (with I. S. Cobb, 1920). *A Poor Wise Man* (1920). *The Truce of God* (1920). *The Breaking Point* (1921). *More Tish* (1921). *Sight Unseen and the Confession* (1921). *The Out Trail* (1922). *Temperamental People* (1924). *The Red Lamp* (1925). *Nomad's Land* (1926). *Tish Plays the Game* (1926). *Two Flights Up* (1926). *Lost Ecstasy* (1927). *The Trumpet Sounds* (1927). *The Romantics* (1929). *This Strange Adventure* (1929). *The Door* (1930). *Mary Roberts Rinehart's Mystery Book* (1930). *The Book of Tish* (1931). *Mary Roberts Rinehart's Romance Book* (1931). *My Story* (1931; rev. ed., 1948). *Miss Pinkerton* (1932). *The Album* (1933). *The Crime Book* (1933). *The State Versus Elinor Norton* (1933). *Mr. Cohen Takes a Walk* (1934). *The Doctor* (1936). *Married People* (1937). *Tish Marches On* (1937). *The Wall* (1938). *Writing Is Work* (1939). *The Great Mistake* (1940). *Familiar Faces* (1941). *Haunted Lady* (1942). *Alibi for Isabel, and Other Stories* (1944). *The Yellow Room* (1945). *A Light in the Window* (1948). *Episode of the Wandering Knife* (1950). *The Swimming Pool* (1952). *The Frightened Wife, and Other Mur-*

der Stories (1953). *The Best of Tish* (1955). *The Mary Roberts Rinehart Crime Book* (1957).

BIBLIOGRAPHY: Cohn, J., *Improbable Fiction: The Life of Mary Roberts Rinehart* (1980). Disney, D. C., and M. Mackaye, *Mary Roberts Rinehart* (1948). Doran, G. H., in *Chronicles of Barrabas* (1935). Overton, G., et al., *Mary Roberts Rinehart: A Sketch of the Woman and Her Work* (1921?). Overton, G., in *When Winter Came to Main Street* (1922).

Other references: *American Magazine* (Oct. 1917). Boston *Evening Transcript* (12 June 1926). *Good Housekeeping* (April 1917). *Life* (25 Feb. 1946). *Writer* (Nov. 1932).

JAN COHN

Anna Cora Mowatt Ritchie

B. 5 March 1819, Bordeaux, France; d. 21 July 1870, Twickenham, England
Wrote under: Helen Berkeley, Henry C. Browning, Cora, Isabel, Charles A.
  Lee, M. D., Anna Cora Mowatt, Anna Ritchie
D. of Samuel Gouvernour and Eliza Lewis Ogden; m. James Mowatt, 1834;
  m. William Fouchee Ritchie, 1854

The ninth of fourteen children, R. was descended from old colonial families. Her early years were spent in France, but when she was seven the family moved to New York, where R. was educated in private girls' schools. Although "Lily," as she was called, was not outstanding at her studies, she was considered precocious by her family because of her ability to write and act in home theatricals.

At fifteen she eloped with Mowatt, a wealthy young lawyer, and moved to Melrose, his estate on Long Island. Here she wrote *Pelayo* (1836), a romantic poem in six cantos "founded strictly upon historical facts." R.'s preface to this poem reveals an extensive acquaintance with literature. It was not well received, however, and R. retaliated with *Reviewers Reviewed* (1837), a satiric essay on criticism.

An attack of tuberculosis, her constant enemy, led R. to visit Europe in 1838. Ironically, as her health improved that of her husband began to fail. Nonetheless, they returned to the U.S. and celebrated his "cure" with a ball at which R.'s blank verse melodrama in five acts, *Gulzara; or, The Persian Slave*, was presented with R. in the title role. The play attracted much favorable attention from critics when it was published in the *New World* in 1841.

Her husband's fragile health and the loss of his fortune led R. to give public poetry readings. When she became too ill to perform, she began to write articles for *Godey's Lady's Book, Graham's Magazine, The Democratic Review,* and other magazines. Under the pseudonym "Henry C. Browning," she wrote a life of Goethe, and as "Charles A. Lee, M.D." compiled *Management of the Sickroom* (1844). In 1842, R. won a hundred-dollar prize from *New World* for her novel *The Fortune Hunter* (1842). R.'s play *Fashion* (1845) had an unprecedented three-week run, and was long a favorite of audiences in England and America. The money she earned not only supported her and James, but three orphans she had taken into her childless home.

Even more profitable than writing was R.'s career as an actress. Starting as a star, she remained one for eight years of touring the U.S. and Great Britain.

After Mowatt's death in 1851, R. returned to New York. Again she turned to writing to supplement her income, and her lively *Autobiography of an Actress* (1854) was an immediate success.

In 1854, R. married a prominent Virginian and editor of *The Richmond Enquirer.* In 1861 R. left her husband because of irreconcilable political and personal differences. She went to Florence, where she supported herself by writing novels and sketches. In 1865, R. visited England, became too ill to travel back to Italy, and took a small house in Twickenham, where she died five years later.

Fashion (1845), R.'s most important work, is a bright, witty satire of 19th-c. New York society. The basic plot line is a standard love story with melodramatic elements; but the sharp comedy has kept its freshness. The play reveals a remarkable sense of theater and a grasp of dramaturgy rare in a first effort. The action moves rapidly, the plot turns are cleverly planned, and the climax satisfies the comedic expectations. The first American social comedy, *Fashion* was successfully revived in 1924 and again in 1959.

R.'s early novels, *The Fortune Hunter* (1842) and *Evelyn* (1845), are also contemporary views of New York life; R. draws upon her own experience as a member of upper-class society, giving these works more substance than is usual in such tales. She paints the evils of money marriages and juxtaposes them with marriages based on honesty in values and actions.

Most of R.'s later stories make use of her theatrical experiences in setting and characters; both background and types are recognizable and timeless. Her plots are traditional romantic love stories, and her characters are often embodiments of the sentimentality so prevalent in that time. They are seasoned, however, with humor and a Dickensian awareness of the ridiculous.

R.'s reliance upon action precludes the development of profound characters, but her use of detailed description removes them from the stock types in most popular novels of the time. She also differs from her contemporaries in her treatment of women, for she places a high value on independence. Dependent females in her stories invariably fall victim to circumstances or villains, whereas the heroines not only think for themselves but are usually self-supporting. R. believed women should be wives and mothers, but she contemplated, and in some cases endorsed, the single life. A unique author, combining a European elegance with an American admiration for practical labor, she is, in the truest sense, the first transatlantic writer.

WORKS: *Pelayo; or, The Cavern of Covadongo* (1836). *Reviewers Reviewed* (1837). *The Fortune Hunter* (1842). *Evelyn; or, A Heart Unmasked* (1845). *Fashion; or, Life in New York* (1845). *Armand; or, The Peer and the Peasant* (1847). *The Autobiography of an Actress* (1854). *Mimic Life* (1856). *Twin Roses* (1858). *Fairy Fingers* (1865). *The Mute Singer* (1866). *The Clergyman's Wife, and Other Selections* (1867). *Italian Life and Legends* (1870).

BIBLIOGRAPHY: Barnes, E. W., *The Lady of Fashion* (1954). Bernard, B., *Tallis's Drawing Room Table Book* (1851). Blesi, M., *The Life and Letters of Anna Cora Mowatt* (1938). Harland, Mr., "Recollections of a Christian Actress," in *Our Continent* (1882). Howitt, M., "Memoirs of Anna Cora Mowatt," in *Howitt's Journal* (1848). McCarthy, I., *Anna Cora Mowatt and Her American Audience* (1952).

HELENE KOON

Elizabeth Madox Roberts

B. 30 Oct. 1881, Perryville, Kentucky; d. 13 March 1941, Orlando, Florida
D. of Simpson and Mary Elizabeth Brent Roberts

About 1884, R. moved with her family to Springfield, Kentucky, the town which would become the center of her stories and novels. As a child, R. listened to her father's storytelling. An equally important influence on R. as a child were family legends, including the tale of a great-grandmother who had come to Kentucky by the Wilderness Road.

R. attended a private academy in Springfield and later graduated from high school in nearby Covington, Kentucky. In 1900, she entered the State College of Kentucky but withdrew from school, probably because of ill health and financial problems. In 1917, R. registered at the University of Chicago—a college freshman at the age of thirty-six. R. wrote poetry while at Chicago and took part in a group—including such talented friends as Yvor Winters and Glenway Westcott—which met frequently to discuss one another's work. R. graduated in 1921 with honors in English.

In 1922, R. returned to Springfield, where she was to spend most of her life and devoted herself to writing, even after she learned in 1936 that she had Hodgkin's disease.

The quality of R.'s work is uneven. Few people would claim greatness for *Jingling in the Wind* (1928), an allegorical novel of the courtship of two rainmakers, or *He Sent Forth a Raven* (1935), a highly artificial and contrived novel, but other novels are more successful.

The Time of Man (1926) chronicles the life of Ellen Chesser, a poor white girl who is a descendant of Kentucky pioneers. Ellen is fourteen at the opening of the novel. R. portrays Ellen's early love affair, her marriage to Jasper Kent, and the hardships she suffers as wife and mother. The real strengths of the novel lie in R.'s use of Ellen's consciousness as we see her transcend the bleakness of her life and in the poetic quality of the narrative.

My Heart and My Flesh (1927) traces Theodosia Bell's initial rejection and ultimate acceptance of life. Theodosia, with a good family, wealth, and pride, loses her lover, her friends, her home, and her health. She is driven to suicide, but at last reaffirms her love for life.

The power of the self to transcend external forces is the controlling thesis of *The Great Meadow* (1930), set during the revolutionary-war period in Virginia and Kentucky. R.'s central characters are Berkeleian idealists whose lives appear as spiritual dramas deriving their substance from the mind of God. The protagonist, Diony Hall, chooses to leave the order and safety of her family's farm to enter the wilderness of the frontier. The most notable element of the novel is the mental or spiritual ordering Diony exerts over the chaos of her life and her surroundings.

R. wrote poetry throughout her life—her first important volume, *Under the Tree* (1922), was poetry—and, although her output in verse is slim in comparison with her prose, she wrote several first-rate poems, including "Love in the Harvest" and "Sonnet of Jack." R. also published two volumes of short stories—*The Haunted Mirror* (1932) and *Not by Strange Gods* (1941)—but they are less successful than her novels.

R. deserves further study and analysis. A fine prose writer whose experiments in stream-of-consciousness narration and feminine characterization seem far ahead of her time, she is of especial interest today for her penetrating analysis of the female consciousness.

WORKS: *In the Great Steep's Garden* (1915). *Under the Tree* (1922). *The Time of Man* (1926). *My Heart and My Flesh* (1927). *Jingling in the Wind* (1928). *The Great Meadow* (1930). *A Buried Treasure* (1931). *The Haunted Mirror* (1932). *He Sent Forth a Raven* (1935). *Black Is My Truelove's Hair* (1938). *Song in the Meadow* (1940). *Not by Strange Gods* (1941).

BIBLIOGRAPHY: Auchincloss, L., *Pioneers and Caretakers: A Study of Nine Women Writers* (1965). Campbell, H. M., and R. Foster, *Elizabeth Madox Roberts: American Novelist* (1956). McDowell, F. P. W., *Elizabeth Madox Roberts* (1963). Rovit, E. H., *Herald to Chaos: The Novels of Elizabeth Madox Roberts* (1960).

Other references: *Kentucky Historical Society Review* (April 1966). SatR (2 March 1963).

ANNE ROWE

Jane Roberts

B. 8 May 1929, Albany, New York
D. of Delmar and Marie Burdo Roberts; m. Robert F. Butts, Jr., 1954

R. dedicated herself early to writing, beginning with poetry in her teens and later writing fiction. Nothing in R.'s life, however, foreshadowed the development of her mediumistic abilities or the messages from Seth—"an energy personality essence no longer focused in physical reality"—which form the backbone of her literary production.

R.'s first novel, *Bundu,* was published in 1958 and her second, *The Rebellers,* in 1963. In September 1963, R. had her first psychic experience, during which she wrote almost automatically while simultaneously feeling the conditions about which she was writing. Shortly after this event, R. and her painter husband began research for *How to Develop Your ESP Power* (1966), using a Ouija board. In 1963, Seth introduced himself via the Ouija board and soon afterward R. started speaking as Seth's voice. Since then, more than one thousand similar sessions have taken place, providing the material for R.'s five Seth-dictated books and for seven books associated with the Seth communications. Virtually all the Seth dictations have been recorded in shorthand by Butts. Butts is also author of the running commentary which provides background and framework for the Seth-dictated material in the Seth books.

The cosmology voiced through R. by Seth is vastly different from the usual "spirit messages." Seth depicts a monist creation of which this universe is only a small fraction. Everything has consciousness. God is "All That Is" and, as a whole and in all Its parts, is constantly evolving.

As well as being parts of All That Is, humans are also parts of entities greater than themselves; humans have free will nonetheless. They have existed before birth as individuals and, after death, will continue to do so. The Seth teachings emphasize the power and potential of the individual human. "You create your own reality" is a basic tenet of his message.

Since Seth's advent, R. has not limited herself to material dictated by him. R.'s books depicting her own experiences in attempting to understand and apply Seth's philosophy add a poignantly personal dimension to the Seth communications. R. has also written two fast-paced novels about Oversoul 7, which embody and vivify Seth's teachings. A more recent development in R.'s career is her work on the "after-death journal." Two of these have been published, one received from the painter Paul Cézanne, and the other from the psychologist William James (*The Afterdeath Journal of an American Philosopher*, 1978).

The Seth teachings are complex, intellectually demanding, and not for everyone. Readers of like mind will find R.'s Seth books uniquely challenging, expanding, and—if fortune smiles—deeply satisfying.

WORKS: *Bundu* (1958). *The Rebellers* (1963). *How to Develop Your ESP Power* (1966; reissued as, *The Coming Of Seth*, 1976). *The Seth Material* (1970). *Seth Speaks: The Eternal Validity of the Soul* (1972). *The Education of Oversoul 7* (1973). *The Nature of Personal Reality: A Seth Book* (1974). *Adventures in Consciousness: An Introduction to Aspect Psychology* (1975). *Dialogues of the Soul and Mortal Self in Time* (1975). *Psychic Politics* (1976). *The Unknown Reality: Volume One of a Seth Book* (1977). *The World View of Paul Cézanne* (1977). *The Afterdeath Journal of an American Philosopher* (1978). *The Unknown Reality: Volume Two of a Seth Book* (1979). *The Further Education of Oversoul 7* (1979). *Emir's Education in the Proper Use of Magical Powers; The Nature of the Psyche: Its Human Expression: A Seth Book* (1979). *The Individual and the Nature of Mass Events: A Seth Book* (1981). *The God of Jane: A Psychic Manifesto* (1981). *If We Live Again; or, Public Magic and Private Love* (1982).

BIBLIOGRAPHY: Andreae, C., *Seances and Spiritualists* (1974). Bentov, I., *Stalking the Wild Pendulum* (1977).

Other references: *New Realities* 1 (1977). *VV* (9 Oct. 1978; 16 Oct. 1978).
LUCY MENGER

Harriet Jane Hanson Robinson

B. 8 Feb. 1825, Boston, Massachusetts; d. 22 Dec. 1911, Malden, Massachusetts
Wrote under: Harriet J. Hanson, Harriet H. Robinson, Mrs. W. S. Robinson
D. of William and Harriet Browne Hanson; m. William Stevens Robinson, 1848

R.'s father, a carpenter, died in 1831, and her mother took her four children to Lowell, where she managed a factory boardinghouse. R. began working as a bobbin-doffer at ten. After working a fourteen-hour day, she went to evening schools until she was able to attend Lowell

High School for two years. At fifteen her regular formal education ceased. She tended a spinning frame and then became a "drawing-in girl"—one of the most skilled jobs in the mill. Taking private lessons in German, drawing, and dancing, R. read widely and began publishing poetry in newspapers, annuals, and *The Lowell Offering.*

One of her verses caught the attention of William Stevens Robinson, assistant editor of the *Lowell Courier;* after a two-year courtship, in which R. was torn between love and literary ambition, they were married. W. S. Robinson published *The Lowell American,* one of the first free-soil papers, from 1849 to 1854. R. joined him in his support of abolition and worked as editorial assistant while becoming the mother of four children. (Her elder girl became the second woman admitted to the bar in Massachusetts.) After the Civil War, R. and her husband worked for woman suffrage until his death in 1876. R. became the Massachusetts leader of Susan B. Anthony's National Woman Suffrage Association and a strong organizer and supporter of women's clubs.

All of R.'s books were published after her husband's death. Her first is *"Warrington" Pen-Portraits* (1877), which combines her memoir of her husband with a collection of his works. (The title refers to the name under which his militant abolitionist writings had been published.) It gives valuable pictures of abolitionist circles of the 1850s and of two eras in Concord, Massachusetts, where W. S. Robinson grew up and the couple lived from 1854 to 1857. "Among his schoolmates were John and Henry D. Thoreau; 'David Henry,' as he was then called. Of the elder, John, Mr. Robinson was very fond. He was a genial and pleasant youth, and much more popular with his schoolmates than his more cele-brated brother. Mr. Robinson had a high opinion of his talents and said that he was then quite as promising as Henry D." *Pen-Portraits* also records impressions of John Thoreau, Sr., as "the most silent of men, particularly in the presence of his wife and gifted son," and of Cynthia Dunbar Thoreau as "one of the most graphic talkers imagin-able, [who] held her listeners dumb."

In *The New Pandora* (1889), a verse drama, R. writes, "A woman should no more obey a man / Than should a man a woman. . . . My mate's no more my slave than I am hers;" and "Sex cannot limit the im-mortal mind. / We are ourselves, with individual souls, / Still struggling onward toward the infinite." Her pleas for equality of the sexes and the equal representation of women in councils of state, however, bog down in archaic verbs and verb forms and poetic diction.

Loom and Spindle (1898), R.'s most important work, adds personal history, anecdotes, and detail to the account she already had given in *Early Factory Labor in New England* (1883) of life in the cotton mills and corporation boardinghouses. *Loom and Spindle* provides analyses of the social hierarchy of Lowell and unforgettable vignettes, such as that of backwoods Yankee farm girls arriving to work in the city. R. also provides a full account of *The Lowell Offering* and biographical sketches of its chief contributors, carried through to 1898 whenever possible. R. admits that her account of "the life of every-day working-girls" may omit a darker side of their existence, but says, "I give the side I knew best—the bright side!"

R.'s play may be only a relic of feminist propaganda, but her lucid first-person accounts of Lowell life in the 1830s and 40s, of *The Lowell Offering*, and of Concord will always be valuable to literary and social historians as well as enjoyable reading.

WORKS: "*Warrington*" *Pen-Portraits* (edited by Robinson, 1877). *Massachusetts in the Woman Suffrage Movement* (1881). *Early Factory Labor in New England* (1883). *Captain Mary Miller* (1887). *The New Pandora* (1889). *Loom and Spindle; or, Life among the Early Mill Girls* (1898).

BIBLIOGRAPHY: Eisler, B., ed., *The Lowell Offering: Writings by New England Mill Women* (1977). Foner, P. S., *The Factory Girls* (1977). Josephson, H. G., *The Golden Threads: New England's Mill Girls and Magnates* (1949). Merk, L., "Massachusetts and the Woman-Suffrage Movement" (Ph.D. diss., Radcliffe College, 1961). Rothman, E., "Harriet Hanson Robinson: A Search for Satisfaction in the Nineteenth Century Woman Suffrage Movement" (Ph.D. diss., Radcliffe College, 1973).

For articles in reference works, see: *American Literary Manuscripts*, Ed. J. A. Robbins (1977). *NAW* (article by G. Blodgett).

SUSAN SUTTON SMITH

Anna Katharine Green Rohlfs

B. 11 Nov. 1846, Brooklyn, New York; d. 11 April 1935, Buffalo, New York
Wrote under: Anna Katharine Green
D. of James Wilson and Catherine A. Whitney Green; m. Charles Rohlfs, 1884

R. was the youngest child of a lawyer father and a mother who died when R. was three. R. received a B.A. from the Ripley Female Seminary in Poultney, Vermont, and began publishing poetry in *Scribner's, Lippincott's,* and other journals.

Although not the first American detective novel, *The Leavenworth Case* (1878) has been our most famous early mystery. Because of the decided success of *The Leavenworth Case,* R. gradually turned away from poetry writing. Only two of her forty books are not mysteries: a volume of verse, *The Defense of the Bride, and Other Poems* (1882), and a verse drama, *Risifi's Daughter* (1887).

In 1884, R. married a tragedian turned furniture designer. They made their home in Buffalo, New York. Over the next eight years, R. produced three children and eight books. The last two decades of the century were her most fertile writing years. She produced twenty-two published volumes between 1880 and 1900—for an ever-widening audience.

R.'s popularity grew with each new published thriller. She soon became the grande dame of the American mystery novel. R.'s international fame made her an effective lobbyist for international copyright.

The Leavenworth Case was, for many years, considered both the first American detective novel and the first detective novel by a woman, although it is neither. It is, however, a well-plotted, vastly entertaining murder puzzle of a type now classic. The rich Mr. Leavenworth is found murdered in his locked study. The suspects include his servants, employees, and two nieces. The sleuth is Ebenezer Gryce—a kind, rheumatic man and G.'s most frequently used detective. *The Leavenworth Case* was very popular. The Pennsylvania legislature even debated its authorship, consensus being that "the story was manifestly beyond a woman's powers."

Miss Hurd: An Enigma (1894) is a powerful mystery-melodrama in which the woman is the mystery to be solved. Vashti Hurd had wanted a "broad, free life." Instead, she was forced to marry the rich Mr. Murdoch. The murder puzzle that eventually develops is a subplot to the greater problem of Vashti's hatred for her husband and her need for freedom. Contemporary male critics found Miss Hurd an unsympathetic character. But feminist readers will find Vashti both sympathetic and heroic. Despite its rather sensational plot elements, the novel transcends its identity as a mystery novel and becomes a women's novel.

That Affair Next Door (1897) introduces R.'s prototype spinster sleuth, Miss Amelia Butterworth. A sharp, independent woman, Miss Butterworth works both with and against the police, as personified by the now-elderly Mr. Gryce. Amelia's own, rather satirical, narration makes the book a delight. It is also one of R.'s most challenging mysteries. Miss Butterworth would make two more appearances: a starring role in *Lost Man's Lane* (1898) and a cameo appearance in *The Circular Study* (1900).

The Golden Slipper, and Other Problems for Violet Strange (1915) is a short-story collection featuring a professional woman detective. Violet Strange is worthy of respect both as an investigator specializing in women's "problems" and for her motivation in becoming an investigator—to support a dearly loved but disinherited older sister.

R. brought detective fiction to a more "cultured" reading public. She frankly and proudly wrote for a popular audience, but her books were published in hardbound editions by respected houses. No longer was the American mystery relegated to dime-novel status. Prime ministers, presidents, and honored writers were avowed fans.

R.'s long and prolific career spanned from the infancy of the genre to its "golden age." But changing tastes within this fast-growing fiction formula dealt harshly with R. at the end of her career. Soon her poetic touches, her fondness for melodrama, her Victorian verbiage, were judged worthless by the jaundiced eye of the interwar reading public. The genre became rigidly formularized, lean, and cynical. By the 1940s, R.'s work was forgotten, or remembered only to ridicule.

R. is worthy of reexamination, both as a female forerunner in a largely female genre and as a writer with a real respect for women. R.'s female characters are strong, brave, and resolute against evil and largely male violence. There is a recurrent theme of sisterhood in R.'s works among women who pool their energies for survival. R. gave us some of the first female sleuths, both amateur and professional. Unlike many 20th-c. mystery writers who think of women only as victims or secondary characters, R. portrayed women as characters of primary importance who refused to be victimized.

WORKS: *The Leavenworth Case* (1878). *A Strange Disappearance* (1880). *The Sword of Damocles* (1881). *The Defense of the Bride, and Other Poems* (1882). *Hand and Ring* (1883). *X.Y.Z.* (1883). *The Mill Mystery* (1886). *Risifi's Daughter* (1887). *7 to 12: A Detective Story* (1887). *Behind Closed Doors* (1888). *The Forsaken Inn* (1890). *A Matter of Millions* (1890). *The Old Stone House* (1891). *Cynthia Wakeham's Money* (1892). *Marked 'Personal'* (1893). *Miss Hurd: An Enigma* (1894). *The Doctor, His Wife, and the Clock* (1895). *Dr. Izard* (1895). *That Affair Next Door* (1897). *Lost Man's Lane* (1898). *Agatha Webb* (1899). *The Circular Study* (1900). *A Difficult Problem* (1900). *One of My Sons* (1901). *Three Women and a Mystery* (1902). *The Filigree Ball* (1903). *The Amethyst Box* (1905). *The House in the Mist* (1905). *The Millionaire Baby* (1905). *The Woman in the Alcove* (1906). *The Chief Legatee* (1906). *The Mayor's Wife* (1907). *The House of Whispering Pines* (1910). *Three Thousand Dollars* (1910). *Initials Only* (1911). *Dark Hollow* (1914). *The Golden Slipper, and Other Problems for Violet Strange* (1915). *To the Minute / Scarlet and Black* (1916). *The Mystery of the Hasty Arrow* (1917). *The Step on the Stair* (1923).

BIBLIOGRAPHY: Harkins, E. F., and C. H. L. Johnson, *Little Pilgrimages among the Women Who Have Written Famous Books* (1901). Overton, G., *The Women Who Make Our Novels* (1928).

Other references: *Bookman* 70 (1929). *Reading and Collecting* 2 (1938). *The Writer* 2 (1888).

KATHLEEN L. MAIO

Constance Mayfield Rourke

B. 14 Nov. 1885, Cleveland, Ohio; d. 23 March 1941, Grand Rapids, Michigan
D. of Henry Button and Constance E. Davis Rourke

R. was an only child; her father was a lawyer, her mother a kindergarten teacher. R. moved to Grand Rapids, Michigan, at age seven when her father died. Her close relationship with her mother, who passed on to R. an appreciation for painting and handicrafts, probably encouraged R.'s later concern for native American folk arts. In addition, R.'s professional interest in the details of ordinary life may have been a midwestern inheritance. This regard for the near-at-hand was never mere provincialism, however; for R. understood, as have all the best mid-western writers and critics, the profound relationship between local de-tails and national myth, between particular experience and its more universal implications.

R. attended Vassar College (B.A. 1907); her primary interests were aesthetics and literary criticism. From 1908 to 1910, R. was a researcher at the Bibliothèque Nationale in Paris and the British Museum in London. She became an English instructor at Vassar in 1910, but in 1915 resigned from Vassar to live with her mother in Grand Rapids, and to do free-lance research and writing on American history and culture.

R. is best known for her advocacy of a native American culture, her use of popular culture and other "living research" sources and meth-ods, and her popular, highly readable prose style. R. argued from a social and anthropological view of history against a belief that the quality of American society made it difficult for "culture" to live and prosper in the U.S. She saw a significant relationship between low and high cul-tures, and believed that America had a robust cultural tradition wherein unique native arts grew and flourished. R. proposed that American cul-ture, woven from a great number of low- and high-culture strands, was more unified and vigorous than some scholars had believed.

Implicit in R.'s work, especially in *American Humor: A Study of the American Character* (1931), is the belief that American culture need not be judged against European models. Rather, it has its own charac-teristics, resulting from the particular conditions of the national history that produced it. The first part of *American Humor* recreates the rich climate in which this culture arose. R. traveled widely and used personal interviews, oral history, and popular culture documents as well as tra-ditional historical materials to present a vivid picture of the rise of Amer-ican humor. She saw this humor as an essential element in the definition of American character and culture. The second part of the book ana-lyzes mainstream- or high-culture American writers in relationship to their antecedents in native American humor.

In *American Humor*, R. demonstrates a remarkable harmony between style and thematic approach. She writes in a lively, unacademic prose, often using fictional narration and the present tense, which makes history come alive and which celebrates ordinary American experiences and the common man.

Although *American Humor* and *The Roots of American Culture* (1942) include the most explicit statements of R.'s ideas, *Charles Sheeler: Artist in the American Tradition* (1938) is also a convincing application of R.'s theories about the interrelations between the popular American cultural experience and the mainstream art it produces. Similarly, *Troupers of the Gold Coast; or, the Rise of Lotta Crabtree* (1928) exemplifies R.'s approach. This is the lively biography of two women: Mary Ann Crabtree and her actress-comedienne daughter, Lotta. Like all of R.'s social histories, it provides a myriad of everyday details from America's past. Lotta Crabtree's story is not only the chronicle of an important life, but the vital dramatization of San Francisco in the later days of the gold rush, and of the popular theater and American humor on the Gold Coast.

Critics have attacked R. for overstating her case on behalf of American culture and the interdependence of popular and so-called "high" arts; however, R.'s reputation has been sustained not only by later studies that support her views, but by the increased use of R.'s popular-culture research methods and by the continuing influence of her readable, scholarly books.

WORKS: *Trumpets of Jubilee* (1927). *Troupers of the Gold Coast; or, The Rise of Lotta Crabtree* (1928). *American Humor: A Study of the American Character* (1931). *Davy Crockett* (1934). *Audubon* (1936). *Charles Sheeler: Artist in the American Tradition* (1938). *The Roots of American Culture* (Ed. V. W. Brooks, 1942).

BIBLIOGRAPHY: Brooks, V. W., Preface to *The Roots of American Culture* (1942). Hyman, S. E., *The Armed Vision* (1948). Rubin, J. S., *Constance Rourke and American Culture* (1980).

For articles in reference works, see: *CB* (May 1941). *Contemporary American Authors*, F. B. Millett (1940). *DAB*, Suppl. 3. *NAW* (article by K. S. Lynn). *NCAB*, 32.

Other references: *Nation* (17 Sept. 1938; 24 Oct. 1942). *NewR* (31 Aug. 1942). *WF* (April 1967).

NANCY POGEL

Susanna Haswell Rowson

B. 1762, Portsmouth, England; d. 2 March 1824, Boston, Massachusetts
Wrote under: Mrs. Rowson, Susannah Rowson, Susannah Haswell
D. of William and Susanna Musgrave Haswell; m. William Rowson, 1786

The English-born R. was raised in America after 1868. By age twelve, she was considered remarkably well-read in the Classics. Due to her father's Tory allegiances, R.'s family was "interned" during the Revolutionary War but finally allowed to return in poverty to England. R. worked as a governess until 1786, the year she published her first novel, *Victoria*, and married a hardware merchant and musician.

When her husband's business failed, R. assumed the role of primary economic provider. During the five-year theatrical career which brought her back to America in 1792, she demonstrated considerable versatility as an actress, dancer, dramatist, and popular-song writer. She spent the next twenty-five years in the Boston area successfully running one of the first schools to offer girls an education above the elementary level. R. also wrote more than a dozen plays and novels, several books of poetry, a collection of tales, and several textbooks. She was contributing editor to the *Boston Weekly Magazine* for several years and also wrote for other magazines. In addition, the childless R. managed a household consisting of her husband's younger sister and his illegitimate son, her own niece, and an adopted daughter.

R.'s fame in literary history rests on her highly successful novel *Charlotte Temple: A Tale of Truth* (1791), a sentimental story about an English schoolgirl seduced by a British officer. He abandons her in America, where she dies after the birth of a daughter. Despite its wooden characters, this popular classic's appeal probably lies in its sensational portrayal of the dangerous power of the sexual impulse. For an early American novel, it displays a surprising unity of purpose and protest, albeit indirect, against the dependent status of women and the disloyalty of women to other women.

Although the didactic sentimentality of Richardson and Fanny Burney permeates her novels, R. could be considered an incipient realist in her use of colloquial dialogue, homely detail, and her own and others' experiences. R. claimed that her two seduction novels, *Victoria* and *Charlotte Temple*, were taken from "Real Life," and it has been suggested that

R. drew upon her frustrations with her own marriage in the moving descriptions of Charlotte's responses to her unfaithful lover. Certainly, *Rebecca; or, The Fille de Chambre* (1792), her second best novel, is semi-autobiographical in its presentation of the shipwreck and poverty faced by the friendless but virtuous heroine, as is *Sarah; or, The Exemplary Wife* (1813), a novel about the struggles of a woman who, like herself, raises her husband's illegitimate son. In the frontispiece to *Mentoria; or, The Young Ladies Friend* (1791), a collection of essays and moral tales on similar themes, R. advises, "From my experiences, *dearly* bought, / Blush not, my Anna, to be taught."

R.'s contributions as an early American dramatist and feminist writer have been largely ignored. Her only extant play, *Slaves in Algiers; or, A Struggle for Freedom* (produced in 1794), which was inspired by the crisis of Americans held hostage by Barbary pirates, dramatizes the escape of freedom-loving American women from the submissive harem of the Dey of Algiers. Several scenes satirize the macho postures of male captors and a would-be rescuer, and in a clever epilogue, R. imagines the women in the audience approving the good sense of her women's rights theme. Unlike most of her contemporary dramatists, R. evidently exploited American materials also in her lost plays.

Feminist themes are also present in R.'s otherwise undistinguished poetry. In "The Choice"—written more than a hundred years before Virginia Woolf's *A Room of Ones Own*—R. asks for "a competent estate, / . . . About five hundred pounds a year" and that "One little room should sacred be / To study, solitude, and me." Although "Rights of Woman" argues that women should have domestic rights only, R.'s domestic woman is an active, productive, and assertive person who refuses the passive role of sex object. Her collected poems also include patriotic odes, naval songs, and nature lyrics.

R.'s contributions to early American literature need to be reassessed. Not only did she write America's first bestseller, but she was a significant early American dramatist who should rank with the best of that period. In addition, her entire canon deserves to be reexamined for its early development of feminist themes in American literature.

WORKS: *Victoria* (1786). *The Inquisitor; or, Invisible Rambler* (1788). *A Trip to Parnassus; or, The Judgment of Apollo on Dramatic Authors and Performers: A Poem* (1788). *Mary; or, The Test of Honor* (1789). *Charlotte Temple: A Tale of Truth* (1791). *Mentoria; or, The Young Ladies Friend* (1791). *Rebecca; or, The Fille de Chambre* (1792). *Slaves in Algiers; or, A Struggle for Freedom* (1794). *Trials of the Human Heart* (1795). *Reuben and Rachel; or, Tales of Old Times* (1798). *Miscellaneous Poems* (1804). *Sarah; or,*

The Exemplary Wife (1813). *Biblical Dialogues between a Father and his Family: Comprising Sacred History from the Creation to the Death of our Savior* . . . (1822). *Lucy Temple; or, The Three Orphans: A Sequel to Charlotte Temple* (1828).

BIBLIOGRAPHY: Kirk, C. M., and R. Kirk, Introduction to *Charlotte Temple* (1964). Loshe, L. D., *The Early American Novel* (1907). Mates, J., *The American Musical Stage before 1800* (1962). Nason, E. A., *A Memoir of Mrs. Susanna Rowson* (1870). Quinn, A. H., *A History of American Drama: From the Beginnings to the Civil War* (1943). Rourke, C., *The Roots of American Culture* (1942).

For articles in reference works, see: *AA. DAB*, XVI. *NAW* (article by R. D. Birdsall). *NCAB*, 9.

KATHLEEN L. NICHOLS

Anne Newport Royall

B. *11 June 1769, near Baltimore, Maryland; d. 1 Oct. 1854, Washington, D.C.*
D. *of William and Mary Newport; m. William Royall, 1797*

R. began her long and colorful life in Maryland, but moved with her family to Westmoreland County, Pennsylvania, when she was three. The family lived in a rude cabin where William Newport taught his daughter to read and write. Newport, a Tory in those prerevolutionary days, died a few years later, and Mary Newport remarried. After the death of her second husband, she and R. moved to Sweet Springs, now in West Virginia. A planter, Major William Royall, took them in and gave Mary domestic work. R., then eighteen years old, had access to the gentleman's ample library and to his tutelage. Ten years later Anne married her benefactor and mentor, who was then in his mid-fifties. When he died in 1812, he left Anne wealthy, and she began to travel.

If a nephew had not broken Royall's will, charging R. with forgery and "barbarous treatment" of her husband, the world probably would not have heard of this strong-minded woman. Because she was without income, R. turned to writing as a livelihood. *Sketches of History: Life and Manners in the United States by a Trœveller* (1826) is the product of R.'s trip from Alabama to New England in 1823, containing sketches of well-known and unknown people, descriptions of landscape and cities, and personal reflections. R.'s blend of documentary material with gossipy tidbits fulfills the promise of the book's subtitle. Although R.'s books have limited literary value, they contribute to our knowledge of the social history of America.

In spring 1824, R. arrived in the District of Columbia, a sprawling community that would eventually become her home. Her first activity there was to lobby Congress for a commutation-of-pay resolution that would give her an income from her husband's military service in the Revolutionary War. R., in near-rags, solicited political, literary, and financial support from whomever she could interview, including Secretary of State John Quincy Adams. During the next seven years, R. continued to crusade, travel, write, and interview influential people.

When age forced R. to stop traveling in 1831, she settled in Washington, where she founded and printed, in her kitchen, a weekly newspaper, *Paul Pry*. R. served not only as editor and printer but also as reporter, writer, and solicitor of subscriptions. For years R. had been attacking anti-Masons and fundamentalists, and she continued her propaganda against them in *Paul Pry*. One of her best-known conflicts with the "Holy Willies," as she called evangelicals, resulted in her conviction as a "common scold." R. was fined ten dollars.

Deciding that *Paul Pry* sounded too much like a gossip sheet, R. changed the name to *The Huntress* in 1836. In the prospectus for the new paper, R. vowed to "expose corruption, hypocrisy and usurpation, without favor or affection." Among the causes R. championed were states' rights on the issue of slavery, justice for the American Indian, separation of church and state, tolerance for foreigners and Roman Catholics, and abolition of the United States Bank monopoly. She interspersed editorials and diatribes against Congress with gossip and with stories and poems written by others. R.'s crusading journalism continued in *The Huntress* for eighteen years.

WORKS: *Sketches of History: Life and Manners in the United States by a Traveller* (1826). *The Tennessean: A Novel Founded on Facts* (1827). *The Black Book: A Continuation of Travels in the United States* (3 vols., 1828–29). *Mrs. Royall's Pennsylvania* (2 vols., 1829). *Mrs Royall's Southern Tour* (3 vols., 1830–31). *Letters from Alabama* (1830).

BIBLIOGRAPHY: Dodd, D., and B. Williams, " 'A Common Scold': Anne Royall," *American History Illustrated* 10 (1976). Griffith, L., Introduction to *Letters from Alabama, 1817–22* (1969). Jackson, G. S., *Uncommon Scold: The Story of Anne Royall* (1937). James, B. R., *Anne Royall's U.S.A.* (1972). Porter, S. H., *The Life and Times of Anne Royall* (1909).

LYNDA W. BROWN

Muriel Rukeyser

B. 15 Dec. 1913, New York City; d. 12 Feb. 1980, New York City
D. of Lawrence B. and Myra Lyons Rukeyser

R. was educated at the Fieldston schools, Vassar College, and Columbia University. She was vice-president of the House of Photography, New York (1946–60), taught at Sarah Lawrence College (1946, 1956–60), and later served as a member of the Board of Directors of the Teachers-Writers Collaborative in New York, a member of the National Institute of Arts and Letters, and president of PEN.

R. wrote and published a play, TV scripts, a novel, juveniles, biographies, criticism, translations, and fourteen volumes of poetry. R.'s poems have been translated into European and Asian languages, and her readings from *Waterlily Fire* (1962) have been recorded for the Library of Congress. R.'s first book of poems, *Theory of Flight* (1935), won the Yale Series of Younger Poets competition in 1935.

From R.'s poems we can study much that has happened in modernist and postmodernist poetry in the last fifty years—from distance to confession, social protest, and feminism; from Yeats and Eliot to Ginsberg, Bly, and Levertov.

R.'s personality is manifest in the exuberant, hyperbolic, and generally optimistic tone that dominates her work. R. insists on experiencing and feeling *everything*, private or social, from the smallest physical sensation to transcendence of the physical. She treats sex, a cockroach, social injustice, and mystical self-dissolution with equal exuberance; *being* is its own excuse.

The result is that R.'s poetry, but not the individual poems, is multidimensional. Some poems are almost pure sensation ("Stroking Songs"); some are explanation ("Written on a Plane"); some are vituperation ("Despisals"); and some are pure fun ("From a Play: Publisher's Song"). Both her personal and artistic credos are expressed in the poem "Whatever."

For each mood or concept, R. selects or creates a perfectly suitable form. She is skillful enough so that her forms embody rather than contain their meanings: "Afterwards" is a poem that reaches into the unconscious for a "deep-image" ("We are the antlers of that white animal") expressed in breath rhythm. "Flying There: Hanoi" uses the incremental repetition and the rhythm of nursery rhyme to rededicate a poet. "Two Years" uses three terse stream-of-consciousness lines to express the dislocation of grief. "Rational Man" is a list of man's tortures of his kind in the rhythm of a dirge, ending in a prayer.

R.'s temperament and talent are best suited for writing the Dionysian sort of poems written by Bly and Levertov at their best—sensation, the concrete and physical, in ecstasy, rage, or prayer. R. weakens when she philosophizes and explains, and she frequently explains more than is necessary.

For a poet whose published volumes of poetry spanned more than forty years, R.'s range and energy were remarkable. Her changes were toward greater variety and flexibility and personal involvement.

WORKS: *Theory of Flight* (1935). *Mediterranean* (1938). *U.S. 1* (1938). *A Turning Wind: Poems* (1939). *The Soul and Body of John Brown* (1940). *Wake Island* (1942). *Willard Gibbs* (1942). *Beast in View* (1944). *The Children's Orchard* (1947). *The Green Wave* (1948). *Elegies* (1949). *The Life of Poetry* (1949). *Orpheus* (1949). *Selected Poems* (1951). *Come Back Paul* (1955). *One Life* (1957). *Body of Waking* (1958). *I Go Out* (1961). *Waterlily Fire: Poems 1932–1962* (1962). *Selected Poems of Octavio Paz* (translated by Rukeyser, 1963). *Sun Stone* by O. Paz (translated by Rukeyser, 1963). *The Orgy* (1966). *Bubbles* (1967). *The Outer Banks* (1967). *Selected Poems of Gunnar Ekelöf* (translated by Rukeyser, with L. Sjöberg, 1967). *Three Poems by Gunnar Ekelöf* (translated by Rukeyser, 1967). *Poetry and Unverifiable Fact: The Clark Lectures* (1968). *The Speed of Darkness* (1968). *Mayes* (1970). *Twenty-nine Poems* (1970). *The Traces of Thomas Hariot* (1971). *Breaking Open* (1973). *Brecht's Uncle Eddie's Moustache* (translated by Rukeyser, 1974). *The Gates* (1976). *The Collected Poems of Muriel Rukeyser* (1978). *More Night* (1981).

BIBLIOGRAPHY: Jarrell, R., *Poetry and the Age* (1953). Kertesz, L., *The Poetic Vision of Muriel Rukeyser* (1979). Rexroth, K., *American Poetry in the Twentieth Century* (1971).

For articles in reference works, see: *Contemporary Poets*, Eds. J. Venison and D. L. Kirkpatrick (1975).

Other references: *Carolina Quarterly* (Spring 1974). *Christian Century* (21 May 1980). *LJ* (1 Oct. 1976). *Ms.* (April 1974). *Nation* (19 March 1977; 8 March 1980). *NR* (24 Nov. 1973). *NYTBR* (25 Sept. 1977). *Poetry* (Oct. 1974).

ALBERTA TURNER

Adela Rogers St. Johns

B. 20 May 1894, California

D. of Earl and Harriet Greene Rogers; m. William Ivan St. Johns, 1914; m. (?), 1930s

The diversity of S.'s reporting may well have been anticipated by her unusually sophisticated childhood. She was the daughter of a renowned criminal lawyer and a displaced Southern Belle—a woman S. has described as having been extremely unhappy and violently cruel. Her parents' tumultuous relationship proved a daily trial, and their marriage, divorce, and remarriage frequently placed her with relatives or at boarding schools in various parts of California. She charts her father's career and his tremendous influence on her in *Final Verdict* (1962). In 1913, when she was eighteen, he introduced her to William Randolph Hearst, and until 1918 she worked for the Hearst papers in San Francisco and Los Angeles.

During these early years, S. also began writing for Hollywood. In order to work at home when her children were young, she wrote and collaborated on several scripts. She became "Mother Confessor to the Stars" for *Photoplay Magazine* and later wrote biographies of movie stars for a Hearst series called "Love, Laughter, and Tears" (a title she would use for her memoirs of this period).

S.'s journalism began setting precedents in the 1920s when she became the country's first woman sports writer. But it was in the 1930s, while an International News Service reporter, that she created her best stories. Among them is her Depression series on the plight of unemployed women. These articles are largely based on personal experiences. Despite the artificiality of the premise—S. set out to look for a job with only a dime in her pocket—they dramatize the misery of these women and expose the uncharitableness of several charitable institutions.

S.'s fiction shares with her journalism a heavily emotive style (she was known as a "Sob Sister") and topical subject matter and background. She writes about Prohibition and WWII, and sometimes bases her plot on a publicized crime or incident. She can write engagingly, but the predominant concerns of her fiction can be traced to a few fixed themes. One of these themes, that of the "modern woman," is treated with some depth in her autobiography, *The Honeycomb* (1969), but in her fiction it appears as a much less complex phenomenon. It is often merely a decorative element in stories that are largely examples of women's escape fiction.

Several of her novels are romances set in Hollywood or in "high society." Women protagonists may, in fact, possess the characteristics of modern women—they may be important executives (*Field of Honor*, 1938) or women who freely engage in affairs (*The Single Standard*, 1928)—but as one critic put it, they are ultimately unconventional heroines too faithful to the conventions of their type. Characterizations are superficial and limited in depth and originality by the author's moralizing. Nonetheless, S.'s novels and more than two hundred short stories appealed to a large readership. She published in all the leading fiction and women's magazines of her time. This commercial success was in all likelihood the motivation for her 1956 book, *How to Write a Story and Sell It.*

Unlike some of the characters in her fiction, the people she describes and the persona she reveals in her autobiographies are vivid, authentic, and moving. Her memoirs ramble sentimentally, but they are candid and provide lively insights into political and cultural history. S. discusses her professional progress as well as such traumas as the death of a child, divorce and custody trials, and her alcoholism; her personal philosophy emerges as the distillation of family values, religious faith, and her self-consciousness as a modern woman.

This consciousness, however, has little to do with any overt alliance with feminist issues. In her opinion, a "single standard" for men and women will remain unattainable so long as women are mothers. S. approaches her ideal of modern woman through speculation on the moral integrity women should maintain in the flux of modern society. She sees this ideal most inspiringly realized in such admirable individuals as Eleanor Roosevelt and Anne Morrow Lindbergh.

In recent years, S.'s writing has explored her deepening religious faith and her belief in the afterlife. *First Step up toward Heaven* (1959), is the account of the founder of Forest Lawn Cemetery; *Tell No Man* (1966) is a novel of a religious conversion, and her latest book, *No Goodbyes: My Search Into Life Beyond Death* (1981), relates her communications with her deceased son.

S. is one of this century's most famous women journalists. In 1970, she was awarded the Medal of Freedom by President Richard Nixon, her former newspaper boy in Whittier, California.

WORKS: *A Free Soul* (1924). *The Skyrocket* (1925). *The Single Standard* (1928). *Field of Honor* (1938). *The Root of All Evil* (1940). *Never Again, and Other Stories* (1949). *Affirmative Prayer in Action* (1955). *How to Write a Story and Sell It* (1956). *First Step up toward Heaven: Hubert Eaton and Forest Lawn* (1959). *Final Verdict* (1962). *Tell No Man* (1966). *The Honeycomb* (1969). *Love, Laughter, and Tears: My Hollywood Story* (1978). *No Goodbyes: My Search into Life Beyond Death* (1981).

BIBLIOGRAPHY: *Collier's* (24 Jan. 1924). *Foremost Women in Communications* (1970). *Newsweek* (27 June 1936). *NYTBR* (7 June 1925; 28 Aug. 1927) 3 June 1928; 7 Aug. 1938; 12 June 1949; 10 April 1966).

ELINOR SCHULL

Lucy Maynard Salmon

B. 27 July 1853, Fulton, New York; d. 14 Feb. 1927, Poughkeepsie, New York
D. of George and Maria Clara Maynard Salmon

S.'s father was a staunch Presbyterian and a Republican with abolitionist sentiments. Her mother was head of the Fulton Female Seminary from 1836 until her marriage to George Salmon. With this strong heritage of female education, it is not surprising that S. received an excellent education for a woman of her day and age. She attended grammar school in Oswego, New York, and the coeducational Falley Seminary, formerly the Fulton Female Seminary.

S. was one of only fifty women at the University of Michigan. Under the tutorship of Charles Kendall Adams, she majored in history and graduated with a B.A. degree in 1876. She received her M.A. degree in 1883, after several years as assistant principal and principal of a high school in MacGregor, Iowa. While teaching at the Indiana State Normal School, S. published her first significant historical work, *Education in Michigan during the Territorial Period* (1885). After further graduate study in American history at Bryn Mawr College, S. accepted a position as the first professor of history at Vassar College in 1887. Except for a time spent studying in Europe (1898–1900), she remained at Vassar the rest of her professional career.

S. became a recognized leader within the Vassar College community. She believed the student should be the principal agent in her own education (S. taught her history courses in a seminar format, with emphasis placed on student research) and that the heart of any college is its library. She also anticipated future trends in historical research and methodology when she encouraged the development of a collection of periodical literature at the Vassar college library. Her personal contribution to the periodical collection was the guide *The Justice Collection of Material Relating to the Periodical Press in the Vassar College Library* (1925).

S. was a charter member of the American Historical Association. From 1896 to 1899, she served as a member of the association's "Committee of Seven," whose report *The Study of History in Schools* (1915), formed the guide for teaching history in secondary schools for generations. In addition to her professional activities, S. was an active supporter of woman suffrage and an advocate of world peace.

As a scholar, S.'s work followed no developmental pattern until her later years. Her most important early work is the volume *History of the Appointing Power of the President* (1886), which investigates the creation of the appointing power of the president by the Constitutional Convention, its precedents in English law, and the experience of the states under the Articles of Confederation. While this work is dated, and while S.'s hopes for a future when presidents would again make appointments based on merit, as they had during the Federalist era, were certainly not borne out by history, it is still a significant historical work for anyone interested in presidential use and abuse of power.

Domestic Service (1897) and *Progress in the Household* (1906) document S.'s increasing interest in what are considered today to be nontraditional subjects and methods of writing history. *Domestic Service* is based on a survey conducted in 1889 and 1890. It presents an analysis of household employment within a historical perspective, beginning with a discussion of domestic service in colonial America. S. suggests that there should be specialization of the work of domestic servants—paralleling the division of labor in other fields—and that servants be compensated fairly for their work, through higher wages and profit-sharing plans.

Progress in the Household is, in essence, a supplement to *Domestic Service*, as the essays outline "recent progress in the study of domestic service." These books are dated, and the institutions and problems described by S. are for the most part nonexistent today. Still, they present the modern reader with a picture of domestic life and service in the years before the technological revolution of the 20th c. and express the issues of concern to American women at that time.

S.'s departure from the then-current traditional school of history, which emphasized study of the political institutions of America, led to the writing of her most important historical works, *The Newspaper and the Historian* and *The Newspaper and Authority*, both published in 1923.

The Newspaper and the Historian discusses the advantages and limitations of newspapers and other periodicals as sources in the writing of history. S. points out how the periodical press reveals the personality of its time or environment. The companion volume, *The Newspaper and Authority*, is international in scope and investigates the press with reference to its external government controls.

Just three months prior to her death, S. completed *Why Is History Rewritten?* (1929). "History must be continually rewritten because there is always a new history. To the end of time, as far as the human mind can see, history will need to be rewritten and in that very fact the historian finds one of its greatest interests." S. was a pioneer in liberating the study of history from the narrow confines of a political perspective and introducing historians to a new range of sources for historical study.

WORKS: *Education in Michigan during the Territorial Period* (1885). *History of the Appointing Power of the President* (1886). *Domestic Service* (1897; rev. ed., 1901). *History in the German Gymnasia* (1898). *Progress in the Household* (1906). *Some Principles in the Teaching of History* (1908). *Patronage in the Public Schools* (1908). *History in the Back Yard* (1913). *The Dutch West India Company on the Hudson* (1915). *"Is This Vassar College?"* (1915). *Main Street* (1915). *What Is Modern History?* (1917). *The Newspaper and the Historian* (1923). *The Newspaper and Authority* (1923). *The Justice Collection of Material Relating to the Periodical Press in the Vassar College Library* (1925). *Why Is History Rewritten?* (1929). *Historical Material* (1933).

BIBLIOGRAPHY: Brown, L. F., *Apostle of Democracy: The Life of Lucy Maynard Salmon* (1943).

For articles in reference works, see; *DAB*, VIII, 2. *NAW* (article by V. Barbour).

PAULA A. TRECKEL

Mari Sandoz

B. *1896, Sheridan County, Nebraska; d. 10 March 1966, New York City*
Wrote under: Marie S. Macumber, Mari Sandoz
D. of Jules Ami and Mary Elizabeth Fehr Sandoz

S. grew up in northwest Nebraska, in a frontier area at the edge of Indian country. Despite little formal education and much opposition from her father to a literary career, S.'s life was dedicated to writing. In both fiction and nonfiction she depicted the difficulties of frontier life and its violence, the harsh beauty of the country, the changes that have come to the area as Indians have been pushed aside and whites have imposed their way of life, the effects of political and social corruption upon the lives of the people, and the relations between ranchers, farmers, and Indians.

S.'s first published book was *Old Jules* (1935), a biography of her father; three years of research and two years of writing went into it. The book's subject is a vigorous frontiersman, opinionated and cruel as well as creative and foresighted; S.'s mixture of fear and admiration for him are ably conveyed. In his story S. epitomized the recent history of her part of the West.

Five other works later joined *Old Jules* as parts of the Great Plains series. *Crazy Horse* (1942) is a biography of the Oglala chief, stories of whom S. had heard in her girlhood from old traders, frontiersmen, and Indians; *Cheyenne Autumn* (1953) tells of an epic flight of the northern Cheyenne Indians. *The Buffalo Hunters* (1954), *The Cattlemen* (1958), and *The Beaver Men* (1964) study aspects of the economic history of the West, evoking people, landscape, and events and showing their interactions through several hundred years. Two projected volumes were never written; one, the introduction to the series, would have dealt with stone-age people, the other with the impact of oil upon the history of the region. S. considered this series the contribution upon which her reputation would rest. As history the books are flawed by lack of documentation and by fuzzy handling of dates and chronology; as evocative recreations of their time and place they are unsurpassed.

S.'s fiction uses similar materials. Of her novels, only *Capital City* (1939) is set in the present. One of many antifascist novels of the period, it analyzes a thinly disguised Nebraska and is flawed by its lack of a clear central character and focus.

The four novels set in the past are firmly rooted in historical fact. *Slogum House* (1937), the story of a woman who ruthlessly uses her family to build an empire, vividly depicts frontier violence. Murders, prostitution, and the castration of a man she perceives as an enemy are incidents in the growth of the central character's power. *The Tom-Walker* (1947) follows three generations of war veterans (of the Civil War, World War I, and World War II) from their return home, wounded in body and spirit, through their disillusioning attempts to adjust to a corrupt society. *Miss Morissa* (1955), the story of a young woman doctor who makes a life for herself on the frontier, is dedicated to three actual women doctors of the period. *Son of the Gamblin' Man* (1960) is a fictionalized biography of the painter Robert Henri, son of a frontier gambler and community builder. Through her imaginative recreation of the complicated relationship between father and son, S. mirrored the development of a section of Nebraska.

In her late years, S. received many honors, both as novelist and as historian. Her brutally realistic depictions of frontier violence and lawlessness and her penetrating analyses of western history give her a secure place among those who have tried to understand that region both as it actually was and as a mythic force in the American consciousness.

WORKS: *Old Jules* (1935). *Slogum House* (1937). *Capital City* (1939). *Crazy Horse, the Strange Man of the Oglalas: A Biography* (1942). *The Tom-Walker* (1947). *Cheyenne Autumn* (1953). *The Buffalo Hunters: The Story of the Hide Men* (1954). *Winter Thunder* (1954). *Miss Morissa: Doctor of the Gold Trail* (1955). *The Horsecatcher* (1957). *The Cattlemen: From the Rio Grande across the Far Marias* (1958). *Hostiles and Friendlies: Selected Short Writings* (1959). *Son of the Gamblin' Man: The Youth of an Artist* (1960). *Love Song to the Plains* (1961). *These Were the Sioux* (1961). *The Far Looker* (1962). *The Story Catcher* (1963). *The Beaver Men: Spearheads of Empire* (1964). *Old Jules Country: A Selection from Old Jules and Thirty Years of Writing since the Book Was Published* (1965). *The Old Jules Home Region* (1965). *The Battle of the Little Bighorn* (1966). *Sandhill Sundays, and Other Recollections* (1966). *The Christmas of the Phonograph Records: A Recollection* (1966).

BIBLIOGRAPHY: *American West* 2 (Spring 1965). PrS (40, 1966; 41, 1967; 42, 1968; 45, 1971).

MARY JEAN DeMARR

Margaret Sanger

B. *14 Sept. 1879, Corning, New York;* d. *6 Sept. 1966, Tucson, Arizona*
D. *of Michael and Anne Purcell Higgins;* m. *William Sanger, 1902;*
    m. *J. N. H. Slee, 1922*

S.'s mother died, leaving eleven children, when S. was seventeen. Profoundly affected by her mother's death, S. would later refer to women like her as "breeders," and would dedicate *Women and the New Race* (1920) to her.

S. trained as a nurse, married Sanger, an architect, had three children, and lived in suburban Hastings-on-Hudson for ten years. After the destruction of their new home (an event which S. was later to see as symbolic), the Sangers moved to New York City and became involved in socialist and union activities. This activity and her earlier experiences led to S.'s feminist writings. The Sangers' 1913 trip to Europe spelled the end of their eleven-year marriage. After visiting Glasgow to research an article on the benefits of municipal ownership for women and children, S. went to France where she discovered that, in contrast to Scotland and America, contraceptive information was available and poverty was limited. After some time of "inactive, incoherent brooding," S. returned to America, with her three children but without her husband.

On her return S. took up the cause of woman suffrage, linking it loosely to birth control. In 1914, she founded the journal *The Woman Rebel*, written by women and for women. Contributors included Voltairine De Cleyre and Emma Goldman. The first issue was an unfocused burst of rage, with a rather sharp statement of feminist community and less concern for birth control than for emancipation. Although *The Woman Rebel* never included much birth-control information, sending any through the mail was illegal, so S. was arrested and forced to flee to Canada and Europe until the charges were dropped.

In 1916, S. opened the first birth-control clinic in America in the Brownsville section of Brooklyn. She also established the *Birth Control Review*, a publication greatly superior to *The Woman Rebel*. S.'s feminist rage had become sharply focused on the problem of birth control. *Birth Control Review* continued until 1928.

S.'s greatest successes came with her association with America's health professionals in achieving the legalization and availability of birth control. With physicians, social workers, and technicians to staff it, she opened the Clinical Research Bureau. When the police raided the clinic in 1929 and seized the confidential physicians' records, the medical profession defended its right to dispense birth-control information. In 1936, a U.S. District Court upheld that right, which had been denied previously by the Comstock Law. In 1932, S. had rallied individuals across the nation to join the National Committee on Federal Legislation for Birth Control, and in 1937—one year after the court decision—the American Medical Association publicly endorsed birth control, bringing American physicians and their prestige to the side of S.'s cause. The National Birth Control League and S.'s clinics were combined in 1942 to form the Planned Parenthood Association of America.

S.'s many publications consistently express her view that women are victim and need to "free themselves from involuntary motherhood." Concerned mainly for working-class women, S. believed that they were victimized by their husbands, their doctors, and their priests. They suffered from the sexual appetites and insensitivity of the first, from the passivity of the second, and from the doctrine of the third. S. writes in *Woman and the New Race* (1920): "Women are determined to decide for themselves whether they shall become mothers, under what conditions and when. This is the fundamental revolt. . . . It is for woman the key to the temple of liberty."

In *Happiness in Marriage* (1926), S. claims that men are the sexual aggressors, while women are sexually passive. Female sexuality, she maintains, has not been expressed; if it were, it could become a creative force; and birth control is the means by which it could be released.

Even after her marriage to Slee, a wealthy industrialist, S. continued to address the problems of working-class women. *Motherhood in Bondage* (1928) is based on five thousand of the two hundred and fifty thousand letters she claimed to have received in response to *The New Woman*. The letters are arranged in chapters entitled "Girl Mothers," "The Problem of Poverty," "The Trap of Maternity," "The Struggle of the Unfit," and "The Sins of the Fathers."

To S., the birth-control movement meant not only prevention of unwanted babies and abortions but, more importantly, the rational control of the individual woman's body and spirit, synthesized into female sexuality, as well as the subsequent lessening of war and of suffering. Her numerous publications, starting from the premise that women had always been the victims of men and society, are devoted to changing that role.

WORKS: *What Every Girl Should Know* (1913). *Family Limitation* (1914). *What Every Mother Should Know* (1914). *Dutch Methods of Birth Control* (1915). *Woman and the New Race* (1920). *Appeals from American Mothers* (1921). *Sayings of Others on Birth Control* (1921). *The Pivot of Civilization* (1922). *Happiness in Marriage* (1926). *Problems of Overpopulation* (1926). *Religious and Ethical Aspects of Birth Control* (1926). *What Every Boy and Girl Should Know* (1927). *Motherhood in Bondage* (1928). *My Fight for Birth Control* (1931). *Woman of the Future* (1934). *Margaret Sanger: An Autobiography* (1938).

BIBLIOGRAPHY: Dash, J., *A Life on One's Own: Three Gifted Women and the Men They Married* (1973). Douglas, E. T., *Margaret Sanger: Pioneer of the Future* (1970). Kennedy, D., *Birth Control in America: The Career of Margaret Sanger* (1970).

JULIANN E. FLEENOR

May Sarton

B. 3 May 1912, Wondelgem, Belgium
Given name: Eléanore Marie Sarton
D. of George and Mabel Elwes Sarton

S. is an only child. Her father was a noted historian of science; her mother, an artist and designer. S. became a naturalized U.S. citizen in 1924. She originally planned a career in the theater and served a valuable apprenticeship in Eva LeGallienne's Civic Repertory Theater. She founded and was director at the Apprentice Theatre (New School for Social Research) and was director of the Associated Actors Theatre in Hartford, Connecticut. From her mid-twenties, however, S. has devoted herself to the craft of writing.

S.'s autobiographical writings achieve a clear, candid, conversational tone and are significant explorations of the life of the mind and of the writer at work. It is S.'s belief that genuinely valid autobiography must move beyond reportage of event or even feeling and extend into an examination of motive, impulse, thought, and belief; and her journals are enriched by miniature informal essays which provide these explorations.

I Knew a Phoenix (1959) closely traces S.'s early life. In *Plant Dreaming Deep* (1968), S. uses her renovation of an old house in Nelson, New

Hampshire, as an effective metaphor for the establishment of roots and nourishment of the spirit. *Journal of a Solitude* (1973) deals frankly with the pain, frustration, and rage of the human experience. *A World of Light* (1976) is a series of fascinating character sketches of S.'s friends and relatives. In *The House by the Sea* (1977), S.'s home in York, Maine, is a symbol of the joys of productive solitude. S.'s recuperation from a mastectomy becomes the symbol for overcoming emotional deprivation and despondancy caused by harsh reviews in *Recovering* (1980), one of her most effective journals.

S.'s poetry often discusses the balance growing from difficult human choices. Her tenet that "form is freedom" accounts for the frequent employment of traditional poetic forms, although she also works in free verse. S. believes that the "white heat" of inspiration fuses the poet's critical and emotional selves to trigger artistically productive revision. "Prayer before Work," from *Inner Landscape* (1939), is an evocation of such inspiration.

In both poetry and fiction, S. treats the social and political questions of the day. "Night Watch," from *A Grain of Mustard Seed* (1971), compares human sickness and social ills. *Faithful Are the Wounds* (1955) fictionalizes the political witch hunts of the 1950s with force, wisdom, and understanding. *Crucial Conversations* (1975) includes comments about the Watergate scandal.

Mrs. Stevens Hears the Mermaids Singing (1965) is the story of an elderly, successful writer who reviews her life and work during an important interview and in preparation for helping a young friend at odds with himself and his sexuality. Frank, direct, powerful, this novel ranks among S.'s best work and is an example of why S. is often hailed as a spokesperson for women writers.

Death is a topic S. treats in all the genres she employs, and the tonal and philosophical span is generous, ranging from the contemplative comments of *The House by the Sea* through the furious protest of Caroline Spencer, the protagonist of *As We Are Now* (1973), who transforms her death into an indictment of society's attitudes toward the aged and the infirm. Brief, spare, blunt, the splendid characterizations of *As We Are Now* elevate it far above most protest fiction.

One of S.'s constant and most compelling themes is friendship, as in *The Birth of a Grandfather* (1957), in which the terminal illness of a close friend engenders a middle-aged man's reconsideration of himself and his values, and *Kinds of Love* (1970), a character study of two lifelong women friends.

The Small Room (1961) compares and contrasts Lucy Winter's growth as a teacher with her developing ability to function as an independent person. Her many committed colleagues serve as Lucy's mentors as she seeks to understand not only herself but also a brilliant student who has broken under the demands of personal pride and faculty pressure. Honest, compassionate, discerning, *The Small Room* is a major novel, its treatment of the student-teacher relationship singularly effective.

Steadily productive, unusually successful in her explorations of both isolation and union, S. is a serious writer who has won great popularity, with significant achievements in three major genres.

WORKS: *Encounter in April* (1937). *The Single Hound* (1938). *Inner Landscape* (1939). *The Bridge of Years* (1946). *The Underground River: A Play in Three Acts* (1947). *The Lion and the Rose* (1948). *Leaves of the Tree* (1950). *Shadow of a Man* (1950). *A Shower of Summer Days* (1952). *The Land of Silence* (1953). *Faithful Are the Wounds* (1955). *The Birth of a Grandfather* (1957). *The Fur Person* (1957). *In Memorium* (1957). *The Writing of a Poem* (1957). *In Time Like Air* (1958). *I Knew a Phoenix* (1959). *Cloud, Stone, Sun, Vine* (1961). *The Small Room* (1961). *The Design of a Novel* (1963). *Joanna and Ulysses* (1963). *Mrs. Stevens Hears the Mermaids Singing* (1965). *Miss Pickthorn and Mr. Hare* (1966). *A Private Mythology* (1966). *As Does New Hampshire* (1967). *Plant Dreaming Deep* (1968). *The Poet and the Donkey* (1969). *Kinds of Love* (1970). *A Grain of Mustard Seed* (1971). *A Durable Fire* (1972). *As We Are Now* (1973). *Journal of a Solitude* (1973). *Collected Poems (1930–1973)* (1974). *Punch's Secret* (1974). *Crucial Conversations* (1975). *The Leopard Land: Alice and Haniel Long's Santa Fé* (1976). *A Walk through the Woods* (1976). *A World of Light* (1976). *The House by the Sea* (1977). *A Reckoning* (1978). *Selected Poems* (Eds. S. Hilsinger and L. Byrnes, 1978). *Halfway to Silence* (1980). *Recovering* (1980). *Writings on Writing* (1981).

BIBLIOGRAPHY: Anderson, D. H., in *Images of Women in Fiction*, Ed. S. K. Cornillon (1972). Bakerman, J. S., "May Sarton's *The Small Room*: A Comparison and an Analysis," *Chrysallis* 1 (Summer 1975). Blouin, L. P., *May Sarton: A Bibliography* (1978). Sibley, A., *May Sarton* (1972).

Other references: *Hollins Critic* (June 1974). *NewR* (8 June 1974). *PW* (24 June 1974).

JANE S. BAKERMAN

Alma Sioux Scarberry

B. 24 June 1899, Carter County, Kentucky
Writes under: Beatrice Fairfax, Annie Laurie, Alma Sioux Scarberry
D. of George Washington and Caledonia Lee Patrick Scarberry; m. Theodore
  A. Klein, 1930

S. is the daughter of a Kentucky fundamentalist minister. Her early home life was difficult; her father, a stern disciplinarian, remarried several times, and S. often had to support herself as a child. She began to write prose and poetry at an early age, and writing always seemed natural to her.

After working her way through a semester at New Bethlehem Business College in Pennsylvania, S. moved in 1917 to New York City, selling varnish to pay her way. S. first found a sales job in a Brooklyn department store, but soon enlisted in the Navy, serving a year as one of the first Yeomanettes. S. took a position with King Features in 1920, first writing daily love columns under the names Beatrice Fairfax and Annie Laurie, but soon writing under her own byline for the New York *American, Graphic*, and *Mirror*. She won fame for her feature articles and daring publicity stunts. S. also appeared on Broadway in Irving Berlin's Music Box Revue (1922–23) and in the Shubert revival of *The Mikado* (1924).

In 1926, S. moved to Pittsburgh to write a daily column and features for the Pittsburgh *Sun Telegraph*. On her editor's dare, she wrote her first novel. The tremendous popularity of *Make Up* (1931) won her a contract as columnist and serial writer with Central Press in 1928. After her marriage, S. moved to Chicago, where her first radio drama, *The Girl Reporter*, was purchased and produced by NBC. In 1930, she began to write for the Bell Syndicate and North American Newspaper Alliance. The next fourteen years would see all twenty-one of her romances published serially; only twelve were republished in book form. S.'s son was born in 1930.

In 1940, S. took a publicity job with Columbia Broadcasting System in Hollywood, soon moving to head the writing department of the Mutual Don Lee Network to write radio dramas and general continuity. From 1944 to 1946, S. directed the Radio Bureau of the National War Fund in New York. The years after 1946 were productive; she wrote features, columns, and songs for films. *The Doofer Family*, a serial fantasy for children which was inspired by songs and jokes she enjoyed with her young son and is S.'s own favorite, appeared through General Features (1955–56).

During the Korean War, S. was a soldier show technician for the U.S. Army, stationed at Fort Chaffee, Arkansas. S. worked as public relations director for Columbus Plastics in Columbus, Ohio, from 1959 until 1965, when she moved to Austin, Texas. Since 1965, she has handled public relations for good causes and has contributed columns to magazines and newspapers. S. is currently featured in a local radio talk show and writes and stars in television commercials.

S.'s romances are readable, with interesting characters, rapidly developed action, and lively dialogue. The serials reflect the author's experiences and views. Like Janet James of *Make Up* and Rosalie March of *Dimpled Racketeer* (1931), S.'s heroines are often attractive and talented country girls who come to the city naive but eager to get ahead. But like singer Elanda Lee of *High Hat* (1930), determined to get a break in radio, or dancer Jan Keats of *Rainbow over Broadway* (1936), determined to become a Broadway star, S.'s heroines are characterized by independence, hard work, and a refusal to compromise values and expectations. After finding independence and success, they can make room in their lives for love, happiness, and a home with a reliable, honest, and sensitive man. All offer readers the vicarious experience of the best of both a brilliant career and a loving family. Each novel climaxes with the happy marriage of hero and heroine, a marriage that resolves all subplots.

For S., writing has always meant the use of a particular kind of talent for profit. Inspiration usually begins with characters. When these are fully developed, a plot forms around them. From the plot outline, the writing comes quickly. As S. puts it: "Writing takes three things. It requires an active creative imagination which leads to a pattern, a formula. And it requires a market. Without a market, a writer really has no purpose." The great popularity of S.'s serial fiction indicates her success and understanding in creating for the market of her choice.

WORKS: *The Flat Tire* (1930). *High Hat: A Radio Romance* (1930). *Dimpled Racketeer* (1931). *Make Up: A Romance of the Footlights* (1931). *Flighty: A Romance of Gypsy O'Malley—A Girl Who Lived Down Her Family* (1932). *Puppy Love: A Hollywood Romance* (1933). *Penthouse Love* (1934). *Too Wise to Marry* (1935). *Rainbow Over Broadway* (1936). *Too Many Beaus* (1936). *Thou Shalt Not Love* (1937). *The Lady Proposes* (1941).

KATHERINE STAPLES

Dorothy Scarborough

B. 27 Jan. 1878, Mount Carmel, Texas; d. 7 Nov. 1935, New York City
D. of John B. and Mary Adelaide Ellison Scarborough

S. came from a prosperous southern background—both grandfathers owned large plantations, and her father was a lawyer and judge. S. received her B.A. (1896) and M.A. (1898) from Baylor University, where she taught from 1905 to 1914. She did advanced graduate work at the University of Chicago, Oxford University, and Columbia University (Ph.D. 1917). She joined the faculty of Columbia, specializing in teaching short-story writing.

S.'s doctoral dissertation, *The Supernatural in Modern English Fiction* (1917), is an important scholarly work. She establishes the Gothic romance and French, Italian, German, and Russian works as primary influences on the use of the supernatural in modern literature. She discusses the supernatural by categories: modern ghosts, the devil, folktales, and supernatural science. S. concludes that the war was the cause for the contemporary interest in the supernatural and that American writers are essentially responsible for combining humor and the supernatural.

S. contributed book reviews, sometimes covering more than twenty works in a single review, to publications such as the New York *Sun*, *The Bookman*, and *The Dial*. She attacks writers who use fiction as a vehicle for propaganda or didacticism. Unfortunately, as many reviewers have noted, this criticism is applicable to her own novels and short stories. S. is praised for her realistic presentation, but condemned for her editorializing.

Many of S.'s novels use the Texas farmlands as setting. The plots revolve around romance, but love is frequently hampered by the problems facing the tenant farmer, the economics of the cotton industry, the threat of drought, flood, and the boll weevil. The depiction of natural forces in *The Wind* (1925) has been compared with that of Conrad (*Times Literary Supplement*, 5 Nov. 1925); the 1928 film, starring Lillian Gish, was, however, criticized for excessive use of nature imagery.

Impatient Griselda (1927) is one novel not flawed by propagandizing. Again the setting is a small Texas town with its typical inhabitants: the minister and his wife and children, the doctor, the do-gooder, the busybody, the Negro cook. S. contrasts two types of women: the seductress

(Lilith) and the wife (Irene). The novel opens with the death of one Lilith as she gives birth to a second. Irene marries Lilith's widower (Guinn the minister) and raises the stepdaughter Lilith and her own four children, but feels she never replaces either Lilith in her husband's heart. The book closes with the death of the second Lilith as she gives birth to a third-generation Lilith. Irene sees the cycle continuing as her own daughter must stand in for another Lilith. The types remain unreconciled.

S. did important research in collecting folk songs and ballads; her interest dated back to her early teaching career in Texas. In *On the Trail of Negro Folk-Songs* (1925) and *A Song Catcher in Southern Mountains* (sponsored by "Project 41" at Columbia University and published posthumously in 1937), S. discusses origins, influences, instruments, and variations and provides melodies for many songs. (Ola Lee Gulledge collected and transcribed the music in the first book.) *On the Trail of Negro Folk-Songs* includes a chapter on the blues based primarily on a visit with W. C. Handy. S. uses these songs extensively in her novels and the autobiographical *From a Southern Porch* (1919).

Humor pervades S.'s writings; she employs informal language, coins words, and puns. A modern reader may be annoyed by S.'s facile stereotyping of races (she shows blacks as a happy people singing while they toil in field or kitchen) or amused by her genteel treatment of passion and illegitimate birth, but her novels are entertaining. A scholar may be frustrated by the lack of scholarly apparatus in *The Supernatural in Modern English Fiction*, but S. has made significant contributions to scholarship with her dissertation and folk-song collecting.

WORKS: *Fugitive Verses* (1912). *The Supernatural in Modern English Fiction* (1917). *From a Southern Porch* (1919). *Famous Modern Ghost Stories* (edited by Scarborough, 1921). *Humorous Ghost Stories* (edited by Scarborough, 1921). *In the Land of Cotton* (1923). *On the Trail of Negro Folk-Songs* (with O. L. Gulledge, 1925). *The Wind* (1925; film version, 1928). *Impatient Griselda* (1927). *Can't Get a Red Bird* (1929). *The Stretch-berry Smile* (1932). *The Story of Cotton* (1933). *Selected Short Stories of Today* (edited by Scarborough, 1935). *A Song Catcher in Southern Mountains: American Folk-Songs of British Ancestry* (1937).

BIBLIOGRAPHY: Overton, G., *The Women Who Make Our Novels* (1928). For articles in reference works, see: *DAB*, Suppl. 1. *20thCA*.
Other references: *Bookman* 50 (Jan. 1920). *PW* (16 Nov. 1935). *NYT* (8 Nov. 1935). *NYTBR* (11 Nov. 1917; 14 Aug. 1927; 27 Oct. 1929; 14 Feb. 1932; 11 April 1937). *TLS* (15 Nov. 1917; 5 Nov. 1925; 20 Nov. 1937).

NANCY G. ANDERSON

Evelyn Scott

B. 17 Jan. 1893, Clarksville, Tennessee; d. 1963, New York City
Given Name: Elsie Dunn
Wrote under: Evelyn Scott, E. Souza
D. of Seely and Thomas Dunn; common law marriage, Frederick Creighton
  Wellman (Cyril Kay Scott), 1919; m. John Metcalf, 1928

Although S.'s family no longer held the moneyed position it enjoyed before the Civil War. S. was trained the values of the southern aristocratic
tradition. At fifteen, she rejected the role of the southern woman and
became an ardent feminist. The Dunn family moved to New Orleans when
S. was eighteen. She enrolled in Sophie Newcomb College, but never
finished her studies there; instead, she educated herself.

In 1913, S. ran away to Brazil with the dean of the School of Tropical
Medicine of Tulane University. They changed their names to Evelyn and
Cyril Kay Scott. One son was born of this union in Brazil.

The Scotts returned from Brazil in 1920, lived in Greenwich Village
and Cape Cod, and separated in Bermuda. In 1928, S. married British novelist John Metcalf.

Escapade (1923) is an account of S.'s six-year exile with her lover in
Brazil. It is written in a subjectively impressionistic style, controlled by a
conception: the entanglement of life and death in a conflict between the
lush tropical growth soaring above villages of earthy natives and S.'s
deathlike isolation. By selecting images that express feelings and actions, S.
balances emotionalism with understanding, and avoids immersion in sub-
jectivity. S. endured hunger, squalor, severe illness, and a fearful pregnancy. Each episode or carefully composed moment is imbued with S.'s
belief that only in the presence of death do we discover life.

Background in Tennessee (1937) is an autobiographical history in
which S. discusses the sociological, economic, religious, and cultural
growth of the South, integrating her own experiences and judgments. S.
believed the slow growth of culture in the South was due to the short
span of time between the Revolution and the Civil War; most of the important men of the South were orators and politicians, not artists.

S. wrote several triologies of novels. *The Narrow House* (1921), *Narcissus* (1922), and *The Golden Door* (1925) are about three generations

of a family attempting to hold on to their self-made ideals and hollow beliefs. *Migrations* (1927), *The Wave* (1929), and *A Calendar of Sin* (1932) cover American history from 1850 to 1918. In *The Wave*, set during the Civil War, S. combined over one hundred episodes in a deliberately structured mosaic, illustrating the conflict of individuals with society and with themselves. S. equated the perversion of war with the perversion of love lying in the heart of each individual.

The range of S.'s other publications is broad. *Precipitations* (1920), her first book, is of imagist poetry. *The Winter Alone* (1930) contains poetry more varied in subject and techniques. *Love*, a play, was performed by the Provincetown Players in 1930. S. wrote a mystery, *Blue Rum* (1930), under the name E. Souza, and three juvenile books: *In the Endless Sands* (1925), *Witch Perkins* (1928), and *Billy, the Maverick* (1934).

S. possessed the rare combination of emotional intuition and an artistic genius for style and technique. She was a fervent intellectual, sensitive but analytical. She had no strict philosophy, but she consistently strove in her life and work for freedom from every limitation. S. believed in authorial intrusion and wrote all her fiction from an omniscient point of view, a technique which gave her the freedom she desired. S.'s major works can be read and studied simultaneously on psychological, philosophical, and artistic levels.

WORKS: *Precipitations* (1920). *The Narrow House* (1921). *Narcissus* (1922). *Escapade* (1923). *The Golden Door* (1925). *In The Endless Sands* (1925). *Ideals* (1927). *Migrations* (1927). *Witch Perkins* (1928). *The Wave* (1929). *Blue Rum* (1930). *The Winter Alone* (1930). *A Calendar of Sin* (1932). *Eva Gay* (1933). *Breathe upon These Slain* (1934). *Billy, the Maverick* (1934). *Bread and a Sword* (1937). *Background in Tennessee* (1937). *Shadow of a Hawk* (1941).

The papers of Evelyn Scott and two unfinished novels are in the possession of Robert L. Welker.

BIBLIOGRAPHY: Scott, C. K., *Life Is Too Short* (1943). Welker, R. L., "Liebestod with a Southern Accent," *Reality and Myth* (1964).

For articles in reference works, see: *America Now*, Ed. H. E. Stearns (1938). *Living Authors*, Ed. D. Tante (1935).

PEGGY BACH

Catharine Maria Sedgwick

B. 28 Dec. 1789, Stockbridge, Massachusetts; d. 31 July 1867, West Roxbury, Massachusetts
Wrote under: Miss Sedgwick
D. of Theodore and Pamela Dwight Sedgwick

S.'s father was from a family of New England farmers and tavern keepers. He served in both houses of Congress and as Massachusetts Supreme Court chief justice. Her mother belonged to one of the wealthiest colonial families. Because she was sickly, her seven surviving children were raised by a black servant, Elizabeth Freeman, whom they called "Mumbet."

Education was an important part of the Sedgwicks' daily life. All the children were required to read Hume, Butler, Shakespeare, and Cervantes. S. attended the local grammar school at Stockbridge and was sent to Mrs. Bell's School in Albany and Payne's Finishing School in Boston. S. later commented that the greatest influence on our characters is our childhood home.

Shortly before her father's death in 1813 he unexpectedly confided his liberal religious beliefs to a close friend, the Unitarian minister William Ellery Channing. At this time, S. began to express in her journals and letters her own disapproval of Calvinism, the predominant religion of her Berkshire community. Several years later she joined the Unitarian church in New York. Her brothers Theodore and Henry, both noted lawyers and advocates of social reform, also joined the Unitarian church, but other of her relatives objected to S.'s conversion. An aunt told S., "Come and see me as often as you can, dear, for you know, after this world, we shall never meet again."

In 1822, S. began to write a small pamphlet protesting religious intolerance. This work evolved into a full-length novel entitled *A New England Tale*, which was published anonymously that year. The book is set in the New England countryside, and includes characters who speak in the local dialects. It is the story of a virtuous orphan girl, Jane Elton, who is reduced to extreme poverty. The heroine is mistreated by ostensibly pious relatives until she marries a Quaker gentleman and lives happily ever after. The book exposes the hypocrisy of certain church officials, and includes subplots concerning corrupt lawyers, dueling, and gambling. It was an immediate success. At that time, most books read in the U.S. were British imports or American imitations of British works. *A New England Tale* was recognized as one of the first novels to include authentic American settings, situations, and characters. It was soon a bestseller on both sides of the Atlantic.

With the publication of her second novel, *Redwood* (1824), S. became as popular as her contemporaries Cooper and Irving. *Redwood* was translated into German, Swedish, Italian, and French. The novel is about the marriage of a Southern gentleman to the daughter of a Vermont farmer. It also has a subplot involving the Shaker sect and a charter study of a strong, outspoken New England spinster.

With her third novel, *Hope Leslie* (1827), S. became the most famous American woman writer of her day. S.'s own mother had nearly been a victim in an Indian raid, and one of the family ancestors had married an Indian. The book contains lengthy discussions of Mohawk customs and colonial history. It is the story of three American women: Faith Leslie, who is captured by Indians, marries into the tribe, and adopts its way of life; her sister Hope, who is pursued by a villainous English admiral until his ship sinks in Boston harbor; and Madawisca, an Indian woman who saves Hope's fiancé when Mohawks attack him, and loses her arm in the process. *Hope Leslie* was hailed by critics as an American masterpiece.

S.'s next novel, *Clarence* (1830), discusses fashionable New York society. *The Linwoods* (1835) is a historical romance set during the Revolutionary War. S.'s last novel, *Married or Single?* (1857) was designed, in her words, "to lessen the stigma placed on the term 'old maid.'"

S., who never married, divided her time among the Sedgwick family homes in Stockbridge, Lenox, and New York City. She also toured Europe. Her tea parties were attended by Cooper, Hawthorne, Bryant, Emerson, and Melville. S. kept a journal for most of her life; it describes her spiritual quest, her travels, and her daily activities. She was an active social reformer: she founded the Society for the Aid and Relief of Poor Women and organized the first free school in New York, primarily for Irish immigrant children.

During the second half of her career, S. became famous as the author of didactic stories intended for children and working-class people. She hoped to convince her readers of the importance of education, democracy, and a close-knit family life. She believed that in America social mobility was largely determined by manners. Her most famous didactic novels were the trilogy consisting of *Home* (1835), *The Poor Rich Man and the Rich Poor Man* (1836), and *Live and Let Live* (1837). These books went through fifteen, sixteen, and twelve editions respectively.

S. lived to the age of seventy-eight and was buried next to her nurse Mumbet in Stockbridge. Her contemporary Hawthorne called S. "our most truthful novelist." Her finely crafted writing is more direct than the embellished style of most novels of her time. She was one of the creators of the American literary tradition, and one of the first American novelists to achieve international popularity.

WORKS: *A New England Tale* (1822). *Redwood* (1824). *Hope Leslie* (1827). *Clarence* (1830). *Home* (1835). *The Linwoods* (1835). *The Poor Rich Man and the Rich Poor Man* (1836). *Live and Let Live* (1837). *Letters from Abroad to Kindred at Home* (1841). *The Boy of Mount Rhigi* (1848). *Married or Single?* (1857). *Memoir of Joseph Curtis* (1858).

BIBLIOGRAPHY: Dewey, M., ed., *The Life and Letters of Catharine Maria Sedgwick* (1871). Foster, E. H., *Catharine Maria Sedwick* (1971).
   For articles in reference works, see: *NAW* (article by R. E. Welch, Jr.).

JANE GILES

Anya Seton

B. *1916, New York City*
Writes under: *Anya Seton*
D. *of Ernest Thompson and Grace Gallatin Seton; m. Hamilton Chase, 1934 (?)*

S.'s father was a nature writer; her mother was a feminist, explorer, and writer. S. was educated in England, France, and the U.S. She is married and the mother of two children. She has written thirteen novels, all historical, although her preferred term is "biographical." The variety of periods depicted is remarkable, but the settings are generally either British or American. All tell exciting stories, usually from the point of view of a female protagonist.

   The heroines of the fictionalized biographies are related in some way to men who made history. *My Theodosia* (1941), S.'s first novel and the story of Aaron Burr's only child, dramatizes an obsessive, almost unnatural relationship between father and daughter. *Katherine* (1954) sympathetically recreates the life of Katherine Swynford, mistress and then wife of

John of Gaunt and sister-in-law of Geoffrey Chaucer. *The Winthrop Woman* (1958) centers on Elizabeth Fones Winthrop, niece and daughter-in-law of Jonathan Winthrop, a settler with him of the Massachusetts Bay Colony but a rebel against harsh Puritan rule. *Devil Water* (1962) studies Jenny Radcliffe, daughter of an English Jacobite nobleman who was executed for his participation in the rebellions of 1715 and 1745; her conversion to participation in his cause and her life in England and in Virginia are recreated.

Among the novels not centered on actual events is S.'s best-known work, *Dragonwyck* (1944). Set among Dutch patroons on the Hudson River in the mid-19th c., it contains an effective portrait of a Gothic villain and a heroine who is his innocent accomplice, for her passion and ambition have unconsciously helped cause his crimes. *The Turquoise* (1946), set in late 19th-c. New Mexico and New York, shows its destitute heroine's rise to the top of New York society, inadvertently causing a catastrophe. Her repentance and later life of contrition are movingly depicted. *The Hearth and the Eagle* (1948), set in 19th- and 20th-c. Marblehead, with a flashback to the 17th c., contains another strong heroine whose passionate and impulsive behavior leads her to a series of disappointments, then to ultimate acceptance of values she had earlier rejected.

In recent years, S.'s interest in the occult has led her to the theme of reincarnation. In *Green Darkness* (1972), contemporary characters redress evils that occurred in 1552–1559. *Smouldering Fires* (1975), a mixture of popular psychology and the occult, depicts an ungainly high-school girl who must, through hypnosis, relive the anguish of her Acadian ancestress in order to exorcise it and become a normal young woman.

The Mistletoe and the Sword (1955), set in Roman Britain, tells of the relationship between a Celtic girl and a Roman soldier, their initial enmity gradually being transformed to love. *Avalon* (1965), which moves through the British and Norse worlds of the late 10th c., follows the relationship of a Cornish girl and a French-English prince, whose lives are intertwined but who are always at cross-purposes. These two novels are unusual for S. in that male and female protagonists are balanced against each other, both angles of vision being used about equally.

Foxfire (1950) is the only one of S.'s novels that is not clearly historical. It is set in Arizona in the 1930s and combines the common western myth of the fabulous lost mine with the motif of a Shangri-la.

S.'s female protagonists are passionate and ambitious. In their youthful romantic idealism, they often rush into relationships that are doomed to disaster. The novels generally end with the heroines recognizing their responsibility for their fates and either doing penance or making a new beginning. In the process, they become "strong to endure." The historical backgrounds are based on thorough research. In her afterword to *Avalon*, S. stated her goal as being the attempt "to tell an accurate story, and to illuminate a shadowy corner of the past." That goal she has succeeded in accomplishing in many of her novels.

WORKS: *My Theodosia* (1941). *Dragonwyck* (1944; film version, 1946). *The Turquoise* (1946). *The Hearth and the Eagle* (1948). *Foxfire* (1950; film version, 1954). *Katherine* (1954). *The Mistletoe and the Sword: A Story of Roman Britain* (1955). *The Winthrop Woman* (1958). *Washington Irving* (1960). *Devil Water* (1962). *Avalon* (1965). *Green Darkness* (1972). *Smouldering Fires* (1975).

BIBLIOGRAPHY: NY (6 Feb. 1946). NYTBR (16 March 1941; 16 Feb. 1958; 21 Nov. 1965). SatR (9 Oct. 1954; 15 Feb. 1958; 3 March 1962).

MARY JEAN DeMARR

Anne Sexton

B. 2 Nov. 1928, Newton, Massachusetts; d. 4 Oct. 1974, Weston, Massachusetts
D. of Ralph and Mary Staples Harvey; m. Alfred M. Sexton II, 1948

Although her childhood included winters with her beloved great-aunt at the spacious family residence in Weston, Massachusetts, as well as happy seaside summers in Maine, S. was a demanding, rebellious child who felt rejected by her upper middle-class parents. Her impulsive marriage in 1948 to Alfred Sexton weathered many years of crises before it ended in divorce in 1973. S.'s sudden bouts of suicidal depression, which for several years necessitated separating her from her two small daughters, continued throughout her life, as did her psychiatric care in and out of mental hospitals. All of these problematic relationships form the basis of much of her poetry.

Discovering her poetic interests at age twenty-eight, this attractive housewife from the suburbs of Boston began studying under mentors such as Robert Lowell. S. taught at Boston University from 1970 until she took her life at the age of forty-five.

In *To Bedlam and Part Way Back* (1960), S. probed the intensely personal terrain of madness, guilt, and loss. As she undertakes her poetic journey from madness to partial sanity, her most frequent voice is that of the helpless, dependent child searching into the past for the lost parents and the disinherited self. Her two most famous *Bedlam* poems, "You, Doctor Martin" and "Ringing the Bells," capture the helpless childishness of mental patients who are "like bees caught in the wrong hive."

While many readers objected to her subject matter, the raw power of the *Bedlam* poetry quickly established S. as a new and significant "confessional" poet.

In the Pulitzer Prize–winning *Live or Die* (1966), religious parallels tend to universalize the dilemma of the "mad" persona. Thus, in "For the Year of the Insane," S. tries to overcome the passivity which keeps her "locked in the wrong house" but fumbling for a fragmented prayer to Mary, the "tender physician" who could heal the spiritual sickness of the "unbeliever." A new voice of awareness and self-irony is also heard. In one of her best poems, "Flee on Your Donkey," S. realizes that her madness has lost its "innocence." All the years of "dredging" dreams, "like an old woman with arthritic fingers, / carefully straining the water out," have only brought her back to the same "scene of the disordered senses," the "sad hotel" or mental institution from which she urges herself to flee. This book ends on an affirmative note: "I say *Live, Live* because of the sun, / the dream, the excitable gift."

Probably most notable are her poems on womanhood. In "Those Times . . .," S. remembers childhood humiliations and how she "hid in the closet" waiting "among shoes / I was sure to outgrow" while she "planned my growth and my womanhood." The joyous lyric "Little Girl, My Stringbean, My Lovely Woman" is addressed to her daughter who is about to discover that "women are born twice." The frustrations of being female are the focus of poems like "One for My Dame," "Man and Wife," and "Menstruation at Forty," frustrations which, in "Consorting with Angels," culminate in S.'s weariness with the "gender of things"—her own and that of the "men who sat at my table, / circled around the bowl I offered up."

S.'s interest in the religious drama of self led to an only moderately successful psychodrama, the one-act play *Mercy Street* (produced at the American Place Theatre, New York City, 1969) as well as several experimental short stories. More successful was Conrad Susa's free-form operatic adaptation of *Transformations* (1971), S.'s colloquially rendered poetic fairy tales, which was produced by the Minneapolis Opera Company in 1973 and televised in 1978. These experiments foreshadow some of the characteristics of S.'s later poetry: the looser poetic-prose line, the bold image, and the informal interpretations of mythic characters and situations.

Although S.'s poetry has sometimes been labeled bathetic or hysterical, the startling force of the hyperbolic image is her forte. In her best poetry,

S. explores the intensely personal but also universal conflict between the creative and self-destructive selves, a schizophrenic drama controlled by formal metrical patterns and casually placed rhymes. The elegaic voice searches for the lost, original self that has been tainted with experience and repressed in shame.

Although the frankness of her approach and the rather limited range of her autobiographical themes will continue to alienate some readers, S. has attained a significant ranking among contemporary confessional poets.

WORKS: *To Bedlam and Part Way Back* (1960). *All My Pretty Ones* (1962). *Eggs of Things* (with M. Kumin, 1963). *More Eggs of Things* (with M. Kumin, 1964). *Live or Die* (1966). *Selected Poems* (1967). *Poems* (with D. Livingston and T. Kinsella, 1968). *Love Poems* (1969). *Transformations* (1971). *Joey and the Birthday Present* (with M. Kumin, 1971). *The Book of Folly* (1972). *O Ye Tongues* (1973). *The Death Notebooks* (1974). *The Awful Rowing toward God* (1975). *The Wizard's Tears* (with M. Kumin, 1975). *45 Mercy Street* (Ed. L. G. Sexton, 1976). *Anne Sexton: A Self-Portrait in Letters* (Ed. L. G. Sexton, 1977).

BIBLIOGRAPHY: Fields, B., in *Poets in Progress: Critical Prefaces to Thirteen Modern American Poets*, Ed. E. Hungerford (1967). Fields, B., in *American Poets in 1976*, Ed. W. Heyen (1976). Lacey, P. A., *The Inner War: Forms and Themes in Recent American Poetry* (1976). McClatchy, J. D., ed., *Anne Sexton: The Artist and Her Critics* (1978). Mills, Jr., R. J., *Contemporary American Poetry* (1966). Nicholas, K. L., "The Hungry Beast Rowing Toward God: Anne Sexton's Later Religious Poetry," *NMAL*3 (Summer 1979). Northouse, C., and Walsh, R. P., *Sylvia Plath and Anne Sexton: A Reference Guide* (1974). Phillips, R., *The Confessional Poets* (1973). Rizza, P., "Another Side of This Life: Women as Poets," in *American Poetry Since 1960: Some Critical Perspectives*, Ed. R. Shaw (1973). Rosenthal, M. L., *The New Poets: American and British Poetry Since World War II* (1967).

Other references: *CentR* 19 (Spring 1975).

KATHLEEN L. NICHOLS

Mary Elizabeth Wilson Sherwood

B. 27 Oct. 1826, Keene, New Hampshire; d. 12 Sept. 1903, New York City
D. of James and Mary Lord Richardson Wilson; m. John Sherwood, 1851

S. was the oldest of seven children of a distinguished family of Scotch-Irish origin. She attended a fashionable private school for girls in Boston, where the training focused on good manners, not academic studies. S. became part of Washington social life as a hostess during her father's term in Congress (1847-50). Upon her mother's death in 1884 S. also assumed the duties of family management.

After her marriage to a New York lawyer, S. settled in Manhattan. She had four sons. Robert Sherwood, the playwright, was a grandson.

S. first began to sponsor literary events in a fund-raising effort for the restoration of Mount Vernon. By the 1870s, the Sherwood residence had become an establishment in New York literary and philanthropic circles. S. served as president of the Causeries, a literary gathering of distinguished New York women and was a member of several benevolent societies.

The drain on the family resources induced by entertaining persuaded S. to turn her efforts toward writing professionally. She had already published short stories and occasional verse in New York and Boston magazines. *A Transplanted Rose* (1882), her second novel, about the acceptance of a western girl into New York society, and a later, similar novel, *Sweet-Brier* (1889), were well-received. S. also published a volume of poetry and two autobiographical books, *An Epistle to Posterity* (1897) and *Here & There & Everywhere* (1898). Her style is lively, idiomatic, and touched with humor. S.'s most notable works, however, are in the field of etiquette. S.'s experience in Washington and Europe, where she traveled extensively, gave her great familiarity with a variety of styles of manners. Her articles on manners appeared in *Atlantic, Scribner's, Harper's, Appleton's Journal,* and *Frank Leslie's Weekly. Manners and Social Usages* (1884) was the most successful of S.'s books.

S. wrote popular manuals of style treating such standard topics as table manners and the art of conversation. Like later 20th-c. philosophers of social convention such as Emily Post, Amy Vanderbilt, and Peg Bracken, S.

pointed to kindness and regard for others as the universal law of manners. S. was, however, keenly aware of class differences. She was frank and firm in advocating the leadership of society by a class possessing talent and money. This was largely in reaction to the "upstarts" of the lower orders who were coming into sudden fortunes and social prominence.

S.'s several books on etiquette are addressed to a *status quo* of domestic women in the roles of wives and mothers—ladies of leisure and some means, whose main duties were, in S.'s belief, to temper the uncivilized tendencies of men and to serve as exemplars of congenial and decorous interpersonal relations. Like those social arbiters following her, S. sees women as the directors and managers of social setting and action.

Although S. can be criticized for not using her talents for more serious ends, and although her assessment of the role of good manners and the position of women in society was conservative, she should be remembered as the author of the most influential etiquette book of her time.

WORKS: *The Sarcasm of Destiny; or, Nina's Experience* (1878). *Amenities of Home* (1881). *A Transplanted Rose* (1882). *Etiquette* (1884). *Home Amusements* (1884). *Manners and Social Usages* (1884). *Royal Girls and Royal Courts* (1887). *Sweet-Brier* (1889). *The Art of Entertaining* (1892). *Poems by M.E.W.S.* (1892). *An Epistle to Posterity: Being Rambling Recollections of Many Years of My Life* (1897). *Here & There & Everywhere: Reminiscences* (1898).

BIBLIOGRAPHY: For articles in reference works, see: *AW. NAW* (article by B. A. Weller).
   Other references: *NYT* (15 Sept. 1903).

                                        MARGARET J. KING

Lydia Howard Huntley Sigourney

B. 1 Sept. 1791, Norwich, Connecticut; d. 10 June 1865, Hartford, Connecticut
D. of Ezekiel and Zerviah Wentworth Huntley

S. was christened "Lydia Howard," in memory of her father's deceased first wife. As a child, she was favored by the widow of Dr. Daniel Lathrop, who employed S.'s father as a gardener. Mme. Lathrop made a pet of the clever, bookish girl, read with her and nurtured her sentimental tastes. After Mme. Lathrop's death in 1806, S. became acquainted with Lathrop's relatives, the Wadsworths of Hartford, and with their assistance, she and a friend—Nancy Maria Hyde—opened a school in Hartford in 1814. In 1815 Daniel Wadsworth helped her publish her first volume of poetry, *Moral Pieces*. In the following year, S. published her first elegiac volume, a tribute to her former colleague, Nancy Maria Hyde.

In 1819, S. gave up teaching to marry Charles Sigourney, a widower with three young children. Five children were born to her, of whom two survived infancy. When her husband's hardware business began to fail in the 1820s, S. turned to writing as a source of income and quickly became successful. A book of her poems was published by Samuel Goodrich ("Peter Parley") in 1827. By 1830, according to her biographer Gordon Haight, more than twenty periodicals were regularly accepting her occasional verse.

S. was early labelled "the American Hemans," a reference to her English counterpart, Mrs. Felicia Hemans, a popular writer of elegiac verse. S.'s work was indeed derivative and, like Heman's, unstintingly sentimental. Best known as a contributor to the "graveyard school" of popular verse, her "tributes," sometimes written at the request of unknown admirers, combine stilted rhetoric, conventional Christian consolation, and commonplace references to the condition or character of the deceased. Collections of her verse catalogue occasions on which the mourning note may be sounded. In one such volume, "The Anniversary of the Death of An Aged Friend" is followed by other verses lamenting deaths—"The Faithful Editor," "The Babe Who Loved Music," "The Good Son," "A Sunday

School Scholar," and "The Original Proprietor of Mount Auburn" (a well-known rural cemetary near Boston). Despite the individualized titles, the verses are almost interchangeable evocations of genteel religiosity and the postures of decorous sorrow. Such collections, prettily printed and illustrated, were republished throughout S.'s lifetime. Their popularity reflects conventional attitudes toward death, the quality of popular piety, and the widespread admiration for cultured refinement in Victorian America.

Always a popular writer, S. was never respected by contemporary literati. Edgar Allan Poe condemned her imitation of Hemans and her "gemmy," or over-colored, diction. (S. described her home, for example, as a "domain . . . beloved by flowers" where life "in its varied forms, biped and quadrupedal, leaped and luxuriated among us.") Bayard Taylor in *Diversions of the Echo Club* (1876) parodied her verse "to see whether a respectable jingle of words, expressing ordinary and highly proper feelings, can be so imitated as to be recognized." The best known parody of S.'s style and its imitators is Mark Twain's "Ode to Stephen Dowling Bots, Dec'd" in *The Adventures of Huckleberry Finn* (1884). However meagre its merits, S.'s verse is an important index of an era in American taste, and she herself was hailed by Taylor as "good old Mother Sigourney" who had once been "almost our only woman-poet." John Greenleaf Whittier, in a memorial verse of 1887, also noted that "She sang alone, ere womanhood had known / The gift of song which fills the air today."

WORKS: *Moral Pieces* (1815). *The Writings of Nancy Maria Hyde* (1816). *The Square Table* (1819). *Traits of the Aborigines of America* (1822). *Sketch of Connecticut Forty Years Since* (1824). *Poems* (1827). *Female Biography* (1829). *Biography of Pious Persons* (1832). *Evening Readings in History* (1833). *The Farmer and Soldier* (1833). *How to Be Happy* (1833). *The Intemperate* (1833). *Letters to Young Ladies* (1833). *Memoir of Phebe P. Hammond* (1833). *Report of the Hartford Female Beneficient Society* (1833). *Poems* (1834). *Poetry for Children* (1834). *Sketches* (1834). *Tales and Essays for Children* (1835). *Memoir of Margaret and Henrietta Flower* (1835). *Zinzendorff, and Other Poems* (1835). *History of Marcus Aurelius* (1936). *Olive Buds* (1836). *Poems for Children* (1836). *History of the Condition of Women* (1837). *The Girl's Reading-Book . . .* (1838). *Letters to Mothers* (1838). *The Boy's Reading-book . . .* (1839). *The Religious Souvenir for 1839* (1839). *Memoir of Mrs. Mary Ann Hooker* (1840). *The Religous Souvenir for 1840* (1840). *Letters to Young Ladies* (1841). *Pocahontas, and Other Poems* (1841). *Poems, Religious and Elegiac* (1841). *Pleasant Memories of Pleasant Lands* (1842). *The Pictorial Reader . . .* (1844). *The Lovely Sisters* (1845). *Poetry for Seamen* (1845). *Scenes in My Native Land* (1845). *Myrtis, with Other Etchings and Sketchings* (1846). *The Voice of Flowers* (1846). *The Weeping Willow* (1847). *Water-drops* (1848). *The Young Ladies Offering* (with others, 1848). *Illustrated Poems* ... (1849) *Poems for the Sea* (1850). *Whisper to a Bride* (1850). *Letters to My Pupils* (1851). *Examples of Life and Death* (1852). *Margaret and Henrietta* (1852). *Olive Leaves* (1852). *Voices of Home* (1852). *The Faded Hope* (1853). *Memoir of Mrs. Harriet Newell Cook* (1853). *Past Meridian* (1854).*The Western Home, and Other Poems* (1854). *Sayings of the Little Ones, and Poems for their Mothers* (1855). *Examples from the Eighteenth and Nineteenth Centuries* (1857). *Lucy Howard's Journal* (1858). *The Daily Counsellor* (1859). *Gleanings* (1860). *The Man of Uz, and Other Poems* (1862). *Selections from Various Sources* (1863). *Sayings of Little Ones* (1864). *Letters of Life* (1866). *The Transplanted Daisy: Memoir of Frances Racilla Hackley* (n.d.).

BIBLIOGRAPHY: Haight, G. S., *Mrs. Sigourney: The Sweet Singer of Hartford* (1930).

JANE BENARDETE

Bertha Muzzy Sinclair

B. *15 Nov. 1871, Cleveland, Minnesota; d. 23 July 1940, Los Angeles, California*
Wrote under: B. M. Bower
D. *of Washington and Eunice A. Miner Muzzy; m. Clayton J. Bower, 1890;*
m. Bertrand W. Sinclair, 1906; m. Robert Ellsworth Cowan

S. moved to Montana as a youngster, where she gained expertise in ranching and acquaintance with cowboys, which she would later use in her novels. S. lived in the West most of her life. She was married three times and was the mother of four children.

S. wrote nearly sixty Westerns from 1904 to 1940. Her use of initials as a pseudonym led many to assume that her works were written by a man. In this guise she was probably the first woman, and certainly the most prolific, to write in the genre of the "formula" Western.

Chip of the Flying U (1904) furnishes the basic plot for S.'s writing and introduces characters for later works. "The Happy Family," the cowboys of the Flying U Ranch, appear in several subsequent novels and furnish prototypes for others. Chip is the first of many young heroes predictably tall, handsome, taciturn, and, by modern standards, remarkably naive about his emotions. Della, the heroine, is petite and dimpled, and has the tiny hands and feet so admired in the 19th c. Their love affair suffers many vicissitudes before it reaches its foregone conclusion, with intimations that they will live happily ever after. Later books sometimes offer more violence and villainy, but in most of the novels the happy outcome is predictable.

S.'s detailed descriptions of ranch life in the early 20th c. make her books attractive. The habits—down to the typical gestures—of the cowboys are well depicted, from the back-hand twist the practiced roper uses to catch a calf to the apparently eternal preoccupation of all cowboys with their cigarettes. The men's affection for their horses is an inevitable part of the Western, but, in addition, the actions of horses often affect the stories, with scenes in which the individual characteristics of horses play a major role. Dialogue especially reflects both the western setting and the period in which S. wrote. When a man declares his love it is apt to be in terms of a card game: "It's my deal . . . do you want to know what's trump?"

Characterization of males is, on the whole, weak, with one hero almost indistinguishable from another and supporting characters flat. S.'s women, on the other hand, are often accomplished and independent, indicating S.'s interest in unconventional roles for women. She introduces two women doctors in *Chip of the Flying U*, for example, in which the heroine is not only a doctor, she is also a crack shot and brave in the face of danger. Housewifely skills assume little importance in other books as well. In *The Five Furies of Leaning Ladder* (1935), five orphan girls run their ranch in the face of many obstacles; the one sister who is domestic is relegated to a minor role.

The suffering young mother in *Cabin Fever* (1918), whose little boy has been kidnapped, is much more interesting than the male hero in this mining story. The heroine of *The Heritage of the Sioux* (1916) is an Indian. She travels a long distance alone to find the man she loves. Later, when she learns the man she promised to marry has betrayed her friends, she kills herself.

S.'s books read like early Western scenarios, and with good reason. The uncluttered scenery and rapid uncomplicated actions of her characters lend themselves easily to film. Several of S.'s novels were made into movies. Some books, written in the 1910s, in the early days of the film industry, portray the cowboys forming their own film company and making Westerns in New Mexico.

S. brought a fairy-tale West to life for her readers. In spite of the realism of her descriptions of western life and specific details of ranch scenes, S.'s description of the larger scene is vague and ephemeral. The background, no matter what state is named, is simlpy "the West," and her books are typical formula Westerns. There are many weaknesses in S.'s writing; nevertheless, her stories are fun—warm and full of humor.

WORKS: *Chip of the Flying U* (1904). *The Lure of the Dim Trails* (1907). *Her Prairie Knight* (1908). *The Lonesome Trail* (1909). *The Long Shadow* (1909). *The Happy Family* (1910). *The Range Dwellers* (1910). *Good Indian* (1912). *Lonesome Land* (1912). *The Gringos* (1913). *The Uphill Climb* (1913). *Flying U Ranch* (1914). *The Ranch at the Wolverine* (1914). *Flying U's Last Stand* (1915). *Jean of the Lazy A* (1915). *The Heritage of the Sioux* (1916). *The Phantom Herd* (1916). *The Lookout Man* (1917). *Starr of the Desert* (1917). *Cabin Fever* (1918). *Skyrider* (1918). *The Thunder Bird* (1919). *The Quirt* (1920). *Rim o' the World* (1920). *Casey Ryan* (1921). *Cow Country* (1921). *Trail of the White Mule* (1922). *The Parowan Bonanza* (1923). *The Voice of Johnnywater* (1923). *The Bellehelen Mine* (1924). *Desert Brew* (1924). *Black Thunder* (1925). *Meadowlark Basin* (1925). *Van Patten* (1926). *White Wolves* (1926). *The Adam Chasers* (1927). *Points West* (1928). *The Swallowfork Bulls* (1928). *Rodeo* (1929). *Fool's Goal* (1930). *Tiger Eye* (1930). *Dark Horse* (1931). *The Long Loop* (1931). *Laughing Water* (1932). *Rocking Arrow* (1932). *Open Land* (1933). *Trails Meet* (1933). *The Flying U Strikes* (1934). *The Haunted Hills* (1934). *The Dry Ridge Gang* (1935). *The Five Furies of Leaning Ladder* (1935). *Trouble Rides the Wind* (1935). *The North Wind Do Blow* (1936). *Shadow Mountain* (1936). *Pirates of the Range* (1937). *Starry Night* (1938). *The Wind Blows West* (1938). *The Singing Hill* (1939). *The Man on Horseback* (1940). *The Spirit of the Range* (1940). *Sweet Grass* (1940). *The Family Failing* (1941).

BIBLIOGRAPHY: For articles in reference works, see *20thCA*.
Other references: *NYHT* (24 July 1940). *NYT* (24 July 1940).

HELEN STAUFFER

Cornelia Otis Skinner

B. 30 May 1901, Chicago, Illinois; d. 9 July 1979, New York City
D. of Otis and Maud Durbin Skinner; m. Alden S. Blodget, 1928

S. was the only child born to a theatrical couple. Her mother retired from the stage shortly after S. was born, but her father went on to gain national prominence as an actor and matinee idol. Skinner spent much of his time on tour, but the family's desire for a stable and respectable home life led them to settle in Bryn Mawr, Pennsylvania, where S. grew up.

Tall and lanky, S. thought of herself as an ugly duckling. The autobiographical *Family Circle* (1948) underscores the embarrassing contrast between her mother's effortless charm and S.'s adolescent gawkiness. Nevertheless, from an early age S. gravitated toward the theater. After two years at Bryn Mawr, where she proved herself hopelessly unmathematical, S. departed for Paris. There she attended lectures at the Sorbonne while also receiving classical theater training from Jacques Copeau and Émile Dehelly of the Comédie Francaise. S.'s father paved her way onto the Broadway stage by providing a small role for her in his own production of the Spanish novel *Blood and Sand*.

While undertaking small roles in a number of productions, S. wrote a play for her father. Called *Captain Fury*, it opened in December, 1925. Soon S. was using her writing talents for her own benefit, creating lively theatrical monologues, which she performed in the United States and London. The monologues grew into a series of historical costume dramas, with S. herself playing all the roles.

From a sentimental novel of the day, *Edna His Wife*, S. developed a monodrama in which she portrayed three generations of women. This ambitious work toured the country in 1938, generating great public enthusiasm, although the New York critics were less kind. She was much better received by them in the title role of Shaw's *Candida* and in other full-fledged productions.

S. also contributed light verse and humorous essays to *The New Yorker, Harper's Bazaar, Ladies' Home Journal*, and other magazines. The witty depiction of human social foibles is her particular specialty, and her sketches often turn on comic self-deprecation. S. married in 1928 and has one son, and she often wrote of domestic matters. Her satirical treatment of her own ineptness as wife, mother, and social animal is good-natured enough so that readers can identify easily with her tales of woe. Her essays have been collected into a number of genuinely funny volumes, among them *Tiny Garments* (1932), *That's Me All Over* (1948), and *Bottoms Up!* (1955).

S.'s most famous volume is *Our Hearts Were Young and Gay* (1942), an uproarious account of a youthful trip abroad in the company of a schoolmate, Emily Kimbrough. The book details how these two naive young ladies spent the night in a brothel, came down with childhood diseases at inopportune moments, and otherwise found themselves in hot water. It captured the public fancy, and a million copies were sold. Inevitably there was soon a motion picture version (1944), and in 1948 Jean Kerr adapted the book into a popular play. Through all of this, S. did not neglect her own stage career. With Samuel Albert Taylor she wrote a successful Broadway comedy, *The Pleasure of His Company* (1959), and herself played one of the key supporting roles to general acclaim. Her one-woman shows also continued.

S.'s skills as a biographer were first displayed in *Family Circle* (1948), which is as much about her parents as herself. Her major work on Sarah Bernhardt, *Madame Sarah* (1967), was well received, less for its scholarship than for the vivid and affectionate portrait it draws.

S.'s reputation today rests on the grace with which she moved in several directions at once. Both a master of the comic sketch and a serious researcher into theater history, she brought to her writing projects an effortless quality that tends to obscure her very real talent.

WORKS: *Tiny Garments* (1932). *Excuse It, Please!* (1936). *Dithers and Jitters* (1938). *Soap Behind the Ears* (1941). *Our Hearts Were Young and Gay* (with E. Kimbrough, 1942). *Popcorn* (1943). *Family Circle* (1948). *That's Me All Over* (1948). *Nuts in May* (1950). *Bottoms Up!* (1955). *The Ape in Me* (1959). *The Pleasure of His Company* (with S. A. Taylor, 1959). *Elegant Wits and Grand Horizontals* (1962). *Madame Sarah* (1967). *Life with Lindsay & Crouse* (1976).

BIBLIOGRAPHY: *The New Yorker* (21 Nov. 1942). *NYT* (5 Sept. 1948; 10 July 1979). *NYTBR* (8 Jan. 1967). *SatR* (19 Nov. 1938; 14 Nov. 1942; 11 Sept. 1948). *TLS* (27 April 1967).

BEVERLY GRAY BIENSTOCK

Tess Slesinger

B. 16 July 1905, New York City; d. 21 Feb. 1945, Los Angeles, California
D. of Anthony and Augusta Singer Slesinger; m. Herbert Solow, 1928;
m. Frank Davis, 1936

S. could be said to have had everything but time: well-to-do parents who sacrificed in order to give her the best education at the Ethical Culture

Society School in New York, Swarthmore College, and Columbia University; immediate and continued success when she started to write; a happy marriage and children. But her works show that this success was not achieved without pain. Through her first husband she became part of a left-wing circle important in publishing, and she was able to publish her first short-story at age twenty-three; but S. found radical theorizing and intellectualizing insufficient to give meaning to life and divorced Herbert Solow. In 1935, S. went to Hollywood to begin a new career as a script writer.

After working on the screenplay for Pearl Buck's *The Good Earth* (produced in 1937), S. began a collaboration with Frank Davis which led to many successful scripts. She was able to combine a happy marriage to Davis and having two children with full professional activity until her untimely death of cancer at 39. Just a week after her death, *A Tree Grows in Brooklyn*, for which she and her husband had written the script, opened in New York. S. was politically active in helping to make the Screen Writers Guild a viable union and in many other human rights causes.

Received by contemporaries as a realistic portrayal of the "lost generation," *The Unpossessed* (1934) reveals S.'s profound understanding of her own time. The central character Margaret Flinders attempts to please her egotistical husband, even undergoing an abortion in order to "free" him; S. lets us see her act as a violation of her own being in exchange for his pretentious and selfish ambition. S. reveals his attempts to find meaning through endless discussions with other intellectuals, without any commitment to action, as typical of the futilities of the 1930s. Her skillful use of stream-of-consciousness establishes a light tone while revealing her persona's despair; the reader identifies with her because her problems are questions, her attempts to solve them are processes, not authoritative answers. The final chapter, "Missis Flinders," also published as a short story, is a masterpiece of ironic understatement affirming both the pain and the power to endure of her character.

The title of S.'s 1935 collecton of short stories *Time: The Present* is ironic in that its very contemporary concerns are timeless. S. touches on the emptiness of middle-class life, disillusionment with the American dream, the ruthlessness of the struggle to survive brought on by the Depression, the hypocrisy of whites toward blacks, the ambiguities for women of their relationships to their adulterous husbands and to their mothers, the problems of the artist attempting to reduce the felt hugeness of experience into effective form. Her story on this last theme, "A Day in the Life of a Writer," shows S.'s mastery of form and her typical ironic tone. Following the mental ramblings of a male writer trying to overcome a writing-block, she shows his "life in the day"—his self-loathing for not being able to repeat the success of his first book, his childish projection of his failure onto his "deaf-mute" typewriter and his wife. The reader understands both his ambivalence toward writing as a prison and the anger of his wife, who supports him.

S.'s stories about women show particular acuity. "On Being Told that Her Second Husband has Taken his First Lover" focuses on the continuance of the double-bind for women even with the sexual revolution. A wife who did not originate adultery feels she must accept her husband's announced infidelity as his right to freedom but cannot perceive her right to respond in kind as viable. Her only recourse is to accept his decision, with wit and anguish; rejecting him will only be a repetition of the end of her first marriage. "Mother to Dinner" explores the dilemma of a young wife caught between her husband's demands for her entire devotion and her mother's need for emotional support. The character sees no way out. (S., in divorcing her first husband, refused such a commitment and devoted herself to her writing.)

S.'s works show not only promise but accomplishment; her short stories and her film scripts will long outlive her. Although her works have been republished, twenty of her stories remain uncollected. Excerpts from recently discovered notes for another novel, focusing on the real workers of Hollywood, confirm her importance as one who saw through the pretensions and complexities of her own time to basic human issues.

WORKS: *The Unpossessed* (1934). *Time: The Present* (1935; reprinted as *On Being Told That Her Second Husband Has Taken His First Lover, and Other Stories*, 1971). Screenplays produced: *The Good Earth* (1937). *The Bride Wore Red* (1937). *Dance, Girl, Dance* (with F. Davis, 1940). *Remember the Day* (with F. Davis, 1941). *Are Husbands Necessary?* (with F. Davis, 1942). *A Tree Grows in Brooklyn* (with F. Davis, 1945).

BIBLIOGRAPHY: Sharistanian, Janet, in *MQR* (Summer 1979).
   For articles in reference works, see *20thCA. 20thCAS.*
   Other references: *AR* (Spring 1977). *Jewish Social Studies* (Summer 1976). *NYT* (20 May 1934). *Prospects* (1981). *WLB* (Dec. 1934).

MARY ANNE FERGUSON

Agnes Smedley

B. 1892, Missouri; d. 6 May 1950, London, England
D. of Charles and Sarah Ralls Smedley; m. Ernest Brundin, 1912

S.'s life began in the drab rural poverty of northwestern Missouri. She grew to maturity in the squalor of Colorado mining towns, where her father, an uneducated, hard-drinking, defiant man, had hoped to find his fortune and where her mother took in laundry and died of overwork when S. was sixteen.

Determination to avoid her mother's fate led S. to leave home, work at odd jobs throughout the Southwest, and supplement her grade school education with a year at Tempe Normal School in Arizona. A brief "egalitarian" marriage ended in divorce.

Around 1917, S. began a decade of deep involvement, in New York and Berlin, with the efforts of Indian nationalists to free India from British rule. At the same time she wrote in support of socialist and feminist causes, established birth control clinics, and studied Asian history and Marxism. A relationship during the 1920s with exiled revolutionary leader Virendranath Chattopadhyaya drove S. to a nervous breakdown; she wrote her autobiographical novel *Daughter of Earth* (1929) in an attempt to reorient her life.

S. went to China in 1928 and dedicated the rest of her life to the Chinese revolutionary cause. She developed friendships with Communist leaders, traveled with the Red Army as it fought Chiang Kai-Shek's Kuomintang and later the Japanese, and worked unstintingly to secure medical treatment for the wounded. S. wrote prolifically, producing three books during the 1930s and a profusion of articles for European, American, and Asian periodicals.

Ill health forced S. to return to the U.S. in 1941, and in 1943 she published her widely acclaimed *Battle Hymn of China*. Although she had never joined the Communist Party, the forces of McCarthyism hounded S. out of the country in the late 1940s. She died in London enroute to the new People's Republic of China.

Daughter of Earth, S.'s only novel, tells of a working-class woman who develops a feminist and a class consciousness as she pits her determination to be a free person against the traps society lays for women and the poor.

Marie Rogers, the narrator of this first-person account, attains and preserves her independence—the book's plot is taken from S.'s own life right up to the moment of its writing—but the emotional cost is high. Marie must cope with the persistent guilt, confusion, and pain of a woman who refuses to fit into expected roles.

S.'s novel differs from standard proletarian fiction in its outspoken feminism and its emphasis on the psychological. Although it is not reliable autobiography, especially in the concluding sections, the book suffers artistically from its close identification with the still-unfolding events of S.'s own life. But what this startlingly up-to-date novel lacks in balance and perspective it makes up for in emotional power.

Chinese Destinies: Sketches of Present-Day China (1933), the first of S.'s five books about China in upheaval, is a collage of articles, stories, and impressions; it communicates a vivid sense of the corruption and utter wretchedness of life in the old China and the revolutionary fervor of those who hoped to build the new. S. focuses on individual lives, often women's lives; the tales are well told and the effect is moving. *China's Red Army Marches* (1934) follows a similar but less kaleidoscopic format, its sketches relating loosely to the Red Army's historic progress as it widens and secures its territory in inland China. In *China Fights Back: An American Woman with the Eighth Route Army* (1938), S. becomes an active participant in her story, using her journal entries to give the Western world a rare inside account of what life was like in the Red Army as it battled the Japanese invaders. S.'s zeal and haste sometimes lead to simplistic characterizations and inelegant style, but at their best these books display stirring narrative power.

In *Battle Hymn of China*, history, autobiography, war reporting, and story telling intermingle, as S. tries to tell wartime America all she had experienced and learned during her twenty-two years in China. This most comprehensive of S.'s China books is also S.'s comprehensive autobiography. Like all her books, this one is strongly partisan, but its very fervor helps promote an understanding of modern Chinese history by capturing and communicating that spirit which made revolution possible.

The Great Road: The Life and Times of Chu Teh, S.'s enthusiastic biography of the peasant who became commander-in-chief of the Red Army—and S.'s personal friend—was begun in the 1930s and published posthumously in 1956. Despite stylistic inadequacies, the book is strong in its depiction of rural Chinese society and its detailed look at life and politics within the Red Army.

S. saw herself as an interpreter of the Chinese revolution to the West.

Her vivid and sensitive observations from the center of one of the century's great dramas constitute her most important professional achievement. But S. also saw herself as a woman who, as she once wrote, refused to "live the life of a cabbage."

WORKS: *Daughter of Earth* (1929). *Chinese Destinies: Sketches of Present-Day China* (1933). *China's Red Army Marches* (1934). *China Fights Back: An American Woman with the Eighth Route Army* (1938). *Battle Hymn of China* (1943). *The Great Road: The Life and Times of Chu Teh* (1956). *Portraits of Chinese Women in Revolution* (Eds. J. MacKinnon and S. MacKinnon, 1976).

BIBLIOGRAPHY: Howe, F., Afterword to *Portraits of Chinese Women in Revolution* (1976). Huberman, L., and P. M. Sweezy, Publisher's Foreword to *The Great Road: The Life and Times of Chu Teh* by A. Smedley (1956). Lauter, P., Afterword to *Daughter of Earth* by A. Smedley (1973). Lovett, R. M., Preface to *China's Red Army Marches* (1934). MacKinnon, J., and S. MacKinnon, Introduction to *Portraits of Chinese Women in Revolution* (1976 by A. Smedley; a shorter version of this introduction is in *Bulletin of Concerned Asian Scholars*, Jan.–March 1975).

For articles in reference works, see: *CB* (1944, 1950). *DAB*, Suppl. 4 (article by K. E. Shewmaker). *NAW* (article by R. Gottesman). *20thCA. 20thCAS.*

Other references: *Chinese Literature* (Oct. 1980). *Monthly Review* (April 1978). *Nation* (19 Feb. 1949). *NewR* (29 May 1950; 14 Dec. 1974). *New Statesman and Nation* (20 May 1950). *NYT* (9 May 1950; 6 April 1978). *Survey* (Autumn 1974).

PEGGY STINSON

Betty Wehner Smith

B. 15 Dec. 1896, Brooklyn, New York; d. 17 Jan. 1972, Shelton, Connecticut
Wrote under: Betty Smith
D. of John C. and Katherine Hummel Wehner; m. George Smith (1924?);
* m. Joseph Jones, 1943; m. Robert Finch, 1957*

Born and raised in the Williamsburg section of Brooklyn, S. attended public schools until the age of fourteen when, having completed eighth grade, she began working at a series of factory and clerical jobs. An avid reader as a young girl, she also wrote poems and acted in amateur productions at the Williamsburg YMCA. Moving to the Midwest, she met and married George Smith, a law student at the University of Michigan. There her two daughters were born. She audited literature and writing classes at the university and, although not a regular student, had two plays published in a collection of undergraduate work and won an Avery Hopwood prize.

From 1930 to 1934 S. studied with George Pierce Baker and others at the Yale Drama School. S.'s first two marriages ended in divorce. After the first divorce, S. accepted a Rockefeller fellowship in playwriting at the University of North Carolina; she remained in Chapel Hill, writing, occasionally lecturing at the university, and playing small roles in local productions. Her third husband, Robert Finch, a writer with whom she had collaborated on several plays, died about a year and a half after their marriage.

A dramatist by inclination, S. wrote over seventy plays and edited several collections and texts for drama classes. Most of her plays were not published and none received critical acclaim or even major professional performances. Typical of her plays meant for youth groups or schools are *The Boy, Abe* and *First Sorrows*, both about the young Abe Lincoln and the death of his mother. Other one-act plays range in tone from burlesque to sentimentality and in setting from a mid-19th-c. rural political rally (*Freedom's Bird*, written with Robert Finch) to the sidewalk in front of an illegal abortionist's office on a late depression era Christmas Eve (*So Gracious Is the Time*).

Though she preferred drama, S. won fame through her fiction. Drawing upon her own memories and those of her mother, she expanded an earlier work, "Francie Nolan," into *A Tree Grows in Brooklyn* (1943), her most successful novel. It sold millions of copies and was made into a movie and a Broadway musical. Whereas the plot and much of the writing can be criticized for excessive sentimentality, the strength of this highly autobiographical novel lies in the richness of detail with which S. recreates a young girl's childhood and adolescence in the slums of early-20th-c. Brooklyn, including both the pains of a poverty-stricken childhood and the good times. The characters are vivid and three-dimensional; even the minor characters come alive as recognizable types.

S.'s next novel, *Tomorrow Will Be Better* (1948) is set against the same background as her first, but reviewers were not impressed with this effort; they found the dialogue authentic but the book as a whole less spontaneous and more self-conscious than *A Tree Grows in Brooklyn*. In *Maggie-Now* (1958), the character types are similar to those in *A Tree Grows in Brooklyn*—charming, irresponsible men and their long-suffering, hard-working wives and daughters—but this novel too lacks the depth of the earlier one. In her fourth novel, *Joy in the Morning* (1963), S. shifted the locale from Brooklyn to a midwestern college campus. In some ways, this book is a sequel to the first novel, as the heroine, a Brooklyn girl with only a grade school education, marries a law student, audits literature and writing classes, and has her work published in a student collection.

S. obviously drew heavily upon her own experiences for the material for her novels. Her accurate ear for dialogue (a legacy of her dramatic training) is a strength in all of them. But the wealth of detail in *A Tree Grows in Brooklyn* may have exhausted her memories. Each of the succeeding books was less rich in characterization and atmosphere. Her greatest weakness, however, was her inability to shape her novels into realistic and meaningful form; thus they tend to be overly sentimental and to end mechanically or without resolution.

WORKS: (including the novels and a selection of the plays) *Folk Stuff* (1935). *His Last Skirmish* (1937). *Naked Angel* (1937). *Popecastle Inn* (1937). *Saints Get Together* (1937). *Plays for Schools and Little Theaters: A Descriptive List* (edited by Smith, with R. Finch and F. H. Koch, 1937). *Trees of His Father* (1937). *Vine Leaves* (1937). *The Professor Roars* (1938). *Western Night* (1938). *Darkness at the Window* (1938). *Murder in the Snow* (1938). *Silver Rope* (1938). *Youth Takes Over; or, When a Man's Sixteen* (1939). *Lawyer Lincoln* (1939). *Mannequins' Maid* (1939). *They Released Barabbas* (1939). *A Night in the Country* (1939). *Near Closing Time* (1939). *Package for Ponsonby* (1939). *Western Ghost Town* (1939). *Bayou Harlequinade* (1940). *Fun After Supper* (1940). *Heroes Just Happen* (1940). *Room for a King* (1940). *Summer Comes to the Diamond O* (1940). *To Jenny with Love* (1941). *25 Non-Royalty One-Act Plays for All-Girl Casts* (edited by Smith, 1942). *A Tree Grows in Brooklyn* (1943, dramatization by Smith, with G. Abbott, 1951; film version by Tess Slessinger and F. Davis, 1943). *20 Prize-Winning Non-Royalty One-Act Plays* (edited by Smith, 1943). *The Boy, Abe* (1944) *Tomorrow Will Be Better* (English title: *Streets of Little Promise,* 1948). *Young Lincoln* (1951). *Maggie-Now* (1958). *A Treasury of Non-Royalty One-Act Plays* (edited by Smith et al., 1958). *Durham Station* (1961). *Joy in the Morning* (1963).

BIBLIOGRAPHY: For articles in reference works, see: *CA, 5-8* (1969). *CB* (1943, 1972). *20thCAS.*

ELAINE K. GINSBERG

Eliza Roxey Snow Smith

B. 21 Jan. 1804, Becket, Massachusetts; d. 5 Dec. 1886, Salt Lake City, Utah
D. of Oliver and Rosetta Leonora Pettibone Snow; m. Joseph Smith, 1842;
  m. Brigham Young, 1847

When S., the second of seven children, was very young, her parents migrated to Ohio, where her father successfully took up farming. S. received the most liberal education allowed a young woman at the time, attending the local schools of Ravenna, Ohio, and a grammar school taught by a Presbyterian minister. In her early teens, S. began writing poetry. Her first efforts were published in local newspapers and journals under pennames. These verses are typical of her day—sentimental, religious, and didactic.

In the 1820s, S., with her parents, joined the Reformed Baptist or "Campbellite" church, and she began a devoted study of the Bible. S. converted to the Church of Jesus Christ of the Latter Day Saints early in 1835, and that year left her family's home for the Mormon stronghold of Kirtland, Ohio, where she lodged with the Prophet Joseph Smith and his family. In 1838, S. followed Smith and his flock first to Missouri and then to Illinois, where S. began her rise to prominence in the Mormon church. S. probably became the Prophet's fourth or fifth wife when she secretly wed him in 1842.

After the murder of Smith and the dispersal of the followers, S. was among the first pioneering companies to reach the valley of the Great Salt Lake. During the course of the journey west, she kept a diary (published in *The Improvement Era*, 1943-44), and wrote patriotic, religious, and eulogistic poetry. Her poetry served as an inspiration to trail-weary Mormons, and encouraged them to continue on their way to the promised land: "Altho' in woods and tents we dwell / Shout, shout O Camp of Israel. / No Christian males on earth can bind / Our thoughts, or steal our peace of mind." On this trip westward, S., along with several of Smith's widows, was married to Brigham Young.

S. became the most beloved and powerful woman in Utah, as she increased her involvement with charitable, spiritual, and educational projects. In addition to publicly defending polygamy, S. was an ardent feminist. As head of the Women's Suffrage Society, she worked to dispel the myth that Mormon women lived lives subject to their husband's wills. She worked hard to ensure Utah's women the right to political franchise and won success in 1870.

S. continued to write poetry, hymns, and religious essays, published in several Utah journals, as well as practical educational texts while living in Utah. Her first volume of poetry, incorporating many of the poems she had written while on the trail from Illinois, was published in 1856, and a second volume was published in 1877. S. compiled a number of hymnals for the church, containing some of her own hymns, the most popular of which was "O My Father, Thou that Dwellest." She contributed an account of the "assassination" of Smith and his brother and several poems to Lucy Smith's *Biographical Sketches of Joseph Smith* (1853). With her brother Lorenzo Snow, the fifth president of the Mormon church, S. wrote *The Correspondence of Palestine Tourists* (1875), the record of their missionary trip to the Middle East. S. was reticent to write of her own experiences, but she did write an autobiographical sketch, which was published in the *Relief Society Magazine* (1944). S.'s best-known work, and an excellent source for historians interested in the foundations of the Mormon religion, is *The Biography and Family Record of Lorenzo Snow* (1884).

Married in turn to the two most important figures in the history of the Mormon church, S. made a name for herself through her own involvement in church affairs and education, and she pointed with pride to Utah women's right to vote and active participation in church affairs as evidence of Mormon women's freedom and equality. In addition, S. wrote poems and songs for the church; she provided the young Mormon church with its chief hymns.

WORKS: *The Story of Jesus* (1845). *Poems, Religious, Historical, and Political* (2 vols., 1856 and 1877). *The Correspondence of Palestine Tourists* (1875). *Bible Questions and Answers for Children* (1883). *Biography and Family Record of Lorenzo Snow* (1884). *Recitations for the Primary Associations* (edited by Smith, 1887). *Hymns and Songs: Selected from Various Authors for the Primary Associations of the Children of Zion* (edited by Smith, 1888). *Recitations for the Primary Associations in Poetry, Dialogues, and Prose* (edited by Smith, 1891).

A copy of Eliza Roxey Snow Smith's 1847 diary and her autobiographical sketch are in the Bancroft Library, University of California.

BIBLIOGRAPHY: Brodie, F. M., *No Man Knows My History: The Life of Joseph Smith, the Mormon Prophet* (1971). Crocherson, A. J., *Representative Women of Deseret* (1884). Gates, Susa Young, and L. D. Widstoe, *Women of the Mormon Church* (1926). Hill, D., *Joseph Smith: The First Mormon* (1977). Tullidge, E., *The Women of Mormondom* (1877).

For articles in reference works, see: *DAB*, IX, 1. *NAW* (article by M. S. De Pillis).

PAULA A. TRECKEL

Elizabeth Oakes Prince Smith

B. 12 Aug. 1806, North Yarmouth, Maine; d. 15 Nov. 1893, Hollywood, North
Carolina
Wrote under: E., Ernest Helfenstein, Elizabeth Oakes Smith, Oakes Smith,
Mrs. Seba Smith
D. of David and Sophia Blanchard Prince; m. Seba Smith, 1823

As a child, S. lived in the country near the south coast of Maine, where
she spent much time even after her family moved to Portland when she
was eight. At the age of sixteen, S. married Seba Smith, an editor and publisher and the author of the popular Major Jack Downing stories. S.'s first
poems and sketches appeared anonymously in his newspapers. In Portland,
S. had five sons; one died as a young child.

After a series of financial reverses, the Smiths moved to New York in
1837 and took their places in that city's literary circles. S. contributed to
the support of her family through her writing. Her stories, sketches, and
poems appeared in the Ladies' Companion, Godey's Lady's Book, Graham's Magazine, and other popular monthlies of the day, in addition to
her husband's various periodical publications. She contributed to thirty-six
gift books (sentimental annual publications) between 1836 and 1856, editing some of them with her husband and some of them on her own.

From about the midpoint of her life, the "busy devil" with which S.
professed to be afflicted directed her into intense reform activity. She was
an active participant in the women's rights conventions of 1848, 1851,
1852, and 1878. In 1851, as an advocate of the working woman, S., with
Lucretia Mott, sponsored a tailoring cooperative that employed women in
Philadelphia. Under the auspices of the YMCA, she was a social worker in
New York City. In 1868, she became a charter member of New York's
first women's club; she served as its vice-president in 1869. In 1877, after a
lifetime of religious searching and questioning, S. became the minister of
an independent congregation in Canastota, New York.

S.'s early writings draw heavily on her immediate environment and include Indian myths and legends, Down East characters, and stories of
Maine. These early writings also include sketches of women whose lives
were far outside her experience, such as Charlotte Corday and Mme. de
Staël, which reappear in later writings and in her lectures on the Lyceum
circuit.

S. won popular and critical acclaim for "The Sinless Child," a long narrative poem which first appeared in the *Southern Literary Messenger*, to which she was a frequent contributor. In the poem, the unworldly heroine is released from a corrupt world through death. Its publication as the title piece in a collection of her poems in 1843 established S.'s reputation.

S.'s first novel, *Riches without Wings*, was published in 1838. Its themes and values are conventional: the superiority of natural beauty, temperance in all things, modesty, cleanliness. Worldly riches are not to be pursued at the expense of spiritual purity, but wealth and recognition do reward hard work and honesty. Her dialogues and asides to her readers are intended to instruct, and in these, along with the dominant themes, S. occasionally disparages convention, as when the leading female character asserts the value of passion in women as well as in men, and again when she refuses to wear the prescribed mourning dress on the death of a relative.

In her later work, S. continued to use the conventional themes of her first novel. A strong strain of mysticism, present in most of her writing, becomes more marked in the later writing. Patriotism and progress are typical themes. The evils of cities, the romantic theme of the superiority of the natural, or country life, is the major theme in *The Newsboy* (1854), a novel credited with influencing social reform in New York.

S.'s beliefs that women had the right to develop fully as individuals and that the current constraints of the marriage relation inhibited their development, were articulated in a series of essays in the New York *Tribune*, published as a monograph in 1851, under the title *Woman and Her Needs* (reprinted in 1974).

As a writer, S. was spurred always by financial necessity. Her work is remarkable for variety, volume, and inventiveness; it ranges from sonnets to very informal travel sketches and reminiscences, from children's stories to tragic drama. Though in general her characters have the conventional virtues and vices and her intensely romantic themes were chosen to appeal to a wide audience, S.'s fiction, poetry, and essays expose the occasional "burr under the saddle" that placed her among contemporary reformers and made her a significant contributor to the popular literature of the middle third of the 19th c.

WORKS: *Riches without Wings* (1838). *The Western Captive* (1842). *The Sinless Child, and Other Poems* (1843). *The Dandelion, The Rose-bud and The Moss Cup* (1845). *The Lover's Gift* (1848). *The Salamander* (1848). *The Roman Tribute* (1850). *The Good Child's Book* (1851). *Woman and Her Needs* (1851). *Hints on Dress and Beauty* (1852). *Shadowland* (1853). *Old New York* (1853). *The Sanctity of Marriage* (1853). *Bertha and Lily* (1854).

Black Hollow (1864). *The Newsboy* (1854). *Bald Eagle* (1867). *The Sagamore of Saco* (1868). *Selections from the Autobiography of Elizabeth Oakes Smith* (Ed. M. A. Wyman, 1924).

The New York Public Library has a collection of Elizabeth Oakes Smith's unpublished papers, including the manuscript of her autobiography.

BIBLIOGRAPHY: Wyman, M. A., *Two American Pioneers: Seba Smith and Elizabeth Oakes Smith* (1927).

For articles in reference works, see *Appleton's Annual Cyclopedia* (1893). *CAL. DAB, IX,* 1. *FPA, NAW* (article by A. F. Tyler).

Other references: *Broadway Journal* (23 Aug. 1845). *Graham's* (June 1843; Sept. 1853; April 1856). *North American Review* (Oct. 1854).

VIVIAN H. SHORTREED

Hannah Whitall Smith

B. *7 Feb. 1832, Philadelphia, Pennsylvania; d. 1 May 1911, Iffley, England*
Wrote under: H.W.S.
D. *of John Mickle and Mary Whitall; m. Robert Pearsall Smith, 1851*

After a happy childhood in her Quaker home, S. married in 1851 and had four children.

S. departed early from strict Quaker ways, which seemed to her too rigid, to set out on a spiritual pilgrimage. Eventually, she began to preach, alongside her husband. The Smiths preached the "Higher Life" in America, in England, and on the Continent, being particularly active around 1873. Because S.'s husband was suspected of preaching false doctrine and also of improper conduct with female admirers, they returned to the U.S., but they settled permanently in England in 1886.

S.'s preaching was nonsectarian and the influences on her thought were various. After her marriage, S. came under the influence of the Plymouth Brethren, the Baptists, and the Methodists. But she had inherited from her father an attachment to the works of the 17th-c. French quietist Mme Guyon. S. also treated as a guide Mme Guyon's friend Fénelon, whose *Spiritual Letters* she quoted with approval.

Because S. was open to religious enlightenment from any source, she worked out for herself a safeguard against fanaticism, which she offers to her readers in *The Christian's Secret of a Happy Life* (1875). Her message is that God's guidance comes to us in four ways: "through the Scriptures, through providential circumstances, through the convictions of our own higher judgment, and through the inward impressions of the Holy Spirit on our minds." In early editions S. also included a chapter warning against taking emotional states as proof of the baptism of the Holy Spirit.

Both *The Christian's Secret of a Happy Life* and *The God of All Comfort* (1906) are still religious bestsellers today. They owe their appeal to the clarity, simplicity, and directness with which S. expresses her complete trust in God. Of at least equal interest, but out of print, is S.'s spiritual autobiography, *The Unselfishness of God, and How I Discovered It* (1903).

In the end, S. found that she had returned to a basic Quaker principle: that God has power to save us from sin, not only in a legalistic sense but also in a practical way, by preserving us from it and giving us constant guidance. Because of this interest in the practical applications of Christian teaching, S. was also active in the temperance and woman suffrage movements.

S. believed in will power as the chief condition for total trust in God. Her orthodoxy may have been suspect at one time, but her outlook suits the modern Christian.

WORKS: *The Record of a Happy Life: Being Memorials of Franklin Whitall Smith* (1873). *The Christian's Secret of a Happy Life* (1875). *John M. Whitall: The Story of his Life* (1879). *Every-Day Religion* (1893). *The Science of Motherhood* (1894). *The Unselfishness of God, and How I Discovered It* (1903). *The God of All Comfort* (1906). *Religious Fanaticism* (Ed. R. Strachey, 1928). *Philadelphia Quaker: Letters of Hannah Whitall Smith* (Ed. L. P. Smith, 1950).

BIBLIOGRAPHY: Pearsall, C. E., H. M. Pearsall, and H. L. Neall, *History and Genealogy of the Pearsall Family* (1928). Smith, L. P., *Unforgotten Years* (1939). Smith, R. M., *The Burlington Smiths* (1877). Strachey, R., *A Quaker Grandmother: Hannah Whitall Smith* (1914).

For articles in reference works, see: *DAB*, IX, 1. *NAW* (article by E. C. Kaylor, Jr.).

BARBARA J. BUCKNALL

Lillian Smith

B. *12 Dec. 1897, Jasper, Florida; d. 28 Sept. 1966, Atlanta, Georgia*
D. *of Calvin and Anne Simpson Smith*

S. was the seventh of nine children. She tasted the "strange fruit" of racial segregation early in her childhood, when her well-to-do, genteel Methodist parents took in an apparently white orphan found living with a black family. The Smiths welcomed the girl until they learned she was part black. Then the children were hastily separated, leaving S. in conflict over the paradox of a culture that teaches hospitality, democracy, and Christian charity at the same time that it violently denies the humanity of blacks.

S.'s traditional southern upbringing led her to value literature, art, and music and to want to be socially useful. Her education (at Piedmont College and Baltimore's Peabody Conservatory of Music) was repeatedly interrupted by declining family fortunes, which had forced the Smiths to move to their summer home in Clayton, Georgia, in 1915. S. joined the Student Nursing Corps in WWI and, after the Armistice, taught for a year in an isolated mountain school in Georgia. She spent three years teaching music at a Methodist mission school in Huchow, China, and then returned to help run Laurel Falls Camp for Girls, the exclusive summer camp her father founded at their Georgia home, and to act as secretary to her brother Austin, the city manager of Fort Pierce, Florida. In 1928, she attended Columbia University's Teachers College, adding to her already considerable knowledge of child development and Freudian psychology. After her father died in 1930, S. assumed heavy family responsibilities, including the care of her invalid mother. And, in the next five years, she wrote five novels, never published and all lost in a 1944 house fire.

Along with her lifelong companion, Paula Snelling, another young, liberal southern intellectual hired to help run the camp, S. founded *Pseudopodia*, a little magazine heavily influenced by the editors' Freudian persuassion and their antisegregationist political and social views. At first, the magazine concentrated on reviewing works by and about blacks and took a literary stand against, among other things, Margaret Mitchell's *Gone with the Wind* and the Agrarians. It was renamed twice—as the *North American Review* (1937–42) and *South Today* (1942–44)—as the editors broadened their liberal crusade against the consequences of caste in the South and in other countries and as it became a forum also for S.'s fervent views on sexuality and childrearing.

Strange Fruit (1944), S.'s first published novel, sold over three million copies and was translated into sixteen languages. It was banned from the bookstores and libraries of Boston and from the bookstores of Detroit; Eleanor Roosevelt intervened to remove the Post Office ban. Much of the uproar stemmed from the realistic language and the ironic treatment of miscegenation, sexuality, and abortion. Set in racially segregated Maxwell, Georgia, in the years following WWI, the plot traces from its youthful beginning the secret interracial love affair of Tracy Deen—a war veteran, son of the town's respected white doctor and his aristocratic wife—and Nonnie Anderson—a black college graduate who can only find a job as a maid in Maxwell.

As in Theodore Dreiser's *American Tragedy* and Richard Wright's *Native Son*, S.'s fictional world is deterministic. Characters breaking a taboo in this segregated society must suffer violence. Tracy Deen is murdered by the brother of his pregnant lover. A mob lynches the black servant Deen had paid to marry Nonnie so that he could marry as his mother and the town expect him to. S. handles the stream-of-consciousness technique well, aptly combining it with the sensational plot and subject matter to create a strongly moving, finely detailed picture of the tragedy of racism for both black and white southerners.

The furor over *Strange Fruit* created the national publishing and speaking outlet S. needed to wage her campaign against racism. She published a second novel, *One Hour* (1959), and five nonfiction books that preach racial justice and denounce any person or organization that did not seem as liberal as she. Each book contains eloquent stories about her personal life and the lives of those she encountered on her travels through the South and abroad. Her ability to recreate atmosphere through physical detail allows her to carry out the psychological, social, and political analysis that is her purpose.

S. also wrote a column for the Chicago *Defender* and articles and book reviews for such widely read magazines as *New Republic*, *Saturday Review*, *Redbook*, the *Nation*, and *McCall's*.

S.'s contribution to the cause of racial justice in the U.S. won her the reputation as the most liberal white advocate of civil rights in the South in the 1940s. In the 1950s and 1960s, despite recurrent battles with lung cancer, S. continued to fight against the evils of segregation by championing the nonviolent movement of Rev. Martin Luther King, Jr.

Her conviction was deep and sincere, but her view of literature and art was limited by the intensity of her belief in the perfectability of mankind. She took daring stands against segregation, but the impact of her writing is diminished by her moralizing. S. is justifiably recognized as a minor literary figure and a major social reformer.

WORKS: *Strange Fruit* (1944). *Killer of the Dream* (1949). *The Journey* (1954). *Now Is the Time* (1955). *One Hour* (1959). *Memory of a Large Christmas* (1962). *Our Faces, Our Words* (1964). *From the Mountain* (writings from *South Today*, Eds. H. White and R. S. Suggs, Jr., 1972). *The Winner Names the Age* (Ed. M. Cliff, 1978).

BIBLIOGRAPHY: Blackwell, L., and F. Clay, *Lillian Smith* (1971). Sosna, M., *In Search of the Silent South* (1977).
For articles in reference works, see: *CB* (1944).

SUZANNE ALLEN

Margaret Bayard Smith

B. 20 Feb. 1778, near Philadelphia, Pennsylvania; d. 7 June, 1844, Washington, D.C.
D. of John Bubenheim and Margaret Hodge Bayard; m. Samuel Howard Smith, 1800

S. married the editor of the Jeffersonian newspaper the *National Intelligencer* and brought with her to Washington in 1800 a lively curiosity, a warm understanding of human relationships, and an openness to experience.

During her early life in Washington, S. wrote privately, chiefly letters and notebooks. Her public career as a writer began in the 1820s. She published two novels based on Washington life, *A Winter in Washington* (1824) and *What is Gentility?* (1828). She also wrote short stories, essays, and verse for such publications as *Godey's Lady's Book*, the *National Intelligencer*, and the *Southern Literary Messenger*. In addition, S. wrote several biographical accounts for James Herring and John B. Longacre's *National Portrait Gallery of Distinguished Americans*.

S.'s reputation as a writer rests primarily on the collection of her letters and notebook entries edited by Gaillard Hunt in 1906 and published under the title *The First Forty Years of Washington Society*. This miscellany revealed S. as a person of wit, insight, and affection and as a discerning observer of the society of her time.

S.'s Jeffersonian sympathies are evident in her work, but her circle of friends far transcended party lines. She found the transition from Jeffersonian republicanism to Jacksonian democracy a difficult one. Though flexible by nature, S. belonged to an earlier age of gentility and ordered society. Her writing about the pre-Jacksonian period combined the personal world and public political concern; in the latter period, her focus was more on the private side of Washington life.

S. was a novelist whose primary concern was the changing ways and values of society. *A Winter in Washington* had its elements of suspense and mystery, including an abducted child and a murder. But the central theme of this book and of *What is Gentility?* is the clash of moral values and cultural ways. S. saw the Jeffersonian era as a kind of republican golden age, and she sought to convey the values of that period to a later generation.

S. portrayed the political scene as women saw it—as outsiders. For her novels, she drew on some of the sketches of real-life events she had recorded previously in her notebooks as historical memoirs.

On the whole, S. held traditional views about women and their role in society. In *A Winter in Washington* she did voice, through Mrs. Mortimer, perhaps the most original and nonconformist of her female characters, some of the discontent experienced by women of the day. An incipient feminist, Mrs. Mortimer thinks it folly for women to talk of government when they are "slaves to all" or "mill horses" or "captive birds." But S. herself affirmed the theory of separate spheres and home as the "place of highest duties . . . and most enduring pleasures."

As a novelist S. is on soundest ground in depicting the social and political world of which she had been a part. S.'s private papers have proved a storehouse of information about that society. As a letter writer, S. has charm and liveliness. She clearly enjoyed people, and her portraits of the personalities of her age are drawn with an affectionate yet keen-eyed view. It is both the quality of the person S. is and the perceptive insight she brings to bear on her society that give her work its vitality and durability.

WORKS: *A Winter in Washington; or, Memoirs of the Seymour Family* (1824). *What Is Gentility?* (1828). *The First Forty Years of Washington Society* (Ed. by G. Hunt, 1906).

BIBLIOGRAPHY: Green, C. M. *Washington: Village and Capital, 1800–1878* (1962). van der Linden, F., *The Turning Point: Jefferson's Battle for the Presidency* (1962).

For articles in reference works, see: *NAW* (article by L. Mayo).

INZER BYERS

Susan Sontag

B. 16 Jan. 1933, New York City
m. Philip Rieff, 1950

Raised in Arizona and California, S. studied at the University of California at Berkeley and the University of Chicago, from which she received her B.A. when she was only eighteen, a year after marrying sociologist Philip Rieff. Her M.A. and Ph.D. in philosophy are from Harvard University. In the late 1950s, she divorced her husband and settled with her son (born in 1952) in New York City. She spends a good portion of each year in Europe. Through the mid-1960s she taught English and philosophy at several American colleges and universities. She began publishing fiction, critical essays, and reviews when she was twenty-eight. She is also a writer and director as well as a critic of films. The provocative *Duet for Cannibals* (1969) and *Brother Carl* (1971) were both made in Sweden; *Promised Lands* (1974) is a documentary about Israel.

S. is one of our most influential cultural critics. *Against Interpretation, and Other Essays* (1966) is a brilliant expression of the modernist sensibility. Despite the title, she does interpret, making accessible the most striking experiments in avant-garde film and criticism. From her treatment of new-wave critics to her famous "Notes on Camp," she is always provocative and original, so much so that one critic observed: "Perhaps what makes *Against Interpretation* valuable and exciting is not so much its erudition, which is considerable . . . as its passionate irresponsibility, its determined outrageousness."

In *Styles of Radical Will* (1969), S. again investigates the difficulties of confronting new artistic modes. Part of her appeal lies in her ability to move from the world of high culture to low—from Karl Marx to Harpo Marx, for instance. She flirts with the demonic, the underside of human experience. Her "dark and complex vision of sexuality" is not to feminists' taste, but it is worth paying some attention to what she has to say about our impulses towards violence and destruction. Elsewhere, as in "The Third World of Women" (*Partisan Review*, 1973), she shows that she can be a brilliant spokeswoman for feminism.

Politically, S. takes the part of adversary, as in the autobiographical *Trip to Hanoi* (1968). She sees art as something that expands consciousness; thus, in *Styles of Radical Will*, her views on politics and art are related, "for it is sensibility that nourishes our capacity for moral choice."

As a novelist, S. has never been autobiographical. The heroes of her full-length works are male. *The Benefactor* (1963) is about a European man who looks back on his sixty-plus years and on such surrealistic adventures as selling his mistress to an Arab merchant. Despite the brilliance of isolated perceptions, the work as a whole lacks the passionate conviction of those writers (Djuna Barnes, Dostoevsky, Nietzsche) who influenced it. To many readers, the work requires an interpreter to give it meaning.

In *Death Kit* (1967), S. wittily combines mythical, religious, and philosophical elements within the structure of a who-done-it that makes use of the journey-to-hell theme. Despite the high praise of some critics, such as Granville Hicks, most readers are more excited by S.'s criticism than her fiction.

The reader of the short-story collection *I, etcetera* (1978) has a greater sense of the intimate self with all its pain and longing, than is usual in her fiction.

In *Illness as Metaphor* (1977), S. describes "not what it is really like to emigrate to the kingdom of the ill and live there [a theme that would have had autobiographical relevence], but the punitive or sentimental fantasies concocted about that situation: not real geography, but stereotypes of national character." She applies a moralist's scorn to the use of tuberculosis and cancer as metaphor.

Yet S.'s own metaphoric power is freely employed in equally dubious contexts, as when, in *On Photography* (1979), she labels those who take or view photographs as junkies, rapists, and murderers. In some ways, the aesthetic position here is the antithesis of that in *Against Interpretation* and *Styles of Radical Will*: art, at least the art of the photographer, is now an amoral force rather than one which enlivens sensibilities and consciousness. "By getting us used to what, formerly, we could not bear to see or hear, because it was too shocking, painful, or embarrassing, art changes morals. . . ."—for the worse, it is implied.

Like the camera, to which she is addicted at the same time that she bewails it, S. always brings to the reader a new awareness of the world.

WORKS: The Benefactor (1963). *Against Interpretation, and Other Essays* (1966). *Death Kit* (1967). *Trip to Hanoi* (1968). *Styles of Radical Will* (1969). *Duet for Cannibals* (1970). *Brother Carl* (1974). *On Photography* (1977). *I, Etcetera* (1978). *Illness as Metaphor* (1978). *Under the Sign of Saturn* (1980).

ELAINE HOFFMAN BARUCH

Emma Dorothy Eliza Nevitte Southworth

B. 26 Dec. 1819, Washington, D.C.; d. 30 June 1899, Washington, D.C.
Wrote under: Mrs. E.D.E.N. Southworth
D. of Charles LeCompte and Susanna Wailes Nevitte; m. Frederick H. Southworth, 1840

S. and her sister were educated in Washington, D.C., at the school run by her step-father, Joshua Henshaw, whom her mother had married after the death of Captain Nevitte. S. taught school in Washington after her graduation. Deserted by her husband within a few years of their marriage, S. was left with two young children to support. Despite ill health, which plagued her for many years, she returned to teaching in Washington and began to write.

S.'s first publication was a short story, "The Irish Refugee," which appeared in the Baltimore *Saturday Visitor*. This was followed by other short stories. Her first novel, *Retribution* (1849), was serialized in 1847 in the columns of the Washington *National Era*, which published most of her early stories. It is reported that S. never knew how long her serials would be; she would continue on week after week, with characters presumed dead sometimes reappearing. When the serial had reached a certain length, the book publisher would bring out as one volume the work written so far and later publish the rest as a sequel. Many of her works were reprinted in other countries and translated into several languages.

S. produced about three novels per year throughout most of the rest of her life and even at that rate could hardly satisfy the demands of her readers, so popular were her works. *The Hidden Hand* (1888), first published serially in the New York *Ledger*, is said to have been the most popular work that paper ever printed. In book form it sold almost two million copies; it was also transformed into several dramatic versions, one of which starred John Wilkes Booth. *Ishmael* (1876) and *Self-Raised* (1876) sold over two million copies each. Others tried to capitalize on S.'s popularity by writing under names such as S. A. Southworth, Ella Southworth, or Emma S. Southworth; her publishers insisted however that the only genuine novels were those signed with the famous initials E.D.E.N.

A typical theme in S.'s novels is the "rags and riches" romance, exemplified in *The Curse of Clifton* (1853). Clifton, heir to an ancestral fortune, loves a humble mountain girl. Clifton's "curse" is his step-mother—one of S.'s more malignant villains, who in her most furious soliloquies echoes the most evil moments of Lady Macbeth. Some criticis consider *The Hidden Hand* S.'s best work. The heroine, Capitola, is a multi-faceted character, though she is portrayed as thoroughly good. The plot has a great deal of variety, with pranks, outlaws, and much mystery. The villain, Colonel LeNoir, is a model of the type; he grinds his teeth in impotent rage and vows revenge for afronts both real and imagined. S. considered *Self-Made* her best work. It was originally published in 1876 in two parts, the first called *Ishmael; or, In the Depths* and the second *Self-Raised; or, Out of the Depths*. This novel has an interesting rags-to-riches theme, a degenerate villain, and a highborn young woman who refuses to marry the hero, Ishmael, because of his low birth but who is justly punished for her pride. It also has a fine touch of humor and well-handled descriptions of setting and costume.

Villains in S.'s novels are thoroughly evil, heroes and heroines thoroughly pure. The situations in which they are brought together are the familiar fare of most novels written originally in serialized form: sudden catastrophic illnesses, bankruptcies, murders or other calamitous deaths, ancestral secrets revealed, hidden passions unleashed. A voracious reader herself, S. perhaps unconsciously echoes in her work such 19th-c. authors as Scott, Dickens, and Cooper. Some of her favorite settings—wild mountain roads and fearful chasms—are reminiscent of the novels of the Brontës. Finally, however, the enormous popularity of S.'s novels seems to be attributable to the simple black and white morality of her tales, her fine melodramatic touch, and her innate storytelling ability.

WORKS: *Retribution* (1849). *The Deserted Wife* (1850). *The Mother-in-Law* (1851). *Shannondale* (1851). *The Discarded Daughter* (1852). *The Curse of Clifton* (1853). *Old Neighborhoods and New Settlements* (1853). *The Lost Heiress* (1854). *India: The Pearl of Pearl River* (1855). *The Missing Bride* (1855). *Vivia; or, The Secret of Power* (1857). *Virginia and Magdalene* (1858). *The Lady of the Isle* (1859). *The Haunted Homestead* (1860). *The Gipsy's Prophecy* (1861). *Hickory Hall* (1861). *The Broken Engagement* (1862). *Love's Labor Won* (1862). *The Fatal Marriage* (1863). *The Bridal Eve* (1864). *Allworth Abbey* (1865). *The Bride of Llewellyn* (1866). *The Fortune Seeker* (1866). *The Coral Lady* (1867). *The Widow's Son* (1867). *Fair Play* (1868). *The Bride's Fate* (1869). *The Changed Brides* (1869). *The Family Doom* (1869). *How He Won Her* (1869). *The Prince of Darkness* (1869). *The Christmas Guest: A Collection of Stories* (1870). *The Maiden Widow* (1870). *Cruel as the Grave* (1871). *Tried for Her Life* (1871). *The Artist's Love*

(1872). *The Lost Heir of Linlithgow* (1872). *A Noble Lord* (1872). *A Beautiful Fiend* (1873). *Victor's Triumph* (1874). *The Mystery of Dark Hollow* (1875). *The Spectre Lover* (1875). *Ishmael; or, In the Depths* (1876). *Self-Raised or, Out of the Depths* (1876). *The Fatal Secret* (1877). *The Red Hill Tragedy* (1877). *The Phantom Wedding* (1878). *Sybil Brotherton: A Novel* (1879). *The Hidden Hand* (1888). *A Leap in the Dark* (1889). *Nearest and Dearest* (1889). *Unknown* (1889). *For Woman's Love* (1890). *The Lost Lady of Lone* (1890). *Broken Pledges* (1891). *David Lindsay* (1891). *Gloria: A Novel* (1891). *Lillith* (1891). *The Unloved Wife* (1891). *"Em": A Novel* (1892). *Em's Husband: A Novel* (1892). *Brandon Coyle's Wife* (1893). *Only a Girl's Heart* (1893). *A Skeleton in the Closet* (1893). *Gertrude Haddon* (1894). *The Rejected Bride* (1894).

BIBLIOGRAPHY: Boyle, R. L., *Mrs. E.D.E.N. Southworth, Novelist* (1939). Hart, J. D., *The Popular Book* (1950). Mott, F. L., *Golden Multitudes* (1947). Pattee, F. L., *The Feminine Fifties* (1940).
For articles in reference works, see: *AW. DAB*, IX, 1.

ELAINE K. GINSBERG

Elizabeth Spencer

B. *19 July 1921, Carrollton, Mississippi*
D. *of James Luther and Mary James McCain Spencer; m. John Rusher, 1956*

A native of Mississippi and the progeny of a family whose ancestors had lived in Carroll County, Mississippi, since the 1830s, S. spent her childhood in the kind of rural South that she depicts with topographic precision in several of her novels. S. studied English at Belhaven College in Jackson, Mississippi, (B.A. 1942) and Vanderbilt University (M.A. 1943). S. taught for two years, first in Mississippi and then in Tennessee, resigning from teaching to work as a reporter for the Nashville *Tennessean*. In 1946, S. abandoned the craft of the journalist for that of the novelist, and her first novel, *Fire in the Morning*, was published two years later. Recipient of a Guggenheim Fellowship in 1953, S. traveled to Italy, the scene of two later novels, *The Light in the Piazza* (1960) and *Knights and Dragons* (1965). She has served as writer-in-residence at several colleges and universities in the U.S. and Canada.

Fire in the Morning, published with the encouragement of the Fugitive poet Donald Davidson, reveals S.'s first-hand knowledge of the intricate workings of a small Southern town—its layers of intrigue and the complexities of relationships that span several generations. With the Southerner's sense of local story as possessing the power of myth, S. delineates the history and works out the fate of two antagonistic families in Tarsus, Mississippi, in a fashion that recalls the conflicts in various "houses" of Greek drama. The movement of the novel is predicated on a young man's gradual discovery of the interwoven affairs of love, fraud, and violence which underlie one family's dominance of the town. In the process of uncovering the private histories which link together the inhabitants of Tarsus, he comes to terms with the town, his own family, and himself in relationship to what had seemed an inexplicable past.

In *Fire in the Morning*, S. suggests that there are sociological differences between the regions of Delta and hill country in Mississippi. In *This Crooked Way* (1952), these regions provide symbolic points of reference for charting Amos Dudley's odyssey from poverty to riches and from damnation to salvation. Convinced as a consequence of a religious experience that God will support him in his opportunistic endeavors, Dudley leaves the Yocona hills, striding into the Delta in Colonel Sutpen fashion to wrest a plantation out of the overgrown land. His success, however, leaves destruction in its wake; and it is not until he brings the remnants of his hill-country family to the Delta to share his affluence that he finds a measure of peace and is able to reconcile himself with his past.

S.'s third novel, *The Voice at the Back Door* (1956), which treats of politics and the cost of equal justice for blacks and whites in a Southern town, is the last to deal with the Mississippi South. She returns in *The Snare* (1972) to a southern locale; but in this novel it is to the New Orleans atmosphere of the French Quarter, where her heroine becomes involved in the city's underworld of jazz musicians.

In 1960, with the publication of *The Light in the Piazza*, S. shifts locales, delineating in this novella the crisis of conscience of an American woman who decides to allow her beautiful but mentally retarded daughter to marry her young Italian suitor. S. treats such a dilemma, which might otherwise be too ponderous, with grace and charm; and her evocation of the Florentine atmosphere and its impact upon the Americans makes the city a powerful force in the story.

In *Knights and Dragons*, S. again utilizes the Italian scene; but in her recounting of an American divorcee's love involvement there, Rome and Venice are only backdrops for a story dealing essentially with Americans.

She expands both the concern of failing marriages and the setting in *No Place for an Angel* (1967), a novel which focuses upon the complexities of a pair of marital relationships against backgrounds as diverse as Texas, Washington, New York, Rome, and Sicily.

S.'s seven novels, moving as they do from the fixed geography and traditions of the South to an international scene, demonstrate the scope of a writer who may have begun under the shadow of the mythic South but whose vision is not regionally limited. She explores in several contexts and with considerable artistry the individual as an outsider to the environment, whether that environment be the Mississippi Delta or the Italian city.

WORKS: *Fire in the Morning* (1948). *This Crooked Way* (1952). *The Voice at the Back Door* (1956). *The Light in the Piazza* (1960; film version, 1962). *Knights and Dragons* (1965). *No Place for an Angel* (1967). *Ship Island, and Other Stories* (1968) *The Snare* (1972). *The Stories of Elizabeth Spencer* (1981).

BIBLIOGRAPHY: Bradbury, J. M., *Renaissance in the South: A Critical History of Literature, 1920–1960* (1963). Burger, N. K., in *South Atlantic Quarterly* 63 (Summer 1964). Pugh, D. G., in *The Fifties: Fiction, Poetry, Drama*, Ed. W. C. French (1970). Sullivan, W., "The Continuing Renascence: Southern Fiction in the Fifties," *South: Modern Southern Literature in its Cultural Setting*, Eds. L. D. Rubin, Jr., and R. D. Jacobs (1961).

GUIN A. NANCE

Harriet Elizabeth Prescott Spofford

B. *3 April 1835, Calais, Maine; d. 14 Aug. 1921, Deer Island, Massachusetts*
Wrote under: Harriet Prescott, Harriet Prescott Spofford
D. *of Joseph Newmarch and Sarah Jane Bridges Prescott; m. Richard Smith Spofford, 1865*

S. was born into a distinguished New England family that had suffered economic reversals since the War of 1812. S. spent most of her early years in a household of women, including her mother and four Prescott aunts, while her father sought his fortune in the West. In 1849, she settled with her mother in Newburyport, Massachusetts, where she attended Putnam Free School, finishing her education later at the Pinkerton Academy in Derry, New Hampshire. In 1856, when her father returned an invalid and her mother soon was stricken, Harriet became the support of the family. She turned to writing, one of the few lucrative careers open to women in her day. This early work, published anonymously in Boston family story-papers in the 1850s, remains uncollected and unacknowledged. Quantity was demanded rather than quality, as each piece earned S. between two dollars and fifty cents and five dollars. Only with the publication of her short story "In a Cellar," in the young *Atlantic Monthly* (February 1859) did her career really begin.

S.'s marriage to Spofford, a Newburyport lawyer, was long and successful, although their only child died as an infant in 1867. They lived briefly in Washington (*Old Washington*, 1906, is based on S.'s memories); traveled abroad twice; and finally settled on Deer Island, a five-acre island in the Merrimac River near Newburyport. The scenery, legends, and people of her New England home supplied much of the material for S.'s writing, especially her poetry. In "June on the Merrimac," John Greenleaf Whittier called attention to the setting in which "Deer Island's mistress sings." S. lived on Deer Island for the rest of her life, often visited by and visiting a circle of women writers in Boston that included Sarah Orne Jewett, Elizabeth Stuart Phelps Ward, and Julia Ward Howe.

From the 1860s until her death, S. was one of the most widely published of American authors. Many stories, essays, and poems appeared in *Harper's Bazar*, *Atlantic Monthly*, the *Knickerbocker*, the *Cosmopolitan*, and in juvenile magazines such as *Youth's Companion*.

Two strengths save S. from being dismissed as merely a popular-magazine contributor producing only "romantically frothy tales." The first, for which she is alternately highly praised and condemned, is her vivid and often graphic description. In *Sir Rohan's Ghost: A Romance* (1860), for instance, her description of a wine cellar was so convincing and memorable that connoisseurs sent her tributes of wine for years afterward. In a century when woman's sphere was domestic, S. utilized her special knowledge to make textures, jewelry, even furniture definitive of character. In *Art Decoration Applied to Furniture* (1878), S. observed that furniture is "emblazoned, as one might say, with the customs of a people and the manners of a time." Her ability to capture character through setting and inanimate objects is nowhere more stunning than in the title story of *The Amber Gods* (1863), where the two women, Yone and Lu, are defined by the jewels they wear ("This amber's just the thing for me, such a great noon creature!") and the materials that suit them ("I never let Lu wear the point at all; she'd be ridiculous in it,—so flimsy and open and unreserved; that's for me.").

S.'s second strength is that although she too divides her women into opposites reminiscent of the fragile blondes and passionate brunettes who represent saint and sinner for most romantics—and only too accurately represent the roles in which contemporary women were cast—S. reveals the woman within the role. If she takes sides, her vibrant heart urges her to admire the passionate Yones over the dutiful Lus; but Lu, too, is always loved. In "Desert Sands," for instance, the submissive wife Eos has artistic talent that is recognized immediately and appreciated by the seductive Vespasia, and her cousin Alain berates her husband for suppressing it: "This aptitude, this power, this whatever you choose to call it, genius or inspiration, for which you refuse her utterance, this has produced a spiritual asphyxia."

Beginning her career in the 1850s, S. found herself caught between the dying school of romanticism and the newly-vociferous advocates of realism. Her discerning eye and ability to capture the character of her New England neighbors in dialect and description earned the praise of W. D. Howells and the young Henry James, but they were both bothered by her romantic lushness and discouraged her from "fine writing." Although her realistic talent would culminate in her last collection, *The Elder's People* (1920), it could at best earn her recognition as a strong minor writer scarcely comparable to Mary E. Wilkins Freeman. It is in her romantic tendencies that the uniqueness of S.'s writing can be found, even though in response to the fickle changes in popular taste and literary approach, she often either abandoned (always reluctantly) or failed to develop and control the poetic promise of her early romantic work.

WORKS: *Sir Rohan's Ghost: A Romance* (1860). *The Amber Gods, and Other Stories* (1863). *Azarian: An Episode* (1864). *New England Legends* (1871). *The Thief in the Night* (1872). *Art Decoration Applied to Furniture* (1878). *The Servant Girl Question* (1881). *Hester Stanley at St. Marks* (1882). *The Marquis of Carabas* (1882). *Poems* (1882). *Ballads about Authors* (1887). *House and Hearth* (1891). *A Lost Jewel* (1891). *A Scarlet Poppy, and Other Stories* (1894). *A Master Spirit* (1896). *In Titian's Garden, and Other Poems* (1897). *An Inheritance* (1897). *Stepping-Stones to Happiness* (1897). *Hester Stanley's Friends* (1898). *Priscilla's Love-Story* (1898). *The Maid He Married* (1899). *Old Madame, and Other Tragedies* (1900). *The Children of the Valley* (1901). *The Great Procession, and other Verses for and about Children* (1902). *That Betty* (1903). *Four Days of God* (1905). *Old Washington* (1906). *The Fairy Changeling: A Flower and Fairy Play* (1911). *The Making of a Fortune: A Romance* (1911). *The King's Easter* (1912). *A Little Book of Friends* (1916). *The Elder's People* (1920).

BIBLIOGRAPHY: Cooke, Rose Terry, *Our Famous Women* (1883). Halbeisen, E. K., *Harriet Prescott Spofford* (1935). Hopkins, A. A., *Waifs, and Their Authors* (1879). *The Development of the American Short Story* (1923). Pattee, F. L., *A History of American Literature since 1870* (1915). Ward, Elizabeth Stuart Phelps, "Stories that Stay," *The Century Magazine*, N.S. 59 (Nov. 1910). Richardson, C. F., *American Literature (1607–1885)* (1902).

For articles in reference works, see: *NCAB*, IV.

Other references: *Bookman* 62 (Nov. 1925).

THELMA J. SHINN

Elizabeth Cady Stanton

B. 12 Nov. 1815, Johnstown, New York; d. 26 Oct. 1902, New York City
D. of Daniel and Margaret Livingston Cady; m. Henry Brewster Stanton, 1840

S. was the fourth of six children. Her father was a lawyer, politician, and judge. Listening to his clients and reading his law books, she learned at an early age of the injustices women suffer. When the family's only son died in 1826, she resolved to take his place. She was tutored in Greek by her Presbyterian minister and later studied Latin and mathematics at the Johnstown Academy. She graduated from Emma Willard's Troy Female Seminary in 1832.

A strong advocate of the reforms of the day—temperance, abolition, and women's rights—she had the word "obey" omitted from the ceremony at her marriage to Stanton, an antislavery lecturer. On their honeymoon, the couple attended a world anti-slavery convention in London, where S. met Lucretia Mott, a delegate the convention refused to seat because she was a woman. After the European tour, they settled in Johnstown, where the first of their seven children was born in 1842. They moved to Boston shortly thereafter and, in 1847, to Seneca Falls, New York. S. and Lucretia Mott organized the first convention for women's rights there in 1848. S. was commissioned to draft the Declaration of Principles, in which she included a most controversial resolution demanding suffrage.

S. met Susan B. Anthony in 1851, and the two formed a very fruitful collaborative friendship which spanned the next half century. S. was the writer and speaker whenever possible; Anthony the strategist, organizer, and intrepid traveler. In the years after the Civil War there were increasing divisions in the women's movement, due partly to differing assessments of priorities. S. campaigned against the Fourteenth and Fifteenth Amendments because they did not extend rights to women. This alienated many reformers who argued that "this is the Negro's hour." In 1868, S. and Anthony published a magazine, *Revolution,* financed by erratic entrepeneur George Francis Train, in which they included his controversial views on economics and labor unions as well as their own radical views on marriage and divorce. In 1869, S. and Anthony formed the National Woman Suffrage Association, which S. led as president for twenty-one years. Other reformers, generally more conservative, formed the American Woman Suffrage Association. When the two suffrage associations merged in 1890, she served as president for two years.

In order to finance her children's education, S. spent many years delivering lectures, on subjects such as the education of women and divorce, for the New York Lyceum Bureau. Throughout a half-century career, she wrote many letters and articles, not only on suffrage but on a wide range of social and political questions affecting women, for feminist and general newspapers. In addition to numerous tracts and pamphlets reprinting her speeches and articles, she published three major works.

With Anthony, she edited the first three volumes of the monumental *History of Woman's Suffrage* (1881–86), covering the years from 1848 to 1885. Admittedly one-sided, their history contains a rich store of speeches, summarized debates, letters, and evaluations of the early women's rights conventions, both national and state.

S.'s most controversial work is *The Woman's Bible* (2 vols., 1895–1898). Her unorthodox views had been known for years, through essays like "The Effect of Woman Suffrage on Questions of Morals and Religion," included in pamphlets such as *The Christian Church and Women* (1881) and *Bible and Church Degrade Women* (1885). She believed that "whatever the Bible may be made to do in Hebrew or Greek, in plain English it does not exalt and dignify woman." Although she invited a panel of women scholars to assist her, most declined. The bulk of the brief notes on each book are S.'s, and the results are eclectic and sketchy. Despite an appeal from Anthony for tolerance of differing opinions, the 1896 national convention of the National American Woman Suffrage Association passed a resolution dissociating the organization from the work.

S.'s autobiography, *Eighty Years and More* (1898), contains the candid and delightful reminiscences of a woman who, at eighty-three, was still trying to expand the frontiers for her sisters.

WORKS: *History of Woman Suffrage* (with S. B. Anthony, Vols. 1–3, 1881–86). *The Woman's Bible* (2 Vols., 1895–98). *Eighty Years and More* (1898). *Elizabeth Cady Stanton as Revealed in her Letters, Diary, and Reminiscences* (Eds. T. Stanton and H. S. Blatch, 2 vols., 1922).

BIBLIOGRAPHY: Blatch, H. S., and A. Lutz, *Challenging Years: The Memoirs of Harriot Stanton Blatch* (1940). Lutz, A., *Created Equal* (1940), Lutz, A., *Susan B. Anthony: Rebel, Crusader, Humanitarian* (1959).

NANCY A. HARDESTY

Gertrude Stein

B. 13 Feb. 1874, Allegheny, Pennsylvania; d. 27 July 1946, Neuilly-sur-Seine, France
D. of Daniel and Amelia Keyser Stein

S., the youngest of seven children, spent her early years in Europe, before her intense, restless, argumentative father settled his family in Oakland, California. Both her parents died while she was an adolescent. Her principal companion until she was well into her thirties was her brother Leo, a brilliant but erratic lifelong student of the arts.

She studied at Radcliffe College (1893–97), with William James, and then studied neurology at Johns Hopkins Medical School, where she completed two satisfactory years before becoming undisciplined in her work. She did not receive her degree.

In 1903, S. joined Leo in Paris at 27, rue de Fleurus, the site of her now legendary salon, and under his guidance she began to collect modern art. She and Alice B. Toklas established the love relationship that would endure for the remainder of their lives in 1907. Two years later, Toklas moved to the rue de Fleurus, where she remained with S. after the brother and sister formally separated in 1913.

Except for a visit to America (1934–35), S. spent the rest of her life in Europe. She and Toklas did war-relief work during WWI. During the 1930s, S.'s reputation grew, especially with the extensive promotion of

The Autobiography of Alice B. Toklas (1933). With Toklas, she spent much of WWII in the French countryside, where their fellow villagers protected them as Jews during the Nazi occupation.

The range of her work is great, and her innovations in style make strict classifications difficult and misleading. She wrote poems, plays, novels, autobiography, theory, and criticism; and, in addition, she created new kinds of works, such as the "portraits."

Her first full-length work charts the dynamics of a lesbian love triangle. *Q. E. D.* was written in 1903 and published posthumously in 1950 as *Things as They Are.* Adele, the principal character, is modeled in S.'s own image, and the plot is patterned after her thwarted love affair at medical school. The novel is largely realistic, with an established set of characters and a sequential plot line. S. is most concerned with the revelation of character through plot and believes character determines events. In this respect, she differs from contemporary naturalistic and realistic writers and their concern with the effects of deterministic forces external to the individual.

Written between 1903 and 1911 but not published until 1925, *The Making of Americans; or, The History of a Family's Progress* is S.'s most voluminous and possibly most accomplished prose work. Her original intention was to write a history of every American "who ever can or is or was or will be living," but her goal changed in the course of writing the novel. It begins in the realistic mode, with attention to delineation of time, place, and character, but swiftly becomes an autobiographical record in which she meditates on partially transformed aspects of her past and the movement of her consciousness at the moment of composition. S. seeks to express the "bottom nature"—that rhythmic movement of consciousness that is what one essentially is, that makes up one's identity. As a consequence, the work becomes increasingly abstract, for narrative is abandoned and associative patterning determines the ordering of word and phrase and sentence.

Three Lives (1909) contains three stories of lower-class women. The heroines of "The Good Anna" and "The Gentle Lena" are lightly sketched, flat characters. "Melanctha," the most accomplished work of *Three Lives*, represents a great change and advance in S.'s style. Ostensibly, "Melanctha" concerns the relationship between a young mulatto woman and a black doctor; the fairly sympathetic portrayal of black characters is remarkable for the time. The work also concerns the same love triangle S. had written of earlier. Now the focus is on Jeff Campbell, who shares the cerebral, bourgeois quality of S.'s alter ego Adele in *Q. E. D.*; Melanctha, a vibrant, sensual woman corresponds to Adele's beloved. S. later contended that the detailed and complex characterization was the result of writing in the spirit of a Cézanne portrait, for she accords substantial attention to each aspect of her characters' composition. She was praised for using sentence forms that reflect her characters' mode of dealing with reality. For example, compound declarative sentences, replete with participial modifiers, represent Jeff Campbell's habitual recoiling from experience into endless rumination.

During the years from 1908 to 1913, S. wrote one- to three-page prose "portraits" of her friends and acquaintances. The portraits were published in a variety of places: Alfred Stieglitz published "Picasso" and "Matisse" in *Camera Work* (1912); many were included in *Portraits and Prayers* (1934). In far shorter works than "Melanctha," S. continues her study of how sentence forms can express character.

The portraits are helpful in charting the increasing abstraction of S.'s style, the change from the minimal narrative and direct characterization of *Three Lives* to the hermetic style of *Tender Buttons* (1914). Instead of portraying the character of others, in the latter she meditates on her own individual mode of perceiving and reacting to experience. Virtually without referents and narrative, *Tender Buttons* is unified by a single consciousness.

S.'s early plays, some of which are included in *Geography and Plays* (1922), use conventional dramatic elements in an idiosyncratic way to call attention to their mere conventionality. "Counting Her Dresses," for example, contains numerous "parts" and "acts" randomly assigned; most have one line, only one has three. Yet the subject is fairly accessible: the eccentricities, frailties, and vanities of women who identify with their outward appearance.

Composition as Explanation (1926) builds on the substance of talks S. addressed to the literary societies of Oxford and Cambridge universities. By "composition" she means both the world as a set of phenomena perceived in any moment of time and the expression of this perception in a work of art. The artist creates an impression of what is seen in her time, but because her realization is far more sensitive and acute than that of others, her work is termed ugly by contemporaries. The greater the masterpiece, the more surely it will be judged ugly. Only in the future will the validity and beauty of such a work be established.

Operas and Plays (1932) contains works spanning the years 1913 to 1931, including S.'s best-known opera, "Four Saints in Three Acts" (1927), for which Virgil Thomson composed the music. It deals with the condition of being a saint—of being constant in faith, of sustaining internal balance, of knowing one's identity clearly and truly.

The Autobiography of Alice B. Toklas is S.'s most popular work and also her most stylistically accessible. By writing as if she were Toklas, she distances herself from her material and creates her own legend, and she takes advantage of a certain latitude with the truth allowed by the semifictional mode that results from her innovative use of narrative voice. It remains unclear to what degree Toklas herself contributed to the work's composition and editing. S. recounts with sympathy and wit Toklas's life in San Francisco and arrival in Paris in 1907, relates her own early years (not necessarily accurately), and then treats the women's lives in Paris.

Lectures in America (1935) is S.'s theoretical explanation and justification of her work. It is fairly straightforward, highly egocentric, and thoroughly charming. Her assessment of her place in the history of literature must be looked at in the light of her intense sense of self-importance, but the lectures are significant because in them she sets up the critical framework (relating her writing to the goals of cubist painters) that is the most frequent means of explaining her innovative style. *The Geographical History of America; or, The Relation of Human Nature to the Human Mind* (1936) is S.'s formal treatise on the nature and operation of consciousness.

In *Paris France* (1940), S. attempts to justify remaining in France despite the specter of war. For her, politics is irrelevant; she retreats into the security of a harmoniously composed and ordered everyday life and asserts its viability against imminent physical danger. "I cannot write too much upon how necessary it is to be completely conservative that is particularly traditional to be free."

Of particular interest in *Wars I Have Seen* (1945) is S.'s almost exclusive focus on domestic affairs and her acceptance of the Vichy regime. Her placid attitude may be the result of her age—she was then seventy—her consistently conservative political views, and her lifelong need to bring events within the spectrum of her personal philosophy, often at the expense of the truth.

S.'s forty-three-year career was as prolific as it was long. It is however, her lot to be remembered primarily for her support and encouragement of other artists, and neglected for her own accomplishments as a writer. Undoubtedly, S.'s patronage of abstract painters encouraged and supported Picasso, Matisse, and others in their work. Her friendship with and close reading of such writers as Ernest Hemingway and Sherwood Anderson clearly affected the direction of their writing. Her own work was read by American and European writers, and the simplicity and purity of her language was well appreciated by a number of them. S.'s salon was a site of intellectual ferment at a time when Americans and Europeans were forging an artistic community in Paris. Still, S. was accomplished as a writer herself, and it is time that increased critical attention is paid her and the measure of her innovative work made.

S.'s work rests firmly on autobiographical features and on her attempt to find a stylistic equivalent for her philosophy of perception. Her first writings are fairly traditional in form, but swiftly convention gives way to innovation. All of her works are difficult if the reader demands conventional stylistic devices, because S. employs them only to ask: what purpose do they serve? what limits do they place on expression and comprehension? When she innovates in style, it is to sharpen her own scrutiny of language: its sounds, its meanings, its sequence. Hence, her writing is essentially metalinguistic, for the subject of her work is the work itself.

WORKS: *Three Lives* (1909). *Tender Buttons* (1914). *Geography and Plays* (1922). *The Making of Americans* (1925). *Composition as Explanation* (1926). *Useful Knowledge* (1928). *Lucy Church Amiably* (1930). *Operas and Plays* (1932). *The Autobiography of Alice B. Toklas* (1933). *Matisse, Picasso, and Gertrude Stein, with Two Shorter Stories* (1933). *Four Saints in Three Acts* (1934). *Portraits and Prayers* (1934). *Lectures in America* (1935). *Narration* (1935). *The Geographical History of America* (1936). *Everybody's Autobiography* (1937). *Picasso* (1938). *The World Is Round* (1939). *Paris, France* (1940). *What Are Masterpieces?* (1940). *Ida: A Novel* (1941). *Wars I Have Seen* (1945). *Brewsie and Willie* (1946). *Four in America* (1947). *Blood on the Dining Room Floor* (1948). *The Gertrude Stein Reader and Three Plays* (1948). *Last Operas and Plays* (1949). *Things as They Are* (1950). *The Unpublished Works of Gertrude Stein* (8 vols., 1951–58). *Gertrude Stein: Writings and Lectures, 1909–1945* (1967). *Gertrude Stein on Picasso* (Ed. E. Burns, 1970). *Fernhurst, Q. E. D., and Other Early Writings* (1971). *Sherwood Anderson/Gertrude Stein: Correspondence and Personal Essays* (1972). *A Book Concluding with As a Wife Has a Cow: A Love Story* (1973). *Reflections on the Atomic Bomb* (1973). *How Writing Is Done* (1974). *In Savoy; or, "Yes" Is for Yes for a Very Young Man* (1977; produced, 1949).

BIBLIOGRAPHY: Bridgman, R., *Gertrude Stein in Pieces* (1970). Brinnin, J. M., *The Third Rose: Gertrude Stein and Her World* (1959). Gallup, D., ed., *The Flowers of Friendship: Letters Written to Gertrude Stein* (1953). Gass, W. H., *The World within the Word* (1978). Hobhouse, J., *Everybody Who Was Anybody: A Biography of Gertrude Stein* (1975). Hoffman, F., *Gertrude Stein* (Univ. of Minnesota Pamphlets on American Writers, 1961). Hoffman, M., *The Development of Abstractionism in the Writings of Gertrude Stein* (1965). Hoffman, M., *Gertrude Stein* (1976). Katz, L., "The First Making of *The Making of Americans:* A Study Based on Gertrude Stein's Notebooks and Early Versions of Her Novel (1902–1908)" (Ph.D. diss., Columbia Univ., 1963). Kawin, B., *Telling It Again and Again* (1972). Klaich, D., *Woman +*

Woman: Attitudes towards Lesbianism (1974). Mellow, J. R., *Charmed Circle: Gertrude Stein & Company* (1974). Miller, R., *Gertrude Stein: Form and Intelligibility* (1949). Reid, B. L., *Art by Subtraction* (1958). Sprigge, E., *Gertrude Stein: Her Life and Work* (1957). Stein, L., *Journey into the Self* (1950). Stewart, A., *Gertrude Stein and the Present* (1950). Sutherland, D., *Gertrude Stein: A Biography of Her Work* (1951). Thomson, V., "A Very Difficult Author," in *NYRB* (8 April 1971). Thomson, V., *Virgil Thomson* (1966). Toklas, A. B., *Staying on Alone: Letters of Alice B. Toklas* (1973). Toklas, A. B., *What Is Remembered* (1963). Wilson, E., *Axel's Castle* (1931). Wilson, E., *The Shores of Light* (1952).

Other references: *AL* 45 (1973). *Ascent* 18 (Autumn 1958).

JANIS TOWNSEND

Elizabeth Gertrude Levin Stern

B. *14 Feb. 1889, Skedel, Poland; d. 9 Jan. 1954, Philadelphia, Pennsylvania*
Wrote under: Eleanor Morton, Leah Morton, E. G. Stern, Elizabeth Stern,
  Elizabeth Gertrude Stern
D. *of Aaron and Sarah Leah Rubenstein Levin; m. Leon Thomas Stern, ca. 1911*

The infant S. emigrated with her parents in 1890 from Poland to Pittsburgh, where she was raised and educated, graduating from the University of Pittsburgh in 1910. After a year at the New York School of Philanthropy, she married penologist Leon Stern, and began a career that successfully combined marriage and motherhood with social work and writing. S. was a night school principal in New York and Galveston, supervised welfare work for Wanamaker's in Philadelphia, and directed two New York settlement houses. A journalist from 1914 to 1937, S. included features in the *New York Times* and a regular column in the Philadelphia *Inquirer* among her accomplishments. In the 1940s she wrote, lectured, and was active in many Quaker and philanthropic organizations. She died at sixty-four after a long illness.

S.'s best works are fictionalized autobiographies that focus on her movement from Polish-Jewish ghetto to American mainstream. Theodore Roosevelt introduced S.'s first book, *My Mother and I* (1917), which poignantly describes how education loosens bonds between an immigrant mother and her daughter. While the young protagonist is proud of her achieved status as middle-class housewife, she regrets her mother's alienation from the world maternal self-sacrifice helped her reach. In *I Am a Women—and a Jew* (1926), S. explores the confrontation between a rebellious daughter and her rabbi-father, with the mother as mediator. The first-person narrator's rejection of both orthodox Judaism and feminine domesticity is complicated by a lingering sense of responsibility to both traditions, and inability to escape anti-Semitism and sexism.

S. also used her work experience as raw material for fiction. With her husband, she wrote *A Friend at Court* (1923), the "casebook" of an idealized female probation officer. The work is marred by a predictable romantic subplot and panegyrics on probation as a social panacea. The middle-aged social worker in *When Love Comes to Woman* (1929) provides no such pat answers to women involved in unconventional living arrangements; S.'s ideal is a dual-career marriage promising lifelong friendship. Her telling comparisons between the sexual experimentation of the "new women" of the 1920s and the seriousness of the suffragists of her youth offer insights into important and still-contemporary issues.

Family relationships are central to S.'s other novels. In *A Marriage Was Made* (1928), a mother's domination of her daughter thwarts the girl's promising career by making her too passive to express emotion in her music or life. The mother-daughter theme is also important in *Gambler's Wife* (1931), which traces a strong but self-sacrificing woman from her youth in the Arkansas hills, through her elopement with a drifter who repeatedly abandons her, to her last years with her grown, but immature, children.

Later in life, S. moved from fiction to essay and biography. A collection of her newspaper columns, *Not All Laughter* (1937), reveals her consuming interest in relationships, and her version of woman's true role: the thinking wife, the comrade. S. wrote biographies of a businesswoman (*Memories: The Life of Margaret McAvoy Smith*, 1943) and a Quaker inventor (*Josiah White: Prince of Pioneers*, 1946). In her last book, *The Women behind Gandhi* (1953), S. concentrates on Gandhi's wife and his Indian and European female disciples, highlighting the women's rights phase of his movement for India's full liberation.

In her works, S. accurately accounts the costs and benefits of both the Americanization process and the application of feminist principles to life.

Her books may appear dated by their romanticism and frequent concentration upon battles considered long won (particularly on the right of married women to work), but S.'s emphasis upon the sacrifices involved in family relationships complicated by cultural change is of continuing interest, and her perspective as a daughter of immigrants makes her insights especially important.

WORKS: *My Mother and I* (1917). *A Friend at Court* (with L. T. Stern, 1923). *I Am a Women—and a Jew* (1926). *This Ecstasy* (1927). *A Marriage Was Made* (1928). *When Love Comes to Woman* (1929). *Gambler's Wife* (1931). *Not All Laughter: A Mirror to Our Times* (1937). *Memories: The Life of Margaret McAvoy Scott* (1943). *Josiah White: Prince of Pioneers* (1947). *The Women behind Gandhi* (1953).

BIBLIOGRAPHY: Baum, C., P. Hyman, and S. Michel, *The Jewish Woman in America* (1976).

For articles in reference works, see: *NCAB*, 39.

Other references: *Bookman* (Aug. 1917). *NYT* (8 July 1917; 24 April 1929; 19 Feb. 1928; 12 April 1931; 10 Jan. 1954). *SatR* (18 Dec. 1926; 7 Sept. 1929; 8 Aug. 1953). *Survey* (15 Oct. 1923; Feb. 1947).

HELEN M. BANNAN

Annis Boudinot Stockton

B. *1 July 1736, Darby, Pennsylvania; d. 6 Feb. 1801, Burlington County, New Jersey*
Wrote under: "Emelia" (sometimes spelled "Amelia")
D. of Elias and Catherine Williams Boudinot; m. Richard Stockton, ca. 1755

Although few records of S.'s childhood remain, her extant manuscripts and Stockton family histories leave a considerable body of material for reconstructing her adult life. Born to a tradesman of French Huguenot descent, S. apparently received a more substantial education than was common for girls of her time. Her first poems were written before her marriage to Stockton, a well-known New Jersey lawyer, landowner, and future signer of the Declaration of Independence. Some of these poems celebrate their courtship: " . . . I find on earth no charms for me / But what's connected with the thought of thee!" After her marriage, S. moved to the Stockton estate near Princeton, naming her home "Morven," after the imaginary land of Ossian's (James Macpherson's) Fingal. The romance of that title and the elaborately stylish gardens S. cultivated at Morven reflect the impulses of much of her verse: pastoral, sentimental, and imitative of popular British modes.

The quiet life at Morven was interrupted by the Revolutionary War. Because both S. and her husband were committed patriots, Morven was occupied by the British under Cornwallis during the Battle of Princeton in December, 1776. The estate was sacked; plate and papers (including some of Stockton's early poems) were stolen. And although the family had been evacuated, Richard Stockton was taken prisoner soon after their escape. Washington's quick recapture of Princeton allowed S. and her children to return to their ruined home. Richard Stockton was released later in 1777, but ill treatment in prison probably hastened his death in 1781. S.'s watch by her husband's deathbed occasioned two of her most moving elegies: "But vain is prophesy when death's approach, / Thro' years of pain, has sap'd a dearer life, / And makes me, coward like, myself reproach, / That e're I knew the tender name of wife." S. continued to live at Morven until the marriage of her eldest son, at which time she left the estate to him and moved to the home of her youngest daughter, Abigail Field of Burlington County, where she died in 1801.

Much of S.'s life had been occupied with the raising of her six children and the managing of a sizeable household. But however demanding those responsibilities became, she continued to make time for her verse. Richard Stockton encouraged her work, and S.'s audience gradually expanded beyond the family circle. She exchanged verses, for example, with Philadelphia poet Elizabeth Graeme Fergusson. Noting the support she found in her "sister" poet, S. addressed Fergusson directly in "To Laura" (Fergusson's pseudonym): "Permit a sister muse to soar / To heights she never try'd before, / And then look up to thee. . . ." Additionally, S. became a close friend of Esther Burr, who preserved two of S.'s poems in her journal. She wrote a number of odes to George Washington, many of them warmly acknowledged in his letters to her. Such encouragement from family and friends may have suggested to S. the possibility of an even wider audience: her first known publication, "To the Honorable Colonel Peter Schuyler," appeared in the *New-York Mercury* for 9 January, 1758, and in the *New American Magazine* for January, 1758. Although other Philadelphia, New York, and New Jersey periodicals printed S.'s verse from time to time, most of her work remained in manuscript.

Throughout her life, S. continued to work in the couplets and alternately rhymed quatrains of Pope, Young, Thomson, and Gray. Using these models, she developed themes of courtship, marriage, nature, friendship, patriotism, old age, and grief. But even as she imitated conventional forms, S. worried about the propriety of her activities: she confided to her brother Elias in a letter dated 1 May, 1789, about one of her odes to Washington, that "if you think it will only add one sprig to the wreath the country twines to bind the brows of my hero, I will run the risk of being sneered at by those who criticize female productions of all kinds." Fearful for her reputation, yet wishing recognition for her work, S. faced a dilemma common to colonial women poets. The number of her publications and the size of her extant manuscript collection may indicate that the desire to write finally outweighed her fear of impropriety.

WORKS: Poems by Stockton were published in the *New-York Mercury*, the *New American Magazine*, the *Pennsylvania Magazine*, the *Columbian Magazine*, and the *New Jersey Gazette*. Some poems are appended to the Reverend Samuel Stanhope Smith's *Funeral Sermon on the Death of the Hon. Richard Stockton . . .* (1781). Manuscripts are in Princeton University Library, Historical Society of Pennsylvania, and Library of Congress, and several poems from this collection were reprinted in *PULC* (Nov. 1944; Nov. 1945).

BIBLIOGRAPHY: Bill, A., *A House Called Morven* (1954). Cowell, P., *Women Poets in Pre-Revolutionary America, 1650–1775* (1981). Ellet, E., *Women of the American Revolution* (1850). Glenn T., *Some Colonial Houses and Those Who Lived in Them* (1899). Green H. C., and M. W. Green, *Pioneer Mothers in America* (1912). Stockton, J., *A History of the Stockton Family* (1881). Stockton, T. C., *The Stocktons of New Jersey, and Other Stocktons* (1911).

PATTIE COWELL

Harriet Elizabeth Beecher Stowe

B. 14 June 1811, Litchfield, Connecticut; d. 1 July 1896, Hartford, Connecticut
Wrote under: Christopher Crowfield, Harriet Beecher Stowe
D. of Lyman and Roxana Beecher; m. Calvin Stowe, 1836

S. was the daughter, sister, wife, and mother of New England Calvinist clergymen. Instead of speaking from the pulpit as a man could do, she used her pen to offer moral guidance on contemporary issues. She began writing as a child and first published (primarily contributions to gift books) while teaching at the school of her sister, the famous educator Catharine Beecher, in Cincinnati.

Her husband, a theology professor, did not earn much to support their family as they moved from Ohio to Maine, to Massachusetts, and to Connecticut, where S. had been raised. She bore seven children. In the early years of her marriage, she occasionally wrote short stories and sketches, and the income provided some relief from her domestic drudgery. Her commitment to writing increased after a collection of stories, *The May-flower*, was published in 1843.

Her first novel, *Uncle Tom's Cabin* (1852) became one of the most popular novels of the century, and it gave her widespread recognition in the U.S. and Great Britain. S. wrote ten novels, short stories for children and adults, travel sketches of Europe and Florida, religious poems, biographies of Civil War heroes, a book on Lady and Lord Byron's marriage (which is critical of Byron), and numerous articles on homemaking and other subjects. Throughout her life, S. wrote quickly and prolifically under the pressure of meeting the financial needs of her husband and children, even long after they had become adults. Many lesser works were published under the name Christopher Crowfield.

Like her sister Catharine, she contributed to the 19th-c. cult of domesticity and gospel of womanhood. S. rejected the intellectual formula for salvation propagated by the overly speculative male clergy of New England and substituted a belief in the function of women as spiritual redeemers of husbands and sons necessarily involved in worldly struggles. As one of her characters explains, "I believe it is woman who holds faith in the world. I'd rather have my wife's . . . opinion of the meaning of a text of Scripture than all the doctors of divinity."

Literary romanticism, such as that of Byron, Scott, Burns, and Goethe, provides a framework for her glorification of women who trust their hearts more than their minds and favor nature over urban environments. Her novels are simple, romantic, and sentimental. The plots are formulas, involving the redemptive power of love, and usually culminate in both marriage and salvation of the soul. The heroine frequently saves the hero through the purity of her sentiment. S.'s novels are often set in the colonial era, which she believed to be wholesomely moral in contrast to 19th-c. urban decadence.

Her best-known novel, *Uncle Tom's Cabin*, did much to stir northern indignation against slavery. It has been suggested by various biographers that there were personal motivations behind S.'s response to slavery. She herself explained that "much that is in that book . . . had its root in the awful scenes and bitter sorrows of that summer" of 1847, when her infant son died in a cholera epidemic. She learned what a slave mother felt when her child is taken from her, and she also identified with black women because of her own heavy domestic duties, her never ending labors to take care of her children on a meager income and with a melancholy husband.

The slavery novels are significant in the development of S.'s belief in women as saviors. Uncle Tom is portrayed as motherly, submissive, feminine; Little Eva's death saves onlookers moved by her angelic innocence; Rachel, the Quaker mother, is a model of piety. A mature woman, however, is not yet central. She wrote two additional books to show the disastrous effect of slavery on the family—*The Key to Uncle Tom's Cabin* (1853) and *Dred: A Tale of the Great Dismal Swamp* (1856)—and then turned to her major theme of women as agents of salvation.

In *The Minister's Wooing* (1859), the heroine, Mary Scudder, is described as a "pure priestess of a domestic temple" who had a "strange power" to inspire boys. Mary lives in the late 18th c.; Agnes of *Agnes of Sorrento* (1862) lives in 15th-c. Italy, but is also a divinity to the nobleman she married. Mara, in *The Pearl of Orr's Island* (1862) is yet another fairy princess, angel, and saint, whose pious death brings salvation to Moses, the young man who loves her. Tina, in *Oldtown Folks* (1869), is "one of the species of womankind that used to be sought out as priestesses to the Delphic Oracle."

Lillie, in *Pink and White Tyranny* (1871), is an exception to S.'s archetypal heroine, although her husband is a "romantic adorer of womanhood." She illustrates the power of the environment: Lillie's beauty causes her to be shallow and spoiled by men. Only her suffering during illness and her husband's compassion save her soul at the end of the story.

S.'s last novel, *Poganuc People* (1878), is semiautobiographical. The heroine, Dolly, reflects S.'s struggle with the conversion requirements established by New England theology, which she could not meet. Like S., Dolly turns to the Episcopal church, which granted membership to any sincere believer. Dolly is another soul-saver; S. describes her as "exhorting with a degree of fervor and fluency in reciting texts of Scriptures."

S.'s novels aroused great feeling against slavery and popularized the notion of woman's place as guardian angel of the home. She said that she wrote her books so that children as well as adults could read them. Perhaps it is for this reason that they are cast in repetitious formulas of angelic heroines, absurd male clergy tangled in the inconsistencies of their theological systems, and well-meaning sons and husbands dependent on mothers and wives for spiritual inspiration. Her readers found in her books what they read sentimental fiction for; they were titillated by scenes of her characters' struggles, such as the passionate death of the young, virginal heroine—most famous being Little Eva's death in *Uncle Tom's Cabin*.

She does not often develop her characters beyond the obvious typologies, but the reader identifies with their problems nevertheless, perhaps because S. did herself. She was not a complex or sophisticated writer, but she mirrored and evoked common beliefs and concerns of her era: the desire to sanctify woman and the family to provide solutions, first, to the problem of slavery and, then, to the corruption of industrial urban life.

WORKS: *An Elementary Geography* (1835). *The Mayflower; or, Sketches of Scenes and Characters of the Descendants of the Pilgrims* (1843; rev. ed., 1855; English title, *Let Every Man Mind His Own Business*). *The Two Altars* (1852). *Uncle Tom's Cabin* (2 vols. 1852). *The Key to Uncle Tom's Cabin* (1853). *Uncle Tom's Emancipation* (1853). *Sunny Memories of Foreign Lands* (2 vols., 1854). *Dred: A Tale of the Dismal Swamp* (2 vols., 1856; reissued as *Nina Gordon*, 1866). *My Expectation* (1858). *My Strength* (1858). *Our Charlie and What to Do with Him* (1858). *Strong Consolation* (1858). *Things that Cannot Be Shaken* (1858). *A Word to the Sorrowful* (1858). *The Minister's Wooing* (1859). *Agnes of Sorrento* (1862). *The Pearl of Orr's Island* (1862). *House and Home Papers* (1865). *Little Foxes* (1865). *Stories about Our Boys* (1865). *Religious Poems* (1867). *Daisy's First Winter, and Other Stories* (1867). *Queer Little People* (1867). *The Chimney Corner* (1868). *Men of Our Times* (1868). *The American Woman's Home* (with C. E. Beecher, 1869). *Oldtown Folks* (1969). *Lady Byron Vindicated* (1870). *Little Pussy Willow* (1870). *My Wife and I* (1871). *Pink and White Tyranny* (1871). *Sam Lawson's Old Town Fireside Stories* (1872). *Palmetto Leaves* (1873). *Women in Sacred*

History (1873; reissued as *Bible Heroines*, 1878). *Deacon Pitkin's Farm* (English, 1875; similar American collection, *Betty's Bright Idea, and Other Tales*, 1876). *We and Our Neighbors* (1875). *Footsteps of the Master* (1876). *Poganuc People* (1878). *A Dog's Mission; or, The Story of Old Avery House, and Other Stories* (1881). *Nellie's Heroics* (1888). *Our Famous Women* (1884). *The Collected Works of Harriet Beecher Stowe* (16 vols., 1896).

BIBLIOGRAPHY: Adams, J., *Harriet Beecher Stowe* (1963). Ashton, J. W., *Harriet Beecher Stowe: A Reference Guide* (1977). Cross, B., ed., *Autobiography of Lyman Beecher* (2 vols., 1961). Crozier, A., *The Novels of Harriet Beecher Stowe* (1969). Fields, Annie Adams, *Life and Letters of Harriet Beecher Stowe* (1897). Foster, C. H., *The Rungless Ladder* (1954). Gerson, N. B., *Harriet Beecher Stowe: A Biography* (1976). Gilbertson, C., *Harriet Beecher Stowe* (1937). Johnston, J., *Runaway to Heaven* (1963). Kimball, G., *The Religious Ideas of Harriet Beecher Stowe: Her Gospel of Womanhood* (1982). McCray, F. T., *The Life-Work of the Author of Uncle Tom's Cabin* (1889). Stowe, C. E., and L. Stowe, *Harriet Beecher Stowe: The Story of Her Life* (1911). Stowe, L., *Saints, Sinners, and Beechers* (1934). Wagenknecht, E., *Harriet Beecher Stowe: The Known and the Unknown* (1965). Wilson, F., *Crusader in Crinoline* (1941).

GAYLE KIMBALL

Gene Stratton-Porter

B. 17 Aug. 1863, Wabash City, Indiana; d. 6 Dec. 1924, Los Angeles, California
D. of Mark and Mary Shellabarger Stratton; m. Charles Dorwin Porter, 1886

S. was the youngest of twelve children. She married in 1886; there was one daughter. From early childhood, S. spent most of her time outdoors with her father and brothers and was fascinated by plants and birds. From her father, S. learned her first lessons as a naturalist.

Few authors claim to write so directly from life. S. stressed that she based fictional characters on her beloved family and admired friends, insisting that true-to-life portraits need not focus on undesirable human traits. Similarly, the three areas in which she lived—the Wabash River Basin, the Limberlost Swamp in northeastern Indiana, and Southern California—figure importantly in her work.

Although S. was enormously popular and successful at several types of imaginative writing (magazine articles, short stories, poetry, and novels), she considered herself primarily a naturalist. In natural history as in fiction, S. relied wholly on her own observations, devoting enormous energy and facing considerable danger to achieve veracity. Largely self-educated, S. also trained herself as an expert photographer and polished her drawing skills to illustrate the nature books. Although critics have questioned the accuracy of some of her observations, S. had total confidence in her field work as in her personal experience.

S.'s aim was to teach love of nature, God, and one's fellow man, and these themes regulate all her fiction. An equally important motif is familial heritage and relationships. Often a mystery about the family's background lends tension. Another powerful pattern is the consistent strength and capability of the females. Although these characters believe that their first obligation is to run a perfect home and to nurture husband and children, they are also frequently committed to a life work of their own. They are able, productive citizens, usually equal partners in their marriages, who value the money earned for the independence it represents.

S.'s enduring popular reputation is based largely on her novels. *Freckles* (1904), the story of a maimed orphan who works his way to fame, position, and wealth through honesty, bravery, and tremendous effort, is a prime example of the pluck-makes-luck school of American fiction. The sequel, *A Girl of the Limberlost* (1909), portrays Elnora Comstock, born in the Limberlost and dedicated to studying and earning her way out of it and to resolving a severely damaged relationship with her mother. Some of the values the Limberlost youngsters share—the desires for urban life, fine clothing, wealth, and social position—have been sharply criticized, but for S., these were the logical rewards of ability and extremely hard work. These two novels celebrate the swamp's danger as well as its beauty and are surprisingly little concerned with conservation; S. depicts the area as a natural prey to progress.

Other novels clearly reflect S.'s lifelong commitment to conservationism, and their protagonists value money in part as a means of serving humanity. David Langston in *The Harvester* (1911) and Linda Strong in *Her Father's Daughter* (1921) earn their livings from the flora, but they also make deliberate efforts to harvest wisely and to save threatened species.

Though accused of preoccupation with happy endings and the sunny side of life, S. intended thoughtful examination of serious human problems. *At the Foot of the Rainbow* (1907) and the long narrative poem,

Euphorbia (*Good Housekeeping*, Jan.–Mar. 1923) treat serious marital discord, and *The Magic Garden* (1927) explores problems faced by children of divorced parents. In *Michael O'Halloran* (1915), S. examines the work ethic as spiritual salvation for both Mickey, a slum child, and Nellie Minturn, a woman whose inherited wealth has barred her from genuine love. Mahala, of *The White Flag* (1923), struggles for self-definition as well as purity. Always, the S. formula prevails: central love stories embellished by nature lore, a pattern devised deliberately to make nature study and moral guidance palatable and salable.

More than twenty films were based on the novels, and S. organized her own company, Gene Stratton-Porter Productions, to protect the moralistic tone of her work. The movies she produced were popular but not landmark productions.

Perhaps the most widely read female American author of her day, S. is generally considered somewhat limited in her world view, but she is an author of power, invention, and strong narrative ability.

WORKS: *The Song of the Cardinal* (1903). *Freckles* (1904). *At the Foot of the Rainbow* (1907). *What I Have Done with Birds* (1907). *Birds of the Bible* (1909). *A Girl of the Limberlost* (1909). *Music of the Wild* (1910). *After the Flood* (1911). *The Harvester* (1911). *Moths of the Limberlost* (1912). *Laddie* (1913). *Birds of the Limberlost* (1914). *Michael O'Halloran* (1915). *Morning Face* (1916). *Friends in Feathers* (1917). *A Daughter of the Land* (1918). *Homing With the Birds* (1919). *Her Father's Daughter* (1921). *The Firebird* (1922). *Jesus of the Emerald* (1923). *The White Flag* (1923). *Wings* (1923). *The Keeper of the Bees* (1925). *Tales You Won't Believe* (1925). *Let Us Highly Resolve* (1927). *The Magic Garden* (1927).

BIBLIOGRAPHY: Bakerman, J. S., "Gene Stratton-Porter: What Price the Limberlost?" *The Old Northwest* 3 (June 1977). MacLean, D. G., *Gene Stratton-Porter: A Bibliography and Collector's Guide* (1976). Meehan, J. P., *The Lady of the Limberlost: The Life and Letters of Gene Stratton-Porter* (1928). Overton, G., *American Night's Entertainment* (1923). Richards, B., *Gene Stratton-Porter* (1980). S. F. E. [E. F. Saxton], *Gene Stratton-Porter: A Little Story of the Life and Works and Ideals of "The Bird Woman"* (1915).

Other references: *Harper's* (Oct. 1947). *Smithsonian* 7 (April 1976).

JANE S. BAKERMAN

Anna Louise Strong

B. *14 Nov. 1885, Friend, Nebraska; d. 29 March 1970, Peking, China*
Wrote under: "Anise," Anna Louise Strong
D. of Sydney and Ruth Tracy Strong; m. Joel Shubin, 1932

S. descended from Puritan families who arrived in New England in 1630. Her father was a Congregational minister; her mother an important figure in the church's missionary organizations. S. completed secondary schooling by the age of fourteen, studied languages in Germany and Switzerland, and obtained her bachelor's degree at Oberlin. Her first writing, poetry and stories, was published in *Youth's Companion* during her teens.

After college, S. took her first journalism position as an associate editor and writer for a fundamentalist weekly, the *Advance*, where she was overworked and fired by the publisher as soon as she had increased circulation. "As for their exploitation of myself, I was only eager to do more work for the salary than anyone else could do; this seemed the road to advancement." Partially to save face, she enrolled in a philosophy program at the University of Chicago. At the age of twenty-three, S. defended her doctoral thesis on the psychology of prayer before the combined theology and philosophy faculties and became the youngest student ever awarded such a degree at the university.

For several years, S. worked in urban social-reform projects, including organizing child-welfare exhibits in cities across America. She began to combine political activism and journalism after rejoining her father in Seattle, Washington, in 1915. S. was elected to the Seattle School Board, but was recalled in 1918 because of her activism in antiwar groups and her reportage (under the pseudonym "Anise") for the Seattle *Daily Call* and the Seattle *Union Record*, both socialist newspapers. Her first major article was a rather detached, "impartial" account of the Everett Massacre (New York *Evening Post*, 4 Feb. 1919). As events led to the Seattle General Strike of 1919, S. became their major chronicler. After the strike, she analyzed what happened and the lessons to be learned in a pamphlet, *The Seattle General Strike* (1918). Roger Sale, a historian of Seattle history, considers the chapter on the strike in S.'s autobiography, *I Change Worlds: The Remaking of an American* (1935), as the "best single work on Seattle in one of its most critical periods."

In 1921, S. did publicity work on the famine in Poland and Russia for the American Friends Service Committee, and she reported on the famine in both countries for the International News Service. From Moscow she wrote in defense of the Bolsheviks' new government and made several trips to the U.S. to lecture and raise money for projects aimed at promoting friendship between the two nations. In 1930, S. founded the *Moscow News,* an English-language newspaper for foreigners in Russia. Despite working as hard as she once did for the *Advance,* S.'s ultimate inability to reconcile her American view of the proper style and philosophy of reporting with the perspectives of the Russian staff, caused her to leave the newspaper. Eventually concluding that she would always remain an "outsider," S. ceased to dream of "becoming a creator in chaos. . . . I would organize no more. . . . I could always write." For the next forty-five years, S. reluctantly embraced a life of "roving to revolutions and writing about them for the American press."

In addition to her coverage of Russia from the 1920s through the 1940s, S. reported on the course of revolutionary change in Mexico, the civil war in Spain, the advance of the Red Army against the Germans in Poland—her only novel, *Wild River* (1943), is a celebration of the courage shown by Russians during the German invasion—and, most regularly, on the revolution in China. S.'s most famous single piece of reportage is "The Thought of Mao Tse-Tung" (*Amerasia,* June 1947), an article she based on an interview with the leader at the Chinese Revolutionary Army's headquarters in Yenan in 1946. Mao's first use of the phrase "paper tiger" is found here. Perhaps the most widely read of S.'s writing among intellectuals, academics, and government officials is *Letter from China,* a monthly newsletter which she published from 1962 until January 1969. During this period, it represented one of the few reliable sources of information about life in China and the position of the Chinese leadership on their rift with the Soviet Union.

Besides her China reportage, S.'s best works are her only book on the U.S., *My Native Land* (1940), and her autobiography, *I Change Worlds.* The first belongs to the genre of documentary reportage in which American intellectuals sought to "discover America." Her account is moving, filled with human interest stories, and governed by a simple—although not reductive—vision of the world. S. condemns the failures of the American capitalist system; yet, she does not entirely deny the past, but rather affirms a kind of populist democracy.

Most of S.'s journalism is flawed by a consistent naiveté, a disinterest in explaining theory, and an overabsorption in portraying personality and action. The best of her work, however, is informative and meaningful "for the great middlewestern masses," because of S.'s well-constructed images, dialogue, and use of the human-interest story.

WORKS: *The Psychology of Prayer* (1909). *Child Welfare Exhibits: Types and Preparation* (1915). *The Seattle General Strike* (1918). *The First Time in History: Two Years of Russia's New Life* (1924). *Children of Revolution* (1925). *China's Millions* (1928). *Red Star in Samarkand* (1929). *The Soviets Conquer Wheat* (1931). *The Road to the Grey Pamir* (1931). *I Change Worlds: The Remaking of an American* (1935). *The Soviet World* (1936). *My Native Land* (1940). *The Soviets Expected It* (1941). *Wild River* (1943). *The Chinese Conquer China* (1949). *Cash and Violence in Laos and Vietnam* (1962). *Letters From China, Nos. 1–10* (1963). *Letters From China, Nos. 21–30* (1966).

The papers of Anna Louise Strong are at the University of Washington, Seattle.

BIBLIOGRAPHY: Chen, P., *China Called Me* (1979). Friedham, R. L., *The Seattle General Strike* (1967). Milton, D., and N. Dall, *The Wind Will Not Survive* (1976). Nies, J., *Seven Women: Portraits from the American Radical Tradition* (1977). Ogle, S. F., "Anna Louise Strong: Seattle Years" (M.A. Thesis, Seattle Univ., 1973). Ogle, S. F., in *Notable American Women: The Modern Period*, Eds. B. Sicherman and C. H. Green (1980). Pringle, R. W., "Anna Louise Strong: Propagandist of Communism" (Ph.D. diss., Univ. of Virginia, 1972). Sale, R., *Seattle: Past to Present* (1976).

Other references: *Eastern Horizon* (1970). *NewR* (25 April 1970). *Newsweek* (13 April 1970). *NYT* (30 March 1970). *Survey* (Oct. 1964).

JENNIFER L. TEBBE

Mary Alsop Sture-Vasa

B. *10 July 1885, Cape May Point, New Jersey; d. 15 Oct. 1980, Chevy Chase, Maryland*
Given name: *Mary O'Hara Alsop*
Wrote under: *Mary O'Hara*
D. *of Reese Fell and Mary Lee Spring Alsop; m. Kent Kane Parrott, 1905; m. Helge Sture-Vasa, 1922*

S. was privately educated, with the emphasis on languages and music. She traveled widely during her youth in the eastern U.S., and she also lived in California and Wyoming, locales important to her career as popular novelist, screen writer, and composer. For example, *The Catch Colt* (1964), a musical drama, blends all these influences. S. was married twice and had two children.

In *Wyoming Summer* (1963), a fictionalized autobiography, S. defines a story as "a reflection of life plus beginning and end (life seems not to have either) and a meaning." She applied her definition to ranch life as recorded in her journals to create this book and her best-known works, the Flicka series. Like the straight autobiographical works, *Novel-in-the-Making* (1954) and *A Musical in the Making* (1966), *Wyoming Summer* conveys a clear sense of the artist, writer, and composer at work. Episodic but smooth, highly personal but detached, it includes poignant comments about women and their careers and is embedded with tiny, insightful essays about adversity, loneliness, religion, creativity, happiness, and love.

Now regarded as young people's classics, the very popular series *My Friend Flicka* (1941), *Thunderhead* (1943), and *Green Grass of Wyoming* (1946) shares these themes and reflects S.'s knowledge and love of animals. These novels trace the maturation of Ken McLaughlin and his development of a line of horses destined to realize his family's dreams. In the first novel, Ken's struggle to master the filly is clearly the symbol for his efforts to discipline himself. The parallelism continues in the next two books, where Ken's development is symbolized by the difficulty of training Flicka's colt, Thunderhead, a promising but wild stallion. Ken learns to differentiate between absolute freedom and freely exercised responsibility, between dream and reality, and is thus prepared for his role as young man and young lover. The characterization is well wrought, persuasive, and sound.

Thunderhead and *Green Grass of Wyoming* are more intricately plotted than *My Friend Flicka* and more appealing to adults, for in each an important subplot explores the sometimes strained marriage (complicated by possessiveness, financial worries, and parenthood) of Rob and Nell McLaughlin. Nell's portrait is particularly strong in its presentation of the tensions engendered by traditional women's roles. Defining herself only as Rob's wife, the mother of Ken and Howard, Nell learns to subordinate herself to her husband in *Thunderhead*. In *Green Grass of Wyoming*, she finds herself at a stage of life she has always desired—she has at last borne a daughter, has taught her sons to be self-reliant young men, and has helped her husband achieve some financial security. But Nell is unprepared for this new era, and it precipitates a physical and emotional breakdown. Her resolution of these difficulties remains traditional and is honestly depicted; she does not alter her self-definition, but she does learn to invest herself in herself as well as in others. Beautifully rendered natural settings and details of ranch life underscore the realism of all three works.

Christian faith is a major theme in S.'s work. *Let Us Say Grace* (1930) explains the Trinity in a fable framing a parable. The parable compares the function of the monetary system to the relationships within the Trinity. In the Flicka series, Nell's musings and her talks with her sons often concern religion. *The Son of Adam Wyngate* (1952), a less well-received novel, portrays a clergyman whose faith is tested when he confronts his wife's adultery.

S. is considered a talented, careful writer who reveals a genuine understanding of human nature and a fine ability to project into animal "mentality" without anthropomorphizing.

WORKS: *Let Us Say Grace* (1930). *My Friend Flicka* (1941; film version, 1943). *Thunderhead* (1943; film version, 1945). *Green Grass of Wyoming* (1946; film version, 1948). *The Son of Adam Wyngate* (1952). *Novel-in-the-Making* (1954). *Wyoming Summer* (1963). *The Catch Colt* (1964). *A Musical in the Making* (1966).

BIBLIOGRAPHY: Witham, W. T., *The Adolescent in the American Novel, 1921–1960* (1964).

Other references: *NYTBR* (24 Aug. 1941; 27 Oct. 1946). *SatR* (1 Nov. 1941; 17 May 1952).

JANE S. BAKERMAN

Ruth Suckow

B. 6 Aug. 1892, Hawarden, Iowa; d. 23 Jan. 1960, Claremont, California
D. of William John and Anna Mary Kluckhohn Suckow; m. Ferner Nuhn, 1929

The second daughter of a Congregational minister, S. grew up in Iowa. A moving and useful account of her childhood, which examines many of the materials used in novels and stories, is "A Memoir," published in *Some Others and Myself* (1952). She was educated in Iowa schools, Grinnell College, the Curry School of Expression in Boston, and the University of Denver (B.A. 1917; M.A. 1918—her thesis dealt with woman novelists). Learning the apiary business, she later supplemented her earnings by beekeeping. In 1929, she married Ferner Nuhn, another Iowa writer. Arthritis eventually necessitating a dry climate, she spent her last years in Southern California.

A regional realist, S. created fiction that is remarkably even in quality and consistent in theme and tone, although her stories treat a wider variety of character types than are fully portrayed in the novels; they also tend to end less hopefully. Her almost invariable setting is rural Iowa. Early reviewers praised her knowledge of her characters and her skill in description; often they also accused her of stressing the unpleasant side of Iowa life and of the indiscriminate piling up of detail. In mid-career, she was praised for her realism and for the warmth now seen in her work. Critics found the late novels nostalgic and less pessimistic than the early works. But today they seem very much of a piece: all show disappointed lives but end on a positive note. What changed was not S.'s view of her world but the critical expectations of her.

Country People (1924) tells the story of August Kaetterhenry, dour son of German immigrants. Years of toil, leading finally to prosperity, leave him unable to enjoy the results of his labor. After his death, however, his wife discovers an unsuspected independence in herself and lives more happily than before. This novel seems static, as it is presented almost entirely through narration; dialogue and dramatized action are lacking.

The next four novels, *The Odyssey of a Nice Girl* (1925), *The Bonney Family* (1928), *Cora* (1929), and *The Kramer Girls* (1930), make effective use of dramatized scenes and of accurately rendered and functional dialogue. All are concerned with family relationships, but most particularly with women. Their fully and sympathetically drawn characters are ordinary people about whom S. makes us care.

The Odyssey of a Nice Girl and *Cora* follow the lives of two Iowa girls from childhood into adulthood. In the first, Marjorie is a middle-class girl; while "nice," she is also shallow. Her marriage strikes many readers as an unsatisfactory, conventional ending to a pointless "odyssey." Cora is from working-class backgrounds; her success in a career and her failed marriage leave her facing the future with courage; although not happy, she is strong and would not change her life. The experiences of both women are so presented as to be typical for their time and place.

The Bonney Family and *The Kramer Girls* deal with families. The Bonney family consists of parents, two sons, and two daughters; in the novel, the initially happy family is followed to its eventual breakup. The final focus is on Sarah, the oldest daughter, as she sets out on a new career. In *The Kramer Girls*, the central family group is three sisters, the two eldest sacrificing themselves to give the youngest a chance. All three lead narrow lives, but the youngest, after years of struggle, eventually reaches a balance, content in her marriage and in her job. The depictions of the mannish Georgie and feminine Annie, the two older sisters, breathe new life into the stereotype of the "old maid."

The Folks (1934), S.'s most ambitious novel, shows a natural progression from earlier themes and techniques. Fred Ferguson, his wife Annie, and their children are all developed fully and believably. Each of the children is given a section of the novel, while the opening and closing sections focus on their parents. All four children ultimately disappoint the parents: Carl, the most apparently successful, is trapped in an unhappy marriage, and Bunny marries a young woman whom his parents can neither approve nor understand. Dorothy, conventionally pretty and popular, makes an apparently ideal marriage; her section, set near the center of the novel, describes her wedding as a perfect moment against which everything else is measured. Margaret's section, the longest, follows her from college, through a Bohemian period in New York City, into an obsessive affair with a married man. The novel's structure is thematic rather than chronological, presenting some key events from several viewpoints. Margaret is the most complex of the characters; the depiction of her rebellion against middle-class midwestern standards is well handled.

Only two more novels followed. They continue S.'s earlier themes but are more heavily symbolic, abstract, and moralistic. *New Hope* (1942) is a parable of the American experience. The town of New Hope is presented in the first optimism of its early years. But the settlers bring their old sins with them, and S. makes it clear that New Hope will never become more than a village. The novel centers around two families, those of a businessman and a minister. The minister's arrival and departure several years later give the novel its form; events are seen through the perspective of the little son of the businessman. A central theme is the loss of innocence. Like *The Folks*, *New Hope* is organized thematically, though without any complication of chronology or point of view.

The John Wood Case (1959) studies the effects on family, church, and community of the revelation that a trusted small-town business and church leader is an embezzler. The town's hypocrisy is revealed, but some characters behave well under the pressure. The novel ends hopefully, as the culprit's son is shown courageously facing the future.

While never considered a major writer, S. has always been deservedly respected for her contributions to regional realism, her sensitive characterizations of Iowa women and men, and her honest, unflinching studies of decent people meeting the disappointments of their lives with dignity. Her fiction is always carefully crafted; to read her work is to be carried to rural Iowa as it was not long ago.

WORKS: *Country People* (1924). *The Odyssey of a Nice Girl* (1925). *Iowa Interiors* (1926). *The Bonney Family* (1928). *Cora* (1929). *The Kramer Girls* (1930). *Children and Older People* (1931). *The Folks* (1934). *Carry-Over* (1936). *New Hope* (1942). *Some Others and Myself* (1952). *The John Wood Case* (1959).

BIBLIOGRAPHY: Kissane, L. M., *Ruth Suckow* (1969). McAlpin, S., "Enlightening the Commonplace: The Work of Sarah Orne Jewett, Willa Cather, and Ruth Suckow" (Ph.D. diss., Univ. of Pennsylvania, 1971). Omreanin, M. S., *Ruth Suckow: A Critical Study of Her Fiction* (1972). Stewart, M. O., "A Critical Study of Ruth Suckow's Fiction" (Ph.D. diss., Univ. of Illinois, 1960). Other references: *BI* 13 (Nov. 1970). *Palimpsest* 35 (Feb. 1954).

MARY JEAN DeMARR

May Swenson

B. *28 May 1919, Logan, Utah*
D. *of Dan Arthur and Anna Margaret Hellberg Swenson*

One of a large family, S. grew up and was educated near the State University in Logan, where her father was professor of mechanical engineering. After graduation, S. worked as a reporter on the Salt Lake City *Deseret News* and then moved to New York where she held various jobs, becoming an editor for New Directions in 1959. In 1966 she resigned to devote full time to her writing, with interludes as poet-in-residence at several American and Canadian universities. S. has received numerous honors for her poetry, including Guggenheim and Rockefeller Fellowships, the Shelley Memorial Award, and an Award in Literature from the National Institute of Arts and Letters. In 1970 she was elected to membership in the Institute.

Though S. has done translations from the work of the Swedish poet Tomas Tranströmer and has written a play and some prose, she is best known as a poet. Her first book, *Another Animal* (1954), indicated the directions and methods much of her later work would follow; it demonstrates the qualities of freshness, vitality, and keen and often unusual observations of natural phenomena and a magical balancing of surface and interior meanings. Often the balancing takes the form of metaphor as in the equation between landscape and the human body in "Sketch for a Landscape." In this book she begins, too, the riddling pattern often followed later of refusing to name lest naming interfere with the observer's truly identifying the object.

S.'s second book, *A Cage of Spines* (1958), a solid volume both in length and quality, continues the pressure upon the things of this world, turning them into emblems of other, deeper structures. For example, in "Promontory Moment," the poet evolves from the image of a yellow pencil tilted in sand like the mast of a ship, the whole relationship of the works of man, nature, the sea, and sun where "little and vast are the same to that big eye / that sees no shadow." But S.'s cosmic images are rarely solemn, so interspersed are they with vivid accounting of the immediate world. Depth and wit come together in this book described by Richard Wilbur as "happy throughout in both senses of the word."

To Mix with Time: New and Selected Poems (1963) reproduces most of the poems of her first two volumes, along with an entire new collection. Some of the poems came as a response to France, Italy, and Spain, which S. visited in 1960 and 1961 with an Amy Lowell Travelling Scholarship. Of particular interest is "Death Invited," in which S. combines an awareness of the ongoingness of death with the ritual of the bullfight.

Half Sun Half Sleep (1967) continues the search for "the clarities of Being" through the landscapes of city, country, and the sea. She continues also her experiments with unusual typography suited to the material of the poem which has marked her work from the beginning.

All the poems in *Iconographs* (1970) are in such shapes. It is important to notice, however, that S. has never sacrificed the sense of the poem to its iconography; the shapes are imposed upon the poems after composition. *Iconographs* marks too a further expression of passion in such poems as "Feel Me," "A Trellis for R.," "Wednesday at the Waldorf," and "The Year of the Double Spring." Here S. releases some of the intense feeling that remained as a strong undercurrent in many of the earlier poems.

New & Selected Things Taking Place (1978) marks a return to more conventional typography while the poet carries on her exact, often witty, exploration of the world, together with more somber remembrances of family and aging. Here is a complete collection of new poems, with a large selection from the earlier books as well.

Besides her six volumes of original verse, S. has published three books for young readers. Most of the poems in the first two of these, *Poems to Solve* (1966) and *More Poems to Solve* (1971), have been chosen from her already published work.

S. has carried the perception of visual detail farther than any other contemporary poet, and probably none so successfully joins freshness of vision with serious undercurrents of ideas. Moreover, she is aware of the textural connotations of sound, consistently using them to enhance meaning. Wit, too, enlivens poem after poem in the metaphysical sense, being a play between intellect and object in a serious sleight of hand. As Richard Howard has said, "her attention is to the quality of being itself in order to encounter, to espouse form as it *becomes* what it is." S.'s poetry is unique in such encounter and well deserves the high praise it has from the beginning received.

WORKS: *Another Animal* (1954). *A Cage of Spines* (1958). *To Mix with Time: New and Selected Poems* (1963). *Poems to Solve* (1966). *Half Sun Half Sleep: New Poems* (1967). *Iconographs: Poems* (1970). *More Poems to Solve* (1971). *Windows and Stones: Selected Poems* by Tomas Tranströmer (translated by Swenson, 1972). *The Guess & Spell Coloring Book* (1976). *New & Selected Things Taking Place* (1978).

BIBLIOGRAPHY: Stanford, Ann, "The Art of Perceiving," *SoR* (Winter 1969).
Other references: *American Poetry Review* (March–April 1978). *Nation* (10 Aug. 1963; 28 Feb. 1972). *NYTBR* (7 May 1971). *Poetry* (Nov. 1971; Feb. 1979). *PrS* (Winter 1960; Spring 1968). *TriQ* (7 Fall 1966).

ANN STANFORD

Jane Grey Cannon Swisshelm

B. 6 Dec. 1815, Pittsburgh, Pennsylvania; d. 22 July 1884, Sewickley, Pennsylvania
Wrote under: Jennie Deans, J. G. S., Jane Grey Swisshelm
D. of Thomas and Mary Scott Cannon; m. James Swisshelm, 1836

When S. was seven, her father died of tuberculosis. Her mother, who had previously lost four children to the disease, disregarded the doctor's prescription when S. showed symptoms, treating her with fresh air, fresh food, and exercise. S. recovered, and at the age of fourteen was teaching in the public school in Wilkinsburg, Pennsylvania. S. joined the church of her Scotch Covenanter parents at the age of fifteen, after a period of torment. The church provided her with a sense of purpose and a source of conflict throughout her life. In 1836, she married James Swisshelm, entering upon a marriage that was stormy and intermittent.

A short stay in Louisville, Kentucky, where her husband went into business, provided S. with material for her later writing against slavery. She started a school for blacks, but gave it up when threats were made to burn her house. From 1840 on, S.'s articles attacking capital punishment, advocating woman suffrage and the right of women to hold property, and urging the abolition of slavery appeared, at first anonymously, in newspapers in and around Pittsburgh. She contributed stories and poems as well. When Pittsburgh was left without an abolitionist paper in 1847, S. resolved to edit one herself. S. delighted in the criticism she drew as a woman editor with pronounced political views. She continued to write for the Pittsburgh *Saturday Visiter* after it merged with Robert Riddle's *Journal* in 1852. Her zeal for reform included advocacy of the "water-cure treatment," advice on woman's health, dress, reading, and education.

An opponent of the Mexican War, S. went to Washington, D.C., in 1850 to observe the debate over disposition of Mexican territory acquired through the War. At that time Horace Greeley engaged her as a Washington correspondent to the New York *Tribune*. The first woman to have such a regular assignment, she sought and secured a seat in the Congressional reporters' gallery.

In 1857, S. severed her connection with the *Family Journal and Visiter*, left her husband, and took her small daughter to northern Minnesota. There she agreed to revive and edit a defunct Democratic newspaper, which had as a major purpose attracting immigration to Minnesota. Her agreement with its proprietor included, however, the right to express her own views. The St. Cloud *Visiter* readily offended one of the leading political powers in the territory, and in March, 1858, three men broke into her office and destroyed her press. S. first discovered she had an aptitude for public speaking at a meeting to raise funds to procure a new press, and for some years afterward made a lecture tour each year. As she traveled, she sent vivid letters to the St. Cloud *Democrat*, the weekly which had emerged under her editorship in July, 1858, when, in order to avoid a libel suit, she had promised never again to use the *Visiter* as a political organ.

In 1863, following a revolt by the Sioux Indians, S. went on a lecture tour through the East to arouse opinion in favor of sterner treatment of the Indians. At this time, she characterized the Washington scene as "treason, treason, treason all around about—paid treason—official treason." She served as a nurse in military hospitals around Washington, while waiting to begin her duties as a clerk in the War Department. Her letters continued, castigating all whose conduct she disapproved: public officials, the Sanitary Commission, women who knit in the office.

Her last journalistic venture, the *Reconstructionist* (1865), was a radical newspaper, outspoken in its criticism of Andrew Johnson. Johnson responded by dismissing her from her post in the War Department, and without this source of income, she could not continue publication of the *Reconstructionist*.

S.'s autobiography, *Half a Century* (1880), is unquestionably flawed by her biases. In addition, it was reconstructed from memory, as she had systematically destroyed letters and diaries during her unhappy marriage. It is, nevertheless, an important first-hand account of events of her time, as well as of her struggle as a woman. The last third of the book contains her picture of her experiences nursing the sick and wounded during the Civil War, putting to use her powers of keen observation, willingness to sacrifice herself, her sense of humor, her strong will, and her personal warmth.

A journalist who espoused many reform causes, S. was best known as an abolitionist. Her unrestrained style often provoked violent response, physical as well as verbal. Her writing is simple and direct, distinguished by dramatic narrative, graphic description, and vivid characterization. Although S. is noted and remembered for her ruthlessness, invective, and sarcasm, her brilliant style is equally effective in describing men and women she admired, and in conveying her warmth and her sense of pride in places and events which, to her, meant progress.

WORKS: *Letters to Country Girls* (1853). *True Stories about Pets* (1879). *Half a Century* (1880). *Crusader and Feminist: The Letters of Jane Grey Swisshelm, 1858–1865* (Ed. A. J. Larsen, 1934).

Files of the St. Cloud *Visiter* and the St. Cloud *Democrat* and a partial file of the Pittsburgh *Saturday Visiter* are in the Minnesota Historical Society. A file of the Pittsburgh *Saturday Visiter* and a few issues of the *Reconstructionist* are in the Carnegie Library in Pittsburgh.

BIBLIOGRAPHY: McCarthy, A., in *Women of Minnesota*, Ed. B. Stuhler and G. Kreuter (1977). Thorp, M. F. *Female Persuasion* (1949).

For articles in reference works, see *DAB* IX, 2. *NAW* (article by A. F. Tyler).

Other references: *Abraham Lincoln Quarterly* 6 (Dec. 1950). *American Historical Review* 37 (July 1932). *Minnesota History* 32 (March 1951). *Mississippi Valley Historical Review* 7 (Dec. 1920). *NYT* (23 July 1884). *Western Pennsylvania Historical Magazine* 4 (July 1921).

VIVIAN H. SHORTREED

Gladys Bagg Taber

B. 2 April, 1899, Colorado Springs, Colorado; d. 11 March 1980, Hyannis,
  Massachusetts
D. of Rufus Mather and Grace Raybold Bagg; m. Frank Albion Taber, 1922

T. was born in the West, grew up in the Midwest, and lived her
adult life in Virginia, New York, and New England. She graduated from
Wellesley in 1920; took an M.A. at Lawrence College, Appleton, Wisconsin, in 1921; and did graduate work at Columbia University. In 1922, she
married a professor of music at Randolph-Macon College in Virginia, who
lost his hearing and had to leave his profession. T. had one daughter.

T.'s early work includes a play and a book of poems, but most of it is
popular romance, sometimes serialized in magazines such as the *Ladies'
Home Journal*. Her fiction is light and uplifting; her heroines usually find
true love despite an unsympathetic father or class differences. In later novels, her heroines are long-suffering middle-aged housewives. T.'s fiction
shows a remarkable concentration on her own life, with the same themes
and characters appearing again and again, and, as often happens with popular writers about whom the public is very curious, she became increasingly open about her own life when she turned completely to nonfiction
after publishing her last novel, a barely disguised autobiography, in 1957.

T.'s father is a perennial character in her books, fiction or autobiography. She wrote one book about him, *Especially Father* (1949), and portrays him in detail again in *Harvest of Yesterdays* (1976). He is harshly
dealt with in her fiction, where he is the tyrant who keeps his daughter
from marrying the man she loves, but in T.'s nonfiction she tries to sym-
pathize with him. Nevertheless, T. always portrays him as a hyperactive
domestic tyrant with the social responsibility of a sand flea. T.'s literary
treatment of her father is an interesting case history in the making of capital from one of life's burdens.

T.'s fiction is not the work which gained her the loyal fans that she has
attracted over the years; rather, her magazine columns and the books she
made from them are the cornerstone of her success. From November 1937
to December 1957, her column, Diary of Domesticity, ran in the country's
leading women's magazine, the *Ladies' Home Journal*, where S. was also
assistant editor (1946–58). Then for ten more years the column continued,

in *Everywoman's Family Circle*, the supermarket magazine, as Butternut Wisdom. These columns, and the books she made from them, chronicle the life of T. and her family at Stillmeadow, a farmhouse built in 1690, near Southbury, Connecticut. The first Stillmeadow book, *Harvest at Stillmeadow*, was published in 1940. There is a lot of repitition in the Stillmeadow books, which are organized seasonally, but these are the most popular mid-20th-c. examples by a woman of the subgenre of semiautobiographical books about country life.

Sharing Stillmeadow with T. and her daughter is Jill (Eleanor Mayer), T.'s beloved "life-long friend," and her two children. Jill was widowed in 1943. T.'s husband is seldom mentioned; he died in 1964. Throughout the series, the reader follows the changes that come to the lives of T. and Jill as their children grow up and they struggle with the usual problems of country life. Jill is portrayed by T. as the stereotyped demon gardener. Her death in 1960 was acknowledged in T.'s columns and became the subject of a book on coping with grief, *Another Path* (1963). T. characterizes herself, like the usual middle-aged heroines in her later novels, as timid and incompetent in mechanical things, unable to use the telephone or the vacuum cleaner.

Like other women who write for the popular audience, T. portrays herself as much more of an average housewife than she could have been. In *Mrs. Daffodil* (1957), an autobiographical novel in which the heroine is a columnist who lives in an old house in New England, an interviewer asks Mrs. Daffodil why she is so successful as a writer. "I think it's because I am not a special person at all. . . . I am just any woman with a house and a family and dogs and a garden. So if I put down what I feel, others feel the same way. I've often wished I were a literary writer, like Virginia Woolf, but I'm just the common garden variety." Such is indeed the nature of popular appeal; the readers want to read what they already think.

WORKS: *Lady of the Moon* (1928). *Lyonesse* (1929). *Late Climbs the Sun* (1934). *Tomorrow May Be Fair* (1935). *The Evergreen Tree* (1937). *Long Tails and Short* (1938). *A Star to Steer By* (1938). *This is For Always* (1938). *Harvest at Stillmeadow* (1940). *Nurse in Blue* (1943). *The Heart Has April Too* (1944). *Give Us This Day* (1944). *Give Me the Stars* (1945). *Especially Spaniels* (1945). *The Family on Maple Street* (1946). *Stillmeadow Kitchen* (1947). *The Book of Stillmeadow* (1948). *Especially Father* (1949). *Stillmeadow Seasons* (1950). *When Dogs Meet People* (1952). *Stillmeadow and Sugarbridge* (with B. Webster, 1953). *Stillmeadow Daybook* (1955). *Mrs. Daffodil* (1957). *What Cooks at Stillmeadow* (1958). *Spring Harvest* (1959). *Stillmeadow Sampler* (1959). *Stillmeadow Road* (1962). *Another Path* (1963). *Stillmeadow Cookbook* (1965). *Stillmeadow Calendar* (1967). *Especially Dogs* (1968). *Stillmeadow Album* (1969). *Amber: A Very Personal Cat* (1970). *My*

Own Cape Cod (1971). *My Own Cook Book* (1972). *Country Chronicle* (1974). *Harvest of Yesterdays* (1976). *Conversations with Amber* (1978). *Still Cove Journal* (1981).

BIBLIOGRAPHY: *Ladies' Home Journal* (Oct. 1946). *NYT* (9 Oct. 1955). *WLB* (April 1952).

BEVERLY SEATON

Genevieve Taggard

B. *28 Nov. 1894, Waitsburg, Washington; d. 8 Nov. 1948, New York City*
D. *of James Nelson and Alta Gale Arnold Taggard; m. Robert Wolf, 1921;*
  m. Kenneth Durant, 1935

T. was the eldest child of schoolteacher-missionaries, whose Scots-Irish pioneer ancestors had migrated to Washington from Vermont. Feeling alienated from the spiritual and cultural sterility of eastern Washington, T.'s devout parents moved the family to Hawaii when she was two. Except for two traumatic returns to Washington necessary for her father's health, T. lived eighteen years in what she later idealized as innocent, exotic poverty.

The contrast between Hawaii, where caste, race, and wealth seemed irrelevant, and Waitsburg's small-town prejudice and rude materialism, focused T.'s moral vision. Her social conscience was a logical extension of her parents' preachings, but their faith as fundamentalist Disciples of Christ allowed only biblical reading; Keats and Ruskin were illicit pleasures. Defiantly, T. embarked upon her writing career at age twelve.

By the time she graduated from the University of California at Berkeley (1920), T. was both poet and socialist. Nationally published, T. was offered work in New York by Max Eastman at the *Liberator*. She took a leading role in the literary and social developments of the 1920s and 1930s, working first for B. W. Huebsch's avant-garde *Freeman* and helping found and edit the *Measure*, a lyric poetry journal. T. taught at several colleges, traveled in Europe and Russia, raised a daughter, and was active in humanitarian and proletarian causes. Her two husbands were also radical writers. T. retired in 1946 in Vermont; she died in 1948 of the effects of hypertension.

Known primarily to scholars for her biography of Emily Dickinson (1930), a passionate, bold interpretation of the father-daughter relationship and Dickinson's psychology, T. received wide recognition throughout her career as a literary activist and poet, who was published and reviewed in journals ranging from *The New Yorker* to *New Masses*.

Her first book of poetry, *For Eager Lovers* (1922), established her unique idiom as a metaphysical Marxist, a lyric intellectual who incorporates Hawaiian exotica into poems about revolution and a woman's experience in love. Even such Marxist visions of doomed decadence as "Twentieth Century Slave-Gang" eschew rhetoric and combine modern directness ("the ants are hurried") with extraordinary images: oaks bend knotted knees in labor, a pond is wrinkled with velvet oil, wasps carry spider-spoil to where crude honey hangs in mud.

While this volume commemorates a first year of marriage, and T. occasionally speaks as an "eager lover," she insists on the necessary independence—even defiance—of soul, voice, whole being, especially in the potentially compromising love relationship. Her resolute quest for freedom (personal, artistic, social, and political) is the dominant theme of T.'s poetry; here the tone is "caged arrogance" as the voice celebrates its emancipation.

In *Collected Poems, 1918–1938*, T. juxtaposes early and late poems to show their essential continuity, that love of beauty and hatred of oppression are not contradictory. T. brings her modernist and ideological rebellion against romanticism to the lives of "mothers, housewives, old women" to capture with compassion, "the kitchens they knew, sinks, suds, stew-pots, and pennies . . . / Dull hurry and worry, clatter, wet hands and backache."

In *Slow Music* (1946), T. is still working to support her lifelong conviction that the desire to be socially relevant and the belief that art obeys its own laws must coexist.

Charges that her poetry lacks a "unified sensibility" point to what makes T.'s poetry unusual: the lifelong synthesis of her experience and vision as sister, daughter, mother, wife, lover, professor, activist, and poet, whose words were heard on records and on the radio, sung at Carnegie Hall to music of Copland and Schuman, and read in Moscow and in bean fields. T. lived paradox as naturally as she wrote metaphysical verse. The synthesis of mangoes, metaphor, and Marx makes T.'s poetry complex. But her passion for precision makes abstract idea and mood arresting and accessible: T. renders psychological and social states through metaphors of the physical world.

WORKS: *For Eager Lovers* (1922). *Hawaiian Hilltop* (1923). *Continent's End* (edited by Taggard, with G. Sterling and J. Rorty, 1925). *May Days* (edited by Taggard, 1925). *Words for the Chisel* (1926). *The Unspoken, and Other Poems* by Anne Brenner (edited by Taggard, 1927). *Travelling Standing Still* (1928). *Circumference: Varieties of Metaphysical Verse, 1459-1928* (1929). *The Life and Mind of Emily Dickinson* (1930). *Remembering Vaughan in New England* (1933). *Ten Introductions* (with Dudley Fitts, 1934). *Not Mine to Finish* (1934). *Calling Western Union* (1936). *Collected Poems, 1918-1938* (1938). *Long View* (1942). *Falcon* (1942). *A Part of Vermont* (1945). *Slow Music* (1946). *Origin Hawaii* (1947).

BIBLIOGRAPHY: Aaron, D., *Writers on the Left* (1961). Lins, K. L., "An Interpretive Study of Selected Poetry by Genevieve Taggard" (M.A. thesis, Univ. of Hawaii, 1956). Mossberg, B.A., and C. L. Mossberg, *Genevieve Taggard* (Western Writers Series, forthcoming). Peck, D. R., "Development of an American Marxist Literary Criticism: The Monthly New Masses" (Ph.D. diss., Temple University, 1968). Wilson, E., "A Poet of the Pacific," in *The Shores of Light* (1952).

For articles in reference works, see: *DAB*, Suppl. 4. *NAW* (article by B. Rauch). *The Oxford Companion to American Literature*, James D. Hart (1965). *20th CA*.

Other references: *Masses and Mainstream* (Jan. 1949). *Ms.* (1979). *Nation* (19 Jan. 1927). *New Masses* (Jan. 1927). *Poetry* (Dec. 1934; May 1936; Feb. 1947). *SatR* (7 Nov. 1936; 14 Dec. 1946). *Scholastic* (17 May 1938). *Time* (22 Nov. 1948). *WLB* (Jan. 1930).

BARBARA ANTONINA CLARKE MOSSBERG

Ida Minerva Tarbell

B. 5 Nov. 1857, Erie County, Pennsylvania; d. 6 Jan. 1944, Bridgeport, Connecticut
D. of Franklin Sumner and Esther Ann McCullough Tarbell

T. grew up in what was then the heartland of America's oil region. As a child, T. evinced considerable intellectual curiosity and independence, which her parents (both former teachers) encouraged. The Tarbell family was closely knit and espoused the typical virtures of the early American Dream: hard work, honesty, thrift, and moral good. To the end of her life, T. tended to judge all character (of person or corporation) on the basis of its adherence to what she called "the fair and open path." It was this high moral sense that animated her best writing.

An adolescent struggle to reconcile the Holy Writ with scientific fact (T. found a solution in theories of evolution) led T. to study biology at Allegheny College, as the sole female in a freshman class of forty. After graduating in 1880, T. took an onerous and poorly paid teaching position with a Poland, Ohio, seminary (like her college, not far from her family home). In 1882, she returned home and soon became a staff member of the *Chautauquan*, a monthly magazine connected with the Chautauqua movement and its home studies program. Beginning as an editorial secretary, T. advanced, during her eight-year employment on the magazine, to writer and annotator.

At the age of thirty, T. decided she was "dying of respectability" and gave vent to her need for adventure by quitting her job and going to Paris to write a biography of a French revolutionary, *Madame Roland: A Biographical Study* (1896).

Despite her own (and others') assessment of her ability as "not a writer but a dead scholar," T. supported herself in France by writing for American magazines. In this manner she was noticed by S. S. McClure, publisher of the fledgling *McClure's* magazine. Her contribution on Napoleon, in 1894, boosted the magazine's popularity and T.'s reputation as a journalist of note. From 1894 until 1906, T. was a writer for *McClure's*; from 1906 to 1915, for *American Magazine*. In this twenty-one-year period as a staff writer, T. produced the works which support her journalistic reputation. Almost all resulted from assignments for articles, which later were published separately as books; they are either biographies (not critical or analytical but thoroughly researched) or studies of complex issues (such as the oil corporations or tariffs), which T. could explain in concepts and language understandable to the average person. These studies, however, are not purely objective analyses but reflect the attitudes and values of her background. T. was one of the investigative journalists popular in the early 20th-c. who were given the name "muckrakers" by Theodore Roosevelt.

Like many others, T. was profoundly affected by WWI and its alteration of traditional beliefs; this is reflected in her focus, from 1911 until the 1920s, on war and peace and resultant social problems. Her writings after WWI are fewer; in these years, T. was more active as lecturer or delegate to various national and international conferences. She herself considered her postwar writings "musty"; it seems probable that she no longer was able to write from the fierce certainties of youth and that the concerns of the reading public had been altered substantially by the war.

Perhaps T.'s best writing from the later years of her life is her autobiography, *All in the Day's Work* (1939), written when she was eighty-two. She relates that at fourteen, she had prayed never to be married; as a college student, she avoided "entangling alliances." The phrase (hers) is telling; throughout her autobiography, T. repeatedly notes her need for independence and freedom—freedom from marriage and from groups, especially the suffragists or other women's groups.

T. was not a feminist; indeed, she opposed the woman suffrage movement because she felt the suffragists belittled women's contributions to society. As her autobiography, her study of Mme Roland, and her two treatises on "womanhood"—*The Business of Being a Woman* (1912) and *Ways of Woman* (1915), reveal, T. answered "the woman question" with the cliché that the hand that rocks the cradle rules the world. The home, which T. felt to be a sufficient and necessary sphere in which women could operate, was to T. the most vital unit in a healthy society. Thus she approved patriarchial practices by big business (such as Henry Ford's workers communities) and she herself flourished under the direction of patriarchal males.

T. deserves recognition, however, for her pioneering role in journalism and especially for her classic study of the oil industry, *The History of the Standard Oil Company*, a two-volume work first published in 1904. H. H. Rogers, a Standard Oil executive, guided T. through selected corporate documents during her two-year research effort, but she consulted other sources, as the massive documentation reveals. The *History* does not by any means whitewash Standard Oil; T. frankly regards the corporation as guilty of "commercial sin." But she is equally honest in recognizing the genius of John D. Rockefeller: he early understood that control of the oil industry depended on control of the transportation of that oil. While he embodied the industry and verve she had been taught to admire, he created the corporate entity she recognized as death to the individual businessman—a clear negation of the American dream. *The History of the Standard Oil Company* is a landmark in both business and journalism because it represents Standard Oil's first serious attempt at public relations and because it was in the vanguard of serious investigative reporting by American periodicals.

WORKS: *A Short Life of Napoleon Bonaparte* (1895). *Early Life of Abraham Lincoln* (1896). *Madame Roland: A Biographical Study* (1896). *The Life of Abraham Lincoln* (2 vols., 1900). *Napoleon's Addresses* (1902). *The History of the Standard Oil Company* (2 vols., 1904; re-issued in one volume, 1963; abridged, by David Chalmers, 1966). *He Knew Lincoln* (1907). *Father Abraham* (1909). *Selections from the Letters, Speeches, and State Papers of*

Abraham Lincoln (1911). *The Tariff in Our Times* (1911). *The Business of Being a Woman* (1912). *Ways of Woman* (1915). *New Ideals in Business: An Account of Their Practice and Their Effects upon Men and Profits* (1916). *The Rising of the Tide: The Story of Sabinsport* (1919). *In Lincoln's Chair* (1920). *Boy Scout's Life of Lincoln* (1922). *He Knew Lincoln, and Other Billy Brown Stories* (1922). *Peacemakers, Blessed and Otherwise: Observations, Reflections, and Irritations at an International Conference* (1922). *In the Footsteps of the Lincolns* (1922). *Life of Elbert H. Gary: The Story of Steel* (1925). *A Life of Napoleon Bonaparte* (1927). *A Reporter for Lincoln: Story of Henry E. Wing, Soldier and Newspaper Man* (1927). *Owen D. Young: A New Type of Industrial Leader* (1932). *The Nationalizing of Business, 1878–1898* (Vol. 9, A History of American Life series, 1936). *Women at Work: A Tour Among Careers* (1939). *All in the Day's Work: An Autobiography* (1939).

T.'s papers are in the collections of the Reis Library of Allegheny College and the Sophia Smith Collection at Smith College.

BIBLIOGRAPHY: Chalmers, D., *The Social and Political Ideas of the Muckrakers* (1964). Filer, L., *Crusaders for American Liberalism* (1939). Fleming, A., *Ida Tarbell: First of the Muckrakers* (1971). Hamilton, V., "The Gentlewoman and the Robber Baron," *American Heritage* 21 (April 1970). Marzolf, M. *Up from the Footnote* (1977). Tomkins, M., *Ida M. Tarbell* (1974).

SALLY BRETT

Phoebe Atwood Taylor

B. *18 May 1909, Boston, Massachusetts; d. 8 Jan. 1976, Boston, Massachusetts*
Wrote under: Phoebe Atwood Taylor, Alice Tilton
D. *of John D. and Josephine Atwood Taylor; m. Grantley Walden Taylor*

T.'s parents were both natives of Cape Cod; her father was a physician. T. graduated from Barnard College in 1930. She published her first detective novel in 1931 and published up to three detective novels a year every year afterwards for almost twenty years. She wrote between midnight and 3:00 A.M., "after housekeeping all day," "beginning three weeks before the deadline for the novel to be delivered to her New York publishers." (Her Leonidas Witherall novels include heartfelt depictions of the harried popular author, besieged by telegrams from his publisher, struggling to meet his deadlines.) T. married a prominent Boston surgeon of the same surname and lived in Newton Highlands and then in Weston, suburbs of Boston, always keeping a summer home at Wellfleet on Cape Cod. She died of a heart attack.

T.'s first book, *The Cape Cod Mystery* (1931), features her most famous detective, Asa Alden (Asey) Mayo. A "man of all work" to the wealthy Porter family, he is a "fine and bleak" Cape Cod native who chews tobacco and must be sixty but could be anything from thirty-five to seventy. Using what he calls "common sense," he extricates a Porter scion suspected by incompetent local officials of murdering a popular novelist and identifies the actual killer—the three-hundred-pound widow of a Boston minister who bashed the writer with an advance copy of his latest book, a sensational account of her husband's life.

By the last of the Cape Cod mysteries, *Diplomatic Corpse* (1951), the hero's character has evolved and, like many of his fellow series detectives, he has become a superman. "Tall, lean, salty Asey Mayo" has changed from chewing tobacco, as in the first two books, to smoking a pipe, and from being the Porters' handyman to being Chairman of the Board of Porter Motors. In intervening novels he has been revealed as a more and more expert marksman, knife-thrower, hand-to-hand fighter, driver, sailor, and cook.

The charm of the Cape Cod novels lies not only in Asey's role as the wryly humorous Yankee, but also in their settings. T.'s eye for detail and lively sense of place combine with many glimpses of the daily life of the times, and now increase the historical interest and fun of her novels.

Leonidas Xenophon Witherall, hero of the mysteries T. wrote under the pen name of Alice Tilton, solves crimes that take place in a recognizable prewar and wartime Boston and its suburbs. He is a master, then headmaster and owner of Meredith's Academy, a private boys' school. His escapades are even crazier and more convoluted, if possible, than Asey Mayo's. *The Hollow Chest* (1941) concerns a samurai sword as murder weapon, an antique horse car, a Lady Baltimore cake, a papier-maché lion's head, and the manuscript of a treatise on the "eleventh-century vowel shift," and requires a massive suspension of disbelief.

Many of T.'s works are notable for their brisk, even breathless, pace. Both detectives encounter problems and solve them within a day or two, and their chases—by car, on foot, by plane, by motorboat, or via antique horsecar—often make their adventures tests of physical stamina and agility as well as mental ability. This pace and T.'s zany plots rife with eccentric characters and odd props often make her mysteries seem the literary equivalents of the classic screwball film comedies of the 1930s.

T.'s mystery comedies also incorporate many elements of the classic detective story. Asey has a trio of Dr. Watsons and a Lestrade. T. includes one case of young love per story: the ingénue is never guilty, nor is the young man who falls in love with her. Like many British detective stories of the same era, T.'s works are touched with xenophobia, racism, and anti-Semitism. Some of this narrowness is of the "Napoleon was a great man and a great general, but he was an off-Islander" variety and goes with T.'s regional-comedy territory.

T.'s mystery-farces will never appeal to those who want realism in their criminal fiction, but they have withstood the passage of time at least as well as those of her Golden Age sisters, Agatha Christie and Ngaio Marsh. T.'s characters, settings, and historical interest still provide excellent entertainment, and explain why the novels have been reissued in the 1960s and again in the 1980s.

WORKS: *The Cape Cod Mystery* (1931). *Death Lights a Candle* (1932). *The Mystery of the Cape Cod Players* (1933). *The Mystery of the Cape Cod Tavern* (1934). *Sandbar Sinister* (1934). *Deathblow Hill* (1935). *The Tinkling Symbol* (1935). *The Crimson Patch* (1936). *Out of Order* (1936). *Beginning with a Bash* (1937). *Figure Away* (1937). *Octagon House* (1937). *The Annulet of Gilt* (1938). *Banbury Bog* (1938). *The Cut Direct* (1938). *Cold Steal* (1939). *Spring Harrowing* (1939). *The Criminal C.O.D.* (1940). *The Deadly Sunshade* (1940). *The Left Leg* (1940). *The Hollow Chest* (1941). *The Perennial Boarder* (1941). *The Six Iron Spiders* (1942). *Three Plots for Asey Mayo* (1942). *File for Record* (1943). *Going, Going, Gone* (1943). *Dead Ernest* (1944). *Proof of the Pudding* (1945). *The Asey Mayo Trio* (1946). *Punch with Care* (1946). *The Iron Clew* (1947). *Diplomatic Corpse* (1951).

T.'s manuscripts are collected in the Mugar Memorial Library, Boston University.

BIBLIOGRAPHY: Haycraft, H., *Murder for Pleasure* (1941).

For articles in reference works, see: *A Catalogue of Crime*, Barzun, J., and W. H. Taylor, eds. (1971). *Encyclopedia of Mystery and Detection*, Steinbrunner, C., and O. Penzler, eds., (1976). *20th CA. 20th CAS. Twentieth-Century Crime and Mystery Writers*, Reilly, J. M., ed. (article by M. H. Becker, 1980).

Other references: *Barnard Alumnae Monthly* (Oct. 1932; March 1936). *NYT* (12 Jan. 1976). Washington *Post* (17 Jan. 1976).

SUSAN SUTTON SMITH

Sara Teasdale

B. 8 Aug. 1884, St. Louis, Missouri; d. 29 Jan. 1933, New York City
Given name: Sarah Trevor Teasdale
D. of John Warren and Mary Elizabeth Willard Teasdale;
  m. Ernst B. Filsinger, 1914

The youngest of four children, T. was born into comfortable circumstances provided by her father, a prominent businessman, and her independently wealthy mother. Because of her nervous temperament, she was educated at home until she was nine. After attending Mary Institute (founded by T. S. Eliot's grandfather) for a year, she completed her education at Hosmer Hall, a school designed to prepare young women for college. She was already writing poetry, and she received much encouragement from her teachers; she also read Heine and Sappho, who, along with Christina Rossetti, were the greatest influences on her own work.

Following graduation in 1902, T., together with several of her friends, published a manuscript magazine, *The Potter's Wheel*, in which many of her early poems appeared. Her first professional publication came in May, 1907, when her dramatic monologue "Guenevere" appeared in *Reedy's Mirror*. The poem attracted much attention, as did *Sonnets to Duse, and Other Poems* published that same autumn, though the book was not a financial success.

T. literally sacrificed herself to poetry, and therein lay her tragedy. Frail and high-strung, she lived perforce a disciplined life which brought both unhappiness and loneliness, for she was innately an outgoing person, capable of great emotional depth. Her line, "O, beauty, are you not enough? Why am I crying after love?" reveals her constant ambivalence. She experienced two major romantic involvements, one with the poet Vachel Lindsay, and the other with Ernst Filsinger, a St. Louis businessman whom she married in December, 1914. But the demands of poetry brought about a gradual estrangement, and the marriage was dissolved in 1929, by T.'s decision. After courageously enduring four years of rapidly deteriorating health and acute depression, exacerbated by the fear that she might become a helpless invalid, she took an overdose of barbiturates, and died in 1933.

At first glance, T.'s poetry appears to be simple, but its simplicity is deceptive. Although it does not lend itself to involved critical exegesis, its highly connotative language can imply deeply felt emotion which evokes an equal response. T. treads a fine line between revelation and reticence. *Sonnets to Duse* and *Helen of Troy, and Other Poems* (1911) reveal her experimentation to find her own poetic voice, and successive volumes demonstrate her constant striving to speak from her own experience, honestly and without sentimentality. Her constant theme is love, its joys, and, as her own life grew more difficult, its tragedies. The source of her imagery is invariably nature, which serves equally well for moments of exaltation—"I am the pool of gold / Where sunset burns and dies / You are my deepening skies, / Give me your stars to hold,"—or, as in her posthumous volume *Strange Victory* (1933), for moments of deepest pain: "Nothing but darkness enters this room, / Nothing but darkness and the winter night, / Yet on this bed once years ago a light / Silvered the sheets with an unearthly bloom; / It was the planet Venus in the west / Casting a square of brightness on this bed, / And in that light your dark and lovely head / Lay for a while and seemed to be at rest." Here the controlled objectivity of the language deepens the sense of anguish and desolation; the words must be read for implication and nuance, as well as for obvious meaning. In T.'s poetry, every word is important.

Though deprecated by critics of the post-*Wasteland* generation, T. continues to be read and admired. One reason for her popularity doubtless derives from her ability to write about bitter experience without bitterness, and to laugh wisely, especially at herself. But even more important is a sense of that inner courage and integrity, which compelled her to write in her own way, uninfluenced by the work of her contemporaries: "Let the dead know, but not the living see— / The dead who loved me will not suffer, knowing / It is all one, the coming or the going— / If I have kept the last essential me. / If that is safe, then I am safe indeed. . . ." She recognized that her way inevitably incurred suffering. Even at her moments of deepest despair, however, T. exercises a control born of a conscious choice, and the ultimate effect of her poetry is one of confident affirmation: "If this be the last time / The melody flies upward / With its rush of sparks in flight, / Let me go up with it in fire and laughter. . . ."

WORKS: *Sonnets to Duse, and Other Poems* (1907). *Helen of Troy, and Other Poems* (1911). *Rivers to the Sea* (1915). *The Answering Voice: Love Lyrics by Women* (edited by Teasdale, 1917). *Love Songs* (1917). *Flame and Shadow* (1920). *Rainbow Gold* (edited by Teasdale, 1922). *Dark of the Moon* (1926). *Stars To-Night* (1930). *Strange Victory* (1933). *Collected Poems* (1937).

BIBLIOGRAPHY: Brenner, R., *Poets of Our Time* (1946). Carpenter, M. H.,

Sara Teasdale: A Biography (1960). Sprague, R., *Imaginary Gardens: A Study of Five American Poets* (1969). Untermeyer, L., *The New Era in American Poetry* (1919).

ROSEMARY SPRAGUE

Tabitha Gilman Tenney

B. 7 April 1762, Exeter, New Hampshire; d. 2 May 1837, Exeter, New Hampshire
Wrote under: Tabitha Tenney
D. of Samuel and Lydia Robinson Giddinge Gilman; m. Samuel Tenney, 1788

T. was descended from early pioneers in New Hampshire who had raised themselves to prominent social positions in the town of Exeter. She was the oldest of the seven children, and probably remained at home with her mother to help raise her younger siblings after the death of her father. T. was somewhat older than was typical for her time and social class when she married. The couple had no children. Her husband, who served as a physician in the Revolutionary army, later directed his attention chiefly to politics and scientific inquiry.

Although T. was described as an "accomplished lady," it is unlikely that her formal schooling differed greatly from that of other respectable 18th-c. American women, or from that form of "female education" which she satirizes in her novel, *Female Quixotism: Exhibited in the Romantic Opinions and Extravagant Adventures of Dorcasina Sheldon* (1801). Her education, like Dorcasina's, would have provided her with a command of the fine points of fashion and household management, some acquaintance with the classics, and a fuller knowledge of contemporary novels. While married, T. produced two books which largely derived from her reading. After her husband's death in 1816, she spent the remainder of her life concentrating on her needlework, which was renowned for its intricacy.

T.'s first publication was *The Pleasing Instructor* (1799), an anthology of classical literature addressed to young women. It was intended to "inform the mind, correct the manners, or to regulate the conduct" while at the same time blending, in best classical fashion, "instruction with rational amusement."

T. dedicated *Female Quixotism* "to all Columbian Young Ladies, who Read Novels and Romances." But unlike most novels so dedicated, T.'s book satirizes both sentimentality and sentimental fiction in general. *Female Quixotism* is roughly modeled on Charlotte Ramsay Lennox's *The Female Quixote; or, The Adventures of Arabella* (1752), but T. alters the pattern of her model to emphasize a different message. In the earlier book, the main character is basically innocent but is corrupted by the ideals of the sentimental fiction she reads. T., however, portrays a character who rationalizes her foolishness by blaming it on the novels that she has read.

This change gives *Female Quixotism* an effective focus. Dorcasina, who is an adolescent when we first see her, remains frozen in the kind of prolonged adolescence that sentimental fiction requires. She is intelligent, occasionally witty, but entirely blind to the increasing disparity between her own life and the sentimental life she envisions for herself. Dorcasina early rejects a sensible suitor, Lysander, because his letter proposing marriage fails to use words like "angel" or "goddess." Ironically, Lysander is as close as Dorcasina ever comes to making the sentimental match she aspires to.

Over the years, Dorcasina is duped by, and deceives herself about, men who seek to humiliate her or gain her fortune. Finally, the malicious ridicule of Seymour, a most despicable character who intends to marry the toothless, white-haired Dorcasina and then have her committed to a mental institution so that he can enjoy her fortune unhindered by her company, leads Dorcasina to recognize the folly of her life and warn her young readers "to avoid the rock on which I have been wrecked."

The novel is a satire, but it is written with a sensitivity to its main character seldom encountered in satire. As silly as Dorcasina's version of reality is, it is in many ways preferable to the world she faces. Most of the men she meets are singularly cruel, spiteful, misogynistic creatures, and, on this level, T.'s novel covertly warns women that they must be particularly cautious in a world where they have little place and little power. T.'s satire is also effectively double-edged in another sense. While she criticizes the women who get their education from fiction, she equally criticizes a social system that denies women any real education.

F. L. Pattee once described *Female Quixotism* as the most popular novel written in America before *Uncle Tom's Cabin*. This is not the case, but T.'s novel did run through at least six separate editions between the time of its publication and 1841. However, no current edition of the novel is available. Ironically, *Female Quixotism* fell into obscurity by the middle of the last century, while novels it satirized, such as Susanna Rowson's

Charlotte Temple (1791), continued to be popular into our own century, and even now are available in modern editions.

WORKS: *The Pleasing Instructor* (1799). *Female Quixotism: Exhibited in the Romantic Opinions and Extravagant Adventures of Dorcasina Sheldon* (1801).

BIBLIOGRAPHY: Bell, C.H., *History of the Town of Exeter* (1888). Brown H. R., *The Sentimental Novel in America, 1789–1860* (1940). Gilman, A., *The Gilman Family* (1869). Loshe, L. D., *The Early American Novel, 1789–1830* (1907). Petter, H., *The Early American Novel* (1971). Tenney, M. J., *The Tenney Family; or, The Descendants of Thomas Tenney of Rowley, Massachusetts, 1638–1890* (1891).

For articles in reference works, see: *CAL. NAW* (article by O. E. Wilson).

CATHY N. DAVIDSON

Mary Virginia Hawes Terhune

B. *21 Dec. 1830, Dennisville, Virginia; d. 3 June 1922, New York City*
Wrote under : Marion Harland
D. *of Samuel Pierce and Judith Anna Smith Hawes; m. Edward Payson Terhune, 1856*

T. was tutored at home and began contributing regularly to Richmond papers at fourteen. She wrote a version of her first published novel at sixteen and had published two very successful novels when she married a Presbyterian minister at twenty-six. She continued to write while she successively moved with her husband to Newark, New Jersey; Springfield, Massachusetts; and Brooklyn, New York. He assisted her in her work, providing "the first reading and only revision of her MSS., before they are given into the hands of the printer." She bore six children, three of whom survived childhood. Christine Terhune Herrick and Virginia Terhune Van de Water followed their mother as writers on domestic matters, and Albert Payson Terhune became "the collie's Balzac," an enormously popular author of dog stories.

Alone (1854), the first of T.'s many novels and her most popular, follows the trials of Ida Ross, who must live "alone" at fifteen after the death of her widowed mother, "a being more than human—scarcely less than divine." The first scene of the book depicts Ida throwing herself upon her

mother's coffin as it is lowered into the grave. She must leave her plantation home and live in Richmond with a cynical, worldly guardian who has
raised his daughter to be as cold-hearted as himself. For a time, under their
influence, Ida becomes almost misanthropic, but she blossoms again when
she meets the loving and merry Dana family. She finds and loses and finds
again her true love, the Reverend Morton Lacy, and they are happily
married at the novel's end. *Alone* depicts life in Richmond and a prewar
plantation—slaves are all happy, devoted family "servants." In a closing
scene Ida strikes the book's keynote: "A woman is so lonely without a
home and friends! They are to us—I do not say to you [men]—
necessaries of life."

Many of T.'s twenty-five novels and three collections of short stories
have the same antebellum southern background and sentimental message:
women can and should be educated and able to support themselves, but
their truest position is dependence and their proper sphere the home.

T.'s most famous book on household affairs, *Common Sense in the
Household: A Manual of Practical Housewifery* (1871), became a best
seller and was translated into French, German, and Arabic. She advocates
learning by doing, attention to the presentation of food and a varied
menu, and she deprecates the "vulgar prejudice against labor-saving ma-
chines." Here, the housewife can consult a thirteen-page essay on how to
handle her servants; she can find out how to clean and cook a catfish or
restore luster and crispness to black alpaca and bombazine. The style is informal, the advice practical.

T.'s twenty-five books of advice are by no means confined to the culi-
nary and domestic. *Eve's Daughters; or, Common Sense for Maid, Wife,
and Mother* (1892) covers all facets of the growing girl's physical, mental,
and moral health, including the way in which a mother should educate her
daughter about sex: "Get some good familiar treatise upon Botany,—I
know of none better than Gray's 'How Plants Grow,'—and read with her
of the beautiful laws of fructification and reproduction."

Eve's Daughters also counsels women through marriage and motherhood to menopause—the "climacteric"—and a postmenopausal "Indian
Summer." In the chapter "Shall Baby Be?" T. voices her convictions on
the sin of childlessness; she believed that American mothers had a duty to
bear "troops" of boys and girls to withstand the invasion of "massed filth"
—"Irish cottiers and German boors, and loose and criminal fugitives from
everywhere."

T.'s ideas on woman's role seem as dated today as her methods for healing cuts, but her cookbooks and domestic advice profoundly influenced Americans for half a century.

WORKS: *Alone* (1854). *The Hidden Path* (1855). *Nemesis* (1860). *Miriam* (1862). *Husks* (1863). *Moss-Side: Husbands and Homes* (1865). *Colonel Floyd's Wards* (1866). *Sunnybank* (1866). *The Christmas Holly* (1867). *Phemie's Temptation* (1869). *Ruby's Husband* (1869). *At Last* (1870). *Common Sense in the Household: A Manual of Practical Housewifery* (1871). *The Empty Heart: "For Better, for Worse"* (1871). *True as Steel* (1872). *Jessamine* (1873). *From My Youth Up* (1874). *Breakfast, Luncheon, and Tea* (1875). *My Little Love* (1876). *The Dinner Year-Book* (1878). *Loiterings in Pleasant Paths* (1880). *Our Daughters: What Shall We Do with Them?* (1880). *Handicapped* (1881). *The Cottage Kitchen* (1883). *Judith: A Chronicle of Old Virginia* (1883). *Cookery for Beginners* (1884). *Common Sense in the Nursery* (1885). *Country Living for City People* (1887). *Not Pretty, but Precious* (1887). *Our Baby's First and Second Years* (1887). *A Gallant Fight* (1888). *House and Home* (1889). *Stepping-Stones* (with Virginia F. Townsend and Louise Chandler Moulton, 1890). *With the Best Intentions* (1890). *Eve's Daughters* (1892). *His Great Self* (1892). *The Story of Mary Washington* (1892). *Mr. Wayt's Wife's Sister* (1894). *The Premium Cook Book* (1894). *The Royal Road* (1894). *Home of the Bible* (1895). *Talks upon Practical Subjects* (1895). *Under the Flag of the Orient* (1895). *The Art of Cooking by Gas* (1896). *The National Cook Book* (with Christine Terhune Herrick, 1896). *The Secret of a Happy Home* (1896). *An Old-Field School-Girl* (1897). *Ruth Bergen's Limitations* (1897). *Some Colonial Homesteads and Their Stories* (1897). *The Comfort of Cooking and Heating by Gas* (1898). *Where Ghosts Walk* (1898). *Charlotte Brontë at Home* (1899). *Cooking Hints* (1899). *Home Topics* (1899). *More Colonial Homesteads and Their Stories* (1899). *William Cowper* (1899). *Dr. Dale* (with Albert Payson Terhune, 1900). *Hannah More* (1900). *John Knox* (1900). *In Our County: Stories of Old Virginia Life* (1901). *Marion Harland's Complete Cook Book* (1903). *Everyday Etiquette* (with Virginia Van de Water, 1905). *When Grandmamma Was Fourteen* (1905). *The Distractions of Martha* (1906). *Marion Harland's Cook Book of Tried and Tested Recipes* (1907). *The Housekeeper's Week* (1908). *Ideal Home Life* (with Margaret E. Sangster et al., 1910). *Marion Harland's Autobiography* (1910). *The Story of Canning and Recipes* (1910). *Home Making* (1911). *The Helping Hand Cook Book* (1912). *Should Protestant Ministers Marry?* (1913). *Looking Westward* (1914). *A Long Lane* (1915). *The Carringtons of High Hill* (1919). *Two Ways of Keeping a Wife* (n.d.).

BIBLIOGRAPHY: Baym, N., *Woman's Fiction: A Guide to Novels by and about Women in America, 1820–1870* (1978). Griswold, W. M., *A Descriptive List of Novels and Tales, Dealing with the History of North America* (1895). Halsey, F. W., *Women Authors of Our Day in Their Homes* (1903). Pattee, F. L., *The Feminine Fifties* (1940).
For articles in reference works, see: *AA. The Living Female Writers of the*

South, Ed. I. Raymond (1872). *The Living Writers of the South*, Ed. J. W. Davidson (1869). *NAW* (article by M. Cross). *Southland Writers*, Ed. I. Raymond (1870). *Women of the South Distinguished in Literature*, Ed. M. Forrest (1861).

Other references: *Harper's* (Nov. 1882). *NYT* (4 June 1922).

SUSAN SUTTON SMITH

Celia Laighton Thaxter

B. 29 June 1835, Portsmouth, New Hampshire; d. 26 Aug. 1894, Appledore
  Island, Isles of Shoals, Maine
D. of Thomas B. and Eliza Rymes Laighton; m. Levi Lincoln Thaxter, 1851

Raised on a lighthouse island in the Isles of Shoals ten miles off the New Hampshire coast, T. grew up within the sound and sight of the sea and early learned to appreciate its beauty and its cruelty. This dual awareness became a major theme in her poetry, which established her literary reputation at a relatively young age.

T.'s father became the lighthouse keeper when she was four years old. T., her father, mother, and two brothers were the sole human inhabitants of the island for many years. In 1841, the family moved to another of the islands, Smutty-Nose, where they began receiving paying summer guests. As this proved a successful venture, Thomas Laighton in 1847 began building a resort hotel on Appledore Island, the largest of the Shoals island group. This he completed the following year with the help of Levi Lincoln Thaxter, a young Harvard graduate.

The Appledore House opened the following year and became a major summer resort attracting artists and writers including Hawthorne, Thoreau, Emerson, Whittier, Lowell, Mark Twain, Charlotte Cushman, Ole Bull, Lucy Larcom, Sarah Orne Jewett, Annie Adams Fields, and Childe Hassam. Hassam completed a series of remarkable paintings of the islands, including some of T. in her garden (1892), which are now in the Smithsonian. Many of these artists were attracted by T. as well as by the scenery, and she established a kind of literary salon on the islands beginning in the 1860s.

Levi Thaxter had become T.'s tutor in her early teens, and in 1851 they married. The couple had three sons. The marriage was not successful, as T. pined for her island home when, off and on in the 1850s, they lived on the mainland, in several Massachusetts towns. Levi, on the other hand, began to resent her literary success. By the end of the 1860s, T. and her husband lived essentially separate lives, although they never divorced. She remained on Appledore with her mother and her oldest son Karl, who was retarded.

The death of her mother in 1877 was a severe shock to T., precipitating a religious crisis wherein she attempted to communicate through seances with her mother. This endeavor may have inspired a similar experience described fictionally by Sarah Orne Jewett in her spiritualistic story, "The Foreigner" (1900). Although a religious skeptic in her early years, T. did turn to spiritualism, theosophy, and Eastern religions in her later years.

T. was an extraordinarily accomplished water-colorist; this is an overlooked aspect of her considerable talent. Her prose publications, *Among the Isles of Shoals* (1873) and *An Island Garden* (1894), also remain as gems of descriptive prose.

T.'s first poem, significantly entitled "Land-Locked," appeared in the *Atlantic Monthly* in March 1861. She continued to publish poems in the major literary journals of her day, namely *Scribner's*, *Harper's*, the *Independent*, the *Century*, and the *Atlantic*. She also published juvenile material in *Our Young Folks* and *St. Nicholas Magazine*. The first collection of T.'s poetry, *Poems*, appeared in 1871. Many subsequent revised editions were printed.

Most of T.'s poetry deals with nature, not the benign nature of the Romantics, but a harsh, indifferent ocean. Several poems deal with actual shipwrecks that occurred on the Isles of Shoals while she was there. In "The Wreck of the Pocohantas," T. asks: "Do purposeless thy children meet/Such bitter death? How was it best/These hearts should cease to beat?" She returns often in her poetry to this basic theological question. T.'s tones is sometimes bitter and despairing, and occasionally somewhat cynical about traditional religious explanations. At times her austere, harsh imagery anticipates that of 20th-c. poets such as Anne Sexton and Sylvia Plath. Probably some of T.'s bitterness, like theirs, stemmed from the frustrations she encountered trying to play the many and conflicting roles of wife, mother, and artist. These conflicts are apparent in T.'s letters, published in 1895.

WORKS: *Poems* (1871). *Among the Isles of Shoals* (1873). *Drift-Weed* (1878). *Poems for Children* (1884). *The Cruise of the Mystery* (1886). *Idyls and Pastorals* (1886). *My Lighthouse, and Other Poems* (1890). *An Island*

Garden (1894). *Stories and Poems for Children* (1895). *The Letters of Celia Thaxter* (Eds. Annie Adams Fields and Ruth Lamb, 1895). *The Heavenly Guest, and Other Unpublished Writings* (Ed. O. Laighton, 1935).

BIBLIOGRAPHY: Faxon, S., et al., *A Stern and Lovely Scene: A Visual History of the Isles of Shoals* (1978). Hawthorne, Nathaniel, *The American Note-books* (1881). Laighton, O., *Ninety Years at the Isles of Shoals* (1930). Spofford, Harriet Prescott, *A Little Book of Friends* (1916). Thaxter, R., *Sandpiper: The Life and Letters of Celia Thaxter* (1962). Westbrook, P. D., *Acres of Flint, Writers of Rural New England 1870–1900* (1951).

JOSEPHINE DONOVAN

Dorothy Thompson

B. 9 July 1894, Lancaster, New York; d. 30 Jan. 1961, Lisbon, Portugal
D. of Peter and Margaret Grierson Thompson; m. Josef Bard, 1923; m. Sinclair Lewis, 1928; m. Maxim Kopf, 1943

T. was the daughter of an English clergyman who married an American woman and settled in upper New York State. Left motherless when she was still a child, T. turned early to history, literature, and languages for pleasure as well as study. She attended the Lewis Institute in Chicago, and received the B.A. degree from Syracuse University in 1914.

T. began her writing career as a publicist for woman suffrage groups and the Red Cross. This work took her abroad, where she secured free-lance writing assignments and made influential friends among the overseas press corps. Within a few years she had become a regular correspondent for the Philadelphia *Public Ledger* and the New York *Evening Post*. Later, she became a bureau chief in Berlin.

T. was fluent in German and thoroughly at ease with German culture and politics—which was perhaps why she was among the first, and among the most perceptive and persistent, critics of Nazism. Her enduring repu-tation rests chiefly on the worldwide recognition and respect she won as the plain-speaking reporter who, through her widely syndicated New York *Herald Tribune* column On the Record, alerted the English-speaking world to the brutality and menace of the Hitler regime.

Although she broke with the *Herald Tribune* over her support for Pres-ident Franklin Roosevelt in 1940 (she had originally favored the paper's candidate, Wendell Willkie), T. continued writing until virtually the end of her life. In addition to her newspaper column, she contributed a monthly article to the *Ladies' Home Journal* and did regular radio broadcasts. A series of wartime talks sent by short wave to Germany was published under the title *Listen, Hans* (1942). *Let the Record Speak* (1939) was culled from her political columns. *The Courage to be Happy* (1957), drawn from T.'s *Journal* pieces and dealing mainly with personal and social topics, reflects the rigorous, work-centered ethic of her Methodist childhood.

By the 1940s, T. was one of the most widely read columnists in the country, and the press of travel and speaking engagements made her writing of necessity a collaborative effort with researchers and editorial aides. Critics should look to her early work for the full flavor of her journalistic style. In *The New Russia* (1928), for example, she combines cogent political analysis with vivid personal detail to give a memorable picture of the Soviet Union after ten years of Communist rule. T. compares the pioneering work of the Soviet experiment to the development of the American frontier. She is, however, astute and clear-sighted in her recognition of the ways in which classical communist ideals have been jettisoned for practical political purposes.

Perhaps T.'s greatest gift as a journalist was her ability to maintain an enthusiastic receptivity to her subject while tempering enthusiasm with objective judgment. T. was considered a highly opinionated writer, but in general, her opinions represent moral convictions which the reader can easily detect and allow for. In *I Saw Hitler* (1932) T.'s scorn for the subject of her interview is everywhere apparent, yet personal antipathy does not lead her to underestimate the leadership potential of the Nazi dictator.

One of T.'s biographers suggests that she felt keenly her failure to produce a body of writing that would transcend the topical. In particular, she seems to have wanted to write her own autobiography, and she made several efforts, which she abandoned as unsatisfactory. T. seems to have been a writer with greater powers than her subjects called forth.

WORKS: *Depths of Prosperity* (with P. Bottome, 1925). *The New Russia* (1928). *I Saw Hitler* (1932). *Refugees* (1938). *Political Guide* (1938). *Let the Record Speak* (1939). *Listen, Hans* (1942). *The Courage to be Happy* (1957).

BIBLIOGRAPHY: Sheean, V., *Dorothy and Red* (1963). Sanders, M., *Dorothy Thompson: A Legend in Her Time* (1973).
    Other references: *Atlantic* (July 1945). CB (1940). *Colliers* (June 1945). *Newsweek* (20 Oct. 1944). NY (20 April 1940; 27 April 1940).

                                        ANN PRINGLE ELIASBERG

Mabel Loomis Todd

B. *10 Nov. 1856, Cambridge, Massachusetts; d. 14 Oct. 1932, Hog Island, Muscongus, Maine*
D. *of Eben Jenks and Mary Alden Wilder Loomis; m. David Todd, 1879*

T., an only child, was a descendant of Priscilla and John Alden of Plymouth Colony. T.'s father, astronomer at the U.S. Naval Observatory, poet, and naturalist, was a friend of Asa Gray, Henry David Thoreau, and Walt Whitman. Educated at private schools in Cambridge and Georgetown, D.C., T. later studied at the New England Conservatory of Music. She married an astronomer, and their one child was born in 1880. They moved to Amherst College in 1881, when her husband became director of the observatory and a member of the faculty. Upon his retirement in 1917, they made their winter home in Coconut Grove, Florida, where T. fostered the movement to establish the Everglades National Park; her Maine island, where they had a summer house, became a National Audubon Society wildlife sanctuary.

T., who was responsible for the publication of the first volumes of Emily Dickinson's poetry, undertook the editorial work at a time when no one else would. The Todds had been initially well-received, when they moved to Amherst, by Susan Gilbert Dickinson and her husband Austin, treasurer of the College and the poet's brother. A liaison developed between T. and Austin in the fall of 1882 and continued until his death in 1895. Although the men remained friends, animosity between the wives extended to family imbroglios over T.'s legitimate claims as the editor, at the request of the poet's family, of Dickinson's verse and selected letters.

The editing was a formidable job. Dickinson's handwriting was idiosyncratic; her grammar and punctuation were not always conventional. There were tentative words, alternate lines, or different versions of the same poem between which to choose. The labor required a sure grasp of the poet's intentions, but also anticipation of readers' resistance to an original and imaginatively daring language. T. enlisted the help of her husband, of Austin, and of the reluctant T. W. Higginson, editor of the *Atlantic*, with whom Dickinson had begun correspondence as early as 1862. A modest selection, *Poems by Emily Dickinson*, appeared in 1890, with a preface by Higginson, who assisted in securing a publisher and launching the book. "You," he told T., "did the hardest part of the work."

T. is less well known for the books she wrote. She first published *Footprints* (1883), which in retrospect seems fictionalized autobiography. The story of a quiet, lonely man—a forty-year-old physician for whom life's mysteries are cold and bleak—ends as he comes to know a spirited young woman who shares his sense of the autumnal beauty of the New England seacoast and they glimpse a promise of joy together. Lyrical descriptions of an austere landscape with its granite cliffs, wild flowers, and expanse of sky and ocean suggest emotions that are not overtly described in the narrative.

T. wrote *Total Eclipses of the Sun* (1894), the first volume in the Columbian Knowledge series, edited by her husband. She traces the separation of modern scientific astronomy from the inaccurate poetic views characterized by mysticism, superstition, and terror of the past. Authoritative without being pedantic, T. writes a muted poetry describing an eclipse she witnessed with her husband in Japan during 1887. "A startling nearness to the gigantic forces of nature," she concludes, "seems to have been established," and personalities, hates, jealousies, even mundane hopes "grow very small and very far away."

T. also collaborated with her husband in other scientific writing. She published informal essays, reviews of new books, three serialized novels, and a sonnet sequence. T. wrote two travel books. *Corona and Coronet* (1898) is a leisurely account of a yacht trip to Japan to view the total eclipse of the sun in 1896. *Tripoli the Mysterious* (1912) describes Libya's ancient desert city, its changeless etiquette, sand-blown ruins, architecture, crafts, trades, and the people T. met on two "eclipse trips" in 1900 and 1905. In the tour de force, *A Cycle of Sunsets* (1910), she observes changes of light, hues, tones, and atmosphere at the end of every day throughout a year as attentively as an artist like J. M. W. Turner studies sky and land. Sixty of her paintings are in the Hunt Institute for Botanical Documents, Carnegie-Mellon University.

T.'s judgments are apt to be aesthetic rather than conventionally moral; her condescension toward "village" insularity is tempered if not tolerant. Her tensions are disciplined, her feelings cultivated. Graceful in manner, she values decorum appropriate to occasions and is sensitive to the nuances of the moment. Human presences rarely dominate the scenes or subjects to which T. responds with subtlety, composure, and intelligent interest.

WORKS: *Footprints* (1883). *Poems by Emily Dickinson* (edited by Todd, with T. W. Higginson; First Series, 1890; Second Series, 1891). *Letters of*

Emily Dickinson (edited by Todd, 1894; enlarged edition, 1931). *Total Eclipses of the Sun* (Columbian Knowledge Series No. 1, 1894). *A Cycle of Sonnets* (1896). *Poems by Emily Dickinson* (edited by Todd; Third Series, 1896). *Corona and Coronet* (1898). *Steele's Popular Astronomy* (edited by Todd, with D. P. Todd, 1899). *A Cycle of Sunsets* (1910). *Tripoli the Mysterious* (1912). *Bolts of Melody: New Poems of Emily Dickinson* (edited by Todd, with Millicent Todd Bingham, 1945). *The Thoreau Family Two Generations Ago* (Thoreau Society Booklet No. 13, 1958).

BIBLIOGRAPHY: Bingham, Millicent Todd, *Ancestor's Brocades* (1945). Blake, C. R., and C. F. Wells, eds., *The Recognition of Emily Dickinson* (1967). Sewall, R. B., *The Life of Emily Dickinson* (1974).

For articles in reference works, see: *NAW* (article by D. Higgins).

ELIZABETH PHILLIPS

Amélie Rives Troubetzkoy

B. 23 Aug. 1863, Richmond, Virginia; d. 16 June 1945, Charlottesville, Virginia
Wrote under: Amélie Rives
D. of Alfred and Sarah Macmurdo Rives; m. John Chanler, 1888; m. Pierre
  Troubetzkoy, 1896

Both of T.'s parents were of prominent Virginia families. Her father was a colonel of engineers on Robert E. Lee's staff. Soon after her birth, T. and her mother were moved to Castle Hill, the home of her father's parents, a gracious colonial estate in the foothills of the Blue Ridge not far from Charlottesville. Her grandparents took a great interest in T.'s education, and she developed sophisticated tastes in the rich cultural milieu of Castle Hill. It became a center of security for her throughout her active life and provided the setting for a number of her novels.

By all accounts, T. was a beautiful and dynamic woman; and many of her heroines are reflections of herself in their vivacity, intelligence, sensitivity—and their luxuriant blond hair. She traveled widely and maintained contacts with many outstanding English and American authors of her time. Her first marriage proved incompatible and ended, amicably, in divorce in 1895. Her second marriage, to Prince Pierre Troubetzkoy, a young portrait painter who had given up his wealth and position in Russia, was long and happy.

T.'s long writing career spanned several American literary movements and several trends in American reading tastes. Frequently, the fiction that appealed most strongly to the public was not her strongest work. T.'s first published story, "A Brother to Dragons" (*Atlantic*, March 1886), is a romantic, sentimental tale written in Elizabethan diction. Weak novels that appealed to the public primarily for their exotic settings or melodramatic situations are interspersed throughout her career; still, the strength and development of T.'s talents can be seen.

In *Virginia of Virginia* (1888), we can see the beginning of the strong T. heroine. Most critics praised its realism and dialogue while pointing out that it is an uneven work. It was the novel *The Quick or the Dead?* (1888) that caused a public furor. The heroine is a young widow. Her debating whether to remarry shocked propriety; most shocking were the scenes of sensuality, especially the implications that they were instigated by Barbara herself. But the novel is more than a deliberately sensational one; it is a sincere portrayal of the painful self-questioning that Barbara undergoes as she considers the conflict between what she sees as her duty and feels as her need for fulfillment. Tinged with sentimentality and flowery diction, it is not consistently realistic; but in many ways *The Quick or the Dead?* is a more open, honest statement of the sexuality of women than the major realists of the period allowed.

The Quick or the Dead? became a bestseller as a result of its notoriety. In its sequel, *Barbara Dering* (1893), Barbara continues to show a conflict between her true nature and her expected role. In both novels, T. uses nature imagery to reveal this conflict.

Another strong heroine is Phoebe, the protagonist of *World's End* (1914), a novel that won high critical praise and had large sales. Phoebe, like earlier heroines, is a young woman of feeling and intellect; but she is less perfect and more realistic and develops more as a character than her predecessors. In this novel, for the first time, the heroine is matched by a fully developed, strong male character. T.'s later works move more and more to sympathetic, less stereotyped male characters, possibly because of her years of happy marriage with Pierre. In *World's End*, the conflict is resolved in the sense that the heroine comes to some self-knowledge; but, as is usual in T.'s novels, there is no totally happy ending.

Shadows of Flame (1915)—reflecting her own experience with drug addiction—*The Queerness of Celia* (1926), and her last novel, *Firedamp* (1930), are all among T.'s best works, but do not quite equal the achievement of *World's End*.

In addition to her novels, T. wrote drama and poetry throughout her career. She published several plays written in blank verse and a long narrative poem, *Seléné* (1905), which shows a skillful handling of sustained verse, with many fine sensuous passages.

During and after WWI, T. wrote a series of plays which had successful Broadway runs, including *Allegiance*, *The Fear Market* (of which a movie version was made), and an adaptation of Mark Twain's *The Prince and the Pauper*. *Love-in-a-Mist* (1927) was an effective comedy of manners, and her only commercially successful play to be published after its Broadway run. Her last play, *The Young Elizabeth* (1938), shows her admiration for the young queen who is torn between love and duty; Elizabeth becomes a true T. heroine.

T. has been called a realist, a fine local colorist, and an important social historian; she has also been called a semierotic, a sensationalist, a romantic who revels in morbid scenes and hysterical passions. Both strengths and weaknesses can be found in her work. T. did not always use her many talents to their best artistic effect; her active life and spontaneity may have led her away from careful revision. But the vitality and sincerity of much of her work remain fresh and significant for modern readers.

WORKS: *A Brother to Dragons, and Other Old-Time Tales* (1888). *Herod and Mariamne* (1888). *The Quick or the Dead?* (1888). *Virginia of Virginia* (1888). *The Witness of the Sun* (1889). *According to Saint John* (1891). *Athelwold* (1893). *Barbara Dering* (1893). *Tanis, the Sang-Digger* (1893). *A Damsel Errant* (1898). *Seléné* (1905). *Augustine, the Man* (1906). *The Golden Rose: The Romance of a Strange Soul* (1908). *Trix and Over-the-Moon* (1909). *Pan's Mountain* (1910). *Hidden House* (1912). *World's-End* (1914). *Shadows of Flames* (1915). *The Ghost Garden* (1918). *As the Wind Blew* (1920). *The Sea-Woman's Cloak and November Eve* (1923). *The Queerness of Celia* (1926). *Love-in-a-Mist* (1927). *Firedamp* (1930).

BIBLIOGRAPHY: Clark, E., *Innocence Abroad* (1931). Longest, G., *Three Virginia Writers: Mary Johnston, Thomas Nelson Page, and Amélie Rives Troubetzkoy: A Reference Guide* (1978). Manly, L., *Southern Literature from 1579–1895* (1895). Meade, J., *I Live in Virginia* (1935). Painter, F., *Poets of Virginia* (1907). Taylor, W., *Amélie Rives (Princess Troubetzkoy)* (1973).

For articles in reference works, see: *LSL*, 10 (article by R. Duke).

Other references: *Lippincott's* (Sept. 1888). *Mississippi Quarterly* (Spring 1968). *Virginia Cavalcade* (Spring 1963).

ANNE NEWMAN

Barbara Tuchman

B. 30 Jan. 1912, New York City
Writes under: Barbara Tuchman, Barbara Wertheim
D. of Maurice and Alma Morgenthau Wertheim; m. Lester Reginald
Tuchman, 1940

T.'s grandfather was Henry Morgenthau, Sr., the businessman and diplomat; her uncle was Henry Morgenthau, Jr., Roosevelt's secretary of the Treasury; and her father was an international banker and owner of the *Nation*. T. was educated at Radcliffe College. Her first job, with the Institute of Pacific Relations, took her to Tokyo in 1935. One of her earliest works is an essay on the Japanese character published in the prestigious *Foreign Affairs* when she was only twenty-three. T.'s work as a journalist during the next seven years, reporting from the war in Spain and writing in London for the magazine *The War in Spain*, led to the publication in England of her first book, *The Lost British Policy: Britain and Spain Since 1700* (1938).

T. is the mother of three daughters. She is now divorced.

Bible and Sword: England and Palestine from the Bronze Age to Balfour (1956) argues that the support for the Jewish homeland in Palestine had a double root: on the one hand, imperial strategy in a part of the world vital to the defense of Suez, India, and the oil fields of the Mideast; and, on the other hand, the attitude toward what Thomas Huxley called the "national epic of Britain," the Bible.

The Zimmerman Telegram (1958) is a work of history that aroused both professional respect and popular notice. It tells the story, only partly known until then, of efforts made by German Foreign Minister Arthur Zimmerman, before America's entrance into WWI, to bring about an alliance with Mexico in return for territorial concessions in the U.S. *The Zimmerman Telegram* is an artful narrative offering both the excitement of action and the color of personalities.

The Guns of August (1962), which brought T. a Pulitzer prize, applied a similar technique to a broader and more significant moment in WWI. Beginning with the description of the funeral of Edward VII, T. sketches the familial and political ties of Germany, England, and France and makes clear the interrelatedness of their world on the eve of its dissolution. It is typical of the T. style in its mix of detail and long view, character and event. She aims at an account of the way things happen rather than seeking the underlying causes or attempting to convert events into arguments for historical theory.

Nevertheless, in her next book, *The Proud Tower* (1966), T. describes her interest in writing about the decade before WWI as coming in part from a desire to understand the war. Although the individual chapters—for example, on the Dreyfus case—are beautifully done, it is not easy to see how these particular parts of a social history support a coherent conception of the origins of the war. T. admits to a certain arbitrariness in her choice of chapter subjects.

In *Stilwell and the American Experience in China, 1911–45* (1970), the career of General Joseph W. Stilwell becomes the central focus of an examination of the relationship of America and China. T. sees Stilwell as quintessentially American and his career in China as a "prism of the times," representing America's greatest effort in Asia as well as the "tragic limits" of America's experience there. T. believes that the efficiency and aggressiveness Stilwell brought were like the Christianity and democracy he also represented—all foreign to Chinese society and not assimilable. T.'s conceptual framework is equal to the complex narrative and able to raise it to a higher order of historical writing.

While the response of professional historians to *Stilwell and the American Experience in China* was very positive, *A Distant Mirror* (1975) has been the most criticized of any of T.'s books. However, it has received the same enthusiastic greeting from the layman eager to read well-shaped narrative about an unfamiliar period. T. regards the 14th c. as a period like our own, "a distraught age whose rules were breaking down under the pressure of adverse and violent events." Her original plan to follow the effects of the bubonic plague was changed to allow her to explore the marriage alliances and treaties that made up medieval diplomacy and to examine the code of chivalry. Whatever professional questions have been raised about the book's overarching concept, its sense of time and place are as brilliant as in any of T.'s works.

Practicing History (1981) is a collection of essays in which T. discusses the techniques and role of the historian. She also comments on some crucial events of her own day: the Six Day War, Watergate, and Vietnam.

WORKS: *The Lost British Policy: Britain and Spain since 1700* (1938). *Bible and Sword: England and Palestine from the Bronze Age to Balfour* (1956). *The Zimmerman Telegram* (1958). *The Guns of August* (1962). *The Proud Tower: A Portrait of the World Before the War, 1890–1914* (1966). *Stilwell and the American Experience in China, 1911–45* (1970). *Notes from China* (1972). *A Distant Mirror* (1975). *Practicing History* (1981).

BIBLIOGRAPHY: *Nation* (26 April 1971). *NYT* (19 Oct. 1958). *NYTBR* (28 June 1962; 3 Feb. 1968; 28 Sept. 1978).

LOIS HUGHSON

Jane Turell

B. 25 Feb. 1708, Boston, Massachusetts; d. 26 March 1735, Medford, Massachusetts
D. of Benjamin and Jane Colman; m. Ebenezer Turell, 1726

T.'s father was minister of the innovative Brattle Street Church and an influential figure in Boston's cultural and religious life. Like the fathers of other notable 18th-c. New England women, Colman carefully attended to his daughter's education, so that by the time T. was four she had amassed amounts of knowledge remarked upon by her father's peers. She began writing poetry under her father's guidance when she was about eleven years old. Throughout her life, Colman remained her mentor in spiritual and literary matters, partly through a lively, intimate exchange of letters and poems.

T.'s husband, a Congregationalist minister, had a pastorate in Medford, Massachusetts, where the couple settled. Of their four children, three died in infancy; one survived to age six, dying eighteen months after his mother. T. suffered from bouts of illness and depression for many years and died at age twenty-seven.

T. wrote poetry and prose throughout her adolescent years, and her poetic ambitions were not diminished by domestic duties and pregnancies. Her reading ranged from divinity to history, medicine, public debates, and poetry. After her death, her husband wrote a short biography, interspersed with selections from her works, to illustrate her talent and piety. He wished her life and work to serve as examples for young New England women. First published in Medford in 1735 as *Reliquiae Turellae et Lachrymae Paternal*, the slim volume contains correspondence, diary extracts, short religious essays, and verse—the only extant samples of T.'s writing. Unfortunately, because he published her work to illustrate her piety, her husband excluded material, such as her humorous verse, that he judged unsuitable.

It is probable that, even before her death, T.'s works circulated in manuscript form among her friends and acquaintances, as was customary in
18th-c. New England. She achieved enough contemporary fame as a
writer to warrant a second edition of the biography, published in 1741 as
*Memoirs of the Life and Death of the Pious and Ingenious Mrs. Jane
Turell.*

Like many of her female contemporaries, T. had no wish to compete
with male writers or to be published; she wrote privately, discussing personal events and religious ideas. She read widely in the neoclassic English
poets and copied their style, adapting it to her religious subjects. Even her
eulogies of other writers find their meaning in religious themes. She
praises the English moralist poet Elizabeth Singer because Singer attacked
evil: "A Woman's Pen Strikes the curs'd Serpents Head, / And lays the
Monster gasping, if not dead."

T.'s neoclassicism is evident in a poetic enticement to her father to pass
the hot summer months in Medford. "An Invitation into the Country in
Imitation of *Horace*" is exactly what the title indicates. She compares
harsh city life to the joys of innocent country living, transforming her
small New England village and rural domicile into a model Arcadia. She
lures her father with pastoral descriptions of "soft Shades" and "balmy
Sweets / of Medford's flow'ring Vales, and green Retreats" and an occasional New England touch: "Yet what is neat and wholsom . . . Curds and
Cream just turn'd."

She again mixed the neoclassic, religious, and personal in what is perhaps her most moving work, a lament for her dead children, written during her last pregnancy. She recollects the pains of childbirth in vivid
tropes, but ends the poem with a reaffirmation of faith in Christ, as she
pledges her next child to God's service.

The major portion of T.'s verse consists of skillful paraphrases of psalms
and canticles, which reveal her understanding of Puritan ideas and histo-
riography. For example, she transforms Psalm 137 to dramatize the Puritan's experiences in the New World, changing a Babylonian landscape
into American wilderness.

Most of T.'s prose pieces are simple meditations on religious subjects,
often expressing doubts and fears over the state of her soul. In letters to
her father, she repeatedly sought comfort from anxiety. Often, in more
serene moments, she wrote short, essaylike letters to her younger sister,
guiding her towards a life of virtue and pietry and advising her to abandon the frivolities of youth. Her prose works are thoughfully serious, although undisinguished in style and content.

Since only fragments of T.'s work are available, a thorough assessment remains impossible. Clearly, she imitated her father's style and ideas, and she followed the prescriptions of early-18th-c. poetics. Religious themes are ever present, and abstractions and personifications are common in her poetry. Much of her later verse indicates a potential never realized.

WORKS: *Reliquiae Turellae et Lachrymae Paternal* (Ed. E .Turell, 1735; reissued as *Memoirs of the Life and Death of the Pious and Ingenious Mrs. Jane Turell . . . Collected Chiefly from Her Own Manuscripts*, 1741).

BIBLIOGRAPHY: Brooks, C., *History of the Town of Medford* (1855). Evans, C., *American Bibliography* (1912).
For articles in reference works, see: *NAW* (article by O. E. Winslow).
JACQUELINE HORNSTEIN

Agnes Sligh Turnbull

B. *14 Oct. 1888, New Alexandria, Pennsylvania; d. 31 Jan. 1982, Livingston, New Jersey*
D. *of Alexander Halliday and Lucinda Hannah McConnell Sligh; m. James Turnbull, 1918*

Of Scots Presbyterian background, T. grew up in western Pennsylvania and was graduated from Indiana (Pennsylvania) State College in 1910. She then attended the University of Chicago for one year. She was married in 1918 and has one daughter.

T.'s fiction is varied and uneven. She began with a number of sentimental and undistinguished narratives about actual and imagined Biblical women. Scattered throughout her career are a few children's books: *Elijah the Fishbite* (1940), *Jed, the Shepherd's Dog* (1957), *George* (1965), and *The White Lark* (1968).

Her best fiction deals with Scottish settlers in the coal country of western Pennsylvania. Major concerns are the difficult lives of pioneer women and the effect upon them of their strict Presbyterianism. Her attitude toward that faith is ambivalent. While she dramatizes the psychological damage done by adherence to the Calvinistic doctrine of predestination and portrays Episcopalianism as gentler (see especially *The Rolling Years*, 1936, and *The Bishop's Mantle*, 1947), she also shows the comfort and sense of community given by the faith. In some books (notably *The Gown of Glory*, 1952, and *The Nightingale*, 1960) set in the early years of this century, she writes nostalgically of small-town life centered around the local Presbyterian church. Her women are strong and self-reliant, but they also are traditionally home and family centered.

Two of T.'s finest novels are set on the Pennsylvania frontier during the Revolutionary War. Vividly depicting the joys and hardships of the frontier, *The Day Must Dawn* (1942) tells of a gently bred pioneer woman who schemes to have her daughter go east to an easier life. The novel climaxes with an Indian raid, based on an actual incident, and ends with her dying acceptance of the fact that her daughter will marry a frontiersman and go west to still wilder country, postponing the dream for another generation.

The King's Orchard (1963), set in the same period and using some of the same historical material, is a fictionalized biography of James O'Hara, who came to this country shortly before the Revolution, traveled west to Indiana, became Washington's quartermaster during the war, and was prominent in the early history of Pittsburgh. Many other historical personages, of minor as well as major importance, figure in its pages. It effectively contrasts settled Philadelphia, rough young Pittsburgh, and the wilderness that would become Indiana and Illinois.

For other novels T. turned to the late 19th and early 20th centuries. The most ambitious of these, *The Rolling Years*, studies three generations of Scots Presbyterian women in western Pennsylvania. Sarah McDowell bears twelve children (of whom five survive) to her dour Calvinistic husband; her bitterness about her repeated, difficult confinements is effectively shown. Her last child, Jeannie, has an easier and yet more restricted life. A gay and loving girl, she marries a minister and moves to town. As a young widow, she rears her daughter, Constance, with the help of her spinster sisters, who are also strikingly portrayed. Engaged to a Presbyterian divinity student, Constance faces her crisis when he denies some of the tenets of their faith. Thus the novel dramatizes the gradual weakening of the strict Calvinism of the Scottish immigrants as their life grows increasingly easy.

Remember the End (1938) tells of Alex MacTay, a poetic young Scotsman who comes to Pennsylvania in 1890. Suppressing his aesthetic interests, he rises to great wealth and power, but at the cost of deeply wounding his wife and alienating his only son. Sympathetically portrayed, he typifies the strengths and weaknesses of the great tycoons of the period, such as his own model, Andrew Carnegie.

Much of T.'s fiction tends toward the sentimental and some of her novels seem written to inculcate an easy and conventional morality. In addition, her novels tend to use trite plot devices. But at her best, in the novels studying her Scottish background in western Pennsylvania, she has created moving and believable pictures of women's joys and sufferings.

WORKS: *Far above Rubies* (1926). *The Wife of Pontius Pilate: A Story of the Heart of Procla* (1928). *In the Garden: A Story of the First Easter* (1929). *The Four Marys* (1932). *The Colt that Carried a King* (1933). *Old Home Town* (1933). *This Spring of Love* (1934). *The Rolling Years* (1936). *Remember the End* (1938). *Elijah the Fishbite* (1940). *Dear Me: Leaves from the Diary of Agnes Sligh Turnbull* (1941). *The Day Must Dawn* (1942). *Once to Shout* (1943). *The Bishop's Mantle* (1947). *The Gown of Glory* (1952). *The Golden Journey* (1955). *Jed, the Shepherd's Dog* (1957). *Out of My Heart* (1958). *The Nightingale: A Romance* (1960). *The King's Orchard* (1963). *Little Christmas* (1964). *George* (1965). *The Wedding Bargain* (1966). *The White Lark* (1968). *Many a Green Isle* (1968). *Whistle and I'll Come to You: An Idyll* (1970). *The Flowering* (1972). *The Richlands* (1974). *The Winds of Love* (1977).

BIBLIOGRAPHY: NYHTB (26 Oct. 1947). NYTBR (9 Feb. 1936; 27 Nov. 1938; 25 Oct. 1942; 26 Oct. 1947; 16 March 1952). SatR (17 Oct. 1942; 19 Nov. 1955).

MARY JEAN DeMARR

Anne Tyler

B. 25 Oct. 1941, Minneapolis, Minnesota
D. of Lloyd Parry and Phyllis Mahon Tyler; m. Taghi Mohammad
   Modaressi, 1963

T. was raised in North Carolina. She graduated from Duke University with a major in Russian (1961) and pursued graduate work at Columbia (1962). She served as Russian bibliographer at Duke University Library and as assistant to the librarian at McGill University Law Library, Montreal. In 1963, T. married a child psychiatrist, and they now live in Baltimore with their two daughters.

T. has been prolific: she has written eight novels in sixteen years and numerous short stories, which appear in diverse magazines from *McCalls* to *The New Yorker*.

T. introduces most of the major characteristics of her novels in her first, *If Morning Ever Comes* (1964). Plots involve the complexities of family life and are geographically bound to small towns in North Carolina or to withering row houses or more fashionable Roland Park in Baltimore. The title of each novel appears in the text and focuses on a major theme. Humor, often bittersweet, is important. Characterization is T.'s greatest strength, especially of old people who are presented with compassion and of invincible and usually eccentric women. T. uses diction and grammar that establish characters' backgrounds and imagery that reflects characters' problems and traits: "Pieces of Emerson were lodged with Elizabeth like shrapnel." She has established herself, particularly with her last four novels, as a writer of unquestioned talent.

Jeremy Pauling, of *Celestial Navigation* (1974), is a sensitive and shy artist who lives in his own mind and who finds forays into the real world puzzling and, finally, destructive. The chapters centering on him employ a narrative voice, but the six chapters devoted to four women in Jeremy's life all use first-person voices. Ironically, Jeremy experiences his greatest happiness and creativity after his mother's death (an event his sisters thought would devastate his life) and after Mary and their children depart, leaving only a note on the refrigerator door. Both Jeremy—"Wasn't that what life was all about: steadfast endurance?"—and Mary—"I don't know which takes more courage: surviving a lifelong endurance test because you once made a promise or breaking free, disrupting your whole world"—embody the trait that T. insists on for most of her characters: endurance.

Searching for Caleb (1975) juxtaposes the comic and the serious, chronicling three generations of a Baltimore family of Roland Park. Family strife climaxes when the first cousins, Justine and Duncan, marry each other. These two set out on adventures best symbolized by the Mayflower truck that moves their rosewood chests and crystal from Roland Park and by the orange U-Haul van that, much later, moves only their books and clothes to a circus's winter trailer park. Like *Celestial Navigation*, this novel brings characters into Chekhovian scenes where people talk to unlistening ears, Daniel and Caleb Peck, T.'s most endearing old people; Justine, Daniel's fortune-telling, nomad-like granddaughter; other Pecks; and eccentric strangers make up this comic novel, which details man's foibles, charms, mores, weaknesses, and flaws.

In *Earthly Possessions* (1977), Charlotte Emory gives a minute account of being kidnapped in a Maryland bank and abducted to Florida. In alternate chapters she tells the history of her own life (a struggle to dispossess herself of encumbering possessions) and the histories of the peculiar and unhappy families of her mother and husband. Richly humorous, this novel epitomizes in Charlotte a woman T. frequently portrays—a woman denied the autonomous existence she craves. No shrill feminist cries rise from T.'s fiction, but an existential longing for freedom does.

Eccentric characters are prominent in T.'s work; they settle into a private world, unconcerned with the day-to-day activities that dominate the lives of others. *Morgan's Passing* (1980), her most recent novel, presents a highly eccentric character, Morgan Gower, in fascinating detail. The reader, however, is left somewhat at a loss, never completely sure of the character or of his personae.

A skillful writer, T. treats serious and often tragic themes without sacrificing the comic. Her prose, as some critics charge, is not stylistically daring, and her concerns are not with depressed minorities or with mythic ghosts. Instead, she writes truly about the lives of middle-class Americans, and her characters dwell, as John Updike has said, "where poetry and adventure form as easily as dew."

WORKS: *If Morning Ever Comes* (1964). *The Tin Can Tree* (1965). *A Slipping-Down Life* (1970). *The Clock Winder* (1972). *Celestial Navigation* (1974). *Searching for Caleb* (1975). *Earthly Possessions* (1977). *Morgan's Passing* (1980). *Dinner at the Homesick Restaurant* (1982).

BIBLIOGRAPHY: *Atlantic* (March 1976). *NY* (29 March 1976; 6 June 1977). *NYTBR* (15 July 1965). *SoR* 14 (Jan. 1978).

ELIZABETH EVANS

Dorothy Uhnak

B. *1931, Bronx, New York*

For fourteen years, U. served as a member of the New York City Transit Police, achieving the rank of detective first class. She is married and the mother of one daughter.

Her first book, *Policewoman* (1964) is a partially fictionalized account of the transformation of the narrator (who shares U.'s name and background) from applicant to fullfledged, working member of the New York City Police Department. No attempt is made to gloss over the frustrations engendered by tedious procedures, the reluctance of citizens to testify against offenders, the use of influence to free criminals justly apprehended, or the hardening process through which a beginning officer must pass. In contrast, however, the excitement of the work and the sense of service rendered and assignments well done is also dramatized, making *Policewoman* a strong, compelling first book.

U. then introduced a cast of continuing characters who appear in a series of three novels. The protagonist, Detective Christie Choriopoulos Opara, works for the district attorney's Special Investigations Squad. The problems common to working mothers—Opara is a young widow whose husband, also a policeman, was killed while on duty—and the presence of Opara's family, which serves as a support group, both contribute to the realism of the series. The developing personal and professional relationships between Opara and her boss, Casey Reardon, one of fiction's best realized "tough cops," provide subplots throughout the trilogy. Other members of the squad lend depth, color, comic relief, and effective detail.

The plot of *The Bait* (1968) springs from an arrest Opara unwillingly makes while on her way to the culmination of a seemingly more important undercover assignment. U.'s development of the background and motivation of the murderer enhances the suspense and offsets the book's dependence on coincidence. The organization and the machinations of the Secret Nation, a black religio-political gang, form the subplot of *The Witness* (1969); seen through the eyes of initiate Eddie Campion, the scenes involving the Nation are especially powerful. Elena Vargas of *The Ledger* (1970) is one of U.'s most vibrant and complex characters, and her attitudes and history are fully explored. Vargas and Opara engage in a long, absorbing battle of wills which contributes enormously to the book's success.

Law and Order (1973) is not a crime novel but rather the panoramic saga of a family of New York policemen, their connections, their work, their sense of self and place. The central character, Brian O'Malley, is a study of an essentially decent man struggling to master himself, his work, and the necessarily shady world into which that work takes him.

Sergeant Joe Peters, the officer investigating the murder of two little boys, is the protagonist and narrator of *The Investigation* (1977). Both the police and public opinion point to Kitty Keeler, the children's mother, as the killer, and Peter solves a double mystery to achieve the book's climax. Much of the tension springs from the contradictory and intense appraisals other characters make of the accused. She is believed by some to be nearly saintly in her generosity, warmth, and kindness; believed by others to be a sensual, self-indulgent, fiendish woman. Kitty Keeler's real motivations and personality are the plot's true mystery. *The Investigation* is U.'s best novel to date.

False Witness (1981) portrays two women who have achieved success in professions dominated by men. Sanderalee Dawson, model, television personality, and political activist, is the victim of rape and attempted murder; Lynne Jacobi, a bureau chief in the New York City District Attorney's Office, investigates the crime, forcing the two women into an uneasy alliance. The extreme violence of the attack on Sanderalee underscores the brutality of the struggles for power and control the protagonists experience professionally. *False Witness* is a superior novel whose characterizations are expecially strong.

Remarkably well able to convey tellingly the ambiences of home, squad room, and mean streets, U. is a good writer noted for her mastery of realistic detail in plot, setting, and characterization.

WORKS: *Policewoman* (1964). *The Bait* (1968). *The Witness* (1969). *The Ledger* (1970). *Law and Order* (1973). *The Investigation* (1977). *False Witness* (1981).

BIBLIOGRAPHY: *Best Sellers* (1 Feb. 1964). *Mystery Fancier* (Jan. 1978). *Newsweek* (13 April 1973).

JANE S. BAKERMAN

Frances Jane Crosby Van Alstyne

B. *24 March 1820; Putnam County, New York; d. 12 Feb. 1915, Bridgeport, Connecticut*
Wrote under: *Fanny Crosby, etc.*
D. *of John and Mercy Crosby; m. Alexander Van Alstyne, 1858*

At the age of six weeks, V. was permanently blinded as a result of an eye infection treated by hot poultices that destroyed the optic nerves. This trauma was compounded when her father died before she was one year old, but as an eight-year-old she wrote the lines: "O what a happy soul am I! / Although I cannot see, / I am resolved that in this world / Contented I will be!" V. spent her childhood studying the Bible and developing the powers of her memory. In fact, she later told friends that she had memorized the first five books of the Bible, the Psalms, and most of the New Testament.

At the age of fifteen, V. enrolled in the New York Institution for the Blind, where she remained as a student for the next eight years. Here she developed her poetic talents by reciting topical poems for visitors, such as Jenny Lind and Henry Clay. She also recited on fund-raising tours for the institution from 1842 to 1844. One of her favorites on such occasions began: "Contented, happy, though a sightless band, / Dear friends, this evening we before you stand." After graduating at the age of twenty-three, V. stayed at the institution and taught a number of subjects for the next fifteen years.

V.'s first volume of poetry, *The Blind Girl, and Other Poems* (1844), was published when she was twenty-four. Ironically, the preface states that "any pecuniary advantage" to the authoress will be appreciated since she is in "declining health." V. died at the age of ninety-five. The volume concentrates on the extremely morbid subjects so popular at the time. Typical poems are "My Mother's Grave," "Ida, the Broken-Hearted," and "On the Death of a Child."

In her next volume of poetry, *Monterey, and Other Poems* (1851), V. again appeals to her readers' sympathy: she states that her health is "sadly impaired," while she hopes her "declining years" will be supported by the sale of this volume. The contents are even more maudlin, including "The Dying Daughter," "Let Me Die on the Prairie," "Weep Not for the Dead," "The Stranger's Grave," and "Reflections of a Murderer."

A Wreath of Columbia's Flowers (1858) is a collection of short fiction. Although V. claims that her writings are "natural and true to life," this volume contains the story "Annie Herbert," about a girl who hears flowers talking to her.

Her final volume of poetry, *Bells at Evening, and other Verse* (1897), includes a biographical sketch by Robert Lowry. V. considered *Bells at Evening* her finest poetic effort. It contains such secular poems as "A Tribute to Cincinnati" and other patriotic fare. The final section includes some sixty-five of her most famous hymns.

Hymn writing was V.'s major claim to fame. She began writing popular songs with the composer George F. Root in 1851, and the two collaborated on about fifty songs, including "Rosalie, the Prairie Flower," which

earned three thousand dollars in royalties. In 1864, V. began writing
hymns with William B. Bradbury, generally considered the father of Sunday-school music in America. Over her long career, she wrote around
eight thousand hymns. Not even she could remember the exact figure,
since so many were published under her more than two hundred pseudo-
nyms. Her most successful hymns include "Rescue the Perishing" and "Safe
in the Arms of Jesus," used by Dwight L. Moody and Ira D. Sankey in
their missionary work and by Frances E. Willard in her temperance work.

V.'s final literary efforts were two versions of her autobiography, *Fannie Crosby's Life-Story* (1903) and the more detailed volume, *Memories
of Eighty Years* (1906). In the latter volume she gives one paragraph to
her marriage to another blind teacher at the institution. The two moved
to Brooklyn, where V. continued to write hymns and her husband
worked as a music teacher until his death in 1902. One suspects, from V.'s
autobiographical volumes, that beneath her saccharine surface she was a
shrewd businesswoman who prospered by presenting to the public the
popular sentiments they wanted to hear.

WORKS: *The Blind Girl, and Other Poems* (1844). *Monterey, and Other
Poems* (1851). *A Wreath of Columbia's Flowers* (1858). *Bells at Evening, and
Other Verses* (1897). *Ode to the Memory of Captain John Underhill* (1902).
Fanny Crosby's Life-Story (1903). *Memories of Eighty Years* (1906).

BIBLIOGRAPHY: Van Alstyne, F. C., *Fanny Crosby's Life-Story* (1903).
Van Alstyne, F. C., *Memories of Eighty Years* (1906).
    For articles in reference works, see: *NAW* (article by C. E. Rinehart).
                                            DIANE LONG HOEVELER

Marie Van Vorst

B. 23 Nov. 1867, New York City; d. 16 Dec. 1936, Florence, Italy
D. of Hooper Cumming and Josephine Treat Van Vorst;
m. Count Gaetano Gaiati, 1916

V. was the daughter of a financially prosperous and socially prominent
family, and she was educated by private tutors; but most of her best-
known writings are animated by a conscious dedication to social reform.
She most likely inherited this commitment to reform from her father who,

during his tenure on the New York City Superior Court, was involved in an investigation of urban corruption which contributed to the demise of the Tweed Ring.

V. began writing short stories, poems, and nofiction essays for periodical publication during the late 1890s. Shortly after the death of her brother, John, she and her sister-in-law, Bessie, moved to France where they both served as correspondents for American journals. With only occasional visits to the U.S., primarily to gather research material for her writing, V. lived in various European cities until her death in 1928. Although she wrote for many American, French, and British periodicals, her association with *Harper's* was the most sustained and significant. One of her most important assignments for *Harper's* was a cultural series, "Rivers of the World" (1906–09), which included information gathered at the Seine, Tiber, and Nile.

V. began writing before her sister-in-law, but it was their collaboration on a novel and, particularly, on an exposé of women factory workers that initially brought the work of both women public attention. After the two ceased actively writing together, Bessie remained V.'s most constant friend, critic, and consultant.

V. and Bessie returned to the U.S., assumed aliases, and worked in factories to gather information for *The Woman Who Toils* (1903). As "Bell Ballard," V. worked in a shoe factory in Lynn, Massachusetts, and in cotton mills in South Carolina. Describing herself as a "mirror, expositor and mouthpiece" for working women, she was more sympathetic to her co-workers than Bessie. Although she never identified herself with these women, she was more understanding in her estimation of their values. Where Bessie criticized the women for their frivolity, V. saw in it an incipient rebellion against the deadening limitations of their lives. Similarly, she was more hopeful of reforms coming within the industrial workplace rather than by removing the women from the mills. Although sharply critical of "the abnormality, the abortion known as Anarchy, Socialism," she championed the cause of labor unions: "Organize labor, therefore, so well that the work-woman who obtains her task may be able to continue it and keep her health and self-respect."

V.'s experiences in the cotton mills provided her with enough information to write a fictionalized account of the situation in one of her better novels, *Amanda of the Mill* (1905). She presents both the history of how the hill people came to work in the mills and the world they found there, primarily through two characters—the somewhat idealized, but none the less interesting heroine, Amanda Henchley, and the man she loves, Henry

Euston, a drunkard whose reformation is effected through the dual inspi-rations of Amanda and reform-oriented labor organizing. The novel is memorable for its accurate and concerned reporting of industrial issues.

In *Amanda of the Mill*, V. leads her characters through a series of crises that seemingly could be resolved only through economic revolution. She avoids this conclusion through a propitious natural disaster, which clears the way for a new era without requiring confrontation with the problems the narrative so carefully raises. Although a tendency to equivocate also occurs in the later novels—in which dilemmas posed by marital incompati-bility and illicit sexual passion predominate, and spouses conveniently die before virtue is endangered—these books are entertaining and occasionally of more lasting interest.

The most significant of the later novels is *Mary Moreland* (1915), the story of a stenographer in love with and loved by her employer, a married Wall Street financier. In *Mary Moreland*, V. writes her most sophisticated discussion of the moral issues surrounding marital dissatisfaction and infi-delity and creates her most complex and admirable heroine. Mary, a self-supporting suffragist dedicated to her career while searching for a passion-ate love that is neither compromising nor limiting, is a memorable fictional portrait of a young American woman seeking her identity in a world of shifting social and sexual values.

Although V.'s fiction fails to fulfill the promise engendered by her vivid moral and economic observations, the novels, especially *Amanda of the Mills* and *Mary Moreland*, deserve some renewal of critical interest. Per-haps because of her continued inability to solve the problems she raises without resorting to catastrophe and coincidence, V.'s writings provide a remarkable record of the turmoil of a society in transition. Although she never abandoned the traditional codes of behavior, she raised penetrating questions about their viability.

WORKS: *Bagsby's Daughter* (with B. Van Vorst, 1901). *Philip Longstreth* (1902). *The Woman Who Toils* (with B. Van Vorst, 1903). *Poems* (1903). *Amanda of the Mill* (1905). *Miss Desmond* (1905). *The Sin of George Warre-ner* (1906). *The Sentimental Adventures of Jimmy Bulstrode* (1908). *In Am-bush* (1909). *First Love* (1910). *The Girl from His Town* (1910). *The Broken Bell* (1912). *His Love Story* (1913). *Big Tremaine* (1914). *Mary Moreland* (1915). *War Letters of an American Woman* (1916). *War Poems* (1916). *Fairfax and His Bride* (1920). *Tradition* (1921). *The Queen of Karmania* (1922). *Sunrise* (1924). *Goodnight Ladies!* (1931). *The Gardenia* (1933).

BIBLIOGRAPHY: Blake, F., *The Strike in the American Novel* (1972). Filler, L., *The Muckrakers* (1976). Hill, Vicki Lynn, "Strategy and Breadth: The So-cialist-Feminist in American Fiction" (Ph.D. diss., State Univ. of New York at

Buffalo, 1979). Maglin, N., "Rebel Women Writers, 1894–1925" (Ph.D. diss., Union Graduate School, 1975). Rose, L., "A Descriptive Catalogue of Economic and Politico-Economic Fiction in the United States, 1902–1909" (Ph.D. diss., Univ. of Chicago, 1936). Taylor, W., *The Economic Novel in America* (1942).

For articles in reference works, see: *NAW* (article by L. Filler).

Other references: *Athenaeum* (18 April 1908). *Bookman* (May 1902; April 1903; June 1905; Jan. 1910). *Critic* (Jan. 1902; Oct. 1903). *Dial* (1 Sept. 1906). *Overland* (May 1903). *SatR* (18 August 1906).

VICKI LYNN HILL

Frances Fuller Victor

B. 23 May 1826, Rome, New York; d. 14 Nov. 1902, Portland, Oregon
Wrote under: Frances Barritt, Dorothy D., Florence Fane, Frances Fuller,
  Frances Fuller Victor
D. of Adonijah and Lucy A. Williams Fuller; m. Jackson Barritt, 1853;
  m. Henry Clay Victor, 1862

V. was the eldest of five daughters, descended from an old colonial family. V. and her sister Metta, with whom she wrote poetry, received their schooling at a young-ladies seminary in Wooster, Ohio. At the age of nine she wrote verses on her slate and directed her fellow students in plays she had written. The publication of her verses in the Cleveland *Herald* in 1840 marked the beginning of a long writing career.

V.'s turbulent private life frequently interrupted her prolific writing career. When her father died in 1850, she stopped writing poetry and returned home to live with her family, who by then had moved to St. Clair, Michigan. Her first marriage broke up after a period of homesteading in Omaha, but V. didn't obtain a divorce until March, 1862, two months before she married her sister's brother-in-law, Henry Clay Victor, a navy engineer. V. and her husband moved to the West Coast, but his position in the navy often took him away for long periods of sea duty. Left alone, V. embarked on a successful career as a historian, and continued it after her husband was drowned in 1875 in the wreck of the *Pacific*.

As teenagers, V. and her sister Metta together wrote poetry and published it locally and, eventually, in the New York *Home Journal*. In 1848, they moved to New York, and in 1851 they published *Poems of Sentiment and Imagination*, a collection of descriptive and highly melodramatic poetry. The remainder of their poetry was written and published separately. After V. moved west in 1862, she wrote numerous poems of a more descriptive quality for western magazines.

In 1848, V. published her first melodramatic romance, *Anizetta, the Guajira; or, The Creole of Cuba*. She abandoned this genre when she discovered she had more talent as a realistic dime novelist. For her brother-in-law's editions of Beadle's Dime Novels, V. wrote *East and West; or, The Beauty of Willard's Mill* (1862) and *The Land Claim: A Tale of the Upper Missouri* (1862), both realistically treating Nebraska farm life, especially the hardships faced by women. Her short stories, published in the western magazines, reflect this same concern for the hard lot of frontier women; the regional writing of Bret Harte was a major influence on these realistic short stories.

V.'s work as a satirist and crusader began when she moved to the West Coast in the 1860s. As Florence Fane, she took satiric pokes at all levels of society in regular contributions to the San Francisco *Bulletin* and the *Golden Era*. Her brief crusade as a temperance supporter resulted in one temperance tract, *The Women's War with Whiskey* (1874). She also served as a columnist for the *Call-Bulletin* under the name of Dorothy D.

The thirty years V. spent as a historian and folklorist proved the most successful aspect of her writing career. She discovered history was her forte in 1864 when she began studying local Oregon history. She interviewed many western pioneers and researched family papers and archives. *The River of the West* (1870), based on an interview with Joseph Meek, is his first-person account of life as a Rocky Mountain trapper. V. acknowledges in her introduction her debt to Washington Irving's *Astoria* (1836) and *Captain Bonneville* (1837), which reveal a romantic attachment to historical places.

V.'s second attempt at this new genre, *All Over Oregon and Washington* (1872) contains less folklore than *The River of the West*. The book covers the discovery, early history, natural features, resources, and business and social conditions of these two states. V.'s response to rapid social and economic change is nostalgic. She emphasizes her disappointment at the close of the frontier, but points with pride to the cultural developments of the Northwest Coast.

V.'s major historical endeavor was her contribution to Hubert Howe Bancroft's voluminous *History of the Pacific States* (1890); she contributed to all but two of the twenty-eight volumes. V. joined the staff as a chief assistant and its only woman in 1878, three years after the death of her husband. By this time, she had accumulated a wealth of journalistic, literary, and historic experience. As a member of Bancroft's staff, she prepared all of the two-volume history of Oregon, Washington, Idaho, and Montana and was the major writer and researcher for the history of Utah. She also wrote over half of the two California volumes and researched *Northwest Coast* and *California Inter Pocula*. The series is written in textbook style, but V.'s volumes, like her other historical works, exhibit a sensitive response to the aesthetics of the land and a nostalgia for the past.

V.'s historical accounts reflect a keen understanding of the economic and social elements of a slowly diminishing frontier; these works also reveal a seemingly contradictory perception of the West as a land of hardships and cherished memories. Her main contribution to American letters rests with these history and travel books and their blend of fact and romance. Her realistic dime novels and short stories, her sentimental and descriptive poetry, and her satiric and crusading pieces, however, also earn a place for her in American letters.

WORKS: *Anizetta the Guajira; or, The Creole of Cuba* (1848). *Poems of Sentiment and Imagination* (with M. F. Victor, 1851). *The Land Claim: A Tale of the Upper Missouri* (1862). *East and West; or, The Beauty of Willard's Mill* (1862). *Border Law; or, The Land Claim* (1862). *The River of the West* (1870). *All Over Oregon and Washington* (1872; revised edition, *Atlantis Arisen*, 1891). *The Women's War with Whiskey* (1874). *The New Penelope, and Other Stories and Poems* (1877). *Eleven Years in the Rocky Mountains* (1879). *History of the Pacific States* (with H. Bancroft et al., 1884-90). *The Early Indian Wars of Oregon* (1894). *Poems* (1900). *Letters to Matthew P. Deady, F. G. Young, and Others, 1866–1902* (1902).

BIBLIOGRAPHY: Caughey, J. W., *Hubert Howe Bancroft: Historian of the West* (1946). Morris, W. A. "Historian of the Northwest: A Woman Who Loved Oregon," *In Memoriam: Frances Fuller Victor; Born May 23, 1826; Died November 14, 1902* (1902). Morris, W. A., "The Origin and Authorship of the Bancroft Pacific States Publications," *Oregon Historical Society Quarterly* 5 (1903).

For articles in reference works, see: *AW. NAW* (article by F. Walker).

DONNA CASELLA KERN

Metta Victoria Fuller Victor

B. 2 March 1831, Erie, Pennsylvania; d. 26 June 1885, Hohokus, New Jersey
Wrote under: George E. Booram, Corinne Cushman, Eleanor Lee Edwards,
  Metta Fuller, Walter T. Gray, Louis LeGrand(?), Rose Kennedy, Mrs. Mark
  Peabody, Seeley Regester, the Singing Sybil, Mrs. Henry J. Thomas, Metta
  Victor
D. of Adonijah (Adanigh?) and Lucy Williams Fuller; m. Dr. Morse, 1850(?);
  m. Orville J. Victor, 1856

Five years younger than her sister Frances, V. was eight years old when
the family moved to Wooster Village, Ohio. Soon thereafter, she began
her writing career. By the age of thirteen she was publishing in journals
and papers. By fifteen, she had published *The Last Days of Tul: A Romance of the Lost Cities of Yucatan* (1846). That same year V. began
publishing as "The Singing Sybil" in Willis and Morris' *New York Home
Journal.* Her poetry was much praised, but after producing one joint poetry volume with her sister, she turned her greatest energies to the writing
of stories and novels.

V.'s early novels are often moralistic as well as melodramatic and focus
on a particular social ill. One example, *The Senator's Son* (1853; sometimes called *Parke Madison*), is a temperance novel. It was also V.'s first
bestseller, running to ten editions in the U.S., and selling some thirty thousand copies in pirated British editions.

There is some evidence (see Johansen) that, by 1851, while living in
Michigan, V. was married to a Dr. Morse. Nothing is known about this
marriage, which does not appear in records for St. Clair, Washtenaw, or
Oakland County, Michigan. Her first marriage is even more mysterious
than that of her sister to Jackson Barritt. It is known that in 1856 V.
married Orville J. Victor, a young journalist who would soon become one
of the architects of the Beadle Dime Novel empire. Besides untold poems,
stories, articles, manuals, and novels, V. produced nine children. She was
still an active writer when she died, at age fifty-four, of cancer.

Not surprisingly, V. was one of Beadle's prime resources. She edited
their journal, the *Home*, and was the author of manuals and cookbooks as
well as fiction. She produced more than twenty books for Beadle. Dime
Novel Number Four was V.'s *Alice Wilde* (1860). Her most popular Beadle novel was *Maum Guinea and Her Plantation Children*, first published

in 1861. This impassioned story of slave life is said to have been praised by both President Lincoln and Henry Ward Beecher. It sold some one hundred thousand copies in the U.S. and was also reprinted widely in Britain.

Although V. is perhaps best known for sensationalist sermons on issues like temperance and slavery, her most important contribution is probably her landmark work in the American detective novel. Under the pseudonym Seeley Regester, V. produced *The Dead Letter*. First published by Beadle in 1866 (but believed to have been originally published two years earlier), *The Dead Letter* is one of the first detective novels. It antedates, by at least twelve years, Anna Katharine Green (Rohlf's) *The Leavenworth Case*, which was long believed to be the first American detective novel.

Still a highly readable tale of treachery, true love, and murder, *The Dead Letter* features a professional gentleman sleuth named Mr. Burton. Besides the help of the young hero, Redfield, Burton also relies on the considerable talents of his young daughter, a psychic. V. produced a second novel as Seeley Regester, *The Figure Eight; or, The Mystery of Meredith Place* (later called *A Woman's Hand*) in 1869. Other novels by V. during this period, although not pure detective puzzles, certainly feature violent crimes and their detection. One example, *Too True: A Story of Today* (1868), was published under V.'s real name and features a good deal of detection by a woman artist.

V. deserves recognition as one of the earliest creators of the detective novel and as a writer with facility in any formula of popular fiction. She wrote romance, pioneer adventure, detective, sensation, and social issue novels. Late in her career she also created a comic realm populated by bad boys, bashful men, and prosperous pork merchants. During the heyday of the American dime novel and serial V. was in great demand. At one point in the 1870s, V. received twenty-five thousand dollars for exclusive story rights from the *New York Weekly*.

V. could easily be labeled a hack writer. But she was also a writer of undeniable skill whose inventiveness anticipated the needs of her reading public. Sensational thrillers like *The Dead Letter* opened new frontiers in popular fiction and have the power to entertain even a modern reader.

WORKS: *The Last Days of Tul* (1846). *Poems of Sentiment and Imagination* (with F. F. Victor, 1851). *Fresh Leaves from Western Woods* (1852). *The Senator's Son* (1853). *Fashionable Dissipation* (1854). *Mormon Wives* (1856). *The Arctic Queen* (1858). *Miss Slimmen's Window* (1859). *The Dime Cook Book* (1859). *The Dime Recipe Book* (1859). *Alice Wilde: The Raftsman's*

Daughter (1860). *The Backwood's Bride* (1860). *Myrtle: The Child of the Prairie* (1860). *Uncle Ezekiel and his Exploits on Two Continents* (1861). *Maum Guinea and Her Plantation Children* (1861). *The Emerald Necklace* (1861). *The Unionist's Daughter* (1862). *The Gold Hunters* (1863). *Jo Daviess' Client* (1863). *Laughing Eyes* (1868). *The Country Cousin* (1864). *The Two Hunters* (1865). *The Housewife's Manual* (1865). *The Dead Letter* (1866). *Who Was He?* (1866). *Too True: A Story of Today* (1868). *The Betrayed Bride* (1869). *The Figure Eight* (1869). *Black Eyes and Blue* (1876). *Passing the Portal* (1876). *Brave Barbara* (1877). *The Hunted Bride* (1877). *Guilty or Not Guilty* (1878). *The Locked Heart* (1879). *A Wild Girl* (1879). *A Bad Boy's Diary* (1880). *The Black Riddle* (1880). *Madcap: The Little Quakeress* (1880). *The Mysterious Guardian* (1880). *Pretty and Proud* (1880). *Pursued to the Altar* (1880). *The Blunders of a Bashful Man* (1881). *At His Mercy* (1881). *Miss Slimmen's Boarding House* (1882). *A Woman's Sorrow* (1882). *The Bad Boy Abroad* (1883). *Morley Beeches* (1883). *Naughty Girl's Diary* (1883). *Abijah Beanpole in New York* (1884). *Mrs. Rasher's Curtain Lectures* (1884). *The Bad Boy at Home* (1885). *A Good Boy's Diary* (1885). *The Brown Princess* (1888). *The Phantom Wife* (1888). *Born to Betray* (1890). *The Gay Captain* (1891). *Who Owned the Jewels?* (1891). *The Georgie Papers* (1897).

BIBLIOGRAPHY: Johannsen, A., *The House of Beadle and Adams*, Vol. 2 (1950).

Other references: *Cosmopolitan Art Journal* (March 1857).

KATHLEEN L. MAIO

Mary Heaton Vorse

B. *9 Oct. 1874, New York City; d. 14 June 1966, Provincetown, Massachusetts*
D. *of Hiram and Ellen Cordelia Blackman Heaton; m. Albert White Vorse,
1898; m. Joe O'Brien, 1912; m. Robert Minor, 1920*

V. was born to an old New England family. As a child, she spent her summers in the college town of Amherst, Massachusetts, and her winters in New York City and Europe. Although seemingly cosmopolitan, V. wrote, in later life, about how the sheltered academic atmosphere of her youth enabled her to acquire a dedication to intellectual speculation, but left her isolated from the industrial and economic changes that characterized late 19th-c. America.

V. was married three times and had three children. After the death of her first husband, V. supported herself through her writing.

V.'s earliest published writings were short sketches, which appeared in diverse periodicals including *Criterion, Critic, Woman's Home Companion,* and *Atlantic Monthly*. Both *The Very Little Person* (1911) and *The Prestons* (1918) include short fiction excerpted from these early publications. V. drew on the experiences of her first years of marriage to Albert Vorse in her first novel, *The Breaking-in of a Yachtsman's Wife* (1908). *The Autobiography of an Elderly Woman* (1911), an anecdotal and entertaining narrative, is told from the point of view of a woman her mother's age who resents the circumscriptions youth imposes on the aged.

In 1906, V. moved to Greenwich Village, where she and her husband founded the A Club, an experimental cooperative living arrangement frequented by Mark Twain, Theodore Dreiser, Mother Jones, Maxim Gorky, and others. Primarily a collection of liberal reformers who flirted with varieties of socialism, the participants in the A Club were devoted to a thoughtful and stimulating analysis of American society. V. wrote favorably about her experiences in the club. Still, she affectionately satirizes the Greenwich Village lifestyle in the novel *I've Come to Stay* (1915). The heroine, Camilla Deerfield, justifies the excesses and absurdities of the village residents as a necessary and long overdue response to their Calvinist heritage: "We are the flaming shadows cast by unfulfilled joys which died unborn in our parents' souls. We come of people who lived in the ordinary hypocrisies so long that some of us cast away even the decencies in our endaevor not to be hypocritical."

From 1906 through the mid-1940s, V. spent a portion of each year in Provincetown, Massachusetts, as did other members of the Greenwich Village radical intelligentsia. It was here that V., prompted by a series of articles on infant education she had researched in Italy for *Woman's Home Companion*, organized a Montessori school. More importantly, here V. was among the founding members of the experimental theater group, the Provincetown Players, that staged Eugene O'Neill's earliest plays.

In *A Footnote to Folly* (1935), an autobiographical account of the years 1912 to 1922, V. identified the 1912 Lawrence, Massachusetts, textile strike as the single most significant event in her political and literary development. She described how her experiences at Lawrence led both her and Joe O'Brien, the labor reporter who became her second husband, to active identification with the problems and struggles of the American working class. Henceforth, V. was to write the bulk of her work in explicitly politicized terms.

This dedication is reflected in the prolific writing of her major phase. For more than thirty years she was a tireless reporter of current events on labor and battle fronts throughout the U.S., Europe, and the Soviet Union. Most of this writing is ephemeral; it appeared in Hearst newspapers, *Harper's* the *Nation, New Republic, Advance, World Tomorrow, Outlook,* and the *Masses* (which she edited) and was never collected. As a war correspondent during WWI, V. covered the 1915 International Congress of Women in Amsterdam and the International Woman Suffrage Convention in Budapest. Her journalism was enhanced by personal involvement with the Red Cross, the American Relief Association, and the Committee for Public Information; her coverage of the war, like that of labor disputes, often focused on the ignored victims—women and children.

With the exception of *The Ninth Man* (1918), a novel set in 12th-c. Italy, all of V.'s book-length publications spring from her experiences as a radical journalist. They vary from compilations recording her coverage of actual events, such as *Men and Steel* (1920) and *Labor's New Millions* (1938), to fictionalized accounts of actual strikes, such as *Passaic* (1926) and *Strike* (1930), and novels springing from her impressions of a world in turmoil, such as *Second Cabin* (1928), based on an ocean voyage from inflation-ravaged postwar Germany to the U.S., after a visit to "optimistic" postrevolutionary Russia.

For the contemporary reader, unfamiliar with the events V. so passionately described throughout her lengthy career, the best introduction to her writing and sensibilities probably will be found in either *A Footnote to Folly*—in which she effectively describes the relationship between personal identity and political commitment and growth—and *Of Time and the Town* (1942). The latter deals with her years in Provincetown; the legends and traditions of the fishing village provide a background for her history of the Provincetown Players and cultural attitudes during the first half of the 20th c. Both books reflect the perspective V. acknowledges in *A Footnote to Folly*: "Indeed, my book is the record of a woman who in early life got angry because many children lived miserably and died needlessly."

WORKS: *The Breaking-in of a Yachtsman's Wife* (1908). *The Whole Family* (with others, 1908). *The Very Little Person* (1911). *The Autobiography of an Elderly Woman* (1911). *The Heart's Company* (1913). *I've Come to Stay* (1915). *The Ninth Man* (1918). *The Prestons* (1918). *Growing Up* (1920). *Men and Steel* (1920). *Fraycar's Fist* (1923). *Wreckage* (1924). *Passaic* (1926). *Second Cabin* (1928). *Strike* (1930). *A Footnote to Folly* (1935). *Labor's New*

Millions (1938). *Of Time and the Town: A Provincetown Chronicle* (1942). *Here Are the People* (1943).

The Mary Heaton Vorse Collection is in the Archives of Labor History and Urban Affairs, Wayne State University, Detroit, Michigan.

BIBLIOGRAPHY: Aaron, D., *Writers on the Left* (1961). Blake, F., *The Strike in the American Novel* (1972). Hill, Vicki Lynn, "Strategy and Breadth: The Socialist-Feminist in American Fiction" (Ph.D. diss., SUNY at Buffalo, 1979). Overton, G., *The Women Who Make Our Novels* (1918). Rideout, W., *The Radical Novel in the United States, 1900–1954* (1956). Sochen, J., *The New Woman in Greenwich Village, 1910–1920* (1972). Sochen, J., *Movers and Shakers* (1973). "The Reminiscences of Mary Heaton Vorse" (transcript of interviews conducted for the Oral History Research Office of Columbia University, 1957).

For articles in reference works, see: *American Women*, Ed. D. Howes (1939). *20th CA*.

Other references: *Nation* (4 June 1908; 15 Jan. 1936). *NewR.* (13 July 1942). *Time* (23 Dec. 1935).

VICKI LYNN HILL

Margaret Walker

B. 7 July 1915, Birmingham, Alabama
D. of Sigismund and Marion Walker; m. M. Alexander, 1943

W.'s middle-class parents were both university graduates; her father was a Methodist minister, and her mother a musicologist and third-generation educator. W. graduated from Gilbert Academy (1930) and studied at Northwestern University (B.A. 1935) and the University of Iowa (M.A. 1940; Ph.D. 1965).

After working on the federal government's Writers Project in Chicago and as a newspaper and magazine editor, she began teaching. Since 1949, W. has been a professor of English at Jackson State College, Mississippi. She is director of the Institute for the Study of History, Life, and Culture of Black People and has organized black culture and writers' conferences, notably the Phillis Wheatley Poetry Festival (in November 1973), at which twenty blackwomen poets read. W. has four children.

W. began writing poetry at the age of twelve. She is the first of her race to receive the Yale Younger Poets Award for her first volume of poetry, *For My People* (1942), and other awards have followed. Her work is widely published in periodicals.

For My People is an early indication of W.'s poetic talent. She experiments with traditional and modern poetic forms. There are ten occasional poems, written in unmistakably black poetic rhythms; ten ballads with superimposed jazz rhythms or blues metrics; and six sonnets, the most traditional of her poetry in substance and structure. The volume begins at a dramatic, intense pitch, continues in a relaxed tone, and ends in contemplative modulation.

In *Prophets for a New Day* (1970), W. limits her subject to the often fatal struggle to secure human rights—chiefly for blacks. Substance clearly dominates form, whether sonnet or ballad.

W. dedicates *October Journey* (1973), a volume of ten poems, to two of her greatest influences: her father and Langston Hughes, her "friend and mentor." Her verse is at its most melodramatic here. The first poem, "October Journey," establishes the volume's tone: "A music sings within my flesh / I feel the pulse within my throat." The final piece, "A Litany from the Dark People," is a skillful, rhythmic composition.

Jubilee (1966), W.'s gripping novel, spans several genres: Civil War epic, historical fiction, and the slave narrative. It is the story of Vyre, daughter of a slave and her master. She experiences simultaneously the rite of passage to womanhood and the change from slavery to freedom. W. frees her epic from the traditional male-oriented sense of the heroic, structuring her novel around Vyre, her maternal great-grandmother. Vyre's first husband, a free and literate Negro, functions only in a supportive role to underscore Vyre's heroism. W.'s poetic style is evident in *Jubilee*'s rhythmic prose and biblical overtones.

In all her poetry, W. reveals an emotional depth as lyrical and spiritual as her personal convictions about her identity and her Protestantism. But despite her political polemics and deep racial sensitivities, W. always maintains a reasonably critical objectivity.

WORKS: *For My People* (1942). *Jubilee* (1966). *Prophets for a New Day* (1970). *How I Wrote Jubilee* (1972). *October Journey* (1973). *A Poetic Equation: Conversations with Nikki Giovani* (1974).

BIBLIOGRAPHY: Untemeyer, L., in *Yale Review* (1943).

For articles in reference works, see: *CB* (Nov. 1943). *Ebony Success Library* 1 (1973).

Other references: *Black World* (Dec. 1971).

ADRIANNE BAYTOP

Elizabeth Stuart Phelps Ward

B. 3 Aug. 1844, Boston, Massachusetts; d. 28 Jan. 1911, Newton, Massachusetts
Given name: Mary Gray Phelps
Wrote under: Mary Adams, E. S. Phelps, Elizabeth Stuart Phelps
D. of Austin and Elizabeth Stuart Phelps; m. Herbert Dickinson Ward, 1888

W. was the oldest child and only daughter of the popular author, Elizabeth Stuart Phelps. Her father was professor of sacred rhetoric at Andover Theological Seminary in Massachusetts. She identified strongly with her mother, who wrote of frustration with the role of a minister's dutiful wife. At some point after her death when W. was eight, W. adopted her mother's name. She attended Abbot Academy and Mrs. Edwards' School for Young Ladies, both in Andover.

By 1868, W. had written eleven undistinguished Sunday-school works and her first story to receive literary recognition, "The Tenth of January" (*Atlantic*, 1868), conceived under the influence of Rebecca Harding Davis. During the next two decades, W. found strong support from many other women writers, such as Lucy Larcom, Mary Bucklin Claflin, Annie Adams Fields, Harriet Prescott Spofford, and Harriet Beecher Stowe.

In the late 1870s and early 1880s, W.'s "boon companion" was Dr. Mary Briggs Harris, a physician in Andover. W.'s female characters during this period were innovatively independent. But with the deaths of her brother [Moses] Stuart Phelps and Dr. Harris in the mid-1880s, the ever-declining health of her father, and her own increasing invalidism, W.'s desire for male companionship increased, and her female characters showed decreased self-confidence. Letters suggest that W. hoped for literary companionship from the much younger man she married in 1888. Although the couple continued to summer together in Gloucester, Massachusetts, after 1900 she and her husband spent their winters apart.

W.'s career as a writer was established with the immediate and international popularity of *The Gates Ajar* (1868). As commonly interpreted, it offers the consolation of a heavenly afterlife to those bereaved by Civil War deaths. This, however, was the first of a series of books presenting W.'s major theme of women's right to self-fulfillment. *The Gates Ajar* shows the quality of female support required for women to gain fulfillment; *Beyond the Gates* (1883), the social and cultural institutions needed; and *The Gates Between* (1887), the behavior required of husbands and fathers. In 1901, W. recast the last book as a play—*Within the Gates*, which was never produced—strengthening the wife-mother role. The Gates series suggests that if earthly society—including a misguided clerical establishment—could not meet the rightful demands of women and the poor, then surely a heavenly society must exist as compensation for such earthly deprivation. These books antedate the outpouring of Utopian literature that followed Edward Bellamy's *Looking Backward* (1888).

From 1869 until her marriage in 1888, W. actively supported women's rights. In the early 1870s, she wrote feminist articles, published in *The Independent* and reprinted in the *Woman's Journal*. They dealt with the sexual double standard, women's economic and emotional independence, the sources of women's ill health, the "true woman" stereotype, and the problems of women in traditional marriages. She also used these themes in fiction for youth and adults. Early fictional examples include *Hedged In* (1870), about the social constraints placed on an unwed mother, and *A Silent Partner* (1871), dealing with men's prejudice against making a woman a business partner. Both novels emphasize women's not men's reliable support for women and women's persistent innovation of social structures designed to meet, rather than frustrate, people's basic needs.

In *The Story of Avis* (1877), W. tackled an imaginative reworking of her mother's life and fiction as well as of her own life. It is her most interesting work and contains her favorite heroine. W. shows that marriage has a devastating effect on a woman's artistic potential: Avis is expected to be dedicated only to her husband and children. *The Story of Avis* was praised by such literati as James T. Fields, Henry Wadsworth Longfellow, and John Greenleaf Whittier. But it aroused indignation in others. In 1879 and 1881, W.'s father opposed her support for women by publishing two essays decrying woman suffrage. They were later collected in *My Portfolio* (1882).

Two humorous books draw on W.'s experience as owner of a summer seaside cottage in Gloucester. *An Old Maid's Paradise* (1879), a series of sketches, shows women enjoying typically masculine pleasures, unhampered by male protection. *Burglars in Paradise* (1886), a spoof of detective fiction, reveals men's protection of women to be a mere charade and suggests that the most insidious burglar of all is the suitor.

W.'s only male protagonists appear in works written during her courtship and marriage. After her father's death in 1890, W. memorialized him in *Austin Phelps: A Memoir* (1891), then based her favorite hero, Emanuel Baynard of *A Singular Life* (1895), on her father's youthful ideals.

W. also supported antivivisection legislation, a cause that two novels connect with social wrongs against women: the vivisectors are men experimenting callously on dogs and women alike in *Trixy* (1904) and *Though Life Us Do Part* (1908).

W.'s autobiography, *Chapters from a Life* (1896), is as tantalizing for what it omits as it is useful for its revelations. In addition to some twenty-five novels, she wrote poetry and short stories for the leading magazines of her day. The poetry is mediocre, but some of the stories are outstanding. They are collected in five volumes.

Although W.'s work frequently lacks aesthetic merit, its importance lies in her ability to translate the psychological and sociological realities of her own life into literary figures. She was pulled in opposite directions by a woman's movement urging the self-fulfillment for which her mother yearned and a conservative Calvinist tradition adovacting the "feudal views" of women her father held.

WORKS: *Mercy Gliddon's Work* (1865). *Up Hill; or, Life in the Factory* (1865). Gypsy series (1866–67). *The Gates Ajar* (1868). *Men, Women and Ghosts* (1869). *Hedged In* (1870). *The Trotty Book* (1870). *The Silent Partner* (1871). *Trotty's Wedding Tour and Story-book* (1873). *What to Wear?* (1873). *Poetic Studies* (1875). *The Story of Avis* (1877). *My Cousin and I* (1879). *An Old Maid's Paradise* (1879). *Sealed Orders* (1879). *Friends: A Duet* (1881). *Doctor Zay* (1882). *Beyond the Gates* (1883). *Songs of the Silent World, and Other Poems* (1885). *Burglars in Paradise* (1886). *The Gates Between* (1887). *The Struggle for Immortality* (1889). *Austin Phelps: A Memoir* (1891). *Fourteen to One* (1891). *Donald Marcy* (1893). *A Singular Life* (1895). *Chapters from a Life* (1896). *The Story of Jesus Christ: An Interpretation* (1897). *The Successors of Mary the First* (1901). *Within the Gates* (1901). *Avery* (1902). *Confessions of a Wife* (1902). *Trixy* (1904). *The Man in the Case* (1906). *Walled In: A Novel* (1907). *Though Life Us Do Part* (1908). *The Oath of Allegiance, and Other Stories* (1909). *A Chariot of Fire* (1910). *The Empty House, and Other Stories* (1910). *Comrades* (1911).

BIBLIOGRAPHY: Bennett, M. A., *Elizabeth Stuart Phelps* (1939). Coultrap-McQuin, S. M., "Elizabeth Stuart Phelps: The Cultural Context of a Nineteenth-Century Professional Writer" (Ph.D. diss., Univ. of Iowa, 1979). Douglas, A., *The Feminization of American Culture* (1976). Hart, J. D., *The Popular Book* (1950). Kelly, L. D., " 'Oh the Poor Women'–A Study of the Works of Elizabeth Stuart Phelps" (Ph.D. diss., Univ. of North Carolina, 1979). Kessler, C. F., *Elizabeth Stuart Phelps* (1982). Phelps, A., *My Portfolio* (1882). Smith, H. S., ed., *The Gates Ajar* by E. S. P. Ward (1964). Stewart, G. B., *A New Mythos* (1979). Welter, B., *Dimity Convictions: The American Woman in the Nineteenth Century* (1976).

For article in reference works, see: *AW. DAB*, X, 1. *NAW* (article by B. K. Hofstadter).

Other references: *AQ* 29 (1977). *Frontiers: A Journal of Women Studies* 5 (Fall 1980). *MR* 13 (1972). *PMLA* 91 (1976). *Regionalism and the Female Imagination* 3 (Fall 1977). *Women's Studies* 6 (1978).

CAROL FARLEY KESSLER

Susan Bogert Warner

B. *11 July 1819, New York City; d. 17 March 1885, Highland Falls, New York*
Wrote under: Susan B. Warner, Elizabeth Wetherall
D. *of Henry Whiting and Anna Bartlett Warner*

W.'s family was prosperous during her childhood, but the depression of 1837 saw the collapse of their fortunes. Thereafter, W. and her sister Anna were responsible for the support of themselves, their father (their mother had died young), and a paternal aunt. Their father had purchased Constitution Island, in the Hudson River opposite West Point, as a summer retreat, but the family was forced to make it their permanent home. The sisters cooked, gardened, chopped wood, and fished.

At her aunt's suggestion, and because of a great need for money, W. wrote *The Wide, Wide World* (1850), which went through many editions in many languages. She and her sister were among the century's most prolific writers, but their earnings were small, partly due to literary piracy.

A sensitive, rather morbid personality distinguished W. from her younger sister socially, but hers was the greater talent. Although poverty and hard work narrowed her world, she managed to travel some, meeting Emerson and other New England literary figures in Boston. She spent almost every winter in New York, where she knew such writers as Alice and Phoebe Cary.

The Wide, Wide World, which had been rejected by several publishers, was a literary phenomenon. Its basic appeal is to girls and women. After her mother dies, Ellen Montgomery must live with other relatives —first an old-maid aunt who runs her own farm and then a worldly Scottish family who claim her for a time. Ellen finds that they try her Christian patience—and they disapprove of her priggish ways. No matter what the issue, Ellen expresses herself by bursting into tears. (Biographers say that W. was apt to cry frequently herself.) However sentimental this novel appears today, W.'s ability to tell a story and to involve the reader in the lives of her characters is superior.

W.'s second novel, *Queechy* (1852), almost as popular as her first, tells how, after the death of her grandfather and the business failure of her uncle, young Fleda Ringgan helps support her family by selling flowers and garden produce. Throughout the novels of both sisers, young women in financial difficulties are commonplace; they are often furnished with a father, uncle,or guardian who cannot function once his money is gone. The autobiographical element is obvious. While the sisters preserved a pious respect for their father (who lived unttil 1875), their books reveal their annoyance with such helpless characters. In *Queechy* even the resourceful heroine feels faint if she must answer the door or eat with the hired girl, but the late novel *Nobody* (1882) shows a family of sisters who do their own work and thrive on it. Presumably, as the years passed, W. became more accustomed to her status in life.

By herself and in collaboration with Anna, she wrote many children's books. Most of them are highly didactic and were popular in the Sunday-school libraries of the time. Although both sisters were evangelical Presbyterians—they disapproved of the theater, but not of *all* novels—W.'s books are centered on accepting and serving Christ, with little interest in doctrinal or controversial themes.

Most of her adult novels are what she called "true stories" (she didn't like the word "novel"). The books usually have a good Christian heroine (or hero) who overcomes poverty and becomes successful. Meals of bread and molasses are to be found in these books, but generous meals are much more common.

In *Diana* (1877), W. attributes her fascination with writing about food to her intimate knowledge of is preparation. "Sympathy and affection and tender ministry are wrought into the very pie crust, and glow in the brown loaves as they come out of the oven; and are specially seen in the shortcake for tea and the favourite dish at dinner and the unexpected dumpling." W. had a gift for describing the material things of life; a reading of her novels will give the modern reader a close look into 19th-c. American kitchen cupboards, desk drawers, and clothes closets.

Interest today in W.'s books is mainly historical. She is one of the best of the "damned mob of scribbling women" of her time, however, and deserves serious consideration from literary scholars.

WORKS: (The following is a list of Susan Bogert Warner's more important works. A complete bibliography is included in *They Wrote for a Living,* compiled by D. H. Sanderson, 1976). *The Wide, Wide World* (1850). *Queechy* (1852). *The Law and the Testimony* (1853). *The Hills of the Shatemuc* (1856). *The Old Helmet* (1863). *Melbourne House* (1864). *Daisy* (1868). *Walks from Eden* (1870). *The House in Town* (1872). *A Story of Small Beginnings* (1872). *Willow Brook* (1874). Say and Do Series (1875). *Bread and Oranges* (1877). *Diana* (1877). *Pine Needles* (1877). *The Broken Wall of Jerusalem and the Rebuilding of Them* (1878). *The Flag of Truce* (1878). *The Kingdom of Judak* (1878). *My Desire* (1879). *The End of the Coil* (1880). *Nobody* (1882). *The Letter of Credit* (1882). *Stephen, M.D.* (1883). *A Red Wallflower* (1884). *Daisy Plains* (1885).

BIBLIOGRAPHY: Sanderson, D. H., *They Wrote for a Living* (1976). Stokes, O. E., *Letters and Memoirs of Susan and Anna Bartlett Warner* (1925). Warner, Anna, *Susan Warner* (1909).
  Other references: *N. Y. History* 40 (April 1959).

BEVERLY SEATON

Mercy Otis Warren

B. 25 Sept. 1728, Barnstable, Massachusetts; d. 19 Oct. 1814, Plymouth, Massachusetts
D. of James and Mary Allyne Otis; m. James Warren, 1754

W. was the third of thirteen children. Her father, a staunch Whig, was a district judge whose life revolved around politics. Although women were customarily denied formal education, her father permitted W., his eldest daughter, to be tutored with her brothers by their paternal uncle, Rev. Jonathan Russell. Russell encouraged her to take lessons in all fields except Greek and Latin, so her elder brother James, an exceptionally brilliant young man, instructed her in these languages. Theirs was an unusually close relationship. He introduced her to Locke's *Essay on Government*, which became the foundation of the political theory they shared. Her writing shows the influence of Raleigh, Pope, Dryden, Milton, Shakespeare, and Molière, but she learned the art of writing from her study of her uncle's sermons.

W.'s husband, like her brother James, was a Harvard graduate. In this cultured and politically astute man she found a husband she loved and respected, who returned her feelings, and they enjoyed a long and happy life together. She bore five sons to him between 1757 and 1766, all of whom survived to adulthood. Warren took much pride in his wife's intelligence and literary talents. He not only brought stimulating guests like John and Samuel Adams regularly into their home but he himself gave her companionship and stability.

During the early years of marriage, W. served her literary apprenticeship, writing verse on every subject considered proper for poetry. She also wrote many letters. Perhaps her favorite correspondent was Abigail Adams, but she exchanged letters with many distinguished people on both sides of the Atlantic.

During the 1770s, W. became active in politics, along with her husband, father, and brother. "Be it known unto Britain even American daughters are politicians and patriots," she wrote. She began writing political satires in the form of plays. None of them has plot or women characters. They are not stage-worthy pieces, but they were not intended to be. They accomplished their task, firing their readers' imaginations and urging them to turn the depicted events into reality and punish the easily recognized villains.

The Adulateur (1772), published anonymously in two installments in the *Massachusetts Spy*, presents "Rapatio, the Bashaw [ruler] of Servia whose principal mission in life is to crush the ardent love of liberty in Servia's freeborn sons," who clearly is the colony's Governor Thomas Hutchinson. The classical names of her characters do not obscure their identities: for example, Brutus is James Otis, Jr., champion of the patriots. The "play" was so well received that the names W. had given the characters were widely and gleefully used in the community.

Her second play, *The Defeat* (1773), published by the *Boston Gazette*, continued Rapatio (Hutchinson) as arch villain. It pictures Rapatio planning to charge the improvements he has made on his house to the public taxes. Together with his self-incriminating letters then being circulated among the patriots, it brought about Hutchinson's disgrace and recall.

The Group (1775), the most popular of W.'s political satires, appeared in pamphlet form only two weeks before the clash of "Minutemen" and British soldiers at Lexington. John Adams himself arranged its printing and, years later, personally verified that W. was its author. Almost pure propaganda, the play has only villains, the Tory leaders who are the group of the play's title. Chief is Brigadier Hate-All, really the American-born Tory Timothy Ruggles, a longtime enemy of the Otis family. Other characters include Hum Humbug, Esq.; Crusty Crowbar, Esq.; Dupe; and Scrblerius Fribble.

After the collapse of the Confederation, W. wrote *Observations on the New Constitution, and on the Federal Conventions* (1788), under the pen name "A Columbian Patriot," opposing the Constitution as it was originally proposed. She was an anti-Federalist who believed, as she said, in "a union of the states on the free principles of the late Confederation." The pen name caused some confusion, and the author's identity was in dispute until 1930.

History of the Rise, Progress, and Termination of the American Revolution, Interspersed with Biographical and Moral Observations (1805) was published in three volumes nearly seventeen years after W. finished it. By that time, other histories of the Revolution had appeared. However, hers is the only contemporary history told from a Republican point of view. Much of its value lies in the fact that more than ten percent of the work is devoted to character analyses of the people she knew. John Adams broke off their long friendship over her analysis of him, but a number of years later a mutual friend brought them together again. Her history did not enjoy the success she had expected or that it deserved; yet it has endured, and her reputation survives principally upon its merits.

W. was given a chance—rare for a woman—to use her talents, and she made the most of them. Although she was much respected in her own time, her reputation has dimmed somewhat, perhaps because so much of her writing was published in pamphlets and newspapers, perhaps because so much of it is topical, and perhaps because so much of it reflects the classical pretensions of the time. Her history of the Revolution, however, is viewed by modern scholars as having enduring value, as being, according to M. Curti, "a realistic history of the struggle for independence."

WORKS: *The Adulateur: A Tragedy* (1772). *The Defeat: A Play* (1773). *The Group: A Farce* (1775). *Observations on the New Constitution, and on the Federal Conventions* (1788). *Poems, Dramatic, and Miscellaneous* (1790). *History of the Rise, Progress, and Termination of the American Revolution, Interspersed with Biographical and Moral Observations* (3 vols., 1805).

BIBLIOGRAPHY: Anthony, K., *First Lady of the Revolution: The Life of Mercy Otis Warren* (1958). Brown, A., *Mercy Warren* (1896). Fritz, J., *Cast for a Revolution: Some Friends and Enemies 1728–1814* (1972). Smith, W., *History as Argument: Three Patriot Historians of the American Revolution* (1966).

Other references: *New England Magazine* (April 1903). *PMHS* 64 (March 1931). *WMQ* (July 1953).

BILLIE W. ETHERIDGE

Jean Webster

B. *24 July 1876, Fredonia, New York; d. 11 June 1916, New York City*
Given name: Alice Jane Chandler Webster
D. *of Charles Luther and Annie Moffett Webster; m. Glenn Ford McKinney,*
1915

W. was a grandniece of Mark Twain; her father was Twain's partner in has ill-fated publishing ventures. She attended the Lady Jane Grey School in Binghamton, New York, and was graduated from Vassar College in 1901. She was a frequent contributor to college publications and literary editor of the yearbook. W.'s friend and roomate at Vassar, Adelaide Crapsey, was probably the inspiration for Patty in her books *When Patty Went to College* (1903) and *Just Patty* (1911). W. became a freelance writer, lived in Greenwich Village, and traveled extensively, touring the world in 1906–07. After her marriage in 1915 to a lawyer, she and her husband lived in New York City and the Berkshires. She died a day after the birth of her only child, a daughter.

When Patty Went to College collects sketches W. began writing while still at Vassar. It depicts the escapades of Patty Wyatt and Priscilla Pond, seniors in a turn-of-the-century women's college where the students surreptitiously brew afternoon tea and evening cocoa on alcohol stoves in their rooms, receive gentleman callers in the parlor after a maid has carried up cards, dine in evening dress, evade obligatory chapel, and study Greek and ethics. A sequel, *Just Patty*, concerns the innocent adventures of Patty and Priscilla as seniors at a high-church boarding school.

The epistolary novel *Daddy-Long-Legs* (1912) presents a modern Cinderella, Jerusha Abbot ("Judy"), who leaves her life-long home in a depressing orphanage to attend a women's college. She must report her progress to her nameless benefactor, whom she christens "Daddy-longlegs" and whom she marries four years later. W.'s dramatization became highly successful on Broadway, starring Ruth Chatterton, and has since appeared in several film versions, including a silent version with Mary Pickford. A 1915 reviewer criticized the drama on the ground that "the chief object of the play" was to provide "sentimentalism sentimentally interpreted, turnip smothered in sugar offered as an apple of life." The novel, however, largely avoids sentimentalism, and the brisk irreverence and piquancy of its humor have made it a perennial favorite with both adults and children.

Dear Enemy (1914), an epistolary sequel to *Daddy-Long-Legs*, follows Judy's college friend Sallie McBride as she arrives to reform the old-fashioned orphanage from which Judy had escaped and stays to fall in love with its dour Scotch doctor. Once again, a potentially sentimental story is saved from stickiness by the practical point of view and the lively prose of its narrator.

Both *Daddy-Long-Legs* and *Dear Enemy* have remained constantly in print for almost seventy years. Their strong stories and charming characters, together with W.'s real interest in reforms in the care of dependent children, will secure them an audience for many years to come.

WORKS: *When Patty Went to College* (1903). *The Wheat Princess* (1905). *Jerry, Junior* (1907). *The Four Pools Mystery* (1908). *Much Ado about Peter* (1909). *Just Patty* (1911). *Daddy-Long-Legs* (1912; dramatization by Webster, 1914). *Asa* (1914). *Dear Enemy* (1914).

The papers of Jean Webster are collected in the Lockwood Library of Vassar College. An authorized biography is being written by Alan Simpson and Mary McQueen Simpson.

BIBLIOGRAPHY: For articles in reference works, see: *Junior Book of Authors*, Eds. S. J. Kunitz and H. Haycraft (1951). *NAW* (article by R. Salisbury, 1971). *20thCA*.

Other references: *NewR* (13 March 1915). *NYT* (9 Nov. 1914; 13 Dec. 1914; 12 June 1916). *Vassar Quarterly* (Nov. 1916).

SUSAN SUTTON SMITH

Carolyn Wells

B. *18 June 1869, Rahway, New Jersey; d. 26 March 1942, New York City*
Wrote under: Carolyn Wells, Rowland Wright
D. of William E. and Anna Wells; m. Hadwin Houghton, 1918

A precocious child, W. hated formal schooling and refused to attend college. Scarlet fever, suffered at the age of six, caused her to become hard of hearing. Reared in New Jersey, she made her home in New York City after her marriage. She loved puzzles, bridge, chess, charades, and detective stories (her discovery of a mystery by Anna Katharine Green was pivotal, inspiring her both to read voraciously and to write voluminously in that genre). Her literary career began almost by accident, with the contribution of jingles to humorous periodicals. She considered 1902 an important date in her career: by then she had written eight books and had begun composing juveniles; after that date she consistently published at least three or four books annually. From 1909 on she wrote mysteries, and she claimed in an autobiographical work (*The Rest of My Life*, 1937) to have written 170 books, including seventy detective stories—"so far." Her other main literary activity was as an anthologist, but she was also an important collector and bibliographer of the works of Walt Whitman. Her parody of Sinclair Lewis' *Main Street* (*Ptomaine Street*, 1921), in which Carol Kennicott becomes Warble Petticoat, is funny and full of witty puns. Sometimes it misses its mark because both locale and social class are changed, but it wickedly refashions a number of episodes from the original.

W.'s juveniles are intended for young girls; different series are aimed at different age groups. Marjorie is in her early teens, for example, and is presented as a child, sometimes mischievous though generally a model little girl (in *Marjorie's Vacation*, 1907, and five other novels through 1912). Patty, on the other hand, is in her later teens, and the final books in her series lead to her marriage (in *Patty Fairfield*, 1901, and sixteen other novels through 1919). In the middle are "two little women", who are fifteen when their series begins (see *Two Little Women*, 1915, and two other novels through 1917). All these novels are seriously dated by their intense concern for the social conventions of the early 20th c. For example, Patty's main problems and decisions grow from situations in which she has (either apparently or actually) been led to behave in an unconventional manner (such as going out without a chaperone).

Although also clearly limited by its time and place, W.'s detective fiction holds up somewhat better. She claimed the title of "Dean of American Mystery Writers" and was widely considered an authority. *The Technique of the Mystery Story* (1913; rev. ed. 1929), heavily larded with quotations of both primary and secondary materials, is a thorough survey of the field, written for aspiring authors. Unfortunately, W.'s own style is undistinguished; dialogue and dialect are often clumsily handled. Characterization is flat, characters often being hard to distinguish from each other. Her women are often irritatingly coy, shallowly coquettish ingenues—whom the reader is clearly expected to find charming—and she made it a rule that a woman could never be the murderer (though women were sometimes the victims in her stories). Although male figures are more varied, heroes and detectives are consistently well educated and wealthy. Plotting, however, is inventive, and W. made interesting use of such conventional types as the "locked room" mystery.

W. created a number of detectives, the best known and most frequently used (in sixty-one novels) being Fleming Stone, a professional detective who is a cultivated gentleman, moving easily in the elevated social circles in which W.'s mysteries occur. He was her first creation (*The Clue*, 1909), and she continued to use him until the end of her career (*Who Killed Caldwell?*, 1942). Similar to Stone in characterization and methods of detection is Kenneth Carlisle, but he is distinguished by being a former screen star and matinee idol (in *Sleeping Dogs*, 1929, and two other novels). More interesting is the team of Pennington ("Penny") Wise and Zizi (in *The Man Who Fell Through the Earth*, 1919, and five other novels). His approach to detection is rational while hers is intuitive; both are fallible, although Zizi is more often right. She is presented as a mysterious young sprite of a girl who seems to have no background or past. W.'s other detectives are Lorimer Lane (in *More Lives Than One*, 1923, and another novel) and Alan Ford (in *Faulkner's Folly*, 1917, and two other novels). W.'s sleuths often work wonders of detection, but they occasionally err and thus illustrate her distaste, often expressed, for the "omniscient detective."

Once well known and highly respected, W.'s works now languish unread. She was too prolific, wrote too easily and rapidly, reflected her age too uncritically, and restricted herself too narrowly to popular genres and formulas. Her importance thus is largely historical, and is most clearly found in her practice of the detective novel.

SELECTED WORKS: At the Sign of the Sphinx (1896). *The Jingle Book* (1899). *Patty Fairfield* (1901). *A Nonsense Anthology* (edited by Wells, 1902). *A Parody Anthology* (editied by Wells, 1904). *The Rubaiyat of a Motor Car* (1906). *A Whimsey Anthology* (edited by Wells, 1906). *Fluffy Ruffles* (1907). *Marjorie's Vacation* (1907). *The Clue* (1909). *A Chain of Evidence* (1912). *The Techniques of the Mystery Story* (1913; rev. ed., 1929). *Two Little Women* (1915). *Faulkner's Folly* (1917). *Vicky Van* (1918). *The Man Who Fell through the Earth* (1919). *The Book of Humorous Verse* (edited by Wells, 1920). *Ptomaine Street: The Tale of Warble Petticoat* (1921). *More Lives than One* (1923). *The Fleming Stone Omnibus* (1932). *The Rest of My Life* (1937). *Murder Will In* (1942). *Who Killed Caldwell?* (1942).

BIBLIOGRAPHY: For articles in reference works, see: *Encyclopedia of Mystery and Detection*, Eds. C. Steinbrunner and O. Penzler (1976). *NCAB*, 13.
Other references: *NYT* (27 March 1942). *NYTBR* (4 Dec. 1937).

MARY JEAN DeMARR

Emmeline Blanche Woodward Wells

B. *29 Feb. 1828, Petersham, Massachusetts; d. 25 April 1921, Salt Lake City, Utah*
Wrote under: *Amethyst, "Aunt Em," Blanche Beechwood, E.B.W., Emmeline B. Wells*
D. *of David and Deiadama Hare Woodward; m. James Harvey Harris, 1843; m. Newell K. Whitney, 1845; m. Daniel H. Wells, 1852*

W. converted to Mormonism when she was fourteen, married James Harris at fifteen, and moved the following year to Nauvoo, Illinois, then the Mormon headquarters. Deserted by Harris, W. married Whitney and joined the exodus of Mormons to Salt Lake City. After Whitney's death in 1850 she married Wells. Five daughters were born of W.'s last two marriages.

An ardent suffragist and women's rights advocate, W. was a member of numerous national and state woman-suffrage and other (especially literary) organizations. As president of the Utah Woman's Suffrage Association, she successfully lobbied for the inclusion of woman suffrage in Utah's constitution in 1895. In 1910, at age eighty-two, W. was appointed general president of the Mormon woman's Relief Society, serving until three weeks before her death in 1921. The *Woman's Exponent*, a Mormon woman's journal that W. edited from 1877 to 1914, gave her an influential voice in women's affairs. She used its editorial page to promote equal rights for women, and also to defend the Mormon practice of plural marriage.

W.'s only collection of poetry, *Musings and Memories*, (1896), is aptly named. The poems are reflective and personal, most of them a sentimental backward look at a past both pleasant and painful. "A Glance Backward" illustrates the portentous mood pervading much of her retrospective verse. The festive celebration in honor of two young lovers who "plighted their troth" is underscored by ominous intimations. Shadows of a fire creep "like spectres," trees stand "phantom-like," and laughter echoes "in a hollow sound." The lovers are doomed, yet choose to shun the "potent sway of dread" and exchange their vows in "fond expectancy." W. subtly sustains the fateful mood, which she delicately balances on a thin narrative thread that gives the piece its unity.

As a poet, W. fits comfortably under Hawthorne's rubric of "scribbling women." While much of her poetry has definite merit, it occasionally demonstrates the stilted manner and excessive sentiment typical of the period. Poetry, she said, was "a history of the heart." She wrote for a receptive local audience appreciative of her style; a second edition of her poems was published in 1915. W. did not use poetry as a medium for polemics, reserving her feminist arguments for the editorial page. She left a collection of diaries spanning nearly half a century. A prominent figure in the Mormon female hierarchy, she wrote perceptively and intelligently, if not always disinterestedly, of events in Mormon history, especially during the critical period of 1876 to 1896. She is often frustratingly elusive in her references to personal affairs but remarkably informative in her observations of the effect on women of a changing Mormon society.

It is as a journalist that W. is most noted. The majority of her editorials for the *Woman's Exponent* responded to the "woman question" of her century, her rhetoric often echoing the polemics of other feminists. In them she exercised both logic and analysis, sometimes interlacing her premises with poetic imagery. Other editorials dealt with local issues, particularly those centering on the religious and political tensions polarizing Utah and the rest of the nation. Writing initially as a contributor to the *Exponent* under the name of Blanche Beechwood, W. dropped the pseudonym soon after becoming editor. She created another literary identity, however, "Aunt Em," who wrote eighty-seven articles and stories incorporating traditional Victorian values and sentiments. W., the editor, and "Aunt Em," the contributor, symbolize the different views of woman battling for women's allegiance and formed the double dimension of W.'s literary personality.

W. was a woman of her time, her literary products felicitously harmonizing with its concerns and values. While her poetry was addressed to another audience, her editorials are relevant to the contemporary woman's movement. One of the most influential of 19th-c. Mormon women, W. made a literary impact both substantial and effective.

WORKS: *Memorial of the Mormon Women of Utah to the President and Congress of the United States, April 6, 1886* (1886). *Charities and Philanthropies: Women's Work in Utah* (1893). *Songs and Flowers of the Wasatch* (edited by Wells, 1893). *Musing and Memories* (1896).

BIBLIOGRAPHY: Anderson, R., "Emmeline B. Wells: Her Life and Thought" (M.A. thesis, Utah State Univ., 1975). Burgess-Olson, V., *Sister*

Saints (1978). Crocheron, A. J., *Representative Women of Deseret* (1884). Gates, S. Y., *History of the Young Ladies Mutual Improvement Association, 1869–1910* (1911). Madsen, C. C., " 'Remember the Women of Zion': A Study of the Editorial Content of the *Woman's Exponent,* a Mormon Woman's Journal" (M.A. thesis, Univ. of Utah, 1977). Whitney, O.F., *History of Utah,* vol. 4 (1904).

For articles in reference works, see: *Latter-day Saint Biographical Encyclopedia.* Ed. A. Jenson (1914). *NAW* (article by M. DePillis).

Other references: *Improvement Era* (June 1921). *NYT* (27 April 1921). *Relief Society Magazine* (Feb. 1915; Feb. 1916). *Sunset* (May 1916). *Utah Historical Quarterly* (Fall 1974). *Young Woman's Journal* (April 1908).

CAROL CORNWALL MADSEN

Eudora Welty

B. *13 April 1909, Jackson, Mississippi*
D. *of Mary Chestina Andrews and Christian Webb Welty*

Although she is thoroughly southern, W.'s family came from Ohio (her father's home) and West Virginia (her mother's home, which figures prominently in *The Optimist's Daughter*). W.'s childhood in Jackson was in a household of readers and in a town not yet industrialized, where schools and parks and grocery stores were all within walking distance of her home. W. attended Mississippi State College for Women from 1925 to 1927, received her B.A. in 1929 from the University of Wisconsin, and spent 1930 to 1931 at Columbia University, studying advertising. With jobs scarce in Depression days, and with her father's death in 1931, W. returned to Jackson where she has continued to live. Various jobs with local newspapers, Jackson radio station WJDX, and the Works Progress Authority (WPA) occupied her in the mid 1930s; but all the while she was writing, and her first story, "Death of a Traveling Salesman," appeared in *Manuscript* (May–June 1936).

W. possesses the coveted honors America awards its writers: the National Medal for Literature, the American Academy of Arts and Letters Howells Medal, the National Institute of Arts and Letters Gold Medal for the Novel, the Presidential Medal of Freedom, and numerous honorary degrees.

Predictably, it was not easy to convince an editor to publish a collection of W.'s short stories before a novel appeared, but Doubleday, Doran did bring out *A Curtain of Green, and Other Stories* in 1941. The volume, distinguished in having an introduction by Katherine Anne Porter, brought W. critical acclaim, and readers still find that it contains many favorite stories—"Petrified Man," "Why I Live at the P.O.," "Keela, the Outcast Indian Maiden." These stories establish W.'s voice in portraying lower-middle-class characters with convincing dialogue, in her lyrical descriptive power, and in her sense of place.

Reviewers generally were puzzled by *The Wide Net, and Other Stories* (1943), finding the stories (except "Livvie") radically different and less accessible than those in the first collection. "First Love," "A Still Moment," and "The Wide Net" show W.'s ability to use historical background, explore the mystery of human relationships, and incorporate levels of myth.

W.'s third collection, *The Golden Apples* (1949), presents seven interrelated stories based on three generations of families in Morgana, Mississippi, whose lives intertwine publicly and privately. It is a work that draws heavily on myth to give added dimension to the lives and deeds of characters whose daily activities are of great interest. The MacLain, Morrison, Stark, Rainey, and Carmichael families undergo the many experiences of life and the reader is drawn into the generations of this fictional world.

The Collected Stories of Eudora Welty (1980), containing work published from 1936 to 1966, confirms that W. is among the great practitioners of the short story. It includes stories from the four earlier collections and two previously uncollected stories, excluding only five published stories. By the inclusion of *The Golden Apples*, her own favorite, W. denies that this volume should be classified as a novel, as many critics have argued. Anne Tyler has noted that the early stories are left unrevised, although W. has privately made changes by hand on her own printed copies. Recently, W. has commented on her first published story, "Death of a Traveling Salesman." She sees some weaknesses in it, but declares her respect for it because it still presents a challenge to writer and reader.

W.'s first novel, *The Robber Bridegroom* (1942), is a short work that integrates stories of the Old Natchez Trace and remnants of Grimms' fairy tales and American frontier humor to relate the story of Clement Musgrove, his fair daughter Rosamond, and Jamie Lockhart, her "robber bridegroom." As W. has pointed out, this work is not a *historical* historical novel and many critics see it as "an examination of the theme of disenchantment in the pursuit of a pastoral, and fundamentally American,

Eden." *Delta Wedding* (1946), W.'s first full-length novel, had its origin in a short story, "The Delta Cousins." The novel is set in 1923, a year chosen for its relative calm so that domestic concerns in the Fairchild household might take precedence over outside involvements in a narrative that presents a southern demiparadise on the verge of social change. W.'s comic masterpiece, *The Ponder Heart* (1954), has enjoyed success as a short novel and as a Broadway play (adapted by Joseph Fields and Jerome Chodorov) in which the antics of Uncle Daniel and Bonnie Dee Peacock, Miss Teacake Magee, Mr. Truex Bodkin, the Peacock clan, and the populace of Clay, Mississippi, combine with the firm narrative voice of Edna Earle Ponder to form a work of boundless humor.

Two more novels appeared much later. After a virtual silence of fifteen years, W. published *Losing Battles* in 1970. A work of brilliant parts, *Losing Battles* is a long novel and has not pleased all readers; its diffusion and loose structure, however, are for many compensated by its comic richness —its eccentric characters, amusing situations, and details of places, names, and objects. Telescoped into a day and a half, the novel presents the community of Banner, Mississippi, during the Depression, with kin and neighboring connections joined by choice or chance at the Beecham family reunion. It is an expression of W.'s persistent emphasis on the mystery surrounding human relationships and on the redeeming power of love.

For *The Optimist's Daughter* (1972) W. won the Pulitzer Prize, an award many thought she should have received already. This novel presents both lower-middle-class characters and the upper-middle-class citizens of Mount Salus, Mississippi. The second marriage of Judge Clinton McKelva to Wanda Fay Chisom evokes consternation in the town gossips, forces the Judge's daughter Laurel McKelva Hand to reassess her life, and in the end leaves her able to give up the ties of the past and to live in the present.

The spirit of celebration, of lived life, is of singular importance in much of W.'s fiction. While there are always serious matters at the heart of her fiction, it is also true that the comic spirit is a significant force, not merely entertaining but also conveying thoughtful commentary. Standard comic devices are found: disingenuous characters (Leota in "Petrified Man"), eccentric characters (Aunt Cleo in *Losing Battles*), and homely figures of speech. In "Why I Live at the P.O.," Sister valiantly cooks away, trying "to stretch two chickens over five people and a completely unexpected child into the bargain without one moment's notice." Comedy of situation, comic one-liners, and ironic juxtapositions—used by W. in a variety of stories—confirm the presence of the comic spirit at the base of W.'s fiction. She writes, in the essay "The Radiance of Jane Austen," that comedy "is social and positive, and exacting. Its methods, its boundaries, its *point*, all belong to the familiar." For W., the comic spirit is true and natural.

The recent publication of *The Collected Stories* has given critics the opportunity to reassess three decades of W.'s work. Reviewers were particularly impressed with the range of W.'s work. Indeed, Walter Clemons found her "an experimental writer with access to the demonic. . . . She is bigger and stranger than we have supposed." If some of W.'s prose has occasionally been described as deformed, if she has sometimes been charged with presenting an imprecise landscape and using vague language, most of her fiction challenges our reading power, speaks to our hearts, and convinces us that her world of fiction embodies the best and truest of human experience.

WORKS: *A Curtain of Green, and Other Stories* (1941). *The Robber Bridegroom* (1942). *The Wide Net, and Other Stories* (1943). *Delta Wedding* (1946). *The Golden Apples* (1949). *The Ponder Heart* (1954). *The Bride of Innisfallen* (1955). *The Shoe Bird* (1964). *Losing Battles* (1970). *One Time, One Place: Mississippi in the Depression. A Snapshot Album* (1971). *The Optimist's Daughter* (1972). *The Eye of the Story* (1978). *The Collected Stories of Eudora Welty* (1980).

The manuscripts and papers of Eudora Welty are in the Department of Archives and History, Jackson, Mississippi, and at the University of Texas at Austin.

BIBLIOGRAPHY: Appel, A., Jr., *Eudora Welty* (1965). Bryant, J. A., Jr., *Eudora Welty* (1968). Desmond, J. F., ed., *A Still Moment: Essays on the Art of Eudora Welty* (1978). Dollarhide, L., and A. Abadie, eds., *Eudora Welty: A Form of Thanks* (1979). Howard, Z., *The Rhetoric of Eudora Welty's Short Stories* (1973). Isaacs, N., *Eudora Welty* (1968). Kreyling, M., *The Achievement of Eudora Welty* (1980). Manz-Kunz, M., *Eudora Welty: Aspects of Reality in Her Short Fiction* (1971). Prenshaw, P., ed., *Eudora Welty: Critical Essays* (1979). Vande Kieft, R., *Eudora Welty* (1962).

Other references: *Delta Review* (Nov. 1977). *Eudora Welty Newsletter* (Toledo, Ohio). *Mississippi Quarterly* 26 (1973). *Shenandoah* 20 (1969).

ELIZABETH EVANS

Jessamyn West

B. *18 July 1902, near Butlerville, Indiana*
D. *of Eldo Roy and Grace Anna Milhous West; m. Harry Maxwell McPherson,*
1923

The eldest of four children, W. was reared in Yorba Linda, California. She began writing—novels, short stories, essays, autobiography, articles, reviews—after a severe case of tuberculosis halted her formal education while she was in graduate school. W. is married, and she has adopted an Irish girl.

The female maturation process is a frequent pattern in W.'s fiction, which treats girls' social, emotional, and familial joys and difficulties even-handedly and well. A central problem for the young protagonists is often the mother-daughter relationship: mothers, uneasy with their own rigidly controlled sensuality, teach their daughters to fear sexuality; furthermore, they often insist that the elder daughters help to curb sexual impulses in their younger sisters.

In *The Witch Diggers* (1951) and *South of the Angels* (1960), the maturation stories are embedded in a cluster of subplots. Here, the healthy acceptance of sexuality is the symbol of genuine maturity and the ability to love. The locales, eras, and atmospheres of both books are beautifully wrought. Despite some problems with structure, these novels succeed through the power of the maturation device, and the portraits of the sisters Cate and Em Conboy in the first are splendid.

Leafy Rivers (1967) and *The Massacre at Fall Creek* (1975), both set on the Indiana frontier, provide variations of the female maturation pattern. In W.'s most traditional maturation novel, Leafy comes to terms with her flawed marriage by undergoing the usual *Bildungsroman* journey, presented in flashbacks. The story of the first whites to be executed for murdering Indians is the subject of *The Massacre at Fall Creek*, told largely through the perceptions of Hannah Cape, who learns to accept her own limitations as well as those of her lover. Clearly, this novel compares Hannah's maturation with the coming of age of the frontier; the device is compelling and works well. These books present large casts of characters portrayed with W.'s usual sound insight.

One of W.'s most successful forms is the collection of a series of inter-related short stories into books having the impact of novels. *Cress Dela-hanty* (1953), set in the California of W.'s youth, is the sunniest of the female maturation pieces, the portrait of a gifted girl who learns to value herself and her abilities. *The Friendly Persuasion* (1945) and *Except for Me and Thee* (1969) draw upon the Quaker family background and Indi-ana locale of W.'s mother's memories, which provided W. with "the look of the land, the temper of the people, the manner of speech." Probably the best known of her books, these "Quaker stories," depicting the deep-ening relationship and developing family of Jess and Eliza Birdwell, avoid sentimentality through splendid use of humor. *The Friendly Persuasion* was made into a successful movie in 1956; *To See the Dream* (1957) is W.'s account of her work on the film.

Central to all W.'s work is her basic theme: genuine love is acceptance; the lover may not approve of all the traits and habits of the loved one, but to demand alteration as the price of love is unfair. This theme is stated most overtly in the autobiographical *The Woman Said Yes* (1976), which celebrates Grace West's influence upon her daughters. The emphasis is on Grace's life-enhancing qualities, and W. attributes both her own recovery from tuberculosis and her sister Carmen's capacity to defeat cancer (by choosing suicide) to strength learned from their mother.

A Matter of Time (1966), which is W.'s best novel, also deals with a mother's influence and love, but here redemptive understanding occurs late. As Tassie nurses Blix, her younger sister, through terminal illness, the middle-aged women discuss their mother's use of Tassie to control Blix's behavior. This exploitation has severely damaged the women and their re-lationship, but they now validate their sisterly love by acceptance of themselves and one another. The maturation story appears in flashbacks, its strength completely overshadowing any moral question arising from the fact that Tassie helps Blix commit suicide. This decision is presented as a final affirmation of Blix's humanity and her will.

In *The Life I Really Lived* (1979), Orpha Chase, successful novelist, at-tempts to put her experiences into perspective. She recounts the central events of her Kentucky girlhood and of her later life in California and Hawaii. Each step of the real journey as well as the maturation journey is illuminated by Orpha's analysis of the people—parents, husbands, daugh-ter, lover, friends—who influenced and formed her. As in *A Matter of Time*, the impact of a sibling is especially important. Serious and some-times grim, *The Life I Really Lived* is less successful than *A Matter of Time* and sometimes recalls *The Massacre at Fall Creek*, for it reflects W.'s clear grasp of the danger, difficulty, and complexity as well as the joys and triumphs of the life of her protagonist, who stands for the women whose lives bridged the gap between the frontier and "civilization."

Considered an able, serious craftsperson, W. is noted for her detailed, accurate settings and the careful development of motivation which makes fine characterization a dominant quality in her sound work.

WORKS: *The Friendly Persuasion* (1945; film version, 1956). *A Mirror for the Sky* (1948). *The Witch Diggers* (1951). *The Reading Public* (1952). *Cress Delahanty* (1953). *Love, Death, and the Ladies' Drill Team* (1955). *To See the Dream* (1957). *Love Is Not What You Think* (1959). *South of the Angels* (1960). *The Quaker Reader* (1962). *A Matter of Time* (1966). *The Chilekings* (1967). *Leafy Rivers* (1967). *Except For Me and Thee* (1969). *Crimson Ramblers of the World, Farewell* (1970). *Hide and Seek* (1973). *The Secret Look* (1974). *The Massacre at Fall Creek* (1975). *Violence* (pamphlet, 1976). *The Woman Said Yes* (1976). *The Life I Really Lived* (1979). *Double Discovery: A Journey* (1980).

BIBLIOGRAPHY: Shivers, A. S., *Jessamyn West* (1972).

Other references: *EJ* (Sept. 1957). *Expl* (Dec. 1964). *Indiana Magazine of History* (Dec. 1971). *Nation* (30 March 1957). *NYTBR* (14 Jan. 1951). *SatR* (24 Oct. 1970). *Writers Digest* (May 1967; Jan. 1976).

JANE S. BAKERMAN

Mae West

B. 17 Aug. 1893, Brooklyn, New York; d. 22 Nov. 1980, Los Angeles, California
D. of John and Mathilda Doegler West

W.'s description of her childhood (in the early chapters of her autobiography, *Goodness Had Nothing to Do with It*, 1959) illustrates the qualities that were to become her caricature: She learned early that "two and two are four, and five will get you ten if you know how to work it." She began her performing career at age seven. When, as a young actress and singer, she was criticized for "wriggling" on stage during performances, she realized that it was the "force of an extraordinary sex-personality that made quite harmless lines and mannerisms seem suggestive." Her one marriage was annulled; she had no children.

W. was producer, author, and star of *SEX* (1927). At first, the title scared away both booking agents and theatergoers. Ultimately, however, the play was a success, firmly casting the stylistic idiom in which W., actress, author, and woman, would be known: the tough, street-smart, unashamedly sexual "dame"—no man's fool—whose unrelenting self-promotion is exceeded only by her vanity.

She believed that *The Drag* (1928), in which she did not appear, was a serious approach to a modern social problem, but her sensitivity to the issue of homosexuality is relative to her time. She writes that the homosexual's "abnormal tendencies (have) brought disaster to his family, friends, and himself"; and her message is that "an understanding of the problems of all homosexuals by society could avert such social tragedies."

SEX and *The Drag* ran simultaneously—*SEX* in New York City (for forty-one weeks, before, thanks to efforts by the Society for the Suppression of Vice, W. was arrested and jailed for a short time) and *The Drag* in Paterson, New Jersey. The district attorney in New York had *The Drag* closed and the entire cast arrested after only two performances.

Diamond Lil (1932) was written specifically to attract the female audience her earlier plays had failed to draw. Later filmed (as *She Done Him Wrong*, 1933) and even turned into a novel (1932), it features perhaps the most famous W. character in a "grand Bowery folk play." One critic wrote an appropriately picturesque summation: "It's worth swimming to Brooklyn to see her descend those dance hall stairs, to be present while she lolls in a golden bed reading the *Police Gazette*, murders her girlfriend, wrecks the Salvation Army, and sings as much of 'Frankie and Johnny' as the mean old law allows."

The novel follows the footsteps and idiom of Diamond Lil. The narrative is liberally dosed with "kinda," "an'," and their counterparts in diction. Women are "skirts," policemen are "dicks," and they are all vividly drawn types. It is lively and reasonably well written, given the genre.

In *The Constant Sinner* (originally titled *Babe Gordon*, 1930), a novel, the siren Babe "starts low and ends up high"—reversing everything mothers tell their daughters about the fate of bad girls. Babe is celebrated by the author, in part, for knowing her own mind and keeping the control of her body up to no one but herself. Again, W. deals with subjects (such as interracial sex) socially unmentionable in the U.S. of the 1930s; yet she does it all within the confines of her public's expectations of the W. caricature.

Pleasure Man (1975), W.'s novelization of *The Drag*, is about a bisexual Broadway headliner, Rodney Terrill, "whose wild sex-affairs with women," W. declares, "led to unexpected but well-deserved difficulties."

Again, street talk prevails, but in the novel the prose is often laced with attempts at more eloquent diction—mixed usage with mixed results.

Beginning in 1932, W. appeared in many films. She wrote (or cowrote —as with her plays and novels, her collaborative debts are often unclear) at least six of these. Films such as *She Done Him Wrong, I'm No Angel* (1933), and *My Little Chickadee* (1939)—the last of which was written with her costar, W. C. Fields—are considered comedy classics.

Her novel, stage, and film personae are one and the same, often a mirror of W. herself: the woman who will not conform, in her words, to the "old-fashioned limits" men have "set on a woman's freedom of action." Unfortunately, W.'s sex-personality became legitmate for the American public only as she became more and more a caricature of herself. Her public self was laundered into a distant cousin, twice-removed, from W. the woman, thereby making her frank yet refreshing sexuality laughable and comic, but legitimate.

An extension of American pulp literature, W.'s fiction receives little attention. She is well known, however, as the queen of the reverse-sexist one-liners: Hatcheck Girl: "Goodness, what lovely diamonds!" W.: "Goodness had nothing to do with it, dearie." Her contributions to American culture are immeasurable, yet—perhaps because her outrageous persona commands so much attention—her written work is virtually unrecognized. She was not only the performer but the author of plays and films in which she appeared, and she deserves to be acknowledged as a creative and successful comic playwright.

WORKS: *Babe Gordon* (1930, reissued as *The Constant Sinner,* 1931). *She Done Him Wrong* (alternate title, *Diamond Lil,* 1932). *Goodness Had Nothing to Do with It* (1959). *The Wit and Wisdom of Mae West* (Ed. J. Weintraub, 1967). *Pleasure Man* (1975).

DEBORAH H. HOLDSTEIN

Edith Newbold Jones Wharton

B. 24 Jan. 1862, New York City; d. 11 Aug. 1937, St. Brice-sous-Forêt, France
Wrote under: Edith Jones, Edith Wharton
D. of George and Lucretia Rhinelander Jones; m. Edward Wharton, 1885

W. was born into the very wealthy and extremely traditional society of "old New York." She had her debut in 1879 and seemed to be well on her way to realizing her ambition—to be, like her mother, the best-dressed woman in New York. Her marriage to a socially prominent Bostonian, however, was not a success; they both suffered nervous breakdowns. After her husband's prolonged bouts with mental illness and his numerous and public infidelities, the Whartons were divorced in 1913.

By this time, partly as a cure for her own illness, she had seriously turned her energies toward writing. She had already established her permanent residence in France; had had an affair that continued intermittently from 1907 to 1910 and was to have a profound effect on her artistic life; had cemented her close friendship with Henry James; and had come to depend on the international lawyer Walter Berry as her most dependable literary advisor and closest personal friend.

During WWI, she organized such an extensive refugee program, helping literally thousands of people, that in 1916 the French government awarded her the Legion of Honor. W. returned to the U.S. only once, for a few days in 1923 to receive an honorary doctorate from Yale. Her last years were spent in a continuous literary and social activity at Pavillon Colombe, her large 18th-c. home near Paris.

W. began writing as early as 1873. She published poetry, short stories, a book on interior decoration, and a novel. All of these works were critically acclaimed, but W. was not recognized as an important writer until the appearance of The House of Mirth in 1905.

The House of Mirth (the title comes from Ecclesiastes) is set in New York's aristocratic society of the first years of the 20th c. It is an outstanding novel of manners focusing on the excruciating social fall and personal rise of its complex, appealing, and somewhat pathetic heroine, Lily Bart. Lily, orphaned as a young woman and now living with her wealthy aunt, has been raised by her mother to abhor the dingy and sordid in life, and is determined to find a husband to keep her in luxury. She is attracted to Lawrence Selden, but he lacks the money she desires. Yet neither is she willing to marry merely for money; "what she craved, and really felt herself entitled to, was a situation in which the noblest attitude should also be the easiest." In the fall of both heroine and hero, we see W.'s attacks on the moral failures of "old New York" and the *nouveaux riches* invading it, and on any society which trains its women to be decorative objects, subject to breakage.

W. followed her 1905 triumph with three years of tremendous productivity, but little artistic success. She published a novella, a full-length novel, a travel book, and two volumes of short stories. Although a few stories in *Tales of Men and Ghosts* (1910) show her brilliance, she did not regain her artistic strength until 1911, with her novella *Ethan Frome*.

In this book, W. left the familiar territory of Fifth Avenue and Europe and went north to the harsh environment and psychological realities of impoverished rural Massachusetts. The narrator is told the story of the young Ethan Frome, twenty-five years earlier. Out of loneliness he marries a sickly wife, Zeena. Her young cousin, Mattie Silver, is hired to help with the chores, and as Mattie and Ethan fall in love, Zeena protests by firing Mattie. During Ethan's trip with Mattie to the train that will take her away, they plan a dual suicide run on a sled, only to have the suicide misfire, sparing them both for a lifetime of crippled endurance. When the narrator encounters Ethan at fifty-two, he is still maimed and prematurely aged by hardship. Zeena is caring for him and the once lovely, now ugly, querulous, and paralyzed Mattie. This tale of unremitting isolation, loneliness, intellectual starvation, and mental despair is among W.'s very best.

W. followed this bleak story with her most Jamesian, and some say her most autobiographical novel, *The Reef* (1912). This tale of the courtship of Mrs. Leath and her old admirer George Darrow and of the subsequent trials caused by Darrow's previous brief affair with a governess is a problem to readers and critics alike. The James circle loved it. More recently, however, Louis Auchincloss has written: "it is a quiet, controlled, beautiful novel, but its theme has always struck me as faintly ridiculous."

In her text on aesthetics, *The Writing of Fiction* (1925), W. acknowledges her debt to James. *The Reef* is proof positive of direct literary influence, but W. did better when she avoided James's subtle, speculative, indirect style. The narrative line in her best works—*The House of Mirth, Ethan Frome, The Custom of the Country* (1913), and *The Age of Innocence* (1920)—is more direct than his, her sense of life more despondent.

"I want to get a general view of the whole problem of American marriages," says Mrs. Fairford in W.'s next novel, *The Custom of the Country*. She is promptly told that the main problem is "that the average American looks down on his wife . . . "; it is the "custom of the country" for the American man to keep his wife totally ignorant of "the real business of life." In this story of Undine Spragg, W. returns to New York of the turn of the century, and caustically satirizes its burgeoning aristocracy of wealth and its values, especially those pertaining to marriage. Armed with beauty, money, and confidence, Undine leaves the security of Apex City (W. displays her prejudice against the Midwest) and assails New York, directing her energies at the only market open to women, the marriage mart. Undine's rise in society is as rapid as Lily Bart's fall, for Undine is not troubled by morality.

The Age of Innocence is W.'s retrospective self-confrontation with the world of her childhood. She is deadly in her attack on this world which dreaded scandal worse than disease, which kept its women encased in invincible innocence. But W. also saw the social order as the domain of life's most important values: decency, honesty, moral commitment. To defy the social ethic was to threaten the very fabric of a moral universe. Archer opts for a stable society and the dullness of May, but he does so at what was most probably great personal loss. Yet the alternative would also extract a great price, one that most of us, says W., lack the strength to pay.

W.'s later works, the eight novels and novellas that follow *The Age of Innocence*, are not as strong as her previous fiction. Indeed, her next, *The Glimpses of the Moon* (1922) is generally considered her worst book. *Hudson River Bracketed* (1929) and *The Gods Arrive* (1932), companion novels, are valuable because the central character, Vance Weston, is W.'s self-portrait of an artist who voices the aesthetic theories she had earlier presented in *The Writing of Fiction*, but as fiction these two books are negligible. Some attribute the falling-off to haste, others to diminished powers. The latter theory is weak, for her unfinished last novel, *The Buccaneers* (1938), shows a return to her old powers. Whatever the reason for these last failures, the novels evidence what Irving Howe has called a "hardening of the moral arteries," a somewhat mean-spirited dismissal of a younger generation she could not understand.

W.'s themes are eclectic, and perhaps as hard to categorize as their author, who has variously been called a novelist of manners, a psychological realist, and a naturalist. She wrote out of her conviction that the true drama of life takes place within the soul. Old New York provided a manageable backdrop for these dramas, and early in her career its flaws were the object of her detached irony. Over the years, as she remarks in *A Backward Glance* (1934), she mellowed enough to grant that New York society, in its three hundred years of "consecrated living up to long-established standards of honour and conduct, of education and manners," has contributed enough to the "moral wealth of our country" to justify itself. Despite this mellowing, her vision throughout the novels remains dark. Her juvenilia is especially morbid, and although she later tempers this pessimism, human beings always remain inadequate and seem consistently to fail each other. Men especially fare poorly, disappointing their women less out of malice than inertia and insensitivity.

W. has been criticized for so often limiting herself to a small social range and narrow historic span—from the 1870s to the 1920s—but even her detractors admit that she depicts her own sphere with consummate skill. Contemporary reviewers of her work repeatedly admired her "perfect plots" or her "graceful, felicitous language." Like her life, her style is formal, and at its best it is terse, caustic, epigrammatic, with sparse use of dialogue and little first-person narration (*Ethan Frome* is the only novel told in the first person). W. has also been criticized for her aloof tone. She was painfully shy, a person who covered her insecurity with what could be an imposing frigidity supported by an undeviating sense of her own social class; but this aloofness can become, in her writing, acid satire motivated by a truly humanistic empathy with the victims of the society she attacks.

The new scholarship resulting from the opening of the Yale University collection of W.'s papers in 1968 is reversing much of the impression of her as haughty, snobbish, and limited, as we see the humanity beneath the glacial reserve bred into her class. So too has the new interest in women's writing led to a broader understanding and more perceptive critical account of her fiction. With increasing admiration, critics and readers alike continue to recognize the consummate craft and sensitivity with which she takes us on an intimate visit into the drawing rooms of society and the mind.

WORKS: *Verses* (1878). *The Decoration of Houses* (1897). *The Greater Inclination* (1897). *The Touchstone* (1900). *Crucial Instances* (1901). *The Joy of Living*, by H. Suderman (translated by Wharton 1902). *Valley of Decision* (1902). *Sanctuary* (1903). *The Descent of Man, and Other Stories* (1904). *Italian Villas, and Their Gardens* (1904). *The House of Mirth* (1905). *Italian Backgrounds* (1905). *Fruit of the Tree* (1907). *Madame de Treyms* (1907). *The Hermit and the Wild Woman, and Other Stories* (1908). *A Motor Flight through France* (1908). *Artemis to Actaeon, and other Verses* (1909). *Tales of Men and Ghosts* (1910). *Ethan Frome* (1911). *The Reef* (1912). *The Custom of the Country* (1913). *Fighting France, from Dunkerque to Belfort* (1915).

The Book of the Homeless (1916). *Xingu, and Other Stories* (1916). *Summer* (1917). *The Marne* (1918). *French Ways and Their Meaning* (1919). *The Age of Innocence* (1920). *In Morocco* (1920). *The Glimpses of the Moon* (1922). *A Son at the Front* (1923). *Old New York* (1924). *The Mother's Recompense* (1925). *The Writing of Fiction* (1925). *Here and Beyond* (1926). *Twelve Poems* (1926). *Twilight Sleep* (1927). *The Children* (1928). *Hudson River Bracketed* (1929)). *Certain People* (1930). *The Gods Arrive* (1932). *Human Nature* (1933). *A Backward Glance* (1934). *The World Over* (1936). *Ghosts* (1937). *The Buccaneers* (1938). *Eternal Passion in English Poetry* (1939). *The Collected Short Stories of Edith Wharton* (2 vols., Ed. R. W. B. Lewis, 1968).

BIBLIOGRAPHY: Auchincloss, L., *Edith Wharton* (1961). Bell, M., *Edith Wharton and Henry James: The Story of Their Friendship* (1965). Howe, I., ed., *Edith Wharton: A Collection of Critical Essays* (1962). Lawson, R. H., *Edith Wharton* (1977). Lewis, R. W. B., *Edith Wharton: A Biography* (1975). Lubbock, P., *Portrait of Edith Wharton* (1947). Lyde, M., *Edith Wharton: Convention and Morality in the Work of a Novelist* (1959). Maxwell, D. E. S., *American Fiction: The Intellectual Background* (1963). Mc-Dowell, M., *Edith Wharton* (1976). Nevius, B., *Edith Wharton: A Study of Her Fiction* (1953). Springer, M., *Edith Wharton and Kate Chopin: A Reference Guide* (1976). Tuttleton, J., *The Novel of Manners in America* (1972). Walton, G., *Edith Wharton: A Critical Interpretation* (1970). Wolff, C. G., *A Feast of Words: The Triumph of Edith Wharton* (1977). Ammons, E., *Edith Wharton's Argument with America* (1980).

MARLENE SPRINGER

Phillis Wheatley

B. 1753 (?), Senegal, Africa; d. 5 Dec. 1784, Boston, Massachusetts
M. John Peters, 1778

Facts about W.'s birth are unknown. The speculation of biographers that she was seven years old in 1760, when she was sold as a slave in Boston, is based on the condition of her teeth at the time. Susannah Wheatley, the wife of a prosperous Boston tailor, bought the frail, asthmatic child. It is inferred from her later recollection of a sunrise ritual and familiarity with Arabic script that her African background was that of a Senegalese Moslem.

W.'s nurturing with the Wheatley's two eighteen-year-old twins was remarkably pleasant and unique to the period. Struck by her sharp intellect, the Wheatleys, contrary to the law and the accepted morality of the times, immediately began to teach her to read and write. In sixteen months, W. was reading the Bible, and at the age of twelve, she began to learn Latin and read the classics of English literature.

Greatly influenced by Pope, W. began poetry at thirteen. After she started publishing at seventeen, she received the attention of Boston society and was invited to social gatherings. Whether to advance their social status or to further W.'s career, the Wheatleys greatly supported her success among the Boston elite. Her fame soon spread from Boston to New York, Philadelphia, and England. She became a freedwoman in 1772. In 1773, the Wheatleys financed her trip to England, where—on a visit cut short by Mrs. Wheatley's illness—W. was presented to London society. In 1776, W. was warmly received by General Washington, with whom she had corresponded and to whom she had addressed a forty-two-line poem, published in the *Pennsylvania Magazine*, edited by Thomas Paine (April 1776).

By 1778, the Wheatleys were either dead or had moved to England; W. fended for herself as a poet and seamstress. After marrying Peters, she moved to Wilmington, Massachusetts, and lived in poverty for the rest of her life. According to the Massachusetts Historical Society record, when Peters was jailed for debts, W. experienced drudgery for the first time in her life, working in a boarding house for blacks in Boston. She bore three children. Two had died by 1783; the third died a few hours after her own death in 1784.

Poems on Various Subjects, Religious and Moral was first published in England in 1773; the first American edition did not follow until 1784. It includes thirty-nine poems of varying merit, some published earlier in magazines. Most of the poems are occasional; some are elegies. "Niobe in Distress for Her Children Slain by Apollo" and "Goliath of Gath," both long poems, reveal the two all-encompassing passions in W.'s life, for the Bible and the classics. The first, along with short poems such as "An Hymn to Morning" and "An Hymn to Evening," exhibits her characteristic classical allusions and use of heroic couplets. A very few poems, such as her odes to Washington and Major General Charles Lee reflect her response to the war.

W. has been criticized for not being concerned enough with her own background and the problems of her race. Only two poems, "On Being Brought from Africa" and "To S. M., a Young African Painter, on Seeing

His Works," deal with African subjects. There are clear references to Africa in only another nine poems. Richard Wright suggests that W.'s lack of racial protest must be explained by her acceptance in Boston society. It may well be that what we consider weaknesses in the collection of her poetry are the results of the temper of contemporary New England and the literary tastes of W.'s time.

W. was celebrated by her contemporaries as a child prodigy and poet and regarded as a skillful letter writer and entertaining literary conversationalist. Her poetry is impersonal, with a self-effacement that subordinates her racial and sexual identities to her identities as Christian and poet. She retains, however, the distinction of being the first famous black woman poet.

WORKS: *Poems on Various Subjects, Religious and Moral* (1773; American edition, 1784). *Letters of Phillis Wheatley, the Negro-Slave Poet of Boston* (Ed. C. Deane, 1864).

BIBLIOGRAPHY: Hughes, L., *Famous American Negroes* (1954). Mason, J., Introduction to *The Poems of Phyllis Wheatley* (1966). Odell, M. M., *Memoir and Poems of Phillis Wheatley* (1834). Richmond, M. A., *Bid the Vassal Soar: Interpretive Essays on the Life and Poetry of Phillis Wheatley and George Moses Horton* (1974). Robinson, W. H., *Phillis Wheatley in the Black American Beginnings* (1975).

ADRIANNE BAYTOP

Frances Miriam Berry Whitcher

B. 1 Nov. 1813 (?), Whitesboro, New York; d. 4 Jan. 1852, Whitesboro, New York
Wrote under: Aunt Maguire, Frank, Widow Bedott, Widow Spriggins
D. of Lewis Berry and Elizabeth Wells; m. Benjamin Whitcher, 1847

The eleventh of fifteen children, W. was the daughter of a prominent Whitesboro innkeeper. Deemed a precocious child, she was educated both at home and at a local academy. In spite of close family ties, she recalled having a lonely childhood because of her keen sense of the ridiculous; the neighbors sternly disapproved of her cariacutures of them. As a young woman, however, she participated in many community activities.

In her mid-thirties, W. married an Episcopal minister and moved with him to his new pastorate in Elmira, New York. Although her marriage was happy, her life in Elmira apparently was not. In 1848, her husband resigned his pastorate and returned to Whitesboro, where she gave birth to her only child, Alice Miriam. W. died of tuberculosis at the age of thirty-nine.

W.'s first humorous sketches (published posthumously as *The Widow Spriggins*, 1867), written to entertain a literary society, are burlesques of a popular English sentimental novel, *Children of the Abbey* (1798), by Regina Maria Roche. The sketches ridicule both sentimental fiction and women who attempt to imitate literary heroines; W.'s persona, Permilly Ruggles Spriggins, is an uncouth sentimentalist who models her language and her every action on Roche's Amanda.

W.'s most famous series of sketches, written at the request of Joseph Neal of the *Saturday Gazette* (1846–47), are dramatic monologues presented entirely in the malapropian vernacular language of the Widow Bedott, who is a parody of a small-town gossip. The sketches are laced with references to contemporary fads, such as phrenology lectures and literary-society meetings.

Bedott devotes considerable energy to a search for a second husband. The first widower she shamelessly pursues seems about to propose, but instead asks for permission to court her daughter. Her second major effort succeeds when she encourages the rumor that she is a woman of means; she succeeds in marrying the Reverend Sniffles, who is as pompous as Bedott is conniving.

After W.'s move to Elmira, she began a third series of sketches for the widely popular *Godey's Lady's Book* (1847–49). Her new persona, Aunt Maguire, is more compassionate than her fictive sister Bedott and speaks a more colloquial language. Inspired by her own observations and experiences as a minister's wife, W. satirizes the residents of small towns for their uncharitable conduct and genteel pretensions.

In one sketch, "The Donation Party," W. satirizes the custom whereby parishioners augment their minister's meager salary by giving him "donations" of substantial commodities. In her story, the minister's guests bring only trifling gifts, break the wife's heirloom china, eat more food than they contribute, and exhibit crude and socially reprehensible behavior. At the end, the fictive minister resigns, declaring that one more donation party would ruin him financially.

W.'s most controversial Aunt Maguire sketches focus on a fictional sewing society that was created ostensibly for charitable purposes, but whose participants turn the meetings into malicious gossip sessions. The series ends when Aunt Maguire travels to a neighboring village where the inhabitants mistakenly believe it is their sewing society that served as the model for the story in *Godey's* and their minister's wife who is the offending author.

Although W.'s responsibility for the sketches had been a closely guarded secret, rumors persisted that the author lived in Elmira. So realistic and biting were the sketches that when Benjamin Whitcher confirmed that his wife was indeed "Aunt Maguire," he was threatened with a law suit and ultimately forced to resign his Elmira pastorate. Not since Frances Trollope's *Domestic Manners of the Americans* (1832) had readers been so stung by a woman's social satire. W. responded by abandoning humorous writing.

Following the tradition of writers such as Seba Smith (who created Jack Downing), W. used first-person vernacular humor as a medium for social criticism. She was unique in humorously depicting small-town life from a woman's perspective, and she thus became one of America's first significant woman humorists. Her work was widely popular in the 19th-c., and modern readers will find much to admire and enjoy in W.'s humor.

WORKS: The Widow Bedott Papers (1856; containing also the Aunt Maguire sketches). *The Widow Spriggins, Mary Elmer, and Other Sketches* (1867).

BIBLIOGRAPHY: Curry, J. A., "Woman as Subjects and Writers of Nineteenth-Century American Humor" (Ph.D. diss., Univ. of Michigan, 1975). Derby, J. C., *Fifty Years among Authors, Books, and Publishers* (1884). Hart, J. D., *The Popular Book: A History of America's Literary Taste* (1961). Morris, Linda A. Finton, "Women Vernacular Humorists in Nineteenth-Century America: Ann Stephens, Frances Whitcher, and Marietta Holley" (Ph.D. diss., Univ. of California, Berkeley, 1978). Neal, A., Introduction to *The Widow Bedott Papers* (1856). Whitcher, Mrs. M. L. Ward, Introduction to *The Widow Spriggins, Mary Elmer, and Other Sketches* (1867).

For articles in references works, see: *NAW* (article by M. L. Langworthy). Other references: *Godey's* (July 1853: Aug. 1853). *New York History* (1974).

LINDA A. MORRIS

Elizabeth White

B. ca. 1637; d. 1699
M. 1657

W. was born in New England, possibly in or near Boston, around 1637, and married in 1657; she had at least one child. There are apparently no extant records of her life, except for these sketchy details which she put into the one published work, her spiritual autobiography.

The Experience of God's Gracious Dealing with Mrs. Elizabeth White, published as a short pamphlet in 1741, is a notable example of early American women's spiritual autobiography. It contains imaginative and personally revealing details about the psychic life of a Puritan woman in 17th-c. New England. This work was discovered after her death in W.'s "closet," a small room used for private meditation and writing. Although it was probably circulated among friends and relatives for many years, as was the practice, it was not published until four decades after W.'s death, during a period of religious revival in New England; her confession would have evoked for its readers an earlier, much admired pious period.

The lack of polish and sophistication in W.'s autobiography is made up for by spontaneity and vividness as she reveals the internal landscape of the darkest recesses of her soul in an attempt to express her redemptive experience. Three experiences of deepest despair about her soul's destiny occurred, concurrently with her marriage, the birth of her first child, and the weaning of this infant. A month before her marriage, she relates, her father desired her to take communion; but she suddenly had grave doubts about her preparedness for taking part in the sacrament. Similarly, she experienced a crisis three days after delivering her first child; she was tempted by the devil with a vision of the Trinity, but escaped Satan's clutches through the suckling of her infant and finally through sleep in which she dreamt of her assured place in heaven, a place secured for her after death in childbirth. A third great trial coincided with weaning, and relates directly to W.'s stated feelings of guilt for the affection she lavished on her first born. Tempted to believe that the Bible is not God's word, she was uplifted by Christ, and the darkness about her soul dispelled.

Although she felt renewed after this final experience, moments of doubt continued to plague her. But she felt secure enough in her salvation and regeneration to commit to writing her account of repentance and trust in Christ. In talking about the trials and religious doubt in the period of early womanhood, W. reveals the deep-seated conflicts and uncertainties felt by a Puritan woman when facing the responsibilities and struggles of marriage and motherhood. As a Puritan, she views these external events only as markers by which she identifies moments of acute spiritual awareness. For the modern reader, the conjunction of W.'s internal and external experiences provides thought-provoking clues to the psychic life of Puritan women.

WORKS: *The Experiences of God's Gracious Dealing with Mrs. Elizabeth White* (1741).

BIBLIOGRAPHY: Shea, D., *Spiritual Autobiography in Early America* (1968).

JACQUELINE HORNSTEIN

Ellen Gould Harmon White

B. 26 Nov. 1827, Gorham, Maine; d. 16 July 1915, St. Helena, California
Wrote under: Ellen G. White
D. of Robert and Eunice Harmon; m. James White, 1846

The daughter of a hatter, W. had only a third-grade education. Although baptized in the Methodist church, by the age of seventeen she was enthusiastically involved with the activities of William Miller—an itinerant preacher who believed the Second Coming of Christ, and the end of the world, would occur during the fall of 1844. In that year, W. had the first of a series of over two thousand visions, which revealed to her why Miller's prediction failed and what God intended her to accomplish.

W. married a fellow "Millerite," and together they spread the message of the coming of Christ to the New England area. She had four children; the first died at sixteen and the last in infancy, but the other two boys became active in the church their mother helped found.

The Whites moved to Battle Creek, Michigan, in 1855, and W., prompted by her visions, preached and wrote on the significance of the imminent (if unknown) coming of Christ, the validity of biblical prophecies, fundamental Christianity, and the divine desire for observing the Sabbath not on Sunday but on the seventh day of the week, Saturday. The Seventh Day Adventist church was eventually established on those principles in 1863. When her husband died in 1888, W. increased her writing and speaking activities, campaigning for Adventist Christianity, health reform, and temperance. As many as twenty thousand people gathered to hear her orations against alcohol. Her travels included two years touring Europe and ten years as a missionary to Australia. In 1902, W. moved the Adventist headquarters from Battle Creek to a suburb of Washington, D.C., and she settled in California. She died at the age of eighty-seven from complications following a hip fracture.

It has been estimated that W. wrote over one hundred and five thousand pages of published and unpublished materials. She maintained that, because of her poor health and lack of education, only God's visions enabled her to produce this literary corpus. Much of her writing was done late at night or in the early morning when domestic tasks were completed.

The foundation of the Seventh Day Adventist church rests on the belief that the Bible reveals the ultimate truth concerning the nature of God, the origin and purpose of human life, and the future of the world. Divine inspiration was not sufficient to convince most 19th-c. Americans that Adventist doctrine was the ultimate truth; W. wanted to show the continuity of biblical prophecy and the course of historical events. Five books, the Conflict of Ages series, are devoted to tracing the history of the battle between God and Satan as predicted in the Old and New Testaments. Four books tell the biblical story from Genesis to the Pauline epistles. *The Great Controversy* (1888), although actually written first, continues the story into the European and American historical settings. W. used the history of Western civilization to underline certain central themes in Adventist belief: the reality of Satan, the evil of Roman Catholicism, and the redemptive quality of William Miller's proclamation.

Much of W.'s writings were composed during a period of general social reform in the U.S. Women's rights, prison reform, the settlement-house movement, and prohibition were important issues at grassroot and national levels. Such late 19th-c. reforms were a part of the "social gospel movement," which emphasized the role of Christianity as a force for social change, rather than as a promoter of the status quo. W. fueled this movement with her tracts on health, education, temperance, and diet; and she encouraged her followers to adopt a life-style encompassing many of the contemporary reforms.

According to W., God intends humans to lead a simple life: pure air, deep breathing, regular sleeping and eating habits, and good sanitation promote moral as well as physical well being; tobacco, coffee, alcohol, meat, and sugar are all detrimental to the body, soul, and mind. Her views on dress reform echo some of the earlier sentiments of Amelia Bloomer and Elizabeth Cady Stanton. In *The Ministry of Healing* (1905), she condemns the restrictive and overly decorative style of contemporary dress: "Every article of dress should fit easily, obstructing neither the circulation of the blood nor a free, full, natural respiration. Everything should be so loose that when the arms are raised, the clothing will be correspondingly lifted."

Educational reform also figures prominately in W.'s writings. Education must include not only the Biblical and historical basis of Adventism but also a foundation in physiology, diet, health, and medicine. Traditional secular education should be limited to basic English, arithmetic, and history ("from the Divine point of view"). She sought to purge from Adventist education "pagan" languages and literature, modern literature by immoral authors, frivolous fiction writers, non-Christian science, biblical criticism, spiritualism, and anarchy. Seventh Day. Adventist education included girls as well as boys and even encouraged some fluidity in sex-role education: "Boys as well as girls should gain a knowledge of household duties. . . . it is a training that need not make any boy less manly; it will make him happier and more useful."

W.'s writings on practical reforms have antecedents in the work of earlier reformers, but she was able to institutionalize them in the doctrine of the Seventh Day Adventist church. She remains a unique woman in the history of American religions, for her writings act as a foundation not only for a growing religious organization but for that religion's extensive system of schools, hospitals, and sanatoriums.

WORKS: *Sketches from the Life of Christ and the Experience of the Christian Church* (1882). *The Great Controversy Between Christ and Satan During the Christian Dispensation* (1888). *Christian Temperance* (1890). *Gospel Workers; Instructions for the Minister and the Missionary* (1892). *Steps to Christ* (1892). *The Story of Patriarchs and Prophets; the Conflict of the Ages Illustrated by the Lives of Holy Men of Old* (1890). *Christ Our Savior* (1895). *The Desire of Ages* (1898). *Christ's Object Lessons* (1900). *Testimonies for the Church* (1901). *Education* (1903). *The Ministry of Healing* (1905). *The Acts of the Apostles in the Proclamation of the Gospel of Jesus Christ* (1911). *Counsel to Teachers, Parents and Students Regarding Christian Education* (1913). *Life Sketches of Ellen G. White, Being a Narrative of her Experience to 1881 as Written By Herself* (1915). *The Captivity and Restoration of Israel; the Conflict of Ages Illustrated in the Lives of Prophets and Kings* (1917). *Christian Experience and Teachings of Ellen G. White*, vol. 1 (1922). *Counsels on Health and Instruction to Medical Missionary Workers* (1923). *Spiritual and Subject Index to the Writings of Mrs. Ellen G. White* (1926). *Principles of True Science* (1929). *Message to Young People* (1930). *Medical Ministry* (1932). *An Appeal for Self-Supporting Laborers* (1933). *A Call to Medical Evangelism* (1933). *Selections from the "Testimonies"* (1936). *Counsels on Sabbath School Work* (1938). *The Sanctified Life* (1937). *Counsels on Diet and Food* (1938). *Counsels to Editors* (1939). *Counsels on Stewardship* (1940).

BIBLIOGRAPHY: Noorbergen, R., *Ellen G. White: Prophet of Destiny* (1972). Numbers, R., *Prophetess of Health: A Study of Ellen G. White* (1976). Spalding, A. W., *There Shines a Light* (1976). White, A., *Ellen G. White: Messenger to the Remnant* (1969).

For articles in reference works, see: *Comprehensive Index to the Writings of Ellen G. White* (3 vols., 1962–63). *NAW* (article by C. C. Goen).

M. COLLEEN McDANNELL

Rhoda Elizabeth Waterman White

Wrote under: Uncle Ben of Rouses Point, N.Y. Uncle Ben, Rhoda E. White
D. of Thomas G. and (?) Whitney Waterman; m. James W. White

No biographical data on W. appears in the standard 19th-c. sources; however, some general information about her background can be abstracted from *Memoir and Letters of Jenny C. White Del Bal* (1868), a book she wrote following her daughter's death. W. was the oldest daughter of General Waterman, a New York state lawyer who married the eldest daughter of General Joshua Whitney, founder of Binghamton, New York. Her parents were socially prominent Episcopalians. She married a member of an explemplary Irish Catholic family. W. converted to Catholicism in 1837, and the Catholic religion was one of the major influences in her life.

Her husband, a wealthy lawyer, became a judge of the Superior Court of New York City. She traveled in fashionable New York society, vacationed at Newport and Saratoga, and enjoyed the privileges of the rich, but her life was not idle. She studied throughout her marriage and received private lessons in all subjects from the best teachers. The mother of eight children, including six daughters, she tutored her family at their home, "Castle Comfort."

The title page of *Jane Arlington; or, The Defrauded Heiress: A Tale of Lake Champlain* (1853) lists *The "Buccaneer" of Lake Champlain* as an earlier work of Uncle Ben. Any prior publications, however, have been lost. *Jane Arlington*, a short novel, is the story of a "young lady perfect and accomplished in every aspect" who, after she is orphaned, is deceived by her kindly step-father's villainous brother into leaving home and finding employment in the frontierlike Lake Champlain region. The plot is predictable; Jane receives both charity and cruelty from employers and others she encounters, but her moral fortitude and personal goodness enable her to survive and regain her rightful inheritance. W. does make use of the unprincipled scoundrel, but her premise is that villainy, or virtue, is frequently disguised and unanticipated. As a corollary, W. exposes class pretensions and distinctions as inadequate measures of individual merit. In developing her theme of false class consciousness, she reveals a keen comic talent that emerges most fully in the caricatures of Mrs. Prim and her family.

W. extends her humorous portrayal of human foibles in *Portraits of My Married Friends; or, A Peep into Hymen's Kingdom* (1858), a series of six sketches narrated by a wry old bachelor, Uncle Ben, who terms his married acquaintances "more fortunate" than he, but who mainly tells of the problems of marital discord and unhappy matches. Most of the portraits, whether comic or tragic, are slight, melodramatic treatments, but the most effective integrate character and theme with moral vision and social consciousness. One of these, "Jerome and Susan Daly," idealizes the love between a village couple and their children, while at the same time it contrasts childrearing practices in the village with those in the city, depicts Scotch and Irish servant girls in the homes of the rich, and proposes "cultivated hearts" as a means of leveling class distinctions. Another effective portrait, "Kate Kearney," combines social realism—including graphic descriptions of tenement life and the plight of abused wives—with a strong story line.

W.'s main concern in *Mary Staunton; or, The Pupils of Marvel Hall* (1860), the most fully realized of her fiction, is the detrimental effects of poor training and environment on young girls, even if their natures are gentle, loving, and sensitive. The novel is an exposé of a fashionable boarding school in New York City, whose pupils acquire little meaningful education and only superficial training in social amenities. Mary is an unlikely heroine; mean, vengeful, and "coarse," she has been neglected by Mrs. Marvel, who is satirized for her false values. Deprived throughout her childhood of affection as well as of religious and moral instruction, she receives a chance for a different life when her long-absent father returns from India and attempts to repair the damage done to his motherless daugher. Although the novel is weakened by W.'s penchant for exaggerating virtues and faults, it is for the most part refreshingly frank and unsentimental.

Two ideas dominate W.'s fiction—Catholicism and education. Her recurrent theme is that children, regardless of their socio-economic status, develop best when they are instilled with faith and love. Her style is at times stilted and melodramatic, and she uses dialogue excessively in forwarding plots. Nevertheless, W. captures voices accurately, particularly immigrant brogues and regional dialects, and she is skillful in rendering realistic scenes of both lower- and upper-class life. Her treatment of New York tenement dwellers and their living conditions, though neither extensive nor primary, is a forerunner of the work of Stephen Crane and Jacob Riis. All of W.'s writing stems from a sense of ethical and social responsibility, but her view of conventional situations is generally from an unexpected angle. Her humorous perspective raises even her most commonplace subjects from the level of cliché and stereotype.

WORKS: *Jane Arlington; or, The Defrauded Heiress: A Tale of Lake Champlain* (1853). *Portraits of My Married Friends: or, A Peep Into Hymen's Kingdom* (1858). *Mary Staunton; or, The Pupils of Marvel Hall* (1860). *Memoir and Letters of Jenny C. White Del Bal* (1868). *From Infancy to Womanhood: A Book of Instructions for Young Mothers* (1881). *What Will the World Say? An American Tale of Real Life* (1885).

THADIOUS M. DAVIS

Lilian Whiting

B. 3 Oct. 1847, Olcott, New York; d. 30 April 1942, Boston, Massachusetts
D. of Lorenzo Dow and Lucretia Calista Clement Whiting

W. was an only daughter and the eldest of three children. While she was still very young, her parents moved to a farm near Tiskilwa, Illinois, where both parents served as principals of the local school. W., however, was educated privately and at home, where she became acquainted early with literary classics. With the assistance of her mother, her father became editor of the Bureau County *Republican*, published in Princeton, Illinois. A leader in the Grange movement and a fighter against the expansion of the railroads and for the expansion of waterways, he served as both representative and senator in the state legislature and assisted in framing the state constitution.

W.'s writing career started when her articles were accepted by the local newspaper, of which she later became editor. In 1876, she went to St. Louis as a journalist and soon became associated with the idealist Philosophic Club. In 1879, she went to work for the Cincinnati *Commercial*, after it published two papers W. had written on Margaret Fuller. The following year, she moved to Boston to become the art editor—and later literary editor—of the Boston *Traveler*.

In 1890, she became editor-in-chief of the Boston *Budget*, to which she also contributed literary reviews (among them, favorable commentary on Emily Dickinson's poems) and a column, "Beau Monde," credited with helping to break down the artistic parochialism of contemporary Boston.

In Boston, W. was a member of a circle that included James Russell Lowell, Lucy Stone, Mary Livermore, Frances Willard, Oliver Wendell Holmes, and many others active in the intellectual life of the time. She visited Bronson Alcott's School of Philosophy and attended Thomas Wentworth Higginson's Round Table. She went to Europe for the first time in 1895 (to do research for the first of several biographies, *A Study of Elizabeth Barrett Browning*, 1899) and thereafter made eighteen pilgrimages abroad. While there, she became the friend of artists such as Auguste Rodin, Harriet Hosmer, and Rosa Bonheur and the theosophist

Annie Besant. Benjamin O. Flower, editor of the *Arena*, said of her that she "knew more men and women of letters than any other woman in America."

So widespread was W.'s reputation as a writer and critic and as a spiritual influence that in 1897 a Lilian Whiting Club was formed in New Orleans with the aim of inspiring its members in matters relating to the arts and sciences.

W.'s spiritualist leanings had deep roots: her father was a descendent of Cotton Mather and her mother of a long line of New England Episcopalian ministers. She wrote ten inspirational books and became one of the most popular of New Thought writers. (William James called New Thought the "religion of healthy-mindedness.") Liberal in her acceptance of a variety of religious sects—in *Life Transfigured* (1910), she discusses spiritualism, theosophy, Christian Science, the Vedantic philosophy, psychotherapy, and Bahai, all as means of salvation—her philosophy is optimistic. She believed in the primacy of the spiritual world and referred to death merely as "change"; she viewed the time she lived in as the "dawn of a new perfection." The death of the journalist Kate Field, a close friend, led W. to write *After Her Death: The Story of a Summer* (1897), which she considered her best work. It spells out her belief in communication between the living and the dead. The essays, such as "Success as a Fine Art," collected in the World Beautiful series (three volumes, 1894–96, which ran to fourteen editions) are typical of W.'s approach to living.

Boston Days: The City of Beautiful Ideals (1902) was the first of her eight books dealing with places she visited in North America, Europe, and Africa. The chatty tone of her accounts of popular landmarks and works of art as well as the liberal sprinkling of names of her famous acquaintances no doubt were the chief sources of the popularity of her travel writing.

W.'s third-person autobiography, *The Golden Road* (1918), is effusive rather than factual. She published one volume of poetry, *From Dreamland Sent* (1895). The poems are largely personal in subject and traditional in form and tone.

W. is of interest to those studying popular taste rather than excellence and originality in the literary arts. It is worth noting, however, that she achieved fame and success as a professional among professionals and moved freely in an international society of artists in a way few women of her time were privileged to do.

WORKS: *The World Beautiful* (3 vols., 1894–96). *After Her Death: The Story of a Summer* (1897). *Kate Field: A Record* (1899). *A Study of the Life and Poetry of Elizabeth Barrett Browning* (1899). *The Victory of the Will* (edited by Whiting, 1899). *The Spiritual Significance; Or, Death As An Event in Life* (1900). *The World Beautiful in Books* (1901). *Boston Days: The City of Beautiful Ideals* (1902). *The Life Radiant* (1903). *The Florence of Landor* (1905). *The Joy That No Man Taketh From You* (1905). *The Outlook Beautiful* (1905). *From Dream to Vision of Life* (1906). *Italy, the Magic Land* (1907). *Paris, the Beautiful* (1908). *The Land of Enchantment* (1909). *Life Transfigured* (1910). *Louise Chandler Moulton: Poet and Friend* (1910). *The Brownings: Their Life and Art* (1911). *Athens, the Violet-Crowned* (1913). *The Lure of London* (1914). *Women Who Have Ennobled Life* (1915). *The Adventure Beautiful* (1917). *Canada, the Spellbinder* (1917). *The Golden Road* (1918). *Katherine Tingley* (1919). *They Who Understand* (1919).

BIBLIOGRAPHY: Flower, B. O., *Progressive Men, Women, and Movements in the Past Twenty-Five Years* (1914). Gardner, W. E., *Memorial* (1942).

For articles in reference works, see: *AW. NCAB* IX.

Other references: *Arena* (April 1899). Boston *Globe* (1 May 1942). Boston *Herald* (1 May 1942). *NYT* (1 May 1942).

VIRGINIA R. TERRIS

Sarah Helen Power Whitman

B. *19 Jan. 1803, Providence, Rhode Island; d. 27 June 1878, Providence, Rhode Island*
Wrote under: Helen, Sarah Helen Whitman
D. of Nicholas and Anna Marsh Power; m. John Winslow Whitman, 1828

Both W.'s parents were from old Rhode Island families. Her father was absent from home for many years when, after being captured at sea by the British in 1813, he chose to continue his seafaring career until 1832. W. was educated, for brief periods, at private schools in Providence and at a Quaker school in Jamaica, Long Island, where she lived with an aunt. Although a taste for poetry and novels was thought pernicious, she preferred them to lessons and read the classics and French and German literature in the library of another aunt, in Providence. She lived in Boston with her husband, an attorney, editor, and writer, but returned to Providence after his death in 1833. She traveled in Europe in 1857.

W.'s first published poem was "Retrospection," signed "Helen" (*American Ladies Magazine*, 1829). The editor, Sarah Josepha Hale, encouraged further contributions. W. wrote scholarly essays on Goethe, Shelley, and Emerson and served as a correspondent for the New York *Tribune* and the Providence *Journal.*

W. was an advocate of educational reforms, divorce, the prevention of cruelty to animals, the liberal ethics of Fourier, women's rights, and universal suffrage. Opposing the materialism of the Protestant churches, she subscribed to the intellectual and spiritual idealism of the Transcendentalists. She was also noted for her belief in prenatal influences and occult and psychic phenomena.

A woman of unusual intelligence and charm, W. knew many prominent people, but today she is best known as a friend of Edgar Allan Poe. Following their first meeting on 2 September 1848, exchanges of poems, and a romantic correspondence, they were engaged to be married by the end of the year, but the engagement was broken at the time the banns were to be published. After Poe's death in 1849, W. cherished his memory and worked to exonerate the maligned author when, in many circles, it was not considered respectable to have been associated with him. She searched for and located materials and, lent valuable items in her possession, and as the Poe controversy became international, she answered all inquiries about him.

W.'s one volume of verse, *Hours of Life, and Other Poems* (1853) is more carefully composed than the work of most women who were her contemporaries, but it is too genteel and restrained to be of moment by comparison with rougher, more original writers. The subjects are typical for the period: dreams and memories of love, the reality of death, visions of paradise, and the comforts of serene religious faith. Her voice is subdued or languorous; her eyes are sensitive to light and color; her heart is tender. Sixteen poems are the record of her love for Poe; they constitute a structure of illusions for reconciling the "orient phantasies," the experience of mundane and rather ugly stresses, the shame and guilt, the grief, and what she calls the "silent eyes of destiny." The reconciliation freed her for the most radical writing of her career, *Edgar Poe and His Critics* (1860).

Having witnessed a decade of what she calls "remorseless violation" to the memory of Poe, W. wished her vindication of him to be impersonal and authoritative. She refrains from discussing her troubled romance with Poe but does take advantage of having known him, of long familiarity with what he wrote, and a scrupulous reading of all that had been written about him. She draws legitimately on the recollections of others who knew him and her own trenchant knowledge of literature and familiarity with the national scene.

Finally, taking into account Poe's mental desolation and periodic insanity, W. views his "unappeased and restless soul" in relation to an era when a prevailing skepticism and "divine dissatisfaction everywhere present" showed that the age was moving feverishly through processes of transition and development, "yet gave no idea of where they were leading us." Poe was, for W., one of the men of "electric temperament and prophetic genius" who anticipate those latent ideas about to unfold themselves to humanity. Nothing would have been gained, she observes, had he been another Wordsworth or Longfellow.

W. was a woman of courage, independent mind, tact, and dignity—and one of the most impressive of American literary critics of the 19th c.

WORKS: *Hours of Life, and Other Poems* (1853). *Edgar Poe and His Critics* (1860). *The Life and Poems of Edgar Allan Poe,* by E. Didier (introduction by Whitman, 1877).

BIBLIOGRAPHY: Harrison, J. A., ed., *The Last Letters of Edgar Allan Poe to Sarah Helen Whitman* (1909). Miller, J. C., *Building Poe Biography* (1977). Miller, J. C., *Poe's Helen Remembers* (1979). Osgood, F. S., *Poems* (1849). Ostrom, J. W., ed., *The Letters of Edgar Allan Poe* (1966). Robertson, J. W., *Edgar A. Poe: A Psychopathic Study* (1923). Ticknor, Caroline, *Poe's Helen* (1916).

For articles in reference works, see: *American Female Poets,* Ed. C. May (1849). *NAW* (article by J. G. Varner).

ELIZABETH PHILLIPS

Phyllis Ayame Whitney

B. 9 Sept. 1903, Yokohama, Japan
Writes under: Phyllis A. Whitney
D. of Charles Joseph and Lillian Mandeville Whitney; m. Lovell F. Jahnke, 1950

Born of American parents, W. first came to the U.S. at the age of fifteen, after living in Japan, China, and the Philippines. She was graduated from high school in Chicago. She married a business man in 1950 and has one daughter. She lives in Staten Island, New York, and northern New Jersey.

W. has written more than fifty novels, which she divides into three groups: novels for young people, mysteries for young people, and adult novels. Almost all of the last are gothic romances. During her long career, she has reviewed books for newspapers and has taught courses, lectured, and written widely on the business and craft of writing fiction. Two novels, *Mystery of the Haunted Pool* (1960) and *Mystery of the Hidden Hand* (1963) have received Edgars from the Mystery Writers of America.

The novels for young people (all except one from the years between 1941 and 1949) appeal to young girls rather than boys. Many of them carry girls' names in the title: *A Place for Ann* (1941), *A Star for Ginny* (1942), *A Window for Julie* (1943), *Linda's Homecoming* (1950), *Nobody Likes Trina* (1972). Many of these didactic novels have been favorably reviewed by educators and librarians, and W.'s success in this field has made her an authority. She has published two text books, *Writing Juvenile Fiction* (1947; rev. ed., 1960) and *Writing Juvenile Stories and Novels* (1976).

Her mysteries for young people can be easily recognized because, with the exception of *The Vanishing Scarecrow* (1971), each of them has a title beginning with "mystery" or "secret." These too are primarily written for girls, although the adventure aspect is strong. They are all characterized by vivid backgrounds.

W.'s early life abroad provided exotic background material for many of her novels. In recent years, she has made each of her many trips serve a double purpose: she uses the background material gathered for one juvenile novel and one adult gothic romance. Thus a trip to the Virgin Islands produced both *Secret of the Spotted Shell* (1967) and *Columbella* (1966). She has set novels in Turkey, Norway, Japan, Greece, South Africa, and a wide variety of places in the U.S.

W.'s first adult novel was *Red is for Murder* (1943), a straightforward mystery novel set in a department store. She did not return to adult fiction until some time later; the next adult book, *The Quicksilver Pool* (1955), is a historical novel set on Staten Island during the Civil War draft riots. Although there is a domestic mystery, the most important aspect of the plot is a love story, a pattern she also uses in a number of novels in the late 1950s and early 1960s.

After the successful contemporary romantic adventures *Seven Tears for Apollo* (1963) and *Black Amber* (1964), W. only once, in *Sea Jade* (1964), uses a historical setting for her novels. The mystery element becomes a more important part of the plot than it had been before.

W.'s preoccupation with women and their identities in these novels is often very sophisticated. (She has written that she relies on Karen Horney for psychological insight about women.) In novels such as *Columbella*, *Silverhill* (1967), *Lost Island* (1970), *Listen for the Whisperer* (1972), *The Turquoise Mask* (1974), and *The Golden Unicorn* (1976), she is increasingly concerned with relationships between mothers and daughters and with questions of feminine identity as they relate to the past—with the problems of women trying both to come to terms with and transcend their family background. In recent years, most of her heroines are seeking their own identities through returning to their ancestral home or through a reconciliation with another woman in the family. The solution of the mystery provides both a conclusion for the plot and an answer to the significant questions asked by the heroine of her past.

Although each of these books ends with clear answers, the process of finding them is arduous and uncompromising. The mystery genre imposes limits on the ambiguity W. can allow in the resolution, but it does not keep her from an honest and rigorous development of the issues. Her women make mistakes: they marry the wrong man, they misjudge character, one of them has an illegitimate child. But they are allowed the opportunity to see what they have done and to change it and themselves. Many authors write gothic romances; very few write them with the sophistication and wisdom of W.

WORKS: *A Place for Ann* (1941). *A Star for Ginny* (1942). *A Window for Julie* (1943). *Red Is for Murder* (1943; alternate title, *The Red Carnelian*). *The Silver Inkwell* (1945). *Willow Hill* (1947). *Writing Juvenile Fiction* (1947; rev. ed., 1960). *Ever After* (1948). *Mystery of the Gulls* (1949). *Linda's Homecoming* (1950). *Island of the Dark Woods* (1951; alternate title, *Mystery of the Strange Traveler*). *Love Me, Love Me Not* (1952). *Step to the Music* (1953). *A Long Time Coming* (1954). *Mystery of the Black Diamonds* (1954). *Mystery of the Isle of Skye* (1955). *The Quicksilver Pool* (1955). *The Fire and the Gold* (1956). *The Highest Dream* (1956). *The Trembling Hills* (1956). *Mystery of the Green Cat* (1957). *Skye Cameron* (1957). *The Moonflower* (1958). *Secret of the Samurai Sword* (1958). *Creole Holiday* (1959). *Mystery of the Haunted Pool* (1960). *Thunder Heights* (1960). *Secret of the Tiger's Eye* (1961). *Blue Fire* (1961). *Mystery of the Golden Horn* (1962). *Window of the Square* (1962). *Mystery of the Hidden Hand* (1963). *Seven Tears for Apollo* (1963). *Black Amber* (1964). *Sea Jade* (1964). *Secret of the Emerald Star* (1964). *Mystery of the Angry Idol* (1965). *Columbella* (1966). *Secret of the Spotted Shell* (1967). *Silverhill* (1967). *Hunter's Green* (1968). *Secret of Goblin Glen* (1968). *Mystery of the Crimson Ghost* (1969). *Secret of the Missing Footprints* (1969). *The Winter People* (1969). *Lost Island* (1970). *The Vanishing Scarecrow* (1971). *Listen for the Whisperer* (1972). *Nobody Likes Trina* (1972). *Mystery of the Scowling Boy* (1973). *Snowfire* (1973). *The Turquoise Mask* (1974). *Secret of the Haunted Mesa* (1975). *Spindrift* (1975). *The Golden Unicorn* (1976). *Writing Juvenile Stories and Novels* (1976). *Secret of the Stone Face* (1977). *The Stone Bull* (1977). *The Glass Flame* (1978). *Domino* (1979). *Poinciana* (1980). *Vermillion* (1981).

BIBLIOGRAPHY: CA 1–4 (1967). NYTBR (2 July 1967). Time (12 April 1971). Writer (Feb. 1960; Feb. 1967).

KAY MUSSELL

Kate Douglas Smith Wiggin

B. 28 Sept. 1856, Philadelphia, Pennsylvania; d. 24 Aug. 1923, Harrow-on-Hill,
England
Wrote under: Mrs. Riggs, Kate Douglas Wiggin
D. of Robert and Helen Dyer Smith; m. Samuel Wiggin, 1881; m. George
Riggs, 1895

W. was born to a prosperous Philadelphia lawyer and his wife, a native of
Maine. Her childhood was spent in the village of Hollis, Maine, after the
death of her father and her mother's remarriage. She was educated at
home and then at various schools in New England. In the mid-1870s, she
moved with her family to California, where they came on hard times.

W. became interested in the new kindergarten movement and took a
course under Emma Marwedel in Los Angeles, and then opened the Silver
Street Kindergarten in a slum in San Francisco, the first free kindergarten
in California. For a number of years, she was a national leader in the kindergarten movement, and she began her own training school in San Francisco in 1880. To raise money for the free-kindergarten movement, W.
published privately two short sentimental novels, The Story of Patsy
(1883) and The Bird's Christmas Carol (1887).

Her first husband, a lawyer, died in 1889. W. had given up kindergarten
work in 1884, and she began writing full-time after the successful commercial publication of The Birds' Christmas Carol in 1889. She returned to
the East Coast and lived in New York City and Hollis, giving readings
from her works and traveling to Europe. Her second husband was a businessman. Among her New York circle were William Dean Howells, Mary
E. Wilkins Freeman, and Carolyn Wells. W. suffered periodically from
nervous exhaustion; the opening chapters of Rebecca of Sunnybrook
Farm (1903) were written in a sanatorium.

The Birds' Christmas Carol became a seasonal classic, published in multiple editions in various languages. In this edifying tale, Carol Bird, a
wealthy but sick ten-year-old, gives a Christmas dinner for the children of
a poor family in the neighborhood, the Ruggles. Although the heroine
dies after the children leave on Christmas night, the book's popularity did
not rest on sentiment alone; the portrayal of the Ruggles family is realistic
and humorous.

Two children's novels set in California, *A Summer in a Canon* (1889) and *Polly Oliver's Problem* (1893), are not very good, and the same may be said of a series of travel novels, most of which have Penelope Hamilton as the heroine. W. is best known for stories set in Maine, and these are undoubtedly her best work.

Timothy's Quest (1890) and some early short stories have Maine backgrounds, but W. only began to concentrate on regional material after the success of *Rebecca of Sunnybrook Farm*. Today this is considered a children's book, but it was first a best-selling adult novel. Set in a village similar to Hollis, in the Saco River valley, the story is a classic orphan story without the orphan: Rebecca, the daughter of a poor widow, is sent to live with two maiden aunts in order to be "made." In traditional fashion, she wins their hearts, even that of the stern Aunt Miranda. A spirited child, Rebecca accomplishes many things in the course of the story, including the saving of her family fortunes. She graduates from boarding school in a cheesecloth dress, but her time at school has been a success—she is class president. Rebecca's character and the local color of her background are both appealing. This story did not end with a marriage, but with only the hint of an attachment. There was no sequel, only a volume of "missing chapters," or stories about Rebecca set in the time of the first novel: *The New Chronicles of Rebecca* (1907).

Mother Carey's Chickens (1911) is another of W.'s popular New England novels. A more saccharine story than *Rebecca of Sunnybrook Farm*, it tells how the Carey family, under the leadership of young Nancy, manages to survive economically after the death of their father. Other Maine stories with good regional description are another Christmas story, *The Old Peabody Pew* (1907), and *Susanna and Sue* (1909), which features a Shaker colony. *The Story of Waitstill Baxter* (1913) shows more mature character development than the average W. novel. Set in the early 19th c., this novel of Saco-valley life features an historical figure, the traveling evangelist Jacob Cochrane, and describes the disruption he brings to a family.

W.'s autobiography, *My Garden of Memory* (1923), is a charming and valuable document, revealing its author as a woman of spirit and sense. Several of her novels were filmed more than once. These movies mirror the popular modern conception of W. as a silly sentiment a list, but her novels, slight as they are, belie that reputation. She was a chronicler of the romance of real life, not a romanticist. And while there is sentimentality in her earlier works, her major novels are free of it. Most of her heroines —Rebecca, Nancy Carey, Polly Oliver, Waitstill Baxter—are active, intelligent young women, unlike the Little Eva stereotype, Carol Bird. W.

argued for wholesomeness, not hypocrisy, in fiction, and her point of view was that of a sophisticated professional writer, not that of a sheltered matron. She was a popular writer who expressed what her contemporaries themselves thought of as "real life."

WORKS: *The Story of Patsy* (1883). *The Birds' Christmas Carol* (1889). *A Summer in a Canon* (1889). *Timothy's Quest* (1890; film versions, 1922 and 1936). *Polly Oliver's Problem* (1893). *A Cathedral Courtship and Penelope's English Experiences* (1893). *The Village Watch-tower* (1895). *Marm Lisa* (1896). *Penelope's Progress* (1898). *Penelope's Irish Experiences* (1901). *Diary of a Goose Girl* (1902). *Rebecca of Sunnybrook Farm* (1903; film versions, 1917, 1932, 1938). *Rose o' the River* (1905). *New Chronicles of Rebecca* (1907). *The Old Peabody Pew* (1907). *Susanna and Sue* (1909). *Mother Carey's Chickens* (1911; film versions, 1938 and, as *Summer Magic*, 1963). *The Story of Waitstill Baxter* (1913). *Penelope's Postscripts* (1915). *The Romance of a Christmas Card* (1916). *Ladies in Waiting* (1919). *My Garden of Memory* (1923). *Creeping Jenny, and Other New England Stories* (1924). Fifteen books, some collection of stories and some about kindergartens, written with her sister, Nora Archibald Smith.

BIBLIOGRAPHY: Benner, H., *Kate Douglas Wiggin's Country of Childhood* (1956). Smith, N., *Kate Douglas Wiggin as Her Sister Knew Her* (1925).

Other references: *Bookman* (32, 1910; 59, 1924). *Lamp* 29 (1905). London *Bookman* 38 (1910). *NEQ* 41 (June 1968).

BEVERLY SEATON

Ella Wheeler Wilcox

B. 5 Nov. 1850, Johnstown Center, Wisconsin; d. 30 Oct. 1919, Short Beach, Connecticut
Wrote under: Ella Wheeler, Ella Wheeler Wilcox
D. of Marcus Hartwell and Sarah Pratt Wheeler; m. Robert Marius Wilcox, 1884

W. was the youngest of four children born to a music teacher turned farmer and a mother who had strong literary ambitions. She claimed that her mother's extensive reading of Shakespeare, Scott, and Byron was a prenatal influence that shaped her entire career. Her mother helped her to find time to read and write rather than work on the bleak Wisconsin farm.

W. was influenced early by the romantic melodramas of Ouida, Mary J. Holmes, May Agnes Fleming, and Mrs. Southworth. At the age of ten she wrote a "novel" in ten chapters, printing it in her childish hand on scraps of paper and binding it in paper torn from the kitchen wall. The New York *Mercury* published an essay when she was fifteen. In 1867, she enrolled at the University of Wisconsin, where, however, she remained only a short time. She begged her family to be allowed to remain at home and write.

By the time she was eighteen, she was earning a substantial salary, which aided her impoverished family. People from Madison, Milwaukee, and Chicago began to seek out the little country girl with the "inspired pen," and she in turn was delighted to visit their city homes. By 1880, the "Milwaukee School of Poetry" was at its height with W. as its shining light; the poets were all well known throughout the West, and some had even gained recognition in the East.

Maurine (1876), a narrative poem, introduces two types of women W. often wrote about: Helen, a weak and passive person who bears a daughter and soon dies, and Maurine, an aggressive and highly intelligent artist who eventually marries an American poet-intellectual. Maurine travels to Europe, where her paintings are favorably received. Helen and Maurine reappear in more complex form as Mabel and Ruth, two of the characters in *Three Women* (1897).

When W. attempted to publish *Poems of Passion* (1883), a collection of poems that had appeared previously in various periodicals, the book was rejected because of the "immorality" of several poems, and its author became the subject of unpleasant notoriety. When a Chicago publisher brought out the book, however, it was an immediate success, and W.'s reputation was made. In this work, she brought into her love poetry the element of sin. By 1888, she was a leader in what was called the "Erotic School," a group of writers who rebelled against the stricter rules of conventionality. By 1900, a whole feminine school of rather daring verse on the subject of the emotions followed W.'s lead.

The symbolism of sexual passion is depicted throughout her poems as a tiger who is "a splendid creature," as in "Three and One" (*Poems of Pleasure*, 1888); sex for W. is "all the tiger in my blood." In "At Eleusis," motherhood is praised and welcomed, a common theme of her poetry.

W. wrote editorials and essays for the New York *Journal* and the Chicago *American* as well as contributing to *Cosmopolitan* and other magazines. In 1901, she was commissioned by the New York *American* to write a poem on the death of Queen Victoria and was sent to London, where she was presented at the court of St. James. During WWI, she toured the army camps in France, reciting her poems and counseling young soldiers on their problems.

Throughout her life, W. enjoyed great popularity, and she took her work most seriously. In defending her poetry against critics, she maintained that "heart, not art" is most important in poetry and pointed out that her poems comforted millions of weary and unhappy people.

WORKS: Drops of Water (1872). Shells (1873). Maurine (1876). Poems of Passion (1883). The Birth of the Opal (1886). Mal Moulee: A Novel (1886). Perdita, and Other Stories (1886). Poems of Pleasure (1888). The Adventures of Miss Volney (1888). A Double Life (1891). How Salvatore Won (1891). The Beautiful Land of Nod (1892). An Erring Woman's Love (1892). A Budget of Christmas Tales (1895). An Ambitious Man (1896). Custer and Other Poems (1896). Men, Women, and Emotions (1896). Three Women (1897). Poems of Power (1901). The Heart of the New Thought (1902). Kingdom of Love (1902). Sweet Danger (1902). Around the Year (1904). Poems of Love (1905). A Woman of the World (1905). Mizpah (1906). New Thought Pastels (1906). Poems of Sentiment (1906). New Thought Common Sense and What Life Means to Me (1908). Song of Liberty (1908). Poems of Progress (1909). Sailing Sunny Seas (1909). The New Hawaiian Girl (1910). Yesterdays (1910). The Englishman, and Other Poems (1912). Gems (1912). Picked Poems (1912). The Art of Being Alive (1914). Cameos (1914). Lest We Forget (1914). Poems of Problems (1914). World Voices (1916). The Worlds and I (1918). Poems (1918). Sonnets of Sorrow and Triumph (1918). Collected Poems (1924).

BIBLIOGRAPHY: Ballou, J., Period Piece: Ella Wheeler Wilcox and Her Time (1940). Brown, N., Critical Confessions (1899). Town, C. H., Adventures in Editing (1926). Watts, E. S., The Poetry of American Women, 1632–1945 (1977). Wheeler, M. P., Evolution of Ella Wheeler Wilcox and Other Wheelers (1921). Wilcox, E. W., "Literary Confessions of a Western Poetess," in Lippincott's (May 1886). Wilcox, E. W., "My Autobiography," in Cosmopolitan (Aug. 1901).

For articles in reference works, see: AA. NAW (article by J. T. Baird, Jr.).

Other references: American Mercury (Aug. 1934). Bookman (Jan. 1920). Cosmopolitan (Nov. 1888). Harper's (March 1952). Literary Digest (22 Nov. 1919). London Times (31 Oct. 1919). NYT (31 Oct. 1919). Poetry and Drama 1 (March 1913).

ANNE R. GROBEN

Laura Ingalls Wilder

B. 7 Feb. 1867, Pepin County, Wisconsin; d. 10 Feb. 1957, Mansfield, Missouri
D. of Charles and Caroline Quiner Ingalls; m. Almanzo Wilder, 1885

Born in a cabin in the Wisconsin woods, W. is perhaps America's best-known female pioneer. While her books do not follow the pattern of her early life exactly, they are very close. Her parents moved their family many times, searching for a better life for W. and her three sisters. After living in Missouri, Kansas, Iowa, and Minnesota, they settled in De Smet, South Dakota, where W. met and married her husband. After a difficult early married life, in which one daughter, was born and a baby son died, the W.'s bought a farm near Mansfield, Missouri, where they lived the rest of their lives.

At Rocky Ridge Farm, W. raised chickens and made butter, helped her husband build their home, and began to write articles for various rural papers and a column, As a Farm Woman Thinks, for the Missouri *Ruralist*. She stopped writing for the papers in 1924, but her daughter, Rose Wilder Lane, a writer herself, encouraged her to write about her early life. So, in 1930 at the age of sixty-three, W. began to write the Little House books.

The seven autobiographical volumes published during W.'s lifetime cover the years from about age four to her marriage and reflect the changing point of view of the maturing heroine. *Little House in the Big Woods* (1932) describes life in a log cabin in the forest, as seen by a young child. This volume features stories about Pa's adventures in the woods, a jolly Christmas, and a maple sugaring dance. *Little House on the Prairie* (1935) takes the Ingalls family across the Mississippi into Indian lands, where they create a homestead but are forced by the government to leave. Minnesota is the scene of *On the Banks of Plum Creek* (1937) where Laura goes to school and first encounters Nellie Oleson, a tiresome brat who appears in later books as well. The Ingalls life in Minnesota is dominated by the plague of grasshoppers.

By the Shores of Silver Lake (1939) takes the family to South Dakota, where they live at a railroad camp, then spend the winter in the surveyor's house so they will be on hand when the town is established. *The Long*

Winter (1940) describes the severe winter of 1881, which the Ingalls spend in a house in De Smet. The book ends with the arrival of the train (snowbound since fall) and the celebration of Christmas in May. *Little Town on the Prairie* (1941) gives scenes of Laura's life as a teenager in town. At the end of the book, she is given a certificate to teach school, although she is only fifteen. The final volume, *These Happy Golden Years* (1943), tells of her teaching and her courtship with Almanzo W. They are married at the end of the volume. One other volume of the Little House books, *Farmer Boy* (1933), does not deal with her own life but with her husband's boyhood on a large farm near Malone, New York.

The other three books published under her name are all posthumous. *The First Four Years* (1971) covers the early, difficult years of her marriage, ending with the death of her baby boy and the burning of their home. *On the Way Home* (1962) is a journal she kept during their trip to Missouri and the beginning of their life at Rocky Ridge Farm. *West from Home* (1974) is a group of letters written to her husband from San Francisco when visiting Rose there in 1915.

The only major award won by W. was a special award given at the Newbery-Caldecott dinner in 1954, but her Little House books are among the most popular children's classics. The Children's Library Association set up the Laura Ingalls Wilder Award, of which she was the first recipient, to be given every five years. A popular television series has been based on her work, although the scripts depart a good deal from the themes and spirit of the original books, giving more emphasis to exciting and unusual events. Many of the places W. lived have memorials of some sort, and Rocky Ridge Farm is now a museum.

The Little House books' description of everyday life in pioneer times appeals to both children and adults. As children's fiction, their greatest achievement is the ease and grace with which W. speaks to children. She never patronizes, yet she retains a suitable perspective. Laura and her sisters are not glamorized; Laura is adventurous, but in contrast to children in other books about pioneer life, she performs no heroic deeds. Of course, these novels are cosmetic reality, for only a few of the harsher aspects of pioneer life are depicted, as a study of those parts of W.'s life left out of the story reveals. No doubt the romance of pioneer life, aided by the appeal of a series, is no small part of the success of the Little House books, but the heart of W.'s achievement is the literary artistry with which she uses a simple, declarative style and shapes her narrative around ordinary events.

WORKS: Little House in the Big Woods (1932). *Farmer Boy* (1933). *Little House on the Prairie* (1935). *On the Banks of Plum Creek* (1937). *By the Shores of Silver Lake* (1939). *The Long Winter* (1940). *Little Town on the Prairie* (1941). *These Happy Golden Years* (1943). *On the Way Home* (1962). *The First Four Years* (1971). *West from Home* (1974).

BIBLIOGRAPHY: Erisman, F., in *Studies in Medieval, Renaissance, and American Literature: A Festschrift,* Ed. B. Colquitt (1971). Zochert, D., *Laura* (1976).

Other references: *Atlantic* (Feb. 1975). *Children's Literature: The Great Excluded* 4 (1975). *Horn Book* (Sept. 1943; Dec. 1954; Oct. 1965).

BEVERLY SEATON

Emma Hart Willard

B. 23 Feb. 1787, Berlin, Connecticut; d. 15 April 1870, Troy, New York
D. of Samuel and Lydia Hinsdale Hart; m. John Willard, 1809; m. Christopher Yates, 1838

W. was the sixteenth of her father's seventeen children, the ninth born to his second wife. Books were the center of life on the Hart family farm. Captain Hart had served in the Revolution, and in addition to Chaucer, Milton, and Shakespeare, the family savored stories of Washington and Lafayette.

W. attended the Berlin Academy (where within two years she was teaching younger children), but she was extensively self-taught. She took advantage of the medical books of her husband—a fifty-year-old physician and politician who had four children from two previous marriages—and the books of his nephew—a student at Middlebury College who lived in their home in Vermont. W. had been preceptress of a school in Middlebury before her marriage, and in 1814—to aid family finances—she opened the Middlebury Female Seminary, where she began to introduce "higher subjects," such as mathematics, history, and languages, in addition to the "ornamental" subjects usually deemed proper for women.

W. realized that private means were too limited to provide suitable housing, adequate libraries, and the necessary apparatus for quality education. She presented New York governor DeWitt Clinton with her *Plan for Improving Female Education* (1819), published at her own expense and sent to prominent men throughout the country. It received enthusiastic response from all quarters, but the legislature voted no funds. In 1821, however, the Troy, New York, Common Council voted to raise four thousand dollars for female education. Five years before the first public high schools for girls opened in New York (and closed shortly thereafter) and sixteen years before Mary Lyon founded the Mount Holyoke Female Seminary, W. was offering women a serious course of study equivalent to the best men's high schools and sometimes superior to their college work.

She was supported in her work by her husband (until his death in 1825), her sister, Almira Hart Lincoln Phelps, and later by her one son and his wife. Her brief second marriage (to a man who turned out to be a gambler and fortune hunter) was not successful, but W. had had the foresight to draw up an unusual prenuptial financial agreement that protected her property, income, and school.

The work that established W.'s reputation is her *Plan for Improving Female Education*. Incisive as any lawyer's brief, it argues that the current system of privately financed education was inadequate because most proprietors saw schools only as money-making ventures and because many schools, particularly girls' schools, had no entrance requirements, few regulations, and a shallow curriculum. She declares that education "should seek to bring its subjects to the perfection of their moral, intellectual, and physical nature, in order that they may be of the greatest possible use to themselves and others" and concludes by noting that since women give society its moral tone, the country would benefit from quality female education. In 1833, W. expanded these ideas in a series of lectures published as *The Advancement of Female Education* to promote a female seminary in Greece.

Even while running the seminary herself, W. found time to write several textbooks, which made her financially independent. The first is *A System of Universal Geography* (1822), written with William Channing Woodbridge. Older texts had been written as if London were the center of the world and emphasized rote learning. W. encourages students to study and draw maps and to use a globe. She describes the climate, customs, and history of different countries.

W. is best known for her history texts. *Republic of America* (1828) begins with a chronological table dividing American history into ten epochs and concludes with the "political scriptures" she learned as a child. Lafayette endorsed her account of the Revolution, and Daniel Webster wrote, "I keep it near me as book of reference, accurate in facts and dates." It was popular for both the student and the general reader.

Her Episcopal faith gave the books a popular moral tone. *A System of Universal History in Perspective* (1837) details the "virtues which exalt nations and the vices which destroy them." In 1844, she published *Temple of Time*, the first in a series of books in which she charted world history as a multi-storied temple, in which each floor is held up by groups of ten pillars on which are engraved the names of the principal sovereigns of each century. Each floor contains various groupings of nations and the roof displays the names of heroes. Although these books may appear stilted and moralistic today, they were hailed as educationally innovative, making history exciting in their time.

W. never participated in women's rights activities, but she opposed Almira's Anti-Woman Suffrage Society. She wrote to Celia Burr Burleigh in support of her career as a feminist lecturer: "After all, you have only entered now upon a work that I took up more than half a century ago—pleading the cause of my sex. I did it in my way, you are doing it in yours, and as I have reason to believe that God blessed me in my efforts, I pray that he will bless you in yours."

WORKS: *An Address to the Public, Particularly to the Members of the Legislature of New York, Proposing a Plan for Improving Female Education* (1819). *Universal Peace, to Be Introduced by a Confederacy of Nations Meeting at Jerusalem* (1820; rev. ed., 1864). *A System of Universal Geography on the Principles of Comparison and Classification* (1822; alternate title, *Ancient Geography*). *Geography for Beginners; or, The Instructor's Assistant* (1826). *Republic of America; or, History of the United States* (1828). *Advancement of Female Education* (1833). *Journal and Letters from France and Great Britain* (1833). *A System of Universal History in Perspective, Accompanied by an Atlas, Exhibiting Chronology in a Picture of Nations and Progressive Geography in a Series of Maps* (1937). *Temple of Time; or, Chronographer of Universal History* (1844). *Chronographer of Ancient History* (1846). *Chronographer of English History* (1846). *Historic Guide to the Temple of Time* (1846). *A Treatise on the Motive Powers which Produce the Circulation of the Blood* (1846). *Respiration and Its Effects, Particularly as Respects Asiatic Cholera* (1849). *Last Leaves of American History* (1849 enlarged ed., *Late American History: Containing a Full Account of the Courage, Conduct, and Success of John C. Fremont*, 1856). *Astronomy; or, Astronomical Geography* (1853). *Morals for the Young; or, Good Principles Instilling Wisdom* (1857). *Appeal to South Carolina* (1860). *Via Media* (1862).

BIBLIOGRAPHY: Lord, J., *The Life of Emma Willard* (1873). Lutz, A., *Emma Willard: Daughter of Democracy* (1929; rev. ed., *Emma Willard: Pioneer Educator of American Women*, 1964). Woody, T., *A History of Women's Education in the U.S.* (1929).

For articles in reference works, see: *NAW* (article by F. Rudolph).

NANCY A. HARDESTY

Frances Elizabeth Caroline Willard

B. 28 Sept. 1839, Churchville, New York; d. 17 Feb. 1898, New York City
Wrote under: Frances E. Willard
D. of Josiah Flint and Mary Thompson Hill Willard

In 1840, W.'s family moved from New York to Oberlin, Ohio, where both parents attended classes at the then-young college. In 1846, they moved further west, to a homestead on the Wisconsin frontier. W. had very little formal education before college. After graduating from North Western Female College in 1859, she taught in local schools and at female seminaries and colleges and then spent two years traveling in Europe, Russia, and the Near East, meeting expenses by writing weekly articles for Illinois papers.

She was president of Evanston College for Women from 1871 to 1873, when it was absorbed by Northwestern University. She then became dean of women and professor of English and Art. Her career as an educator ended with her resignation in 1874, probably due to conflicts with the university's president, who happened to be W.'s ex-fiancé.

That same summer, W. was asked to lead the Chicago Women's Christian Temperance Union (W.C.T.U.). In October, she became secretary of the state organization, and one month later, at the Cleveland convention that founded the national W.C.T.U., she was chosen as corresponding secretary. She was elected national president in 1879 and remained in that position until her death in 1898, leading for over two decades the largest organization of American women in the 19th c.

From 1876 to 1879, she was head of the publications committee, and she used the W.C.T.U. journal, Our Union, to promote her own views on the necessity of linking the temperance cause with other political issues, particularly woman suffrage. She lectured widely across the country and became a nationally known figure.

The W.C.T.U. advocated not temperance but prohibition. W. was herself responsible for their slogan, "For God, Home, and Native Land," and regularly rang that theme in pamphlets such as Home Protection Manual (1879). This was to some extent a means to retain the support of a basically middle-class and conservative movement for the aims of the more radical W., but it is also a reflection of the fact that alcoholism was not only an individual problem, but a threat to women and children who, in the 19th c., had little protection against the financial and physical exploitation of drunken husbands. In the 1890s, she became interested in socialism and argued that poverty is the cause of intemperance. Long before this country's experiment with prohibition she came to believe that education, not prohibition, is the solution of the problem of alcohol abuse. After her death, however, the W.C.T.U. limited its attention to prohibition and abstinence.

With Mary A. Livermore, W. edited *A Woman of the Century* (1893), the most important 19th-c. biographical reference work on American women. In their preface, the editors draw attention to the "vast array of woman's achievements here chronicled, in hundreds of new vocations and avocations." The articles are laudatory, but also concise and factual.

Nineteen Beautiful Years (1864), W.'s first book, is a brief account of the life of her sister, who died in 1861. It is certainly sentimental, but considerably less so than the flowery preface by John Greenleaf Whittier to the second edition (1885). Her sentimentality is particularly evident in *What Frances Willard Said* (1905), a collection of aphorisms and brief exhortations such as the following appeal for woman suffrage: "by the hours of patient watching over beds where helpless children lay, . . . I charge you, give mothers power to protect, along life's treacherous highway, those whom they have so loved." In fact, W. developed a clear and fairly simple style in which, as in her organizational work, appeals to the ideals of piety, domesticity, and patriotism—although still unpleasant to the modern reader—are connected with a usually well-reasoned argument about the needs of women.

In *Glimpses of Fifty Years* (1889), W.'s sentimental tendencies are used to good effect in the autobiography of a feminist who did not mean to undervalue the "household arts or household saints": "All that I plead for is freedom for girls as well as boys, in the exercise of their special gifts and preferences of brain and hand." For personal and political reasons, W. did not choose to dissociate herself from the sentimental or the domestic modes in either her writing or her organizational work.

WORKS: *Nineteen Beautiful Years; or, Sketches of a Girl's Life* (1864; rev. ed., 1885). *Hints and Helps in Our Temperance Work* (1875). *History of the Women's National Christian Temperance Union* (1876). *Home Protection Manual: Containing an Argument for the Temperance Ballot for Woman and How to Obtain It as a Means of Home Protection* (1879). *Woman and Temperance; or, The Work and Workers of the Women's Christian Temperance Union* (1883). *How to Win: A Book for Girls* (1886). *Woman in the Pulpit*

(1888). *Glimpses of Fifty Years: The Autobiography of an American Woman* (1889). *The Year's Bright Chain: Quotations for the Writings of Frances E. Willard* (1889). *A Classic Town: The Story of Evanston by "an Old Timer"* (1891). *A Woman of the Century; Fourteen Hundred-Seventy Biographical Sketches Accompanied by Portraits of Leading American Women in All Walks of Life* (1893; rev. ed., *American Woman*, 1897). *A Great Mother: Sketches of Madam Willard* (with M. B. Norton, 1894). *Do Everything: A Handbook for the World's White Ribboners* (1895?). *A Wheel within a Wheel: How I Learned to Ride the Bicycle, with Some Reflections by the Way* (1895). *Occupations for Women* (with H. M. Winslow and S. J. White, 1897). *What Frances Willard Said* (Ed. A. A. Gordon, 1905).

BIBLIOGRAPHY: Earhart, Mary, *Frances Willard: From Prayers to Politics* (1944). Strachey, R., *Frances Willard: Her Life and Work* (1912).

For articles in reference works, see: *DAB*, X, 2. *NAW* (article by Mary Earhart Dillon). *NCAB*, 1.

LANGDON FAUST

Catharine Read Arnold Williams

B. *31 Dec. 1787, Providence, Rhode Island; d. 11 Oct. 1872,*
    Providence, Rhode Island
D. *of Alfred and Amey Read Arnold; m. Horatio N. Williams, 1824*

W.'s father was a sea captain. Because her mother died when she was a child, W. was raised and educated by two religious aunts. She did not marry until her mid-thirties, after which she and her husband moved to western New York. Two years later, W. returned to Providence with her infant daughter, Amey, and secured a divorce, although she continued to call herself "Mrs. Williams." W. opened a school, but soon abandoned teaching for health reasons. It was then that she turned to writing.

W.'s first book, *Original Poems on Various Subjects* (1828), sold by subscription, contains some poems that had been published previously. Her next book, *Religion at Home* (1829), was quite successful and went through several editions. During the next two decades, W. wrote histories, biographies, and fiction. About 1849, she moved to Brooklyn, New York, to care for an aged aunt. When her aunt died, she returned to Rhode Island, but never to writing.

In theme and choice of subject, W. always expressed patriotic, republican sentiments. *Tales, National and Revolutionary* (2 vols., 1830–35) and *Biography of Revolutionary Heroes* (1839) reflect her belief in American democracy and her desire to encourage good citizenship. In W.'s opinion, both men and women need to know about and emulate the heroism of Americans in defense of liberty; both need to understand the political and judicial systems. She praises the virtues of patience, industry and self-control, not the display of wealth and aristocratic style, as the marks of a good citizen.

Religion is also a major theme in her works. According to W., dignified and sincere religious expression, not showy religious fervor, was appropriate in the new nation. In *Fall River* (1833), for example, W. argues that the religious display at camp meetings and revivals threatens people's morality, health, and self-control; genuine religion, accordingly, is practiced at home and expressed in the heart. Good manners and useful accomplishments blossom from pure religious sentiment.

There are admirable characters of both sexes in W.'s works. In *Religion at Home, Aristocracy, or, The Holbey Family,* (1832) and other works, "true women" and admirable men are intelligent, sincerely pious, and courageous; they have good natures and even tempers. The men are distinguished from the women principally by their responsibilities and occupations. Honor and admiration characterize men's relationships with their wives; therefore, husbands frequently ask their wives, opinions on public matters. W. is critical of aristocratic pretentions in both sexes, but evil doing is mostly a male trait. When a reader pointed out to W. that her worst characters are male, she responded in the preface to the second volume of *Tales, National and Revolutionary* that she only told stories as they were told to her.

W. insists on the truth and high moral purpose of all her works. To prove that her stories are based on fact, she inserts written "proof" into the text, alluding to her personal acquaintance with the characters, explains where her information was gathered, or gives an historical account of the events behind her story. Sometimes this documentation becomes pedantic, as in *The Neutral French* (1841), but the attention W. gives to historical truth is still impressive. To emphasize the moral of a story, W. sometimes embellishes the facts, as she admits in *Tales, National and Revolutionary*, but she insists she never distorts them. Through her historical fiction, W. warns her readers against errors in personal habits and governmental practices.

W. described her own life as quiet; she said she excluded herself from gaiety not only to have time to earn a living, but also out of a sense of propriety. Prefatory remarks in *Aristocracy; or, The Holbey Family* and elsewhere indicate that W. was somewhat self-conscious about being a *woman* writer on political, legal, and historical topics, yet she never hid the fact of her sex from her readers. In recognition of her talents in those areas, W. was elected to several state historical societies.

For contemporary readers, it is not W.'s moralistic fiction, but her histories that are most interesting. *Fall River* is a fascinating study of ministerial corruption, female textile workers, and legal abuses in the early Republic. *The Neutral French* is a gold mine of carefully collected information on the Acadians. *Tales, National and Revolutionary* and *Biography of Revolutionary Heroes* contain much information about Americans in Revolutionary times. One can't help but regret that this intelligent woman stopped publishing books some twenty-five years before her death.

WORKS: Original Poems, on Various Subjects (1828). *Religion at Home: A Story Founded on Facts* (1829). *Tales, National and Revolutionary* (2 vols., 1830–35). *Aristocracy; or, The Holbey Family: A National Tale* (1832). *Fall River: An Authentic Narrative* (1833). *Biography of Revolutionary Heroes, Containing the Life of Brigadier General William Barton, and also of Captain Stephen Olney* (1839). *The Neutral French; or, The Exiles of Nova Scotia* (1841). *Annals of the Aristocracy, Being a Series of Anecdotes of Some of the Princpal Families of Rhode Island* (2 vols., 1843–45). *Rhode Island Tales* (Ed. H. R. Palmer, 1928; including 5 stories by Williams).

BIBLIOGRAPHY: Rider, S. S., *Biographical Memoirs of Three Rhode Island Authors* (Rhode Island Tracts, no. 11, 1880).
For articles in reference works, see: *DAB.*
Other references: Providence *Daily Journal* (14 Oct. 1872).

SUSAN COULTRAP-McQUIN

Helen Maria Winslow

B. *13 April 1851, Westfield, Vermont; d. 27 March 1938*
Wrote under: Aunt Philury, Helen M. Winslow
D. of Don Avery and Mary Salome Newton Winslow

Educated at the Westfield Vermont Academy, the Vermont Normal School, and the New England Conservatory of Music, W. began her literary career writing pastoral poems and short fiction for such children's periodicals as *Youth's Companion, Wide Awake,* and *Cottage Hearth.* Although she continued to write poetry and children's fiction sporadically throughout her life, she is best remembered not for these "Aunt Philury Papers," but for her newspaper and club work

Early in W.'s career as a journalist, after the death of her parents, she lived in the Boston area with her three sisters. During the 1880s, she wrote for numerous Boston papers, including the *Beacon,* the *Transcript,* the *Advisor,* and the *Saturday Evening Gazette.* Her first novel, *A Bohemian Chapter* (1886), the story of a struggling woman artist, was serialized in the *Beacon.* Her journalistic experiences led her to help form the New England Woman's Press Association (which she served as first treasurer) and the Boston Author's Club (which she served as secretary); she was also vice-president of the Women's Press League.

W.'s most sustained activity resulted from her involvement with the General Federation of Woman's Clubs. In the early 1890s, she was assistant editor of the *Woman's Cycle,* the federation's first official journal, and editor and publisher of its second journal, The *Club Woman.* She also edited the *Delineator's* "Woman's Club" department for thirteen years and was founder and editor of the "Woman's Club Column" in the Boston *Transcript.* From 1898 through 1930, W. annually published the official *Woman's Club Register.* In addition to her direct affiliation with the club movement and its numerous publications, W. wrote numerous articles celebrating club women and their work in journals such as the *Arena,* the *Critic,* and the *Atlantic Monthly.* The most significant of these articles was her extensive history of American woman's clubs, "The Story of the Woman's Club Movement," (*New England Magazine,* June and October 1908).

Among the more interesting of W.'s generally forgotten novels is *Salome Shepard, Reformer* (1893), an indictment of industrial working conditions with suggestions for reform. Salome, a young society woman, awakens to a sense of social responsibility after discovering the unsafe working and intolerable living conditions in the mills she has inherited from her father. Almost single-handedly, Salome initiates a series of reforms, including a model dormitory for the women workers, a social hall for the families of workers, and profit sharing.

W. partly duplicates this plot in *The President of Quex* (1906). In this novel, written in response to Agnes Surbridge's strident denunciation of club women in "The Evolution of a Club Woman—A Story of Ambition Realized" (*Delineator,* 1904), W.'s heroine, the president of a woman's club concerned with municipal reform, becomes aware of abusive child-labor conditions in her factories. Again, the women, this time through their club work, initiate and effect the necessary reforms, with no sacrifice to their home lives.

A Woman for Mayor (1909) is W.'s most effective dramatization of the political sensibilities and capabilities of middle-class women. Written in support of the "municipal-housekeeping" concept of social reform, moderate women's rights, and the Progressive-era concept of expanded social services in local government, the novel relates the story of a young woman who is elected mayor on a platform dedicated to the eradication of political graft and corruption.

Despite both her own achievements and those of her many heroines, W. showed a lifelong ambivalence about the public role of women. In each of her novels, the heroine, after ably demonstrating her superiority, retires willingly to marriage; she claims that marriage will not bring an end to her public activism, although her primary forcus will necessarily be on her home life. In no novel, however, does W. present her heroine after marriage. It is unclear whether this seeming ambivalence results from W.'s desire to defend club women and meet the demands of a literary public in search of the happy ending or from an uncertainty about her own life-style—as her article "Confessions of a Newspaperwoman" (*Atlantic*, February 1905) might suggest. Whatever the reason, W.'s fiction provides useful material for any reader interested in the ongoing debate about the public and private roles of women.

WORKS: *A Bohemian Chapter* (1886). *Salome Shepard, Reformer* (1893). *Mexico Picturesque* (with M. R. Wright, 1897). *Occupations for Women* (with F. Willard, 1898). *Concerning Cats* (1900). *Concerning Polly* (1902). *Little Journeys in Literature* (1902). *Literary Boston of Today* (1903). *Confessions of a Club Woman* (1904). *The Woman of Tomorrow* (1905). *The President of Quex* (1906). *The Pleasuring of Susan Smith* (1908). *Spinster Farm* (1908). *A Woman for Mayor* (1909). *The Road to a Loving Heart* (1926). *Keeping Young Gracefully* (1928).

BIBLIOGRAPHY: Blair, K., "The Clubwoman as Feminist: The Woman's Culture Club Movement in the United States, 1868–1914" (Ph.D. diss., State Univ. of New York at Buffalo, 1976). Blake, F., *The Strike in the American Novel* (1972). Hill, Vicki Lynn, "Strategy and Breadth: The Socialist-Feminist in American Fiction" (Ph.D. diss., State Univ. of New York at Buffalo, 1979). Taylor, W., *The Economic Novel in America* (1942).

For articles in reference works, see: *American Women*, Ed. Howes (1939). *NCAB*, B. *National Cyclopaedia of American Biography* (1927).

Other references: *Atlantic* (Dec. 1894). *Godey's* (Nov. 1893). *Independent* (26 Nov. 1893). *Literary World* (17 June 1893). *Picayune* (7 May 1893).

VICKI LYNN HILL

Sally Sayward Barrell Wood

B. 1 Oct. 1759, York, Maine; d. 6 Jan. 1855, Kennebunk, Maine
Wrote under: Sally Keating
D. of Nathaniel and Sarah Sayward Barrell; m. Richard Keating, 1778; m. Abiel
  Wood, 1804

The first of eleven children, W. was born into a colonial New England family while her father was serving with General James Wolfe, British leader of the attack on Quebec. Her mother was the daughter of Judge Jonathan Sayward, with whom W. lived until she was eighteen. During the American Revolution, Judge Sayward was a Loyalist, and much of his conservatism is evident in W.'s work.

Her first husband was a clerk in her grandfather's office. The Judge gave them a house as a wedding present, and they settled into the cultivated social life that had surrounded her childhood. Two daughters and a son were born before Keating died suddenly in 1783. W. turned to writing, not from any pressing financial need, but because it "soothed many *melancholy*, and sweetened many *bitter* hours." Her work was well received, and she gained a considerable literary reputation.

She stopped writing when she married General Abiel Wood, in 1804. "Madam Wood," as she was then known, took up writing again, after his death in 1811.

Following in the path of such early American novelists as Sarah Wentworth Morton, Susannah H. Rowson, and Hannah Webster Foster, W. occupies an important niche in the development of American fiction, although her work does not mark a radical break from the traditions imported from England. In accordance with her 18th-c. upbringing, she was serious, moralistic, and sentimental. Her stories generally follow a Cinderella pattern centering on a virtuous young woman who either is, or is reputed to be, a poor orphan but who after severe trial is rewarded with a wealthy marriage. Virtue, for W., is more than chastity; it is linked to intelligence and education with a strong infusion of patience and submission. Her heroines redeem, reform, or blunt the evil of the world by the example of their behavior, and if they are passive in suffering vicissitudes, they are strong in the face of vice.

Julia and the Illuminated Baron (1800) is perhaps her best-known work. Certainly it is the most complex, and Julia's progress from nameless orphan to respectably pedigreed wife and mother involves a set of characters (all related by blood) in a series of Gothic adventures. The baron of the title is a member of the Illuminati, a secret society that shocked W.; she presents him as an atheist, anarchist, and mystic who announces proudly, "I am to myself a God, and to myself accountable. . . . if anyone stands in my way, I put him out of it, with as little concern as I would kick a dog." The setting is France, but the characters are clearly recognizable as Americans in their actions and values.

Amelia; or, The Influence of Virtue (1802) states her most constant theme. The gentle heroine, married to a rake, prefers death to divorce and meekly bears the taunts of her husband's mistress and rears his illegitimate children without complaint. She is rewarded in the end with a repentant husband, adoring children, and a respectable position in society. As in all her works, W. does not plumb psychological depths, and the solution is simplistic, but the action is rapid, and her gift for creating melodramatic moments holds the reader's attention.

Ferdinand and Elmira (1804) is an adventure tale, again with intertwined lives of a single family, in a Russian setting that gives an exotic flavor to a moral tale. As it opens, Elmira is a captive in a mysterious castle, and the explanation of this circumstance leads to another mystery. This pattern (of one mystery following the solution of another) is consistent throughout, and the resultant suspense is the primary means of moving the action forward. The ending resolves all, pairs the heroine and hero, rewards the good, and permits the villains an extravagant repentance. W.'s focus is on the morality of the simple life as opposed to the corruption of courts; and, despite her Loyalist grandfather, the tale is clearly antiroyalist in tone.

W. is one of the first writers to embody distinctly American ideals. She does not admire aristocratic idleness; indeed, one of her heroes is praised for his ambition to go into trade, and her young lovers rarely end with titles of nobility. She reflects strongly the responsibilities of freedom so uppermost in the consciousness of the young nation. Typical of her time in sentimental morality and her view of woman's place in society, her work nevertheless reveals an inquiring and imaginative mind searching for new horizons.

WORKS: *Julia and the Illuminated Baron* (1800). *Dorval; or, The Speculator* (1801). *Amelia; or, The Influence of Virtue* (1802). *Ferdinand and Elmira* (1804). *Tales of the Night* (1827).

BIBLIOGRAPHY Goold, W., in *Collections and Proceedings of the Maine Historical Society* (1890). Dunnack, H. E. *The Maine Book* (1920). Sayward, C. A. *The Sayward Family* (1890). Spencer, W. D. *Maine Immortals* (1932).

HELENE KOON

Sarah Chauncey Woolsey

B. 29 Jan. 1835, Cleveland, Ohio; d. 9 April 1905, Newport, Rhode Island
Wrote under: Susan Coolidge
D. of John Mumford and Jane Woolsey

W. spent her formative years in a lively household, amusing her three younger sisters, brother, and cousin with games and stories. She was first educated in Cleveland private schools, then sent to a boarding school in Hanover, New Hampshire, nicknamed "The Nunnery." From 1855 to 1870, W. lived with her parents in New Haven, Connecticut, where her uncle Theodore Dwight Woolsey was president of Yale. During the Civil War, she spent one summer working with her friend Helen Hunt Jackson in the New Haven Government Hospital and ten months serving as an assistant superintendent at the Lowell General Hospital, Portsmouth Grove, Rhode Island.

After her father's death in 1870, W. moved to Newport, Rhode Island, a residence interrupted only by journeys to Europe, California, and Colorado and, in her later years, by summers in the Catskills. In 1871, her career as children's author began with the publication of *The New Year's Bargain*. The Katy series (1872–91) brought her fame. She also wrote poetry and magazine articles, served for a time as children's book reviewer for the *Literary World*, and worked as reader and editor for her publishers, Roberts Brothers.

Although *The New Year's Bargain* employs fantasy reminiscent of Andersen in a story of two German children who trick the months into telling them stories, *What Katy Did* (1872) establishes W. as a writer of realistic juvenile fiction, similar to Louisa Alcott in her gift of depicting real American girls in an appealing family setting. Katy Carr, an impulsive, boisterous, and ever-well-intentioned girl who leads her younger sisters and brothers into scrapes, finally matures through suffering and the acceptance of responsibility. Her adventures continue in *What Katy Did at School* (1873) when Katy and her sister Clover become students at a New England boarding school and meet the irrepressible Rose Red, beloved by more than one generation of schoolgirl readers in America and England.

Katy travels to Europe and finds romance in *What Katy Did Next* (1886), where W. uses the travelogue, a popular formula in children's literature of the period, to carry a rather pedestrian plot. The Katy series concludes with *Clover* (1888) and *In the High Valley* (1891), as the six Carrs grow up and marry. The charm of the final books lies less in the portraits of the young people than in the Colorado setting, which W. remembered so vividly from her trips to visit Helen Hunt Jackson.

W.'s other juvenile novels also feature plucky girls in realistic settings, but none of the heroines has Katy's imagination and vitality.

Among the notable collections of W.'s short stories are *Mischief's Thanksgiving* (1874), *Nine Little Goslings* (1875), *Cross Patch* (1881), *A Round Dozen* (1883), and *Just Sixteen* (1889). These volumes illustrate her capacity for invention and her range—stories for children and for adolescents, tales of realism and of fantasy. *Nine Little Goslings* and *Cross Patch* cleverly translate Mother Goose stories into tales peopled with real children in contemporary settings.

Although W. hoped to achieve distinction as a poet, her three volumes of verse for adults, *Verses* (1880), *A Few More Verses* (1889), and *Last Verses* (1906), reveal little more than careful workmanship, a sober acceptance of suffering and death, and a certain flair for the narrative poem.

A talented and versatile writer of children's fiction, W. was once almost as popular as Louisa Alcott in both England and America. Today she is still remembered for her stories of the incomparable Katy Carr.

WORKS: *The New Year's Bargain* (1871). *What Katy Did* (1872). *What Katy Did at School* (1873). *Mischief's Thanksgiving, and Other Stories* (1874). *Nine Little Goslings* (1875). *For Summer Afternoons* (1876). *Autobiography and Correspondence of Mrs. Delany* (edited by Woolsey, 1879). *Eyebright* (1879). *The Diary and Letters of Frances Burney, Madame D'Arblay* (edited by Woolsey, 1880). *A Guernsey Lily; or, How the Feud Was Healed* (1880). *Verses* (1880). *Cross Patch, and Other Stories* (1881). *My Household Pets* by T. Gautier (translated by Woolsey, 1882). *A Round Dozen* (1883). *A Little Country Girl* (1885). *One Day in a Baby's Life* by M. Arnaud (translated by Woolsey, 1886). *What Katy Did Next* (1886). *A Short History of the City of Philadelphia from Its Foundation to the Present Time* (1887). *Clover* (1888). *A Few More Verses* (1889). *Just Sixteen* (1889). *The Day's Message* (1890). *In the High Valley* (1891). *Letters of Jane Austen* (edited by Woolsey, 1892). *Rhymes and Ballads for Boys and Girls* (1892). *The Barberry Bush* (1893).

Not Quite Eighteen (1894). An Old Convent School in Paris, and Other Papers (1895). Curly Locks (1899). A Little Knight of Labor (1899). Little Tommy Tucker (1900). Two Girls (1900). Little Bo-Peep (1901). Uncle and Aunt (1901). The Rule of Three (1904). Last Verses (1906). A Sheaf of Stories (1906).

BIBLIOGRAPHY: Banning, E., Helen Hunt Jackson (1973). Darling, R. L., The Rise of Children's Book Reviewing in America, 1865–1881 (1968). Kilgour, R. L., Messrs. Roberts Brothers, Publishers (1952). Meigs, C., A Critical History of Children's Literature (rev. ed., 1969).
  For articles in reference works, see: NAW (article by F. C. Darling).
  Other references: Horn Book 35 (1959).

PHYLLIS MOE

Constance Fenimore Woolson

B. 5 March 1840, Claremont, New Hampshire; d. 24 Jan. 1894, Venice, Italy
Wrote under: Anne March, Constance Fenimore Woolson
D. of Charles Jarvis and Hannah Cooper Pomeroy Woolson

W. was the sixth of nine children. She was the grand-niece of James Fenimore Cooper. After the death of three older sisters from scarlet fever, W. moved at a very early age with her family to Cleveland. She attended school there until enrolling in Madame Chegary's school in New York City, from which she graduated in 1858. Her childhood summers were spent at the family cottage at Mackinac Island, later to become the setting for a number of her short stories. After her father's death in 1869, she travelled extensively in the South with her mother. Upon her death in 1879, W. and her sister, Clare Benedict, traveled in Europe, where W. spent the remainder of her life. She died in Venice after falling or leaping from her bedroom window. Whether her death was the result of delirium from influenza or of depression has never been determined. At the time of her death she had achieved a moderate degree of recognition as a writer; today her works are virtually unknown.

W.'s first book, The Old Stone House, a book for children, was published in 1872 under the pseudonym of Anne March. Of more importance, however, is the collection Castle Nowhere: Lake-Country Sketches

(1875), which contains nine stories fashioned from her observations of Mackinac Island. *Castle Nowhere* has been compared favorably with Sarah Orne Jewett's *Deephaven* (1877) and Mary Noailles Murfree's *In the Tennessee Mountains* (1884).

Of even better quality is her second volume of short stories, *Rodman the Keeper: Southern Sketches* (1880), which sympathetically treats the Reconstruction period. One of the most skillfully written pieces in this collection, "Old Gardiston," depicts the downfall of an ancient southern family, and concludes with the burning of their mansion before it can be possessed by a northern businessman and his wife.

Anne (1882) was published as a novel shortly after its serialization in *Harper's*. Set in various places, including Mackinac Island, Pennsylvania, and West Virginia, the novel tells the story of Anne Douglas in a somewhat melodramatic plot including a love affair and a murder trial. In the 1880s *Anne* was a popular novel; today it is a forgotten work which deserves renewed attention.

For the Major (1883), set in Far Edgerly, a mountain village in western North Carolina, is a tale of Sara Carroll's return home from a long journey and her discovery that her father, Major Carroll, has become senile and that her stepmother is laboring to shield both the Major and the townspeople from this knowledge. W.'s story provides an excellent blend of comic treatment of the inhabitants of Far Edgerly and a noble portrait of the declining Major and his compassionate wife. It is considered one of W.'s finest works.

East Angels (1886), set in Florida, was also a popular work at the time of its publication. W. brings together a group of wealthy northerners and impoverished southern aristocrats in this postwar novel of reconciliation.

In her novel *Jupiter Lights* (1889), W. incorporates Georgia, the Lake Country, and Italy as settings. Although the plot is contrived and the action melodramatic, the work has been noted for its advances in the psychological complexity of the characters, especially the heroine, Eve Bruce.

W.'s final novel, *Horace Chase* (1894), set in Asheville, North Carolina, after the war, chronicles the marriage of Horace Chase, self-made millionaire, and Ruth Franklin, his headstrong young wife. Ruth becomes infatuated with a young man of her own age, but is forgiven by her husband who says at the close of the novel, "I don't know that I have been so perfect myself, that I have any right to judge you." In a letter to Henry Mills Alden, W. notes that the essence of the novel lies in that last sentence and concludes, "Do you think it is impossible? I do not."

Two volumes of Italian stories, *The Front Yard, and Other Italian Stories* (1895) and *Dorothy, and Other Italian Stories* (1896), as well as a volume of travel sketches, *Mentone, Cairo, and Corfu* (1896) were published after W.'s death. The Italian stories include some of her best work, such as "The Front Yard," the story of Prudence Wilkin, a New England woman who accompanies her wealthy cousin to Italy. Prudence marries an Italian waiter who dies after their first year of marriage leaving her a house inhabited by eight children and other assorted relatives whom Prudence supports until her death sixteen years later.

A minor writer who produced a number of fine stories, W. is to be noted as a pioneer both in local-color writing and in her depiction of a number of female characters—such as Ruth Franklin of *Horace Chase* or Margaret Harold of *East Angels*—which anticipates female characterization of 20th-c. literature.

WORKS: *The Old Stone House* (1872). *Castle Nowhere: Lake-Country Sketches* (1875). *Rodman the Keeper: Southern Sketches* (1880). *Anne* (1882). *For the Major* (1883). *East Angels* (1886). *Jupiter Lights* (1889). *Horace Chase* (1894). *The Front Yard, and Other Italian Stories* (1895). *Dorothy, and Other Italian Stories* (1896). *Mentone, Cairo, and Corfu* (1896).

BIBLIOGRAPHY: Benedict, C., ed., *Five Generations (1785-1923)* (3 vols., 1929-30). James, H., *Partial Portraits* (1888). Kern, J., *Constance Fenimore Woolson: Literary Pioneer* (1934). Moore, R., *Constance F. Woolson* (1963).
Other references: *SAQ* (38, April 1938; 39, June 1940). *Miss Q* 29 (Fall 1976).

ANNE ROWE

Katharine Prescott Wormeley

B. *14 Jan. 1830, Ipswich, England; d. 4 Aug. 1908, Jackson, New Hampshire*
D. *of Ralph and Caroline Wormeley*

W. was descended, on her mother's side of the family, from Boston merchants and, on her father's, from a long line of Virginians. The family lived in England for many years, settling in the U.S. after her father's death in 1852.

At the beginning of the Civil War, W. threw herself into volunteer work. She formed the local chapter of the Woman's Union in Newport, Rhode Island, and headed it until 1862. She also obtained a contract from the federal government to manufacture clothing for the troops, thus giving employment to otherwise destitute soldiers' wives. In April, 1862, W.

began working for the U.S. Sanitary Commission, a private volunteer organization, as a matron on a hospital ship. Later that year, she became
"lady superintendent" of Lowell General Hospital in Portsmouth Grove,
Rhode Island. Her health, however, gave out after a year, and she returned home to Newport.

After the war, W. continued her charitable work. She helped found the
Newport Charity Organization Society in 1874 and served it in various
capacities for the next fifteen years. She also established an industrial
school for girls that offered classes in cooking, sewing, and domestic management.

Besides charity work, W's passion was for literature. Fluent in French,
she translated many of the works of Balzac, Molière, Daudet, and Saint-
Simon. In 1892, she published *A Memoir of Honoré de Balzac*.

In *The Other Side of War* (1889), W. describes her function on the
hospital ship *Daniel Webster*: "Our duty is to be very much that of a
housekeeper. We attend to the beds, the linen, the clothing of the patients;
we have a pantry and store-room, and are required to do all the cooking
for the sick, and see that it is properly distributed according to the sur-
geons' orders; we are also to have a general superintendence over the condition of the wards and over the nurses, who are all men." W. and her
companions were on duty almost constantly; when they could relax, space
and privacy were limited.

When W. was loaned temporarily to the Medical Department of the
Army, she discovered conditions that were, incredibly, worse than what
she had already seen. Accustomed to abundant supplies of food, bandages,
and medications, she found the Army lacked adequate stores of all three.
Because of that, many men died whom, W. believes, the Sanitary Commission might have saved. The commission's example finally shamed the government into reorganizing its medical department in July 1862. Then, W.
claims with pride, the commission could resume its original functions, "in-
specting the condition of the camps and regiments, and continuing on a
large scale its supply business."

The Other Side of War is an appropriate title for W.'s work. As she
notes, it is far too easy, both for her contemporaries and modern historians, to get caught up in the romance and glory of war without fully ac-
knowledging the human suffering which invariably accompanies it. She
and the countless other women, who worked in the hospitals of the Civil
War, in both the North and South, remind us of its true horror.

WORKS: *The United States Sanitary Commission: A Sketch of Its Purpose
and Work* (1863). *The Other Side of War* (1889). *A Memoir of Honoré de
Balzac* (1892).

BIBLIOGRAPHY: Brockett, L. P., and M. C. Vaughn, Woman's Work in the Civil War (1867). Massey, M. E., Bonnet Brigades (1966). Maxwell, W. O., Lincoln's Fifth Wheel (1956).

JANET E. KAUFMAN

Mabel Osgood Wright

B. 26 Jan. 1859, New York City; d. 16 July 1934, Fairfield, Connecticut
Wrote under: Barbara, Mabel Osgood Wright
D. of Samuel and Ellen Murdock Osgood; m. James Osborne Wright, 1884

W.'s father was a Unitarian minister who late in life became an Episcopalian; the Osgood family lived in a large house in lower Manhattan when there were still cows pastured nearby. Educated at home and at a private school, W. was a keen amateur naturalist from her youth, enjoying long summer vacations at the family summer home.

With her husband, a dealer in rare books and art (whom she referred to as "Evan" in her semi-autobiographical Barbara books) she lived in Fairfield, Connecticut. She apparently had no children.

W. was the first president of the Audubon Society of Connecticut and a member of the American Ornithologists' Union and the Connecticut Society of Colonial Dames—a much more exclusive organization than the Daughters of the American Revolution, which she ridiculed in *The Woman Errant* (1904).

W.'s first published books were about nature. Three—*The Friendship of Nature* (1894), *Birdcraft* (1895), and *Flowers and Ferns in Their Haunts* (1901)—were written for adults, but most are for children. As was common in 19th-c. children's nature books, W. taught about nature in story form, creating fictional children to lead the little readers through their lessons. *Tommy-Anne and the Three Hearts* (1896) and its sequel, *Wabeno the Magician* (1899), tell of a young tomboy who discovers the "Magic Spectacles" that combine truth with imagination. Wearing her spectacles she can converse with the grass, flowers, insects, squirrels, and even her dog, Waddles.

Among W.'s most popular works are the semiautobiographical Barbara books, particularly the first, *The Garden of a Commuter's Wife* (1901), which introduces her alter ego, Barbara, who lives in the country with her husband and shares her life with many eccentric friends. W. calls this book and *The Garden, You, and I* (1906) "pages from Barbara's Garden Book"; three other Barbara books bear designations intended to reveal other aspects of Barbara's life. *People of the Whirlpool* (1903) is "from the Experience Book," *Princess Flower-Hat* (1910) is "from the Perplexity Book," and *A Woman Errant* is "from the Wonder Book." W. blends fanciful fiction with social comment, showing that she was an interested observer of the changes taking place in New York society—particularly among her own class of people. Servants provide comic relief.

A Woman Errant is the most serious book of the series. It is a melodramatic statement of W.'s belief that woman lives for and through man. According to W., women who leave their proper sphere for a career become bisexual. She shows a woman doctor who causes her own son's death because of her lack of the right kind of ability. W.'s attack on career women is not atypical of popular writers, even the professional women writers.

W.'s novels, set in the same area as her Barbara stories, are all romances, and in most of them she focuses on marriage as the most important part of life. In her last, *Eudora's Men* (1931), she underlines the importance of men to women by tracing a family from the beginning of the Civil War down to the present, when one of the youngest generation, a woman doctor, almost ruins the life of her husband by her "unnatural" concept of marriage.

In her autobiography, *My New York* (1926), she writes of her life up to the death of her beloved father and her engagement, focusing entirely on the city. It is a beautifully written picture of life in lower Manhattan in the 1860s and 1870s, giving her gift for observation and social comment its best exercize; it memorializes old New York, which had all but vanished when she wrote the book.

While W. is historically an important figure in popular nature writing, she did not make a successful transition to fiction as did Gene Stratton-Porter. But her autobiography is a charming, nostalgic book written without the bitterness she showed in other books when writing of the changes in society.

WORKS: *The Friendship of Nature* (1894). *Birdcraft* (1895). *Tommy-Anne and the Three Hearts* (1896). *Citizen Bird* (1897). *Four-footed Americans and Their Kin* (1898). *Wabeno the Magician* (1899). *The Dream Fox Story Book* (1900). *Flowers and Ferns in Their Haunts* (1901). *The Garden of a Commuter's Wife* (1901). *Dogtown* (1902). *Aunt Jimmy's Will* (1903). *People of the*

Whirlpool (1903). *The Woman Errant* (1904). *At the Sign of the Fox* (1905). *The Garden, You, and I* (1906). *Gray Lady and the Birds* (1907). *The Open Window* (1908). *Poppea of the Post-office* (1909). *Princess Flower Hat* (1910). *The Love that Lives* (1911). *The Stranger at the Gate* (1913). *My New York* (1926). *Captains of the Watch of Life and Death* (1927). *Eudora's Men* (1931).

BIBLIOGRAPHY: NAW (article by R. H. Welker). *NYT* (18 July 1934).

BEVERLY SEATON

Edith Franklin Wyatt

B. 14 Sept. 1873, Tomah, Wisconsin; d. Oct. 1958, Chicago, Illinois
D. of Franklin and Marian La Grange Wyatt

A self-designated "middle-class American," W. spent her earliest years in midwestern towns where her father was a railroad and mining engineer. Settled in a modest, neighborly Chicago home in the 1880s, she and her two younger sisters shared wide-ranging interests with their mother, who was later a privately published poet. W. attended Bryn Mawr from 1892 to 1894 and taught at a local girls' school for five years.

W.'s first publication, "Three Stories of Contemporary Chicago" (1900), caught the attention of William Dean Howells, who publicly praised her early fiction and remained an admiring friend. While teaching at Hull House and participating in The Little Room, Chicago's preeminent salon, she produced most of her fiction during this decade.

After her *McClure's* report on the 1909 Cherry Mine fire, W. was in great demand during the 1910s as a social commentator and Progressive activist, promoting the causes of working-class women, child laborers, victims of the Eastland pleasure-boat disaster, and suffragists. A founding Board member of *Poetry*, her concurrent literary work included a report on working-women's budgets, a documentary play, poems, and literary criticism. Socially conscientious but tempermentally retiring, W. lived with her mother and maintained a few close friendships with people who shared her commitments.

Her creative talent seems to have exhausted itself in 1923, when she published her second novel after a year as assistant editor for *McClure's*.

Her remaining work was mostly retrospective; she memoralized deceased colleagues and Chicago's past and also collected her earlier short stories.

The stories first published in *Every One His Own Way* (1901) demonstrate W.'s attention to the everyday strengths and distinctive mannerisms of urban ethnic types as well as her exposure of genteel intolerance. Recurring characters and neighborhood settings link together stories ranging from tragedy to satire. "A Matter of Taste" is representative: it recounts a literary critic's disdain for the participative, popular musical tastes of a German-American couple, while embodying W.'s own characteristic perspective in the clear-sighted observations of the critic's sister.

A similar dichotomy between conventionality and wholesomeness informs W.'s first novel, *True Love* (1903). Snobbish Norman Hubbard —whose "sepulchral" Chicago home traps visitors in vacuous conversation —engages himself to an equally convention-bound woman, until they can no longer stand each other's narrowness. A second romance between unpretentious Chicagoan Emily Marsh, whose simple family home welcomes friends to billiards and cards, and an equally ordinary country man, leads to marriage.

W. believed that heterogeneous Americans share primarily the experience of migration: "Movement through a variety of country" is, she declares, the unifying theme of the poems in *The Wind in the Corn* (1917). "To a River God" exemplifies her poetry's dynamic attention to geography; unity-in-diversity theme; and ritualistic, chanting rhythms, which occasionally disintegrate into sing-song. Most admired were W.'s urban poems; "November in the City" and "City Equinoctial" epitomize her unconventional portrayal of natural cycles in city as well as country scenes.

Original observation and social perspective mark W.'s literary criticism and social commentary. A well-chosen selection in *Great Companions* (1917) demonstrates her concerns with national literary culture, writers' attitudes toward women, and autobiographies of working people. "The Dislike of Human Interest" clarifies the political basis for her objections to standardized literary stereotypes.

Invisible Gods (1923) tries to combine W.'s fictional talents with her political commitments in a sociological novel about three generations of a Chicago family. But an uncharacteristically loose, episodic structure and wordy prose undercut her uncompromising vision and talent for characterization.

W. combined a pluralistic appreciation of common people and regional integrity with original observation and satiric humor in her fiction, poetry, literary criticism, and social commentaries. Her early fiction and essays represent her best work, as fine as that of Howells and undeservedly ignored by literary historians and critics.

WORKS: *Every One His Own Way* (1901). *True Love: A Comedy of the Affections* (1903). *The Whole Family* (with W. D. Howells, H. James, et al., 1907). *Making Both Ends Meet* (with S. A. Clark, 1911). *Great Companions* (1917). *The Wind in the Corn, and Other Poems* (1917). *The Invisible Gods* (1923). *Art and the Worth While* (with R. M. Lovett, Z. Gale, et al., 1929). *The Satyr's Children* (1939). *Two Fairy Tales: The Pursuit of Happiness and The Air Castle* (n.d.).

The Edith Franklin Wyatt Manuscripts at the Newberry Library, Chicago, Illinois, include a box of correspondance and three boxes of published and unpublished works.

BIBLIOGRAPHY: Boston *Transcript* (22 Dec. 1917). *Harper's* (Oct. 1901). New York *Tribune* (11 March 1923). *North American Review* (May 1903; March 1917). *Poetry* (Jan. 1918).

SIDNEY H. BREMER

Elinor Hoyt Wylie

B. 7 Sept. 1885, Somerville, New Jersey; d. 16 Dec. 1928, New York City
Wrote under: Elinor Wylie
D. of Henry Martyn and Anne McMichael Hoyt; m. Philip Hichborn, 1905; m. Horace Wylie, 1916; m. William Rose Benét, 1923

W., the eldest of five children born into a socially and politically prominent family, grew up and attended private schools in Philadelphia and Washington, D.C. Her elopement in 1910, with a married Washington lawyer, Horace Wylie, and abandonment of her husband and son became a highly publicized scandal. To escape the notoriety, the couple lived for a few years in England as Mr. and Mrs. Horace Waring. There she published—privately and anonymously—her first book of poetry, *Incidental Numbers* (1912). The pair returned to the U.S. before WWI, living first in Boston, then in Augusta, Georgia, and Washington, D.C.

In Washington, W. became friendly with the writers William Rose Benét, Edmund Wilson, and John Dos Passos, who encouraged her to take her writing seriously. After separating from Wylie in 1921, she moved to New York and captivated the literary world with her beauty, elegance, conversation, and acid wit. She married Benét in 1923.

During the eight years from 1921 until her death, W. served as a contributing editor of the *New Republic* and wrote short stories, literary criticism, four volumes of poetry, and four novels. Two of the latter derive from her great interest in the Romantic movement, especially in the poet Shelley. *The Orphan Angel* (1926) is a fantasy of Shelley searching across the expanding American West for a mysterious and beautiful woman. *Mr. Hodge and Mr. Hazard* (1928) recounts the decline of Romanticism in the tale of "the last Romantic poet" confronting the bourgeois world of the Victorians. Much careful scholarship went into the backgrounds of these novels.

W.'s talent is notable, but problematic. A tension between opposing impulses often led her to miss her mark; but when these tensions were confronted and developed, her work achieved its full potential in powerful poems of heightened irony. W.'s technical facility and taste for elegance produced in her novels and some of her verse a polished surface with little sustaining depth. No doubt aware of this, she called her first full-length novel, *Jennifer Lorn* (1923), "a sedate extravaganza." One critic described it as "a dish of curds and cream flavoured with saffron." The book's heroine is such a delicacy herself—elaborately confected, a visual delight, but entirely unsubstantial. One focus of the novel's rather mild satire is society's vision of women as decorative objects.

The Venetian Glass Nephew (1925) concerns itself with the conflicting claims of art and nature, but thematic development is submerged to elegant sensual richness. Rosalba Berni undergoes the painful transformation into glass in order to become a suitable bride for the manufactured Virginio. One of the characters notes: "The result, although miraculous, is somewhat inhuman. I have known fathers who submitted their daughters to the ordeal, husbands who forced it upon their wives."

In her best poetry, W. dealt more pointedly with the conflicts that claimed her attention: the problem of the feeling self smoldering beneath its decorative surface. Statements of this theme appear in "Sleeping Beauty," "Sanctuary," "Where, O Where?" "The Lie," and "Full Moon." In the last poem, the speaker, dressed elegantly in "silk and miniver," cries: "There I walked, and there I raged; / The spiritual savage caged. . . ." Images of falsehood—masks, disguises, and costumes—convey the tension between beautiful exterior and turbulent interior, between felt passion and enforced restraint.

Carl Van Vechten called *Jennifer Lorn* "the only successfully sustained satire in English with which I am acquainted." Praise for her other works was equally adulatory. Recent criticism has been scanty and less favorable. The inclusion of W. in recently published anthologies of women poets indicates a reawakening of appreciation; it is time for her to receive a full-scale literary reappraisal.

WORKS: *Incidental Numbers* (1912). *Nets to Catch the Wind* (1921). *Black Armour* (1923). *Jennifer Lorn* (1923). *The Venetian Glass Nephew* (1925). *The Orphan Angel* (1926). *Angels and Earthly Creatures* (1928). *Mr. Hodge and Mr. Hazard* (1928). *Trivial Breath* (1928). *Collected Poems of Elinor Wylie* (1932). *Collected Prose of Elinor Wylie* (1933). *Last Poems of Elinor Wylie* (1943).

BIBLIOGRAPHY: Colum, M., *Life and the Dream* (1947). Gray, T. A., *Elinor Wylie* (1969). Gregory, H., and M. Zaturenska, *A History of American Poetry, 1900–1940* (1942). Hoyt, N., *Elinor Wylie: The Portrait of an Unknown Lady* (1935). Kazin, A., *On Native Grounds* (1942). Olson, S., *Elinor Wylie: A Life Apart* (1979). Van Doren, C., *Three Worlds* (1936). Van Vechten, C., Introduction to *Jennifer Lorn* (1923). West, R., *Ending in Earnest* (1931). Wilson, E., *The Shores of Light* (1952).

Other references: *The Dial* (June 1923). *ES* 20 (Dec. 1938). *NewR* (5 Dec. 1923; 6 Feb. 1929; 7 Sept. 1932). *PMLA* (1941). *VQR* (July 1930).

KAREN F. STEIN

Anzia Yezierska

B. ca. 1880, Plinsk, Russian Poland; d. 21 Nov. 1970, Ontario, California
D. of Baruch and Pearl Yezierska; m. Jacob Gordon, 1910;
  m. Arnold Levitas, 1911

Y. was born into the poverty and orthodoxy of an East European *shtetl*. When her large family came to the Lower East Side of New York in the 1890s, her father clung to his life of full-time Talmudic study and the wife and children supported the family.

Y. had little opportunity for formal education; she worked in sweatshops and laundries and learned what she could from night-school English classes and borrowed books. A scholarship enabled her to attend a training program for domestic science teachers, and from 1905 to 1913 she taught cooking in an elementary school. Her determination to rise from the dirt and drudgery of poverty to "make from herself a person" led to an early break with her family, the failure of two brief marriages, and the surrender of her daughter to the father's care.

A meeting with John Dewey, then dean at Columbia Teachers College, led to a romantic involvement that Y. wrote about repeatedly, in disguised form, in her later fiction. Dewey wrote a number of poems to Y. during the years 1917 and 1918; two of these recently unearthed poems appear in Y.'s books of 1932 and 1950, attributed only to the Dewey-figures "Henry Scott" and "John Morrow."

Y. published her first short story in 1915; in the next decade her stories appeared in respected magazines. Edward J. O'Brien praised "The Fat of the Land" as the best short story of 1919. When Hollywood bought the film rights to the short-story collection *Hungry Hearts* (1920) and also hired Y. as a salaried writer, the impoverished immigrant became overnight a wealthy celebrity.

But Y. could not write in materialistic Hollywood. She wrote productively in New York for a few more years, but by the time she lost her money in the Depression, she had also lost her creative inspiration. She joined the Work Projects Administration (WPA) Writers Project in the 1930s; published an autobiography in 1950 and then a few stories about old age; and was poor and forgotten long before her death in 1970.

In *Hungry Hearts* (1920), ten stories of Lower East Side life, Y.'s immigrant characters struggle with the disillusioning America of poverty and exploitation while they search for the "real" America of their ideals. The stories, like all of her fiction, are realistic, passionate, occasionally autobiographical, sometimes formless and overwrought; their effusive language suggests the style and intonation of an immigrant speaker. Women are the chief protagonists—women whose bodies are tied to sweatshop or household drudgery but whose spirits hunger for love, beauty, and some measure of independence, self-expression, and dignity.

In *Salome of the Tenements* (1922), her first novel, she exhibits more passion than craftsmanship. It explores the attraction between two of Y.'s stock character types: the "Russian Jewess," idealistic and emotional, and the rational, aloof, "born American" male. Sonya Vrunsky, poor girl of the ghetto, marries wealthy John Manning. But Sonya is not happy; she renounces her marriage and seeks to build an independent life based on her own talents.

Y. prefaces the short-story collection *Children of Loneliness* (1923) with a revealing essay, "Mostly about Myself," in which she discusses her tortured efforts to write. *Bread Givers* (1925) is an autobiographical novel about a dominating, unbending Talmudic scholar and his daughter's struggle to break free of subservient roles and to forge for herself an independent, fulfilling life. It is worth rediscovering.

Arrogant Beggar (1927) mixes social criticism with sentimentality for an effect that is at once trite and moving. Adele Lindner is from a poor neighborhood on New York's East Side; her gratitude to the Hellman Home for Working Girls turns to disgust with the patronizing attitudes and policies of her rich benefactors. She denounces the home and finds true charity and a satisfying life among her own people.

All I Could Never Be (1932), Y.'s last and not very successful novel, is at least a useful companion to her autobiography, *Red Ribbon on a White Horse* (1950). The latter is semifictional and unreliable, but the book is interesting for its discussion of the bureaucratic absurdities of the WPA and for its account of Y.'s painful attempts to come to terms with herself, her values, and her immigrant Jewish heritage, and to find some real happiness and peace.

Y. was not a master of style, plot development, or characterization, but the intensity of feeling and aspiration evident in her narratives often transcends the stylistic imperfections. Her work deserves consideration as one of the few chronicles of the immigrant experience from a woman's viewpoint and as an early attempt in American fiction to present the struggles of women against family, religious injunctions, and social and economic obstacles to create for themselves an independent identity.

WORKS: *Hungry Hearts* (1920; film version, 1922). *Salome of the Tenements* (1922, film version, 1925). *Children of Loneliness* (1923). *Bread Givers* (1925). *Arrogant Beggar* (1927). *All I Could Never Be* (1932). *Red Ribbon on a White Horse* (1950). *The Open Cage: An Anzia Yezierska Collection* (1979).

BIBLIOGRAPHY: Auden, W. H., Introduction to *Red Ribbon on a White Horse* by A. Yezierska (1950). Baum, C., P. Hyman, and S. Michel, *The Jewish Woman in America* (1975). Boydston, J., Introduction to *The Poems of John Dewey* (1977). Harris, A. K., Introduction to *Bread Givers* by A. Yezierska (1975). Harris, A. K., Introduction to *The Open Cage* by A. Yezierska (1979). Henriksen, L. L., Afterward to *The Open Cage* by A. Yezierska (1979). Sullivan, R. M., "Anzia Yezierska: An American Writer" (Ph.D. diss., Univ. of California, Berkeley, 1975).

For articles in reference works, see: *20thCA. 20thCAS.*

Other references: *Bookman* (Nov. 1923). *MELUS* (1980). *NYT* (23 Nov. 1970; 6 April 1978; 27 April 1978; 24 Feb. 1980). *Studies in American Jewish Literature* 1 (Winter 1975).

PEGGY STINSON

Eliza Ann Youmans

B. 17 Dec. 1826, Greenfield, Saratoga County, New York
D. of Vincent and Catherine Scofield Youmans

Y.'s father was a farmer and mechanic. As a young girl, she enabled her brother, Edward Livingston, to pursue his scientific studies despite his near blindness by reading to him and assisting in his experimentation; he founded and edited the *Popular Science Monthly*, and a younger brother became a noted physician.

Like her brothers, Y. worked to disseminate scientific knowledge through writing and education. She hoped to establish botany as a fourth fundamental branch of education (with reading, writing, and arithmetic) to correct the "almost total lack of any systematic cultivation of the observing powers." Botany seemed the most suitable discipline to advance independent analysis and reasoned judgement because of its abundant and ever-varying materials and precise vocabulary.

The First Book of Botany (1870) develops a new method of study founded on systematic observation and independent thought. It is copiously illustrated and written with the assumption that field samples are in hand.

There were six editions of the book and a sequel for more advanced study, *The Second Book of Botany* (1873). This more close and thorough study introduces scientific notation; methods of gathering, pressing, and mounting specimens; and explanation of plant processes. In the introduction, Y. explains her wish to remedy the common faults of "carelessness in observation, looseness in the application of words, hasty inferences from partial data, and lack of method in the contents of the mind." The appendix, "On the Educational Claims of Botany," describes the natural laws of mental growth and their affinity to the study of botany.

To supplement the study of botany, Y. adapted *Henslow's Botanical Charts* (1873) for American use by substituting native plants for English species not found in the U.S. and enlarging the diagram for classroom use.

After the favorable reception of her translations in the *Popular Science Monthly* of the lectures of Armand de Quatrefages de Breau on the newly established field of anthropology, the series was collected in *The Natural History of Man: A Course of Elementary Lectures* (1875). Again, her concern is for a basic discussion of important scientific disciplines. The unity of the human species, the antiquity and origin of man (in which the theory of evolution was refuted), and human races and cultures are covered. Y. includes an essay explaining evolution to present a balanced treatment of a controversial issue.

Y.'s interest in practical self-instruction and the systemization of basic skills led her to adapt the English handbook, *Lessons on Cookery* (1879); she includes an appendix on diet.

In Appleton's series of science textbooks, she combined her earlier works on botany in *Descriptive Botany* (1885) and abridged the series' sequel to her book *Bently's Physiological Botany* (1886).

Y.'s commitment to the application of scientific knowledge to everyday life encompassed kitchen and classroom. She realized the potential value of systematic scientific study at an early age and of a general understanding of basic scientific principles, and her insights into the educational process are incorporated into teaching methods today.

WORKS: *The First Book of Botany* (1870). *The Second Book of Botany* (1873). *Henslow's Botanical Charts* (edited by Youmans, 1873). *The Natural History of Man: A Course of Elementary Lectures by A. de Quatrefages de Breau* (translated by Youmans, 1875). *Lessons in Cookery* (edited by Youmans, 1879). *Descriptive Botany* (1885). *Bently's Physiological Botany* (edited and abridged by Youmans, 1886).

BIBLIOGRAPHY: For articles in reference works, see: *AA. Appleton's Cyclopaedia of American Biography*, Eds. J. G. Wilson and J. Fiske (1889). *CAL. A Critical Dictionary of English Literature and British and American Authors*, Ed. S. A. Allibone (1871). *A Dictionary of American Authors*, Ed. O. F. Adams (1905). *A Dictionary of North American Authors Deceased Before 1950*, Ed. W. S. Wallace (1951). *NCAB*, 5. *A Supplement to Allibone's Critical Dictionary*, Ed. J. F. Kirk (1891).

ELIZABETH ROBERTS

Charlotte Shapiro Zolotow

B. 26 June 1915, Norfolk, Virginia
Writes under: Charlotte Zolotow
D. of Louis J. and Ella Bernstein Shapiro; m. Maurice Zolotow, 1938

When she was young, Z. moved with her parents to New York City, where she attended public schools. As a shy fourth-grader, she discovered that writing was her way to reach out to the world through a persona when she wrote a first person essay "as told by a Boston bull terrier," and she claims that she has been writing for "the child within" ever since. She studied writing at the University of Wisconsin and then returned to work in New York, eventually becoming a senior editor in the children's division at Harper & Row. She worked under Ursula Nordstrom, whom Z. credits not only with building that department from its original staff of three to its present complement of nearly fifty but also with being, as the editor of imaginatively illustrated books dealing with contemporary subjects and problems, a truly seminal force in the development of modern children's literature.

Z. began writing children's books after leaving her editorial job in 1944 to stay home with the first of her two children. She returned to Harper & Row in 1962 and is now publisher of Harper's Junior Books. She was divorced from her husband, also a writer, in 1970.

Many of her best books, considering both their quality and popularity with children, have been those that deal honestly with situations and problems which prior to the "new wave of realism" were not considered suitable subjects for this genre. Three examples would be *The Quarreling Book* (1963), *The Hating Book* (1967), and *The Unfriendly Book* (1975), all of which recognize that children, like adults, can harbor unpleasant emotions, be negatively affected by gloomy weather and gloomy behavior, and be downright antisocial at least some of the time. Earlier literature eschewed discussion of sibling rivalry and the displacement of an older child with the coming of a new baby, but Z. deals frankly with this topic in both *If It Weren't for You* (1966) and *Big Sister and Little Sister* (1966).

One book that has become a special favorite with feminists is *William's Doll* (1972). It's main character is a little boy who wants a real "baby doll," despite all of the negative reactions from his big brother and the boy next door. His father brings home a basketball, which William enjoys, and electric trains, for which William builds model towns. Only his grandmother understands that he wants to "practice being a father." The point is clearly made, although Z. claims that like all her other work, it was not written to "get a point across," but rather to let children feel that other children have shared the same emotions, frustrations, and joys.

Z.'s work is lyrical, but not over-stated. One of the finest examples is *Mr. Rabbit and the Lovely Present* (1962), in which Mr. Rabbit helps a child find the perfect gift for her mother, who is especially fond of red, yellow, green, and blue. Paul Williams identified it as an all-time favorite: "It is a perfect presentation of something rich and rare and untouchable, the time that exists between friends."

In a genre sometimes accorded less importance than it deserves, Z.'s contribution has been tremendous. For more than thirty-five years, she has provided leadership by example with books that are successful both artistically and commercially; she has reached children by communicating with them through the child within herself and has evoked a response in adults as well. In every respect, Z. must be considered a major voice in the area of juvenile literature today.

WORKS: *The Park Book* (1944). *But Not Billy* (1947). *The City Boy and the Country Horse* (1952). *Indian, Indian* (1952). *The Magic Word* (1952). *The Storm Book* (1952). *The Quiet Mother and the Noisy Little Boy* (1953). *One Step Two* (1955). *Not a Little Monkey* (1957). *Over and Over* (1957). *Do You Know What I'll Do?* (1958). *The Bunny Who Found Easter* (1959) *Aren't You Glad?* (1960). *Big Brother* (1960). *In My Garden* (1960). *The Little Black Puppy* (1960). *The Three Funny Friends* (1961). *The Man with the Purple Eyes* (1961). *The Night When Mother Went Away* (1961; reissued as *The Summer Night*, 1974). *Mr. Rabbit and the Lovely Present* (1962). *When the Wind Stops* (1962; rev. ed., 1975). *The Quarreling Book* (1963). *The Sky Was Blue* (1963). *Thomas the Tiger* (1963). *The White Marble* (1963). *I Have a Horse of My Own* (1964). *The Poodle Who Barked at the Wind* (1964). *A Rose, A Bridge, and a Wild Black Horse* (1964). *Someday* (1965). *When I Have a Little Girl* (1965). *Big Sister and Little Sister* (1966). *If It Weren't for You* (1966). *All that Sunlight* (1967). *The Hating Book* (1967). *I Want to Be Little* (1967). *Summer Is* (1967). *When I Have a Son* (1967). *A Father Like That* (1968). *My Friend John* (1968). *The New Friend* (1968). *A Day in the Life of Yani* (1969). *The Old Dog* (1969). *A Day in the Life of Latef* (1970). *Flocks of Birds* (1970). *River Winding* (1970; rev. ed., 1978). *Where I Begin* (1970). *Wake Up and Goodnight* (1971). *You and Me* (1971). *The Beautiful Christmas Tree* (1972). *Hold My Hand* (1972). *William's Doll* (1972). *Janey* (1973). *An Overpraised Season: Ten Stories of Youth* (edited by Zolotow, 1973). *My Grandson Lew* (1974). *The Unfriendly Book* (1975). *It's Not Fair* (1976). *May I Visit?* (1976). *Someone New* (1978). *If You Listen* (1980). *Say It* (1980). *Flocks of Birds* (1981). *The New Friend* (1981).

BIBLIOGRAPHY: Hopkins, L. B., *Books Are by People* (1969). Williams, P., in *Mademoiselle* (Jan. 1973). Wintle, J., and E. Fisher, *The Pied Pipers: Interviews with the Influential Creators of Children's Literature* (1974). Zolotow, C., "The Revolution in Children's Books," in *Prism* (Dec. 1974).

For articles in reference works, see: *Children's Literature Review*, Vol. 2, Ed. C. Riley (1976). *Something about the Author*, Ed. A. Commire (1971).

Other references: Houston *Post* (10 April 1976). New Orleans *Times-Picayune* (30 April 1974). New York *Daily News* (18 May 1971). Palo Alto *Times* (20 Sept. 1976). *PW* (10 June 1976).

EDYTHE M. McGOVERN

Leane Zugsmith

B. Jan. *1903, Louisville, Kentucky*
Writes under: Leane Zugsmith, Mrs. Carl Randau
D. *of Albert and Gertrude Zugsmith; m. Carl Randau, 1940*

Z. spent most of her childhood in Atlantic City, New Jersey. Her formal education consisted of a year each at Goucher College, the University of Pennsylvania, and Columbia University. She has lived in New York since 1924, except for a year in Europe and some months in Hollywood, where she worked as a screen writer for Goldwyn studio. She has also worked as a copy editor for pulp magazines like *Detective Stories* and *Western Story Magazine* and written advertising copy. In the early 1940s, after marrying a newspaperman, she was a special feature writer on the staff of the New York newspaper *P.M.*

Her first novel, *All Victories Are Alike* (1929) is the story of a newspaper columnist's loss of ideals. *Goodbye and Tomorrow* (1931), which Z. said is "shamelessly derivative of Virginia Woolf," is about a romantic spinster who becomes a patron of artists. *Never Enough* (1932) is a panorama of American life during the 1920s. *The Reckoning* (1934) tells the story of a New York slum boy.

A Time to Remember (1936) is concerned with labor troubles and unionization in a New York department store. Its heroine, Aline Weinman, a Dreiseresque, middle-class, Jewish employee of the store, goes out on strike. She pays the price of painful separation from her family for her political ideals because her father, who has lost his job, would disapprove if he knew Aline's politics.

The Summer Soldier (1938) is about a small group of men and women, mostly northerners, who travel by train to a southern county to hold a hearing on the abuse of black workers. Their mission, however, is not successful. The novel is a slick character sketch of different political types.

Home Is Where You Hang Your Childhood (1937) is a collection of short stories. "Room in the World" describes the desperation unemployment causes in a young family. The title story, about a very young high school girl's movement from childish innocence to experience, uses one of Z.'s favorite themes. *Hard Times with Easy Payments* (1941) is another collection of short stories, all from *P.M.*

With her husband, Z. wrote *The Setting Sun of Japan* (1942) about the Randaus' flying trip through the Far East for *PM*; a mystery story, *Visitor* (1944); and "Year of Wrath," a novel serialized in *Collier's* in 1942. Stories by Z. appeared infrequently until 1949 in *Good Housekeeping, The New Yorker,* and *Collier's*.

In the early 1940s, Z. was considered one of the most promising young left-wing novelists. She said her greatest influences were Albert Maltz and Irwin Shaw in the short story and Josephine Herbst in the novel. All of her six novels are political, and her political themes gained considerable sophistication and some cynicism during the decade of her productivity (1929–38). Her sympathetic treatment of Jewish characters is of interest to the history of Jewish-American writers because her Jewish characters solve the problem of assimilation by becoming socialists. Z. belongs with those Jewish writers of the 1930s who attempted to transform ethnic background into meaningful politics. Her work became dated and of historical interest after WWII and the anti-Soviet backlash of the 1950s.

WORKS: *All Victories Are Alike* (1929). *Goodbye and Tomorrow* (1931). *Never Enough* (1932). *The Reckoning* (1934). *A Time to Remember* (1936). *Home Is Where You Hang Your Childhood, and other stories* (1937). *The Summer Soldier* (1938). *Hard Times with Easy Payments* (1941). *The Setting Sun of Japan* (with C. Randau, 1942). *The Visitor* (with C. Randau, 1944).

BIBLIOGRAPHY: Eisinger, C. E., in *Proletarian Writers of the Thirties,* Ed. D. Madden (1968). Smith, B., Introduction to *The Democratic Spirit: A Collection of American Writings from the Earliest Times to the Present Day* (1941).
For articles in reference works, see: *Contemporary American Authors,* Ed. B. Millett (1944). *20thCA. The Universal Jewish Encyclopedia,* Ed. I. Landman (1943-48).

CAROLE ZONIS YEE

INDEX

Names and page numbers in bold face refer to subject articles

Abbott, Edith, I 72, 73
Abel, Annie Heloise, I 3–4
abolition. *See also* slavery
  activists for, I 109–10, 111, 113–14, 228–
    29, 278–79, 295–96; II 71–72, 265–66,
    293–94
    southern, I 278–79, 280
  in drama, II 165–66
  in fiction, I 395; II 165–66, 277–79
  history of, I 444; II 192
  in poetry, I 109
  religious arguments for, I 278–79, 280
  split within movement for, I 278–79
actresses
  film, II 367–68
  stage, I 269–70, 426; II 65, 102, 482, 237–
    38, 366–68
Adams, Abigail Smith, I 5–6; II 352
Adams, Hannah, I 7–8
Adams, Harriet Stratemeyer, I 9–10
Adams, John, I 5–6; II 352, 353
  and M. O. Warren, II 352, 353
Adams, Léonie Fuller, critical comment by, I 57
Adams, Mary. *See* Ward, Elizabeth Stuart
  Phelps
Addams, Jane, I 11–13, 39, 244; II 36
advertising, women in, I 213, 317
advice. *See also* etiquette
  books, I 205, 263, 404; II 310–11
  columns, I 243, 263–64, 289; II 217
aesthetics, philosophy of, I 389–90; II 256,
  370–71
Afro-American studies. *See* black studies
Aiken, Conrad, and Bradstreet, I 69
Akins, Zoë, I 13–15
Alcott, Louisa May, I 15–18, 111, 431; II 36,
  411, 412
Alden, Isabella MacDonald, I 445
Aldington, Richard, and H. Doolittle, I 176
Aldon, Adair. *See* Meigs, Cornelia Lynde
Aldrich, Bess Streeter, I 18–19
Aldrich, Mildred, I 20–21
A.L.F. *See* Henry, Alice

Allen, Samantha. *See* Holley, Marietta
Allen, Sarah A. *See* Hopkins, Pauline Elizabeth
Allingham, Margery, I 192
A.M. *See* Alcott, Louisa May
American Academy of Arts and Letters.
    See also National Institute of
    Arts and Letters
  awards received from, I 238, 360
  grants received from, I 76
  members of, II 62, 95
American Association of University Women, I
  72
American history. *See* United States history
American literature
  development in, I 104, 125, 153, 301, 383; II
    108, 147, 199, 200, 225
  the "left" in, I 405
  literary criticism in (*see* literary criticism)
  naturalism in, I 153
  the novel in, II 199
  poetry in (*see* poetry)
  realism in, I 104, 124, 302, 351, 405
  the short story in, I 124–25; II 20, 21
American Woman Suffrage Association, II 266
  founders of, I 323
Ames, Mary E. Clemmer, I 21–23
Amethyst. *See* Wells, Emmeline Blanche
  Woodward
Anderson, Sherwood, and G. Stein, II 270
Andrews, Eliza Frances, I 23–24
Andrews, Jane, I 25–26
anthologists, I 392; II 28, 220, 244, 248, 356
  of poetry, II 137
  of short stories, I 117; II 115
Anthony, Susan Brownell, critical comment by,
  I 319
anthropology, I 44–46; II 31–34, 116–17,
  130–31. *See also* cultural studies
  scholars in, II 31–34, 130–31
anti-Semitism
  in drama, I 397
  in fiction, I 219, 317
antislavery movement. *See* abolition

antiwar literature. *See under* world peace
Appleton, Victor, II. *See* Adams, Harriet
    Stratemeyer
Arendt, Hannah, I 26–28
Armstrong, Charlotte, I 28–29
Arnow, Harriette Louisa Simpson, I 30–31
artists, II 313, 317. *See also:* illustrators;
    photographers
art, philosophy of, I 389–90
Asmodeus. *See* Atherton,
    Gertrude Franklin Horn
Atherton, Gertrude Franklin Horn, I 32–34
Auchincloss, Louis, critical comment by, II 370
Auden, W. H., critical comment by, II 178–79
Aunt Em. *See* Wells, Emmeline
    Blanche Woodward
Aunt Fanny. *See* Gage, Frances Dana Barker
Aunt Maguire, *See* Whitcher,
    Frances Miriam Berry
Aunt Pilbury. *See* Winslow, Helen Maria
Australian-American writers, II 180–82
aviators, I 416

Bagley, Sarah G., I 200
Baldwin, Faith. *See* Cuthrell, Faith Baldwin
Barbara. *See* Wright, Mabel Osgood
Barnard, A. M. *See* Alcott, Louisa May
Barnes, Djuna, I 34–35
Barnes, Margaret Ayer, I 36–37, 198
Barnett, Ida B. Wells, I 38–39
Barrell, Sarah Sayward. *See* Wood, Sally
    Sayward Barrell
Barton, May Hollis. *See* Adams, Harriet
    Stratemeyer
Beard, Mary Ritter, I 40–41
Beecher, Catharine Esther, I 42–44, 278; II
    277
Benedict, Ruth Fulton, I 44–46; II 32
Benét, Stephen Vincent, and P. Murray, II 242
Benson, Sally, I 46–47
Berkley, Helen. *See* Ritchie, Anna Cora Ogden
    Mowatt
Bernard, Delores. *See* Ridge, Lola
Bernhardt, Sarah, II 238
Betts, Doris, I 48–49
Bible, the
    in poetry, I 147, 149
    stories of, retold, I 402
    studies of, II 380
    and women, II 266
Bierce, Ambrose, and Coolbrith, I 126
Bildungsroman, the, I 294, 350; II 286, 364.
    See also under women in fiction
biography, the, techniques of, I 61; II 270
    and the autobiography, II 214
birth control, advocates of, I 185; II 212–14

Bishop, Elizabeth, I 49–51
black Americans, I 208–9; II 43, 80, 81. *See
    also:* black American writers; black
    fiction; black literature; civil rights
    and the black consciousness, I 77–78
    folklore of, II 116, 117
    as freed slaves, I 321
    music of, II 220
    photographic commentary on, II 140
    in white fiction, II 140
    and the woman's experience, I 77, 128–29,
        352–53; II 30, 115
black American writers
    Barbadian, II 30–32
    feminist, I 128–29, 295–97
    18th-c., II 373–75
    19th-c., I 38–39, 128–29, 295–97; II
        243–44
    20th-c., I 77–78, 208–9, 273–75, 291–
        92, 320–22, 331–32, 352–53; II 80–83,
        141–43, 344–45
black fiction, I 77, 123, 208–9, 296–97, 321–
    22; II 30–32, 141–43
    folklore in, I 331–32
    tradition in, II 83
    thematic, I 208–9; II 142
    women in, I 77, 78, 322; II 30, 345, 364
black literature. *See also:* black fiction; black
    studies
    drama in, I 291–92
    and the Harlem Renaissance, I 208, 352, 353
    magazines of, I 38, 208, 274, 291, 321, 322
    newspapers of, II 82
    poetry in, I 76–78, 208, 296, 352–53; II 80,
        344–45, 374–75
    black studies, I 274–75, 321; II 114–16
Blaine, James G., and A. Dodge, I 173, 174
Blake, Lillie Devereux, I 52–53
Blanchard, P., critical comment by, II 113
blank verse, I 392; II 85, 320
    drama (*see* verse drama)
Bloomer, Amelia Jenks, I 54–56
Bly, Nellie. *See* Cochrane, Elizabeth
Boas, Franz, critical comment by, II 131
Bogan, Louise, I 56–58
Bolton, Ann, critical comment by, I 63
Bonner, Sherwood. *See* McDowell, Katherine
    Sherwood Bonner
book editors, I 105, 228
    of anthologies (*see* anthologists)
    history, II 419
    in-house, I 423; II 290, 428
    of letters, I 5; II 39, 100
    poetry, II 87, 316
    of reference works, II 403. (*see also under:*
        black studies; women's studies)

book publishers, II 428
book reviewers. *See under* literary criticism
Boothe, Clare. *See* Luce, Clare Boothe
Boucher, Anthony, critical comment by, II 9
Bowen, Catherine Drinker, I 60–62
Bower, B. M. *See* Sinclair, Bertha Muzzy
Bowers, Bathsheba, I 62–63
Bowles, Jane Auer, I 64–65
Boyd, Nancy. *See* Millay, Edna St. Vincent
Boyle, Kay, I 66–67
Bradstreet, Anne Dudley, I 68–69
Branch, Anna Hempstead, I 70–71
Branch, Olivia. *See* Parton, Sara Payson Willis
Brawne, Fanny, I 224, 225
Breckinridge, Sophonisba Preston, I 72–74
Breuer, Bessie, I 74–76
British-American writers, I 68–69, 85–86,
    369–70, 407–8, 434–36; II 55–56
Broadway, plays produced on, I 81, 224–25,
    236–37, 291–92, 304–5, 371–72, 428–
    29, 437–38; II 43, 238, 244, 320, 354
Brook Farm, I 161
Brooks, Gwendolyn, I 76–78
Brooks, Maria Gowen, I 78–80
Brooks, Van Wyck, critical comment by, I 124
Brown, Alice, I 80–83
Bryant, William Cullen, and E. A. R. Lewis,
    I 411
Buck, Pearl Sydenstricker, I 83–85
Burke, Fielding. *See* Dargan, Olive Tilford
Burleigh, Celia Burr, II 401
Burnett, Frances Eliza Hodgson, I 85–87
Burns, Lucy, I 333
Burr, Esther Edwards, I 87–89
Butler, Frances Anne. *See* Kemble,

Calhoun, Lucy Monroe. *See* Monroe, Lucy
Campbell, Helen Stuart, I 89–91
Canadian-American writers, I 364–66; II 47–48
Canfield, Dorothy. *See* Fisher, Dorothea Frances
    Canfield
Carey, Alice. *See* Cary, Alice
Carrighar, Sally, I 92–93
Carrington, Elaine Sterne, I 94–96
Carson, Rachel Louise, I 96–98
Cary, Alice, I 21, 22, **98–99**; II 349
Cary, Phoebe, I 98; II 349
Cather, Willa, I 14, **100–103,** 349, 350
Catherwood, Mary Hartwell, I 103–5
Catholic fiction, I 272, 374; II 98–100
Catholic literature, II 10. *See also* Catholic
    fiction
    autobiography in, II 175
    biography in, II 175
    conversion narratives in, I 154, 374
    journalism in, I 374

and socialism, I 155
Catholics, I 272, 281–82, 374; II 10, 98–101,
    174–75, 382–84
    influence of, as reflected in writings (*see:*
        Catholic fiction; Catholic literature)
Catt, Carrie Lane Chapman, I 106–7, 297,
    404
Caulkins, Frances Manwaring, I 107–8
censorship of literature, II 253
Chandler, Elizabeth Margaret, I 109–10
Chandler, Louise. *See* Moulton, Louise
    Chandler
Channing, William E., and Follen, I 228, 229
charity workers. *See* social workers
Cheney, Ednah Dow Littlehale, I 110–12
Chenoweth, Alice. *See* Gardener, Helen
    Hamilton
Child, Lydia Maria Francis, I 112–15
child development
    in primitive cultures, II 33, 34
children's drama, I 214, 402; II 38–39; 244
    and children's theater, I 256
children's fiction, I 111–12, 161–62, 229,
    286–87, 347, 358; II 35–36, 135, 142,
    393. *See also:*
    children's magazines; young adult
    literature
    animal stories in, II 429
    classics adapted for, I 204
    classics in, I 86, 175, 216–17, 430–31
    fairy tales in, I 228; II 38–39
    family stories in, I 228, 401, 402; II 428–29
    folklore adaptations for, I 189
    historical, I 215
    of inanimate objects, I 228–29
    for interracial understanding, I 25–26
    for minority children, II 115
    moralistic, I 228, 334, 336, 357, 358, 385,
        399, 419; II 146–47, 224, 350
    nature stories, I 253–54; II 417
    of other lands and peoples, I 25–26, 189,
        367–68, 406
    pioneer, II 397–98
    regional, I 90, 214–15, 217; II 393
    religious, I 216–17, 228–29, 402; II 146–47
    series, I 9–10, 16–17, 216–17, 286–87,
        356–57, 367–68, 430–31; II 218, 397–
        98, 411–12
    Sunday-school. *See* Sunday-school movement,
        the
    on women, I 162, 356–57
children's literature, I 419; II 313. *See also:*
    children's drama; children's fiction,
    children's poetry; young adult literature
    awards received in, I 399; II 398 (*see also*
        Newbery awards)

children's literature (*cont.*)
  biographies in, I 59–60, 81, 205; II 36
  history of, II 36
  on history, I 7, 108; II 36
  the realistic trend in, II 428–29
  religious education in, I 107; II 78
  suitability for, I 259
  technique in, I 228–29
children's magazines, I 113, 175, 228, 238,
      257–58, 286, 392, 419, 430; II 109, 313
  for black children, I 208
children's poetry, I 214, 229, 238–39, 402; II
      291
Chopin, Kate O'Flaherty, I 115–17
Christian Science, founder of church of, I 193–
      94
Christie, Agatha, I 192
Chubbuck, Emily. *See* Judson, Emily Chubbuck
civil liberties, campaigns for, II 55–56. *See
      also*: civil rights; women's rights
civil rights, I 38–39, 122–23, 208, 274; II 114,
      115, 265, 345. *See also*: abolition; black
      Americans
  for black education, I 77, 296
  for black suffrage, I 39
  against lynching, I 38–39, 77; II 43
  movement, of the 1960's, I 77, 291; II 55–56
  southern activists for, II 252–53
Civil War, the
  and the Confederacy
    life in, I 23–24, 424–25; II 21, 40–41
    social history of, sources for, I 23
  diaries and journals of, I 23
  fictional treatment of, I 153; II 77, 222, 345
  and Native Americans, I 3–4
  nurses in, I 16, 202; II 293, 294, 411, 416
Clark, Eleanor, I 117–18
Clarke, James Freeman, and Ossoli, II 111
Clarkson, Helen. *See* McCloy, Helen
Clavers, Mrs. Mary. *See* Kirkland, Caroline
      Matilda Stansbury
Clemens, Samuel
  and Coolbrith, I 126
  critical comment by, II 233
  and M. M. Dodge, I 175
  and Keller, I 362
Clemmer, Mary. *See* Ames, Mary E. Clemmer
Clemons, Walter, critical comment by, II 363
Cochrane, Elizabeth, I 118–20
Colette, I 223
comedies, II 303–4
  films as, II 368
  novels of manners as, I 266–67, 286
  plays as, I 14, 224, 236, 256, 257, 371–72,
      438
  tragi-, II 101

Commager, Henry Steele, critical comment by, I
      102
communism. *See also* socialism
  American hysteria against, I 303, 406; II 215,
      241
  analysis of, II 315
  and the Communist Party
    fellow travelers of, I 441; II 241–42
    members of, I 226; II 56
  and feminism, II 242
  in fiction, II 121–22, 167–68
  composers, I 273–74; II 285–86
Comstock, Anna Botsford, I 120–22
Comstock, John Henry, and A. Comstock, I
      120, 121
confessional literature, II 53–54, 228–29
Congregationalists, I 124, 200; II 107, 283,
      287, 323–25
  morale among, II 65
Constantia. *See* Murray, Judith Sargent
conversion literature, I 8, 327–28, 438
  fiction in, I 272, 446–47; II 206
  personal accounts in, I 154, 374
Cook, Fannie, I 122–24
Cook, George Cram, and Glaspell, I 268, 269
Cooke, Rose Terry, I 124–26
cookery, II 310, 311, 427
Coolbrith, Ina Donna, I 126–27
Coolidge, Susan. *See* Woolsey, Sarah Chauncey
Cooper, Anna Julia Haywood, I 128–29
Cornelia. *See* Hale, Sarah Josepha Buell
Cott, Nancy, critical comment by, II 127
Cousin Kate. *See* McIntosh, Maria Jane
Crabtree, Mary Ann, II 198
Craddock, Charles Egbert. *See* Murfree, Mary
      Noailles
Craighead, Jean C. *See* George, Jean Craighead
Crapsey, Adelaide, I 130–31
Crocker, Hannah Mather, I 132–33
Croly, Jane Cunningham, I 134–36
Crosby, Fannie. *See* Van Alstyne, Frances Jane
      Crosby
cultural studies. *See also*: anthropology;
      sociology, studies in
  African, I 361
  Afro-American, I 274
  American, II 33, 197–98, 256, 257 (*see also*
      Native American culture)
  Asian, I 360–61
    Chinese, I 284; II 242
    Japanese, I 45, 361
  European, I 222–23
  Jewish (*see* Jewish culture)
  popular, I 222–23, 284, 360–61
  of primitive societies, II 32–34
  travel books as (*see under* travel books)

cultures, foreign. *See also* cultural studies
  in children's literature (*see under* children's
    literature)
  in newspaper correspondence, I 419–20; II
    60, 112, 113
  as portrayed in drama, II 88
  as portrayed in fiction, I 83–84, 284, 360–
    61; II 31, 89
  series on, II 334
  in travel books (*see* travel books)
Cummins, Maria Susanna, I 136–38
Curtiss, Harriot, I 392
Cushman, Corinne. *See* Victor, Metta Victoria
    Fuller
Custer, Elizabeth Bacon, I 138–39, II 39
Custer, George Armstrong, and E. B. Custer, I
    138–39
Cuthrell, Faith Baldwin, I 140–43

Dall, Caroline Wells Healey, I 143–44
dancers, I 157–59
Dargan, Olive Tilford, I 145–47
Davidson, Lucretia Maria, I 147–48, 148, 149
Davidson, Margaret Miller, I 148–49
Davis, Mary Evelyn Moore, I 150–52
Davis, Paulina Kellogg Wright, I 143
Davis, Rebecca Harding, I 152–54; II 346
Davis, Sylvester. *See* Babb, Sanora
Day, Dorothy, I 154–55
Deane, Martha. *See* McBride, Mary Margaret
Deans, Jennie. *See* Swisshelm, Jane Grey
    Cannon
de Cleyre, Voltairine, II 212
Deland, Margaret Wade Campbell, I 156–57
Dell, Floyd, critical comment by, II 50
De Mille, Agnes, I 157–59
Denslow, Grace, I 282
Depression literature
  fiction in, I 345; II 239, 362
    Marxist, I 145–46
  journalistic, II 205
Deutsch, Babette, I 159–60
Dewey, John, and Yezierska, II 424
diaries and journals, I 369–70, 383–84, 417; II
    72, 91, 254, 255
  of the Civil War era (*see under* Civil War)
  of early America, I 88–89
  of frontier life, II 112, 398
  religious, I 88–89
  of travels, I 383–84
Diaz, Abby Morton, I 161–63
Dickinson, Emily, I 163–66; II 298, 316
didactic fiction, II 147, 249, 339–40. *See also*
    under children's fiction
Didion, Joan, I 166–68
dime novel, the, II 105, 337, 338, 339–40

Dinsmore, Herman, critical comment by, I 307
diplomatic history, I 361; II 322
Disney, Doris Miles, I 168–70
Dix, Dorothy. *See* Gilmer, Elizabeth Meriwether
Dixon, Franklin W. *See* Adams, Harriet
    Stratemeyer
Dock, Lavinia Lloyd, I 170–72
Dodge, Mabel. *See* Luhan, Mabel Ganson
    Dodge
Dodge, Mary Abigail, I 173–74, 392
Dodge, Mary Mapes, I 174–75; II 18
domestic literature, I 257–59, 424; II 136
  advice in (*see* advice)
  in history, II 208–9
  humorous, I 258–59, 341, 371–72
  magazine column, II 295–96
  novels in, I 162, 179–80, 229, 306
Doolittle, Hilda, I 176–78
Dorr, Julia Caroline Ripley, I 178–80
Dorr, Rheta Childe, I 180–82
Dow, Caroline, II 49
drama
  critical studies in, I 293; II 127
  innovations in, I 256, 268, 270; II 119, 200
  reviews of (*see:* magazine columns;
    newspaper columns)
  technique in, I 304–5; II 269
dramatic adaptations
  by women, of others' works, I 14, 224, 244–
    45, 255, 404, 426; II 63, 68, 237, 320
  of women's work, I 237; II 15, 238, 258,
    354, 362
dramatic poetry, I 151. *See also* verse drama
  and the monologue, I 70; II 305, 376
DuBois, Shirley Graham. *See* Graham, Shirley
DuBois, W. E. B.
  critical comment by, I 322
  and Fauset, I 208
  and S. Graham, I 274
Dunbar, Alice. *See* Nelson, Alice Ruth Moore
    Dunbar
Duniway, Abigail Scott, I 182–84
Durant, Mrs. Kenneth. *See* Taggard, Genevieve
Dykeman, Wilma, I 184–86

Earle, Alice Morse, I 186–88
Eastman, Elaine Goodale, I 188–90
Eberhart, Mignon Good, I 190–92
E. B. W. *See* Wells, Emmeline Blanche
    Woodward
ecology literature, I 96–97
economics. *See also* financial analysts
  history of, I 40
Eddy, Mary Baker Glover, I 193–94
editors. *See:* book editors; magazine editors and

editors (*cont.*)
    publishers; newspaper editors and
    publishers
education. *See specific areas of education*
  for blacks, I 111, 296
  and curriculum, II 380–81, 426, 427
  day-care centers for, I 261
  of infants, II 342
  internationalism in, I 25
  kindergarten, I 188–89; II 392
  methods in, II 426, 427
  for Native Americans, I 188–89
  reform, I 25, 59, 72–73, 111; II 380–81
  sociology of, I 449
  textbooks in (*see* textbooks)
  for women (*see* education for women)
education for women, II 53, 144–45, 399–400
  advocates of higher, I 42, 55, 143–44, 288,
    290; II 42–43
  schools for, I 42; II 42, 57, 399–400, 416
  studies on, I 59
  textbooks for, II 144, 400
educators, I 24, 128–29, 299; II 82, 143–45,
    399–400, 402
  and administrators, I 24; II 24, 402
  in Asia, II 252
  of Native Americans, I 188–89
  university faculty as, I 44, 121; II 44, 178,
    219, 402
    in education, II 207
    in English, I 407; II 36, 88, 95, 344, 402
    in foreign languages, I 24
    in history, I 448; II 207
    in literature, I 24, 130; II 86
    in natural science, I 120–21
    in philosophy, I 389
Edwards, Eleanor Lee. *See* Victor, Metta
    Victoria Fuller
Egan, Lesley. *See* Linington, Elizabeth
Eliot, Alice C. *See* Jewett, Sarah Orne
Eliot, T. S., critical comment by, I 34; II 62
Ellen Louise. *See* Moulton, Louise Chandler
Ellet, Elizabeth Fries Lummis, I 195–96
Ellis, Anne, I 196–98
Emerson, Ralph Waldo
  and Alcott, I 16
  critical comment by, I 336, 396
  and Ossoli, II 111
emigré writers. *See specific nationalities*
Emilia. *See* Stockton, Annis Boudinot
Episcopalians, I 130, 180, 432; II 376
  influence of, as reflected in writings, I 156; II
    279, 401
  epistolary novel, the, II 354
essayists, I 117, 166–67, 247, 248, 324; II
    174–75, 200, 256–57

ethnic literature, II 420. *See also* ethnology
  black (*see*: black fiction; black literature)
  Jewish, II 273, 424–25
ethnology. *See also*: anthropology; cultural
    studies; folklore
etiquette, classics in, II 162–64, 231
expatriates, I 176–78; II 267–71
  in fiction, I 34–35
  justification for, II 270

Fairbank, Janet Ayer, I 198–200
Fairfield, Flora. *See* Alcott, Louisa May
family saga, the, I 198–99, 374, 411; II 93,
    169, 221, 288–89, 326, 328, 330, 361,
    420
Fane, Florence. *See* Victor, Frances Fuller
fantasy fiction, II 106
Farley, Harriet, I 200–202, 392
Farnham, Eliza Woodson Burhans, I 202–4
Farquharson, Martha. *See* Finley, Martha
Farrar, Eliza Ware Rotch, I 204–6
Faugeres, Margaretta V. Bleecker, I 206–7
Fauset, Jessie Redmon, I 208–10
feminist fiction. *See also* women in fiction
  humorous, I 318–19
  Marxist, I 146; II 242
  mystery, II 194–95
  19th-c., I 53, 115–16, 247–48, 318–19
  20th-c., I 36–37, 74–76, 146, 210–11, 333–
    34, 387, 406; II 242
feminist literature, I 11–12, 180–82, 241, 248,
    263–64, 345–46; II 112, 212–13, 256,
    358–59. *See also under*: woman
    suffrage; woman's experience; women's
    rights; women's studies
  18th-c., II 79
  fiction in (*see* feminist fiction)
  literary criticism in, II 53, 54, 126–27
  magazines of, I 54–55; II 358, 359
  newspapers of, I 54–55, 183
  poetry in (*see* feminist poetry)
  on religion, I 193
  on sexuality, I 241, 263; II 347
  on socialism, II 26–27
  superiority theory in, I 202, 203, 323–24
feminist movement. *See*: woman suffrage;
    women's liberation movement; women's
    rights
feminist poetry. *See also* women in poetry
  contemporary, I 406; II 179–80
  18th-c., II 200
  late 19th-c., I 260
  likenesses to, II 51
  militant, I 406
feminists. *See also under* woman suffrage

contemporary, I 241, 405–6; II 52–54, 179–80
criticism of, I 167
discussion group of, I 180–81 (see also women's clubs)
18th-c., II 200
literature of (see: feminist literature; women; women's studies)
19th-c.
  early, I 54–55, 113–14, 278–79, 280–81; II 72, 112–13
  late, I 59–60, 143–44, 173–74, 247–48, 260–62, 296, 323–24; II 346–48, 358–59, 402–3
  split among, I 241
20th-c., early, I 87–88, 143–44, 180–81, 247–48, 260–62; II 26–27, 212–13, 346–48, 358–59
Ferber, Edna, I 210–12
Fern, Fanny. See Parton, Sara Payson Willis
Field, Kate, I 212–14; II 386
Field, Peter. See Hobson, Laura Keane Zametkin
Field, Rachel Lyman, I 214–16
Fields, Annie Adams, I 281, 349
Fields, James T., critical comment by, II 347
Fillebrown, Charlotte A. See Jerauld, Charlotte Ann Fillebrown
film adaptations, I 237, 317, 329; II 97, 126, 154, 184, 219, 239, 282, 354, 365, 393
  of biographies, II 29
  for children, I 86, 356–57
  of comedies, I 438; II 16, 238
  as documentaries, I 96
  as musicals, I 47; II 244
  of mysteries, I 312
  of plays, I 94, 437–38; II 320, 367
  of westerns, II 235
film critics, II 133
film industry, the
  experience in, I 428–29; II 132–33
  gossip about, II 133
  screenwriters for, I 428–29; II 53, 167, 205, 239, 240, 286, 368
Finley, Martha, I 216–18
Fisher, Dorothea Frances Canfield, I 218–20
Fiske, Sarah Symmes, I 221–22
Fitzgerald, Sally, II 100
Flanner, Janet, I 222–24
Fleeta. See Hamilton, Kate Waterman
Flexner, Abraham, critical comment by, I 224
Flexner, Anne Crawford, I 224–25
Florence. See Osgood, Frances Sargent Locke
Flynn, Elizabeth Gurley, I 225–27
folklore
  American, I 189, 331–32, 406; II 169, 337

black American, I 331–32; II 116–17
for children, I 189
fictional use of, I 332; II 117, 126, 169 (see also under regional fiction)
Native American, I 189
Russian, II 126
Follen, Eliza Lee Cabot, I 228–30
Foote, Mary Hallock, I 230–32
Forbes, Esther, I 232–34
Ford, Ford Madox, critical comment by, I 271
foreign correspondents. See under journalists
Forrester, Fanny. See Judson, Emily Chubbuck
Foster, Hannah Webster, I 234–35; II 409
founders, II 68, 84–85, 224, 241, 415–16
  of churches, I 193–94; II 123, 380–81
  of magazines (see under magazine editors and publishers)
  of the NAACP, I 38
  of NOW, I 241
  of schools (see schools, founders of)
  of settlement houses, I 11–12; II 114
  of suffrage organizations (see under woman suffrage)
  of temperance organizations (see under temperance movement)
  of theater companies, I 268; II 214, 342
  of women's clubs (see under women's clubs)
Frank. See Whitcher, Frances Miriam Berry
Franken, Rose, I 236–38
Freeman, Mary Eleanor Wilkins, I 238–40
freethinkers, I 246
Freud, Sigmund, and Doolittle, I 176
Friedan, Betty, I 240–42
frontier life
  accounts of, I 138–39, 197, 231, 380–81; II 112, 210–11, 397–98
  in fiction, I 18–19, 93, 100–101, 104, 182–83, 231, 269–70, 387, 388; II 138, 210–11, 325–26, 337, 397–98
  histories of, I 195; II 337–38
Fulbright grant, recipients of, II 151, 155
Fuller, Frances. See Victor, Frances Fuller
Fuller, Margaret. See Ossoli, Sarah Margaret Fuller
Fuller, Metta Victoria. See Victor, Metta Victoria Fuller

Gage, Frances Dana Barker, I 242–44
Gale, Zona, I 244–45
Gardener, Helen Hamilton, I 246–48
gardening books. See under nature study
Garland, Hamlin, and Catherwood, I 104
Garrigue, Jean, I 248–50
Garrison, William Lloyd, I 296
Gary, Dorothy Page. See Page, Dorothy Myra

gay liberation movement, the. *See under*
    homosexuality
Gellhorn, Martha, I 250–52
Genêt. *See* Flanner, Janet
George, Jean Craighead, I 253–55
Gerstenberg, Alice, I 255–57
Gilman, Caroline Howard, I 257–59
Gilman, Charlotte Perkins Stetson, I 89, 244,
    260–62, 364
Gilmer, Elizabeth Meriwether, I 262–64
Gish, Lillian, II 219
Glasgow, Ellen Anderson Gholson, I 264–68
Glaspell, Susan, I 268–70
Godey, Louis, and S. J. B. Hale, I 289
Goldman, Emma, II 212
Goodale, Elaine. *See* Eastman, Elaine Goodale
Gordon, Caroline, I 271–73
Gothic fiction
    romance, I 301–2; II 102, 390
    southern, II 98–101
Gottschalk, Laura Riding. *See* Jackson, Laura
    Riding
Graham, Shirley, I 273–75
Grant, Margaret. *See* Franken, Rose
Grau, Shirley Ann, I 275–77
Graves, Robert, and L. R. Jackson, I 338, 339
Gray, Walter T. *See* Victor, Metta Victoria
    Fuller
Greeley, Horace, and Ossoli, II 111
Green, Anna Katherine Rohlfs. *See* Rohlfs,
    Anna Katherine Green
Greenwood, Grace. *See* Lippincott. Sara Jane
    Clarke
Gregory, Horace, critical comment by, II 18
Grimké, Angelina Emily, I 278–79, 280
Grimké, Sarah Moore, I 279, **280–81**
Guggenheim Fellowship, recipients of, I 48, 66,
    96, 117, 271, 293, 308; II 155, 260, 290
Guiney, Louise Imogen, I 81, **281–83**

Hahn, Emily, I 283–85
Hale, Edward Everett, I 286
Hale, Lucretia Peabody, I 285–87
Hale, Sarah Josepha Buell, I 288–90; II 144
Hale, Susan, I 285
Hamilton, Gail. *See* Dodge, Mary Abigail
Hammett, Dashiell, and Hellman, I 303–4
handicapped writers, I 362–63; II 331–33,
    355–57
Hansberry, Lorraine, I 291–93
Hanson, Harriet J. *See* Robinson, Harriet Jane
    Hanson
Hardwick, Elizabeth, I 293–95
Harland, Marion. *See* Terhune, Mary Virginia
    Hawes
Harlem renaissance. *See* black literature

Harper, Frances Ellen Watkins, I 295–97
Harper, Ida Husted, I 297–99
Harris, Bernice Kelly, I 299–301
Harris, Mary Briggs, II 346
Harris, Miriam Coles, I 301–3
Harris, Mrs. Sidney S. *See* Harris, Miriam
    Coles
Harrison, Constance Cary, I 385
Harte, Bret, and Coolbrith, I 126
Hartwell, Mary. *See* Catherwood, Mary
    Hartwell
Hawthorne, Nathaniel, critical comment by, I
    137; II 135, 225
Hay, Elzey. *See* Andrews, Eliza Frances
Hay, Timothy. *See* Brown, Margaret Wise
Hayes, Helen, I 429
H. D. *See* Doolittle, Hilda
Hegan, Alice Caldwell. *See* Rice, Alice
    Caldwell Hegan
Helen. *See* Whitman, Sarah Helen Power
Helfenstein, Ernest. *See* Smith, Elizabeth Oakes
    Prince
Hellman, Lillian, I 303–5
Hemingway, Ernest
    and Gellhorn, I 251
    and Stein, II 270
Hemingway, Martha. *See* Gellhorn, Martha
Henderson, Alice Corbin, II 60
Hentz, Caroline Lee Whiting, I 306–7
Herbst, Josephine, I 366
Herrick, Christine Terhune, II 309
H. H. *See* Jackson, Helen Maria Fiske Hunt
Hicks, Granville, critical comment by, I 239; II
    257
Higgins, Marguerite, I 307–9
Higginson, Ella Rhoads, I 310–11
Higginson, Thomas Wentworth, I 336
    and Dickinson, II 316
Highet, Helen MacInnes, I 312–13
Highsmith, Patricia, I 314–16
Hill, Grace Livingston. *See* Lutz, Grace
    Livingston Hill
historians
    diplomatic, II 322
    of U.S. history, I 3–4, 7–8, 384–86; II
        197–98, 207–9, 210–11, 336–38
historical fiction, I 215, 233–34, 351, 394–95,
    411–12, 431; II 77, 166, 222, 225–27,
    345, 404–6. *See also* regional fiction
    about aboliton (*see under* abolition)
    biographical, I 182–83, 412; II 149
    for children (*see under* children's fiction)
    about the Civil War (*see under* Civil War)
    about frontier life (*see under* frontier life)
    about the Reconstruction era, I 296–97; II
        414

about the Revolutionary War, II 70, 326, 405–6
romance, I 103–4; II 36, 224, 389
about the world wars, I 251–52, 312; II 151, 205
historical poetry, II 70
history. See also: historians; local history; U.S. history; specific subject areas of history
awards received in, I 233
for children (see under children's literature)
diplomatic, I 361–62; II 322
European, I 394–95
fictional (see historical fiction)
of the Middle Ages, II 322
of the Middle East, II 321
popular, I 394–95; II 137
and research, II 207–9
scholars of (see historians)
textbooks, II 400
world, II 401
of World War 1, II 321, 322
Hobson, Laura Keane Zametkin, I 316–17
Holden, Roger. See Guiney, Louise Imogen
Holley, Marietta, I 318–20
Holme, Saxe. See Jackson, Helen Maria Fiske Hunt
homosexuality
in drama, II 367
in fiction, II 268
and lesbianism, II 180, 268
confessional literature of, II 53–54
Hope, Laura Lee. See Adams, Harriet Stratemeyer
Hopkins, Pauline Elizabeth, I 320–22
hostesses
literary-salon, I 98, 352; II 57, 137, 270
society, II 69, 230
House Un-American Activities Committee, the (McCarthyism)
blacklisting by, II 241
in fiction, II 215
Howard, Richard, critical comment by, II 292
Howe, Irving, critical comment by, II 371
Howe, Julia Ward, I 322–25, 394; II 263
critical comment by, I 112
Howells, William Dean
critical comment by, I 260; II 264
and Jewett, I 351
and Wyatt, II 419
Howes, Barbara, I 325–27
Hughes, Langston, and Walker, II 345
Hull House, I 11–12, 72
Hume, Sophia, I 327–28
humorous literature, II 183, 237–38, 347, 361–63, 376–77. See also comedies
domestic, I 341–42; II 16–17

feminist, I 318–19
purpose of, II 361, 362–63
the study of, II 197
Hunt, Helen. See Jackson, Helen Maria Fiske Hunt
Huntley, Lydia Howard. See Sigourney, Lydia Howard Huntley
Hurst, Fannie, I 329–30, 331
Hurston, Zora Neale, I 331–33
H. W. S. See Smith, Hannah Whitall
Hyde, Nancy Maria, II 232
Hyman, Stanley, and S. Jackson, I 340
hymn writers, II 57–58, 247, 332–33

illustrators, I 120, 230–32, 360; II 106, 281
Imagist poetry, I 177–78, 249–50; II 222, 306
and the Imagist movement, I 176–78; II 60
and the Imagists' influence, I 51, 130, 131, 159, 249–50; II 62
immigrant experience, the, II 126, 273, 274
in fiction, I 366–68; II 424, 425
sociological studies on, I 72–73
Indians, American. See Native Americans
industrialization. See labor, industrial
investigative literature
journalism, II 300, 301 (see also under muckraking literature)
studies, II 55–56
Iola. See Barnett, Ida B. Wells
Ione. See Hewitt, Mary Elizabeth Moore
Irish-American writers, II 180–82
Irving, Washington, critical comment by, I 149
Irwin, Inez Haynes, I 333–35
Isabel. See Ritchie, Anna Cora Ogden Mowatt
Iverson, Sade. See Peattie, Elia Wilkinson

Jackson, Andrew, and Hentz, I 306
Jackson, Helen Maria Fiske Hunt, I 335–37; II 411
Jackson, Laura Riding, I 338–40
Jackson, Shirley, I 340–42
Jacobi, Mary Putnam, I 342–44
James, Henry
critical comment by, II 264
and Wharton, II 369
Janeway, Elizabeth, I 344–46
Jarrell, Randall, critical comment by, II 179
Jerauld, Charlotte Ann Fillebrown, I 347–48
Jewett, Sarah Orne, I 349–52; II 263, 312, 414
Jewish-American writers, I 240–41, 303–5, 316–17, 338–39, 396–98; II 42–44, 57–58, 267–71, 272–74, 430–31
East-European, II 423–25

Jewish culture, I 397; II 58, 431
    and anti-Semitism (*see* anti-Semitism)
    ethnic literature of, II 273, 424–25
    history of, I 8
Johnson, Georgia Douglas Camp, I 352–53
Johnson, Josephine Winslow, I 354–56
Johnston, Annie Fellows, I 356–58
Jones, Edith. *See* Wharton, Edith Newbold
    Jones
Josephy, Helen, II 4
Josiah Allen's Wife. *See* Holley, Marietta
journalists. *See also entries beginning* magazine
    and newspaper
    broadcast, II 3, 315
    exposé, I 119, 153
    foreign correspondent, I 66, 181, 251, 284,
        308; II 8, 11, 284, 314, 321, 343
    19th-c., I 119; II 111, 113, 334
    investigative, I 263; II 300, 301
    muckraking, I 180–82, 246–48; II 300
    political, I 21–22, 154, 222–23, 225–27,
        405; II 11, 283–84, 293, 294, 314–15,
        321, 343
journals. *See* diaries and journals
Judson, Emily Chubbuck, I 358–60
June, Jennie. *See* Croly, Jane Cunningham

Kaufman, George S., and Ferber, I 210
Keating, Sally. *See* Wood, Sally Sayward
    Barrell
Keemle, Mary Katherine. *See* Field, Kate
Keene, Carolyn. *See* Adams, Harriet
    Stratemeyer
Keith, Agnes Newton, I 360–62
Keiz, Marcia, critical comment by, II 31
Keller, Helen Adams, I 362–64
Kelley, Edith Summers, I 364–66
Kelly, Bernice. *See* Harris, Bernice Kelly
Kelly, Myra, I 366–68
Kemble, Frances Anne, I 369–71
Kemble, Miss Fanny. *See* Kemble, Frances
    Anne
Kennedy, Rose. *See* Victor, Metta Victoria
    Fuller
Kerr, Jean Collins, I 371–73
Keyes, Frances Parkinson Wheeler, I 373–75
Kilmer, Aline Murray, I 376–77
Kilmer, Joyce, and Kilmer, I 376
Kimbrough, Emily, I 377–79
Kipling, Rudyard, and M. M. Dodge, I 175
**Kirkland, Caroline Matilda Stansbury, I
    380–82**
Knight, Sarah Kemble, I 382–84
Knowles, Sarah. *See* Bolton, Sarah Knowles
Kuhns, Dorothy. *See* Heyward, Dorothy Hartzell
    Kuhns

labor, industrial, I 11. *See also:* labor,
    industrial, and women; labor reform
    child, I 391–92
    history, I 226
    magazines of, I 200–201, 392
    and unionization (*see* unionization)
labor, industrial, and women
    factory, I 200–201, 391–92; II 192–93,
        334–35
    in fiction, I 414–15; II 27
    history of, II 26–27
    reform in, I 90–91, 161, 162, 171–72; II
        334–35
    sociology of, I 181
    and unionization, I 161; II 27, 121, 334–35
labor reform, I 59, 226; II 342–43. *See also*
    unionization
    for women, I 90–91, 161–62; II 334
Lafayette, Marquis de, critical comment by, II
    400
La Flesche, Suzette "Bright Eyes," I 336
Lamb, Martha Joanna Reade Nash, I 384–86
Lane, Rose Wilder, I 386–88; II 397
Langdon, Mary. *See* Pike, Mary Hayden Green
**Langer, Susanne Katherina Knauth, I 389–
    91**
Langstaff, Josephine. *See* Herschberger, Ruth
Lankford, Sarah Worrall, II 123
Larcom, Lucy, I 391–93
Larkin, Maia. *See* Wojciechowska, Maia
Larrimore, Lida. *See* Turner, Lida Larrimore
Latern, M. H. *See* Hazlett, Helen
Lathrop, Julia, II 138
Latimer, Elizabeth Wormeley, I 394–96
Lawson, Delores. *See* Ridge, Lola
lawyers, II 80, 81
Lazarus, Emma, I 396–98
lecturers, I 54–55, 106, 183, 295–96; II 226,
    269, 270, 293
    and literary readings, II 185–86
Lee, Marion. *See* Comstock, Anna Botsford
Lee, Pattie. *See* Cary, Alice
LeGuin, Ursula K., I 398–400
L'Engle, Madeleine, I 401–2
Lennox, Charlotte Ramsay, II 308
Leslie, Frank. *See* Leslie, Miriam Florence
    Folline
Leslie, Miriam Florence Folline, I 403–5
Le Sueur, Meridel, I 405–7
letters, collected, I 5–6, 278–79, 280–81, 283,
    417, 419; II 100, 254–55, 313
    editors of, I 5; II 39, 100
    18th-c., I 5–6
Levertov, Denise, I 407–9
Lewis, Estelle Anna Robinson, I 409–11
Lewis, Janet, I 411–13

Lewis, Sarah Anna. *See* Lewis, Estelle Anna Robinson
Lewis, Sinclair, I 364
L. H. *See* Hooper, Lucy
Libbey, Laura Jean, I 413–15
Lin, Frank. *See* Atherton, Gertrude Franklin Horn
Lindbergh, Anne Morrow, I 416–18
Lindsay, Vachel, and Teasdale, II 305
Lippincott, Sara Jane Clarke, I 418–20
Lisagor, Peter, and M. Higgins, I 309
literary clubs, II 59, 230, 312
literary criticism, I 160, 282, 293; II 24, 74–75, 86–87, 90, 219, 220, 420
  in book reviews, I 56–57; II 128, 137, 219, 252, 253
  on drama, I 20, 293; II 5, 127
  feminist, II 53, 54, 126
  first major American, II 112, 113
  on poetry, I 56–57, 160, 338–39, 433; II 19, 45
  satire on, II 185
  scholars in (*see* literary scholars)
literary prizes and awards, recipients of, I 399; II 62. *See also: under* children's literature; National Book Award; Pulitzer Prize in Letters
  for criticism, I 293
  for drama, I 291; II 118, 244
  fellowships and grants as, I 76–77, 398; II 99, 142, 151, 155, 290 (*see also* Guggenheim Fellowship)
  for fiction, I 31, 84, 118, 238; II 360 (*see also* O. Henry Memorial Prize Stories)
    mystery, I 191, 314; II 9, 390
    science fiction, I 399
  for nonfiction, I 97; II 87
  for poetry, I 50; II 18, 62, 178, 203, 290, 291, 344–45
literary salons, hostesses of, II 57, 137, 312
literary scholars, II 86–87, 388–89
literature. *See:* American literature; literary criticism; literary history
Livingston, Mrs. C. M. *See* Lutz, Grace Livingston Hill
L. M. A. *See* Alcott, Louisa May
local color, fiction of. *See:* regional fiction; regional literature
local history. *See also* regional literature
  of Appalachia, I 31, 184–85
  fiction based on (*see* regional fiction)
  of the midwest, I 405–6
  of New England, I 7–8, 107–8
    sources for, II 193
  of New York City, I 385–86
  of the northwest, II 337–38
  of the south, II 221 (*see also* Civil War, the)
  of the southwest, I 53
  of the west, II 210–11, 337, 338
    sources for, I 197–98, 202–3, 231, 210, 211
Locke, Jane Erminia Starkweather, I 421–23
Logan, Mary Simmerson Cunningham, I 423–25
Logan, Olive, I 426–28
Lola. *See* Ridge, Lola
Longfellow, Henry Wadsworth
  critical comment by, II 347
  and McDowell, II 20
Loos, Anita, I 428–30
Lothrop, Harriet Mulford Stone, I 430–32
love poetry
  contemporary, I 249–50, 413
  early 20th-c., II 51
  19th-c., I 164; II 74–75, 109
Lowell, Amy, I 432–34
Lowell, James Russell, critical comment by, I 398
Loy, Mina, I 434–36
Lucas, Victoria. *See* Plath, Sylvia
Luce, Clare Boothe, I 437–38
Luhan, Mabel Ganson Dodge, I 439–40
Lumpkin, Grace, I 441–42
Lundy, Benjamin, and Chandler, I 109
Lutz, Alma, I 443–45
Lutz, Grace Livingston Hill, I 445–48
Lynd, Helen Merrell, I 448–49
lyric poetry
  contemporary, I 412–13; II 24
  drama, I 145
  early 20th-c., I 282; II 24, 172
  19th-c., II 172

McBride, Mary Margaret, II 3–5
McCarthy, Joseph. *See* House Un-American Activities Committee
McCarthy, Mary Therese, II 5–8
McCloy, Helen, II 8–10
McCormick, Anne O'Hare, II 10–12
McCullers, Carson Smith, II 12–15
MacDonald, Betty Bard, II 16–17
MacDonald, Golden. *See* Brown, Margaret Wise
MacDonald, Jessica Nelson North, II 18–19
MacDonald, Marcia. *See* Lutz, Grace Livingston Hill
McDowell, Katherine Sherwood Bonner, II 20–21
McGinley, Phyllis, II 22–23
MacInnes, Helen. *See* Highet, Helen MacInnes
McKinney, Alice Jean Chandler Webster. *See* Webster, Jean
McKinnon, Edna Rankin, I 185

Macumber, Marie S. *See* Sandoz, Mari
Madeleva, Sister, II 24–25
magazine columns, I 241; II 314. *See also*
    newspaper columns
  correspondence, I 66, 200–201 222, 223, 284
  drama review, II 127
  literary, I 56; II 128
  political, I 373
  woman's, I 289, 297–98; II 295–96
magazine editors and publishers, I 20, 100; II
      199, 252, 339
  art, II 19
  black, I 38, 208, 274, 321, 322
  children's, I 175, 208, 228, 392
  feminist, I 54
  history, I 385
  literary, I 18, 176, 293, 321; II 19, 60–61,
      62, 95, 113, 297
  political, I 155; II 342
  professional, I 171; II 130
  religious, I 155; II 28, 124
  scholarly, II 87
  women's, I 288–90, 377–78, 403; II 295,
      358–59, 407
    factory, I 200–201, 392
    policy of, I 289
  women's movement, I 54–55, 180, 261, 444;
      II 212, 266
magazines. *See: under* magazine editors and
      publishers; *specific subject areas*
Main, John. *See* Parsons, Elsie Worthington
      Clews
Malkiel, Theresa Serber, II 26–28
Mann, Horace, and J. Andrews, I 25
manners
  comedies of, I 266, 286; II 68
  novels of, I 266–67, 286; II 149–50, 163–
      64, 255, 369–73
  poetry of, II 45
Marah. *See* Jackson, Helen Maria Fiske Hunt
March, Anne. *See* Woolson, Constance
      Fenimore
Markey, Dorothy. *See* Page, Dorothy Myra
Marsh, Ngaio, I 192
Marshall, Catherine, II 28–30
Marshall, Paule, II 30–32
Matisse, Henri, and Stein, II 270
maturation novels. *See: Bildungsroman; under*
      women in fiction
M.C.A. *See* Ames, Mary E. Clemmer
Mead, Margaret, II 32–35
medicine. *See also*: nurses; psychiatrists;
      psychology
  doctors of (*see* physicians)
  and women, I 144, 343
medieval studies, II 322

Meigs, Cornelia Lynde, II 35–37
melodramas, II 65–66, 185
Meloney, Franken. *See* Franken, Rose
Meloney, William Brown, and Franken, I 236
Mencken, H. L., and Loos, I 429
Merington, Marguerite, II 37–39
Meriwether, Elizabeth Avery, II 40–41
metaphysics
  and poetry, I 218; II 44–45, 298
  in religion, I 193–94
Methodists, II 315, 344
  leadership of, II 123–25
M.E.W.S. *See* Sherwood, Mary Elizabeth
      Wilson
Meyer, Annie Nathan, II 42–44
Miles, Josephine, II 44–46
Milholland, Inez, II 50
Millar, Margaret, II 47–49
Millay, Edna St. Vincent, II 18, 49–52
Miller, Bertha, critical comment by, II 36
Miller, Elizabeth Smith, I 54
Miller, Henry, critical comment by, II 91
Miller, Joaquin, and Coolbrith, I 126
Miller, Olive Thorne. *See* Miller, Harriet Mann
Millett, Kate, II 52–54
Minerva. *See* Smith, Eliza Roxey Snow
ministers, I 328; II 248, 250–51, 379
missionaries
  biographies of, I 359
  Seventh Day Adventist, II 380
Mitford, Jessica, II 55–57
M.L.P. *See* Putnam, Mary Traill Spence Lowell
Moise, Penina, II 57–58
Monroe, Harriet, II 19, 59–61
Moore, Alice Ruth. *See* Nelson, Alice Ruth
      Moore Dunbar
Moore, Marianne Craig, II 50, 51, 61–64
Moore, Mollie E. *See* Davis, Mary Evelyn
      Moore
Moorhead, Sarah Parsons, II 64–65
Morgan, Carrie Blake, I 310
Morgan, Claire. *See* Highsmith, Patricia
Morison, Samuel Eliot, critical comment by,
      I 69
Mormons, II 246–47, 358–59
  in fiction, I 319
  history of, II 359
    sources for, II 247
  journals of, II 358, 359
  and polygamy, I 319; II 246, 358
Mortimer, Lillian, II 65–67
Morton, Eleanor. *See* Stern, Elizabeth Gertrude
      Levin
Morton, Lea. *See* Stern, Elizabeth Gertrude
      Levin
Morton, Martha, II 67–69

Morton, Sarah Wentworth Apthorp, II 69–71

Morton-Jones, Verina, II 114

motion-picture industry. *See* film industry

Mott, Lucretia Coffin, II 71–73, 248, 265

Moulton, Louise Chandler, II 73–76

Mowatt, Anna Cora. *See* Ritchie, Anna Cora Ogden Mowatt

muckraking literature
    fictional, II 104
    journalistic, I 119, 181–82, 247; II 300

Murfree, Mary Noailles, II 76–77, 414

Murray, Aline. *See* Kilmer, Aline Murray

Murray, Judith Sargent, II 78–79

Murray, Pauli, II 79–81

musical, the
    adaptation of women's works, I 210, 233, 429; II 244
    and music drama, I 273; II 286

musicians, I 273–74; II 286

mystery drama, II 184

mystery fiction, II 330–31, 389, 390
    classics of, II 184, 194
    comedies in, II 47, 106, 303–4
    feminist, II 390–91, 194–95
    genre, development of, II 195, 340
    Gothic, II 102, 389, 390
    psychological, I 169, 314–15, 340–41; II 9, 390–91
    romantic, I 191–92, 385; II 183
    series, I 168–69; II 47, 102–3, 303, 330, 356–57
    and the spy novel, I 312–13
    technique in, I 28, 158–59, 191; II 47–48, 183, 356

Mystery Writers of America, II 9
    awards given by, I 570, 314; II 9, 390

mysticism
    in fiction, II 249
    in poetry, II 181

myth
    in fiction, I 79–80; II 13, 361
    in poetry, I 177–78; II 179
    and womanhood, I 177–78; II 179–80

NAACP. *See* National Association for the Advancement of Colored People

Narcissa. *See* Smith, Eliza Roxey Snow

narrative poetry, II 172–73, 249, 320, 395, 412

National American Woman Suffrage Association, I 52–53, 297. *See also*: American Woman Suffrage Association; National Woman Suffrage Association
    officer of, I 72; II 266

National Association for the Advancement of Colored People (NAACP), I 208; II 115
    advisers to, I 123

founders of, I 38; II 114

National Book Award
    for Arts and Letters, I 118, 303
    for Children's Literature, I 399
    for Nonfiction, I 96, 97
    for Poetry, I 50
    for the Short Story, II 100

National Institute of Arts and Letters, I 76. *See also* American Academy of Arts and Letters
    awards given by, I 117; II 290, 360
    members of, I 156, 238; II 95, 203, 290

National Organization of Women (NOW), I 241; II 52–53

National Woman's Party, I 333

National Woman's Christian Temperance Union. *See* Woman's Christian Temperance Union

National Woman Suffrage Association, I 183; II 192, 266

Native American culture
    for children's reading, I 189
    folklore in, I 189; II 117
    studies on, I 44; II 117, 131

Native Americans. *See also* Native American culture
    abuse of, I 336
    assimilation of, I 189
    education for, I 188–89
    in fiction, I 336–37; II 224
    history of, I 3–4; II 210
        sources for, I 138–39
    rights of, I 336–37
    women, II 234

natural history. *See also*: anthropology; natural science
    educators in, I 120–22
    studies in, I 96–97, 120–22

natural science, II 317
    of biology, I 96–97, 284; II 426–27
    scholars of, I 96–97

naturalism in fiction, I 354; II 142, 143

nature poetry, I 164–65, 326; II 313
    religious, II 24–25

nature study, I 92–93; II 417
    on birds, II 47
    for children, I 253–54
    in fiction, I 102, 350; II 170, 171, 281
    teachers in, I 120–22

Nelson, Alice Ruth Moore Dunbar, II 81–83

Newbery award medals, I 214, 233, 254, 401; II 36

New Criticism, I 271, 272

newspaper columns, II 11, 135, 163, 253, 272, 273, 337, 430. *See also*: magazine columns; newspaper correspondents

newspaper columns (*cont.*)
  advice (*see under* advice)
  gossip, II 133
  political, I 226–27; II 314–15
  reviews, II 385
    book, II 137
    drama, I 20
  syndicated, I 134, 263, 308; II 3, 133, 134
  women's, I 134, 243, 263, 297–98, 311; II 26, 397
newspaper correspondents, I 21; II 205, 388
  cultural, II 59, 111–12, 113
  foreign, I 119, 181–82, 308–9; II 8, 11, 112, 113, 314, 321
  literary, II 74–75
  political, I 21–22; II 11, 293–94, 314–15
  travel, I 213
newspaper editors and publishers, I 213, 243; II 84, 202, 385
  of arts section, II 385
  of drama section, II 132–33
  feminist, I 54–55, 182–83
  labor, I 155
  of literary section, II 84, 385
  political, II 293
  religious, I 59, 115
  of women's section, I 109; II 3
newspaper reporters, I 74, 119, 253, 263, 308; II 3–4, 10–11, 132–33, 205, 272, 283–84. *See also* newspaper correspondents
Nicholson, Eliza Jane Poitevent, II 84–86
Nicolson, Marjorie Hope, II 86–87
Niggli, Josephina, II 88–89
Nin, Anaïs, II 90–92
  critical comment by, I 35
"No Name Author" series novels, I 336
Nobel Prize
  for Literature, I 84
  for Peace, I 11
Nordstrom, Ursula, II 428
Norris, Kathleen Thompson, II 92–94
North, Jessica N. *See* MacDonald, Jessica Nelson North
novel, the. *See also specific types of novels*
  development of early American (*see under* American literature)
  techniques of writing, I 168–69, 234–35; II 6, 90–91, 96, 222, 268–69, 362
novel of manners, the. *See under* manners
NOW. *See* National Organization of Women
nursing, I 170–72; II 212
  history of, I 171, 172
  in the Civil War, I 16, 202; II 293–94, 411, 416

Oates, Joyce Carol, II 95–97

Oberholtzer, Sara Louisa Vickers, II 95–97
O'Brien, Edward J., critical comment by, II 424
Occidente, Maria del. *See* Brooks, Maria Gowen
O'Connor, Flannery, II 21, 98–101
O'Donnell, Lillian, II 102–3
O'Hara, Mary. *See* Sture-Vasa, Mary Alsop
O. Henry Memorial Prize Stories, I 47, 66, 333, 387
Older, Cora Miranda Baggerly, II 104–5
Older, Mrs. Fremont. *See* Older, Cora Miranda Baggerly
one-act plays, I 81, 214, 245, 255–56, 269; II 39, 137–38, 228, 244
O'Neill, Eugene
  and Day, I 154
  and Glaspell, I 268
O'Neill, Rose Cecil, II 106–7
opera, II 228
  by women, I 273; II 269
organizations, professional. *See also under* women's associations
  in history, I 233; II 208
  literary, II 68, 86, 121, 203
  in music, II 68
organizations, special interest and cause. *See also:* organizations, professional; women's associations
  academic, II 86
  civil liberties, II 213
  civil rights, I 38–39, 123, 208, 274; II 114, 115
  Ku Klux Klan, II 41
  nature, II 417
  for refugees, II 369
  for unionization, I 226
ornithology. *See under* nature study
Osborn, Sarah, II 107–8
Osgood, Frances Sargent Locke, II 109–10
Ossoli, Sarah Margaret Fuller II 111–14
Ovington, Mary White, II 114–16
Owen, Mary Alicia, II 116–18
Owens, Rochelle, II 118–20

Packard, Clarissa. *See* Gilman, Caroline Howard
pacifism. *See* world peace
Page, Dorothy Myra, II 120–22
Palmer, Phoebe Worrall, II 123–25
Papashvily, George, II 125, 126
Papashvily, Helen Waite, II 125–27
Parker, Dorothy Rothschild, II 127–29
Parsons, Elsie Worthington Clews, II 130–32
Parsons, Louella Oettinger, II 132–34
Parton, Sara Payson Willis, II 134–36
patriotic literature, I 219; II 405
  poetry in, I 207; II 70
Pattee, F. L., critical comment by, II 308

Paul, Alice, I 333
Peabody, Mrs. Mark. *See* Victor, Metta Victoria Fuller
peace efforts. *See* world peace
Pearson, Norman Holmes, critical comment by, I 178
Peattie, Elia Wilkinson, II 137–39
Peering, Aminadab. *See* Kirkland, Caroline Matilda Stansbury
Pellowski, Ann, critical comment by, II 36
Percy, Mabel. *See* Hatch, Mary R. Platt
Perkins, Maxwell, and Rawlings, II 170
Peterkin, Julia Mood, II 139–41
Peters, Phillis. *See* Wheatley, Phillis
Petry, Ann Lane, II 141–43
pharmacists, II 141
Phelps, Almira Hart Lincoln, II 143–45
Phelps, Elizabeth Stuart, II 146–48, 346
Phelps, Elizabeth Stuart (daughter). *See* Ward, Elizabeth Stuart Phelps
Philenia. *See* Morton, Sarah Wentworth Apthorp
philosophers, I 26–27, 389–90; II 167–68
philosophy
  of aesthetics, I 389–90; II 256–57, 370, 371
  humanistic, I 45
  of human nature, I 390
  Indian, I 406
  of Objectivism, II 168
  of perception, II 269, 271
  political, I 26–27 (*see also under* socialism)
  religious, I 246, 247–48 (*see also* religious literature)
  Transcendental, II 112, 113, 388
physicians, I 342–44
  in fiction, II 43
Picasso, Pablo, and Stein, II 269, 270
Pilbury, Aunt. *See* Winslow, Helen Maria
Pinckney, Josephine Lyons Scott, II 148–50
Plath, Sylvia, II 150–53
Pocahontas. *See* Smith, Eliza Roxey Snow
Poe, Edgar Allan
  critical comment by, I 148, 381, 410, 411; II 109, 233
  and Whitman, II 388, 389
poetry
  criticism of (*see under* literary criticism)
  development
    of black American, I 352–53
    of modern American, I 160, 338–39; II 61, 173, 203, 395
  Imagistic (*see* Imagist poetry)
  19th-c., characteristics of, II 232–33
  readings, I 296; II 186
  studies on, I 131, 160, 408
  technique in, I 77, 130–31, 165, 338–39; II 45, 62, 203–4, 215, 290, 292

P. O. L. *See* Guiney, Louise Imogen
political figures
  communist (*see* communism)
  contemporary activist, I 155; II 342–43 (*see also under* feminists)
  18th-c., II 352
  government officeholders as, I 185
  in party politics, I 198, 225, 226, 333; II 26, 56
  persecution of, I 154, 225–27, 303, 406; II 241
  socialist (*see* socialism)
  in women's movements (*see*: feminists; *under* woman suffrage)
political literature. *See also*: communism
  conservative, I 337–38
  18th-c., II 352–53
  fiction in, I 66–67, 145, 146, 199, 265–66, 405–6; II 255, 431
  on foreign politics, I 284; II 241–42, 284, 314–15, 321
  journalistic (*see under* journalists)
  on party politics, I 333; II 293
  and philosophy, I 26–27, 406
  poetry in, I 77, 407–8; II 50, 161, 181, 298
  on war, II 321
  and women (*see under*: feminist literature; woman suffrage)
Porter, Eleanor Hodgman, II 152–54
Porter, Gene Stratton. *See* Stratton-Porter, Gene
Porter, Katherine Anne, II 155–58
  critical comment by, II 117–18
Porter, Rose, II 159–60
Porter, Sarah, II 161–62
Post, Emily Price, II 162–64
Pound, Ezra
  and H. Doolittle, I 176, 178
  and H. Monroe, II 60
Presbyterians, I 156; II 207, 309, 350
  influence of, in fiction, II 325–26
  Sunday-school fiction of, I 216–17
Prescott, Harriett. *See* Spofford, Harriett Elizabeth Prescott
prison reformers, I 202
  and penal systems studies, II 56
prizes and awards, recipients of, I 146; II 86. *See also*: Fulbright grant; Guggenheim Fellowship; literary prizes and awards
  in film, I 317
  government, II 206, 360, 369
  in history, I 233
  medical, I 343
  in natural science, I 97
  for peace efforts, I 11
  women's, I 122; II 28
prohibition. *See* temperance movement, the

"proletarian" fiction. *See* socialist-realism

prosody. *See* poetry

protest literature. *See* social criticism

psychics, II 190–91. *See also* spiritualism

psychological drama, I 256, 257

psychological fiction, I 345; II 91. *See also under* women in fiction
    in mystery/crime novels, I 169, 314–15, 340–41; II 9

psychology. *See also* psychiatrists; psychotherapists
    and anthropology, I 45
    in fiction (*see*: psychological fiction; *under* women in fiction)
    poetic treatment of, II 227–29
    and psychobiographies, I 176, 440; II 91
    and therapy, I 440; II 91
    of women, II 91

psychotherapists, II 90

public relations, careers in, II 218

publishers. *See*: book publishers; magazine editors and publishers; newspaper editors and publishers

Pulitzer Prize in Letters
    for Drama, I 14, 245, 269
    for Fiction, I 276; II 155
    for General Nonfiction, II 321
    for History, I 233
    for the Novel, I 36, 84, 100, 210, 267, 354; II 140, 170
    for Poetry, I 50, 76, 77; II 22, 50, 62, 228

Puritanism. *See also*: Congregationalists; Presbyterians
    and Calvinism, I 125; II 73
    diaries and letters of, I 5–6, 88–89; II 324
    in fiction, I 125
    and the Great Awakening, I 107; II 64–65
    histories of, I 186–87
    in poetry, I 68–69, 164–65; II 64–65, 324–25
    spiritual autobiographies of, II 378–79

Putnam, Mary. *See* Jacobi, Mary Putnam

Putnam, Mary Traill Spence Lowell, II 164–66

Quakers. *See* Society of Friends

Quinn, H. *See* Aldrich, Mildred

racism. *See also* civil rights
    in drama, I 291–92
    in fiction, I 219; II 253
    and interracial understanding, I 185; II 253
        awards for attempts to promote, I 185
        fiction promoting, I 25–26, 321–22; II 253

radio programs, II 163, 315
    hostesses of, II 3, 4, 133

    plays for, II 184, 217
    production of, II 217
    serials, I 94–95, 237

Rand, Ayn, II 167–68

Randau, Mrs. Carl. *See* Zugsmith, Leane

Rank, Otto, and Nin, II 90

Rawlings, Marjorie Kinnan, II 169–71

Ray, John. *See* Carrington, Elaine Stern

realism in American fiction, I 104–5, 125, 302, 351; II 199, 264, 268, 288–89, 337, 338
    critical, I 104
    psychological, I 302
    socialist-, I 104, 354; II 241–42

Redfield, Martin. *See* Brown, Alice

Reese, Lizette Woodworth, II 172–73

refugee relief workers, II 369

Regester, Seeley. *See* Victor, Metta Victoria Fuller

regional fiction
    Appalachian, I 30–31, 184–85, 365; II 76–77
    eastern, II 325–27, 414
    midwestern, I 104, 210–11, 269–70; II 117, 288–89
        frontier, I 18–19, 93, 100, 101, 104, 387
        urban, II 420
    New England, I 81, 82, 124, 214–15, 239, 288, 350, 351; II 223–24, 263–64, 303, 393
    northwestern frontier, I 182–83
    southern, I 145–46, 265–67, 271–72, 276–77, 300; II 12–15, 21, 83, 98–101, 148–50, 169–71, 188–89, 260–62, 361–62, 414
        antebellum, I 257, 307; II 40, 310
        black, I 123, 296, 331–32
        Creole, I 115, 116, 150–51, 211
        plantation, II 139–40, 310
        of poor whites, I 441–42; II 176–77
        of primitives, I 276
    southwestern, I 101, 150–51, 211; II 219
    western, I 310–11, 365; II 234–36
        frontier, I 231; II 104–5, 210–11

regional literature. *See also*: local history; regional fiction
    Appalachian, I 184–86
    drama in, I 93, 239, 300
    frontier (*see* frontier life)
    midwest, I 99, 380–81
    New England, I 258
    poetry in, I 219, 311; II 148, 263
    southern
        domestic, I 258
        pro-Ku Klux Klan, II 41
    southwestern, I 150–51
    western, I 197–98, 202–3; II 16–17

Reid, Christian. *See* Tiernan, Frances Christine Fisher
religious affiliations. *See also* Puritanism
  African Methodist Episcopalian, I 208
  Baptist (*see* Baptists)
  Catholic (*see* Catholics)
  Christian Scientist, I 193–94
  Congregationalist (*see* Congregationalists)
  Disciples of Christ, II 297
  Episcopalian (*see* Episcopalians)
  Jewish (*see* Jewish-American writers)
  Methodist (*see* Methodists)
  Moravian Brotherhood, I 176
  Mormon (*see* Mormons)
  and New Thought, II 386
  Presbyterian (*see* Presbyterians)
  Quaker (*see* Society of Friends)
  Scotch Covenanters, II 293
  Seventh Day Adventists, II 380–81
  Unitarian (*see* Unitarians)
religious educators, I 107; II 379–81
religious fiction, I 84, 101–2; II 287. *See also*: conversion literature; Sunday-school movement
  biblical, I 402; II 162
  Catholic (*see* Catholic fiction)
  for children (*see under* children's fiction)
  Episcopalian, I 156
  Presbyterian, I 216–17; II 325–26
  Puritan, I 124–25
  Unitarian, I 229; II 223
religious literature, II 250–51, 386, 404–5. *See also*: Catholic literature; conversion literature; Puritanism; religious fiction; religious poetry; Society of Friends
  autobiographical, I 63: II 29, 378–79
  biblical studies in, II 380
  biographical, II 29, 247
  Christian Science, I 193–94
  diaries in (*see under* diaries and journals)
  drama in, II 269
  evangelical, I 327–28
  history in, I 7–8
  inspirational, I 141; II 28, 29
  and literary criticism, II 24
  magazines of, I 155, II 28, 124
  meditations in, II 159, 176
  on Mormons (*see* Mormons)
  newspapers of, I 59; II 134
  on philosophy, I 246, 247–48
  psychic, II 190–91
  revivalist, II 123–24
  sermons in, II 72–73
  Seventh Day Adventist, II 379–81
  theology in, I 42–43, 53
  on women (*see under* woman's experience)

religious movements
  the Great Awakening, II 64–65
  and the Holiness-Pentecostal tradition, II 123–25
  and Transcendental philosophy, II 111–13, 388
religious poetry
  autobiographic, I 148–49
  on biblical themes, I 69, 149; II 161–62
  contemporary, II 24–25
  18th-c., II 64–65, 161–62, 324, 325, 374
  hymns as, II 57–58, 247, 332–33
  late 19th- to early 20th-c., I 282–83
  mystic, II 25
  19th-c., I 98–99, 147, 149, 164–65
  17th-c., I 68–69
Religious Society of Friends. *See* Society of Friends
Remitrom, Naillil. *See* Mortimer, Lillian
Repplier, Agnes, II 174–75
Rhoads, Ella. *See* Higginson, Ella Rhoads
Rice, Alice Caldwell Hegan, I 224; **II 176–78**
Rice, Cale Young, II 176, 177
Rich, Adrienne Cecile, II 178–80
  critical comment by, I 57
Rich, Barbara. *See* Jackson, Laura Riding
Ridge, Lola, II 180–82
Riding, Laura. *See* Jackson, Laura Riding
Riggs, Mrs. *See* Wiggin, Kate Douglas Smith
Rinehart, Mary Roberts, II 182–85
Rip Van Winkle. *See* Jackson, Helen Maria Fiske Hunt
Ritchie, Anna Cora Mowatt, II 185–87
Rivers, Pearl. *See* Nicholson, Eliza Jane Poitevent
Rives, Amélie. *See* Troubetskoy, Amélie Rives
Roberts, Elizabeth Madox, II 188–89
Roberts, Jane, II 190–91
Robinson, Harriet Jane Hanson, II 191–93
Robinson, William Stevens, and Robinson, I 192
Rogers, Adela. *See* St. Johns, Adela Rogers
Rohlfs, Anna Katharine Green, II 194–96
romance fiction
  contemporary, II 206, 295, 389–91
  18th-c., II 410
  Gothic (*see* Gothic fiction)
  historical (*see under* historical fiction)
  late 19th-c. to early 20th-c., I 85–86, 121–22, 321–22, 414–15; II 263–64, 319, 320, 337
  mystery in, I 374, 385
  19th-c., I 113, 385, 426; II 224, 258–59, 278–79
  religious, I 446–47
  20th-c., I 94–95, 374, 446–47; II 183–84, 217

Roosevelt, Theodore
  critical comment by, I 161
  and M. Kelly, I 368
Rourke, Constance Mayfield, II 196–98
Rousseau, G. S., II 87
Routley, Erik, critical comment by, II 9
Rowson, Susanna Haswell, II 199–201, 409
Royall, Anne Newport, II 201–2
Rubin, Leslie, II 80
Rukeyser, Muriel, II 203–4
rural fiction, I 300, 354; II 170–71, 248. *See
  also* regional fiction
Russian-American writers, II 26–27, 167–68

Sacco and Vanzetti, poetic response to, II 50,
  181
Sagas. *See* family saga, the
St. Johns, Adela Rogers, II 205–7
Salmon, Lucy Maynard, II 207–9
Sandoz, Mari, II 210–11
Sanger, Margaret, II 212–14
Sappho, I 410, 411
Sarton, May, II 214–16
satire. *See* social satire
Sayers, Dorothy L., I 192
Sayers, Frances, critical comment by, II 36
Scarberry, Alma Sioux, II 217–18
Scarborough, Dorothy, II 219–20
schools, founders of, II 224, 232
  kindergartens, II 392
  for women, I 42; II 42, 57, 416
  for writing, I 140
science fiction, I 398–400
  for children, I 399
  the "New Wave" in, I 399
Scott, Evelyn, I 366: II 221–22
Scott, Julia. *See* Owen, Mary Alicia
screenwriters, I 236, 237; II 205, 239, 240,
  286, 368
sculptors, II 52, 54
Seaman, Elizabeth Cochrane. *See* Cochrane,
  Elizabeth
Sedges, John. *See* Buck, Pearl Sydenstricker
Sedgwick, Catharine Maria, I 148; II 223–25
sentimental literature
  fiction, I 53, 296, 337; II 199–200 (*see also*
    romance fiction)
  poetry, II 70
series fiction, I 237; II 218, 418
  children's (*see under* children's fiction)
  mystery, I 169; II 47–48, 102, 330, 357
Seton, Anya, II 225–27
settlement houses
  affiliations with, I 70, 89
  founders of, I 11–12; II 114
Sexton, Anne, II 227–29

Shannon, Dell. *See* Linington, Elizabeth
Sheehan, Marion, II 11
Sheldon, Ann. *See* Adams, Harriet Stratemeyer
**Sherwood, Mary Elizabeth Wilson, II 230–
  31**
short story, the
  development of, I 125
  technique in, II 156, 269
Shuler, Nettie Rogers, I 106
Sidney, Margaret. *See* Lothrop, Harriet Mulford
  Stone
**Sigourney, Lydia Howard Huntley, I 58; II
  232–34**
Sinclair, Bertha Muzzy, II 234–36
Sinclair, Upton, and E. S. Kelley, I 364
Singing Sybil, The. *See* Victor, Metta Victoria
  Fuller
Singleton, Anne. *See* Benedict, Ruth Fulton
Skinner, Cornelia Otis, I 378; II 236–38
slavery. *See also*: abolition; slaves
  in fiction, I 289, 307; II 40, 278, 345
  and the Native American, I 3
  in poetry, I 109, 296
  pro-, I 258; II 40–41
slaves
  owners of, I 23
  writers who were born, I 128–29; II 373
  writers who were children of, I 38–39
Slesinger, Tess, II 238–40
Smedley, Agnes, II 241–43
Smith, Betty Wehner, II 243–45
Smith, Eliza Roxey Snow, II 246–47
Smith, Elizabeth Oakes Prince, II 248–50
Smith, Hannah Whitall, II 250–51
Smith, Josephine Donna. *See* Coolbrith, Ina
  Donna
Smith, Lillian, II 252–54
Smith, Lula Carson. *See* McCullers, Carson
  Smith
Smith, Margaret Bayard, II 254–55
Smith, Mrs. Seba. *See* Smith, Elizabeth Oakes
  Prince
Smith, Seba, II 377
Snow, Eliza Roxey. *See* Smith, Eliza Roxey
  Snow
soap opera, the, for radio, I 94–95
social criticism, II 55–56, 104, 256, 257, 270,
  284. *See also*: social reformers; social
  satire
  in fiction, I 145–46, 315, 365–66, 441–42;
    II 6–7, 95–96, 104, 142, 215, 370–71,
    372, 383–84, 424–25
  in literary criticism, I 294–95
  in poetry, I 207; II 181–82
social history. *See also*: folklore; sociology
  American, I 40–41, 205; II 197–98

Appalachian, I 31, 184–85
black (*see under* black Americans)
Jewish (*see under* Jewish culture)
Native (*see under*: Native American culture;
    Native Americans)
of New York, I 385; II 418, 424–25
of the south, I 23–24
sources of, I 23–24, 73; II 192–93, 202, 424
European, I 205
of woman suffrage, I 299
socialism. *See also* communism
anti-, I 387–88
in communes, I 364–65
and feminism, II 26–27
fiction of, I 146; II 27, 121, 430–31
newspapers of, I 154, 155, 226
poetry of, II 298
political activists in, I 154–55, 170–72, 225–
    27; II 26–27, 121, 241, 283–84, 297–98,
    342–43
and religion, I 155; II 26, 27
and unionization (*see* unionization)
socialist-realism, I 104, 354–55; II 241–42
social protest. *See*: social criticism; *specific
    subject areas of protest and reform*
social reformers, I 11–13, 70–73, 90–91; II
    72–73, 283, 293–94, 419. *See also*:
    civil liberties, campaigns for; social
    criticism; social workers
in birth control, I 185; II 212–13, 241
for black Americans (*see* civil rights)
in education, I 25, 59
in labor (*see* labor reform; unionization)
for Native Americans, I 188–89, 336–37
prison, I 202
in religion (*see* religious movements)
in sex education, I 171
for temperance (*see* temperance movement,
    the)
for women (*see*: woman suffrage; women's
    liberation movement; women's rights)
social satire, II 186–87, 337, 376–77
development of, I 383–84
in drama, I 256, 426
feminist, I 426
in fiction, I 338; II 6, 9, 308, 371, 383–84
in poetry, I 260
social welfare. *See* social workers
social workers, I 11–13, 72–73; II 248, 272,
    283
with black Americans, II 82, 114–15
in charities, I 154–55; II 416
education for, I 72–73
fictional treatment of, II 273
with the handicapped, I 363
Society of Friends (Quakers), II 272, 365

and the Great Separation, II 71
members of, I 109, 204, 222, 230, 327; II
    250–51
ministers of, I 62–63
reform among, I 328
sociology, studies in. *See also*: anthropology;
    cultural studies
of black Americans, II 115
of the family, II 130
of industry, I 11
of penal systems, II 56
scholars of, II 130
urban, I 11–12
of women, II 115, 130–31
sonnets
contemporary, II 345
19th-c., I 347; II 75, 172
20th-c., early, I 71, 145; II 39, 50, 56, 182,
    306
Sontag, Susan, II 256–57
Southey, Robert, critical comment by, I 147
**Southworth, Emma Dorothy Eliza Nevitte, II
    258–60**
Spencer, Elizabeth, II 260–62
spiritual autobiographies, I 221–22; II 107–8,
    378–79
spiritualism, II 206, 313, 386. *See also* psychics
**Spofford, Harriet Elizabeth Prescott, I 283; II
    262–65**
Squier, Miriam. *See* Leslie, Miriam Florence
    Folline
**Stanton, Elizabeth Cady, I 53, 54, 298, 299,
    443, 444; II 40, 72, 265–67**
critical comment by, I 247
Stedman, Edmund Clarence
and J. C. R. Dorr, I 179
and H. Monroe, II 59
Stein, Gertrude, II 267–72
Stella. *See* Lewis, Estelle Anna Robinson
Stephens, Margaret Dean. *See* Aldrich, Bess
    Streeter
Stern, Elizabeth Gertrude Levin, II 272–74
Sterne, Elaine. *See* Carrington, Elaine Sterne
Stevens, Wallace, critical comment by, I 102
Stewart, Eleanor. *See* Porter, Eleanor Hodgman
Stockton, Annis Boudinot, II 274–76
Stoddard, George, critical comment by, I 127
Stokeley, James, and Dykeman, I 184, 185
Stokely, Wilma Dykeman. *See* Dykeman,
    Wilma
**Stowe, Harriet Beecher, I 42, 58, 260, 286,
    306, 307, II 134, 147, 277–80, 346**
Stratton-Porter, Gene, II 280–82
Strong, Anna Louise, II 283–85
Sture-Vasa, Mary Alsop, II 285–87
Suckow, Ruth, I 366; II 287–90

suffrage
  for black Americans, I 39
  for women (*see* woman suffrage)
Sullivan, Anne, I 362, 363
Summers, Edith. *See* Kelley, Edith Summers
Sunday-school movement, the, fiction of, I
  216–17, 228; II 146–47, 346, 350
suspense fiction. *See* mystery fiction
Sweet, Sarah O. *See* Jewett, Sarah Orne
Swenson, May, II 290–92
Swisshelm, Jane Grey Cannon, II 292–94
Sylvia. *See* Smith, Anna Young

Taber, Gladys Bagg, II 295–97
Taggard, Genevieve, II 297–99
Tarbell, Ida Minerva, II 299–302
Tate, Allen, I 271
Taylor, Bayard, critical comment by, II 233
Tate, Caroline. *See* Gordon, Caroline
Taylor, Phoebe Atwood, II 302–4
Teasdale, Sara, II 305–7
television programs, I 292, 314
  adaptations of women's work for, II 184, 398
  situation comedies for, I 372
temperance movement, the
  activists in, I 54–55, 58, 243; II 337, 402–3
  in fiction, I 243, 319; II 205, 339
Tenney, Tabitha Gilman, II 307–9
Terhune, Albert Payson, II 309
Terhune, Mary Virginia Hawes, II 309–12
Terry, Rose. *See* Cooke, Rose Terry
textbooks, I 219; II 199
  in cookery, II 427
  in history, I 40–41
  in the sciences
    natural, I 24; II 144, 400, 426–27
    sociological, II 130
  in writing, II 133
Thaxter, Celia Laighton, II 312–14
theater. *See also* actresses
  children's, I 256
  directors, II 102, 214
  experience, I 426; II 199, 244, 366
    fictionalized, II 186–87
  experimental, I 268; II 342
  founders of groups in, I 268; II 214
  and the little-theater movement, I 256–57
theology. *See under* religious literature
Thomas, Caroline. *See* Dorr, Julia Caroline
  Ripley
Thomas, Mrs. Henry J. *See* Victor, Metta
  Victoria Fuller
Thompson, Dorothy, II 314–15
Thomson, Virgil, and Stein, II 269
Thorndyke, Helen Louise. *See* Adams, Harriet
  Stratemeyer

Tietjens, Elizabeth, critical comment by, II 18
Todd, Mabel Loomis, II 316–18
tragedy
  blank-verse, I 207
  and comedy, II 101
  historical fiction as, I 412
Transcendentalism, I 15, 110, 162; II 111–13,
  388
  and Brook Farm, I 161
translators, I 219; II 290, 426–27
  from the French, I 396; II 63, 416
  from the German, I 397; II 112
travel books
  African, II 317, 386
  on the Americas, II 386
  Asian, I 387; II 317
  for children, I 419
  as cultural studies, I 184–85, 263, 404
  diaries as, I 383–84
  and early American means of travel, I 383–
    84
  European, I 117–18, 179, 213, 378–79, 419;
    II 385–86
  guidebooks, I 378
  journalistic, I 213, 419
  personal impressions in, I 117–18, 258–59,
    419; II 201–2, 415
  as social documents, II 4
  in the U.S., regional, I 184–85, 336, 383–
    84, 404; II 201–2, 386
Tremaine, Paul. *See* Johnson, Georgia Douglas
  Camp
Troubetzkoy, Amélie Rives, II 318–20
Trusta, H. *See* Phelps, Elizabeth Stuart
Truth, Sojourner, I 243
Tuchman, Barbara, II 321–23
Turell, Jane, II 323–25
Turnbull, Agnes Sligh, II 325–27
Twain, Mark. *See* Clemens, Samuel
Tyler, Anne, II 327–29
  critical comment by, II 361

Uhnak, Dorothy, II 329–31
Ullman, Doris, II 40
Umsted, Lillie Devereux. *See* Blake, Lillie
  Devereux
Uncle Ben. *See* White, Rhoda Elizabeth
  Waterman
unionization, II 334
  fictional treatment of, I 123; II 27, 334–35,
    343, 430
  organizers for, I 226; II 26, 239
  for women, I 72, 161; II 27, 121, 334
Unitarians, I 134, 228, 257; II 223
United States history, II 137, 301. *See also*:
  Civil War, the; local history; Native

Americans; *specific subject areas of history*
of the cavalry, sources for, I 138–39
colonial, I 7–8, 186–87
  sources for, I 5–6; II 224 (*see also* Puritanism)
cultural, II 196–98
domestic, I 186–87, 195–96, 385; II 208
  sources for, I 257–59; II 350
economic, I 40
fictionalized (*see* historical fiction)
from a foreign viewpoint, sources for, I 369–70
magazines of, I 385
of pioneers (*see* frontier life)
of presidential social circles, I 196
of the Reconstruction era, I 4
of the Revolutionary War, I 40, 385; II 353
  sources for, II 275, 405–6
social (*see under* social history)
of travel, sources for, I 258–59, 383–84
in the Vietnam War (*see* Vietnam War)
women in (*see* women's studies)
in the world wars (*see* World War I *and* II)
United States presidents, I 5–6, 161, 368; II 275, 352, 353, 374
  social circles of, I 196
  wives of, I 5–6; II 253, 352
Untermeyer, Louis, and J. Untermeyer, I 131
Updegraff, Alan, and Kelley, I 364
Updike, John, critical comment by, II 329
utopian communities, I 161, 162
utopian fiction, II 93, 347

Valentine, Jo. *See* Armstrong, Charlotte
Van Alstyne, Frances Jane Crosby, II 331–33
Van Buren, Abigail, II 164
Van de Water, Virginia Terhune, II 309
Van Vorst, Marie, II 333–36
Vechten, Carl Van, critical comment by, II 422–23
verse drama, I 70, 207, 397, 410–11; II 185–86, 192, 194
Victor, Frances Fuller, II 336–38
Victor, Metta Victoria Fuller, II 336, 337, 339–41
Victorian literature, characteristics of, I 21–22; II 74–75
Vietnam War, the
  activists against, I 407
  history of, I 309
  war correspondents of, I 251, 308–9
Vorse, Mary Heaton, II 341–44

Walker, Margaret, II 344–45
war correspondents, I 181–82, 251, 308; II 321

in the Korean War, I 308
in Vietnam, I 251, 309
in World War I, I 181, 182; II 343
in World War II, I 251–52
Ward, Elizabeth Stuart Phelps, II 263, 346–49
Warner, Susan Bogert, II 349–51
Warren, Mercy Otis, I 5; II 351–53
Watergate scandal, the, II 215
Watkins, Frances Ellen. *See* Harper, Frances Ellen Watkins
WCTU. *See* Woman's Christian Temperance Union
Webster, Daniel, critical comment by, II 400
Webster, Jean, II 354–55
Weeks, Helen C. *See* Campbell, Helen Stuart
Weld, Angelina Grimké. *See* Grimké, Angelina Emily
Wells, Anna Maria Foster, II 109
Wells, Carolyn, II 355–57
Wells, Emmeline Blanche Woodward, II 358–60
Wells, Ida B. *See* Barnett, Ida B. Wells
Welty, Eudora, II 21, 360–63
Wertheim, Barbara. *See* Tuchman, Barbara Wertheim
West, Jessamyn, II 364–66
West, Mae, II 366–68
western novels, I 316; II 234–36
Wetherall, Elizabeth. *See* Warner, Susan Bogert
Wharton, Edith Newbold Jones, I 14; II 369–73
Wheatley, Phillis, II 373–75
Wheaton, Campbell. *See* Campbell, Helen Stuart
Whitcher, Frances Miriam Berry, II 375–77
White, Elizabeth, II 378–79
White, Ellen Gould Harmon, II 379–82
White, Rhoda Elizabeth Waterman, II 382–84
Whiting, Lilian, II 385–87
  critical comment by, II 75
Whitman, Sarah Helen Power, II 387–89
Whitney, Phyllis Ayame, II 389–91
Whittier, John Greenleaf
  critical comment by, I 98; II 233, 347
  and Larcom, II 392
  and F. Willard, II 403
W. H. S. *See* Smith, Hannah Whitall
Wiggin, Kate Douglas Smith, II 392–94
Widow Bedott. *See* Whitcher, Frances Miriam Berry
Widow Spriggins. *See* Whitcher, Frances Miriam Berry
Wilbur, Richard, critical comment by, II 291
Wilcox, Ella Wheeler, II 394–96
Wilder, Laura Ingalls, II 397–99

Wilkins, Mary E. *See* Freeman, Mary Eleanor Wilkins
Willard, Emma Hart, I 443; II 143, **399–401**
Willard, Frances Elizabeth Caroline, I 319; II **402–4**
Williams, Catharine Read Arnold, II 404–6
Williams, Ellen, II 60
Williams, Paul, critical comment by, II 429
Wilson, Mrs. H. L. *See* O'Neill, Rose Cecil
Winslow, Helen Maria, II 406–8
Winters, Yvor, and J. Lewis, I 411
Winthrop, Margaret, I 187
wives of presidents, *See under* United States presidents
Wolf, Mrs. Robert. *See* Taggard, Genevieve
Wolff, Mary Evaline. *See* Madeleva, Sister
woman, superiority of, theory, I 289–90; II 403
woman suffrage
  activists for
    early, I 52–53, 161, 171, 183, 243, 323; II 40, 246, 265–67, 293, 403
    20th-c., I 39, 105–6, 180–82, 198, 297–99, 333; II 192, 212, 314, 358–59
  anti-, II 43, 145, 301
  children's literature for, I 162
  in England, I 333
  in fiction, I 199
  founders of organizations for, I 323, 333; II 265–67
  histories of, I 298, 333; II 266
  journalism for, I 297–99
  lecturers for, I 105–6, 183; II 265–67
  and the 19th Amendment, I 105–6
  periodicals of, I 180; II 266
  in poetry, II 192
  political strategies for, I 105–6, 248
  radical wing of movement for, I 333
  theological arguments for, I 53
Woman's Christian Temperance Union, II 402–3. *See also* temperance movement
woman's columns. *See under*: magazine columns; newspaper columns
woman's experience. *See also*: feminist literature; women in drama; women in fiction; women in poetry; women's rights; women's studies
  Appalachian, I 184, 185
  black (*see under* black Americans)
  frontier (*see* frontier life)
  in health matters, I 144, 171–72, 343
  in history, I 113, 132–33, 187; II 137
  lesbian, II 53–54, 180
  in marriage, I 416–17, 426–27; II 130, 249
  as a moral force, I 42, 171–72, 289–90; II 206, 403
  with motherhood, II 179–80

  and myth, I 345–46
  with oppression, I 280–81, 361; II 53, 212, 213
  in prison, I 227
  psychology of, II 91
  in religion, I 41–42, 53, 261–62; II 246, 247, 266
  and the search for identity, II 91
  with sexual exploitation, I 241; II 53, 213
  with social status, II 130–31, 133, 137
women in drama
  dependence of, I 14
  emancipation of, II 68
  and marriage, II 43
  and the "new woman," I 269; II 42–43
  search of, for identity, I 15; II 68
  sexuality of, II 367, 368
  unflattering portraits of, I 437, 438; II 269
women in fiction, I 191–92, 318–19, 339, 348, 405–6
  aging, II 342
  as artist, I 261, 265
  black (*see under* black fiction)
  frontier, I 185, 269–70, 387, 388; II 138, 211, 325–26, 327, 337
  independence of, I 64–65, 115–16, 211, 269–70, 334; II 26–27, 102, 105, 187, 195, 218, 235, 281, 319, 331, 350, 367–68, 407–8, 425
  and lesbianism, II 268
  and marriage, I 24, 417; II 370–71
    vs. a career, I 141, 317, 350; II 43, 138, 418
    vs. spinsterhood, II 224, 288–89
    status in, I 247; II 347
  muturation of, I 244–45, 293–94, 350; II 30, 188–89, 216, 226–27, 286, 288, 364–65
  failed, II 308, 369–70
  morality of, conventional, I 330, 334, 414
  and motherhood, I 405
  and the "new woman," I 32, 75, 247
  relationships of
    with men, I 167; II 239, 240
    with other women, I 64–65, 167, 345, 350; II 199, 219–20, 263–64, 273, 330–31, 346–47, 364–65, 390–91
  roles of
    conflict of, I 37, 146, 302, 365
    conventional, I 53, 152; II 147, 255, 279, 286, 310, 408, 418
  search of, for identity, II 91, 329, 335, 391
  sexuality of, II 319, 364
  southern, I 146, 266–67, 331–32, 441–42; II 310
  superiority of, I 170–71, 206; II 277–78, 279, 409

survival of, I 441–42
victimization of, I 167–68, 261; II 128–29,
    136
    and passivity, II 96, 128–29, 136
working, I 140–41, 171, 201, 414–15; II
    26–27, 334–35
women in poetry, II 57, 395
common experience of, I 57, 352–53; II 179,
    227–28, 229, 298
creative, II 18–19
and marriage, I 98–99, 435
and motherhood, I 98–99, 421–22, 435; II
    22, 23
mythic structures for, II 179
roles of
    conflict of, II 151
    conventional, I 288, 435
sacrifices of, I 396
suffering of, I 99, 421, 422
women's associations. *See also* women's clubs
colonial, II 417
feminist, I 241; II 52–53
for peace, I 11, 72
professional, I 230; II 85, 407
for unionization, I 220; II 27
woman suffrage, I 52–53, 72, 183, 297, 323,
    333; II 192, 246, 266
women's clubs, I 72, 161; II 248, 407–8. *See
    also* women's associations
federation of, II 407
histories of, I 135; II 407
leaders in, I 98, 134, 135, 323; II 192
literary, I 306; II 59, 230
satirized, in fiction, II 43
Sorosis, I 98, 134, 135
university, I 72
women's columns. *See under*: magazine
    columns; newspaper columns
Women's International League for Peace and
    Freedom, I 11, 72
women's liberation movement, I 346. *See also*:
    feminists; women's rights
history of, I 241; II 53
split within, I 241
women's magazines. *See under* magazine editors
    and publishers
women's rights. *See also*: woman suffrage;
    women's liberation movement
advocates of
    colonial, I 6
    early 19th-c., I 113, 132–33, 278–79,
        280–81, 381; II 72, 136, 246–47, 248–
        49, 293–94
    late 19th- to early 20th-c., I 135, 143–44,
        173, 261–62, 323–24; II 346–48, 358,
        359

anti-, I 290
to birth control (*see* birth control)
for black women, I 128–29, 278, 296
conventions for, II 248, 265
in domestic matters, I 135
for dress reform, I 54
for economic equality, I 143–44, 173, 260–
    61, 381; II 79, 112, 347
to education (*see* education for women)
fiction of (*see under* women in fiction)
history of movement for, I 443–44
for intellectual recognition, I 281; II 79, 112–
    13
lecturers for, I 54–55, 183, 323–24
legislation for, I 52–53, 73, 106
periodicals for, I 54–55, 183, 261
in the professions, II 124–25
religious arguments for, I 280–81; II 72
working (*see* labor, industrial, and women)
women's studies
on women artists, I 284
as biographical sketches, collections of, I 59,
    289, 339, 425, 444; II 273, 403
in literature, I 284; II 126–27
pioneering works in, I 40–41, 195
on professional women, I 73, 171; II 43
on the roles of women in history, I 40–41,
    59, 73, 113, 195
on woman suffrage (*see under* woman
    suffrage)
on women's rights (*see under* women's rights)
Women's Trade Union League, I 72; II 27
Wood, Sally Sayward Barrell, II 409–11
Woodward, Blanche. *See* Wells, Emmeline
    Blanche Woodward
Woolsey, Sarah Chauncey, II 411–13
Woolson, Constance Fenimore, II 413–15
world peace
activists for, I 11, 106, 407; II 401
and the Nobel Peace Prize, I 11
World War I, I 20–21; II 300
activity in, I 387, 424; II 369, 396
advocates of U.S. involvement in, I 81; II
    175
histories of, II 321, 322
nursing in, II 252
peace efforts during (*see* world peace)
war correspondents of, I 181, 182; II 343
World War II
activity in, I 360–61; II 270
in fiction, I 251–52, 312; II 157, 205
in poetry, II 63
war correspondents of, I 251–52
Wormeley, Elizabeth. *See* Latimer, Elizabeth
    Wormeley
Wormeley, Katharine Prescott, II 415–17

Wright, Mabel Osgood, II 417–19
Wright, Richard, critical comment by, II 375
Wright, Rowland. *See* Wells, Carolyn
Wyatt, Edith Franklin, II 419–21
Wylie, Elinor Hoyt, II 421–23

Yezierska, Anzia, II 423–25
Youmans, Eliza Ann, II 426–27
Young, Brigham, wives of, II 246, 247
Young, Eliza Roxey Snow Smith. *See* Smith,
    Eliza Roxey Snow

Young, Maigret. *See* Moore, Marianne Craig
young adult literature
    on adolescent problems, I 254, 399–400
    biographies in, I 274, 378–79; II 122
    dramas in, II 38–39
    historical, II 36
    novels in, I 254, 399–400, 401; II 36, 138,
        154, 159–60, 170, 286, 356, 389–90

Zolotow, Charlotte Shapiro, II 428–30
Zugsmith, Leane, II 430–31